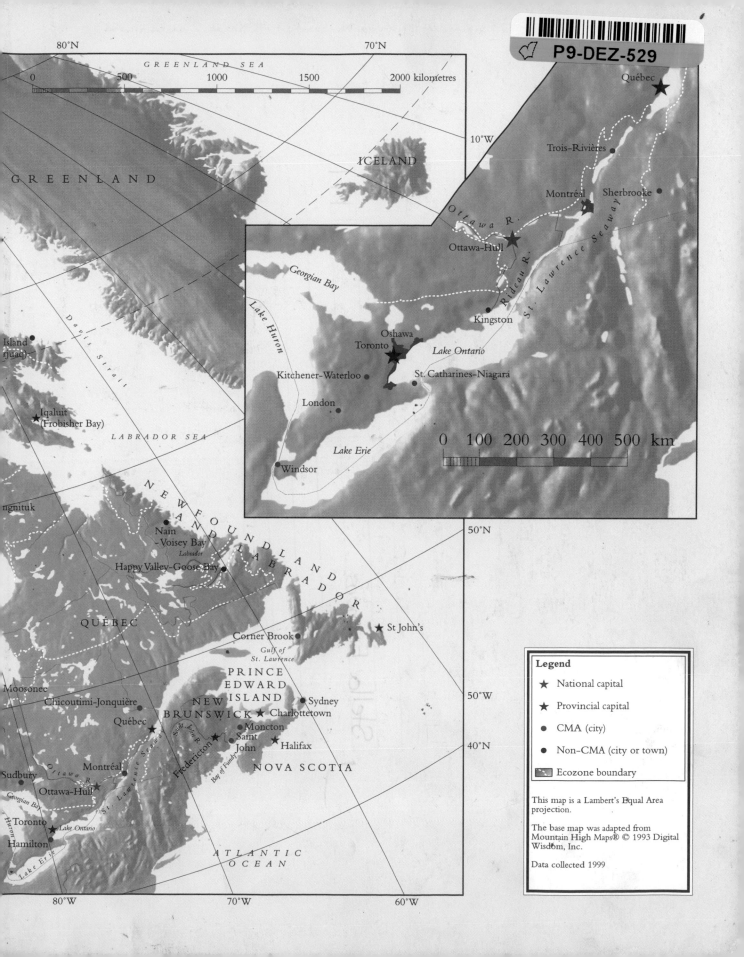

P9-DEZ-529

GREENLAND SEA

0 500 1000 1500 2000 kilometres

ICELAND

10°W

GREENLAND

Québec

Trois-Rivières

Montréal   Sherbrooke

Ottawa-Hull

Ottawa R.

Rideau R.

St. Lawrence Seaway

Georgian Bay

Lake Huron

Kingston

Davis Strait

Island rjuaq)

Iqaluit (Frobisher Bay)

LABRADOR SEA

Oshawa

Toronto

Lake Ontario

Kitchener-Waterloo   St. Catharines-Niagara

London

0 100 200 300 400 500 km

Lake Erie

Windsor

50°N

ngnituk

Nain - Voisey Bay
Labrador

Happy Valley-Goose Bay

NEWFOUNDLAND AND LABRADOR

QUÉBEC

Corner Brook

St John's

Gulf of St. Lawrence

50°W

Moosonee

Chicoutimi-Jonquière

PRINCE EDWARD ISLAND

Sydney

NEW BRUNSWICK

Charlottetown

Québec

Moncton

Saint John

Halifax

40°N

Sudbury

Fredericton

Saint John R.

St. Lawrence Seaway

Montréal

NOVA SCOTIA

Ottawa R.

Ottawa-Hull

Bay of Fundy

Georgian Bay

Lake Huron

Toronto

Lake Ontario

Hamilton

Lake Erie

ATLANTIC OCEAN

80°W   70°W   60°W

05-03

St. Mary Catholic
High School
40 Central Avenue
Brockville, Ontario K6V 4N5
(613) 342-4914

St. Mary Catholic High School - Brockville, Ont.
613-342-4914

Name	Year / Term	Condition	
Lindsey Smith	2005	Great	
Taylor Leeder	2006	G	190
Kendall Murray	2006/2007	Good	136
Stella Emmons	2007		191
Mitchell Beattie	2010		
Erin Brunner			

MAKING CONNECTIONS
Canada's Geography

Bruce W. Clark

John K. Wallace

Prentice
Hall

Toronto

Dedication
To all young Canadians,
especially Graham, Kenyon, David, and Ian

Canadian Cataloguing in Publication Data

Clark, Bruce, 1948-
 Making Connections: Canada's Geography

Includes index.
ISBN 0-13-012635-7

1. Canada – Geography - Juvenile literature. I. Wallace, John K., 1946- II. Title.

FC57.C527 1999 917.1   C99-930984-6
F1011.3.C527 1999

Prentice-Hall, Inc., Englewood Cliffs, New Jersey
Prentice-Hall International, Inc., London
Prentice-Hall of Australia, Pty., Ltd., Sydney
Prentice-Hall of India Pvt., Ltd., New Delhi
Prentice-Hall of Japan, Inc., Tokyo
Prentice-Hall of Southeast Asia (PTE) Ltd., Singapore
Editora Prentice-Hall do Brasil Ltda., Rio de Janeiro
Prentice-Hall Hispanoamericana. S.A., Mexico

ISBN 0-13-012635-7

Publisher: MaryLynne Meschino
Managing Editor: Beverley Biggar
Developmental Editors: Maria Christopoulos,
 Barbara Muirhead, Rena Sutton
Production Editors: Kelly Ronan, Rena Sutton
Research Editors: Tanjah Karvonen, Kendra McKnight
Consulting Editor: Jenifer A. Ludbrook
Permissions/Photo Researcher: Karen Taylor
Production Coordinator: Kathrine Pummell
Design: Julia Hall
Cover Design: Julia Hall

Cover Illustration: Alex Li
Page Layout: Dave McKay
Illustrators: Deborah Crowle, Dave McKay,
 Steven Corrigan
Technical Reviewer: Robert Morrow

Cover Photographs: Photodisc, Tony Stone

Printed and bound in Canada.
 7 8 9 10 11   TP   07 06 05 04

Note From the Publisher
Prentice Hall Ginn Canada, School Division, and the authors of *Making Connections: Canada's Geography*, are committed to the publication of instructional materials that are as bias-free as possible. This text was evaluated for bias prior to publication.

The authors and publisher also recognize the importance of appropriate reading levels and have therefore made every effort to ensure the highest possible degree of readability in the text. The content has been selected, organized, and written at a level suitable to the intended audience. According to research, readability is affected by much more than word or sentence length; factors such as presentation, format, and design also greatly influence the ease with which students read a book. These and many additional features, such as marginal notes and a glossary, have been carefully prepared to ensure maximum student comprehension.

The publisher of this book has made every reasonable effort to trace the ownership of data and visuals and to make full acknowledgement for their use. Web addresses included in the book were accurate at the time of publication but are subject to change. Corrections or suggestions about additional Web sites can be sent to the publisher. If any errors or omissions have occurred, they will be corrected in future editions, providing written notification has been received by the publisher.

A special thank you to ESRI Canada's Schools & Libraries program for contributing ArcVoyager(TM), data and consulting services in this text. ArcVoyager is a trademark provided under a license from Evirontmental Systems Research Institute, Inc. ESRI Canada is a registered trademark of ESRI Canada Limited.

Table of Contents

ACKNOWLEDGEMENTS

The development of *Making Connections: Canada's Geography* required the talents and dedication of many more people than the two whose names appear on the cover. We would like to extend our sincere appreciation to the staff at Prentice Hall, especially the five editors who worked on this text, Beverley Biggar, and MaryLynne Meschino. We would also like to thank our wives, Laurie Wallace and Rosemary Clark, for their editorial suggestions, patience, and tolerance with their often-absent husbands.

Finally, we would like to express our gratitude to our students for field testing the material, and to the many companies, government departments, and individuals who provided materials for this book. Their generosity and cooperation were invaluable.

Bruce Clark and John Wallace

TO THE STUDENT

Geography is a subject that connects both physical and social perspectives to the study of people, places, and environments. Through the use of *Making Connections: Canada's Geography*, you will gain an ecological understanding of local and global events by examining the processes that shape the earth and that show how people and other living things interact with the environment.

Throughout your study of Canada's geography, *Making Connections* will help you to:

• learn about the physical, economic, cultural, and political systems of Canada

• examine the relationships between people and their urban, cultural, and economic environments

• discover Canada's connections with other people and countries around the world

• identify a variety of changing relationships taking place in Canada and the world

• make informed judgements about environmental and social issues

• use a variety of tools such as maps, graphs, satellite images, the Internet, the Global Positioning System (GPS) and geographic information systems (GIS), to gather, organize, and analyze data

HOW TO USE THIS BOOK

Before beginning your study of Canada's geography, you should know how this book is organized and how to use its many parts. This will improve your study skills.

- Six major themes are presented in the book. Each theme is examined in a *Unit* composed of several *Chapters*.

- Unit Two is a special section that can serve as a "reference tool" to be used at any point during your study. It contains activities and information that will help you develop the necessary skills to study the geography of Canada.

- Several chapters in the book contain *Connecting Studies*. These studies examine in detail a specific geographic situation related to the material in the chapter.

- Each chapter, except those in Unit Two, begins with a *Study Guide*. The guide provides you with the most important expectations that you have to meet by the end of the chapter. Use it as a reference for the key ideas of the chapter when you are reviewing and preparing for tests.

- At the beginning of all chapters is a section called *Key Terms*. Major geographical ideas discussed in the chapter are listed here. If you do not know the meanings of the key terms or other terms in **bold face** type, you can look them up in the *Glossary*.

- You will see small blocks of blue type called *marginal notes* in this book:

  i. to facilitate understanding, some words not directly related to geography are explained in the margin

  ii. geographical information and hints are also found in the margin to help explain concepts discussed in the text

- Questions are divided into three groups according to the kind of answers required:

  i. *Check Your Understanding* questions review facts, concepts, principles, and their relationships.

  ii. *Analyze and Apply* questions ask you to use information in the text in new ways. You may be asked to use a number of approaches and tools to problem solve, to express new ideas, combine ideas, reach conclusions, or draw maps, graphs, or diagrams.

  iii. *Think and Communicate* includes questions that encourage you to reflect on the information and ideas provided, discuss and evaluate all points of view, communicate your own opinion, and make recommendations.

- To develop *technological skills*, there are GIS activities that are identified in the margin by a GIS icon. Internet addresses provide you with the opportunity to use the computer to learn more about the topics you are studying. Look for the Internet icon in the margin.

Canadian Connections:
An Introduction

Can you make the connection?

STUDY GUIDE

By the end of this chapter, you will be able to:

- evaluate your knowledge of Canada
- measure your sense of pride in Canada
- compare Canada to other countries using a variety of measures
- understand the concept of population density
- classify countries according to wealth

Key Terms

geographical systems
global connections
mental map

population density
Gross Domestic Product (GDP) per capita

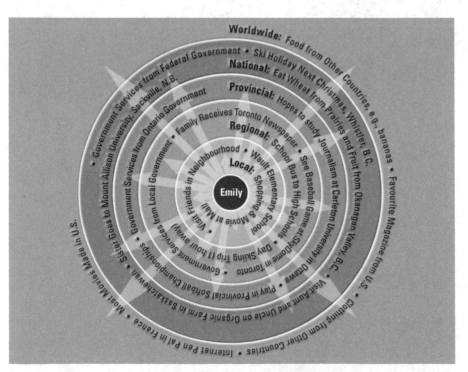

◁ **Fig. 1-1** *Just like this student, every Canadian has connections at many different levels.*

This book, and your study of Canadian geography, is all about connections . . . about who you are and how you relate to the world and, in particular, to our country, Canada. Consider the geographic connections of a Canadian student who lives in Oshawa, Ontario (Fig. 1-1).

She has local, regional, provincial, national, and worldwide connections. Some of these linkages are obvious. For example, she has ties with more distant parts of Canada when she visits her sister at her university in New Brunswick or stays with her uncle and aunt at their farm in Saskatchewan in the summer. She has regional ties when she reads the Toronto newspaper that her family buys every day or goes to the SkyDome in downtown Toronto to see a baseball game.

Other connections are not so clear. For example, a close look at the labels of her clothing would reveal that much of it was made in countries like Malaysia and India. When she broke her leg skiing last year near Barrie, Ontario, the money for her treatment and hospital stay came from taxpayers in Ontario and the rest of Canada. Are you aware of the ways in which you are linked to the rest of the world?

There are five focus areas that are important to geographers in trying to understand all the connections that exist in the world.

If you would like to learn more about careers in geography, check www.muohio.edu/~geocwis/careers/careers_main.html

1. *The reasons things are located where they are*: a geographer might want to study, for example, why McDonald's would choose to locate a new restaurant in a particular place.

2. ***Geographical systems*** *that shape our world*: a study, for example, might be done to try to understand the forces that cause devastating earthquakes or why nations trade with each other.

3. *Interactions between people and the environment within which they live*: by focussing on these links, we can better understand problems such as how we contribute to global warming when driving a sport utility vehicle instead of an economy car.

4. ***Global connections*** *between regions and countries*: for example, in studying trade, we might want to examine the role that Canadians play in the economy of another country when we purchase a new pair of basketball shoes made in that country.

5. *Special tools and skills that geographers use, such as mapping, graphing, and aerial photographing*: in addition to these traditional geographic tools, exciting new developments allow geographers to study the earth's surface from satellites and to analyze and present geographic data using powerful computerized mapping software called **geographic information systems (GIS)**.

YOUR CONNECTIONS

By using *Making Connections: Canada's Geography*, you will have a chance to learn about all of these aspects of geography so that you develop a better understanding of your connections. The activities that follow provide a starting point.

A MENTAL MAP OF CANADA

We use an atlas or road map to help us find the location of a place or discover some missing information. More often, we also make use of a collection of special maps that exist in our minds, what we might call our **mental maps**. These mental maps are very important since they provide the basis on which we make decisions and take actions. Some of these maps are much more complete and accurate than others. For example, your mental map of the house or apartment in which you live is likely to be more precise than your mental map of New York City or New Zealand.

A very important mental map for any Canadian is that of our country. Let's see what is on your mental map of Canada. Take a standard 8 1/2" x 11" sheet of paper and, turning it sideways, draw your mental map of Canada on it. Include any important geographic features of which you are aware such as provinces, main cities, water bodies, and land features. Keep the map you have drawn; you may want to try drawing another mental map later in the course to see what you have learned.

In fact, you will be asked to use your mental maps very often in this book.

AN INTRODUCTORY MAP OF CANADA

Develop a reference map of Canada that you can use and add to during this course. You can create this map in one of two ways: either with pen and paper, or using ArcVoyager software. If you are doing the former, follow the instructions below. If you are using ArcVoyager, your teacher will give you full instructions. Label the following on a blank map of Canada which your teacher will provide:

1. Provinces and territories
2. National, provincial, and territorial capitals
3. Additional cities: Vancouver, Calgary, Saskatoon, Thunder Bay, Windsor, London, Hamilton, Montréal, and Saint John
4. Lakes: each of the Great Lakes, Winnipeg, Great Slave, and Great Bear
5. Rivers: Fraser, Mackenzie, Saskatchewan, St. Lawrence, and Ottawa
6. Large water bodies: Pacific Ocean, Atlantic Ocean, Arctic Ocean, Hudson Bay, and the Gulf of St. Lawrence
7. Neighbours: the United States including Alaska, and Greenland

This logo will tell you where there is an ArcVoyager exercise.

A QUIZ FOR CANADIANS

In the same way that we have a mental image of Canada's map, we have a stock of information about Canada's geography, history, and culture that shapes how we see ourselves as Canadians. In 1998, a survey was conducted by The Dominion Institute, a national charity dedicated to helping Canadians better understand their country. This survey was taken of average Canadians to see what they know about Canada. Let's see how you do on the same survey. Answer the following questions in your notebook. A warning though, the group of Canadian adults who wrote this quiz did not do very well on many of the questions! The percentage of their correct answers is provided at the end of each question. We hope you will do better than they did!

You may be interested to know that the average score of Canadians who wrote this quiz was only 49%. Residents of Manitoba, Saskatchewan, and Ontario did best as did older people, males, people with higher income, and those with higher levels of education. If you did well, congratulations! If you were not pleased with your score, don't be discouraged. In this book there are many opportunities to learn more about Canada and what makes it unique. The answers are provided on p. 16.

INTERNET

To learn more about Canada, check www.macabees.ab.ca/ canada/canada.html

For more surveys on Canadians' knowledge of Canada and related information, check www.dominion.ca

A QUIZ FOR

1. Which of the following slogans is associated with Canada's Constitution? Is it ... (44%)
   a) Liberty, equality, and fraternity
   b) Peace, order, and good government
   c) Life, liberty, and the pursuit of happiness

2. Which Canadian prime minister regularly sought the advice of his dead mother and dog? (30%)

3. Which of the following was Canada's first woman prime minister? (81%)
   a) Audrey McLaughlin
   b) Jeanne Sauvé
   c) Kim Campbell
   d) Flora MacDonald

4. Which river is Canada's longest? Is it ... (32%)
   a) the Mackenzie
   b) the St. Lawrence
   c) the Fraser
   d) the Saskatchewan

5. Who coined the phrase "the global village" and argued that "the medium is the message?" (32%)

6. What is the highest honour that Canada gives to its citizens for outstanding achievement and service to their country or humanity at large? (43%)

7. Which hockey team has won more Stanley Cups than any other? (74%)

8. Which province was the first to introduce medicare? (26%)

9. Sir Louis Hippolyte LaFontaine and Robert Baldwin ... (48%)
   a) were the first Europeans to see the Rocky Mountains.
   b) were French and British military commanders.
   c) formed an alliance of reformers in Lower and Upper Canada.

10. Which of the following Canadian politicians could be called the "last father of Confederation?" (35%)
    a) Lucien Bouchard
    b) Pierre Trudeau
    c) Joey Smallwood
    d) Tommy Douglas

CANADIANS

⑪ In 1992, Roberta Bondar became the first Canadian woman ... (72%)
a) to play in the National Hockey League.
b) to be launched into outer space.
c) to win an Oscar for best actress.
d) to be named president of General Motors of Canada.

⑫ Who composed our national anthem "O Canada?" Was it ... (39%)
a) Sir John A. Macdonald
b) Calixa Lavallée
c) Robert Charlebois
d) Gordon Lightfoot

⑬ What major event happened in Winnipeg in 1919? Was it ... (25%)
a) a general strike
b) the Red River Rebellion
c) a great flood
d) the first Stanley Cup hockey game

⑭ What famous sailboat or schooner, commemorated on the 10-cent coin, was built in Nova Scotia? Was it ... (85%)
a) the *Flying Dutchman*
b) the *Titanic*
c) the *Bluenose*
d) *la Grande Hermine*

⑮ Which of the following people are Canadians? (9%)
a) Hockey player Chris Chelios
b) Country singer Shania Twain
c) Actor Candice Bergen
d) Race car driver Jacques Villeneuve
e) Actor Michael J. Fox
f) Actor Catherine Deneuve

⑯ What is the name of the new territory created in Canada's north in 1999? (13%)

⑰ In 1980, who set out to run across Canada to raise money to fight cancer? (86%)

⑱ On what day do Canadians honour those who served in wartime? (85%)

⑲ Who invented the first practical and commercially successful snowmobile? (60%)

⑳ In which province, famous for its deposits of dinosaur bones, would you find Dinosaur Provincial Park? (60%)

ARE YOU A PROUD CANADIAN?

1. Different factors such as our experiences, personality, and the influences we have felt combine to make us more or less proud to be Canadians. How do you feel about being a Canadian? To measure your sense of pride in Canada, try the following quiz. In your notebook, answer each question using the scale in the margin.

How proud are you of Canada in each of these areas?

a) the way democracy works in Canada
b) Canada's political influence in the world
c) Canada's economic achievement
d) Canada's social security system
e) Canada's scientific and technological achievements
f) Canada's achievements in sports
g) Canada's achievement in the arts and literature
h) Canada's armed forces
i) Canada's history

Total score: _____ Class average score: _____

2. What is your total score on the nine questions?

3. With your teacher's help, calculate a class average for each question and for the entire survey.

4. On this nine-item quiz, scores range from a maximum of 45 for someone *Very Proud* of national achievements in all nine areas, to a minimum of 9 for someone *Not Proud at All* of the nation in all areas. Compare your scores to those from a survey that was done in 23 countries including Canada. As you can see in Fig. 1-2, Canadians were the third most proud of their country's achievements among residents of the countries who took part in this survey. Did you find a similar score in your class? If not, can you account for any differences?

5. When responses to individual questions are considered, some interesting patterns appear (Fig. 1-3). Consider Canada's ranking for each of the nine questions. Remember that overall, Canada was third.

    a) Choose three areas in which Canada was ranked first or second. Why do you think Canadians are particularly proud of achievements in these areas?

    b) Choose three areas in which Canada ranked fifth or worse. Why do you think that Canadians are less proud in these areas?

6. The numbers in brackets next to *Canada* in Fig. 1-3 represent the percentage of Canadians who indicated that they were *Very Proud* or *Somewhat Proud* in this area. Were the responses in your class similar to those shown here? Try to explain any differences that you see.

Use this scale to answer the questions. Record the numbers for each answer.	
Very Proud	5
Somewhat Proud	4
Can't Choose	3
Not Very Proud	2
Not Proud at All	1

social security: government help for those in need, such as the ill, aged, or unemployed

All the countries mentioned in this book are labelled on the world map on the inside back cover of this book.

PRIDE IN COUNTRIES' ACHIEVEMENTS (SCORE OUT OF 45)

Ireland	35.4	Japan	31.1	Italy	27.5
United States	34.7	Spain	29.8	Czech Republic	26.6
Canada	33.8	The Philippines	29.2	Hungary	25.6
Austria	32.9	West Germany*	29.0	Slovakia	25.4
New Zealand	32.8	Sweden	28.4	Poland	25.4
Norway	31.7	Bulgaria	28.3	Russia	25.2
Great Britain	31.2	East Germany*	27.9	Latvia	25.0
The Netherlands	31.1	Slovenia	27.8		

△ **Fig. 1-2** *These scores represent the overall feelings of national pride felt by citizens in many countries.*

*Note that West Germany and East Germany were considered separately in this study even though it was done several years after German reunification. Why might the authors of this survey have made this choice?

COUNTRY RANKINGS ON PRIDE SURVEY

Democracy	Political Influence	Economic Achievement	Social Security
1. Canada (80.7%)	United States	United States	Austria
2. United States	Canada (73.7%)	West Germany	Canada (78.5%)
3. Netherlands	Ireland	Ireland	Netherlands
4. Norway	Norway	Austria	West Germany
5. Ireland	New Zealand	Hungary	Ireland
		12. Canada (59.9%)	

Science and Technology	Sports	Arts and Literature	Armed Forces	History
1. United States	Ireland	Ireland	United States	Ireland
2. Canada (86.8%)	New Zealand	Italy	Great Britain	Bulgaria
3. New Zealand	Bulgaria	New Zealand	Ireland	Czech Republic
4. Austria	Slovakia	Canada (82.6%)	New Zealand	Great Britain
5. Great Britain	Norway	United States	Canada (57.6%)	United States
	11. Canada (80.1%)			7. Canada (81.5%)

△ **Fig. 1-3** *These are the specific levels of pride in the nine areas surveyed. The top five countries for each are listed along with Canada's rank if Canada is not in the top five.*

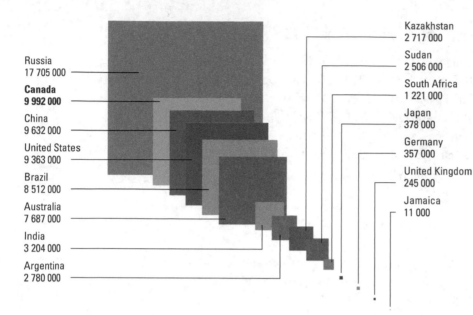

Russia
17 705 000

Canada
9 992 000

China
9 632 000

United States
9 363 000

Brazil
8 512 000

Australia
7 687 000

India
3 204 000

Argentina
2 780 000

Kazakhstan
2 717 000

Sudan
2 506 000

South Africa
1 221 000

Japan
378 000

Germany
357 000

United Kingdom
245 000

Jamaica
11 000

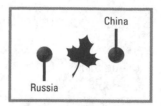

△ **Fig. 1-4** *Canada is the second largest country in the world.*

◁ **Fig. 1-5** *The areas of the 10 largest countries in the world are listed first, followed by the areas of five other countries (in km²).*

CANADA ON THE WORLD STAGE

On what basis would you compare living in Canada to living in another country such as Japan, Ethiopia, Argentina, or any one of the over 180 other countries in the world? To compare Canada to other countries, there are many different types of measurements we could use, including size, population, density, and wealth.

Area

Canada is one of the world's largest countries (Fig. 1-4). Fig. 1-5 compares the areas of the ten largest countries in the world and includes the areas of five other countries.

Population

Compared to many other countries, Canada does not have that many people (Fig. 1-6). In a world with more than 6 billion people, our population of 30 600 000 in 1998 falls far behind that of many countries. In fact, only one out of every 200 people in the world is Canadian. Fig. 1-7 compares Canada to those countries with the largest populations in the world.

Canada's population in 2009 33,739,000

▽ **Fig. 1-6** *Canada's population ranks only 32nd in the world.*

China

Algeria

Tanzania

Population Density

You have just seen that Canada is a very large country with a fairly small population. The relationship between the area and population of a country can be shown using a simple measurement called **population density**. This can be calculated by dividing the country's population by its area. Let's calculate Canada's population density:

30 600 000 people ÷ 9 992 000 km²
= 3.1 people/km² (population density)

This does not mean that there are three people living on each and every square kilometre of Canada. Rather, population density is just a way of making a general comparison of the relationship between the area and the population of a country.

Population densities vary enormously from place to place (Fig. 1-8). The Western Sahara, for example, has 0.8 people/km², while the Falkland Islands has 0.2 people/km². At the other extreme are crowded countries like Singapore (5000 people/km²). If we examine the population densities of countries, we see a smaller, but still significant range of values (Fig. 1-9).

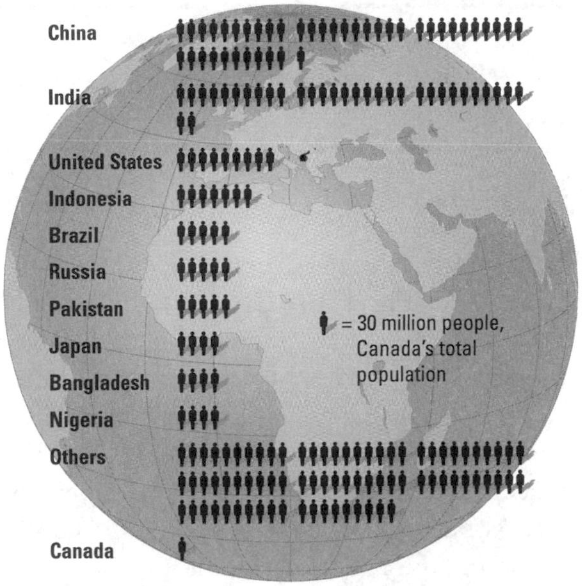

△ **Fig. 1-7** *Showing Canada's population like this clearly indicates how few people we have here compared to countries that have the largest populations.*

▽ **Fig. 1-8** *Canada ranks 206th in the world in terms of population density.*

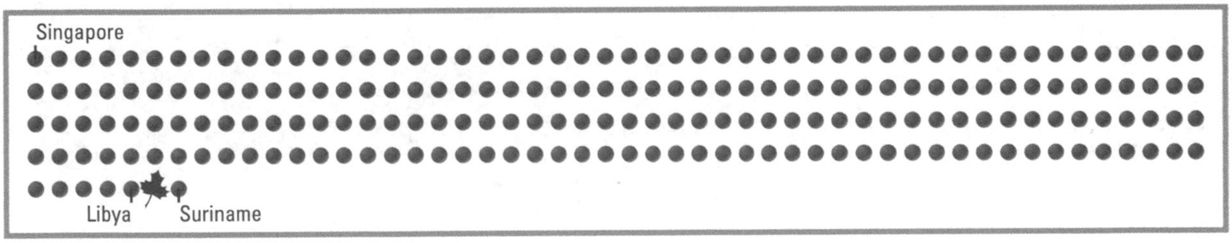

◁ **Fig. 1-9** *What do you notice about Canada's population density compared to those of countries that have the largest populations?*

POPULATION DENSITY (PEOPLE/KM²), 1996

Country	Density	Country	Density
Argentina	13	Jamaica	237
Australia	2	Japan	333
Bangladesh	832	Kazakhstan	6
Brazil	19	Nigeria	112
Canada	3	Pakistan	166
China	127	Russia	9
Germany	229	South Africa	36
India	289	Sudan	12
Indonesia	105	United Kingdom	240
		United States	28

Luxembourg

France

△ **Fig. 1-10** *Canada ranks 11th in the world in terms of GDP per capita.*

Wealth

Canadians have higher average incomes than people in most other parts of the world (Fig. 1-10). Even Canadians with lower incomes might be considered wealthy by many people who live in Asia, Africa, and Latin America. It is not easy to measure a country's wealth in a clear and descriptive way. A commonly used measurement is **Gross Domestic Product (GDP) per capita**. GDP is the value of all of the goods and services produced in the country in a year. As such, it is a measure of the size of the entire economy. When the GDP is divided by the country's population, the result is an indication of the country's wealth.

Per capita means per person.

Many of the citizens of a country with a high GDP per capita are probably better able to afford the basics of life: food, shelter, clothing, and medical care. They may also be able to afford some of the luxuries, such as cars, computers, and trips. Likewise, many citizens of countries with a low GDP per capita might have difficulty affording even basic needs. Of course, no matter what the GDP per capita is in a country, there are people living in various degrees of wealth and poverty in every country of the world.

GDP per capita varies enormously from country to country. If we divide the world into two groups of countries, the wealthier countries have an average GDP per capita of $18 130 while the poorer countries have a GDP per capita of only $1090. A sample of the world's countries reveals the great range of values and a large gap between the richer and poorer countries (Fig. 1-11).

These values are in US dollars. American currency is almost always used to make economic comparisons among countries.

COUNTRY GDP PER CAPITA

◁ **Fig. 1-11** *GDP per capita*

Country	GDP per capita	Country	GDP per capita
Argentina	$8060	Japan	$34 630
Australia	$17 980	Luxembourg	$39 850
Bangladesh	$230	Mexico	$4010
Canada	$19 570	Russia	$2650
China	$530	South Africa	$3010
Egypt	$710	South Korea	$8220
Ethiopia	$130	United States	$25 860
France	$23 470		

SNAPSHOTS: CANADA AND THE REST OF THE WORLD

There are many different ways of measuring where Canada stands compared to other countries, which reflect the different circumstances of its citizens. This section shows how Canada ranks in several other areas.

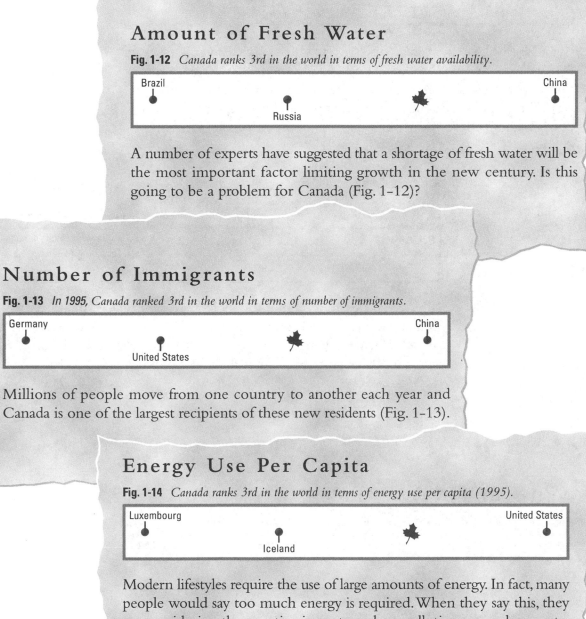

Amount of Fresh Water

Fig. 1-12 *Canada ranks 3rd in the world in terms of fresh water availability.*

Brazil   China
                Russia

A number of experts have suggested that a shortage of fresh water will be the most important factor limiting growth in the new century. Is this going to be a problem for Canada (Fig. 1-12)?

Number of Immigrants

Fig. 1-13 *In 1995, Canada ranked 3rd in the world in terms of number of immigrants.*

Germany   China
             United States

Millions of people move from one country to another each year and Canada is one of the largest recipients of these new residents (Fig. 1-13).

Energy Use Per Capita

Fig. 1-14 *Canada ranks 3rd in the world in terms of energy use per capita (1995).*

Luxembourg   United States
               Iceland

Modern lifestyles require the use of large amounts of energy. In fact, many people would say too much energy is required. When they say this, they are considering the negative impacts, such as pollution or nuclear waste, of energy production and use. In any case, the energy use per capita in a country is a reliable indicator of the level of economic development in the country (Fig. 1-14).

Average Life Expectancy

Fig. 1-15 *Canada is tied for 3rd in the world in terms of average life expectancy.*

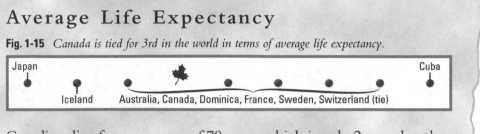

Canadians live for an average of 78 years, which is only 2 years less than the Japanese who have the longest life expectancy (Fig. 1-15). By comparison, residents of some African countries live, on average, for less than 45 years. Why would such large differences exist, and what do the differences indicate about these countries?

Number of Cars and Trucks Produced

Fig. 1-16 *Canada ranks 7th in the world in terms of number of cars and trucks produced.*

Motor vehicle production is the most important type of manufacturing in many countries and can be used as an indicator of the importance of manufacturing in general. Out of over 180 countries, Canada ranks 7th in terms of the number of cars and trucks produced (Fig. 1-16).

Value of Foreign Trade

Fig. 1-17 *Canada ranks 7th in the world in terms of the value of foreign trade.*

The value of foreign trade is an indication of how involved a country is in the growing world economy. Canada is a major "player" in international trade (Fig. 1-17).

QUESTIONS

ANALYZE AND APPLY

1. a) Locate the countries listed in Fig. 1-5. Are these large countries found in any particular part of the world or are they found in all parts of the world?

    b) Group the countries according to size. How many groups did you decide to have? Which countries are similar in size to Canada?

2. a) Fig. 1-18 lists the ten largest countries along with five other major countries. Copy this chart into your notebook and fill in the missing information. You might want to work with a partner to share the calculations. The values for China are shown. (The difference in area between China and Canada is $9\ 632\ 000 - 9\ 992\ 000 = -360\ 000\ km^2$. The percentage of Canada's size can be calculated using the formula $9\ 632\ 000 \div 9\ 992\ 000 \times 100\%$.)

    b) Add together the areas of Canada and the United States.

        i.   How does this number compare to the area of Russia?

        ii. What special problems would the government of a country as large as Russia have?

        iii. Until 1991, Russia was part of a much larger country called the Union of Soviet Socialist Republics (U.S.S.R.). The U.S.S.R. split into 15 new countries, two of which are large enough to appear on this list. Which country, along with Russia, was part of the U.S.S.R.?

    c) Divide the list into four categories based on size (very large, large, medium, and small). To do this, look for natural breaks in the range of numbers. For example, there is an obvious break between Russia and all of the others. Note that there won't be the same number of countries in each group.

    d) Draw four boxes, each 3 cm by 3 cm, in your notebook. Each box represents one square kilometre.

    e) Choose one country from each group in your answer to 2c (be sure to include Canada!) and label one box with the name of each country.

    f) Using the information from Fig. 1-9, within each box, draw the number of dots needed to show the population density of the country. In Canada's box, for example, put three small dots.

    g) Given the range of values represented here, write a brief paragraph to describe Canada's population density situation. In your paragraph, indicate what the advantages and disadvantages are, for Canada, of having this level of population density.

3. a) Using the information from Fig. 1-11, group the countries into 'wealthier' and 'poorer' categories.

    b) Were there any countries that were difficult to classify? What might that mean about the level of economic development in these countries?

    c) Outline at least one shortcoming of GDP per capita as a measure of a country's wealth. (Hint: Think about what this information does not give you.)

THINK AND COMMUNICATE

4. You have decided to become Internet 'pen pals' with a student in Indonesia who knows virtually nothing about Canada and has asked you to describe Canada. Based on what you have learned in this chapter, along with what you knew beforehand, write a brief, point-form description of Canada that you could e-mail to your pen pal.

▽ **Fig. 1-18**

Country	Area (km^2)	Amount larger (+)/smaller (-) than Canada (km^2)	Percentage of Canada's size
Russia	17 705 000		
Canada	9 992 000		
China	9 632 000	-360 000	96.4
United States	9 363 000		
Brazil	8 512 000		
Australia	7 687 000		
India	3 204 000		
Argentina	2 780 000		
Kazakhstan	2 717 000		
Sudan	2 506 000		

Other Countries:

South Africa	1 221 000
Japan	378 000
Germany	357 000
United Kingdom	245 000
Jamaica	11 000

ANSWERS TO CANADA QUIZ (pp. 6-7)

1. b) Peace, order, and good government
2. Sir William Lyon Mackenzie King
3. c) Kim Campbell
4. a) the Mackenzie
5. Marshall McLuhan
6. Order of Canada
7. Montréal Canadiens
8. Saskatchewan
9. c) formed an alliance of reformers in Lower and Upper Canada.
10. c) Joey Smallwood
11. b) to be launched into outer space.
12. b) Calixa Lavallée
13. a) a general strike
14. c) the *Bluenose*
15. b) Shania Twain; d) Jacques Villeneuve; e) Michael J. Fox (you need all three, and only these three to gain credit for this question)
16. Nunavut
17. Terry Fox
18. Remembrance Day occurs on November 11th (either answer is fine).
19. J.-Armand Bombardier
20. Alberta

To find out about other famous Canadians, check alvin.lbl.gov/ terning/Canadians.html

UNIT 2

Methods of
Geographic Inquiry

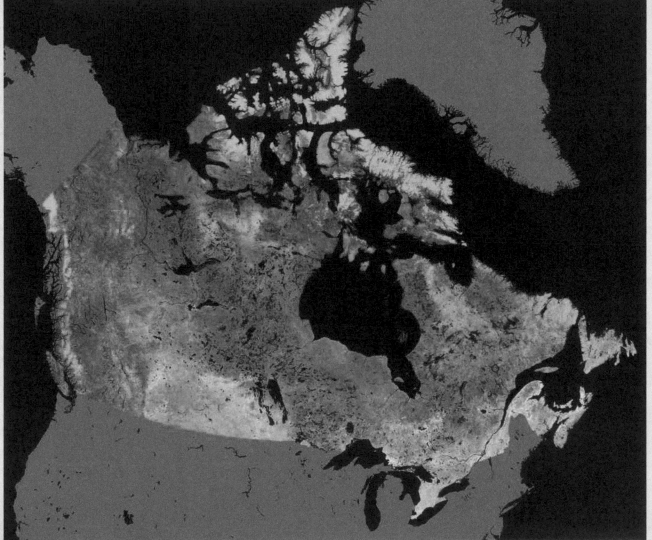

An NOAA AVHRR image of Canada

This unit will familiarize you with the skills that you need to study geography. It should serve as a **reference tool** to be used at any point during your study.

Maps: Geography's Basic Tools

2

Carpenters and dentists need good tools to do their jobs properly. Geographers, too, need good tools to do their job. One of the most important of these is the map. People have used maps for over 4500 years for exploring, determining their location and direction of travel, and describing the shape of the world. You may have consulted a map while camping, canoeing, or hiking. Perhaps, in preparing for a trip, you used a road map to plan your route. Likewise, you may have used a street map to find your way in an unfamiliar neighbourhood or city.

Maps are very useful tools. They help you visualize the shape of countries and locate important features. There are many different types of maps, and each has certain advantages. In this chapter, we will learn about map projections, the key features of maps, and how different types of maps are used.

MAP PROJECTIONS

1. Using a marking pen, draw an outline of the earth's continents on the skin of an orange to create a simple version of a globe.
2. Carefully peel the orange so that the continents are intact.
3. Flatten the skin of the orange on a piece of paper to create your version of a world map.
4. How closely does your world map resemble your globe?
5. Compare your flattened orange peel to those of your classmates.
6. a) What are some advantages of using globes rather than maps?
   b) What are some advantages of using maps rather than globes?

A globe is the only accurate method to represent the earth which, after all, is a ball or sphere. It is not very convenient, however, to carry a globe in your pocket. Maps were created to solve this problem and to provide detailed images of small areas. When the features of a globe are transferred onto a flat surface, a **map projection** is created. There are hundreds of different ways to project the globe onto a flat surface, so there are hundreds of different projections. Think of your orange peel and those of your classmates.

KEY TERMS

map projection

Mercator projection

equal-area projection

Winkel Tripel projection

map

scale

general-purpose map

thematic map

topographic map

When you are done, you can eat the orange as a snack.

INTERNET

To learn more about map projections, www.geosys.com/cgi-bin/genobject/mapskills_project/tig5e6

Most map projections are created on computers, using complex mathematical calculations. Each map projection has certain characteristics that make it useful for a specific purpose. Each one, however, contains distortions such as enlarging some areas and shrinking others, or providing inaccurate directions. Just remember, what you see in a map is not, and cannot be, a true representation of the earth!

distortions: inaccuracies that result when information is twisted or pulled out of its original shape

1. Your teacher will provide you with a world map. This map represents a very famous projection: the **Mercator projection**.

2. On this map, locate, label, and shade the following countries:

   1. Greenland
   2. Canada
   3. Brazil
   4. Argentina
   5. Algeria
   6. Sudan
   7. Saudi Arabia
   8. India

3. In your notebook, rank the countries by size from largest to smallest according to how they appear on your map.

4. Use an atlas to find the actual area of each country. Rank the countries from largest to smallest according to their actual size.

5. Compare your ranking of the countries in question 3 with the actual ranking in question 4. What differences do you notice?

6. a) Why do you think these differences exist?

   b) What do these differences suggest about the Mercator projection and about what it should and should not be used for?

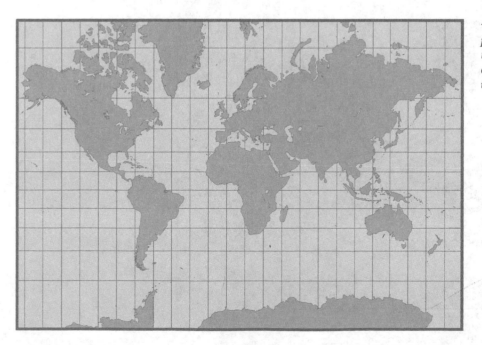

◁ **Fig. 2-1** *The Mercator projection was often used in the past to show the countries of the world in atlases and wall maps.*

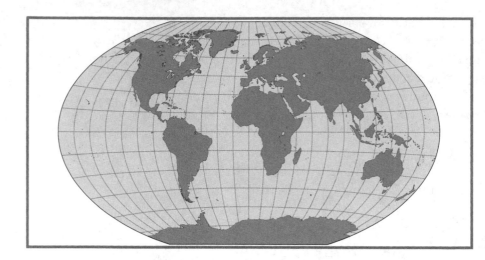

◁ **Fig. 2-2** *The Winkel Tripel projection provides a balance between size and shape.*

A map projection should be used only for the purposes for which it was designed. The **Mercator projection**, for example, is well suited for navigation charts because it gives true compass bearings between points. On the other hand, it greatly distorts the size of land masses (Fig. 2-1). Countries near the equator appear smaller than they actually are while those closer to the poles appear larger.

For more information on compass bearings, see p. 27.

In the past, the Mercator projection was used so widely that it became the standard for world maps. This gave people a mistaken impression about the actual size of countries. At the United Nations, many representatives of tropical countries felt that the importance of their countries had been underestimated because they appeared smaller on the map than their actual size. As a result, most nations and interna-

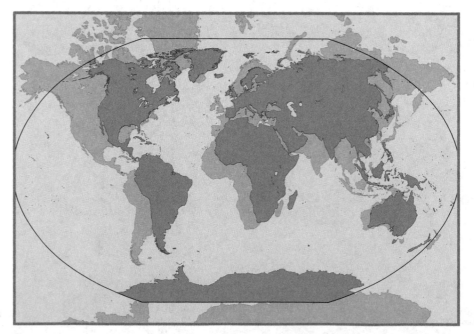

◁ **Fig. 2-3** *The Mercator projection (in green) distorts the earth's surface significantly more than the Winkel Tripel projection (in pink).*

tional organizations now use maps that show the correct size of countries in relation to one other. An **equal-area projection** is one method
of achieving this goal.

In 1998, the National Geographic Society, which produces more maps
each year than any other organization, decided to address the problem of
distortion on world maps. It adopted the **Winkel Tripel** projection for its
standand world reference map. It is a compromise between all types of
distortion. There is still some distortion, but the Winkel Tripel projection provides the best balance between size, shape, distance, and direction.
This projection gives a more realistic representation of the earth (Fig. 2–3).

To see maps of places that you
may hear about in the news,
check www-map.lib.umn.edu/
news.html

WHAT IS A MAP?

A **map** is a representation of the earth's features drawn on a flat surface.
Unlike photographs, maps cannot show you what the land actually looks
like. Instead, maps use symbols and colours to represent the features of an
area. For example, streets may be shown as red lines, and airports may
be shown with a drawing of an airplane.

A map also simplifies the real world; not every tree or telephone pole
is usually shown on a map. The maker of any map must decide which
features to include and which ones to ignore, depending on the map's

▽ **Fig. 2-4** *The basic features
of a map*

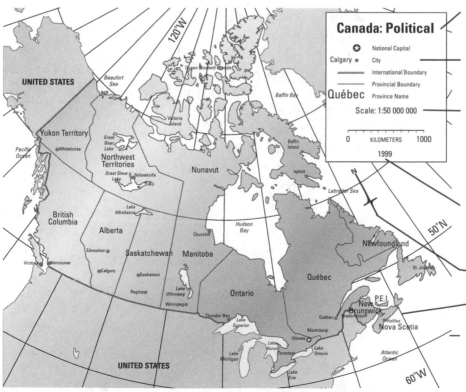

Title:
Identifies area shown and topic,
purpose, or focus.

Legend:
Explains meaning of symbols and
colours.

Scale:
Compares distance between
points on the map with the actual
distance between those points on
the earth's surface. Allows
reader to measure distance and
to calculate area.

Date of Publication:
Indicates if information is recent.

Direction:
Represented in two ways:

i.   by direction arrow or
     symbol

ii. by the use of latitude
     and longitude

Borders:
Set the map apart from other
information.

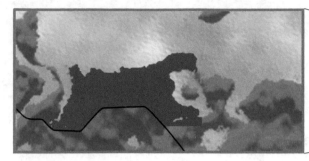

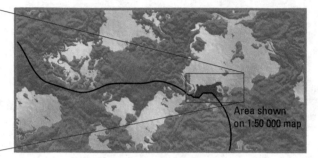

Area shown
on 1:50 000 map

△ **Fig. 2-5** *A large-scale map 1:50 000*   △ **Fig. 2-6** *A small-scale map 1:250 000*

purpose. For example, someone with a sweet tooth might want a map that includes every candy shop in town. A map that includes only those features relating to a distinct purpose is easy to use since it allows the map reader to focus on specific characteristics within an area.

MAP REQUIREMENTS

Whenever you draw a map, certain features should always be included. These features are described in Fig. 2-4. These features help the map reader understand the purpose of the map.

If a map does not indicate direction, assume that the top of the map is north.

LARGE- AND SMALL-SCALE MAPS

The **scale** of a map will vary according to the amount of detail required. Maps may be classified according to two general categories. **Large-scale maps** show a large amount of detail of a small area (Fig. 2-5). Maps with scales of 1:50 000 and 1:25 000 or less are large-scale maps. Maps with these scales are used to show detailed information about a small area for such things as residential planning, hiking, and military purposes.

1:50 000 means that 1 cm on the map represents 50 000 cm (or 500m) on the earth's surface.

On the other hand, **small-scale maps** show a small amount of detail of a large area (Fig. 2-6). Maps with scales of 1:250 000 and 1:500 000 or more are small-scale maps. These maps are used to show general details, such as political, physical, and economic information.

TYPES OF MAPS

Geographers and cartographers make many types of maps. Some examples are political, navigational, topographic, vegetation, and weather maps. Within this vast range, we will examine only a few. We can classify these under three broad headings: general-purpose maps, thematic maps, and topographic maps.

cartographer: a professional map-maker

General-purpose Maps

General-purpose maps provide many types of information on one map. Most atlas maps, wall maps, and road maps fall into this category. Some of the things that might be shown on general-purpose maps are:

- bodies of water
- roads
- railway lines

- parks
- elevations
- towns and cities

When all of these features are combined, a general-purpose map is created. These maps give a broad understanding of the location and features of an area. You can gain an understanding about the type of landscape, the location of urban places, and the location of major transportation routes all at once. Fig. 2-4 is an example of a general-purpose map.

Thematic Maps

If you require very specific information about a place, **thematic maps** are useful. These maps are designed to show information on one particular topic. Because only one type of information needs to be shown, thematic maps tend to be easy to understand. Study the examples in Fig. 2-7.

Topographic Maps

Topographic maps use symbols to show a variety of features (Fig. 2-8). If you want to examine the characteristics of a small area of the earth's surface in detail, these maps are useful (Fig. 2-9).

▽ **Fig. 2-7** *Each of these thematic maps shows a different characteristic of the area shown in Fig. 2-9.*

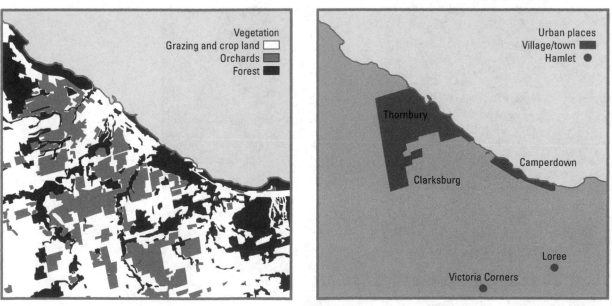

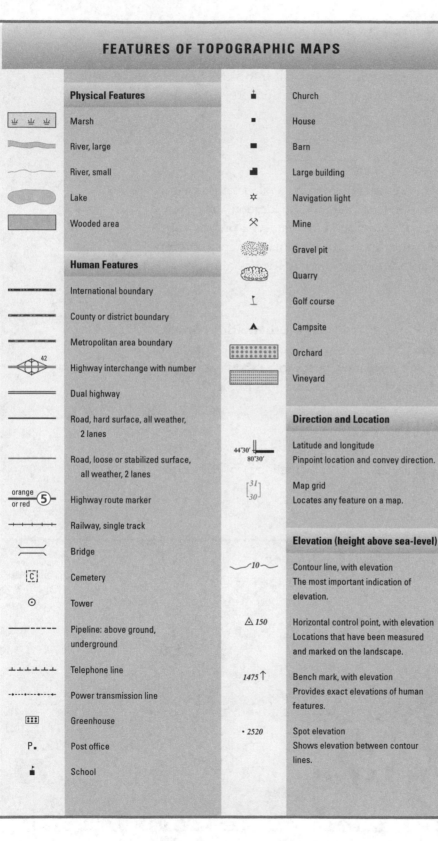

FEATURES OF TOPOGRAPHIC MAPS

Physical Features

Marsh	
River, large	
River, small	
Lake	
Wooded area	

Human Features

International boundary	
County or district boundary	
Metropolitan area boundary	
Highway interchange with number	42
Dual highway	
Road, hard surface, all weather, 2 lanes	
Road, loose or stabilized surface, all weather, 2 lanes	
Highway route marker	orange or red (5)
Railway, single track	
Bridge	
Cemetery	C
Tower	
Pipeline: above ground, underground	
Telephone line	
Power transmission line	
Greenhouse	
Post office	P.
School	

Church	
House	
Barn	
Large building	
Navigation light	
Mine	
Gravel pit	
Quarry	
Golf course	
Campsite	
Orchard	
Vineyard	

Direction and Location

44°30' 80°30'	Latitude and longitude Pinpoint location and convey direction.
31 30	Map grid Locates any feature on a map.

Elevation (height above sea-level)

~10~	Contour line, with elevation The most important indication of elevation.
△ 150	Horizontal control point, with elevation Locations that have been measured and marked on the landscape.
1475 ↑	Bench mark, with elevation Provides exact elevations of human features.
· 2520	Spot elevation Shows elevation between contour lines.

◁ **Fig. 2-8** *Here are some map symbols that are used on topographic maps. Features such as woods, orchards, and lakes, are represented by coloured patterns called* **area symbols. Line symbols** *represent features that are linear in nature, such as roads, railways, and telephone lines. Features that occupy a specific point, such as buildings, bridges, and towers, are represented by* **point symbols**.

Fig. 2-9 ▷
A topographic map of the Thornbury area in the Georgian Bay region of Ontario.

Scale: 1:50 000 (1 cm = 0.5 km) Contour interval: 10m

QUESTIONS

CHECK YOUR UNDERSTANDING

1. Why is a globe the only accurate way to represent the earth?

2. a) Why do all maps have distortions?

   b) What kinds of distortions do maps have?

3. Using the Mercator projection as an example, describe what can happen when a map projection is used for a purpose for which it is not designed.

4. What is the advantage of an equal-area projection?

5. a) What is a map? Use your own words.

   b) Why are maps useful tools?

   c) How do maps help focus the reader's attention on just a few specific things?

6. What are general-purpose maps used for?

7. a) What is the purpose of thematic maps?

   b) Why are thematic maps useful?

   c) Find three examples of thematic maps in this book. Give the page reference and the theme of each map.

8. a) What is the purpose of topographic maps?

   b) List the symbols used for showing elevation on topographic maps.

ANALYZE AND APPLY

9. a) List the essential features of a map.

   b) Draw a sketch map of your classroom. Make sure that all of the features listed above are included on your map.

10. Construct a chart, similar to Fig. 2-10, to compare large-scale and small-scale maps.

▽ Fig. 2-10

	Large-scale Maps	Small-scale Maps
Definition		
Typical Scales		
Purpose		

11. a) What features are found on general-purpose maps?

    b) Examine the road map in Fig. 3-2, p. 28. Which features from your answer to 11a are shown on the road map?

    c) Describe how the features are shown on the road map.

12. Refer to Fig. 2-9.

    a) i. What is the scale of the map?

       ii. What is the straight-line distance, in kilometres, between the intersection in Loree and the arena in Thornbury?

       iii. What is the shortest distance, in kilometres, by road between the intersection in Loree and the main, four-way intersection in Clarksburg?

    b) In which direction does Indian Brook flow? How did you determine this?

    c) What features are found at the following letters?

       i. A   iii. C   v. E

       ii. B   iv. D   vi. F

    d) Calculate the difference in elevation between the top and bottom of the ski run for the following locations:

       i. the ski run between G and H

       ii. the ski run between I and J

    e) Which ski run would be more challenging? Why?

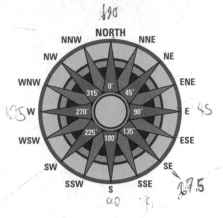

◁ **Fig. 3-1** *A compass rose shows directions (compass points) and bearings (measured clockwise from north).*

To learn more about the compass rose, check www.gisnet.com/gis/notebook/comprose.html

Finding locations is an age-old problem that involves every person in one way or another. While you might use a general location to meet a friend outside a movie theatre, a geologist studying earthquakes might need to measure locations to a tiny fraction of a millimetre. In this chapter, you will learn a variety of ways to locate places on maps.

COMPASS POINTS AND BEARINGS

When giving directions, you need to know where you are and where you want to go. For example, people often use phrases such as "travel south for 1 km, then go west when you reach the traffic lights." For these directions to work, you must know where south and west are located in relation to where you are located. On maps, references to **compass points** (south and west) are shown on the **compass rose** as shown in Fig. 3–1. Most atlas maps do not use a compass rose because direction is indicated by lines of latitude and longitude.

The principal points of a compass are North, East, South, and West. Halfway between the four principal points are points that combine their directions to form North-East, South-East, South-West, and North-West. A further subdivision of the directions between the cardinal points and ordinal points leads to another set of combinations, such as North North-East which, as you can expect, is between North and North-East.

Direction can be given more accurately if degrees (called **compass bearings**) are used rather than compass points. Compass bearings measure

The four principal points of a compass are called the cardinal points.

The secondary points of a compass are called ordinal points.

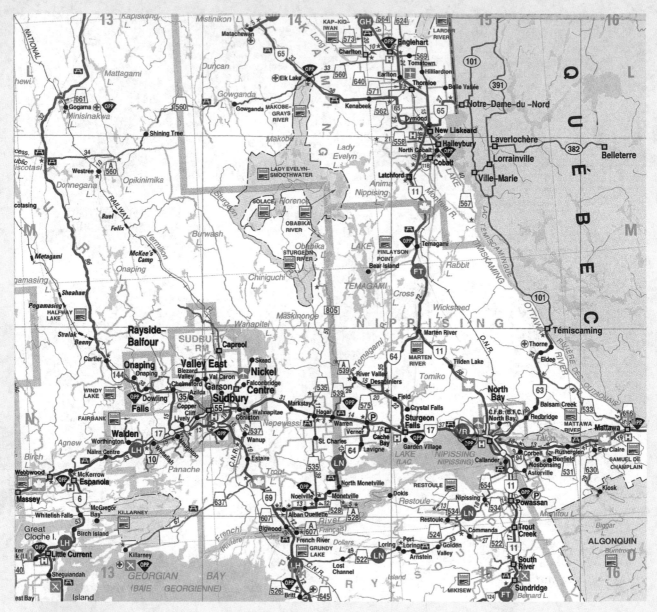

△ **Fig. 3-2** *Find the community of Temagami located in square M15 in this portion of the Ontario road map.*

the angle of a direction in relation to North, moving in a clockwise direction. The use of compass bearings is a more accurate method for stating direction because all points of the compass rose, from 0° to 360°, can be used (Fig. 3–1).

0° and 360° are the same point on the compass.

GRID SYSTEMS

The most common way to locate a place on a map is to use a grid system. In this chapter, we will look at three different grid systems.

L E G E N D *LÉGENDE*

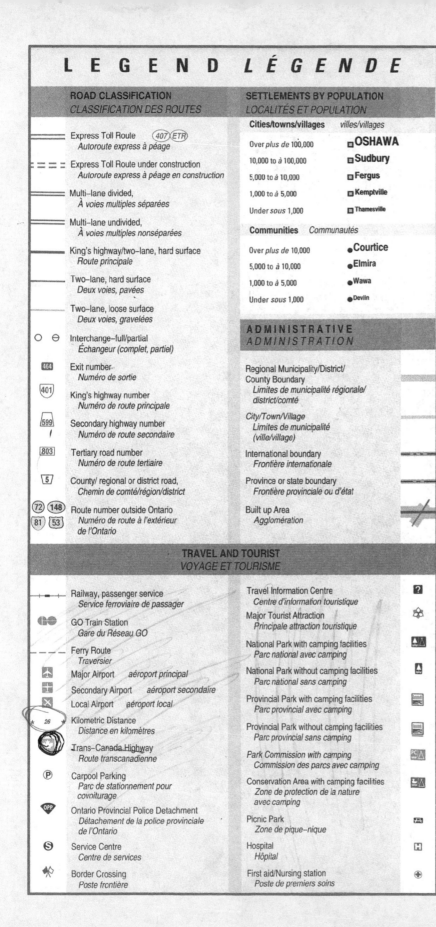

ROAD CLASSIFICATION
CLASSIFICATION DES ROUTES

Express Toll Route (407)(ETR)
Autoroute express à péage

Express Toll Route under construction
Autoroute express à péage en construction

Multi–lane divided,
À voies multiples séparées

Multi–lane undivided,
À voies multiples nonséparées

King's highway/two–lane, hard surface
Route principale

Two–lane, hard surface
Deux voies, pavées

Two–lane, loose surface
Deux voies, gravelées

Interchange–full/partial
Échangeur (complet, partiel)

464 Exit number
Numéro de sortie

401 King's highway number
Numéro de route principale

599 Secondary highway number
Numéro de route secondaire

803 Tertiary road number
Numéro de route tertiaire

5 County/ regional or district road,
Chemin de comté/région/district

72 148 Route number outside Ontario
81 53 *Numéro de route à l'extérieur
de l'Ontario*

SETTLEMENTS BY POPULATION
LOCALITÉS ET POPULATION

Cities/towns/villages   *villes/villages*

Over *plus de* 100,000   OSHAWA

10,000 to *à* 100,000   Sudbury

5,000 to *à* 10,000   Fergus

1,000 to *à* 5,000   Kemptville

Under *sous* 1,000   Thamesville

Communities   *Communautés*

Over *plus de* 10,000   Courtice

5,000 to *à* 10,000   Elmira

1,000 to *à* 5,000   Wawa

Under *sous* 1,000   Devlin

ADMINISTRATIVE
ADMINISTRATION

Regional Municipality/District/
County Boundary
*Limites de municipalité régionale/
district/comté*

City/Town/Village
*Limites de municipalité
(ville/village)*

International boundary
Frontière internationale

Province or state boundary
Frontière provinciale ou d'état

Built up Area
Agglomération

TRAVEL AND TOURIST
VOYAGE ET TOURISME

Railway, passenger service
Service ferroviaire de passager

GO Train Station
Gare du Réseau GO

Ferry Route
Traversier

Major Airport   *aéroport principal*

Secondary Airport   *aéroport secondaire*

Local Airport   *aéroport local*

26 Kilometric Distance
Distance en kilomètres

Trans–Canada Highway
Route transcanadienne

P Carpool Parking
*Parc de stationnement pour
covoiturage*

OPP Ontario Provincial Police Detachment
*Détachement de la police provinciale
de l'Ontario*

S Service Centre
Centre de services

Border Crossing
Poste frontière

Travel Information Centre
Centre d'information touristique

Major Tourist Attraction
Principale attraction touristique

National Park with camping facilities
Parc national avec camping

National Park without camping facilities
Parc national sans camping

Provincial Park with camping facilities
Parc provincial avec camping

Provincial Park without camping facilities
Parc provincial sans camping

Park Commission with camping
Commission des parcs avec camping

Conservation Area with camping facilities
*Zone de protection de la nature
avec camping*

Picnic Park
Zone de pique–nique

Hospital
Hôpital

First aid/Nursing station
Poste de premiers soins

TOURIST ROUTES

DT Deer Trail Route
FT Frontier Trail
GH Golden Highway
GR Great River Road
LH Lake Huron Circle Tour
LN Lake Nipissing Circle Route
VR Voyageur Route

Scale 1 : 1 600 000

Alphanumeric Grid

The **alphanumeric grid** uses letters and numerals to identify squares in a grid pattern. An alphanumeric grid is often used on road maps. Grid squares are identified by a letter on one side of the map and a number on the other (see Fig. 3-2).

Use Fig. 3-2 to answer the following questions.

1. The community of Gogama in square L13 has two symbols beside its name. What do these symbols represent?

2. In which square do you find the intersection of Highway 17 and Highway 144?

3. Which lake would you see to the south when driving the Voyageur Route between North Bay and Sturgeon Falls (N15)?

4. a) Name the town in square M15 that is named after a mineral.

   b) When measured from Sudbury, what is the closest compass direction and bearing of this town?

5. a) Which is larger, Britt (O14) or Sundridge (O15)?

   b) How can you tell?

6. Name each of the highways with the Trans-Canada symbol and list the grid location of each symbol.

7. Name each of the communities with an airport, give the grid location of each community, and indicate the type of airport.

8. a) How is the distance between two points on a road shown on the Ontario road map?

   b) Calculate the distance in kilometres between:

      i. Marten River (N15) and Latchford (M15)

      ii. Killarney (O13) and the intersection where Highway 637 meets Highway 69 (N14)

      iii. Matachewan (L14) and Dymond (L15) following Highway 65

9. There has been an accident in Temagami (M15) and the injured parties need the services of a hospital. What is the name of the nearest community with a hospital?

10. Several minerals are mined in the Sudbury region of Ontario (N14). Determine two of the minerals by examining the map.

Map Grid (Military Grid)

You may have noticed a grid of blue lines on topographic maps. This is referred to as a **map grid**. We can use the lines of this grid to locate any place on a topographic map.

The map grid is also called the military grid because it was developed and used by Britain and its allies during World War I.

IDENTIFYING GRID SQUARES: FOUR-DIGIT GRID REFERENCE

Each vertical line is called an **easting** and runs from the top to the bottom of the map (Fig. 3-3). Each easting is identified by a two-digit number. The easting refers to the column to the right of the line. Now look at the numbered lines that run horizontally across the map. Each line is called a **northing** and refers to the row *above* it. By combining the two digits from the easting and the two digits from the northing, we are able to identify a specific square on the map.

The expression *"Read right up"* will help you remember which numbers go first. This means that first you read to the *right* (of the vertical easting line) and then *up* (from the horizontal northing line).

1. In your notebook, list the four-digit grid reference of each of the shaded squares in Fig. 3-3.

IDENTIFYING LOCATIONS OF POINTS WITHIN GRID SQUARES: SIX-DIGIT GRID REFERENCE

Any point on the map may be located using a six-digit number. Notice in Fig. 3-4 that the grid square 8106 can be divided into tenths. Point A is five-tenths of the way from 81 to 82 so it is located at 815. Point A is also five-tenths of the way from 06 to 07 so it is located at 065. These numbers are combined to get a six-digit reference of 815065.

1. In your notebook, use a six-digit grid reference to identify the location of B, C, D, and E in Fig. 3-4.

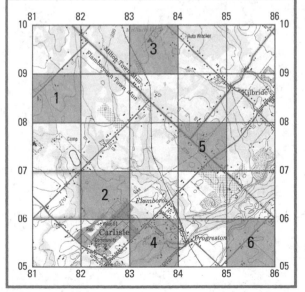

△ **Fig. 3-3**

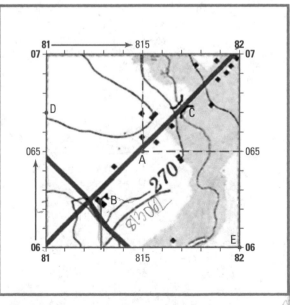

△ **Fig. 3-4**

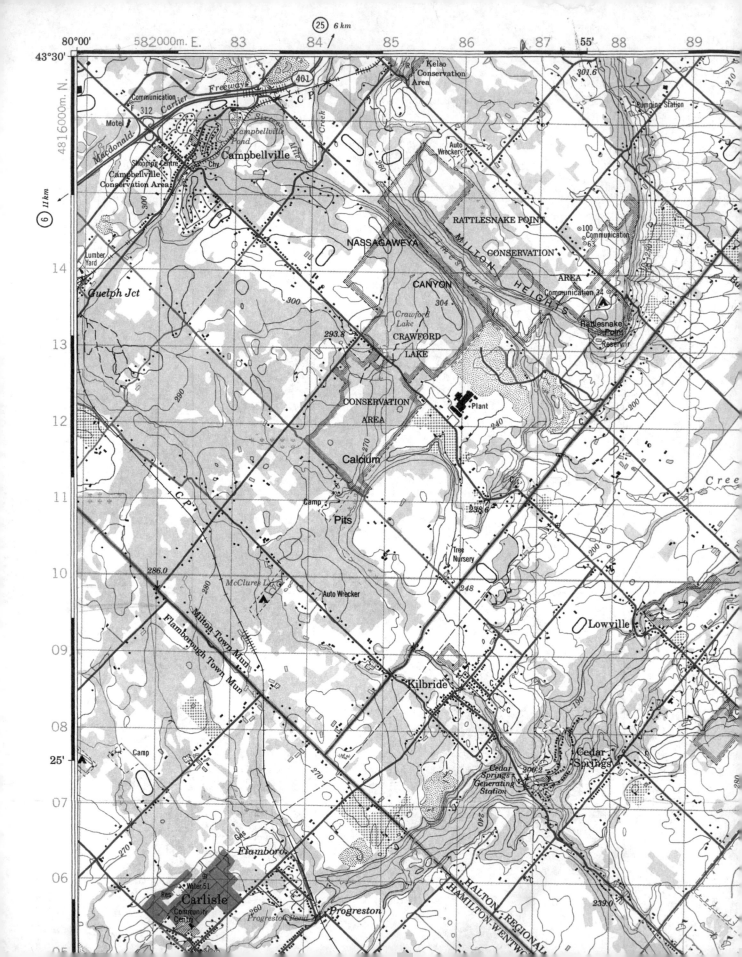

Use this skill in the following activity to interpret some features of a topographic map.

◁ **Fig. 3-5** *A portion of the Hamilton-Burlington topographic map. The contour interval is 10 metres.*

HAMILTON-BURLINGTON TOPOGRAPHIC MAP STUDY

1. In your notebook, use Fig. 3-5 to identify the missing elements in the following essay.

   Your family has decided to visit the area that your ancestors settled when they first came to Canada. Your topographic map shows the highway you are on in square 8316. It is Highway __1__ , which is also known as the __2__ . You exit at interchange 312 and drive northwest to your motel on the left side of the highway. The motel is located at __3__ . You decide to go for lunch in the town of Campbellville, which is located mainly in square __4__ . You are now ready to explore the region and to do a little research about your ancestors. Your first stop is located at 867113, which is a __5__ . You then persuade your parents to take you on a hike at a local conservation area, Rattlesnake Point, which is located to the __6__ of your present location. On the way there, you pass by a __7__ located at 872125. You follow the road that takes you to a reservoir at __8__ . Through the name *reservoir* is a dark brown contour line. The elevation of this contour line is __9__ . You make your way up the escarpment (the Niagara Escarpment) which is known here as __10__ . The name of the conservation area you have entered is __11__ . When you reach the top of Rattlesnake Point, there is another dark brown contour line. Your elevation is __12__ if you are standing at a point along this line looking at the spectacular view. The escarpment is __13__ in height. Just north of the campground area is a communication tower. It is located at __14__ and is __15__ metres in height.

2. On the way back to the motel, you challenge your family to a race to see who can find five features located on the map in the least amount of time.

   Challenge a classmate to this race using the questions listed below. Each of you should take a different challenge to see who answers everything correctly first.

   Your challenge:
   i. What is the human-made feature located at 842098?
   ii. What is the six-digit grid reference of the processing plant in the quarry in the southeastern corner?
   iii. What is the natural feature located at 812110?
   iv. What is the six-digit grid reference of the middle of Crawford Lake? It is located approximately 3 km southeast of Campbellville.

    v.   What is the elevation of the road at 876168?

    Your classmate's challenge:

    i.   What is the human–made feature located at 869061?

    ii. What is the six-digit grid reference of the community centre in Carlisle in the southwestern corner of the map?

    iii. What is the natural feature located at 822086?

    iv. What is the six-digit grid reference of Interchange 312 on Highway 401?

    v.   What is the elevation of the road at 882058?

3. In your notebook, describe the travels and activities of your family on your second day visiting this area. Use the map grid system to help you explain where you went and what you saw.

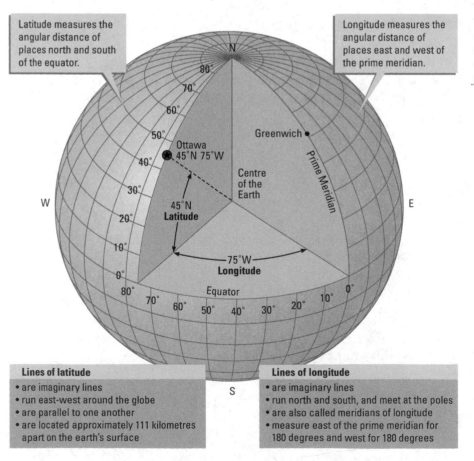

Latitude measures the angular distance of places north and south of the equator.

Longitude measures the angular distance of places east and west of the prime meridian.

◁ **Fig. 3-6** *Latitude and longitude are much easier to understand if you can picture each as an angle measured from the centre of the earth.*

Lines of latitude
- are imaginary lines
- run east-west around the globe
- are parallel to one another
- are located approximately 111 kilometres apart on the earth's surface

Lines of longitude
- are imaginary lines
- run north and south, and meet at the poles
- are also called meridians of longitude
- measure east of the prime meridian for 180 degrees and west for 180 degrees

Latitude and Longitude

The last type of grid system divides the earth into a series of grid squares. No matter where you are in the world, your location can be identified by a latitude and longitude "address."

If you use **latitude** and **longitude**, the geographic centre of the world is in the Gulf of Guinea, off the coast of West Africa. Check in your atlas and you will see that this is 0° latitude and 0° longitude. From here, a gridwork of lines extends north–south and east–west. Using this grid, you can determine the location of any place in the world as the intersection of a line of latitude and a line of longitude.

Latitude and longitude are measured as angles, with the centre of each angle at the centre of the globe (Fig. 3-6). Latitude is measured north and south from the equator and longitude is measured east and west from the **prime meridian**.

You will now "take a trip" around Canada to develop your skills in using latitude and longitude and in using the gazetteer in an atlas. You will also learn some Canadian trivia.

1. Before you begin, check the first page of the gazetteer in your atlas to see what information it contains and how to read the information found in each entry.
2. Divide into groups of two so that you can have a friendly rivalry with your partner. See who can provide all of the missing words below correctly in your notebooks in the least amount of time.

Your trip begins at the base of the Peace Tower located in the _____ Buildings in the city of _____ (45.5°N 75.5°W). From here you head west to Canada's nickel capital, _____ (46.5°N 81°W). You continue to travel west to the railway hub of the west, _____ (50°N 97°W). Following the Trans-Canada Highway, you arrive in a city whose name means *queen* in Latin, _____ (50.5°N 104.5°W). Your next stop is in the city famous for its western fair, called The _____ Stampede (51°N 114°W). With the hope of seeing the famous Ogo Pogo monster in Lake Okanagan, you spend a few days in the community of _____ (49.5°N 119.5°W). You continue to follow the Trans-Canada Highway to Vancouver, located at _____. You take the ferry to Vancouver Island to see the place where the annual bathtub race starts at _____ (49°N 124°W).

Your trip continues northward to _____, located in the Yukon at 64° N 139.5° W. Thousands of people came to this town in 1898 searching for gold. Another town famous for its gold mines is Yellowknife, located on

A gazetteer is an alphabetical index of the places shown in an atlas.

Great Slave Lake at _____. Your next stop is known as the polar bear capital of Canada. At certain times of the year, polar bears are a tourist attraction. This city, _____, located at 58.5°N 94°W, is named after a famous British prime minister. You find that you really have a craving for some seafood from Atlantic Canada. You fly over Québec to the most easterly provincial capital of _____, located at 47.5°N 52.5°W for a serving of cod tongues. These are a rare delicacy since the cod fishery collapsed in the 1990s. After a quick flight to Halifax, located at _____ you find a restaurant that serves freshly cooked lobster with fresh bread and butter. Heading westward, you visit the largest island in the Bay of Fundy, _____, New Brunswick, located at 44.5°N 66.5°W. It is famous for its edible seaweed, called Dulse. Before leaving New Brunswick you visit the Reversing Falls in _____ at 45.5°N 66°W. The centre of French Canada is _____, located at 47°N 71°W. Its old town has been declared a World Heritage Site by the United Nations. Your last stop is a visit to Canada's Museum of Civilization, located in _____ across the river from Ottawa at 45.5°N 76°W.

GLOBAL POSITIONING SYSTEM (GPS)

Imagine that you wake up one morning and discover that your family vehicle has been stolen. The chances of getting it back are slim, unless it happens to be equipped with a satellite tracking device. This device uses the **Global Positioning System (GPS)** and can pinpoint the location of your stolen car anywhere on the planet, 24 hours a day. This may sound like science fiction, but GPS technology can be applied in many ways.

An inexpensive GPS tracking device the size of a mobile phone can give users their position in degrees of latitude and longitude (Fig. 3-7). This information can be transmitted by another device to tell other people where you are and how to find you if you are lost. Environmentalists have been using GPS to track wildlife. Shipping companies use GPS technology to monitor the progress of their delivery trucks. Some automobiles have onboard maps that show users their current location. This location is given to a company which, for a fee, provides information about the fastest or most scenic route to a particular destination.

In the future, mobile phones will be GPS-equipped to trace the source of 911 calls. Pet owners will put GPS devices on their dogs and cats to keep track of their whereabouts. Many of the uses for GPS technology have yet to be invented!

To learn more about GPS, check www.howstuffworks.com/gps.htm

Fig. 3-7

a) ◁ Orbiting satellites provide navigation data around the clock. The satellites send radio signals to earth that a GPS unit uses to calculate its latitude and longitude.

b) ▽ Triangulation: Each satellite's signal contains the exact time it was sent. A GPS unit uses this time to measure and calculate the distance of the satellite. Signals from at least three satellites are needed by a GPS unit to determine its location.

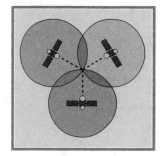

LONGITUDE AND TIME ZONES

The theory behind **time zones** is quite simple:

Since the earth rotates around its axis once every 24 hours, there are 24 time zones around the earth, with 1 hour difference between them. Since the earth rotates through 360 degrees in 24 hours, it must rotate through 15 degrees of longitude in 1 hour ($360° \div 24 = 15°$). Therefore, each of the 24 time zones is 15 degrees wide. Every place within a time zone has the same time, referred to as its **standard time**.

With the development of rapid railway transportation, in the second half of the 1800s, the need for standard time zones became obvious to Sir Sandford Fleming, Canada's most experienced railway surveyor and civil engineer. He wrote to the major governments of the world proposing the use of time zones. In 1884, an international conference was held in Washington, D. C. to approve Fleming's system. It adopted the meridian that runs through the Royal Observatory in Greenwich, England as the prime, or zero, meridian.

The prime meridian is the centre of a time zone that extends 7.5 degrees on either side (Fig. 3-8). Time in this zone is called universal time (UT) and the standard times in other zones are compared to it. Every 15 degrees, on either side of the prime meridian, is the centre of a time zone.

Universal time was formerly called Greenwich Mean Time (GMT). Some people still refer to time in this zone as GMT.

Since the earth rotates from west to east, time zones that are east of the prime meridian have local times that are ahead of UT. Time zones that are west of the prime meridian have local times that are behind UT. For example, if the sun is directly above the prime meridian, the local time in the city of Berlin, which is one time zone east of UT, is 1 p.m. (Fig. 3-9). In Ottawa, which is five time zones west of the prime meridian, the time is 7 a.m. It will be five more hours before the sun appears directly over the 75°W meridian, which is the centre of the time zone where Ottawa is located.

Countries, however, may modify the shape of the time zones and the standard (or legally recognized) time they use. For example, China has one standard time for the whole country despite the fact that it covers more than 60° of longitude. Canada, on the other hand, has six standard time zones, (Fig. 3-10). The boundaries of the zones, however, do not follow exactly the meridians of longitude as discussed above.

△ **Fig. 3-8** *An illustration of the universal time zone.*

▽ **Fig. 3-9** *When it is midnight at the prime meridian, what time is it where you live?*

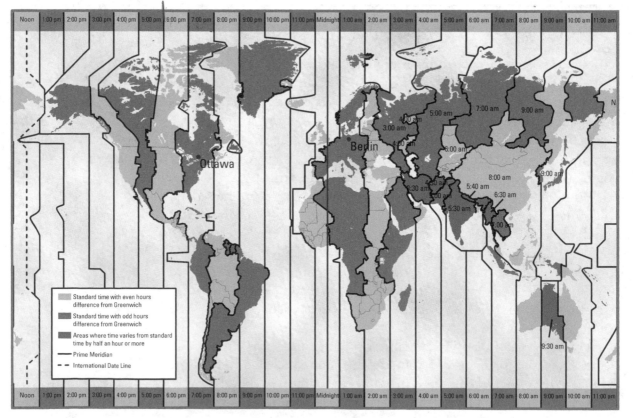

Countries modify the shapes of the time zones for political reasons. For example, it may be more convenient to have all of a province in one time zone. Time zones may also be adjusted so that they do not pass through a city. Imagine the confusion that would arise if half a city was in one time zone and the other half was in another time zone.

Some places are located where time zones meet. St. John's, Newfoundland, at 52.5°W, is located between the third and fourth time zones west of the prime meridian so its time is 3.5 hours behind UT.

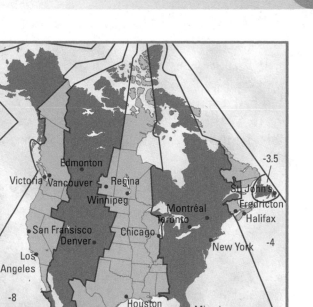

△ **Fig. 3-10** *Canada has six standard time zones. The numbers refer to the number of hours behind Greenwich. If a football game starts in Edmonton at 2 p.m., what time is it on TV in St. John's?*

The International Date Line

When sailors first sailed around the world, they returned home either a day ahead or a day behind those people who stayed. To correct this situation, the **International Date Line** was established. It runs between the North and South Pole, and generally follows the 180° line of longitude through the Pacific Ocean. It zigzags, however, to avoid dividing land masses or island groups that belong to the same country. If you cross the date line moving westward, you add a day. If you cross the date line moving eastward, you lose a day. The time does not change unless the date line corresponds to a time zone boundary.

Daylight-Saving Time

Many parts of the world change their time according to the season. During the summer, **daylight-saving time** is used to extend daylight hours into the evening when most people are awake. For example, the sun would set at 9 p.m. instead of 8 p.m., thereby cutting down on energy use since lights don't have to be turned on until later in the day. In Canada and the United States, daylight-saving time begins on the first Sunday in April and ends on the last Sunday in October. Other countries use different dates.

Remember: *spring forward, fall back*

Longitude and Time

Early sailors determined their latitude by the angle of the sun above the horizon or by the position of the North Star (Polaris), but they had no practical way to find their longitude. In theory, longitude could be calcu-lated if sailors knew their local time and the time in Greenwich. However, the pendulum clocks that were in use at the time did not work on a ship being tossed about by waves.

In 1791, John Harrison, a British inventor, developed his **marine chronometer**. It was a highly accurate spring-loaded clock that could keep time on a moving ship.

The fourth generation of John Harrison's chronometer was used by Captain Cook on his journey around the world.

Longitude was calculated in the following manner:

Exact local time: 7:00 am
Greenwich time: 12:00 noon

Since local time was 5 hours *behind* Greenwich, the location was *west* of the prime meridian

5 hours = 75 degrees (5 x 15)

Current longitude: 75 degrees west of the prime meridian.

Possible locations: Ottawa, Canada; Philadelphia, U.S.A.; Cisneros, Colombia.

You can also find locations on the Internet at www.expe diamaps.com

QUESTIONS

CHECK YOUR UNDERSTANDING

1. How many compass points are shown in Fig. 3-1?

2. What direction is halfway between each of the following directions?
   a) NE and SW
   b) NE and S
   c) WSW and NNW

3. What direction is opposite each of the following directions?
   a) SW
   b) NNE
   c) ESE

ANALYZE AND APPLY

4. Examine Fig. 3-7 and explain how GPS technology works.

5. Give the compass bearing for the following directions (compass points):
   a) N
   b) SSE
   c) NNE

6. What is the direction of the following bearings?
   a) 22.5°
   b) 112.5°
   c) 292.5°

7. Use the information in Fig. 3-11 to determine the direction of each of the numbered arrows.

8. Using a Mercator projection in an atlas and a protractor, calculate the bearing of each of the following locations from Edmonton:

    a) Prince Albert

    b) Medicine Hat

    c) Kelowna

    d) Peace River

9. Using an atlas, draw and label the following major lines of latitude and longitude on the world map provided by your teacher:

    a) Latitude: equator, tropic of Cancer, tropic of Capricorn, Arctic Circle, Antarctic Circle

    b) Longitude: prime meridian, 180° meridian, International Date Line

10. a) From your atlas, determine the name of the major cities at the following locations:

    i.   47°N 52° W

    ii. 39°N 116°E

    iii. 23°S 43°W

    iv. 6°S 106°E

    b) Label each of these places on your world map.

11. a) Use your atlas to determine the location of the following capital cities:

    i.   Ottawa, Canada

    ii. Cairo, Egypt

    iii. Santiago, Chile

    iv. Wellington, New Zealand

    v.   Kampala, Uganda

    b) In which hemisphere is each capital located?

12. What is the straight-line distance in kilometres between each pair of cities? Each pair is located on the same line of longitude.

    a) 20°N and 5°N

    b) 25°N and 17°S

13. Refer to the map of time zones in Canada and the United States (Fig. 3-10).

▽ **Fig. 3-11**

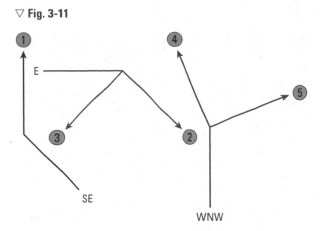

a) If the Vancouver Canucks are playing the Toronto Maple Leafs in Toronto at 8 p.m., what time will the game be seen in Vancouver? 5pm

b) If it is 10 a.m. in Newfoundland and you want to call your uncle and aunt in Winnipeg, what time will it be for them? 7:30 am

c) The Montréal Canadiens are playing in Los Angeles at 8 p.m. At what time will a person in Montréal be watching the start of the game on television?

14. A stockbroker in Toronto must telephone other stockbrokers around the world to discuss the price changes of a particular stock. Each stockbroker is expecting the call from Toronto at 10 a.m. local time. Consult an atlas and Fig. 3-9 to determine what time the stockbroker in Toronto will have to telephone the stockbroker in the following cities:

    a) Frankfurt, Germany

    b) London, England

    c) Vancouver, Canada

    d) Los Angeles, U.S.A.

    e) Hong Kong, China

15. If your local time is 11 a.m. and the time at the prime meridian is 5:30 p.m., what is your longitude?

16. Your local time is 3 a.m. and your longitude is 120 °E. What time is it at the prime meridian?

▽ **Fig. 3-12**

Flight	Departure Time	Flight Duration	Arrival Time Before Time Zone Consideration	Time Zone Difference	Arrival Local Time
Toronto to Calgary	10 a.m.	4h	2 p.m.	-2h	12 noon
Winnipeg to Moncton	8:45 a.m.	5h		+2h	
Quebec City to San Francisco	2:40 p.m.		6:40 p.m.		3:40 p.m.
Victoria to Regina		4h 20m		+2h	6:20 p.m.
Edmonton to St. John's	7 a.m.	10h 30m			

17. You are on a ship that has two chronometers. One gives UT as 3 p.m. and the other gives your local time as 9 a.m. If your latitude has been calculated at 62°N,

  a) what is your longitude?

  b) Consult an atlas to determine in what body of water you are located.

18. Copy Fig. 3-12 into your notebooks and complete the flight information chart. The first calculation has been done for you.

Have you ever made a model of something like an airplane or a building? Every part of the model is in true proportion to the life-size object (Fig. 4-1). This reduction is the basic idea of scale. In Chapter Two, you saw that a map must have a scale. The **scale** shows the relationship between the distance on a map and the actual distance on the earth's surface. A small distance on the map represents a much larger distance on the earth's surface. Scale can be represented in three different ways: direct statement, line scale, and representative fraction.

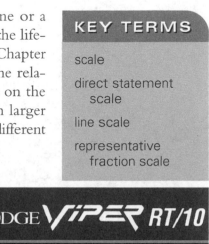

△ **Fig. 4-1** *Every part of this model car is in true proportion to the life-size object that it represents.*

DIRECT STATEMENT SCALE

A **direct statement scale** uses words to describe the relationship between a distance on a map and a specific distance on the earth's surface, for example, 1 cm to 10 km. If you measure the distance between two places on a map and the distance is 1 cm, you would know that the actual distance between them is 10 km.

A direct statement scale is also called a verbal statement.

On the map in Fig. 4-2, the distance between *Here* and *There* is measured and found to be 3 cm. If the scale is 1 cm to 10 km then the distance on the earth's surface is calculated as follows:

1 cm = 10 km

(3 x 1) cm = (3 x 10) km

3 cm = 30 km

Therefore, the actual distance between *Here* and *There* is 30 km.

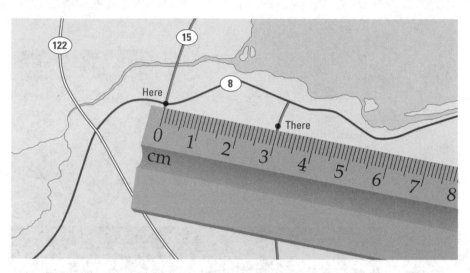

◁ **Fig. 4-2** *To determine the distance on a map with a direct statement scale, measure the distance between two places. Calculate the distance based on the scale.*

◁ **Fig. 4-3** *Follow these steps to find the actual distance between places using the line scale.*

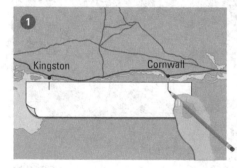

Mark the locations of the two cities on the edge of a sheet of paper.

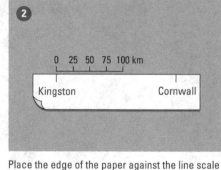

Place the edge of the paper against the line scale with the first mark at 0.

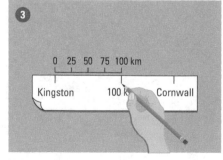

Make a mark on your paper at the right end of the scale.

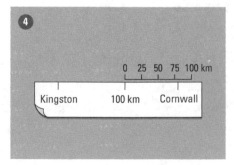

Move the mark from step three to 0 on the line scale and measure the remaining distance.

5 Calculate the total distance between Kingston and Cornwall by adding together the two distances you measured.

The distance between Kingston and Cornwall is 180 km.

LINE SCALE

A **line scale** is like a special kind of ruler that is divided into units of distance. Use a line scale to find the distance between Kingston and Cornwall. Follow the steps illustrated in Fig. 4-3.

A line scale is also called a linear scale.

REPRESENTATIVE FRACTION (R.F.) SCALE

The third method for showing scale is the **representative fraction**. This fraction is a ratio and is shown as follows: 1:50 000. It could also be shown as $\frac{1}{50\ 000}$ but this form is not as common. The R.F. scale means that 1 unit on the map represents 50 000 of the *same* units on the earth's surface. The units may be in any measure, such as centimetres in Canada or inches in the United States. No matter what units are used, the correct distance can be calculated. This is very useful since everyone in the world can use this scale regardless of their language or the units of measurement used in their country.

There are a few properties about this ratio that you should know:

To see examples of different scales, check www.gis.psu.edu/geog121/intro/gorham_24k.html

1:50 000

The first term of the ratio
- is always 1
- represents the distance on the map
- represents the same unit of measurement as the second term of the ratio

The second term of the ratio
- represents the distance on the earth's surface
- represents the same unit of measurement as the first term of the ratio

Therefore, if the R.F. is 1:50 000, then 1 *cm* on the map represents 50 000 *cm* on the earth's surface.

We usually want to know distances in kilometres. To change the centimetres used in the R.F. into kilometres, we must know how to convert one unit of measurement into the other. Continue reading to find out how to do this.

SCALE CONVERSION

The R.F. scale is practical because it can be used by everyone all over the world. It is not very useful, however, when we want to indicate an actual distance between places. For example, if the R.F. is 1:50 000 we know that 1 cm on the map represents 50 000 cm on the earth's surface. What we really want to know, however, is how many kilometres on the earth's surface are represented by 1 cm on the map. For this reason, it is important that we know how to convert from one scale to another.

Converting an R.F. Scale to a Direct Statement Scale

To convert an R.F. scale to a direct statement scale, divide the denominator by 100 000, to change centimetres into kilometres.

Therefore, in order to convert the R.F. 1:50 000 into a direct statement, you would use the following process:

1 km = 1000 m
1 m = 100 cm
1 km = (1000 x 100) cm
　　 = 100 000 cm

　1 cm = 50 000 cm
　1 cm = (50 000 ÷ 100 000) km
　1 cm = 0.5 km or 1 cm to 500 m

Converting a Direct Statement Scale to an R.F. Scale

To convert from a direct statement scale back to an R.F. scale, multiply the number of kilometres by 100 000.

Here is an example which converts the direct statement *1 cm to 2.5 km* into a representative fraction:

　1 cm = 2.5 km
　1 cm = (2.5 x 100 000) cm
　1 cm = 250 000 cm or 1: 250 000

When constructing a map, use the scale that is best suited to the purpose of the map. Make sure that there is a scale on all of your maps.

QUESTIONS

ANALYZE AND APPLY

1. a) What does 1 cm to 0.5 km mean?

   b) Use this scale to recalculate the distance in both kilometres and metres, between *Here* and *There* in Fig. 4-2.

2. The direct statement scale of a map is 1 cm to 35 km. If the map distance between points A and B is 9 cm, what is the real distance?

3. The direct statement scale of a map is 1 cm to 250 km. If two places are 17 cm apart on the map, what is the actual distance between them?

4. Using the scale of 1 cm to 30 km, calculate the road distances between towns X and Y in Fig. 4-4.

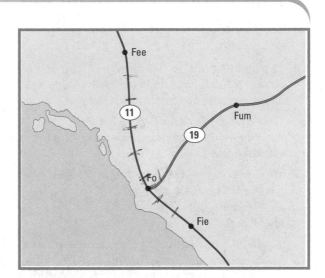

△ **Fig. 4-5** *The scale of this map is 1 cm to 12 km.*

▽ **Fig. 4-4**

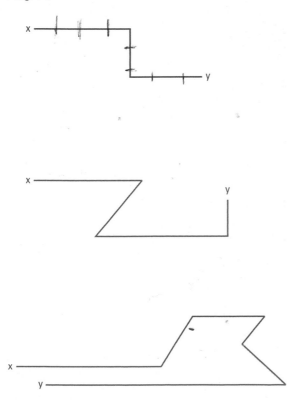

5. Refer to Fig. 4-5 to calculate the road distance between Fee and Fie and between Fo and Fum.

6. Here is a list of distances between Canadian cities:

   a) Calgary to Edmonton   299 km

   b) Fredericton to Montréal   834 km

   c) Regina to Winnipeg   571 km

   Draw straight lines in your notebook to show how each distance would appear on a map. Use a scale of 1 cm to 100 km.

7. a) In an atlas, find a map of a part of Canada that has a line scale.

   b) Use the line scale method to calculate the actual distance between two cities on that map.

   c) Select another pair of cities and repeat the activity.

8. In your own words, what is an R.F. scale?

9. a) What does 1:250 000 mean?

   b) What does 1:3 000 000 mean?

10. Convert the following representative fractions to direct statements.

   a) 1:250 000

   b) 1:1 500 000

   c) 1:63 000 000

11. Use an atlas to find the straight-line distance between the locations listed below. Use the direct statement scale found in the atlas.

   a) Wiarton, Ontario (in the Bruce Peninsula) and Port Dover, Ontario (on Lake Erie)

   b) Gananoque, Ontario (near Kingston on the St. Lawrence River) and Aylmer, Québec (near Ottawa on the Ottawa River)

   c) Sault Ste. Marie, Ontario (between Lake Superior and Lake Huron) and Timmins, Ontario (northeast of Sault Ste. Marie)

12. Find the maps in your atlas that show the following pairs of cities. Measure the straight-line distances between the two cities. Use the R.F. scale shown on the map to calculate the distance in kilometres.

   a) London, England and Rome, Italy (map of Europe)

   b) Havana, Cuba and Miami, Florida (map of the Caribbean)

   c) Prince Rupert and Bella Coola, British Columbia (map of western Canada)

   d) Yarmouth, Nova Scotia and Bathurst, New Brunswick (map of eastern Canada)

13. Convert the following direct statement scales to R.F. scales.

   a) 1 cm to 5 km

   b) 1 cm to 25 km

   c) 1 cm to 160 km

14. The line scale on a map indicates that 4 cm represents 20 km. What is the R.F.?

15. The line scale on a map indicates that 1.5 cm represents 50 km. What is the R.F.?

GIS: Where Geography is Going

We take maps for granted because they are such an everyday part of our lives. Just think about the last time you used a map. Perhaps it was in the newspaper, on television, or while taking a trip. Can you imagine how difficult it would be to give someone the information that is contained in even simple maps, like those on the inside covers of this book, if we could not do so graphically?

Maps of various kinds have been used for thousands of years. Fig. 5-1 is a map of a part of Canada that was made more than 300 years ago. This map was created by an Italian cartographer named Coronelli, and it is considered a work of art. Its purpose, however, was exactly the same as that of modern maps — to portray information in a graphical way about the location of places and things and the relationships that exist among these things.

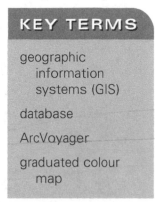

KEY TERMS

geographic
information
systems (GIS)

database

ArcVoyager

graduated colour
map

And in this case, since Coronelli simply created it without accurate information, it is a work of imagination!

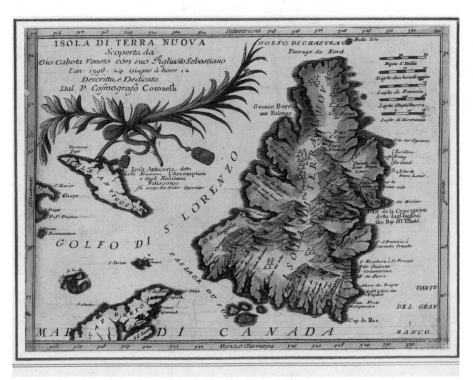

◁ **Fig. 5-1** *This is a map of a part of Canada, made in 1696. Can you tell where this is? Compare it to a current map of the same area. Why are there so many differences?*

In this chapter, you will have an opportunity to learn about the newest kind of mapping technology, that is **geographic information systems,** or, as it is more commonly known, **GIS**. GIS has rapidly come to revolutionize the business of map making and analyzing. It allows the creation of "dynamic maps," made and stored on the computer and able to be easily changed to meet a particular purpose. Enjoy learning about this fascinating new technology!

If you are interested in a career that is related to geography, the rapidly expanding GIS field offers many job opportunities.

HOW GIS IS USED

GIS can be used for three purposes:

1. to organize great masses of data that have a geographic basis
2. to present this kind of data in a clear way
3. to use the data to answer questions

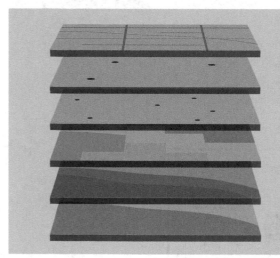

- Roads
- High schools
- Elementary schools
- Census subdivisions
- Landform regions
- Ecozones

◁ **Fig. 5-2** *A GIS map has layers that can be modified and arranged as needed.*

Ecozone	Total Area (km²)	Land Area (km²)	Water Area (km²)	Population	Dominant Cover
Taiga Cordillera	245 865	245 505	360	360	Coniferous forest
Boreal Cordillera	432128	427208	4920	16 000	Coniferous forest
Montane Cordillera	461198	448145	13053	452 000	Coniferous forest
Arctic Cordillera	239216	219499	19717	1000	Perennial snow/ice
Northern Arctic	1433362	1283915	149447	16 000	Barren lands
Southern Arctic	775734	716385	59349	10 000	Arctic/alpine tundra
Atlantic Maritime	196449	176677	19772	2 510 000	Mixed forest
Pacific Maritime	195554	181749	13805	2 504 000	Coniferous forest
Hudson Plains	350318	341322	8996	10 000	Transitional forest
Taiga Plain	563241	496380	66861	21 000	Coniferous forest
Taiga Shield	1268623	1156110	112513	34 000	Transitional forest
Prairie	440537	432108	8429	3 851 000	Agricultural cropland
Boreal Shield	1773894	1609776	164118	1 695 000	Coniferous forest
Boreal Plains	656970	599139	57831	708 000	Coniferous forest
Mixedwood Plains	113431	57422	56009	14 016 000	Agricultural cropland

◁ **Fig. 5-3** *A GIS map combines the capabilities of a database with those of a dynamic map-drawing program.*

GIS is used for many aspects of day-to-day life, without us even realizing it. Here are some uses that may have an impact on your life:

- making sure that 911 emergency services get to your house as quickly as possible
- planning services like water and sewage for a new housing area
- deciding if there are enough children, of the right age, in an area to justify building a new school
- ensuring that the pizza you ordered gets to your house in 30 minutes or less
- illustrating the movement of air masses in the atmosphere in order to better understand critical problems such as global warming

GIS computer programs are very new and are just starting to be used in high schools. Since they are so new, many people have difficulty imagining how they work. Here are two suggestions:

1. Imagine that you have a **base map.** Then imagine overlaying one or more transparent layers, each with specific data, onto the base map (Fig. 5-2). For example, you might want to draw a map that combines layers of information about road patterns (layer #1), the location of high schools (layer #2), and the pattern of census subdivisions (layer #4). This is easily done with GIS.

2. Think of GIS as combining the features of a **database** program (Fig. 5-3) with those of a drawing program. Suppose you want to

To learn more about how GIS works, check www.esricanada.com/k-12/gis/whatisgis.html

base map: a blank map, providing only an outline of the most basic features of the map area

◁ **Fig. 5-4** *An example of a base map created by a drawing program. Red lines indicate ecozone boundaries.*

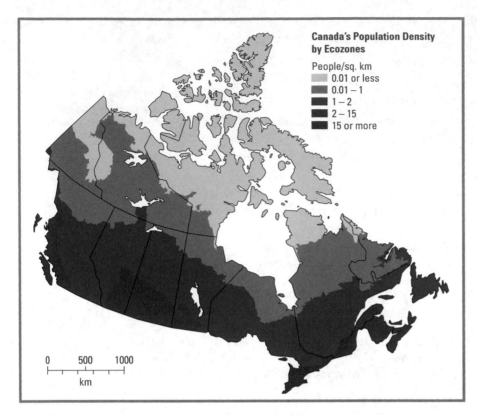

Canada's Population Density by Ecozones

People/sq. km
- 0.01 or less
- 0.01 – 1
- 1 – 2
- 2 – 15
- 15 or more

◁ **Fig. 5-5** *This map of ecozone population densities was created using a GIS program. You will learn how to create this map in Chapter 14. You will learn about ecozones in Chapter 14.*

draw a map of Canada to show the population density by ecozones. You could use a database of information to determine your map, but the results of your selection would still be in the form of a table. With a drawing program, you could create a map (Fig. 5-4), but you would have to shade in each ecozone from the database onto the map individually. A GIS program would automatically create the map and shade in each ecozone for you (Fig. 5-5).

database: a table of information in a computer program that can be searched for particular values or rearranged in some way

What do you need to operate a GIS?

- a powerful computer system along with a printer
- GIS mapping software
- specially created, computerized base maps
- the data that you wish to analyze and map
- most importantly, an imaginative and creative person who wants to analyze and display something — i.e. YOU!

Colour printing is desirable but not essential.

USING GIS IN *MAKING CONNECTIONS*

There are several different geographic information systems on the market. All work in a similar fashion. In *Making Connections: Canada's Geography,* you will have the chance to learn about a GIS program called **ArcVoyager,** from ESRI Canada. ArcVoyager is a demonstration version of a more powerful, commercial program. It will do almost everything that the commercial program does with one important difference — you cannot save your work! You must finish each exercise in one sitting. Your teacher will give you instructions for each of the six ArcVoyager exercises in this book. These exercises are indicated by a special logo (Fig. 5-6).

In ArcVoyager, a project refers to the file within which you create a map. Before you start doing a particular project, it may help you to realize that all projects have many similarities. Creating a map with ArcVoyager consists of three major steps. The first and last steps are the same for all the projects you do. It is only the second step that will vary from project to project, depending on what you want to accomplish in a particular map.

Step #1 —You create a project and set up a base map on which you will work.

Step #2 —You analyze the data you have and decide what layers you will put on your map.

Step #3 —You assemble all of the elements of your map.

△ **Fig. 5-6** *This logo will tell you where there is an ArcVoyager exercise.*

TOOLS YOU CAN USE IN STEP #2

To do the ArcVoyager exercises that are part of this book, you will need to use several different tools (Fig. 5-7). These are

1. *Identifying*: Locations (cities, provinces, lakes, etc.) on ArcVoyager maps usually have a great deal of information associated with them. When you click on a feature of your map, this information is displayed.

2. *Labelling*: When you click, the label command, it automatically adds the name to a highlighted feature of your map.

3. *Charting*: The chart feature allows you to create charts, including pie or bar graphs, from the data with which you are working. The charts you make will appear automatically in the correct locations on your map.

4. *Graduated Colour Mapping*: In a **graduated colour map**, a range of colour shades is used to indicate different values. For example, all areas with a population density between 10 and 20 people per square kilometre will be the same colour shade.

5. *Single-Symbol Mapping*: Single-symbol maps are used to show features like cities and rivers. You might choose symbols seen on traditional maps, such as a cross for churches, or a black line for a highway. You can use different symbols for different purposes.

6. *Zooming*: There may be times when you will want to look at a smaller area in greater detail by enlarging it, or show only part of a

Full instructions for doing ArcVoyager activities will be given to you by your teacher.

Chapter	Project	Tools used
1	Basic location map of Canada	Identifying Labelling
14	Population density in each ecozone	Graduated colour mapping
23	Forest coverage in each ecozone	Charting
31	Canada's foreign aid (2 maps)	Graduated colour mapping
32	Location of North American auto-assembly plants (2 maps)	Single-symbol mapping Zooming Querying
35	World production of carbon dioxide and Kyoto Conference targets (2 maps)	Graduated colour mapping Querying

◁ **Fig. 5-7** *These are the ArcVoyager exercises you can do in Making Connections: Canada's Geography.*

map. With ArcVoyager, you can zoom in to show only part of a map at a larger scale.

7. *Querying:* The query tool allows you to ask questions about your data. For example, suppose you have a database of cities in Ontario. You can use the query tool to find out which cities have populations over 100 000.

8. *Measuring:* This tool allows you to determine the distance between any two places very quickly.

IN CLOSING...

GIS is a revolutionary technology that is changing the way the world looks at geographic information. In this chapter, and in your Canadian Geography course, you will have only scratched the surface of this exciting field. GIS is also becoming increasingly important in your day-to-day lives. Who knows — you may even end up working in GIS when you finish your schooling!

To learn more about ESRI Canada and its products, check www.esricanada.com/products/index.html

6 Air Photos: The View from Above

The first aerial photographs were taken in the 1850s from cameras attached to kites. Later that century, photographs were taken from hot air balloons. Although these early photographs were very crude, they did point out the potential usefulness of photographs taken from a great height.

New techniques have improved the quality of aerial photographs tremendously. Aerial photographs are used to study farm size, crop plantings, soil erosion, and the flow of traffic in cities. They are useful in archaeological studies, geographical research, meteorological observations, and even in crime detection. The result is that, today, aerial photographs are an essential tool for studying geography and other subjects.

WHAT IS A STEREO PAIR?

Although a single **aerial photo** can be useful in the study of an area, the use of a **stereo pair** of photographs is more helpful. These pictures are taken from an aircraft, in rapid succession, by a high-speed camera looking directly down at the ground. The camera is set so that the images overlap from photo to photo. Fig. 6-1 shows how this is done. As you can see, the same area is photographed from a slightly different position in the sky. Any two overlapping aerial photos is a stereo pair.

When you position the photographs properly and view them through an instrument called a stereoscope, your brain sees images in three dimensions. While the height of cliffs, trees, and buildings is exaggerated, this extra dimension allows you to see much more than is possible with a single

KEY TERMS

aerial photo

stereo pair

Stereo pair images may also be taken by satellites.

A stereo pair image is similar to the way your eyes see objects — from two slightly different positions.

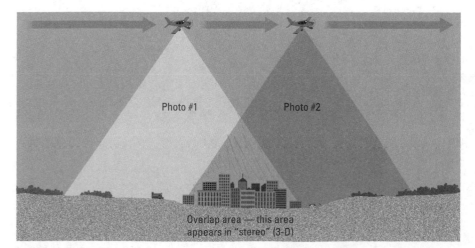

◁ **Fig. 6-1** *An illustration of how aerial photographs are taken*

Photo #1

Photo #2

Overlap area — this area appears in "stereo" (3-D)

photograph. You can learn a great deal about a place without ever having to visit it.

Fig. 6-2 is a stereo pair of photographs showing part of downtown Toronto. What can we learn about Toronto from these photographs? The letters A to M on the stereo pair will allow you to locate items referred to in the analysis that follows. On a piece of tracing paper or clear acetate, you will make an overlay map of this area. Use different colours and/or symbols to show different land uses. Use the photo on the left for all of your tracings.

COMMERCIAL LAND USE

The southern part of Toronto's Central Business District (CBD) is shown in the photographs. The CBD includes many of the city's most important commercial land uses, that is, the major office buildings and shopping areas.

OFFICE BUILDINGS

1. On your tracing paper or acetate, trace the part of the CBD that is bordered by the tallest buildings.

2. Canada's four tallest buildings are all found near the corner of King Street and Bay Street (A). They are First Canadian Place (Bank of Montréal) on the northwest corner, Toronto Dominion Centre (TD Bank) on the southwest corner, Scotia Plaza (Bank of Nova Scotia) on the northeast corner, and Commerce Court (Canadian Imperial Bank of Commerce) on the southeast corner. Which of these buildings appears to be the tallest in the stereo pair? Does it appear to be a light or dark colour?

3. The Toronto Stock Exchange is located in First Canadian Place. What kinds of tenants might you find in the large office buildings nearby? How might the height of buildings be related to the type of business carried on and the wealth of these companies?

The stock exchange is a place where people (like you, if you have the money) can buy shares in companies.

SHOPPING

4. In the past, Yonge Street was the most important shopping street in downtown Toronto. Now, however, many shopping facilities have moved inside or underground. The focus of shopping activity is in the Eaton Centre (B), a multi-level shopping mall. Give one advantage and one disadvantage of this type of development.

5. It is possible to walk from just north of the Eaton Centre to Union Station (F) without going outside. This "underground city" is a series of shopping malls and walkways under the large office towers of the CBD. What are the positive and negative aspects of such a design?

See the map of Toronto's CBD in Chapter 19.

TRANSPORTATION LAND USE

Much of the transportation land use in this area is directly related to commercial activities. Every weekday, hundreds of thousands of people travel to the CBD to go to work or to shop. Most of them do so either by public transit or by car.

PUBLIC TRANSIT

1. a) The most important part of the downtown public transit system is the subway. The subway runs south on Yonge Street (C) and then loops westward along Front Street (E) and up University Avenue (D). Union Station (F) on Front Street is the meeting point of the subway system and the GO train, a commuter railway system. Why do you think this particular route was chosen for the subway? The subway lines appear to have had what affect on the growth of Toronto?

    b) Show the subway routes on your tracing.

2. The other part of the public transit system consists of a fleet of buses and streetcars. Can you suggest where three north-south and three east-west routes might be? Give two reasons why these streets do not have subway lines on them.

STREETS AND ROADS

Two types of roads are shown in the stereo pair: an expressway and city streets.

3. What is the purpose of an expressway? In what directions does the expressway run from the downtown area?

4. What pattern is formed by the city streets? Is this pattern found where you live? How else can a city's streets be arranged?

PARKING LOTS

Because many thousands of cars enter the CBD each day, parking facilities are very important.

5. a) On your tracing, carefully draw and label all of the parking lots you can see.

    b) Describe the location of parking lots in relation to high density developments in the CBD. Why are parking lots found in these locations?

    c) Why might these parking lots be temporary land uses only? Where might new parking lots appear?

    d) How else do you think parking is provided in ways that are not visible on these aerial photographs?

RAILWAYS

6. Freight handling used to be done in the area on the photo indicated by the dotted line. It is now done outside the CBD in suburban locations. Why? Which parts of the railway lands have been redeveloped? Why?

7. On your tracing, show the location of the passenger station, Union Station (F), on Front Street. Why is this a convenient location?

8. The GO train, a commuter railway, runs along the lakeshore tracks to Union Station. Over 300 bi-level (double-decker) coaches carry over 100 000 commuters every day. Show the GO train route on your tracing.

AIRPORT

9. a) Show the location of the Toronto Island Airport on your tracing. How do people get to the airport?

   b) This is not the main airport in the Greater Toronto Area. Its runways are too short for large jets. What kinds of planes would use the island airport? State one advantage and one disadvantage of having an airport near the downtown area.

In 1998, plans were made to build a bridge from the mainland to the island airport.

PUBLIC BUILDINGS

1. Locate Toronto's city hall (G). Describe the shape of this structure. The open space in front of the city hall is used for concerts and special events. Locate this area. In summer, seating is provided around a pond, which becomes a skating rink in winter.

2. Many hospitals are located along University Avenue. The Hospital for Sick Children (H) has a special feature on its roof. Identify this feature.

RECREATIONAL LAND USE

1. On your tracing, locate some of the recreation land use in the downtown area. Include the following:
   a) yacht clubs and marinas
   b) city parks
   c) SkyDome (I)
   d) CN Tower (J)
   e) Roy Thomson Hall (K)
   f) Railway Museum (L)
   g) Air Canada Centre (M)

2. Put a suitable title and legend on your map.

IN CLOSING...

In this exercise, we have only begun to analyze and describe the uses of aerial photographs. As you continue your study of geography, you will discover more and more uses for this valuable tool.

Bonus Question

This question will be a true test of your ability to interpret aerial photographs.

In what season and at what time of day were the stereo pair in Fig. 6-2 taken? Give evidence to support your answer.

7 Remote Sensing: Views from Space

When you watch a weather report on television, you often see a series of **satellite** images that show approaching weather systems (Fig. 7-5 shows such an image). We have become so used to seeing images like these that we take them for granted. The use of satellites to view the earth, however, is a relatively new technology. When your grandparents were your age, they could have seen the image in Fig. 7-1 only in their imaginations. It was taken by a satellite orbiting high above the border between Alberta and Montana. The 49th parallel, the border between Canada and the United States, can be seen quite clearly because the land-use patterns are different in each country. In Canada, most of the land is used for grazing cattle, but south of the border, grain crops are grown in rectangular fields.

The technology for studying earth in this manner is called **remote sensing**. There are two types of remote sensing. One type uses photographs taken from aircraft. Aerial photographs can be used to produce three-dimensional images of the earth's surface. These images

KEY TERMS

satellite

remote sensing

geostationary orbit

false colours

radar

satellite: manufactured object launched by a rocket to circle the earth, for communicating, studying the earth's resources, and helping the military

Remote sensing using aerial photographs is discussed in Chapter 6.

To learn more about remote sensing, check www.ccrs.nrcan.gc.ca/ccrs/imgserv/tour/toure.html

◁ **Fig. 7-1** *In some places, the boundary between Canada and the United States can be seen from space even though it is not marked on the ground in any way.*

can then be used to produce topographic maps. The other type of remote sensing uses electronic images from satellites. Satellite images cover a very large area and show less detail. On the other hand, aerial photographs taken from an aircraft show more detail of a smaller area. By combining information obtained from these two types of remote sensing, geographers can learn about an area without actually visiting it. In fact, they can make observations that wouldn't be possible even if they did visit the area!

INTERNET

To examine satellite images and aerial photographs from around the world, check terraserver.microsoft.com

HOW SATELLITES COLLECT INFORMATION

Since the 1960s, a variety of satellites have been launched to study large areas of the earth's surface. Satellites are placed in one of two kinds of orbits. Several weather satellites are in **geostationary orbit** 36 000 km above the equator. This means they stay over the same spot on the earth since they move at the same speed as the earth's rotation. From this position, they provide almost continuous observations of the earth's changing weather.

Other satellites follow a north–south orbit. Because the earth rotates from west to east below the orbiting satellite, the satellite appears to shift westward with each orbit. The combination of the satellite's orbit and the earth's rotation allows complete coverage of the earth's surface over a period of time. This time period is called the orbit cycle. The satellite passes over a set point on the earth at the same time during each orbit cycle. Information is therefore collected under the same light conditions from season to season.

Different types of satellites are used to collect information about the earth's land surface. The United States has satellites called Landsat (Land Satellite), the Europeans use SPOT (*Satellite Probatoire pour l'Observation de la Terre*), and Canadians use Radarsat. Satellites like Landsat and SPOT examine the earth's surface with different ranges of wavelengths during daylight hours. The wavelengths reveal different characteristics of the earth's surface. For example, some wavelengths are used to identify types of vegetation and other wavelengths are used to identify soil moisture conditions. The collected information is purchased by government agencies and private companies.

The Spot Image Corporation is owned by governments and private companies in France, Sweden, and Belgium.

As these satellites orbit the earth, they collect data which is sent back to earth for analysis (Fig. 7–2). Colours are artificially added to the images to make the patterns more obvious. They are called **false colours** because they are not the colours you would actually see from space.

Features as small as cars are visible in some images. It is rumoured that top secret military satellites are able to pick out the print in a newspaper.

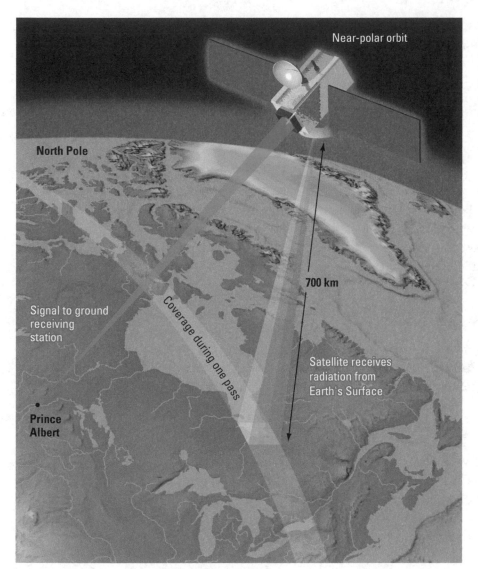

Near-polar orbit

North Pole

700 km

Signal to ground receiving station

Coverage during one pass

Satellite receives radiation from Earth's Surface

Prince Albert

◁ **Fig. 7-2** *Satellites with a north-south orbit fly over the same location at regular intervals. The transfer and processing of satellite data is a complex task involving several steps.*

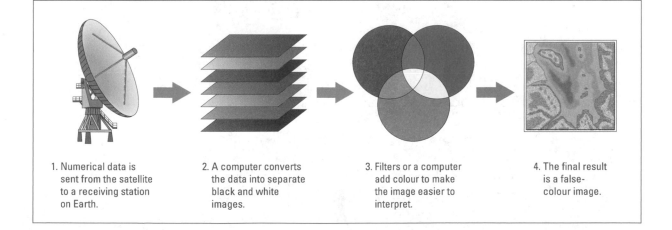

1. Numerical data is sent from the satellite to a receiving station on Earth.

2. A computer converts the data into separate black and white images.

3. Filters or a computer add colour to make the image easier to interpret.

4. The final result is a false-colour image.

Although it takes years of training to fully interpret such images, you can gain some understanding about the earth's surface on satellite images by following this basic guide for the images in this chapter:

- shades of red indicate things that grow (crops and other vegetation)
- shades of blue-green to grey indicate areas where there are few things growing, for example, urban areas or bare soil
- shades of blue to black indicate shallow and deep water

Be aware - both urban areas and rural areas with little vegetation appear as a blue-green colour.

The data from these satellites is received by ground stations around the world. Canada has two such stations: Gatineau, Québec; and Prince Albert, Saskatchewan. Canada has been receiving satellite images since 1972, and has become a world leader in the field. Over the years, Canadian companies have relied on this experience to design and build receiving stations and satellites for several countries around the world.

CANADA'S RADARSAT

Canada's early involvement with remote sensing is not surprising. We have a vast country to study and remote sensing is an efficient and relatively inexpensive way to gather information. It is particularly useful because we can examine even the most remote parts of Canada. Also, since observations are made so frequently, remote sensing provides us with a continuous record of any changes that are occurring.

In 1995, the 3200 kg Canadian satellite Radarsat was launched through public and private funding, at a cost of $620 million. It is Canada's first advanced earth observation satellite and is used to monitor environmental changes and provide information for resource development. NASA and the United States government provided the launch in return for data.

NASA did not want to launch Radarsat-2 since they felt that it might expose American military secrets.

Radarsat was built in Canada by Spar Aerospace with a planned lifetime of five years. It has two liquid-fuel engines to control its path and altitude. Protective padding is used to prevent damage from collisions with space debris and solar flares. Solar energy is converted through solar panels into electrical energy to power the satellite.

Radarsat circles the earth at 7 km/second at an altitude of 800 km. It circles the earth 14 times per day which allows coverage of Canada in only three days. The data that is collected can be sent instantly to three North American ground stations located in Gatineau, Québec; Prince Albert, Saskatchewan; and Fairbanks, Alaska. When it is out of range of a ground station, Radarsat can store data on tape for later transmission.

Other ground stations around the world have been licensed to receive and process this data.

Radarsat sends **radar** (microwave) signals to earth and then records them when they are reflected back, and then transmits the data to a receiving station for processing into images. Radarsat's radar is electronically programmed. There is a choice of seven different beam modes (levels of detail and swath widths). Also, the radar beam can be pointed at different angles (Fig. 7-3). The different beams can be steered so that they can cover different swaths from 50 to 500 km and resolutions from 10 to 100 m. The radar signals can be rotated to examine features of the earth from different angles. This feature allows the production of digital 3-D models of the earth's surface. Radarsat does not rely on sunlight to illuminate the surface, so it can make images of the earth's surface 24 hours a day. It is also able to view the earth's surface under any weather conditions because its signals can penetrate clouds, rain, and fog.

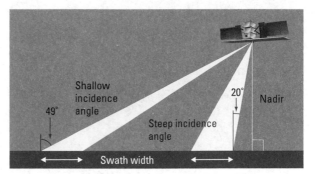

△ **Fig. 7-3** *Both the beam mode (swath width and resolution) and the position of the beam can be changed which makes this a very flexible satellite.*

A swath is the area imaged on the earth's surface. Resolution refers to the size of the object that is visible in the image. For example, a 10 m resolution means that objects as small as 10 m, such as streets and buildings, are visible in the image.

USES OF REMOTE SENSING

In the spring of 1997, one of Canada's worst natural disasters hit southern Manitoba as a result of heavy winter snows that melted rapidly. The Red River flooded its banks. Radarsat images helped officials determine when and where the flood waters would peak. This information was very helpful in evacuating citizens and pinpointing locations where dikes had to be built (Fig. 7-4).

The flooded area was over 100 km in length and up to 40 km wide in places. For a short period, it was the 76th largest lake in the world, and caused 28 000 Manitobans to flee their homes.

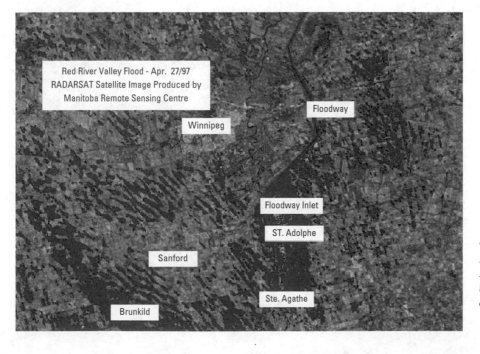

Red River Valley Flood - Apr. 27/97
RADARSAT Satellite Image Produced by
Manitoba Remote Sensing Centre

Floodway

Winnipeg

Floodway Inlet

ST. Adolphe

Sanford

Ste. Agathe

Brunkild

◁ **Fig. 7-4** *During the Red River flood of 1997, Radarsat was used to track the extent of the flood, and assess flood damage.*

There is much that can be done with the data collected through remote sensing. The information may be used

- to study weather and climate, e.g., to follow the development and movement of storms
- for agricultural management, e.g., to examine crop types, growth stages, crop damage from pests and drought, and to predict yields
- for land-cover classification and forest management, e.g., for forest inventory, monitoring cutting, assessing fire damage
- for map making and updating, e.g., to update legal boundaries and urban expansion, and to aid in managing natural resources
- for geology and mineral exploration, e.g., to relate faults and folds to mineral deposits
- for mapping sea ice patterns, e.g., to plan safe ship routes and protect offshore oil platforms
- to monitor the environment, e.g., to track the location and effects of pollution, and to study wildlife habitat
- to monitor the oceans and coastal regions, e.g., to assess fish stock and biological activity, oil spills, and shipping
- to analyze water resources, e.g., to map and monitor floods, determine snow thickness, and to map drainage basins
- to study the impact of geologic events, e.g., earthquakes and volcanic eruptions

yield: an amount produced

forest inventory: a map and related statistics which outline stands of trees of similar type, age

See the Connecting Study in Chapter 25.

The inventory data is stored and managed using geographical information systems, discussed in Chapter 5.

QUESTIONS

CHECK YOUR UNDERSTANDING

1. Define the term "remote sensing."

2. Why are some satellites in geostationary orbits while others are in north-south orbits? Give examples in your answer.

3. a) What are false colours?

   b) Describe the process by which a satellite produces a false-colour image.

   c) Explain the advantage of using false colours rather than real colours in a satellite image.

4. List five important ways that remote sensing information can be used in the study of the earth.

THINK AND COMMUNICATE

5. Satellite images provide information that may be used for many purposes including commercial and political intelligence.

   a) How might a Canadian grain-marketing company use Landsat images that show the wheat-growing areas in other grain-producing countries?

   b) Food production in different countries can be predicted by studying the size of agricultural regions, the impact of drought, disease, or pests, and the expected crop yield. How might an organization like the United Nations Food and Agricultural Organization use this information?

◁ **Fig. 7-5** *For most people, satellite weather maps are the most familiar form of remote sensing.*

USING SATELLITE IMAGES

Let's examine some satellite images to see how they can be used:

- for predicting weather
- for studying environmental pollution
- for making maps

Weather Forecasting

Many of us listen to or watch a weather forecast almost every day, several times a week. These forecasts provide information on temperature, cloud cover, precipitation, winds, and storms. Forecasting weather accurately is a very difficult task because there are so many factors to consider and these tend to change very rapidly. The task is becoming easier, however, because satellites provide almost continuous coverage of the earth.

QUESTIONS

ANALYZE AND APPLY

1. The satellite image in Fig. 7-5 shows southeastern United States and the Gulf of Mexico.

   a) What weather does this image show?

   b) Why are satellite images more useful than local weather radar in this case?

   c) What is the location of the storm? You may wish to consult an atlas.

   d) What information could be gained by comparing this image with one taken a few hours earlier?

Environmental Pollution

Damage to trees and crops from air and water pollution can be detected from satellite images. The false colours in Fig. 7-6 tell us the following about the forest:

- light red indicates new growth and hard-wood trees
- dark red indicates coniferous trees
- blue–green indicates bare soil, or very little or dying vegetation

Fig. 7-6 ▷
A forested area in Northern Ontario

QUESTIONS

ANALYZE AND APPLY

1. What type of tree covers most of this area?

2. What might the small patches of blue-green represent?

3. a) What is the shape of the large blue-green area?

   b) What do you think this blue-green area represents? What might cause it? What would your answer be if you knew that there was a smelter in the area? (In a smelter, metal is separated from ore by melting.)

4. North is at the top of the image. Determine the prevailing wind direction in this area. Explain how you determined this.

5. How could you tell from satellite images taken over a period of time whether the industry causing air pollution has taken measures to reduce it?

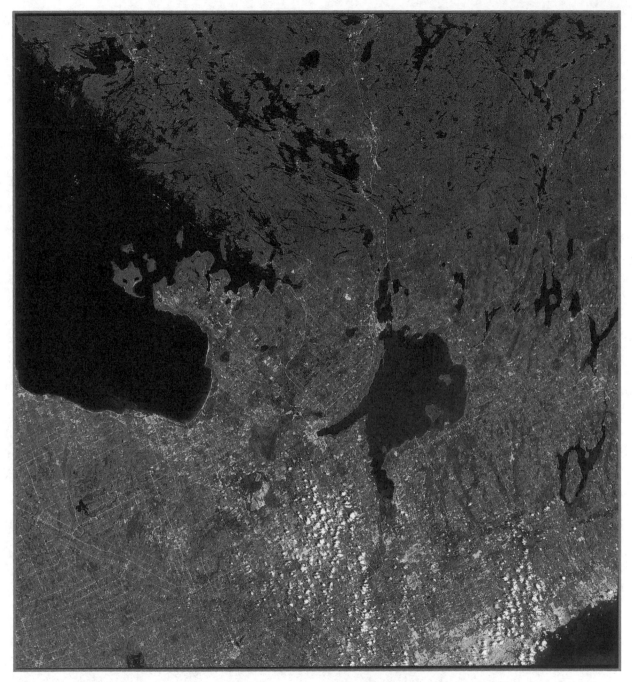

△ **Fig. 7-7** *Southern Ontario. The false colours in this image tell us the following:*

- *dark red/brown indicates dense forest and/or coniferous trees*
- *light red indicates hardwood forest*
- *pink indicates agricultural crops*
- *light blue indicates little vegetation, soil, and urban areas*
- *dark blue indicates water*

Map Making

Satellite images, like aerial photographs, may be used to draw maps. Using the satellite image of Southern Ontario (Fig. 7-7) and an atlas map of the same region, complete the following exercise.

1. Compare this satellite image with the atlas map. What things can you see
   a) on both
   b) only on the atlas map
   c) only on the satellite image

2. On a piece of tracing paper or clear acetate,
   a) draw the border of the satellite image
   b) trace the shoreline of all the lakes
   c) draw the rivers that you can see
   d) label the lakes and rivers

3. Locate and label the following on your map:
   a) the boundary of the urban areas centred on Toronto
   b) the communities of Barrie and Orillia
   c) Highway 11, north of Orillia (Hint: Settlement often occurs along major highways.)

4. a) On your map, draw and shade in the areas that appear as dark red on the satellite image.
   b) What does this colour represent?
   c) Densely forested areas are frequently found in river valleys. What do the river valleys look like in this image?
   d) During the last Ice Age, glaciers shaped the landscape as they moved over this region. By observing the shapes of the lakes northeast of Lake Simcoe and the river valleys between Lake Simcoe and Lake Scugog, determine which direction it appears the glaciers moved.

5. On this image, the Canadian Shield is covered by dense forest but the Great Lakes Lowland is primarily agricultural land with some hardwood and coniferous forests.
   a) Trace the boundary between the Canadian Shield and the Great Lakes Lowland. (Refer to an atlas as well as the image if you are not sure where the boundary may be located.)
   b) How can you tell where this boundary is located?
   c) What might cause the different patterns and colours that you see?

8 Graph It!

Graphs can be extremely useful in helping us to see relationships and patterns in number data. Fig. 8-1 is one of the most famous graphs of all time. It was drawn after Napoleon's disastrous invasion of Russia in 1812-13 and has been called "the best statistical graph ever drawn." It shows an enormous amount of information in a remarkably clear and easily understood manner. Even if you do not read French very well (or at all) you can see that the invasion started with an army of 422 000 soldiers and finished with only 10 000. What other information is given in this graph?

Any time you create a graph, your goal should be the same as Monsieur Minard's (the author of this graph): to present a particular set of numerical information in the most clear and understandable manner. In earlier grades, you probably learned to create two simple types of graphs: bar and line graphs. Your teacher may want to review these with you. In this chapter, you will learn how to create more complicated graphs, how to use the graphing features of a spreadsheet program, and how to avoid some of the pitfalls of graphing.

▽ **Fig. 8-1** *Graph illustrating Napoleon's dwindling army during his invasion of Russia. The months in the dates that appear along the bottom of the graph are as follows:*
X^{bre}=December
9bre=November
8bre=October

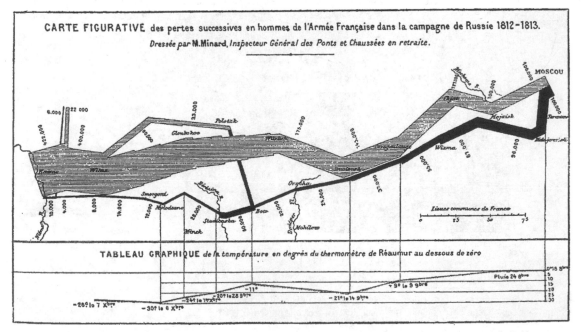

CARTE FIGURATIVE des pertes successives en hommes de l'Armée Française dans la campagne de Russie 1812-1813.

Dressée par M. Minard, Inspecteur Général des Ponts et Chaussées en retraite.

TABLEAU GRAPHIQUE de la température en degrés du thermomètre de Réaumur au dessous de zéro

X^{bre} = December   9bre = November   8bre = October

STACKED BAR GRAPH

A **stacked bar graph** is very much like a simple bar graph, with one important difference. While each bar in a simple bar graph represents one value, a stacked bar can be used to represent several closely related values. Like a simple bar graph, a stacked bar graph can have either horizontal or vertical bars.

In the example below, we chose to make a vertical graph using the data in Fig. 8-2.

In a vertical graph, the horizontal, or x-axis, is used to show the categories, in this case, the regions where fishing occurs. The vertical, or y-axis, is used to show the numerical values. The completed graph is shown in Fig. 8-3, along with suggestions on how to make it.

Examples of groundfish are cod and halibut. Examples of pelagic fish are salmon and herring. Examples of shellfish are lobster and crab. See Chapter 21 for more information on fishing.

VALUE OF FISH CAUGHT IN CANADA, 1994 (IN DOLLARS)

	Groundfish	Pelagic Fish	Shellfish
Atlantic Coast	123 500 000	73 700 000	911 600 000
Pacific Coast	101 000 000	261 300 000	93 600 000
Total	224 500 000	335 000 000	1 005 200 000

◁ **Fig. 8-2** *This data is shown on the stacked bar graph in Fig. 8-3.*

2 Choose the vertical scale. To do this, decide what data will give you the longest bar. In this case, it is the *Total* bar. If a total is not given, you will have to calculate it. Label the scale.

1. Decide on the size of your graph. If you have large amount of data you might want to draw a full-page graph.

◁ **Fig. 8-3** *A stacked bar graph is only slightly more complicated to draw than a simple bar graph.*

5. Add an appropriate legend and title.

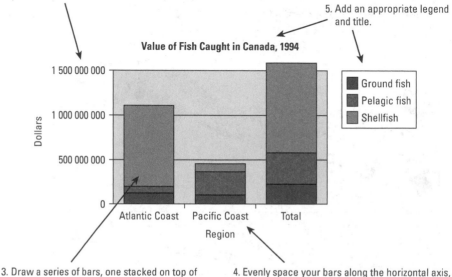

3. Draw a series of bars, one stacked on top of the other, to represent the data for each region.

4. Evenly space your bars along the horizontal axis, and label this axis and the bars.

X/Y SCATTERGRAPH

An **x/y scattergraph** is a very simple and useful way of showing the relationship between two sets of data. For example, you could use a scattergraph to illustrate if there is a relationship between the amount of education of a certain group of people and their salaries, or if there is a relationship between the ages of people and how often they exercise.

We might wonder if there is a relationship between the ability to read and the number of children born in a country, but it is difficult to tell from the numbers in Fig. 8-4. A quick look at the scattergraph produced from this data (Fig. 8-5) shows that there is a clear relationship between these measures.

One question that is often asked about scattergraphs is which variable to put on each axis. A scattergraph is like a line graph in that there is often an **independent variable** that goes on the horizontal axis and a **dependent variable** that goes on the vertical axis. By this we mean that the dependent variable is, to a greater or lesser extent, caused or influenced by the independent variable. In this case, it would be reasonable to think that higher literacy rates would tend to result in smaller families since people would have more access to information about family planning. In some cases, there is no obvious independent/dependent relationship, and it does not matter on which axis you place your information.

▽**Fig. 8-4** *This data is shown on the x/y scattergraph in Fig. 8-5.*

Adult Literacy Rate (%)	Total Fertility Rate
60	3.4
36	5.9
31	7.3
78	5.4
83	2.4
85	4.4
99	1.6
90	3.1
66	4.6
96	2.7
91	1.8
32	6.9
20	6.9

◁ **Fig. 8-5** *Adult literacy rate is the percentage of the adult population who can read and write. Total fertility is the average number of children that would be born to one woman in her lifetime.*

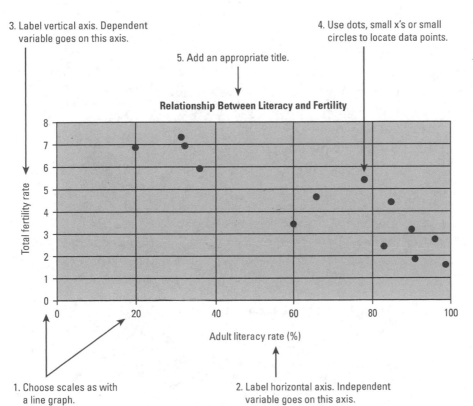

3. Label vertical axis. Dependent variable goes on this axis.

4. Use dots, small x's or small circles to locate data points.

5. Add an appropriate title.

Relationship Between Literacy and Fertility

Total fertility rate

Adult literacy rate (%)

1. Choose scales as with a line graph.

2. Label horizontal axis. Independent variable goes on this axis.

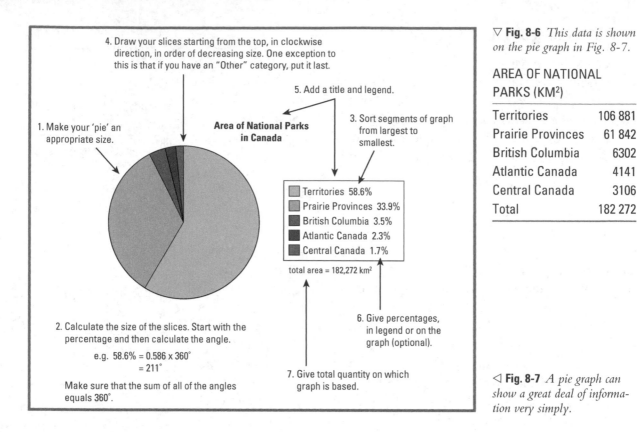

1. Make your 'pie' an appropriate size.

2. Calculate the size of the slices. Start with the percentage and then calculate the angle.

    e.g. 58.6% = 0.586 x 360°
                 = 211°

    Make sure that the sum of all of the angles equals 360°.

3. Sort segments of graph from largest to smallest.

4. Draw your slices starting from the top, in clockwise direction, in order of decreasing size. One exception to this is that if you have an "Other" category, put it last.

5. Add a title and legend.

6. Give percentages, in legend or on the graph (optional).

7. Give total quantity on which graph is based.

Area of National Parks in Canada

- Territories 58.6%
- Prairie Provinces 33.9%
- British Columbia 3.5%
- Atlantic Canada 2.3%
- Central Canada 1.7%

total area = 182,272 km²

▽ **Fig. 8-6** *This data is shown on the pie graph in Fig. 8-7.*

AREA OF NATIONAL PARKS (KM²)

Territories	106 881
Prairie Provinces	61 842
British Columbia	6302
Atlantic Canada	4141
Central Canada	3106
Total	182 272

◁ **Fig. 8-7** *A pie graph can show a great deal of information very simply.*

PIE GRAPHS

Pie graphs are frequently used in newspapers, magazines, and on television news shows since they are very easy to understand and quickly give the viewer a sense of the information being presented. They are not very difficult to draw as long as you remember a few things from math class, like how to use a protractor and how many degrees there are in a circle. Compare the data in Fig. 8-6 with the pie graph produced from this data (Fig. 8-7). Clearly, the graph makes the information much easier to understand.

Remember that a pie graph shows values that are part of a whole, so you could use it to show such things as how many students in your school are in each grade or what percentage of the day you spend sleeping, eating, studying, and so on.

PROPORTIONAL AREA GRAPHS

There are situations when creating a graph, where we want to use shapes or symbols to represent the numerical data. Fig. 8-8 shows the number of unemployed workers in each province in 1995. This infor-

▽**Fig. 8-8** *This data is shown by the circles that appear in the proportional area graph in Fig. 8-9.*

NUMBER OF UNEMPLOYED, 1995

Newfoundland	44 000
P. E. I.	10 000
Nova Scotia	53 000
New Brunswick	41 000
Québec	408 000
Ontario	501 000
Manitoba	42 000
Saskatchewan	34 000
Alberta	116 000
British Columbia	173 000

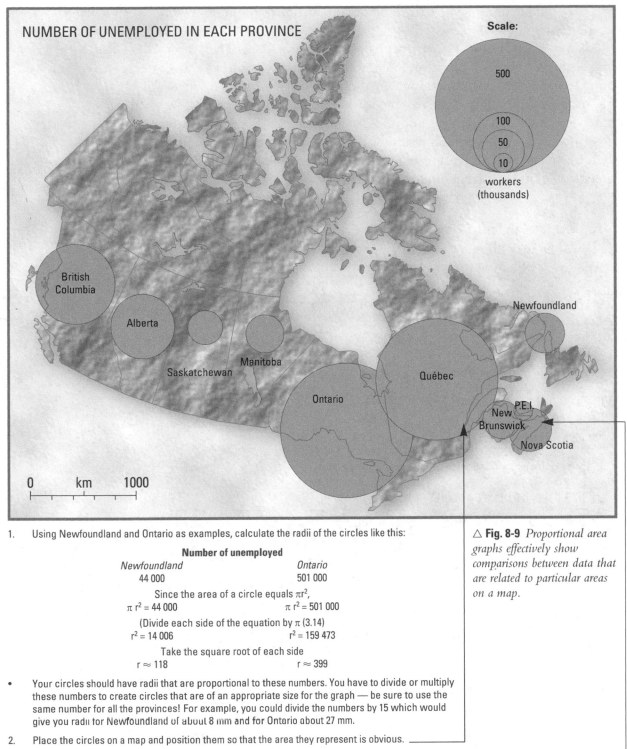

NUMBER OF UNEMPLOYED IN EACH PROVINCE

Scale:

500

100

50

10

workers
(thousands)

British
Columbia

Alberta

Saskatchewan

Manitoba

Ontario

Québec

Newfoundland

New
Brunswick

P.E.I.

Nova Scotia

0   km   1000

1.   Using Newfoundland and Ontario as examples, calculate the radii of the circles like this:

Number of unemployed

Newfoundland   *Ontario*
44 000   501 000

Since the area of a circle equals πr^2,
$\pi r^2 = 44\ 000$ $\pi r^2 = 501\ 000$

(Divide each side of the equation by π (3.14)
$r^2 = 14\ 006$ $r^2 = 159\ 473$

Take the square root of each side
$r \approx 118$ $r \approx 399$

•   Your circles should have radii that are proportional to these numbers. You have to divide or multiply
     these numbers to create circles that are of an appropriate size for the graph — be sure to use the
     same number for all the provinces! For example, you could divide the numbers by 15 which would
     give you radii for Newfoundland of about 8 mm and for Ontario about 27 mm.

2.   Place the circles on a map and position them so that the area they represent is obvious.

3.   Circles may overlap, but remember to place smaller circles on top.

4.   Add an appropriate legend and title.

△ **Fig. 8-9** *Proportional area
graphs effectively show
comparisons between data that
are related to particular areas
on a map.*

mation is graphed in Fig. 8-9, using circles proportional to the numbers in the chart.

While **proportional area graphs** can use many shapes, they most frequently use circles and are often combined with pie graphs to show, not just the amount of something, but also how this quantity is divided. For example, you might draw two proportional circles, one to show how much you spend in one year and the other, somewhat larger, to show how much the richest person in the world, Bill Gates, spends. You could then use these circles to create pie graphs to show how much each student spends on clothes, entertainment, and so on.

1. Examine the four tables of data in Fig. 8-10.
   a) Draw a different type of graph, of the four presented in this chapter, to represent each table of data. Choose a type of graph that suits the characteristics of the data.
   b) Explain why you chose the particular type of graph for each set of data.

▽ **Fig. 8-10**

A) CATEGORIES OF IMMIGRANTS TO CANADA, 1995

Independents	105 809
Refugees	28 400
Family	77 061

*Chapter 17 discusses immigration categories in more detail.

B) SIZE OF CANADIAN FAMILIES, 1991 (THOUSANDS)

No children at home	2580
One child at home	1945
Two children at home	1927
Three children at home	691
Four children at home	165
Five children at home	33
Six or more children at home	15

C) SOURCES OF IMMIGRANTS TO CANADA, 1975-95

	1975	1985	1995
Asia	52 024	39 438	129 001
Europe	68 733	18 530	41 187
Other Countries	67 124	26 334	42 082

D) AREA AND POPULATION OF CENSUS METROPOLITAN AREAS IN CANADA, 1996

	Area (km²)	Population (thousands)
Calgary	5083	822
Chicoutimi-Jonquière	1723	160
Edmonton	9536	863
Halifax	2508	333
Hamilton	1358	624
Kitchener	824	383
London	2105	399
Montréal	4024	3327
Oshawa	894	269
Ottawa-Hull	5686	1010
Québec	3150	672
Regina	3422	194
Saint John	3509	126
St. Catharines-Niagara	1400	372
St. John's	790	174
Saskatoon	5322	219
Sherbrooke	979	147
Sudbury	2612	160
Thunder Bay	2295	126
Toronto	5868	4264
Trois-Rivières	872	140
Vancouver	2821	1832
Victoria	633	304
Windsor	862	279
Winnipeg	4078	667

USING A SPREADSHEET

Some of you may have used a spreadsheet to create the graphs in this chapter.

Figures 8-3, 8-5, 8-7, and 8-9 can be created with AppleWorks, which is a program used in many schools. With this type of program, you will be able to draw most of the graphs you will need. To produce more complex graphs, you can use more sophisticated spreadsheet programs such as Microsoft Excel. Creating graphs on a spreadsheet has several advantages.

- It can be much faster than drawing graphs by hand. This is particularly the case when the data is already in a computer file or if you have to do several graphs with similar formats.

- You can produce more sophisticated, professional-looking graphs.

A spreadsheet is a type of computer program that is designed to assist with numerical calculations and graph creation.

An introduction to graphing with Excel is found at www2.civl.port.ac.uk/ compapps/ssgraphsxl.htm

- If your graphs are to be used in a research paper, a computer-based presentation, or an Internet Web page, they can be easily moved from the spreadsheet to the other program.

While computerized graphing can be very useful, there are some hints that will help you to do the best job possible.

- The most important tip is not to overuse all of the features that a spreadsheet program offers you. Remember that you are trying to communicate ideas to your reader and a complex graph or three-dimensional effects may only make your graph harder to understand.

- The program will automatically do a lot of tasks for you, e.g., label axes, choose symbols, and set scales. You may find that you can achieve a more effective result by doing these things yourself. Experiment with the controls to achieve exactly what you want.

- The arrangement of the numbers on the spreadsheet can have a major impact on how the graph looks. You may want to sort the data or rearrange the order of the columns before you start to graph.

In fact, you may have to move data around to be able to graph it.

QUESTIONS

ANALYZE AND APPLY

1. a) Describe the general characteristics that any graph must have to do its job successfully.

   b) How does Minard's graph of Napoleon's retreat from Moscow meet these requirements?

9 Cruising the Information Superhighway

◁ **Fig. 9-1** *Could this be you?*

The **Internet** is such an accepted part of our lives that it is hard to believe that only a few years ago it did not even exist. The parent of the Internet was created in the 1970s to provide a means of communication for the United States government and military in the event of a nuclear war. The scientists who created it would never have guessed that in approximately 25 years you would be using it to do research for your geography course, let alone to see samples from a new music video. In this chapter, you will have a chance to learn (or improve your ability) to use the Internet as a research tool.

Think of how often you see a Web address listed on television, in the newspapers, or in advertising.

The **World Wide Web** (WWW) is undoubtedly the world's largest cooperative effort. It is an enormous network of millions of sites that contain information on more topics than you could ever imagine. While many of these sites (or **Web pages**) concentrate on somewhat lighter matters — for example, stories about alien abductions, and information about the latest Hollywood movies — there are an enormous number of Web pages that are useful to students of geography and other subjects.

While there are other parts to the Internet, this chapter will concentrate on the World Wide Web, since it is the most valuable element of the Internet for doing research.

The biggest problem with the WWW is finding the Web pages you want among the millions that exist. Let's assume that your family has decided to take a holiday in Canada's new territory, Nunavut. There are few places in the world that are as unspoiled as Nunavut and offer so many opportunities for adventure tourism activities like hiking, ocean kayaking, and whale watching. Your job is to do preliminary research on what is available for your holiday and on who you can contact to make arrangements for your trip. Where do you start? This is where a **search engine** is useful. A search engine is a system that is designed to help you find Web sites on the subject of your choice. Most WWW users are aware of search engines, but few use them effectively. There are many search engines, and they operate in different ways; we will look only at two: **AltaVista** and **Yahoo!**

This exercise is best done at a computer which is connected to the Internet.

www.altavista.com

USING ALTAVISTA

AltaVista uses a series of powerful computers to continually search all of the Web sites on the Internet and record what words are used in each site. This is a remarkable undertaking when you remember that there are millions of Web pages!

To search with AltaVista, you input the terms you are looking for and click on the *Search* button. For your holiday research, enter the words *nunavut tourism* and you will find a total of 428 520 matches or **hits** (Fig. 9–2)! The question becomes how to narrow your search in some way.

There are many techniques to limit your search. A good first step is to require that both of these words be present on the page. If you do this, you get a remarkable decrease in the number of hits. This is easily done by adding a plus (+) sign in front of each term that must appear. Also,

The number of hits which appear for your search may vary from this total (and other totals in this chapter) as new sites are developed and others are deleted from the Web.

◁ **Fig. 9-2**

You can add a minus (–) sign to a word if you want that word *not* to appear on a Web page. For example, you might make the following search +*nunavut* +*tourism* -*government*, if you did not want to find Web pages about the role of government in helping the tourism industry.

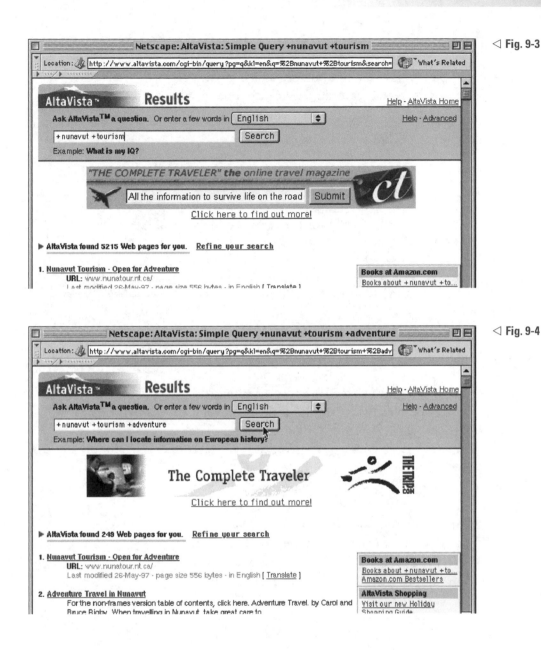

◁ Fig. 9-3

◁ Fig. 9-4

you can specify the language used in the Web pages. In this case, if you choose to look only at English language sites, you get a minor improvement (Fig. 9-3).

You are getting there, but this is still a very large number of hits. Your search can be narrowed even further by adding the search term *+adventure* (Fig. 9-4). While 249 hits is still a large number of Web pages to investigate, you must remember that AltaVista, like most search engines, sorts the Web pages it finds. What you will find is that the pages listed first are the best match to the search terms that you have provided. At this point, you can start scanning the list of sites and visiting any that appear likely to have useful information for planning your vacation.

If you were researching the Swiss banking industry, for example, choosing English-only sites would likely be a big help in reducing the number of hits.

HINTS FOR USING ALTAVISTA

Search engines are a relatively new invention and methods have not yet been standardized. Most search engines will have similar features but may use somewhat different methods for achieving the same results.

1. It is best to put all search terms in lower case. For example, searching for *nunavut* would find *Nunavut* and *NUNAVUT*, while searching for *Nunavut* would not find *NUNAVUT*.

2. You can search for a phrase by putting it into double quotes. For example, "niagara falls" would be more specific than *+niagara +falls*. The first search would look specifically for the name while the latter search might find a Web page about diseased grapes in the Niagara fruit belt falling off their vines!

3. You can also do what is called a wildcard search. For example, if you search for *tour**, you will find all words that start with *tour* like *tourism*, *touring*, and *tourist*.

USING YAHOO!

Yahoo! is a search engine that is based on a tree structure of categories and subcategories. The categories on this figure are the roots of the tree (Fig. 9-5). You move up the tree by clicking on one of these categories. The highest branches of this tree are the actual Web pages. If you are interested in adventure tourism in Nunavut, you could choose the *Outdoors* subcategory of the *Recreation and Sports* category or the *Countries* subcategory of the *Regional* category. This is typical of the sort of choice that you frequently face when using Yahoo! In some cases, you could follow both (or many) possible category linkages but this might mean a great deal of work. In general, you must try to determine which branch is likely to prove most fruitful. In this case, it would make most sense to follow the *Countries* linkages in the *Regional* category.

When you click on *Countries*, you come to a list of all of the countries in the world. A small part of this list is shown in Fig. 9-6. As you can see, there are a huge number of Web sites in Canada. Your job is to determine if any of these sites has information about Nunavut tourism.

When you click on the Canada link, you are taken to a list of all the provinces and territories along with a Canadian topics list (Fig. 9-7).

You keep going in a similar fashion until you reach the Nunavut list.

At this point you have a list, not of subcategories but, of actual Web pages. At least a couple of sites look promising (Fig. 9-8).

If you choose *Nunavut Handbook*, you will get a Web page that promotes a Nunavut guidebook and includes information about travel in the new territory (Fig. 9-9).

The search features of electronic library cataloguing systems, CD-ROM encyclopedias, and magazine and newspaper indexes have similar functions.

To learn more about searching the Internet with AltaVista, check www.learnthenet.com/english/html/78tutorial.htm

www.yahoo.com

Note that if you follow only the Canada linkages, you will not find Nunavut tourism sites that might exist in other countries.

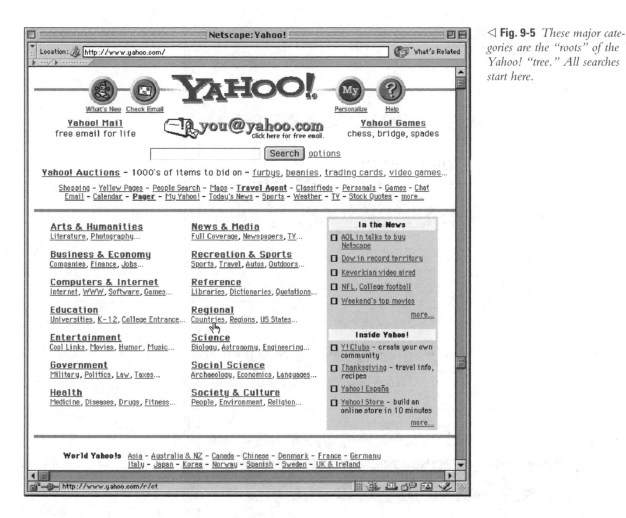

◁ **Fig. 9-5** *These major categories are the "roots" of the Yahoo! "tree." All searches start here.*

◁ **Fig. 9-6** *While the Internet does link the entire world, (Do you know where all of these countries are?) the number of Web sites shown in each country suggest that the Internet is most developed in the richest countries.*

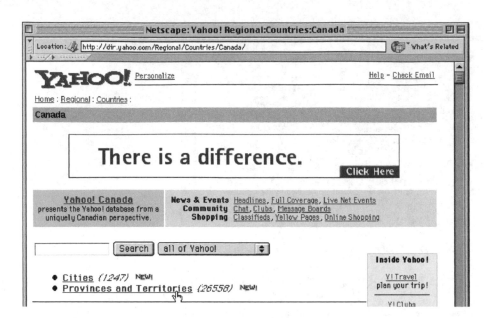

◁ **Fig. 9-7** *You keep moving "up" the tree toward your goal.*

◁ **Fig. 9-8** *At this point, specific Web pages start to appear.*

Please note that the Internet is constantly changing. The Web pages and links you discover may not look exactly like those represented in this book.

HOW DO YOU CHOOSE A SEARCH ENGINE?

Over time, you will come to feel comfortable using one or two search engines that may or may not include AltaVista and Yahoo! Most search engines tend to follow one of the models provided in this chapter, so it

For a comprehensive comparison of Internet search engines, check www.ultranet.com/ ~egrlib/tutor.htm

is easy to switch from one to another. These search engines represent two different ways of approaching a WWW search. It is a good idea to know how and when to use each type. How do you know which one to choose?

- If you have a pretty good idea of what you are looking for, Yahoo! is likely to be faster.
- On the other hand, if you don't know where a particular Web page might be, use AltaVista which is better for "fishing expeditions."

ASSESSING THE VALUE OF WEB PAGES

Let's assume that you find a Web page on the topic that you are researching. How do you know if the information on the page is valid? This is a problem with any information source that you might use. There is, however, an added problem with the information posted on the Internet. When you watch a news program on television, you are usually aware of the **bias** of those who created it. You know that a lot of time and money went into producing the television show. You realize that recognized experts in the field will likely be involved in creating and reviewing the program's content. Finally, if you are offended by the show's content, you can complain to a supervising agency like the Canadian Radio-Television Commission (CRTC).

This is not always the case with the Internet. It is neither difficult nor expensive to post a Web page. Anyone may post any information or personal opinion they wish without a thought about accuracy, or whether someone reading the page will be offended. There is also no agency that hears complaints about something on the Internet.

Many people have said that this is one of the best features of the Internet because it allows ordinary people to express their ideas to the world. Consider the case of the book *Exploring Nunavut*, which you found in your sample Internet search. The publishers used the Internet to inform the world of their book and, in return, help anyone in the world who is planning a visit to Nunavut. On the other hand, the freedom of the Internet also means that people can create Web pages that include the most controversial (and even silly) ideas. As an Internet user, you must be aware of this and be prepared to view everything you see very critically.

△ **Fig. 9-9** *This Web page looks like it will have information to help you plan your vacation.*

QUESTIONS

CHECK YOUR UNDERSTANDING

1. a) What is the World Wide Web, and why is it useful for someone doing research?

   b) Name another element of the Internet.

2. a) What is a search engine?

   b) Yahoo! and AltaVista work in different ways. Compare the two approaches.

ANALYZE AND APPLY

3. a) Choose one of the following topics or a topic given to you by your teacher for the subject of an Internet search.

   Topics for Internet search
   - diamond mining in Canada
   - pollution of the Great Lakes in Canada
   - aquaculture in Canada
   - Hibernia oil project
   - Canadian foreign aid
   - summer theatre in Canada
   - new golf courses in Canada
   - cheese making in Canada
   - archaeology projects in Canada
   - minor league professional baseball in Canada
   - GIS job prospects
   - paper recycling

   b) Do you think that your topic would be easier to research with AltaVista or with Yahoo? Why?

   c) Conduct an Internet search using both AltaVista and Yahoo!

   d) Complete an organizer like the one in Fig. 9-10 to compare the success of each search engine. Was your prediction about the most useful search engine for your topic in 3b accurate? If not, why not?

   e) Choose one of the Web pages you found and comment on its bias by answering the following questions.

      i. Who created the page?

      ii. What was the purpose of the page?

      iii. Did the page attempt to provide a balanced approach to the topic?

▽ **Fig. 9-10**

	AltaVista	Yahoo!
Number of sites found		
Speed of search		
Addresses of five sites found (circle duplicates)		

Physical Connections: Canada's Ecozones

The Solemn Land, by J.E.H. MacDonald

10 Geologic History

STUDY GUIDE

By the end of this chapter, you will be able to:

- explain the theory of plate tectonics
- explain how Canada's physical diversity is a result of geologic development
- explain the rock cycle
- identify the four eras and describe events associated with them

Key Terms

plate tectonics	eras	faulting	sedimentary rock
erosion	Canadian Shield	igneous rock	Ice Age
fossils	folding	metamorphic rock	glaciers
geologic time			

Imagine that it is springtime and you are crossing a frozen lake. As you start out, the ice seems stable and solid, but in fact, it is not. Before you reach the other shore, the ice starts to break up. Large cracks develop, separating the ice into huge plates that are moved by wind and currents in the water below. Some of these ice plates are pulled apart, while others are smashed together forcing one to ride up over the other. Some of the plates drift away to form floating platforms.

What does this have to do with the study of geology? The earth's structure is similar to a frozen lake. The surface of the earth is a thin layer of moving plates, and below these plates is material that is also in motion. Every year around the world, there are about 30 000 earthquakes that are strong enough to be felt. These earthquakes indicate the movement of parts of the earth's rigid upper layer.

Seismologists (scientists who study earthquakes) have discovered that earthquakes occur more frequently in a few specific areas (Fig. 10-1). Earthquakes and volcanoes frequently occur where the edges of the earth's plates are colliding or moving away from one another. Not all seismologists, however, agree on the exact locations of the boundaries of the plates.

To learn more about earthquakes in Canada, check www.seismo.nrcan.gc.ca/english/

◁ **Fig. 10-1** *The global distribution of earthquakes of magnitude 5 or greater on the Richter scale.*

1. On the world map provided by your teacher, colour and label the continents. Lightly shade in the world's oceans.

2. Each dot on the map in Fig. 10-1 represents the location of an earthquake. Which statement best describes the pattern of earthquake distribution?

   a) evenly spaced

   b) scattered

   c) in lines and arcs

   d) in separate groupings

3. On the world map provided by your teacher in question 1, use the pattern of earthquakes to draw lines indicating where you think the boundaries between the plates are located. Most of the earthquakes should take place at the edges of the plates. Since some plate boundaries are not very active, you may find it difficult to find the location of some boundaries, but do your best. (Hint: You should end up with a jigsaw pattern — irregularly shaped pieces that fit together.)

4. a) How many plates did you find?

   b) Compare your results with the results of three of your classmates. Did they put their plate boundaries in the same places? Why or why not?

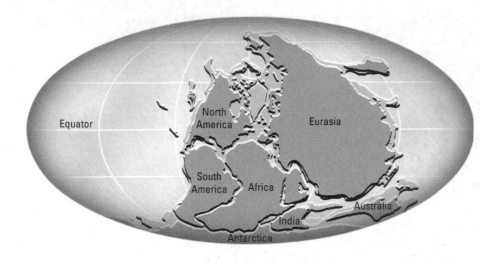

◁ **Fig. 10-2** *About 300 million years ago, the moving land masses came together to form the supercontinent of Pangaea.*

PLATE TECTONICS

If you examine a map of the world, you might notice that the shapes of South America and Africa look like they could fit together. If they were once together, why are they now apart, and what forces could move such large land masses?

In 1915, Alfred Wegener, a German scientist, said that the only possible answer was **continental drift**. He suggested that about 300 million years ago all of the earth's land masses, which were in constant motion, collided to form one supercontinent. He called it **Pangaea**, which means "all land" (Fig. 10-2). About 200 million years ago, the supercontinent of Pangaea started to break up. The pieces drifted in different directions to their present positions.

What proof did Wegener have that the huge continents of the earth could move and that his theory of continental drift was correct (Fig. 10-3)?

Most scientists disagreed with Wegener because he could not explain what mechanism was powerful enough to move huge continents. It was not until the 1960s that the technology existed to further develop Wegener's theory. In fact, it was a Canadian, J. Tuzo Wilson, who helped to spark new interest in the theory of continental drift. By 1968 a new theory, known as **plate tectonics,** was developed.

Plate tectonics is the theory that helps explain most geologic processes. The theory states that the earth's outer shell is made up of about twenty plates (Fig. 10-4). Most of these plates are made up of both a continent and an ocean. They are moving over a weak layer of hot rock, several hundred kilometres below the earth's surface, which flows like slow-moving plastic. No one fully understands the forces that cause the plates to move over this weak layer. It is possible that the unequal distribution of heat within the earth causes **convection currents** to move the plates (Fig. 10-5).

Wegener's theory of continental drift stated that only continents drifted. Today, we know that plates are much larger than continents and contain both continental and oceanic crust.

theory: an explanation based on observation and reasoning

tectonics: relating to the internal forces which deform the earth's crust

convection: a heated fluid rises and carries heat with it, to be replaced by a cool fluid which in turn is heated and rises, creating a current

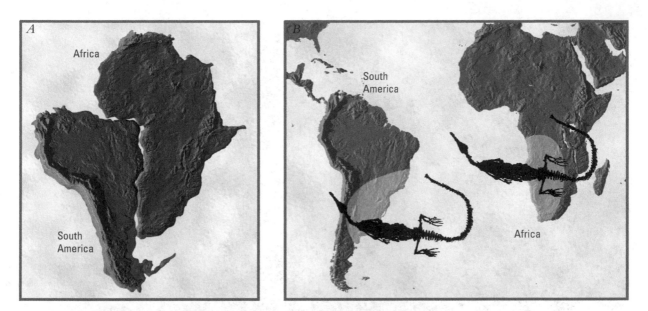

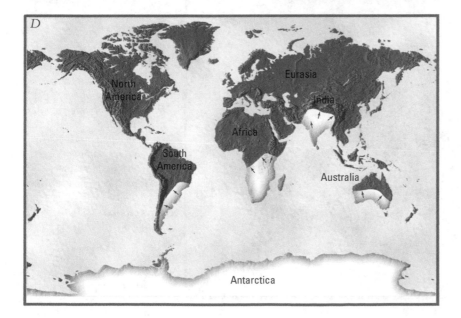

Fig. 10-3

Here is how Wegener tried to prove his theory of continental drift:

A   *He saw the jigsaw fit between South America and Africa.*

B   *He found fossils of the same plants and animals on both continents. He felt that they could only exist in both places if the continents were once joined together.*

C   *There are mountains similar in age and structure on both sides of the Atlantic Ocean — the Appalachians in the eastern United States and Canada, and similar mountains in the northern British Isles and Europe. These mountains formed about 300 million years ago when North America collided with Europe and northern Africa.*

D   *Ice sheets covered southern Africa, India, Australia, and South America about 250 million years ago. How could this ice develop in places that are so warm today? The only explanation seemed to be that at one time the continents were located closer to the South Pole.*

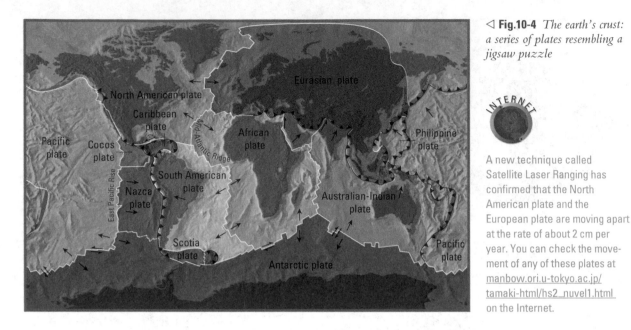

◁ **Fig.10-4** *The earth's crust: a series of plates resembling a jigsaw puzzle*

A new technique called Satellite Laser Ranging has confirmed that the North American plate and the European plate are moving apart at the rate of about 2 cm per year. You can check the movement of any of these plates at manbow.ori.u-tokyo.ac.jp/ tamaki-html/hs2_nuvel1.html on the Internet.

The movement of the earth's plates has shaped Canada in many ways. For example, the mountain chains on the east and west coasts were formed as a result of plates bumping together. Plate tectonics have also played a role in forming Canada's fossil fuels. Oil, gas, and coal were formed as a result of events which took place when Canada's land mass was located in a warmer, tropical climate. Where will Canada be located in the next few hundred million years? Only time will tell.

To learn more about plate tectonics, check www.ucmp.berkeley.edu/ geology/tectonics.html

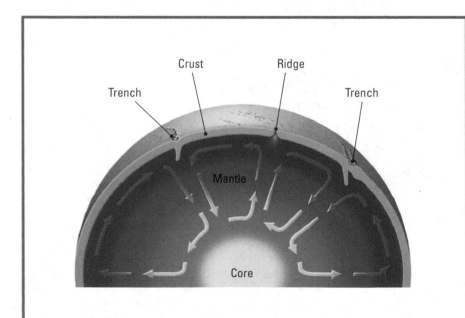

◁ **Fig. 10-5** *Convection cells are caused by the uneven temperatures inside the earth. They are the driving force that moves the plates.*

As two plates move apart, magma comes up from the earth, the sea floor spreads, and a ridge is formed. As two plates collide, one plate descends under the other, creating a trench.

QUESTIONS

CHECK YOUR UNDERSTANDING

1. What was probably the first evidence that led people to think that the continents were once connected?

2. a) What did Alfred Wegener mean by "continental drift"?

   b) What proof did he have to support this theory?

   c) Why did most scientists of his day disagree with his theory?

3. Explain the theory of plate tectonics.

ANALYZE AND APPLY

4. Why are most earthquakes and volcanoes located near plate boundaries?

5. "The movement of the earth's plates has been important to Canada." Explain.

THINK AND COMMUNICATE

6. a) Write a newspaper article describing continental drift that could have appeared when Wegener first published his theory.

   b) Write an editorial that either supports or rejects his theory. Fully explain your reasons.

CANADA'S GEOLOGIC HISTORY

Canada's amazing physical diversity is largely the result of the country's geologic development. Plate tectonics helps to explain part of Canada's geologic history, but there are other forces that come into play. The earth's physical landscape is also partly the result of conflict between forces that build the land higher and those that wear it down. Land that is violently pushed upward by great forces within the earth may form mountains. Mountains, in turn, are slowly and continuously worn down by wind, rain, running water, and ice. This wearing down is called **erosion**.

At different times and in different places, one force has been stronger than the other. This conflict has taken place over hundreds of millions of years, and forms the story of the earth's geologic history. How can we find out about the earth's early physical history? One approach is to carefully analyze landforms, rocks, and **fossils**.

How can we imagine how old the Earth is, when it is estimated to have formed about 4 600 000 000 years ago? Here is a way to help you understand the passing of **geologic time**. Divide your age into a million years. This will tell you how many of your lifetimes equal one million years. For example, if you are 15, you would have to live your life approximately 66 667 (1 000 000 ÷ 15) times before you would live a million years. How many times would the length of your life fit into the earth's lifespan of 4 600 000 000 years?

fossil: the remains or impression of a plant or animal (usually prehistoric) hardened in rock

To learn more about geologic time, check
www.freespace.net/~tnlmcd/internaut/physical/geoltime.html

To make geologic time easier to understand, geologists have divided the earth's history into four time periods called **eras**. Each era represents a time of major sediment deposition and earth movement. While researchers do not all agree on their findings, the following account is widely accepted. An overview of these eras is shown in Fig. 10–6. Complete the following exercise to help you discover what events occurred during which eras.

1. Using the information from Fig. 10–6, answer the questions below.
   a) How old is the earth?
   b) What percentage of the earth's age does each era represent?
   c) What is the name of the era in which we live?
2. a) Draw a line 25 cm long on a piece of paper. Divide it into eras based on the percentages calculated in question 1b.
   b) Using the chart from Fig. 10–6, label the main geological events which occurred in each era along the line.

▽ **Fig. 10-6** *Geologic history is broken down into four major time periods called eras. The eras are separated by major periods of mountain building and, in some cases, mass extinctions.*

Eras	Time Period (millions of years ago)		Major Geological Events	Major Biological Events
	Began	Ended		
Cenozoic (recent life)	66	—	• ice sheets cover much of North America • continents take on their present shape • formation of the Rocky Mountains completed	• human beings develop • age of mammals • modern forms of life evolve
Mesozoic (middle life)	245	66	• formation of Rocky Mountains begins • Innuitian Mountains formed • shallow seas in the interior of North America at various times	• age of reptiles, such as dinosaurs • first flowering plants • first birds and mammals
Paleozoic (ancient life)	570	245	• periods when large parts of North America are covered by shallow seas • Appalachians formed	• age of amphibians and fish • first insects • large swamps-coal formed from this vegetation • first plants and animals appear on land
Precambrian (earliest life)	4600	570	• Precambrian shields, such as the Canadian Shield, Brazilian Shield, African Shield, and Australian Shield are formed	• first multi-celled organisms • first single-celled organisms

Precambrian Era

The earth was formed about 4 600 000 000 years ago. The **Precambrian era** began at this time and lasted for about 4 000 000 000 years, approximately 87% of the earth's history (Fig. 10-6). Many cycles of mountain building and erosion took place during this era (Fig. 10-7). During the Precambrian era, the only part of Canada that existed was the **Canadian Shield** (Fig. 10-8). At times, the peaks of the Canadian Shield were as high as 12 000 m above sea level. These enormous mountains were taller than any that exist today.

The uplifting was accomplished as enormous pressure caused the earth to buckle in a process called **folding**. Other processes such as volcanic action and **faulting**, in which the earth cracks open, also contributed to the formation of these mountain. Over millions of years, these mountains were gradually eroded only to be replaced by new mountains. Areas of land and ocean developed and then disappeared many times.

The rest of Canada, as we know it, did not even form until hundreds of millions of years later. The Canadian Shield is the largest landform region in Canada and the other regions have formed around it. The Shield consists mainly of **igneous** and **metamorphic** rock and some **sedimentary** rock. Igneous rock is created when hot, melted magma

Shields of Precambrian rock form the "core areas" of all the continents. They are called shields because they tend to have the domed shape of a warrior's shield. The centre of the Canadian Shield, however, is lower than its outer rim.

Now, most parts of the Canadian Shield are less than 500 m high.

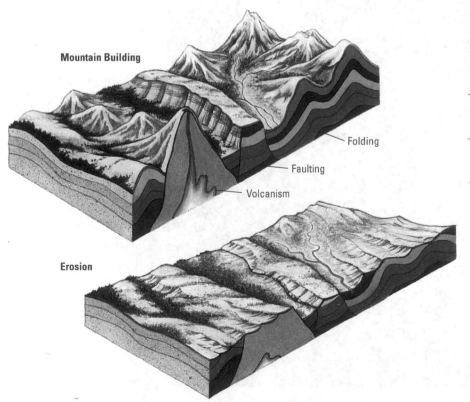

Mountain Building

Folding

Faulting

Volcanism

Erosion

◁ **Fig. 10-7** *The features of the earth are largely a result of the conflict between the forces of mountain building and the forces of erosion. Volcanoes, folding, and faulting are the major forces that build up the landscape. Wind, rain, running water, glaciers, temperature changes, and chemical reactions are the major forces that erode the land.*

Eroded material from shield deposited in ancient seas, hardens into rock.

Erosion wears down the shield mountains.

Precambrian Shield was formed billions of years ago.

◁ **Fig. 10-8** *Over hundreds of millions of years, starting in the Precambrian era, the mountains of the ancient Canadian Shield were eroded. The sediments produced were carried by rivers to nearby seas. The sediments eventually formed sedimentary rock.*

65 million years ago, Western Cordillera formed by collision of plates.

300 million years ago, Appalachians formed by collision of plates.

Western plains emerge from ancient seas.

Eastern lowlands emerge from ancient seas.

Shield greatly reduced by erosion.

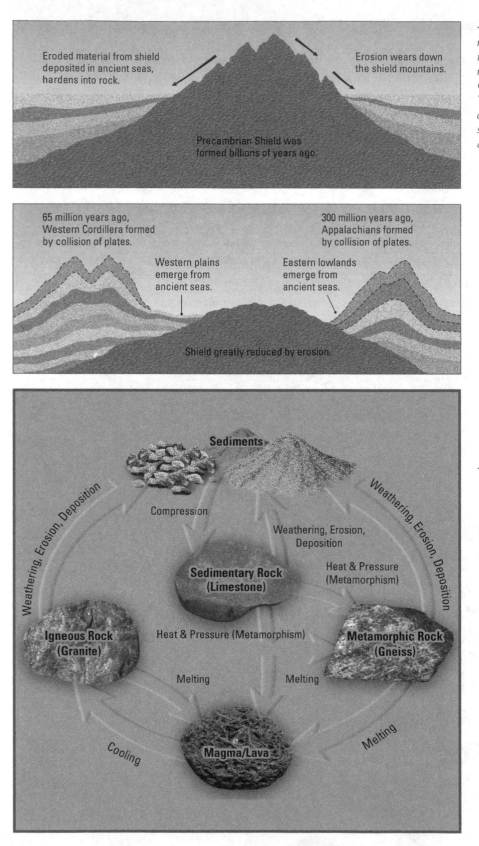

Sediments

Weathering, Erosion, Deposition

Compression

Weathering, Erosion, Deposition

Weathering, Erosion, Deposition

Heat & Pressure (Metamorphism)

Sedimentary Rock (Limestone)

Heat & Pressure (Metamorphism)

Igneous Rock (Granite)

Metamorphic Rock (Gneiss)

Melting

Melting

Melting

Cooling

Magma/Lava

◁ **Fig. 10-9** *The rock cycle*

rises from deep under the earth's crust, then cools and hardens. Igneous rock can either be changed directly into metamorphic rock or break down into particles or **sediments** that harden into sedimentary rock. When pressure and heat melt the sedimentary rock, the result is also metamorphic rock (Fig. 10-9).

There are fossils in the Shield dating back to the middle of the Precambrian era. These are the remains of material deposited by algae, the first single-celled organisms. By the end of this era, more complex organisms had developed.

Paleozoic Era

The next 570 million years are divided into three eras. The longest of these is the **Paleozoic era**. During the 325 million years of this era, Canada's landforms continued to take shape. Sediments were moved by rivers and deposited in the shallow seas that surrounded the Shield. Over millions of years, these sediments were compressed into sedimentary rock. Today these rocks form the **bedrock** of parts of every province.

Geologists believe that North America was located near the equator during the early part of the Paleozoic era, over 400 million years ago. Organisms that eventually produced the great oil and gas deposits of western Canada lived in shallow seas around the ancient Canadian Shield. Huge swamps grew in the warm climate of this tropical location. The swamps eventually produced the coal bearing rocks of Nova Scotia. Sediments deposited in the Paleozoic era also produced the salt beds of southwestern Ontario.

◁ **Fig. 10-10** *The Appalachian Mountains formed during the Paleozoic era.*

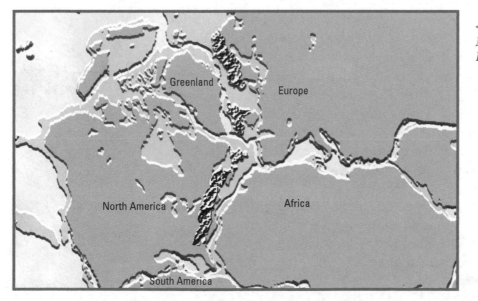

About 300 million years ago, the continents collided to form the supercontinent of Pangaea. This collision caused the eastern part of North America to crumple up and form the Appalachian Mountains (Fig. 10–10).

At the beginning of the Paleozoic era, living organisms existed only in the seas. For the first time, organisms with shells appeared. Later, simple plants appeared on land and eventually forests of trees developed. As time passed, more complex organisms such as fish, insects, and amphibians began to evolve. Amphibians were the first animals to live on land. Remains of these Paleozoic organisms are now found in sedimentary rocks as fossils. Fossils help scientists to estimate the age of the rock in which they are found.

The division between the Paleozoic and the Mesozoic eras was a time when many plant and animal species became extinct. Half of the fossil groups of organisms found in the rocks of the late Paleozoic era are missing in the rocks of the early Mesozoic era. During the past 600 million years, there have been at least five such mass extinctions. During each of these, many of the earth's species disappeared and new and greater numbers of species appeared. The greatest extinction occurred in the late Paleozoic era when at least 80% of life in the seas became extinct and land plants and animal species disappeared in large numbers. The cause of this extinction is not clear but it could be related to the formation of Pangaea and related climate changes.

Mesozoic Era

The **Mesozoic era** lasted about 180 million years and marked the beginning of the breakup of Pangaea. At various times during the Mesozoic period, seas and swamps covered much of central and western Canada. While this area was under water, new layers of sedimentary rock formed on top of those formed in the Paleozoic era.

The Mesozoic era is divided into three periods: the Triassic, Jurassic, and Cretaceous.

As Pangaea broke up, the North American plate moved westward and collided with the Pacific plate. This caused huge amounts of magma to rise to within a few kilometres of the surface of the North American plate. Here it cooled and solidified into a large mass of granite. This granite structure was later uplifted and formed the Coast Range Mountains. The tremendous tectonic forces also began to fold the earth's surface to form the Rocky Mountains toward the end of the Mesozoic era. The Innuitian Mountains were formed in the eastern Arctic as the North American plate moved in a northward direction.

The breakup of Pangaea lasted about 200 million years. It began in the Mesozoic era and continued into the Cenozoic era.

The climate of the land mass that is now Canada was still warm during much of the Mesozoic era. Dinosaurs and other reptiles roamed through huge swamps and forests. Many dinosaurs lived on the shores of the great inland sea to the east of the Rocky Mountains. Evidence of these huge animals has been found in the layers of sandstone along the Red Deer River in southern Alberta. Dinosaur Provincial Park now exists there to protect these 75 million-year-old fossils.

Vegetation in swamps was covered with sand and silt. Layers of sediments compressed the layers of vegetation to form the coal deposits now found in southern British Columbia, Alberta, and Saskatchewan. In the shallow seas that periodically covered the Interior Plains, the remains of tiny sea creatures and plants fell to the sea floor and were covered by sediments. As the sediments piled up they were compressed into sedimentary rock. Pressure from the weight of the rock, bacteria, and heat changed the plant and animal remains into oil and gas.

The end of the Mesozoic era was marked by another mass extinction. More than half of all plant and animal species, including the dinosaurs, became extinct. No one is quite sure of the cause, although scientists have many theories, including the possibility that the earth collided with a giant asteroid.

Dinosaur Provincial Park was declared a UNESCO World Heritage Site. No other place of similar size in the world contains such a wide variety of lifeforms from the late Mesozoic era.

Cenozoic Era

During the **Cenozoic era**, the final changes occurred which gave Canada's landforms their present shape. The continuing collision of the Pacific plate and the North American plate caused the uplifting of the Coast Mountains. Other mountain systems, including the Rockies, which had begun to develop in the Mesozoic era, continued to form through folding, faulting, and the actions of volcanoes. Volcanoes released huge amounts of lava which formed plateaus between the Coast Mountains and the Rocky Mountains. The seas that had occupied the area that is now the Interior Plains disappeared as the land slowly began to rise.

Canada and much of the world experienced an **Ice Age** during the last two million years. The Ice Age consisted of at least four periods of large-scale glacial activity. Huge masses of ice, or **glaciers**, developed as a result of a slight cooling of the earth's climate. As the glaciers moved, their actions were like giant earth-moving machines, scraping and gouging the land they covered. The Appalachian Mountains along the eastern coast and the Canadian Shield were rounded by moving ice that was often more than a kilometre thick. Large amounts of clay, silt, sand, and gravel were dumped on the lowlands surrounding the Shield as the glaciers formed and then melted away. Because this happened very recently (at least in geologic terms!), glaciation had an enormous effect on Canada's geography, setting the current pattern of lakes, rivers, hills, and plains.

The last Ice Age ended for most of Canada as recently as 6000 years ago, but glaciers are still found in some mountain and Arctic areas. Some

An ice age is not an event restricted to modern geologic history. Evidence of glacial activity 300 million years ago helped to prove the existence of the supercontinent of Pangaea.

Glaciers currently occupy about 10% of the earth's land surface.

scientists think it is possible that the Ice Age is not over; that we are in a warm period between the fourth and fifth glacial advance.

The Cenozoic era is the age of **mammals**. When the dinosaurs died out, mammals, including human beings, became dominant. The impact that we have had on the earth is enormous considering the short time that we have been here. For example, we have created huge lakes by building dams, and have increased rates of erosion by cutting forests. However, these changes to the earth's landscape are minor compared to the geologic forces at work.

To ask a geologist a question, check www.nrcan.gc.ca/ess/ esic/cgi-bin/askageol_e.cgi

IN CLOSING...

Many geological events have occurred over hundreds of millions of years to create Canada's diverse landforms. Geological events are still occurring and are slowly changing the appearance and location of the earth's features. Since most people live less than one hundred years, they do not realize that the earth's features are slowly changing. The effects of geologic processes occur over many, many lifetimes.

To find out more about careers in geoscience, check www.science.uwaterloo.ca/ earth/geoscience/careers.html

QUESTIONS

CHECK YOUR UNDERSTANDING

1. "The earth's physical landscape is the result of conflict between forces..." Explain what this means.

2. a) What part of Canada was created during the Precambrian era?

   b) What types of rocks make up this landform?

   c) How did it differ in appearance from today?

3. Where was the eroded material from the Shield deposited and what did this material become?

4. What was the most important geological event of the Paleozoic era?

5. Geologists believe that Canada was located closer to the equator during the early part of the Paleozoic era. Why has this tropical location been important to Canada?

6. Based on the fossil evidence, what life forms existed during the Paleozoic era?

7. What event marks the division between the Paleozoic and Mesozoic eras?

8. During the Mesozoic era, the North American plate collided with the Pacific plate. What resulted from this collision?

9. How were (i) coal deposits and (ii) oil and gas deposits formed in western Canada during the Mesozoic era?

10. a) How many glacial periods have there been during the last two million years?

    b) Describe the effects that glaciers have had on the Canadian landscape.

ANALYZE AND APPLY

11. Most geologic events happen very slowly. What are two geologic events that happen fast enough for people to see?

12. What were the main geologic events that occurred in the area of Canada where you live? In which era did they occur? What evidence of these events can you see?

11   Landform Connections

STUDY GUIDE

By the end of this chapter, you will be able to:

- identify and describe Canada's landforms and regions

- describe the effects of glaciers

- use maps and photos to interpret landform and regional relationships

- describe how art reflects Canada's natural landscape

Key Terms

topography	differential erosion	plateaus	fiord
highlands	escarpment	intrusion	drainage
lowlands	rift valley		

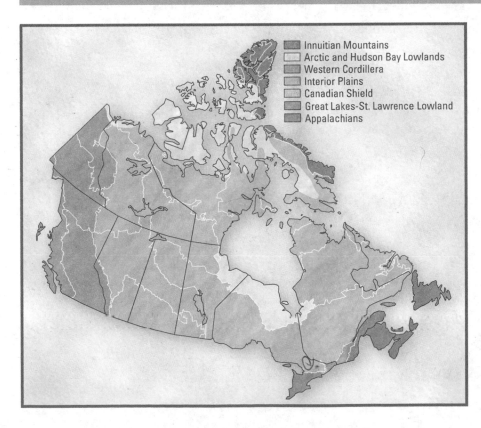

Innituitian Mountains
Arctic and Hudson Bay Lowlands
Western Cordillera
Interior Plains
Canadian Shield
Great Lakes-St. Lawrence Lowland
Appalachians

◁ **Fig. 11-1** *Landform regions of Canada. The white lines indicate ecozone boundaries, which are discussed in Chapter 14.*

To learn more about Canada's landforms, check
sts.gsc.nrcan.gc.ca/landf.htm

Canada is a land of great physical diversity. Perhaps this is not surprising since Canada is the world's second largest country, and has the world's longest coastline. We can look at Canada's **topography** by focusing on landforms.

topography: the earth's surface features including vegetation, soils, and those features shaped by people

Fig. 11-1 shows Canada's landform regions on a map.

1. What is a landform region? Use your own words.
2. How many landform regions are there in Canada?
3. Which landform region is the largest? Which one is the smallest?
4. a) In which landform region do you live?
   b) Describe the landforms in the region in which you live.

Canada is made up of three distinct types of landforms — **shield**, **highlands**, and **lowlands**. The highlands and lowlands are further subdivided into the regions shown in Fig. 11-2.

THE CANADIAN SHIELD

The Canadian Shield is the geographic foundation of Canada. The Shield underlies not only much of Canada but also parts of the United States. More than half of Canada is covered by the Shield, about 4 800 000 km² (Fig. 11-1). Some of the world's oldest rocks (3.96 billion years old) are located in the Shield near Great Slave Lake. Today, most of the Shield is relatively flat with rounded hills of rock which are actually the roots of ancient mountains.

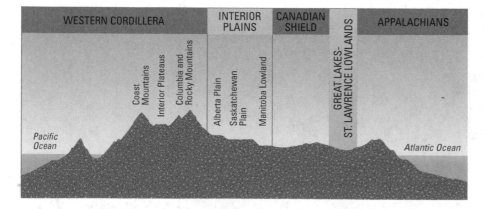

◁ **Fig. 11-2** *Profile of southern Canada's landforms*

Two types of rock, igneous and metamorphic, form most of the Shield. They contain valuable minerals in great quantities. Because of the vast deposits of lead, gold, nickel, copper, zinc, and other important metals, the Canadian Shield is often called the storehouse of Canada's **metallic minerals**. In addition, diamonds have recently been found where ancient volcanoes once existed.

How were mineral deposits formed in the rock of the Shield? Minerals were present in magma (molten rock) beneath the earth's crust. As magma rose toward the surface, it forced its way into cracks and cavities in the shield rock. This process of magma slowly rising toward the surface took thousands or millions of years. As it cooled, some minerals were deposited in the magma itself. Other deposits were formed when minerals, dissolved in very hot water, were forced deep into cracks in the surrounding rock (Fig. 11-3). This process allowed minerals to be deposited in high concentrations which makes mining worthwhile.

As the minerals slowly cooled, they separated into layers according to their density. The lighter ones floated on top of the heavier ones. Those that had similar density floated to the same level. Nickel and copper are often found together because they have similar densities.

Mining companies are attracted to the Shield because of the presence of metallic minerals. Many cities and towns, such as Sudbury in Ontario, Thompson in Manitoba, and Yellowknife in the Northwest Territories, rely on the mining industry for jobs. The mineral ores are smelted to remove waste materials. The concentrated minerals are shipped to factories in Canada and other parts of the world where they are used to manufacture products we use every day.

The Precambrian rocks of the Canadian Shield do not contain fossil fuels (coal, oil, and natural gas). The lifeforms that produced these products did not exist at the time the Shield was created.

A simple experiment will show you how liquids separate into layers.
1. Put 20 ml of vinegar and 60 ml of olive oil into a jar with a lid.
2. Shake well and let stand. What happens? Why?
3. Season, salt, and pour on a salad!

In Sudbury, Ontario, large deposits of nickel and copper are mined.

smelted: when metal is extracted by melting

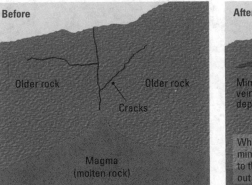

Before

Older rock   Older rock

Cracks

Magma (molten rock)

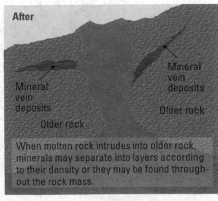

After

Mineral vein deposits

Mineral vein deposits

Older rock

Older rock

When molten rock intrudes into older rock, minerals may separate into layers according to their density or they may be found throughout the rock mass.

◁ **Fig. 11-3** *Minerals may be deposited when molten rock intrudes into existing rock formations.*

While the Shield is well-suited to mining, it is ill-suited to farming because it has very thin soils. However, it is ideal for recreation because of its scenic rivers, waterfalls, lakes, rock outcrops, and vast forests. The action of the glaciers affected the **drainage** of the Shield. The scraping and gouging action of the ice created depressions in the **bedrock**. These depressions filled with water to form the hundreds of thousands of lakes that now dot the Shield (Fig. 11-4). Because the bedrock is **impervious**, water does not pass through it. The glaciers deposited sand, gravel, and clay which dammed rivers or forced them to flow in different directions. The result is a very disorganized pattern of winding rivers, lakes, and swamps. These rivers and swamps are the breeding ground for the many blackflies and mosquitoes found in the Shield. People visit the Shield to canoe, fish, hunt, and "get back to nature." The tourist industry is very important to the towns and cities in the southern parts of the Shield.

The Shield's plentiful water flows have made it an excellent source of water-generated energy, and the pattern of drainage has affected where hydro-electrical plants are located. The centre of the Shield is much lower than its outer portion. This gives it the appearance of a saucer, with Hudson Bay occupying the low-lying centre. As a result, most of the rivers of the Shield flow toward its centre and into Hudson Bay. Hydro-electric generating stations have been built where the rivers tumble from the Shield onto the Hudson Bay Lowlands. The energy produced by these stations is transmitted by power lines to cities and towns both on and off the Shield.

Glaciers removed enormous amounts of soil, clay, rock, and gravel from the Shield. Today, most of the Shield is covered by a thin layer of soil, and the bedrock is visible in many places.

See the Connecting Study on glaciation at the end of this chapter for more information about the effects of glaciation on the Canadian Shield.

▽ **Fig. 11-4** *The Canadian Shield: notice the many lakes, trees, and the exposed bedrock.*

QUESTIONS

CHECK YOUR UNDERSTANDING

1. a) What types of rock make up the platform on which the rest of Canada is built?

   b) What is the topography of the Shield like?

   c) What geologic processes created this topography?

2. Why is the Canadian Shield also referred to as the Precambrian Shield?

3. a) Why is the Shield called Canada's store-house of metallic minerals?

   b) Using your own words, describe how mineral deposits form.

   c) Why are nickel and copper often found together?

4. Describe the effects of glaciers on:

   a) the land's surface material, such as soil, rocks, and gravel

   b) the drainage of the Shield

ANALYZE AND APPLY

5. The natural beauty, the minerals, the rivers, and the forests are the economic backbone of the Shield. How have these resources aided in the economic development of this region?

6. Many products that you use are made from different kinds of raw material that are found in the Canadian Shield. List at least five products and the raw material from which they are made. For example, this book is made of paper that may come from the trees of the Shield.

THINK AND COMMUNICATE

7. a) On an outline map of Canada supplied by your teacher, draw the borders of the Canadian Shield.

   b) On your map, locate and label the major cities (population over 100 000) on the Shield. Consult your atlas for this information. Save this map for another activity later in this chapter.

   c) How many major cities are there?

   d) Discuss the following questions in a small group:

      i. Why are vast areas of the Shield sparsely populated?

      ii. Could this change in the future? Explain.

THE LOWLANDS

There are three lowland regions surrounding the Shield: the Interior Plains, the Great Lakes–St. Lawrence Lowlands, and the Hudson Bay–Arctic Lowlands (Fig. 11–1). The bedrock under these lowlands is formed mainly of sediments eroded from the Shield. The sediments were laid down in the seas that existed at various times millions of years ago. As the rock particles collected, the weight of the upper layers compressed the lower layers into sedimentary rocks.

◁ **Fig. 11-5** *The Interior Plains*

Interior Plains

The Interior Plains of Canada are part of the Great Plains of North America that stretch from the Arctic Ocean to the Gulf of Mexico (Fig. 11-5). The Interior Plains of Canada extend from the 49th parallel north to the Arctic Ocean, a distance of 2700 km. They are about 1300 km wide in the south but only about 275 km wide in the north.

The Interior Plains were often covered by shallow inland seas. Sediments from the Shield and the Rocky Mountains were deposited in these seas over millions of years. Eventually the sediments were compressed by the weight of the layers above into sedimentary rock. Part of the sedimentary rock deposited in these areas consists of coral reefs that formed close to the surface of seas during the Paleozoic era. The rock layers are several thousand metres thick and took millions of years to form. Today, the reefs are thousands of metres below the surface of the land. They contain much of the oil and gas found in Alberta and Saskatchewan.

Mineral deposits also lie below the surface. At various times during the Mesozoic era, shallow seas covered the region that is now Saskatchewan. When they evaporated, thick layers of mineral deposits were left in the dried-out sea beds. These layers are now deep in the earth, covered by newer rocks and glacial deposits. Potash is mined from these layers and used as fertilizer in Canada and overseas. The swamps on the edges of these ancient seas produced plants that were changed eventually into coal which is mined today.

Forces of erosion have also shaped the surface of the landscape. Some sedimentary rocks are hard and resistant; others are quite soft. The softer

Remember that Canada was closer to the equator at this time. Over millions of years, plate movements have placed Canada in its current location.

Potash is the name given to potassium chloride compounds. It is chemically similar to common table salt. Saskatchewan is the world's leading producer of potash.

resistant: able to withstand the forces of erosion

rock erodes more quickly than the harder rock — a process called **differential erosion**. Different rates of erosion have caused three different levels of elevation on the prairies. Each level is separated by a sharp rise called an **escarpment**. Escarpments form when a harder rock layer that overlays a softer layer resists erosion. Although many people think of the Interior Plains as flat, there are relatively few areas where this is true. The landscape is, for the most part, composed of rolling hills, and deep, wide, river valleys. Overall, the land slopes gently downward from west to east.

Glaciation has also marked the landscape in visible ways and affected land use. The Interior Plains, like the rest of Canada, were subjected to glaciation. The glaciers left deposits that produced a rounded, gently rolling landscape in many areas. When the glaciers melted, the meltwater formed a large lake over much of what is now southern Manitoba and Saskatchewan. Later, the land rose, causing most of the water to drain into the ocean. Small portions of the ancient lake remain today as Lake Winnipeg, Lake Manitoba, Lake Winnipegosis and Cedar Lake. The floor of this lake was covered by sediments which made it very flat. The former lake bottom was left as flat land in what is now southern Manitoba and Saskatchewan.

This ancient lake, called Lake Agassiz, was larger than all of the Great Lakes combined.

The soil that developed on these sediments is deep and fertile. Grain is grown in many locations in the southern part of the Interior Plains. The area is known as Canada's "breadbasket" because so much wheat is grown here. Cattle are raised in places where the climate is too dry for crops. Agricultural products from this region are used both in Canada and overseas.

Great Lakes–St. Lawrence Lowlands

South of the Canadian Shield is a smaller landform region, the Great Lakes–St. Lawrence Lowlands. As you might suspect from the name, the region consists of two parts. The parts are separated by a thin wedge of the Canadian Shield that juts across the St. Lawrence River and extends into the United States near Kingston, Ontario. Like the Interior Plains, these lowlands have bedrock formed of sedimentary rock from the Paleozoic era. The Paleozoic bedrock can be seen in several escarpments in the Great Lakes Lowland. The best known is the Niagara Escarpment which extends from Niagara Falls to Manitoulin Island. The Niagara Escarpment was formed by differential erosion.

△ **Fig. 11-6** *The Great Lakes Lowlands*

In the Great Lakes portion of the lowlands, glaciation has created a rolling landscape (Fig. 11-6). The glaciers carried huge amounts of material (soil, sand, and gravel) from the Canadian Shield and dumped them throughout the region. The landscape is characterized by flat plains with glacial hills and deep river valleys. The Great Lakes are located in basins that were gouged out by glaciers. The lakes were even larger than they are

Geographers believe that there were water bodies here before glaciation. The glaciers deepened and widened these depressions.

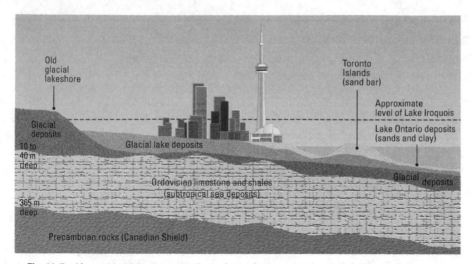

△ **Fig. 11-7** *About 10 000 years ago, the melting glaciers created a glacial lake, Lake Iroquois, that covered the area where Toronto is now situated. The Ordovician was an early part of the Paleozoic era.*

today because of the enormous volume of water from the melting glaciers. They eventually shrank to their present size as the **meltwater** drained into the ocean. The old shorelines of these glacial lakes surround the present-day Great Lakes (Fig. 11-7).

meltwater: water resulting from the melting of glacier ice and/or snow

The St. Lawrence Lowland was formed in a different way from the Great Lakes Lowland. A **rift valley** was formed by faulting (Fig. 11-8). This rift valley was flooded toward the end of the last ice age by a part of the Atlantic Ocean called the Champlain Sea.

The Great Lakes-St. Lawrence Lowlands Region is the most southerly region in Canada. It is well-suited to agriculture because of its excellent soils and warm climate. The flat land is also ideal for transportation routes and the development of cities. Because of these factors, it is the most densely populated region in Canada. About 50% of Canada's population lives in the

▽ **Fig. 11-8** *The cross-section in B shows how the St. Lawrence Lowland was created as a result of double faulting.*

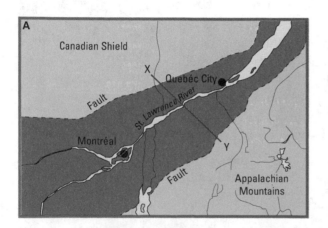

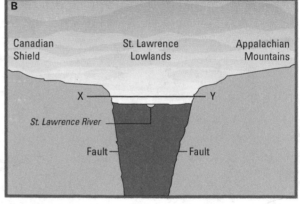

Great Lakes–St. Lawrence Lowlands which comprise only 14% of Canada's area. Canada's two largest cities, Toronto and Montréal, are located here along with 70% of the country's manufacturing industries. Wouldn't you agree that the Great Lakes–St. Lawrence Lowlands could be called "Canada's industrial and **urban** heartland?"

Hudson Bay–Arctic Lowlands

Around the southwestern shore of Hudson Bay and James Bay is a very flat, low area covered by swampy forest (Fig. 11-9). The waters of Hudson Bay covered much of this lowland at the end of the last Ice Age. Known as the Hudson Bay Lowlands, this region has a layer of sedimentary rock which rests on top of the ancient rock of the Shield.

The Arctic Lowlands are made up of a series of islands located in Canada's far north, and have a gently rolling landscape. The harsh climate does not permit farming; the ground remains frozen most of the year. However, the Paleozoic sedimentary rock, from which the Lowlands are formed, contains **lignite** (a form of coal), oil, and natural gas deposits.

▽ **Fig. 11-9** *The Hudson Bay Lowlands*

QUESTIONS

CHECK YOUR UNDERSTANDING

1. How was the bedrock of the lowlands formed?

2. a) How thick is the bedrock in the Interior Plains and why is it so thick?

    b) Why are the ancient coral reefs of the Interior Plains important today?

3. a) Describe the topography of the Interior Plains as you would see it if you were driving across the region from west to east on the Trans-Canada Highway.

    b) Explain the major processes responsible for what you see.

4. Parts of the southern portion of the Interior Plains are often called Canada's "breadbasket." Why?

5. What separates the Great Lakes Lowlands from the St. Lawrence Lowlands? Where does this occur and what is the appearance of this area?

6. Copy the paragraph below into your notebook. Wherever there is an asterisk (*) insert the correct word from this list:

    sedimentary, Escarpment, rift, soft, south, faults, erosion, glaciation, Great Lakes

    To the * of the Canadian Shield is the Great Lakes-St. Lawrence Lowlands. Like the Interior Plains, these lowlands are underlain by * rock. The St. Lawrence Lowlands were created when land between two * collapsed creating a * valley. The landscape of the Great Lakes Lowlands is largely the result of *. The * were carved out by glaciers. The Niagara * is the biggest single feature of the lowlands.

7. a) Describe the characteristics of the Hudson Bay and Arctic lowlands.

    b) What minerals are important in the Arctic Lowlands? How did they get there?

ANALYZE AND APPLY

8. a) Mark the three different lowland regions on the outline map of Canada on which you drew the Shield.

    b) Label the lowlands regions on your map.

    c) On your map, label the major cities (populations of 100 000 and over) in each region. Save your map for another activity later in this chapter.

    d) How many of Canada's major cities are found in the lowlands?

    e) Compare the number of major cities in the lowlands with the number found in the Canadian Shield earlier in this chapter. Which region has more? Why?

9. Examine the photographs of each of the lowland regions (Fig. 11-5, 11-6, and 11-9). Describe the differences you see.

10. a) Name the four lakes in Manitoba and the five Great Lakes which are remnants of glacial lakes.

    b) Why are these lakes smaller than they were in the glacial period? Why did the lakes not disappear completely?

THE HIGHLANDS

Canada's three highland areas lie to the east, north, and west of the Shield and lowlands areas. Each of these three striking, mountainous areas — the Appalachians, the Innuitians, and the Western Cordillera — has a different geological history and appearance (Fig. 11-1).

Appalachian Mountains

The Appalachian Mountains stretch from the state of Georgia in the southern United States through the Maritimes to Newfoundland in the north. They are the oldest highland region in Canada, and formed about 300 million years ago. Layers of sedimentary rock were uplifted and folded at the end of the Paleozoic era when North America collided with Europe and northern Africa during the formation of Pangaea. Rocks found in the Appalachians of Nova Scotia and Newfoundland are similar to rocks found in Wales and Scotland. The layers of sedimentary rock are rich in deposits of **non-metallic minerals** such as coal. Volcanic activity and faulting created igneous and metamorphic rock in certain areas of the Appalachians. **Plateaus** of this rock contain metallic minerals such as iron and zinc.

plateau: elevated, flat area

Millions of years of erosion have reduced the Appalachians' once jagged peaks to rolling mountains and hills (Fig. 11-10). In recent geologic times, glaciation has played a part in this erosion, grinding down the peaks and separating the hills and mountains with wide glacial valleys.

During the last Ice Age, the weight of the ice pressed the Appalachians down. As the land sank, and the ice melted, the small inlets along the east coast were flooded by the sea. The long bays that were created form a "drowned coastline" (Fig. 11-11). These long bays have provided deep harbours for ocean freighters, and some have become today's sites of major cities. Other settlement is located mainly in the fertile river valleys and along the seacoast.

Innuitian Mountains

The Innuitian Mountains stand like icy watch towers in Canada's far north. In some locations they measure over 2500 metres in height. Their present form was shaped in the middle of the Mesozoic era when the North American plate moved northward. The Innuitians contain igneous and metamorphic rocks, but for the most part are composed of sedimentary rock.

They are younger than the Appalachians, and so erosion has not had time to reduce them to rounded hills. They are also barren because trees can neither survive the extremely cold winter temperatures, nor grow during the short summer. Vast areas are covered by ice and permanent snow. The Innuitian Mountains resemble the Appalachians in composition and, as you might expect, contain similar types of minerals. The mineral resources have not been greatly exploited, however, because the region's remote location makes development too costly when cheaper alternatives exist further south.

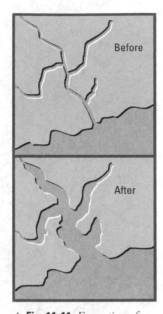

△ **Fig. 11-11** *Formation of a "drowned coastline"*
Former river valleys that were drowned by rising sea levels form deep, irregular inlets.

remote: far away from where most Canadians live

Western Cordillera

The Western Cordillera stands along the western edge of Canada like a great wall: range after range of mountains separated by plateaus and valleys (Fig. 11-12). The great height and rugged appearance of these ranges tell us that they are geologically young. The collision of the North American and the Pacific plates is responsible for uplifting this region into several mountain ranges about 680 km wide. The heavier Pacific plate forced its way under the lighter North American plate causing much folding, faulting, and volcanic activity. The result was the Western Cordillera.

The mountains and valleys of the Western Cordillera run in a north-south direction. This presents an obstacle to transportation because main travel routes across the Cordillera must run in an east-west direction. There are only a few passes, or gaps, in the ranges of the cordillera which are low enough to allow highways and railways to cross over.

In an atlas, find the three major routes through the southern part of the Western Cordillera.

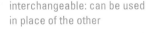
Fig. 11-12 *The Rocky Mountains in the Western Cordillera. The Rockies are the most easterly mountains in the Cordillera.*

Since it is so mountainous, the Cordillera is lightly populated. Most people live in the farming and mining towns located in the river valleys. Vancouver and Victoria, the largest cities in the Western Cordillera, are built on flat land in coastal locations. Towns such as Banff and Jasper thrive because of tourists who come to see the beautiful majesty of the mountains. The glaciers in the mountains of the Western Cordillera are the only remaining glaciers in Canada apart from those in the Arctic. These glaciers add to the beauty for which the Canadian West is famous.

Many people tend to use the name "Rocky Mountains" and "Western Cordillera" interchangeably. This is a mistake. There are three major divisions in the Western Cordillera. The Rocky Mountains and the Columbia Mountains, among others, make up the eastern mountains. The Interior Plateaus to the west of these ranges make up the second division. The Coast Mountains on the western edge of the Cordillera make up the third. Refer to Fig. 11-13 as you read about each division.

interchangeable: can be used in place of the other

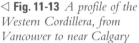
Fig. 11-13 *A profile of the Western Cordillera, from Vancouver to near Calgary*

EASTERN MOUNTAINS

The eastern division of the cordillera consists of two main mountain ranges — the Rocky and the Columbia Mountains — separated by a deep valley. On the east are Canada's youngest, and most famous mountains, the Rockies, formed about 65 million years ago. The Rocky Mountains are formed of folded and faulted sedimentary rock which contains many fossils and deposits of coal. Today, the Rockies stand as much as 4000 m above sea level.

The Rocky Mountain Trench is a deep valley separating the Rockies from the second main range, the Columbia Mountains. This valley was created by erosion along a zone of faults. It is only about 10 km wide, 1600 km long, and almost 2000 m lower than the mountains on either side.

On the western side of the Rocky Mountain Trench in southern British Columbia are three mountain ranges separated by trenches. Together they are known as the Columbia Mountains. At 3000 m, the Columbia Mountains are not as high as the Rockies but they are older. They are made of sedimentary rock but have many metamorphic **intrusions** containing a wide variety of metallic minerals. As a result, there is more mining in the Columbia Mountains than in the Rockies.

intrusion: molten rock injected between or through the layers of rock below the surface

INTERIOR PLATEAUS

In the centre of the Cordillera is a series of rugged plateaus between 1300 m and 2000 m in height among high hills and small mountains. The area is composed of metamorphic and igneous rocks due to past volcanic activity. It contains many valuable metallic minerals such as copper, gold, and zinc. The lava plateaus have been deeply cut by major rivers creating deep valleys that make transportation across them difficult. Glacial and river deposits have, however, made excellent farmland of many of the valleys. One of these is the Okanagan Valley.

COAST MOUNTAINS

Like the eastern mountains, the Coast Mountains are divided into two ranges separated by a deep trough. The Coast Mountain Range is on the mainland, while the Island Mountain Range is located on the offshore islands. The two ranges are separated by a deep trough that is occupied by an area of the Pacific Ocean.

trough: a long narrow depression

The Coast Mountains have been formed by the movement of the North American and Pacific plates. Since the heavier Pacific plate is sinking below the lighter North American plate, the pressure has caused magma to rise into the earth's crust where it has cooled to form igneous rock. The magma also melted some of the overlying crust to form metamorphic rock. The movement of the two plates against one another has uplifted this massive block of igneous and metamorphic rock to form the Coast Mountains.

The continuing movement of the North American and the Pacific plates in this area makes the West Coast of Canada the most active earthquake region in the country. The plates are moving relative to one another at speeds of 2 cm to 10 cm per year. In the past 70 years, the Geological Survey of Canada has recorded more than 100 earthquakes of magnitude 5 or greater under the Pacific Ocean west of Vancouver Island. These are large enough to cause damage if they occur close to shore. In 1949, an earthquake of magnitude 8.1 struck the Queen Charlotte Islands. If such an earthquake were to occur near a major city, the result would be almost total destruction and tremendous loss of life.

The largest earthquakes ever measured had Richter magnitudes near 8.6.

During the last Ice Age, glaciers occupied many coastal valleys. These glaciers eroded the valleys below sea level. When the ice melted, these valleys were flooded by the sea, and became long narrow inlets called **fiords**. The steep sides of these fiords and the towering mountains create spectacular scenery that today attracts thousands of tourists (Fig. 11-14). These tourists, however, must travel by boat or seaplane because there are few roads along the rugged coast of British Columbia. Roads are not very practical because of the long distances around the fiords.

▽ **Fig. 11-14** *A fiord in the Coast Mountains of British Columbia*

IN CLOSING...

The movement of the earth's plates, and the resulting folding, faulting, and volcanic activity, have combined with the forces of erosion and glaciation to create a variety of landscapes that affect the way we live.

"A core of ancient rock, surrounded by lowlands and then highlands on three sides." This may be a simple description, but it summarizes the diversity of Canada's physical landforms.

QUESTIONS

CHECK YOUR UNDERSTANDING

1. Use your own words to describe how the Appalachian Mountains were formed.

2. Why does the Appalachian region have many excellent harbours?

3. a) Describe the composition and appearance of the Innuitian Mountains.

   b) Why has this region not been developed as much as other regions?

4. a) How were the fiords of British Columbia created?

   b) What effect do the fiords have on land transportation along the coast?

5. Explain why the West Coast of Canada has so many earthquakes.

ANALYZE AND APPLY

6. a) Mark the highland regions on the outline map of Canada that you used for the Shield and lowlands.

   b) Name each region.

   c) Locate the major cities (population 100 000 and over) in each highland region.

   d) Compare the number of major cities in these highland regions with the number in the lowlands and the Shield. Why does this pattern exist?

▽ **Fig. 11-15**

Distance from Vancouver

on profile (cm)	Elevation at this point (m)
0.5	350
1.0	1500
1.5	2700
2.5	1800
3.5	2500
4.0	1400
6.0	1200
7.5	1400
8.0	1600
9.0	2200
10.5	3200
11.5	3300
12.0	1000
12.5	2800
13.0	3500
14.0	1800
15.0	1050

7. Examine the photo of the Appalachians (Fig. 11-10) and the photo of the Western Cordillera (Fig. 11-12). Which mountains are older? How can you tell?

8. Draw a profile of the Western Cordillera according to the following instructions.

   a) On a piece of graph paper draw a horizontal line 15 cm long. Label the left end of the line Vancouver and the right end Calgary.

Division	Formation Process	Rock Type	Appearance

Eastern Mountains
    Rocky Mountains
    Rocky Mountain Trench
    Columbia Mountains			

Interior Plateaus			
Coast Mountains			

△ **Fig. 11-16**

Mountain Range	Name of Highest Mountain	Height of Highest Mountain
Rocky Mountains		
Coast Mountains		
St. Elias Mountains		
Appalachians (Québec)		

△ **Fig. 11-17**

b) Draw a vertical scale on the left showing elevations from 0 to 3500 m. The vertical scale should be 1 cm = 700 m.

c) Put dots at the elevations and distances provided in Fig. 11-15. Once all the dots have been placed, join the dots.

d) Label the following features on your profile:

Rocky Mountains, Rocky Mountain Trench, Columbia Mountains, Interior Plateaus, Coast Mountains

e) In your notebook, compare the three major divisions of the Western Cordillera using an organizer like Fig. 11-16.

f) What problems might exist in this region for farming and transportation?

9. a) Construct an organizer in your notebook similar to Fig. 11-17. Complete the information with the help of an atlas.

b) Of these mountains, which one is the highest in Canada?

c) Relate the height of the highest and lowest of these mountains to their age.

THINK AND COMMUNICATE

10. Review the material in this chapter and discuss the following quotation:

"Canada is an east-west country trying to survive in a north-south continent."

Glaciation of Canada

◁ **Fig. 11-18** *Some scientists think that glaciers may cover Canada in the future. During the last Ice Age, which ended less than 10 000 years ago, Canada was covered by ice at least four times. Other scientists think that the glaciers that are left may melt away due to global warming.*

Even though our attention is directed today toward global warming and its consequences, some scientists think that some day we may have a new glacial advance (Fig. 11-18). After all, there have been many times during the earth's geologic history when ice ages have developed after warm periods.

Ice sheets have covered most of Canada several times during the past two million years. This has caused enormous changes in our topography. How did this glaciation happen? What were its effects? Could it happen again soon?

INTRODUCTION

Did you know that ice is one of the hardest substances on earth? This seems strange when we see fragile ice crystals on window panes, or ice cubes floating in cool drinks. Yet ice had the power not only to damage the hull of the Titanic, but also to transform the shape of the land.

The earth has experienced several **ice ages**. About 250 million years ago, parts of South America, Africa, India, Australia, and Antarctica were glaciated when they were part of Pangaea, the supercontinent. North America and Europe were not glaciated at this time because they were located near the equator. There is also evidence that there were several previous ice ages, including one 2 billion years ago and another 600 million years ago. For most of the earth's geologic history, however, glaciers have not covered large parts of the land. The last Ice Age began between one and two million years ago. **Ice sheets** covered almost all of Canada and parts of the United States, Europe, and South America during each of its glacial advances. Enormous volumes of the world's water were frozen in these ice sheets. This caused the level of the oceans to fall well below current levels.

KEY TERMS

ice ages

ice sheets

glacier

advance

retreat

alpine glacier

U-shaped valley

continental glacier

zone of
    accumulation

till

striation

spillway

misfit stream

till plain

moraine

drumlin

erratic

esker

lake plain

The lower ocean levels created a land bridge between North America and Asia where the Bering Strait is today. Find this in an atlas.

During the last Ice Age, **glaciers advanced** and **retreated** at least four times. Between each period of glacial activity, the climate was as warm, or warmer, than today. Why did such a cycle occur? No one is quite sure, but some theories suggest it has to do with changes in the earth's orbit around the sun as well as changes in the tilt of the earth's axis, or changes in the heat output from the sun.

The Ice Age's last period of glacial activity began about 100 000 years ago, and ended in most parts of Canada about 6000 years ago. A period of glacial activity begins when the earth's climate cools, and the snow that falls in the winter does not completely melt in the summer. Over thousands of years, the snow gets deeper and becomes hundreds or thousands of metres thick. The tremendous weight of the snow on top causes the bottom layers to turn to ice. The most remarkable fact about a glacier, other than its tremendous size, is that it can move. Solid ice acts like a very thick liquid, and moves along or flows very slowly.

Glaciers move in different ways, depending upon their location and the climate. In mountainous regions, **alpine glaciers** move down valleys from high elevations to low elevations under the force of gravity. This movement is usually only a few centimetres per day. Alpine glaciers sharpen the upper portions of the mountains and give them a rugged appearance. When they move down valleys, they scrape away the valley walls to produce broad **U–shaped valleys**.

Alpine glaciers exist today in Canada in parts of the Western Cordillera and the Arctic islands. The Columbia Icefield is a mass of ice located along the British Columbia–Alberta border between Banff and Jasper National Parks. It is the largest area of ice in Canada south of the Arctic. It contains 30 glaciers covering about 300 km^2 to depths of 365 m. Waters from this icefield flow into three different oceans. Tourists from all over the world come to our western mountains to enjoy the beauty created by glacial activity.

Canadians appreciate glaciers for more than their beauty. The Cline glacier in Alberta once had an ice mine. Ice was chipped from tunnels in the glacier and shipped to Japan where a 1.5 kg bag sold for about US $30. The glacial ice cubes were much denser than regular ice cubes so they lasted much longer in a drink. The ice was highly prized because it was formed before industrial pollution and acid rain. The mine did not operate for very long because of objections from environmentalists.

Continental ice sheets, or **continental glaciers**, are different from alpine glaciers in that they occupy greater areas of land, and move under their own weight. During the last glacial advance, about 8 million square kilometres of North America were covered by a continental ice sheet. In some spots, this ice sheet reached a thickness of 4 km. The enormous

When the term "Ice Age" is used with capital letters, it refers to the last ice age which occurred during a part of the Cenozoic era called the Pleistocene. When the term is used uncapitalized, it refers to any period of major glacial activity.

For comparison, the CN Tower in Toronto stands only 553 m high.

Alpine glaciers are also known as valley glaciers.

If you would like to learn more about glaciation, check athena.wednet.edu/curric/land/global/climchng.htm#ice

Between 25% and 30% of the earth's surface was covered by glaciers about 20 000 years ago. Today, continental ice sheets occupy less than 10% of the earth's surface.

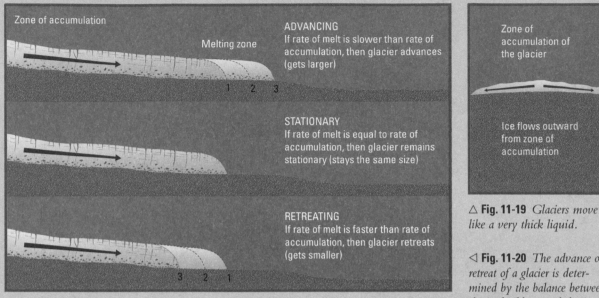

Zone of accumulation

Melting zone

ADVANCING
If rate of melt is slower than rate of accumulation, then glacier advances (gets larger)

1   2   3

STATIONARY
If rate of melt is equal to rate of accumulation, then glacier remains stationary (stays the same size)

RETREATING
If rate of melt is faster than rate of accumulation, then glacier retreats (gets smaller)

3   2   1

Zone of accumulation of the glacier

Ice flows outward from zone of accumulation

△ **Fig. 11-19** *Glaciers move like a very thick liquid.*

◁ **Fig. 11-20** *The advance or retreat of a glacier is determined by the balance between the ice build-up and the ice melt. In all cases the ice continues to move outward from the zone of accumulation.*

You can demonstrate the movement of a continental glacier with a ball of pizza dough. Place the dough on a flat surface and press down on it slowly with your palm. Notice how it spreads outward in all directions.

(Once you have got the dough to the size you want, top it with cheese, sauce, and other toppings and bake in an oven.)

weight of snow and ice causes the ice to spread outward from its centre or **zone of accumulation** (Fig. 11-19). Although the ice of a continental glacier is constantly moving outward, the outer edge or margin of the ice sheet may advance, retreat, or stay in one place. Fig. 11-20 explains the conditions under which each of these movements occur.

Continental glaciers give the landscape a smoother appearance by eroding higher points on the land and filling in lower areas with the eroded material. Today, continental glaciers exist only in Greenland and Antarctica.

THE GLACIATION OF CANADA

Glaciation is the process most responsible for the topography that we see in Canada today. There are two reasons for this:

1. Glaciation is an extremely powerful force.
2. Glaciation happened very recently in geologic terms, and there has not been enough time for the glacial features to be worn away.

Fig. 11-21 shows the maximum extent of glaciation about 20 000 years ago. As the ice sheets spread outward from three locations, they changed the face of the land. The weight of the ice sheets had a dramatic effect on the level of the land. Over a period of thousands of years, the ice compressed the land downward. When the ice melted, the land rebounded upward, but at a relatively slow rate. In fact, this rebound continues today in much of Canada.

The land is rebounding at a rate of approximately 1 to 2 cm per century.

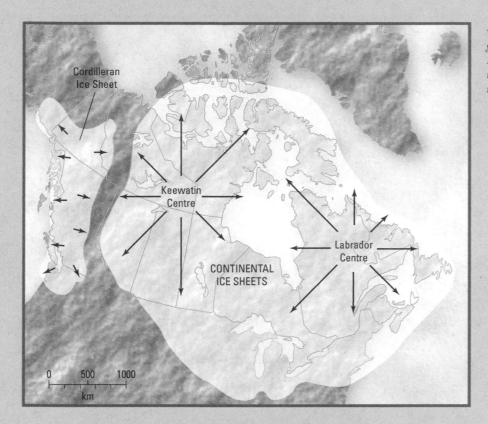

◁ **Fig. 11-21** *Continental glaciation in North America. Notice that the ice sheets did not spread out from polar regions.*

To see the effects that the ice sheets had on the landscape, we will examine

a) features caused by erosion
b) features deposited
   i.   directly by the ice sheets
   ii. by meltwater from the ice sheets

Erosional Features Caused by Glaciation

The continental ice sheets were often several kilometres thick. As they advanced, they expanded existing river valleys. These deeper and wider troughs are known as U-shaped valleys and are similar to those formed by alpine glaciers. The ice also gouged out the basins of existing lakes making them deeper and wider. The Great Lakes were formed in this fashion.

As the ice sheets moved, they eroded huge amounts of soil, sand, gravel, and rock. This material was carried by the ice and acted like sandpaper as it scraped and ground away the surface of the land. Grooves called **striations** were often gouged out in the bedrock under the ice sheet by rocks frozen in the ice (Fig. 11-22). Striations are often visible on the bare rock of the Canadian Shield. They run in the same direction as the movement of the ice sheet, and allow geographers to determine its path.

△ **Fig. 11-22** *The movement of glaciers gouged out scratches called striations in bedrock.*

Have you ever looked at a wide valley with a tiny stream and asked yourself how such a small river could cut such a big valley? Chances are that glacial meltwater formed the valley. Huge volumes of meltwater carved out deep, wide valleys called **spillways** (Fig. 11-23). Once the ice sheets melted away, these spillways became the pathways for small present day rivers, called **misfit streams**.

Depositional Features Created by Glaciation

ICE DEPOSITS

Till is material such as clay, sand, and gravel that is deposited directly by an ice sheet. It is unsorted; that is, large and small particles are all mixed together. The rock fragments have angular or pointed shapes because they have not been rounded by running water.

Sometimes the till deposited under the ice, formed a gently rolling landscape called a **till plain**. Till plains are very good for growing crops because deep, well-drained soil developed here. Sometimes an ice sheet deposited ridges of till at its edge. These ridges of till are known as **moraines** (Fig. 11-23). Moraines are not very good for growing crops

▽ **Fig. 11-23** *Landforms created by continental glaciers*

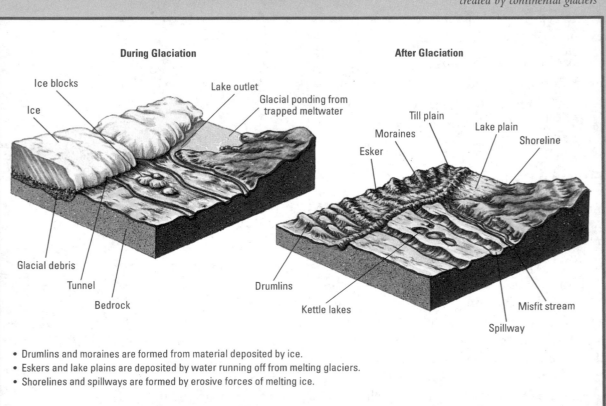

- Drumlins and moraines are formed from material deposited by ice.
- Eskers and lake plains are deposited by water running off from melting glaciers.
- Shorelines and spillways are formed by erosive forces of melting ice.

◁ **Fig. 11-24** *Drumlins are oval-shaped hills formed by materials deposited by glaciers. The steep side of the drumlin faces the direction from which the ice came.*

because they are thin-soiled, hilly, and swampy. Moraines are better suited for grazing and forestry. A well-known moraine runs between Orangeville and Trenton in southern Ontario.

Ice sheets formed other features which are evident today on Canada's landscape. One that is particularly recognizable is a **drumlin**, an egg-shaped hill (as seen from above) with a steep side at the wide end, and a gentle slope on the other. The steep side points in the direction that the glacier came from (Fig. 11-24). Drumlins usually occur in clusters called drumlin fields. A large drumlin field is located near Peterborough, Ontario. Farmers often plant crops on drumlins because the soil is deep and well-drained.

As they moved forward, the ice sheets often picked up large rocks and carried them hundreds of kilometres. These rocks are called **erratics**. For example, rocks from the Canadian Shield were picked up by the ice, carried along, and deposited many kilometres away in the surrounding lowlands. They can often be identified because they are made of rock which is different from the bedrock of the region in which they were deposited.

MELTWATER DEPOSITS

Running water played an important role in the deposition of glacial material. Rivers flowing within or under melting ice carried sand and gravel along with them and laid down this material in the river bed. When the ice sheet melted, the material that had been deposited in the river bed was left as a steep-sided ridge winding across the countryside. This is called an **esker** (Fig. 11-23). The esker follows the path of the river that created it thousands of years ago. Today, eskers are a source of sand and gravel for the construction industry.

Materials carried off the ice sheet by meltwater were sorted, smoothed, and rounded by the running water. The action of the moving water deposited larger rock particles in one layer and the smaller rock particles in another. Today you might find a deposit of coarse gravel where a fast-moving glacial stream once existed, or silt where a glacial lake once was.

About 14 000 years ago, the climate became warmer and the glaciers started to melt. Enormous amounts of meltwater flowed into lakes along the margins of the ice. Some of these lakes, known as glacial ponds, were small. Others, like Lake Agassiz in Manitoba, were larger than any lake in the world today. The Great Lakes were also much larger than their present size. Today, the fertile flat **lake plains** that were once the bottom of ancient glacial lakes are used for agriculture. You may also find fine clay in an area that was once a glacial lake.

As the glaciers melted, the sea rolled in and covered large areas of depressed land in the St. Lawrence River Valley. Today, these areas are dry, but you can see beaches and sand dunes now located far above current sea levels. By about 6000 years ago, the last Ice Age had come to an end, and the Canadian landscape as we know it was visible.

The ancient sea that occupied parts of the St. Lawrence and Ottawa valleys is called the Champlain Sea.

GLACIATION THROUGH THE EYE OF THE ARTIST

Artists portray the world in which we live. It is not surprising that Canadian artists have frequently chosen landscapes shaped by the action

▽ **Fig. 11-25**

White Pine by A. J. Casson, is an artist's view of how glaciation affected much of the Canadian Shield. Notice the bare rocks and the trees bent by the winds blowing across the lake.

▽ **Fig. 11-26**

Hillside, Lake Alphonse by William Goodride Roberts, shows the rolling landscape that was created when glaciers deposited till in many parts of southern Canada.

of glaciers as the subject of their paintings. These landscapes are found throughout most of Canada and some are awe-inspiring in their beauty. Examine Fig. 11-25 to 11-28 to see the variety of landscapes created by glaciers.

IN CLOSING...

For thousands of years, glaciers have sculpted the Canadian landscape, and there is no reason why an ice age should not occur again. We know that average yearly temperatures would need to drop only about 4C°! However, it is safe to say that many questions about ice ages and climate change remain unanswered.

◁ **Fig. 11-27**
No Grass Grows on the Beaten Path *by William Kurelek, shows a flat lake plain created in many parts of Canada under glacial meltwater.*

▽ **Fig. 11-28**
The Glacier *by Arthur Lismer, illustrates the results of alpine glaciation. The rugged triangular mountain peaks are called horns and are created by alpine glaciation.*

QUESTIONS

CHECK YOUR UNDERSTANDING

1. a) How does glacial ice differ from regular ice?

    b) How does a period of glacial activity begin?

    c) What causes snow to turn to glacial ice?

    d) What causes alpine and continental glaciers to flow?

2. During the last Ice Age:

    a) Which parts of the earth were covered by ice sheets?

    b) What happened to ocean levels? Why?

3. "The movement of a glacier is determined by the balance between ice accumulation and ice melt." Consult Fig. 11-20 and draw a series of diagrams to explain this statement.

4. What appearance does a landscape have that was glaciated by an alpine glacier compared to one glaciated by a continental glacier?

5. Construct an organizer in your notebook similar to Fig. 11-29. Complete each column.

6. By observing the deposited materials, how can you tell which materials were deposited directly by a glacier and which materials were deposited by glacial meltwater?

ANALYZE AND APPLY

7. Each of the paintings (Fig. 11-25 to 11-28) depicts a landscape that is the result of glaciation. Analyze each painting using the following questions as a guide.

    a) Describe the physical appearance of the landscape the artist is portraying.

    b) Explain the glacial processes that created this landscape. What evidence is visible to support your explanation?

    c) What economic activities could this glaciated landscape be used for?

8. In Fig. 11-23, there are some glacial features that have not been discussed. Based on your examination of the diagrams, how were the following features formed and what is their appearance:

    a) spillway

    b) kettle lakes

    c) shorelines (from glacial lakes)

THINK AND COMMUNICATE

9. a) Is the use of paintings an effective way to study geography? Why?

    b) What are the advantages and disadvantages of this approach compared to other methods of presenting geographic information?

▽ **Fig. 11-29**

Glacial Feature	How Formed	Appearance	Uses
a) striations			
b) spillways			
c) till plains			
d) moraines			
e) drumlins			
f) erratics			
g) eskers			
h) lake plains			

12 Climate Connections

STUDY GUIDE

By the end of this chapter, you will be able to:

- explain the difference between climate and weather
- understand the factors that effect climate
- explain the differences between maritime and continental climates
- describe the conditions associated with different types of precipitation
- identify and describe Canada's climate regions

Key Terms

continental climate	moderating effect	front	relief precipitation
maritime climate	air mass	jet stream	cyclonic precipitation
temperature range	prevailing winds	convectional precipitation	

INTRODUCTION

The headlines were startling (Fig. 12-1). The most damaging storm in Canada in the 20th Century had hit one of the most heavily populated parts of the country. Yet nature did not reveal its power through the funnel cloud of a tornado nor the driving snow of a blizzard. Instead it showed its power quietly, at first hardly noticeable. Out of a grey sky came a gentle freezing rain that gradually coated everything with a layer of ice more than 80 mm in thickness bringing normal activities to a halt for over a million people and causing many millions of dollars of damage. Why did such a damaging ice storm occur? What impact did it have on people and the environment? Could a storm like this happen again?

Think about what you hear on TV weather reports — details on temperature, precipitation, humidity, wind speed and direction, cloud cover, air pressure, and predictions about weather conditions. **Weather** can be defined as the day-to-day characteristics of these atmospheric conditions. Weather affects each of us in many ways. A rainstorm may wash out a baseball game you were planning to attend. A snowstorm may cancel school for the day. Hot sunny weather makes a day at the beach one

AT LEAST 25 DEATHS

MILLIONS OF DOLLARS OF DAMAGE
to Buildings and Trees

1.5 Million People in
Québec and Ontario Without Power

ICE BRINGS DOWN 120 000 KM OF POWER
LINES AND TELEPHONE CABLES

Over 15 000 Troops Called In For Assistance

◁ **Fig. 12-1** *In 1998, an ice storm in Canada caused massive destruction.*

To obtain current weather conditions and forecasts across Canada, check weather.ec.gc.ca/current.html

of summer's great pleasures. A fresh fall of snow creates great conditions for skiing or snowboarding. In what ways has the weather affected your activities in the past two weeks?

Over the years, records have been kept of the weather in different parts of Canada. These records show weather patterns which have occurred over long periods of time. A long-term pattern of weather is called a **climate**. Climates influence where we live, what farmers can grow, which clothes we wear, and how we construct buildings.

To help you understand why Canada's climate has so much variety, you should remember four basic facts:

1. Canada extends for a great distance from north to south.
2. Different elevations produce different climate conditions.
3. Coastal regions have different climates from inland regions.
4. Wind and pressure systems move weather conditions from one part of the country to another.

Some very large lakes, such as the Great Lakes, also have an effect on climate.

Latitude

The most southerly point in Canada is Pelee Island in Lake Erie at 41°N latitude. The most northerly point of the country is Alert at the northern tip of Ellesmere Island at 83°N latitude. This large range in latitude has a major impact on Canada's climate. Fig. 12-2 shows the **average annual temperature** at these two locations and at Yellowknife, which is about halfway between them at 62°N. What temperature changes occur as the latitude increases?

Distance from the equator is a key factor in whether a region is hot or cold. The size of the land mass in which a region is located is also a factor, but we will discuss this in the section titled Continental and Maritime Environments. In Fig. 12-3, you can see that the energy from the sun that hits the earth at the equator covers a small area. The same amount of energy that hits the earth at a more northerly location is spread over a larger area because of the curvature of the earth. Places closer to the North and South Poles experience colder temperatures than those near the equator because the same amount of energy is spread over a larger area.

Average annual temperature: is the monthly average temperatures, added together and divided by 12. It is used to compare the climates of different places.

Relief and Elevation

Relief refers to differences in elevation of the earth's surface. Mountain ranges act as barriers to the movement of air masses. This is why Vancouver often has warm, rainy weather in winter, while Calgary, on the other side of the Cordillera, has cold, dry weather. Mountains also cause precipitation, this will be discussed in the section titled Relief Precipitation.

If you were to hike from sea level to the top of a high mountain, you would notice that the temperature drops steadily as you climb. As you approach the top, you might even find ice and snow all around you.

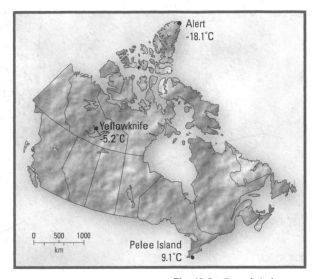

△ **Fig. 12-2** *Canada's large distance from north to south causes a significant difference in the average annual temperatures of various places.*

▽ **Fig. 12-3** *The effects of latitude on climate*

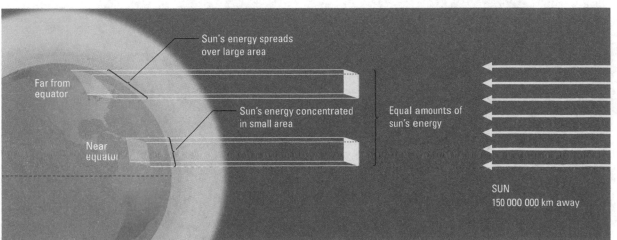

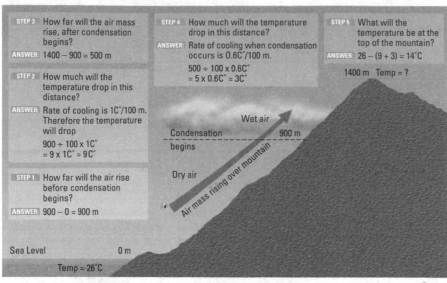

STEP 3 How far will the air mass rise, after condensation begins?
ANSWER: 1400 − 900 = 500 m

STEP 2 How much will the temperature drop in this distance?
ANSWER: Rate of cooling is 1C°/100 m. Therefore the temperature will drop
900 ÷ 100 × 1C°
= 9 × 1C° = 9C°

STEP 1 How far will the air rise before condensation begins?
ANSWER: 900 − 0 = 900 m

STEP 4 How much will the temperature drop in this distance?
ANSWER: Rate of cooling when condensation occurs is 0.6C°/100 m.
500 ÷ 100 × 0.6C°
= 5 × 0.6C° = 3C°

STEP 5 What will the temperature be at the top of the mountain?
ANSWER: 26 − (9 + 3) = 14°C

1400 m Temp = ?

Wet air

Condensation begins   900 m

Dry air

Air mass rising over mountain

Sea Level   0 m

Temp = 26°C

◁ **Fig. 12-4** *Calculating changes in temperature of a rising air mass*

When discussing an actual temperature, use "degrees Celsius." For example, "the temperature today is 20°C." When discussing a temperature change or a range of temperatures, use the term "Celsius degrees." For example, "the temperature fell by 10C°."

To see what the earth looks like from the sun at the present time, check www.fourmilab.ch/cgi-bin/uncgi/Earth/action?opt=-5

You probably know that it gets colder as the elevation gets higher. But why does it get colder even though you are getting closer to the sun? Consider what happens as a mass of air moves up a mountain. Our example in Fig. 12-4 shows what it could be like in the Vancouver area in summer. As air rises, it expands because there is less air pressure. As the air expands, it loses heat. Fig. 12-4 illustrates how you can calculate the temperature of an air mass as it rises up a mountainside.

Continental and Maritime Environments

Areas far from oceans and large lakes in the interior of land masses have a **continental climate** (Fig. 12-5). The **temperature range** is

▽ **Fig. 12-5** *Continental Climate*

▽ **Fig. 12-6** *Maritime Climate*

great because there is no large water body to moderate the hot temperatures of summer and the cold temperatures of winter. On the other hand, coastal locations have a **maritime climate** (Fig. 12-6). This means that the temperature range between the highest average monthly temperature and the lowest average monthly temperature is relatively small and the level of precipitation is higher.

THE MODERATING EFFECT OF WATER

Bodies of water have a **moderating effect** on land temperatures. Oceans and large lakes heat up and cool down more slowly than land masses. In summer, a body of water remains cooler than the land surrounding it. Winds blowing from over the water keep the surrounding countryside cooler than it would be if the water body was not present. In winter, bodies of water retain their heat and are warmer than the land. Winds blowing off the water body warm the surrounding countryside. Therefore, maritime locations near a large body of water, have cooler summers and milder winters than continental locations far from the water body. Maritime temperatures have been "moderated" by the water body.

Hudson Bay, frozen for much of the year, does not significantly moderate the temperatures of the climate regions surrounding it.

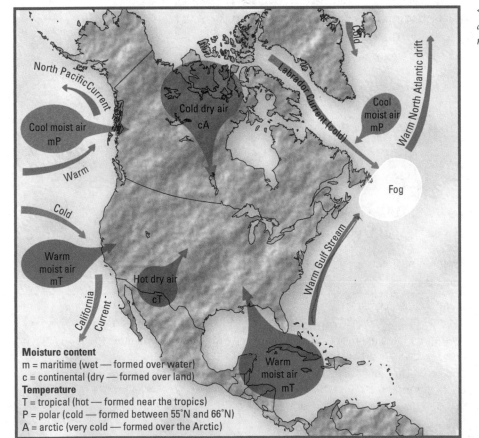

◁ **Fig. 12-7** *Canada's weather and climate are affected by air masses and ocean currents.*

Moisture content
m = maritime (wet — formed over water)
c = continental (dry — formed over land)
Temperature
T = tropical (hot — formed near the tropics)
P = polar (cold — formed between 55°N and 66°N)
A = arctic (very cold — formed over the Arctic)

OCEAN CURRENTS

Climate is affected by ocean currents (Fig. 12-7). The temperature of an ocean current affects the temperature of air that passes over it. On the West Coast, for example, the warm North Pacific Current heats the cool, moist air which passes over it. This gives a mild climate to the coastal regions of British Columbia.

On the East Coast, the cold Labrador Current, which flows southward from the Arctic, cools the air of coastal locations in Labrador and northern Newfoundland. The Gulf Stream, flowing northward from the southern Atlantic, warms the air of coastal areas in Nova Scotia and southern Newfoundland. Where the air above the two currents meets on the Grand Banks, southeast of Newfoundland, the weather is often damp and foggy. It is here that ships must take special precautions to avoid collisions.

AIR MASSES

An **air mass** is a large volume of air with the climate conditions of the area where it is formed (Fig. 12-7). An air mass originating over an ocean contains moisture. As the air passes over land, the moisture is released in some form of precipitation. As a result, a maritime location is likely to receive more precipitation than an inland, or continental location. On the other hand, an air mass originating in a continental climate will be dry because it is far from a large body of water (Fig. 12-8). Landforms also affect the movement of air masses, which was discussed in the section titled Relief and Elevation.

Winds and Pressure Systems

Air, like everything on earth, has weight. This weight is called **air pressure.** Differences in air pressure are created when the earth is heated to different temperatures. Warmed air rising above the heated ground creates an area of low pressure (Fig. 12-9). When the rising air has cooled, it falls toward the earth and creates an area of high pressure.

Temperature of an ocean current in comparison to the surrounding water determines whether it is a cold or warm current. For example, an ocean current of 15°C is a warm current if the surrounding water is 13°C, but it is a cold current if the surrounding water is 18°C.

The meeting of warm air and cold air above these currents produces fog on more than 100 days per year.

The average pressure of air at sea level is 101.3 kilopascales (kPa). If you climbed a mountain, there would be less air above you than at sea level. Therefore, air pressure is less at a high elevation than at a low one.

▽ **Fig. 12-8** *Maritime and continental climate comparison*

Climate	Typical Seasonal Temperatures	Annual Temperature Range	Annual Precipitation
Continental	warm to hot summers; cold winters	25C° to 50C°	200mm to 1000mm (low to moderate)
e.g. Timmins, Ontario	Average annual temperature = 1.2°C	34.5C°	873 mm
Maritime	cool to warm summers; cool winters	20C° to 30C°	1000 mm to 2500 mm (moderate to high)
e.g. Halifax, Nova Scotia	average annual temperature = 6.1°C	24.3C°	1474 mm

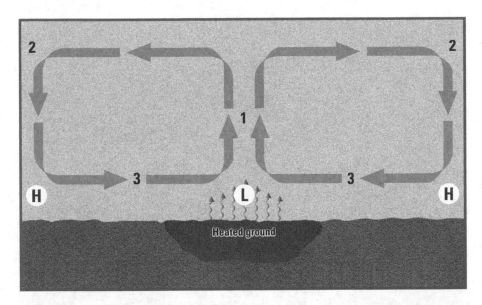

◁ **Fig. 12-9** *Differences in air pressure produce winds.*

1. *Heating of the ground by the sun warms the air above it and causes the air to rise. This produces a low-pressure area.*

2. *The air cools and sinks. This produces a high-pressure area.*

3. *Air at ground level moves from high pressure to low pressure, creating winds.*

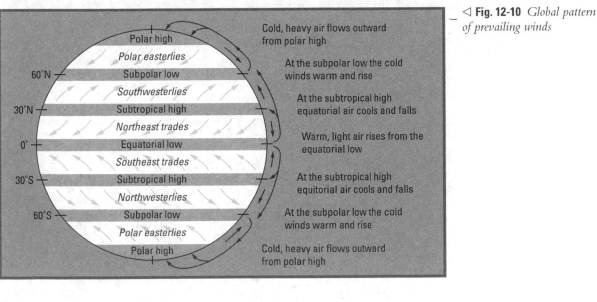

◁ **Fig. 12-10** *Global pattern of prevailing winds*

Air moves along the surface of the earth from high-pressure areas toward low-pressure areas. This moving air causes **wind.** Around the earth, there are high- and low-pressure belts that have created a well-established pattern of **prevailing winds** (Fig. 12-10). Over most of Canada and the United States, the prevailing winds blow from west to east. Called the "westerlies," these prevailing winds move air masses that affect our weather. For example, if an air mass forms over Canada's Arctic in the winter, it will be cold and dry. As it moves southward, its cold, dry conditions are carried across Canada by the prevailing westerly winds. Similarly, if an air mass comes from the Gulf of Mexico, it brings warm, moist conditions to eastern Canada.

As a cold, dry Arctic air mass moves southward, it becomes warmer and picks up moisture. Nevertheless, it remains colder and drier than the air in the region into which it moves.

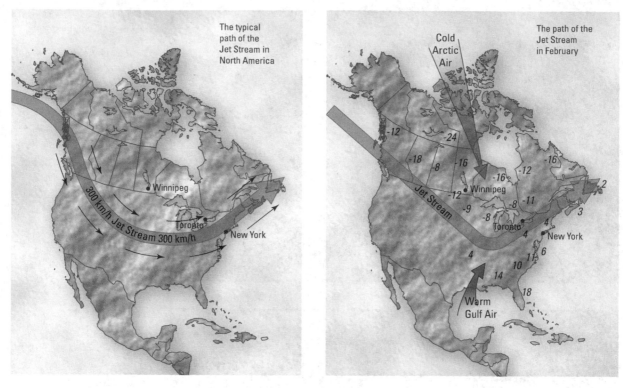

The typical path of the Jet Stream in North America

300 km/h Jet Stream 300 km/h

Winnipeg

Toronto

New York

The path of the Jet Stream in February

Cold Arctic Air

Jet Stream

Winnipeg

Toronto

New York

Warm Gulf Air

The boundary between cold, dry polar air and warm, moist tropical air is called the **polar front**. High in the atmosphere above the polar front is a current of fast-moving air called the polar-front **jet stream** (Fig. 12-11). This current of air flows from west to east at speeds of 300 to 500 km/h, at altitudes between 9000 and 18 000 m. The polar-front jet stream encircles the earth, and changes speed and position with the seasons. In winter this boundary between cold and warm air moves southward, allowing cold arctic air to flow farther southward into the United States. In summer, it moves northward, allowing warm air from the Gulf of Mexico to flow farther northward into Canada's interior. The warm air masses and the cold air masses that meet at the polar front do not mix easily. Instead they often enter into a battle in the sky that we see as a storm.

△ **Fig. 12-11** *The polar-front jet stream separates cold, dry air from warm, moist air.*

There are several jet streams that encircle the earth — two or three in each hemisphere. A pilot needs to consider these high-altitude air currents when calculating the fuel and passenger load that can be carried.

To learn more about air masses and fronts, check ww2010.atmos.uiuc.edu/(Gh)/ guides/mtr/af/home.rxml

PRECIPITATION

You will find it easier to understand why precipitation occurs if you remember these two points:

1. Air cools as it rises.
2. As air cools, water vapour condenses more than it evaporates.

Air may rise for any of the following reasons:

1. It rises to cross an area of high elevation. This causes **relief precipitation**.
2. It rises because it has absorbed heat from the earth's surface. This causes **convectional precipitation**.
3. It rises because there is a cooler, denser air mass flowing beneath it that forces it up. This causes **cyclonic precipitation**.

The type of precipitation that occurs is determined by an area's location and physical features.

Relief precipitation is also called orographic precipitation.

Relief Precipitation

Mountain barriers create relief precipitation. As moist air rises up the **windward** slope of a mountain range, it expands and cools. As air cools, the rate of evaporation decreases while the rate of **condensation** increases. The result is an increase in the number of water droplets in the air. These droplets can combine to form rain drops. As more water vapour condenses, the cloud drops become larger. When they are too heavy to remain suspended in the atmosphere, they fall to the ground as rain. In colder temperatures (below freezing), water vapour condenses into snow.

Features other than high mountains may also cause relief precipitation. For example, Southern Ontario's snowbelt is a result of wind blowing from Lake Huron and Georgian Bay over hilly areas.

- Moisture content is usually measured in terms of relative humidity (RH).
- RH = (amount of moisture in air ÷ moisture-holding capacity) x 100%

Precipitation can also take the form of **dew** or **frost**. On clear nights when the air is calm, surfaces cool down. Invisible water vapour in the air

▽ **Fig. 12-12** *Relief precipitation in the Western Cordillera*

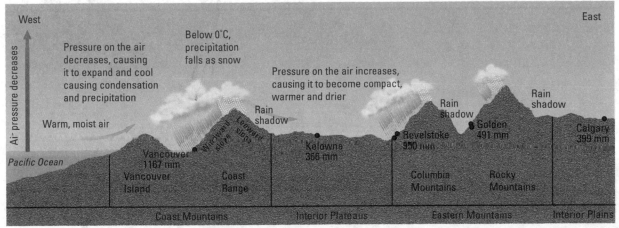

condenses on these cool surfaces forming water droplets called dew. In some desert areas, dew may be the main source of moisture for plants and animals. If the temperature of these surfaces is below freezing, water vapour forms ice crystals called frost.

As cool air descends on the more protected **leeward** slope of a mountain range, it contracts and becomes warmer. More evaporation than condensation takes place, so precipitation and cloud formation decrease. This results in a very dry climate or **rain shadow** on the leeward side of the mountain range. Rain shadows and wet windward slopes are common in the Western Cordillera where air masses pass over a series of mountain ranges (Fig. 12-12).

Convectional Precipitation

Convectional precipitation is very common in summer in continental locations such as the Prairie provinces, Ontario, and Québec. Here, the land is subject to intense heating during the long summer days. As the ground heats up, the air above it rises. The rising air expands and cools,

▽ **Fig. 12-13** *Convectional precipitation in a summer thunderstorm*

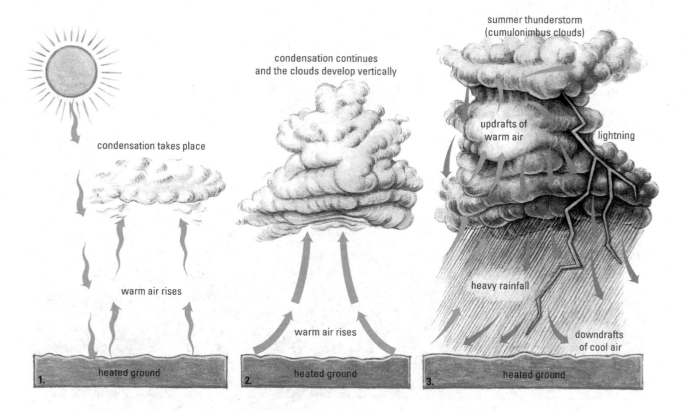

condensation takes place

warm air rises

1. heated ground

condensation continues
and the clouds develop vertically

warm air rises

2. heated ground

summer thunderstorm
(cumulonimbus clouds)

updrafts of
warm air

lightning

heavy rainfall

downdrafts
of cool air

3. heated ground

and the water vapour within it condenses to form the puffy white clouds that we are used to seeing in summer. Sometimes during late summer afternoons you may see these puffy clouds forming into towering clouds with dark bases. These are storm clouds formed by the continuous condensation of water vapour (Fig. 12-13). Small puffy clouds form as the moisture in updrafts of air condenses. The clouds develop vertically throughout the day as more and more moisture condenses and the water droplets get larger and larger. They may even freeze at high altitudes forming ice pellets, called hailstones. By late afternoon or early evening, the weight of the water droplets or hailstones causes them to fall to the ground, often in violent downpours. As they fall to the ground, the rain-drops cool the air and drag some of it downward, creating downdrafts. The strong gusts of wind just before and during a storm are caused by these downdrafts of air. Eventually the cooling effect of the rain on the ground stops more updrafts from forming. At this point, the precipitation-forming process stops and the storm is over. Sometimes the water droplets freeze into hailstones that are uplifted several times by strong updrafts. Each time, another layer of ice is added to their size. Some get as large as golf balls before their weight causes them to fall to the ground. Summer thunderstorms, although short-lived, may cause considerable damage to crops and property because of violent winds, lightning, heavy rainfall, or hail. In extreme cases, even tornadoes may develop in these storm clouds.

If you cut a hailstone in half you will notice that it has rings like a tree. Each ring is a layer of ice and tells you how many times the stone was uplifted within the cloud.

Cyclonic Precipitation

As you learned earlier in this chapter, air masses that are different in moisture content and temperature do not mix easily. Instead, a boundary or **front** forms between them. This front is like a battlefield in the sky, and it is here that cyclonic precipitation develops.

A cyclonic storm is a large, low-pressure system that forms when a warm air mass and a cold air mass collide. This often occurs under the polar-front jet stream which separates cold, dry arctic air from warm, moist tropical air (Fig. 12-11). The rotation of the earth causes the air to circulate in a counterclockwise direction around an area of low pressure.

As the warm air mass moves inward toward the centre of low pressure, it rises and cools creating precipitation (Fig. 12-14). The warm, less dense air is forced to rise above the colder dense air at two locations: the leading edge of the warm air (**warm front**) and the leading edge of the cold air (**cold front**). As shown in Fig. 12-15, a variety of weather occurs as a cyclonic storm passes over an area.

Cyclonic precipitation is also known as frontal precipitation.

The conflict in the sky between air masses was named a "front" during World War I, after the zones of battle along the Western Front in Western Europe.

A cyclonic storm is also called a mid-latitude cyclone.

To learn more about mid-latitude cyclones, check ww2010.atmos.uiuc.edu/(Gh)/guides/mtr/cyc/home.rxml

In North America, these low-pressure storm systems move from west to east throughout the year, and spread precipitation over large areas. Most of the precipitation in the Prairies, Ontario, Québec, and Atlantic Canada, especially in winter, is cyclonic. The ice storm of 1998 was a large cyclonic storm that stalled over eastern North America. Much of the relief precipitation of the West Coast develops out of cyclonic storms that blow in from the Pacific Ocean and rise over the western mountains.

▽ **Fig. 12-14** *Satellite images of cyclonic storms help the weather office to predict our weather. The names of the parts of the storm have been added to help you. In what direction is the storm likely to be moving?*

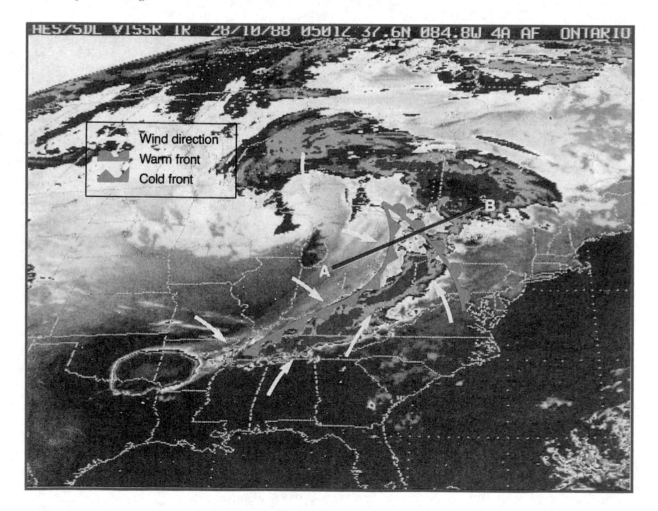

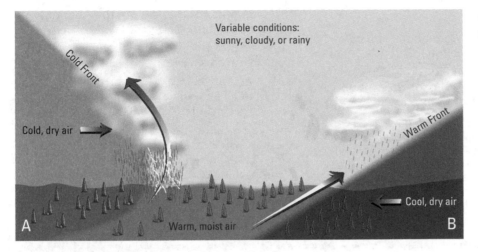

◁ **Fig. 12-15** *Cross section of a cyclonic storm*

Variable conditions: sunny, cloudy, or rainy

Cold Front

Cold, dry air

Warm Front

Cool, dry air

Warm, moist air

A

B

QUESTIONS

CHECK YOUR UNDERSTANDING

1. a) Explain the difference between weather and climate.

   b) Give three examples of how each affects our lives.

2. Examine Fig. 12-3 and describe the effect of latitude on climate.

3. "Bodies of water have a moderating effect on land temperatures." Explain how this is accomplished.

4. a) How do ocean currents affect climate?

   b) The meeting of the cold Labrador Current and the warm Gulf Stream create special weather conditions. What are these conditions and how do they affect ships?

5. How do prevailing winds affect the movement of air masses?

6. How does the polar-front jet stream affect the movement of air masses?

7. What are the two key points that help us understand why precipitation occurs?

▽ **Fig. 12-16**

Label	Interpretation	Where Formed	Characteristics
cA	continental Arctic	over land and frozen water in Canada's Arctic	very cold and dry
mT			
mP			
cT			

8. What three conditions cause air to rise?

9. Explain what happens to the temperature and moisture content of air as it passes over a mountain.

10. a) Explain, in your own words, and with the help of diagrams how convectional precipitation occurs.

    b) Why are some convectional storms so dangerous?

▽ **Fig. 12-17**

Location Within Storm	Temperature	Sky Cover	Precipitation	Wind Direction
Before warm front	Cool	Increasing Cloudiness	Likely	Easterly
At warm front				
Between fronts				
At cold front				
After cold front				

ANALYZE AND APPLY

11. Copy Fig. 12-16 into your notebook and complete it using the information in Fig. 12-7.

12. Using the information in Fig. 12-4, calculate the temperature of air as it rises up a mountainside in the following example:

    Mount Garibaldi, north of Vancouver, is 2700 m high. The temperature at the waterfront in Vancouver is 24°C. What will be the temperature of the air at the mountain top, if condensation starts at 1200 m?

13. The Labrador Current brings icebergs southward from arctic regions to the waters near Newfoundland. This area of the Atlantic Ocean is called "iceberg alley."

    a) What famous marine disaster occurred in 1912 as a result of these icebergs?

    b) What effect might this current have on the oil exploration and development that is occurring off the East Coast of Canada?

14. A cyclonic storm is approaching the area where you live. Using the information in Fig. 12-15 and the headings in Fig. 12-17, compare the weather conditions you will experience as the storm passes over you.

CANADA'S CLIMATE REGIONS

Construct a chart similar to Fig. 12–18 to compare the climate characteristics of the eight **climate stations** in Fig. 12–20. A climate station is any place where climate information is gathered.

a) Complete columns 1 to 5 using the information in the climate graphs on p. 142 and in Fig. 12–19.

b) Now, see where each climate station is located in Fig. 12–21.

Location	1 Average Temperature	2 Temperature Range	3 Total Precipitation	4 Season of Maximum Precipitation	5 Continental or Maritime
A					
B					
C					
D					
E					
F					
G					
H					

◁ **Fig. 12-18**

▽ **Fig. 12-19** *This general guideline will help you to interpret climate graphs of Canadian places.*

Factor	How Determined	Significance
Average annual temperature	• Add together the 12 average monthly temperatures and divide by 12.	• Indicates whether a location has a warm or cool climate e.g. Toronto, Yellowknife.
Temperature range	• Maximum temperature (warmest) - minimum temperature (coldest) indicates whether a place has a continental climate (large range) or a maritime climate (small range). large (>25 C°) = CONTINENTAL small (<25 C°) = MARITIME	• Places that do not have a minimum temperature below 0°C will be on the West Coast.
Total precipitation	• Add monthly precipitation totals. < 1000 mm = CONTINENTAL > 1000 mm = MARITIME	• Indicates whether a place has a dry or wet climate
Seasonal distribution of precipitation	• "WINTER" add precipitation totals for Oct., Nov., Dec., Jan., Feb., Mar. Winter max. = MARITIME (large difference between winter and summer = West Coast) (slight difference between winter and summer = East Coast) • "SUMMER" add precipitation totals for Apr., May, Jun., Jul., Aug., Sep. Summer max. = CONTINENTAL	• Indicates the climate influences at work and therefore different climate types.

The weather and climate of Canada have direct impacts on us. For example, a drought in the Prairies might raise the price of bread in the Maritimes. Heavy snows in the Rockies may lead to avalanches that close highways and railway lines. Weather patterns determine the types of clothing we wear each season. The climates of Canada affect the type of natural vegetation that grows, the soil that develops and the wildlife that lives in the region. The harsh Arctic climate makes mineral exploration costly, and these costs are passed on to customers. As you will see later in *Making Connections: Canada's Geography,* climate affects our agricultural patterns, forestry activities, and population patterns. Areas with similar climates may be grouped together to form a climate region. The climates of Canada may be grouped to create eight climate regions (Fig. 12-21).

To obtain climate information for dozens of places across Canada, check
www.cmc.ec.gc.ca/climate/
normals/eprovwmo.htm

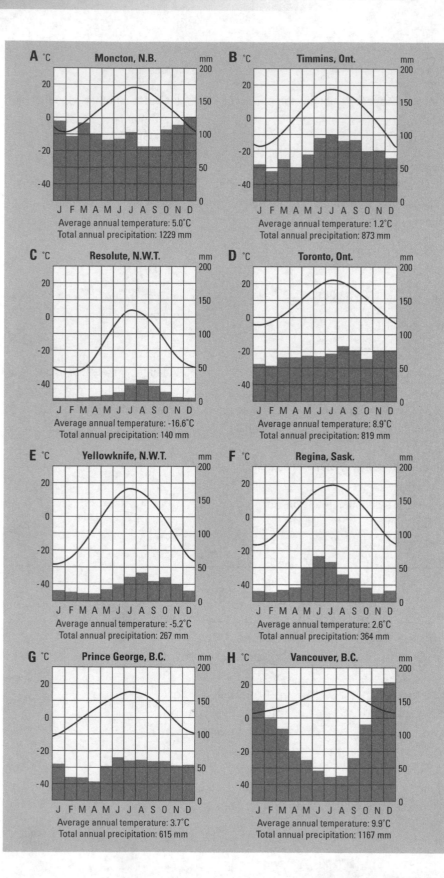

◁ **Fig. 12-20** *Climate graphs for locations in each climate region*

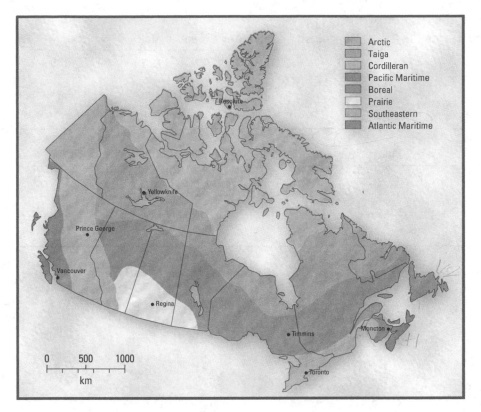

◁ **Fig. 12-21** *Canada's climate regions*

Legend:
- Arctic
- Taiga
- Cordilleran
- Pacific Maritime
- Boreal
- Prairie
- Southeastern
- Atlantic Maritime

QUESTIONS

CHECK YOUR UNDERSTANDING

1. a) In which climate region do you live?

   b) Describe the climate of this region.

ANALYZE AND APPLY

2. Toronto averages about 24 thunderstorms per year whereas Vancouver only has about 4. Why does Toronto experience so many more thunderstorms than Vancouver?

3. a) Using the same headings as in Fig. 12-18, determine the values for each climate station in Fig. 12-22.

   b) In which climate region is each climate station located? Explain how you reached your decision.

4. Examine the climate regions map (Fig. 12-21)

   a) What similarities and differences exist between

      i. the Boreal and the Prairie climate regions?

      ii. the Atlantic and Southeastern climate regions?

THINK AND COMMUNICATE

5. If you could live in any one of Canada's climate regions, which one would you choose? Explain your choice. Compare your choice and reasons with two other classmates.

▽ **Fig. 12-22** *In what region(s) would these climate locations be found?*

STATION A	Jan.	Feb.	Mar.	Apr.	May	June	July	Aug.	Sept.	Oct.	Nov.	Dec.	Year
Average monthly temperature(°C)	-14	-11	-5	4	10	14	16	15	10	4	-6	-12	2.1
Average monthly precipitation (mm)	23	15	16	22	43	76	101	70	47	18	16	19	466

STATION B	Jan.	Feb.	Mar.	Apr.	May	June	July	Aug.	Sept.	Oct.	Nov.	Dec.	Year
Average monthly temperature(°C)	-9	-8	-3	3	9	15	19	18	13	7	2	-6	5.0
Average monthly precipitation (mm)	120	96	117	101	91	93	103	81	81	106	114	126	1229

13 Soil and Natural Vegetation Connections

STUDY GUIDE

By the end of this chapter, you will be able to:

- understand how soil is formed and how it influences vegetation and agriculture
- explain the meaning of natural vegetation
- describe Canada's vegetation zones
- demonstrate the relationship between climate, vegetation and soils

Key Terms

soil	permafrost	coniferous trees	long-grass prairie
tundra	humus	deciduous trees	
leaching	calcification	mixed forest	
transition zone	boreal and taiga forest	short-grass prairie	

THE SOIL BASE

Climate creates wet–and dry–climate soils (Fig. 13-1). True **soil** consists of four main parts. If one of these parts is missing, the material cannot be considered soil.

1. Minerals

The minerals in soil come from rock, known as the **parent material**. The minerals become part of the soil when the rock is broken down by **weathering** into smaller particles of sand, silt, and clay. Many of these minerals, such as calcium, phosphorous, and potassium, are **nutrients** needed by plants for growth.

Parent material can also be materials that have been deposited by a glacier, the wind, or a river.

2. Bacteria and Organic Materials

When plants and animals die, they are decomposed by bacteria in the soil. As bacteria break down the organic matter, nutrients are released. Decaying organic materials form **humus** which provides nutrients and moisture for plants. Humus gives the soil its dark colour.

The process of decay is nature's way of recycling nutrients.

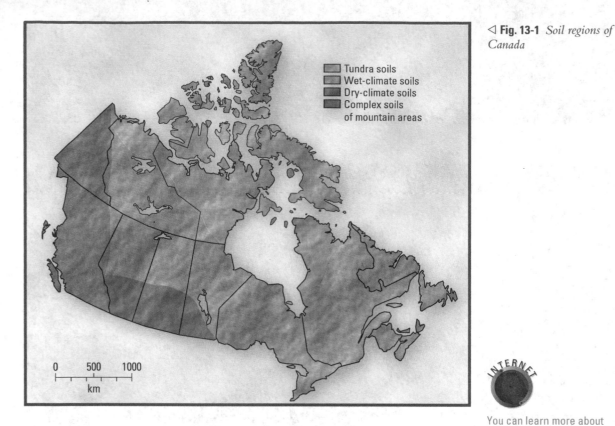

◁ **Fig. 13-1** *Soil regions of Canada*

Legend:
- Tundra soils
- Wet-climate soils
- Dry-climate soils
- Complex soils of mountain areas

0   500   1000
km

You can learn more about Canada's soils at: res.agr.ca/cansis/_overview.html

3. Air

Plants need air around their roots. A high humus level helps produce air in the soil because the loose, decaying materials allow for many air pockets. Air spaces are also created by worms, insects, and small animals which tunnel through the soil.

4. Moisture

Water dissolves nutrients in the soil and is then taken up by plants through their roots. Water is also necessary in the chemical and physical processes that weather rock and decay organic materials.

About half the volume of a high-quality soil is composed of water and air.

A basic **soil profile** is shown in Fig. 13-2. New mineral materials are added at the bottom of the soil by the weathering of the parent material. At the same time, organic materials are added at the top. This top layer of soil containing humus is called **topsoil**. Topsoil formation is a very slow process. Over the last 6000 to 10 000 years, only 15 to 25 cm of topsoil have formed under the forests of Canada. Under the grasslands of the prairies, between 40 and 100 cm of topsoil have developed.

The size of rock particles is an important part of soil structure. The larger particles of sand allow rainwater to drain quickly through the soil, while the smaller particles of clay prevent rapid drainage.

A well-balanced mixture of sand, silt, and clay, plus humus is called **loam.** It is the best soil for growing plants because it encourages root growth and holds moisture, and allows water to pass through it at a rate moderate enough to allow plants to take up nutrients.

Two other processes, which are related to climate, contribute to soil formation. The first is called **leaching**. In areas where there is a great deal of precipitation, there is a continual downward movement of water through the soil (Fig. 13–3). As the water moves down, it dissolves the chemical nutrients in the soil and carries them away. This downward movement of water removes nutrients that plants need. In very wet climates, leaching can take water-soluble minerals so deep that plant roots cannot reach them. You can identify a leached soil by its poor, often thin, topsoil layer. Examine Fig. 13–1 to see how much of Canada is covered with soils that are leached. Leached soils can be developed into excellent farmland by adding fertilizers.

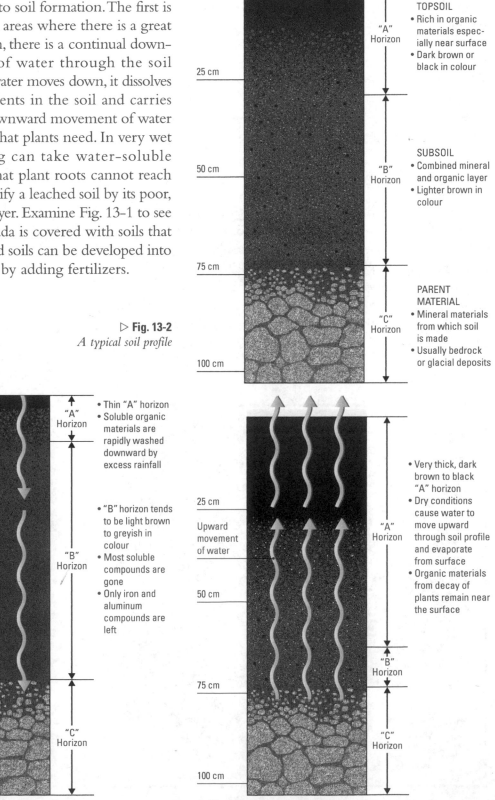

▷ **Fig. 13-2**
A typical soil profile

△ **Fig. 13-3** *A leached soil profile*   △ **Fig. 13-4** *A calcified soil profile*

The second process, known as **calcification** occurs in areas with drier climates (Fig. 13-4). As water in the topsoil evaporates, water from below is drawn up to replace it. This process is called **capillary action**. As the water reaches the surface, it evaporates leaving behind the minerals that were dissolved in it. The result is the creation of a thick topsoil layer which is rich in minerals. This process is called calcification because calcium is the main mineral deposited near the surface. In very dry climates, however, the amount of mineral deposition can be so great that it forms a layer poisonous to plants.

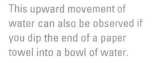

This upward movement of water can also be observed if you dip the end of a paper towel into a bowl of water.

VEGETATION REGIONS

A region's vegetation is determined by its climate and soils. Different types of vegetation require different combinations of climate and soils to grow. The vegetation in turn, affects the character of the soil. Plants must have moisture and heat for their survival. The relative amounts of these two things influence the types of plants that grow. For example, a warm, moist climate may support a forest of large trees; a warm, dry climate may support only short grasses. Areas with different types of natural vegetation are classified as different vegetation regions (Fig. 13-5).

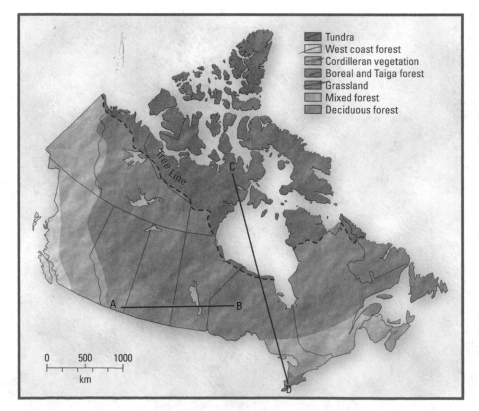

◁ **Fig. 13-5** *Natural vegetation regions of Canada. The A-B and C-D transects are shown in Fig. 13-6 and Fig. 13-7.*

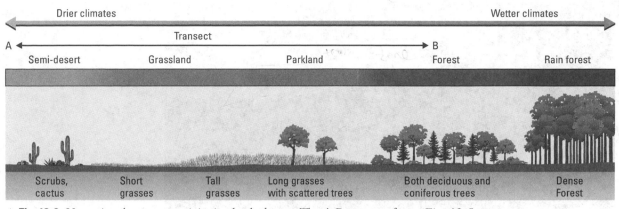

Drier climates   Wetter climates

Transect

A   B

Semi-desert   Grassland   Parkland   Forest   Rain forest

Scrubs,   Short   Tall   Long grasses   Both deciduous and   Dense
cactus   grasses   grasses   with scattered trees coniferous trees   Forest

△ **Fig. 13-6** *Vegetation changes as precipitation levels change. The A-B transect refers to Fig. 13-5.*

▽ **Fig. 13-7** *Vegetation changes as average temperatures change. The C-D transect refers to Fig. 13-5.*

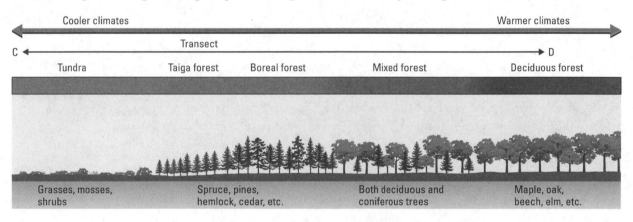

Cooler climates   Warmer climates

Transect

C   D

Tundra   Taiga forest   Boreal forest   Mixed forest   Deciduous forest

Grasses, mosses,   Spruce, pines,   Both deciduous and   Maple, oak,
shrubs   hemlock, cedar, etc.   coniferous trees   beech, elm, etc.

Natural vegetation refers to those plants that grow without any human interference. Natural vegetation is usually quite different from plants that people cultivate for food or for use in industry. Different types of natural vegetation grow in response to different climatic and soil conditions. Fig. 13-6 and 13-7 show the types of natural vegetation that grow as precipitation and temperature change from place to place.

Geographers have identified seven natural vegetation regions across Canada. These regions are composed of three types of natural vegetation: **tundra**, forest, and grassland. Of these, forest vegetation covers most of Canada.

Notice that the vegetation regions in Fig. 13-5 are separated by lines. It is a mistake to think that these lines show an immediate change from one region to another. Instead they represent areas of change called **transition zones**. The characteristics of one region gradually change into those of the next. Some transition zones are so large that they are considered regions in themselves, such as the mixed forest vegetation regions.

◁ **Fig. 13-8** *Tundra vegetation: plants remain small to obtain warmth from the ground.*
Also, low plants are protected from cold, harsh winds.

Tundra

The tundra is the most northerly vegetation region of Canada (Fig. 13-8). It is located above the **tree line**, which marks the northern boundary of tree growth. Trees do not grow in the tundra because the climate is too cold and dry. Most of the tundra has **permafrost**, or permanently frozen ground. Only the top metre or so of permafrost, known as the **active layer**, thaws during the short summer. Water cannot drain downward, so the surface remains water-logged. This thawing permits a very short growing season. Small shrubs, mosses, and lichens grow close to the ground where they soak up as much heat as possible from the earth. Lichens are slow-growing plants that cling to rocks. Tundra plants bloom and mature very quickly to produce their seeds before the cold weather returns. There is very little humus in the tundra's thin layer of soil because of the small amount of vegetation, the water-logged nature of the soil, and the cold climate. The lack of vegetation limits the variety of wildlife as well as the population of each species.

Some stunted trees are able to grow, however, in sheltered valleys in the southern part of this region.

Boreal and Taiga Forest

To the south of the tundra is the **boreal and taiga forest**, the largest vegetation region in Canada (Fig. 13-9). It is separated from the tundra by the tree line. North of this line, it is too cold for trees to grow. **Coniferous trees** grow south of this tree line because there is a longer growing season and more precipitation than in the tundra. Coniferous trees, or evergreens, lose some needles throughout the year but are never bare. Since they don't drop many needles, the humus layer beneath them is very shallow. This gives the topsoil a grey colour. The needles are acidic, so they make the soil acidic. Rainfall and snow melt wash away many soluble minerals

Coniferous trees are also known as needle-leaved trees. The tamarack is an exception. It is a coniferous tree but it is not an evergreen. It drops all of its needles in the fall.

◁ **Fig. 13-9** *Boreal forest: coniferous trees have the following characteristics that allow them to thrive in harsh, northern conditions:*

a)   *They are able to extract nutrients from the poor soil with their long roots.*

b)   *The sticky sap acts as an anti-freeze which prevents the needles from freezing.*

c)   *The waxy needles and thick bark prevent the loss of moisture in times of drought.*

d)   *The needles and flexible branches easily shed snow to prevent damage.*

e)   *The needles are able to conduct photosynthesis on warm days beyond the normal growing season.*

from the topsoil and removes them to deeper levels. The lack of humus, combined with the high acidity, and the leaching effect of water make these wet-climate soils infertile and unsuitable for agriculture.

Coniferous trees have characteristics that make them well suited to this region of cold temperatures and short growing seasons (Fig. 13-9). Trees such as white and black spruce, balsam fir, and pine grow sparsely along the northern edge of the boreal forest, but more densely further south. They are harvested by pulp and paper and lumbering companies. Some **deciduous trees,** such as poplar and white birch, are hardy enough to withstand the harsh winter conditions in the southern portion of the boreal forest (Fig. 13-10).

The cool temperatures and the lack of soil organisms, such as bacteria and earthworms, also slow down the process of humus formation.

The northern part of this coniferous forest is called taiga forest and the southern part is called boreal forest.

Deciduous trees are also known as broad-leaved trees.

◁ **Fig. 13-10** *The leaves of coniferous and deciduous trees*

Mixed Forest

South of the boreal forest in eastern Canada is a **mixed forest** of coniferous and deciduous trees (Fig. 13-11). Spruce, fir, pine, cedar, and hemlock are found in the same forest with maple, beech, ash, oak, and birch. This variety of trees has provided an excellent resource for the lumbering industry. Today, little of the forest remains in the southern part of the region because of farming, lumbering, urban development, and transportation routes. Along the exposed coastlines of the Maritime provinces where the cold winds create a harsher climate, the forest may give way to small shrubs, such as junipers, that grow close to the ground for protection.

The mixed forest is a transition zone between the boreal forest to the north and the deciduous forest to the south. Both coniferous and deciduous trees can survive in the warm summers and cool winters. The regular, abundant precipitation in this region is suitable for both deciduous and coniferous trees. The humus created from the leaves of such a wide variety of trees creates a deep grey-brown topsoil rich in minerals. Because humus holds water, fewer soluble minerals are removed from the topsoil in mixed forest than in boreal forest. Soils in mixed forest regions are suitable for farming.

When settlers first came to this region it was covered in trees. In order to build roads and farms, the forests had to be cleared. This process was so difficult that the forest was often seen as an enemy that had to be defeated.

△ **Fig. 13-11** *Mixed forest: a transition zone*

Deciduous Forest

The only deciduous forest in Canada is found in southwestern Ontario (Fig. 13-12). It is the northern portion of the large deciduous forest regions of the northeastern United States. Only small remnants of this forest remain since most of it has been cleared for farming and urban development.

The summers in southwestern Ontario are long and hot, the winters relatively mild, and the precipitation plentiful. These conditions are ideal for hardwood trees such as maple, beech, hickory, ash, and black walnut. These trees need at least five months of warm weather to store up energy in the form of sap in their roots and trunk to survive the winter.

hardwood trees: broad-leaved deciduous trees that have tough, dense wood

The soils of this region are similar to those of the mixed forest but contain more humus and are less acidic because of the greater number of deciduous trees. The humus-rich topsoil is dark brown in colour. Some of the soluble nutrients are removed from the topsoil by the abundant rain. Still they are the most fertile soils of eastern Canada.

Grasslands

The grasslands, or the prairies, are located in the southern part of Manitoba, Saskatchewan, and Alberta. The climate here is too dry for most species of trees to survive. Some, such as trembling aspen, willow, and spruce, grow

◁ **Fig. 13-12** *Deciduous forest: deciduous trees have the following characteristics that are suitable to the warmer more moist parts of Canada:*

a) *They lose their leaves in the autumn. If they kept their leaves over the winter, the weight of the snow on them might break their branches.*

b) *They are dormant in winter, but with the warmth of the spring, the sap flows to the buds causing new leaves to grow.*

c) *Most deciduous trees need a minimum of five months that have average temperatures above 10°C.*

in river valleys where more moisture is available. Grass, however, is suited to this dry climate. The deep intertwined root system of the grass forms a **sod mat**. This sod mat absorbs and stores moisture, and holds the soil in place. The grass dies off on the surface if it doesn't find enough water, but its roots remain alive. When moisture returns, the grass sprouts again.

When new immigrants first settled on the grasslands they often made their homes out of sod since few trees were available to make a log cabin.

The grasslands consist of three sub-regions. The driest areas of southern Saskatchewan and Alberta make up the **short-grass prairie** (Fig. 13–13). Drought-resistant short grasses, sagebrush, and cactus are the only types of vegetation which can survive here. The warm, dry climate limits the growth of vegetation which, in turn, limits the amount of humus produced in the soil. The limited rainfall and high evaporation have created calcified soils that are unsuitable for crops. The land can be used for grazing animals, particularly cattle.

Sagebrush and cactus are plants that have adapted to growing in dry conditions.

△ **Fig. 13-13** *Short-grass prairie vegetation is found in warm, very dry locations.*

△ **Fig. 13-14** *Tall-grass prairie vegetation is found in warm, dry locations.*

△ **Fig. 13-15** *Cordilleran vegetation: from lush forests to barren tundra vegetation*

△ **Fig. 13-16** *West Coast Forest: a temperate rainforest with the largest trees in Canada*

Surrounding the short-grass prairie is a region where increased precipitation encourages the growth of taller grasses (Fig. 13-14). This **long-grass prairie** is ideal for growing grains and **oil seeds**. Year after year as the tall grasses die in the fall, they produce large amounts of humus that result in a rich, black soil. The rainfall is just enough to keep the minerals within easy reach of the grass roots. This is the richest soil in Canada and produces some of the best grains in the world. Between the warm dry grasslands and the cooler, wetter boreal forest is the third grassland sub-region called **parkland**. This is a transition zone of long-grass prairie dotted with clumps of trees. Coniferous trees are more common in the northern part of the parkland, while deciduous trees dominate in the southern part.

Cordilleran Vegetation

In the Cordillera, temperatures are warmer in the valleys than high in the mountains (Fig. 13-15). The rainfall on the west side of a mountain is more likely to be heavier than on the east side. As a result, Cordilleran vegetation varies greatly. Grasses and cactuses grow in dry, hot valleys on the east side. Here the soils are similar to those found in the prairie grasslands. Irrigation is often required for agriculture.

Vegetation also changes as altitude increases. Forests of coniferous trees grow on lower slopes where precipitation is heavier. These forests are important to the logging industry of British Columbia. The vegetation on the higher slopes of the Cordilleran mountain ranges is similar to that of the tundra. Above the tree line there are only meadows of flowers and shrubs. On the very highest slopes, no vegetation can survive. Here, there is only bare rock, snow, and ice.

Soils of all types are found on the mountains of the Western Cordillera. The distribution of each soil type depends on the particular elevation,

Since winds blow from the west in this part of Canada, the west side of a mountain is the windward side and the east side is the leeward side (see Chapter 12).

slope, rainfall, and vegetation cover of each area within the mountain range. Soil characteristics can change completely in a short distance.

West Coast Forest

Along the West Coast of Canada grow lush forests of Douglas fir, Sitka spruce, red cedar, and western hemlock. The heavy rainfall plus the mild climate of the coastal region provide excellent growing conditions for the trees of this temperate rainforest (Fig. 13-16). Trees more than 1 m in diameter and over 50 m high are common. These splendid trees have played a crucial role in British Columbia's forest industry. Some of the old-growth forests have become the focus of environmental groups who wish to protect these ancient trees. The lush vegetation provides a lot of plant material to make humus but the high rainfall leaches minerals deep into the soil.

temperate: a climate with warm summers and cool winters

rainforest: a forest in an area with very heavy precipitaiton

IN CLOSING...

In southern Canada, there is little natural vegetation left because most of the land has been taken over for farming, lumbering, or the building of cities. In many areas, the large trees of the old-growth forests have been replaced with younger smaller trees.

The different vegetation regions in Canada provide us with many products. The coniferous trees of the boreal forest are the raw materials for pulp, paper, and lumber. Deciduous trees provide wood for eastern Canada's furniture industry. The huge trees of the West Coast forest provide lumber for use in Canada and for export. Beef for your next barbecue may come from cattle raised on the short grasses of the western prairies and may be cooked using charcoal from the hardwood trees of eastern Canada.

QUESTIONS

CHECK YOUR UNDERSTANDING

1. Describe the four components that make up a true soil.

2. a) How is topsoil formed?
   b) How long has it taken to form topsoil in Canada?
   c) Why does the topsoil differ in thickness in different parts of Canada?

3. Why is the size of rock particles important to soil structure?

4. Explain the difference between leaching and calcification.

5. In your own words, explain the meaning of the term "natural vegetation."

6. There are two classes of trees. Which one can survive a harsher climate? Why?

7. Name the Canadian vegetation region which:

   a) is the largest   c) is the wettest

   b) is the smallest   d) is the coldest

8. Explain, in your own words, the term "transition zone." Give an example and explain why this vegetation region is a transition zone.

ANALYZE AND APPLY

9. Fig. 13-17 shows the relationship between precipitation and soil fertility in temperate latitudes. Copy the graph in your notebook, and mark the following on it:

   a) a brown prairie soil

   b) a lightly leached soil

   c) a black prairie soil

   d) a heavily leached soil

   e) the boundary between wet-climate and dry-climate soils

10. "Natural vegetation is usually quite different from plants which people cultivate for food or for use in industry." Explain the differences.

11. Copy Fig. 13-18 into your notebook. Complete the chart using the information in this chapter.

Fig. 13-17 ▷

The relationship between soil fertility and precipitation

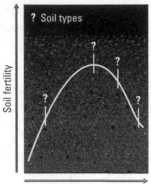

12. a) Using Fig. 13-5 and 12-21, p. 143, match each vegetation region to the corresponding climate region.

    b) The mixed forest and the deciduous forest regions are found in the same climate region. Explain how two vegetation regions can both occur in the same climate region.

13. "If you climb up a mountain, you will find a similar sequence of vegetation to that you would find if you travelled from southern Canada to the high Arctic." Explain why this is a valid statement.

▽ **Fig. 13-18**

Vegetation Region	Types of Natural Vegetation	Temperature Characteristics	Precipitation Characteristics	Soil Characteristics
Tundra	shrubs, mosses, lichens, small flowers	cold — short growing season	very little precipitation, most areas less than 400 mm	thin soils — permafrost
Boreal and Taiga Forest				
Mixed Forest				
Deciduous Forest				
Grassland — short grass — long grass — parkland				
Cordilleran Vegetation				
West Coast Forest				

14 Making the Connections: Canada's Ecozones

STUDY GUIDE

By the end of this chapter, you will be able to:

- identify Canada's ecozones and the criteria by which they were determined

- describe and compare Canada's ecozones

- identify two characteristics that identify why ecozones are useful

- relate the landforms, climate, vegetation, and human activities to ecozones in different parts of the country

Key Term

ecozone

Examine Fig. 14-1. Each of these photographs shows a different part of Canada. The location of each photo is shown on the map. A traveller from a distant country would look at these pictures and quickly realize that each one represents a very different kind of terrain that offers a special combination of opportunities and challenges to the people who live there. In the previous chapters, you had a chance to learn about Canada's geologic history, landforms, climate, soil, and natural vegetation regions. In this chapter, you will have the opportunity to see how these natural regions, together with the ways in which people and other animals live in them, form new kinds of regions called **ecozones**.

Areas can be grouped as separate ecological zones based on the way geologic, landform, soil, vegetation, climate, water, wildlife, and human factors are linked to each other. Change in one part of the system will result in adjustment in the rest of the system. For example, a shift in temperature within an ecosystem will affect the growth of plants which will in turn affect animals' ability to obtain food. Ecozones represent such ecological units.

The idea of dividing Canada into ecozones is fairly recent. In fact, the first map of Canadian ecozones was not published until 1986, so it is very unlikely that your parents or teachers would have learned about them when they were in high school.

Ecology is the study of living things and how they relate to each other and the environment.

You can learn more about ecozones at www1.ec.gc.ca/~vignettes/default.htm

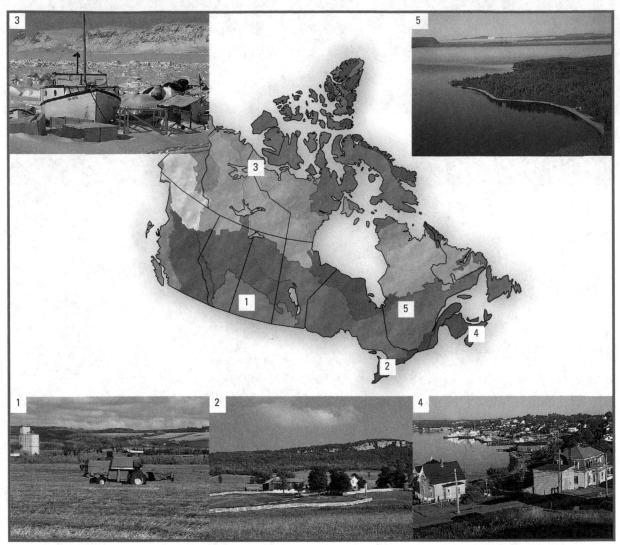

COMPARING REGIONS

Completing Fig. 14-2 may help you to understand how Canada's ecozones were determined. To do this, follow these steps for each of the photos in Fig. 14-1, which represents a sampling of Canada's 15 ecozones.

1. On the map in Fig. 14-1, check the location of each one of the photos.
2. Determine which landform region is located here (see Fig. 11-1). Copy Fig. 14-2 into your notebook and write this information.
3. Repeat this process for climate regions (Fig. 12-21), and soil regions (Fig. 13-1) vegetation regions (Fig. 13-5).
4. Next, list any human activities you see in the photo.

△ **Fig. 14-1** *Clearly there are enormous differences among the different landscapes of Canada. In this chapter, you will have the chance to learn to use the idea of ecozones to organize what we know about Canada's land and how people use it.*

5. Suggest any other human activities you are aware of that would be common in this region.

6. How do you know that each photo represents a different region?

▽ **Fig. 14-2**

Photo	Landform Region	Climate Region	Vegetation Region	Soil Region	Activities Shown*	Other Activities**
1						
2						
3						
4						
5						

* Human activities shown in the photograph

** Other human activities not shown in the photograph

As you have seen, each one of these photos represents a region that is quite distinct, in fact, each represents one of Canada's ecozones.

CANADA'S ECOZONES

Canada has an almost infinite number of different natural environments. How can these be grouped into a manageable number of ecological regions? In doing this, we face a variation of Goldilocks' problem: how many is too many, and how many is too few? We must decide on a number that is "just right." If too few zones are created, the result is inaccurate: any given zone will have environments within it that are very different. On the other hand, if too many zones are created, the result could be confusing: no one could hope to keep 30 or more zones clear in their mind.

Scientists decided on 15 ecozones as a reasonable compromise (Fig. 14-3). Any ecozone differs from its neighbours because of a combination of several factors, including landforms, climate, natural vegetation, soils, wildlife, and human activities. To see how this works, let's compare the Boreal Shield ecozone and the Mixedwood Plains ecozone (Fig. 14-4). We can see significant differences in factors such as the landforms and human activities found in each. For other factors though, such as soil characteristics, there are few, if any, important differences. In other parts of Canada, human activities might be relatively unimportant in establishing ecozone boundaries. This would be the case, for example, with the Northern Arctic and Southern Arctic ecozones. Here, however, there are differences in climate, since the Northern Arctic is colder.

The term "bioregion" is sometimes used in the same way as "ecozone." This is often the case in the United States and other countries.

In addition to the 15 land ecozones discussed here, there are five marine ecozones that cover the oceans that surround Canada.

If you want to examine Canada in more detail, there are more smaller regions called ecoregions, ecoprovinces (as of 2000), and ecodistricts that you can use.

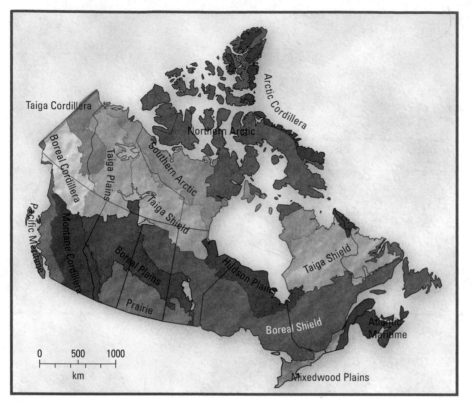

◁ **Fig. 14-3** *Canada's ecozones*

Factor	Boreal Shield	Mixedwood Plains
Landforms	Canadian Shield	Great Lakes Lowland
Climate	Boreal Region	Southeastern Region
Vegetation	Evergreen and mixed forest	Deciduous and mixed forest
Soils	Wet climate, leached soils	Wet climate, leached soils
Wildlife (examples only)	Moose, black bear, lynx, boreal owl, woodland caribou	Raccoon, skunk, great blue heron, grey squirrel
Human activities	Forestry, mining, trapping	Agriculture, urbanization

△ **Fig. 14-4** *The Mixedwood Plains and Boreal Shield ecozones are next to each other, yet are very different in many ways.*

Why Ecozones Are a Useful Idea

Before the concept of ecozones was created, people had a tendency to put the information about a particular place into separate "file folders": one for landform information, another for climate data, a third for facts about the population characteristics, and so on. This book is called *Making Connections: Canada's Geography* to remind you of the importance of the many ways in which these geographic factors are linked (or "connected") to each other. The ecozone concept allows us to bring together a collection of information about unique parts of Canada. Each ecozone can be thought of as a single "information folder" into which we can put all that we learn about an area of Canada. In this chapter, we concentrate primarily on the physical characteristics of the ecozones. Later in the book, we will look at human aspects of Canadian life and geography to add to our knowledge about each ecozone.

A Tour of Canada's Ecozones

Canada's ecozones are described in the following section. You should start your tour of Canada's ecozones with the one in which you live. From there, you can gradually move outward from neighbouring ecozones to more distant ones that may be very different from your own. By using this approach, you will be able to compare the other regions to the area that you know best.

Notes:
- GDP is the value of all economic production in the ecozone.
- Growing season is the average number of days per year when the average temperature is more than 5°C.
- All figures are from 1991, except for city populations which are from 1996.

Mixedwood Plains Ecozone: (Area 113 000 km²)

Landforms: Plains and rolling hills; Great Lakes are an important feature

Climate: Cool, short winters (-7°C); relatively long, mild summers (20°C); precipitation 700 to 1000 mm; growing season 180 to 260 days

Vegetation: Coniferous (white pine, eastern hemlock, red pine) mixed with deciduous (sugar maple, red oak, basswood); little natural vegetation remains

Soils: Leached, wet-climate soils

Human Activities: Total population 14 016 000; GDP $325.2 billion; urbanization, manufacturing, agriculture, recreation

Major Cities: Toronto (4 263 575), Montréal, Ottawa, Québec, Hamilton, Windsor, London

Boreal Shield Ecozone: (Area 1 774 000 km²)

Landforms: Plains and low hills of the Canadian Shield

Climate: Long winters (-15°C); short summers (17°C); precipitation 400 to 1000 mm; growing season 130 to 190 days

Vegetation: Coniferous (black spruce, white spruce, Jack pine, balsam fir) mixed with deciduous (yellow birch, sugar maple, black ash)

Soils: Heavily leached soils; bare rock; swampy areas

Human Activities: Total population 1 695 000; GDP $49 billion; forestry, mining, tourism, recreation, trapping

Major Cities: St. John's (174 051), Chicoutimi, Sudbury, Sault Ste. Marie, Thunder Bay, Thompson

Atlantic Maritime Ecozone: (Area 196 000 km²)

Landforms: Hills and coastal plains

Climate: Long, mild winters (-4°C); moderately warm summers (17°C); precipitation 1000 to 1400 mm; growing season 180 to 210 days

Vegetation: Coniferous (white pine, red spruce, red pine) mixed with deciduous (sugar maple, red oak, yellow birch)

Soils: Leached, wet-climate soils

Human Activities: Total population 2 510 000; GDP $39.9 billion; forestry, agriculture, fishing, tourism, urbanization

Major Cities: Halifax (332 518), Fredericton, Saint John, Charlottetown

Prairie Ecozone:
(Area 441 000 km²)

Landforms: Flat to rolling plains

Climate: Moderately long, cold winters (-15°C); moderately warm summers (18°C); precipitation 250 to 700 mm; growing season 170 to 190 days

Vegetation: Short-grass prairie in drier areas; long-grass prairie in wetter areas; some trees; little natural vegetation remains

Soils: Rich, grassland soils

Human Activities: Total population 3 851 000; GDP $90.8 billion; agriculture, urbanization, oil and gas development

Major Cities: Edmonton (862 597), Calgary, Winnipeg, Regina, Saskatoon

Boreal Plains Ecozone:
(Area 657 000 km²)

Landforms: Level to gently rolling plains

Climate: Long, cold winters (-20°C); short, warm summers (17°C); precipitation 450 mm; growing season 130 to 165 days

Vegetation: Coniferous forests (white spruce, black spruce, balsam fir, Jack pine, and tamarack) mixed with deciduous (aspen, poplar, and white birch); extensive marsh areas

Soils: Rich soils formed under forests; marsh soils in some areas

Human Activities: Total population 708 000; GDP $13.7 billion; forestry, farming, tourism, oil and gas development

Major Cities: Hinton (9961), La Ronge, The Pas, Flin Flon, Peace River, Fort Smith

Montane Cordillera Ecozone:
(Area 461 000 km²)

Landforms: Mountains, plains and plateaus

Climate: Temperatures vary with latitude and elevation; moderate winters (-12°C); moderate summers (15°C); precipitation varies widely with elevation and physical aspects, 500 to 1000 mm; growing season 140 to 240 days

Vegetation: Enormous variations depending on elevation; dominated by coniferous (Engelmann spruce, ponderosa pine, Douglas fir)

Soils: Wide variety of mountain soils

Human Activities: Total population 452 000; GDP $14 billion; forestry, agriculture, tourism

Major Cities: Kamloops (84 914), Prince George, Penticton

Pacific Maritime Ecozone:
(Area 196 000 km²)

Landforms: Mountains with small areas of coastal plains

Climate: Mild winters (3°C); cool summers (15°C); precipitation 600 to 2000 mm; growing season 200 to 260 days

Vegetation: Varies with elevation; coniferous trees (western red cedar, Douglas fir, western hemlock, sitka, spruce)

Soils: Wide variety of mountain soils

Human Activities: Total population 2 504 000; GDP $58.2 billion; forestry, urbanization, agriculture, fish processing

Major Cities: Vancouver (1 831 665), Victoria, Prince Rupert

Boreal Cordillera Ecozone:
(Area 432 000 km²)

Landforms: Mountainous, some hills

Climate: Long, cold winters (-20°C); short, cool summers (12°C); very dry, precipitation 300 to 500 mm; growing season 125 to 150 days

Vegetation: Mainly coniferous (white spruce, subalpine fir)

Soils: Variety of mountain soils

Human Activities: Total population 31 000; GDP $0.9 billion; hunting, trapping, forestry, tourism, mining

Major Cities: Whitehorse (21 808), Dawson

Taiga Cordillera Ecozone:
(Area 246 000 km²)

Landforms: Mountainous

Climate: Long, cold winters (-24°C); short, cool summers (13°C); very dry, precipitation 250 to 400 mm; growing season 90 to 130 days

Vegetation: Tundra of all types; areas of scattered forest

Soils: Variety of poor quality soils; bare rock

Human Activities: Total population 360; GDP $0.005 billion; hunting, trapping, forestry, tourism

Major Cities: Old Crow (300)

Taiga Plains Ecozone:
(Area 563 000 km²)

Landforms: Interior Plains and some foothills

Climate: Long, cold winters (-23 °C); short, cool summers (12 °C); dry, precipitation 200 to 400 mm; growing season 80 days to 150 days

Vegetation: Open forest to dense forest (black spruce, white spruce, Jack pine, tamarack, paper birch, trembling aspen)

Soils: Continuous permafrost in north; scattered permafrost further south; wide variety of poor quality soils

Human Activities : Total population 21 000; GDP $0.5 billion; hunting, trapping, tourism, oil and gas development, agricultural

Major Cities: Hay River (3611), Inuvik, Fort Simpson

Taiga Shield Ecozone:
(Area 1 269 000 km²)

Landforms: Plains and hills of Canadian Shield

Climate: Moderately long, cold winters (-25°C); moderately short, cool summers (12°C); precipitation 300 to 900 mm; growing season 100 to 140 days

Vegetation: Black spruce, jack pine, paper birch, trembling aspen

Soils: Thin, highly-leached soils; bare rock

Human Activities: Total population 34 000; GDP $1.1 billion; tourism, mining, hunting, trapping

Major Cities: Yellowknife (17 275), Uranium City, Happy Valley-Goose Bay

Hudson Plains Ecozone:
(Area 350 000 km²)

Landforms: Low-lying, swampy plains

Climate: Moderately long, cold winters (-17°C); moderately short, cool summers (14°C); precipitation 400 to 700 mm; growing season 90 to 150 days

Vegetation: Ground-hugging tundra; increasingly dense forest in south (white spruce, black spruce, tamarack, Jack pine)

Soils: Scattered permafrost occurs; poorly developed organic and permafrost soils

Human Activities: Total population 10 000; GDP $0.1 billion; hunting, trapping, recreation

Major Cities: Moosonee (1939), Churchill, Attawapiskat

Southern Arctic Ecozone:
(Area 776 000 km²)

Landforms: Plains and hills of Canadian Shield

Climate: Long winters (-25 °C), short summers (10 °C), dry, precipitation 200 to 300 mm; growing season 80 days

Vegetation: Tundra, including shrubs

Soils: Permafrost everywhere; tundra soils, bare rock

Human Activities: Total population 10 000; GDP $0.15 billion; hunting, trapping, tourism, mineral development

Major Cities: Rankin Inlet (2058), Tuktoyaktuk, Povungnituk

Northern Arctic Ecozone:
(Area 1 433 000 km²)

Landforms: Plains and upland areas

Climate: Long winters (-30 °C), short summers (5 °C); precipitation 200 mm; growing season 50 days

Vegetation: Tundra; ground-hugging plants

Soils: Permafrost; tundra soils

Human Activities: Total population 16 000; GDP $0.38 billion; hunting, tourism, some mining

Major Cities: Iqaluit (3500), Cambridge Bay, Resolute

Arctic Cordillera Ecozone:
(Area 239 000 km²)

Landforms: Innuitian Mountains

Climate: Long winters (-40 °C), short summers (0 °C); precipitation less than 200 mm; virtually no growing season

Vegetation: Mostly no vegetation; tundra

Soils: Permafrost; tundra soils; bare rock

Human Activities: Total population 1 000; GDP $0.012 billion; hunting, tourism

Major Cities: Pond Inlet (400), Clyde River, Broughton Island

IN CLOSING...

The concept of an ecozone is an exciting one that may help you to understand Canada better. As you learn about ecozones, remember the two characteristics of ecozones that make them particularly useful. First, they allow you to combine and relate information. For example, they help you to understand why forestry is an important industry in the boreal shield. Secondly they are constantly changing and will continue to grow and change.

QUESTIONS

CHECK YOUR UNDERSTANDING

1. a) What is an ecozone?

    b) Describe the two characteristics of the ecozone concept which make it a useful way to study Canada.

2. a) The population density of each ecozone is shown in Fig. 14-5. Divide these values into four categories on the basis of where you think "natural breaks" occur, for example, between the Mixedwood Plain and the Atlantic Maritime. You do not have to have an equal number of ecozones in each group.

    b) On a base map of ecozones that your teacher will supply, shade each category differently. It will be most effective if you use four different shades of one colour rather than four different colours. For example, you may want to use four shades of red. Always use the darkest shade for the highest value.

    c) Be sure to include a legend and suitable title for your map.

    d) Comment on the pattern of population density that you see. Remember that Canada's overall population density is about 3 people/km^2.

▽ **Fig. 14-5**

Ecozone	Population Density (people/km^2)
Arctic Cordillera	0.005
Atlantic Maritime	12.8
Boreal Cordillera	0.037
Boreal Plains	1.08
Boreal Shield	0.96
Hudson Plains	0.028
Mixedwood Plains	124.03
Montane Cordillera	0.98
Northern Arctic	0.01
Pacific Maritime	12.77
Prairies	8.73
Southern Arctic	0.013
Taiga Cordillera	0.001
Taiga Plain	0.037
Taiga Shield	0.027

Question 2 can also be done using ArcVoyager GIS software. Your teacher will give you instructions on how to do this.

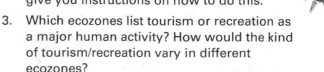

3. Which ecozones list tourism or recreation as a major human activity? How would the kind of tourism/recreation vary in different ecozones?

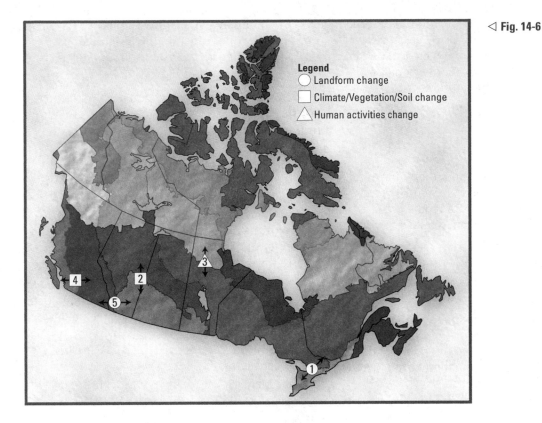

◁ Fig. 14-6

Legend
◯ Landform change
▢ Climate/Vegetation/Soil change
△ Human activities change

ANALYZE AND APPLY

4. a) What is the GDP of an ecozone?

   b) Create a pie graph to show the distribution of Canada's GDP among the ecozones. (Instructions for creating pie graphs are given in Chapter 8.) What does this graph tell you about the location of Canada's economic activities?

   c) Rank the ecozones separately from highest to lowest according to

      i.   GDP

      ii. area

      iii. population

   d) What relationship do you see between GDP and area?

   e) What relationship do you see between GDP and population?

5. Examine the growing seasons found in each ecozone. In what ecozones would you expect to find most of Canada's agricultural activities?

6. a) Ecozone boundaries exist for various combinations of three major factors: landform boundaries, climate/vegetation/soil boundaries, and human activity locations. Examine Fig. 14-6, where boundaries are identified on the map. The general reason for each ecozone boundary is suggested. For each, give the specific reason for the boundary.

   b) Choose any two other ecozone boundaries and explain why they exist.

THINK AND COMMUNICATE

7. a) Collect information about your local ecozone through personal observations, interviews with teachers and local experts, and visits to museums, conservation areas and wildlife organizations. Put this information in an organizer under the headings: Landform, Climate, Vegetation, Wildlife, and Human Activities.

b) Choose three other ecozones in different parts of the country. Draw an organizer using the same headings as 7a. In what ways are the four ecozones similar? In what ways are they different?

c) Choose one of the four ecozones. How do climate and landforms affect the types of wildlife, vegetation, and human activity found there?

8. In this chapter, you learned about the usefulness of ecozones in helping us to understand and explain Canada's geography. Consider how this would apply in each of these cases:

a) solving environmental problems

b) planning how a natural resource should be developed

c) planning a family's holiday trip

9. Complete either question 9a or 9b:

a) If you live in a highly populated ecozone, which lightly populated ecozone would you like to

   i. live in   ii. visit

Give reasons for each choice.

b) If you live in a lightly populated ecozone, which highly populated ecozone would you like to

   i. live in   ii. visit

Give reasons for each choice.

10. In most previous studies of Grade 9 Canadian Geography, the four ecozones Taiga Cordillera, Boreal Cordillera, Montane Cordillera, and Pacific Maritime would have been included in one region called the Western Cordillera. Compare the population densities of these four ecozones. How does this illustrate the difficulty of choosing just the right number of regions?

If you completed question 2, you will have already calculated the population densities. If not, you will have to do these calculations first.

UNIT 4

Cultural Connections

Urban Canada

15 An Introduction to the Study of Population

In the previous unit, you learned about Canada's remarkable physical geography. In this unit, you will learn about Canada's people: who they are, how they got here, and where and how they live. Consider a few numbers. On an average day, about 1070 babies are born in Canada, and 575 people die. As well, about 610 people **immigrate** to Canada and 135 **emigrate** from Canada to live elsewhere. As a result, at the end of the day, there are 970 more people living in Canada than there were at the beginning of the day (Fig. 15-1). In this chapter, you will discover how Canada's population is changing and what these changes mean for Canadians.

$1070 - 575 + 610 - 135 = 970$

CHANGING POPULATIONS

In the introduction to this chapter, we saw that a simple calculation can be done to determine the population growth of a country. This was your introduction to a fascinating subject called **demography**, which is, in simplest terms, the study of human populations. You will find that a knowledge of demography will prove very useful in helping you to understand

To learn more about world population growth, check www.popexpo.net/english.html

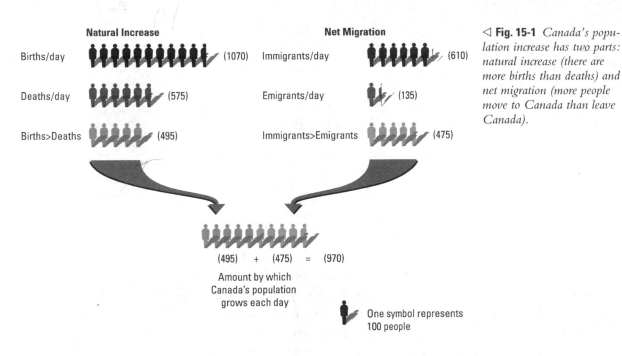

◁ **Fig. 15-1** *Canada's population increase has two parts: natural increase (there are more births than deaths) and net migration (more people move to Canada than leave Canada).*

the geography of Canada and other countries. In the section that follows, be sure that you understand each idea that is presented before moving on to the one that follows.

Use Rates, Not Numbers

We have seen that in Canada about 1070 children are born each day. We can compare these numbers to those in Russia (where about 3600 children are born) and the African country of Togo (with about 600 births). Or can we? Direct comparisons are somewhat pointless since the populations of these countries vary enormously (Canada has about 30 million people, Russia about 148 million, and Togo about 5 million). What really matters is not the number of births, but the relationship between the number of births and the size of the population. A measurement called the **birth rate** demonstrates this (Fig. 15-2). A similar measure can be calculated for deaths: the **death rate**. In Canada's case, the death rate is about 7 per year for each 1000 people.

	Number of Births per Year	Population	Birth Rate (Births per 1000 People)
Canada	390 000	30 000 000	13
Russia	1 329 000	147 700 000	9
Togo	221 000	4 700 000	47

◁ **Fig. 15-2** *A country's birth rate is calculated by dividing the number of births in one year by the population and then multiplying the result by 1000, e.g.,*

$$\frac{390\ 000}{30\ 000\ 000} \times 1000 = 13$$

If you always think about rates rather than about numbers, you will find it much easier to make comparisons between countries and between different periods in a country's history.

Rates That Determine Changes

We can combine the birth rate and death rate into a very useful measurement called the **natural increase rate**. The natural increase rate can be calculated very simply, as shown in the following example of Canada:

natural increase rate = birth rate - death rate
= 13 – 7
= 6

Canada's natural increase rate is therefore 6/1000. Natural increase rates are often given as percentages, which in this case would be 0.6%. In contrast, Togo has a natural increase rate of 3.6% while Russia has an increase of -0.5%. Natural increase is a very important concept since, in most countries, it is the most important reason why a country's population increases (or decreases).

The second reason why a country's population changes, is that people either immigrate to that country or emigrate to live elsewhere. In a similar manner to birth and death rates, you can calculate a country's **immigration rate**, which for Canada is 7/1000 (0.7%), and **emigration rate**, which is 2/1000 (0.2%) for Canada. If we combine these two, we get the **net migration rate** for Canada:

net migration rate = immigration rate - emigration rate
= 7 – 2
= 5/1000 (or 0.5%)

A final useful measurement is a country's **population growth rate**, which combines both natural increase and net **migration**.

population growth rate = natural increase rate + net migration rate
= 6 + 5
= 11/1000 (or 1.1%)

As we shall see, the rate at which a country's population is growing (or declining) has an enormous influence on the lives of people. If a country's population is growing very rapidly, there may be a serious problem providing enough housing, education, healthcare, and jobs for everyone. On the other hand, if a country has a declining population, there may be a shortage of workers (and customers) to meet the needs of the country's businesses.

To convert 6/1000 into a percentage:
6 ÷ 1000 = 0.006
0.006 x 100 = 0.6%

What would this negative natural increase in Russia mean?

Compounding

Imagine that your parents offer you a choice, as a reward for your hard work and success in school. To help pay for your future university costs, you can either choose to receive $1000 for each day in the month of June, or you can receive 1¢ on June 1st, 2¢ on June 2nd, 4¢ on June 3rd, 8¢ on June 4th, and so on.

Which would you choose? If you choose the first option, you will get a total of $30 000. If you choose the second option you will get $10 737 418.23! Such is the power of compounding, since growth occurs on top of the growth that has already taken place. The impact of compounding in demography is not quite as dramatic, but it is still of enormous importance. Consider the following: a French Canadian couple who married in 1660 could theoretically have 16 million descendants today.

If we consider the situation of a country's population, we can see the impact of compounding. Fig. 15-3 shows the impact of compounding on the populations of Canada, Russia, and Togo for the next 100 years, assuming that their population growth rates remain as they are today. Canada's population will grow slowly to about 54 million, but look at what happens to the populations of Russia and Togo. Russia's population drops to only 90 million (about two-thirds of today's population) and Togo's population skyrockets to almost 200 million!

A simple way to think about the impact of population growth is to consider what is called the **doubling time** for the population. As you might expect by the name, this is simply how long it would take for a country's population to double at the country's current population growth rate. You could calculate it with some fancy mathematics or with a spreadsheet, but it can be estimated very easily using something called the

This 16 million figure is based on 30-year generations and the birth of four children to each descendant.

It is very likely that these rates will change for reasons that you will discover in the next few pages.

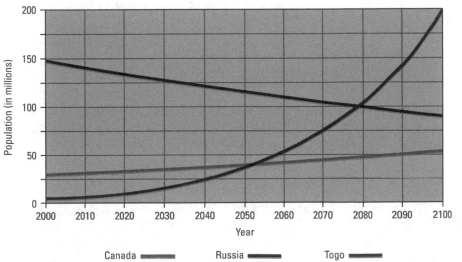

Year

Canada ▬▬   Russia ▬▬   Togo ▬▬

◁ **Fig. 15-3** *Differences among population growth rates appear very small, but compounding allows huge increases or decreases in population to occur.*
Note that these are projected figures for the population.

Rule of 70 — dividing 70 by the population growth rate to estimate how many years it will take. For example, with Canada's 1.1% rate, the population will double in about 64 years (70 ÷ 1.1). With Togo's 3.6% rate, the population doubles in less than 20 years. To understand the significance of this, picture how hard it would be for a rich country like Canada to provide all of the food, housing, healthcare, education, and other items needed, by twice as many people, every 20 years. For a poor country like Togo, the task is almost impossible.

Different Ages — Different Roles

At each stage of our lives, we play different roles. Demographers identify three important stages:

1. Children (up to age 15)
2. Working adults (ages 16 to 64)
3. Older adults (65 and over)

The assumption is that children and older adults are not working and must be supported by the working population. The proportion of the population that must be supported is called the **dependency load**. A high dependency load, of either children or older people, tends to put a great deal of pressure on the society to provide education, housing, health care, old-age homes, and other needs. Canada today has a dependency load of 33% (21% children and 12% older people), while a country like Niger in north Africa has a dependency load of 52% (49% children and only 3% older people). You can imagine the difficulty that a country like Niger would have in trying to support the more than half of its population that is dependent.

Population Pyramids

If someone asked you to examine the two sets of statistics in Fig. 15-4 and compare the percentage of people of different ages, you could probably do it, but it would not be a particularly easy task; you might even miss some important details. As is often the case with statistical data, it is easier to understand what is being shown if it can be graphed. The kind of data we have here is often shown on a special type of graph called a **population pyramid**, which is a series of horizontal bar graphs for the male population placed back-to-back with similar bar graphs for the female population. Fig. 15-5 includes population pyramids for the data in Fig. 15-4. Population pyramids make it easier to see things like the dependency loads of younger and older people.

Togo's natural increase can be considered its population growth rate since it has very little immigration and migration.

1956

Ages	Male	Female
70+	4.7%	5.0%
65-69	2.9%	2.9%
60-64	2.5%	3.5%
55-59	3.0%	4.0%
50-54	4.5%	4.5%
45-49	6.0%	5.5%
40-44	6.5%	6.0%
35-39	7.0%	7.5%
30-34	7.5%	8.0%
25-29	7.5%	8.0%
20-24	7.0%	7.1%
13-19	7.2%	7.3%
10-14	9.0%	8.9%
5-9	11.3%	11.2%
0-4	12.4%	12.3%

1996

Ages	Male	Female
70+	6.9%	10.0%
65-69	3.7%	4.0%
60-64	4.1%	4.2%
55-59	4.5%	4.5%
50-54	5.7%	5.5%
45-49	7.3%	7.2%
40-44	8.1%	8.0%
35-39	8.9%	8.8%
30-34	8.6%	8.5%
25-29	7.1%	7.0%
20-24	6.7%	6.5%
13-19	7.1%	6.5%
10-14	7.2%	6.3%
5-9	7.2%	6.6%
0-4	6.9%	6.4%

△ **Fig. 15-4** *This table shows the percentage of people of each sex and age group in Canada for the years 1956 and 1996.*

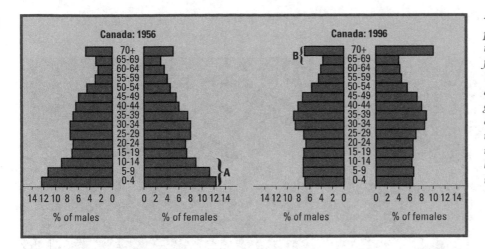

◁ **Fig. 15-5** *Compare these population pyramids to the tables of data in Fig. 15-4 from which they were made. Which is easier to interpret and to compare? At first glance, population pyramids appear complicated but they really aren't. Each consists of no more than 34 individual bar graphs placed in a particular arrangement.*

Population Patterns Change

The pyramids shown in Fig. 15-5 reveal dramatic differences in the population patterns of Canada in 1956 as compared to 1996. Let's consider the most dramatic difference that we see. In 1956, the dependency load of young children (see A on the diagram) is very high; while in 1996, the proportion of children is lower and the percentage of dependent older people has increased dramatically (see B). What significance did these differences have on Canada's society at each of these times?

In 1956, Canadian society's emphasis was on providing schools for the growing number of children (Fig. 15-6). Most of these children were between five and ten years old, so the greatest demand was for elementary schools. Ten years later, as these children grew older, the emphasis was on building secondary schools. During the 1950s, Canada's population was growing rapidly since people had moderately large families and many immigrants were coming to Canada.

By 1996, things had changed dramatically (Fig. 15-7). Except in a few growing suburban areas, there was little need for new schools. In fact, schools were being closed in some areas. Society's emphasis had switched to providing services for an aging population. Children who were in the first grade in 1956 were 46 years old in 1996 and increasingly in need of expanded health care facilities. They were also thinking about retirement. This meant that in 1996, society tended to focus on things like retirement incomes and providing places for leisure activities such as golf. Canada's population in 1996 was growing less than one-third as fast as in 1956, since people were having smaller families and immigration was lower. This meant that fewer schools and housing developments were needed than in 1956. As you can see, changes in population patterns tend to influence almost every part of our lives.

1956 was in the middle of the post-World War II baby boom.

To see population pyramids for various countries, check www.census.gov/ftp/pub/ipc/www/idbpyr.html

Canada's population growth rate in 1956 was slightly over 2%.

Have you ever noticed how many ads there are for RRSPs (Registered Retirement Savings Plans)?

What leisure activities might decline in popularity as the population gets older?

▽ **Fig. 15-6** *In the 1950s, most Canadian families had at least three children.*

▽ **Fig. 15-7** *In the 1990s, Canadian families had an average of 1.6 children.*

What happened to Canada's population has happened, and is happening, to other countries all over the world. A country starts with a high birth rate and an equally high death rate — meaning that the population remains stable. At some point the death rate drops, which means that fewer people die each year. As a result, the population increases quickly since many more people are being born than are dying. This process started in Canada about 200 years ago, but only started in very poor countries in the last 30 years or so.

Canada's 1956 population pyramid shows the population distribution during this stage of population growth. Many years later, the birth rate started to drop. Since this means that the difference between the birth rate and death rate decreased, the rate at which the population increased was slower. Canada's population began to experience this in the early 1960s. This process has not begun in many poorer countries.

A final stage in population growth occurs when the birth rate drops to the point where it is the same as the death rate. This causes the country's population to level off. Canada has not reached this point yet, but a population pyramid for the year 2020 (Fig. 15-8) shows what our population might look like at that time. How will the demands of this population be different from those in 1956 or 1996?

Demographic data, including population pyramids for every country for a range of years, can be found at www.census.gov/ftp/pub/ipc/ www.html

IN CLOSING...

A best-selling book by a Canadian demographer claims that you can understand the directions in which a society is going by understanding the demographic forces that are most powerful at a given time. As you study Canadian geography, and indeed live as a Canadian, you will see there is much truth to this. The ideas presented in this chapter will provide you with a framework for understanding Canada's population and those of other countries.

Boom, Bust, and Echo 2000.
Foot, David K. and Daniel Stoffman. Toronto, Ontario: Macfarlane, Walter and Ross, 1998

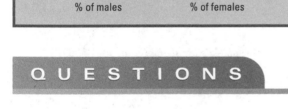

◁ **Fig. 15-8** *This is what Canada's population pyramid will look like in 2020. What will the dependency load be like? How old will you be? How will the dependency load affect you?*

QUESTIONS

CHECK YOUR UNDERSTANDING

1. a) Define: birth rate, death rate, immigration rate, and emigration rate.

   b) Describe, with the help of a numerical example, how these four factors contribute to the rate at which a country's population grows.

2. Ignoring the impact of immigration, Canada's population was relatively stable before the year 1800. Since 1800 our population has grown enormously. However it may stop growing within the next few decades. Some people would say that this pattern is the result of the forces of death control and birth control. Explain what each term means and how each contributed to Canada's population growth.

ANALYZE AND APPLY

3. a) What is the Rule of 70?

   b) Why is the Rule of 70 so useful?

   c) How long would it take for a population to double with each of the following growth rates:

   i. 0.5%   ii. 1.0%   iii. 1.5%

   iv. 2.0%   v. 3.0%

4. a) What is a population's dependency load?

   b) Describe why this would be a useful concept for

   i. a government planner

   ii. the president of a major bank

   c) Consider the ages used in determining the dependency load. For a developed country like Canada, do they accurately describe the dependent population? Why or why not?

5. a) The population growth of a country depends on both natural increase and net migration. Define each of these terms.

   b) Compare the importance of both in determining Canada's population growth over the last 40 years.

   c) Would this also be the case in other countries? Explain.

6. a) Draw a population pyramid using the data in Fig. 15-9.

   b) This data is for Canada in 1881. How is it different from the 1956 and later pyramids given in the text?

7. In this chapter we have looked at the "big picture" of population pyramids. Pyramids also show the impact of specific historical events on population. Examine Canada's population pyramids for 1956, 1996 (Fig. 15-5) and 2020 in Fig. 15-8.

   a) Identify and describe two such events.

   b) Can you follow these events from the 1956 pyramid to the later ones? How?

THINK AND COMMUNICATE

8. a) Your parents (and perhaps some of your teachers) are part of the Baby Boom. Why has their generation had such an enormous influence on Canada's society since the 1950s?

   b) Is this likely to continue?

   c) What effect has the baby boom had on your generation? How will it affect your generation in the future? Hint: Look at the 2020 population pyramid.

9. In the 1950s, the average family had three or four children. By 1997, the average family size had decreased to about 1.6 children.

   a) What is the average number of children each Canadian family must have if Canada's population is to remain

constant over the long-term? What will happen to Canada's population if families continue to have an average of 1.6 children?

   b) The average family size is the result of millions of individual decisions made by every Canadian couple. You probably have not thought about it very much, but how many children do you want to have? Why did you arrive at this family size?

   c) If your decision is typical of the decisions of the majority of people your age, what affect will this have on the Canadian population?

   d) What factors might encourage you to have a larger family? What might cause you to have fewer children?

10. a) What role does immigration play in Canada's population?

    b) How does this compare to most of the world's countries?

▽ **Fig. 15-9** *Canada's population in the year 1881*

Age	Male	Female
70+	2.6%	2.4%
65-69	1.7%	1.5%
60-64	2.4%	2.2%
55-59	2.7%	2.5%
50-54	3.3%	3.3%
45-49	4.0%	3.9%
40-44	4.5%	4.5%
35-39	5.3%	5.4%
30-34	6.1%	6.2%
25-29	7.7%	7.9%
20-24	9.8%	10.3%
15-19	11.0%	11.4%
10-14	12.0%	11.8%
5-9	13.0%	13.0%
0-4	13.9%	13.8%

16 First Nations: The Treaty Process

STUDY GUIDE

By the end of this chapter, you will be able to:

- identify ways in which past treaties failed to meet the needs of the First Nations
- identify and explain factors that affected the traditional lifestyle of the First Nations
- identify what a treaty is and why treaties are signed, both now and in the past
- understand how Nunavut came into being and some of the challenges facing the new territory

Key Terms

treaties

economic base

First Nations

Aboriginal

reserve

self government

Royal Proclamation of 1763

band

residential schools

comprehensive treaties

assimilate

ecotourism

specific claim

Native peoples — descendants of Canada's original inhabitants — have had a complex, and often difficult, relationship with the non-Native peoples (mainly Europeans) who have come to Canada over the last 500 years. As it became obvious to the Native peoples that they were becoming a small minority in their own land, they signed agreements called **treaties** with the Europeans, hoping to accomplish two things. First, they wanted to maintain an **economic base**. This meant having access to or keeping enough land to support themselves by fishing and hunting. They also wanted the right to control their own affairs. As we shall see later in this chapter, most of these treaties have failed miserably, since neither goal was achieved. In recent years, Aboriginal groups and the government have worked to revive the process of treaty making so that fairer settlements can be found.

A **First Nation** is a Native group in which the members share a common culture and history, and wish to be treated as a distinct group on this basis. There are several such cultural groups across Canada, as shown in Fig. 16-1. For legal purposes, the federal government also divides Native peoples into three groups: Indian, Inuit, and Métis. Indians include status Indians, who are entitled to certain rights through treaties made with

The population of about 800 000 people of aboriginal descent in Canada is less than the population of Ottawa-Hull.

A wide range of Aboriginal links can be found at www.bloorstreet.com/300block/aborcan.htm#1

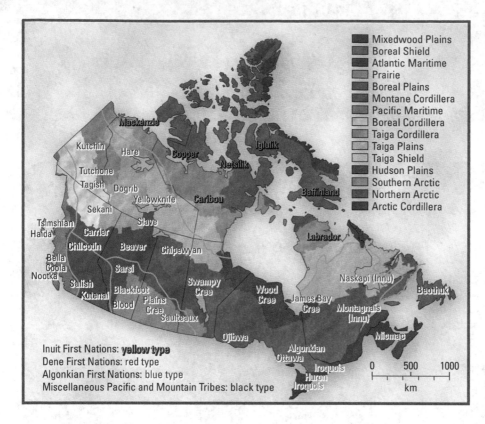

Mixedwood Plains
Boreal Shield
Atlantic Maritime
Prairie
Boreal Plains
Montane Cordillera
Pacific Maritime
Boreal Cordillera
Taiga Cordillera
Taiga Plains
Taiga Shield
Hudson Plains
Southern Arctic
Northern Arctic
Arctic Cordillera

Inuit First Nations: yellow type
Dene First Nations: red type
Algonkian First Nations: blue type
Miscellaneous Pacific and Mountain Tribes: black type

◁ **Fig. 16-1** *Canada's First Nations*

the government, and non-status Indians, who aren't covered by treaties. The federal government has special responsibilities for both status Indians and the Inuit, who include Native people living in the arctic region of Canada. Métis include people of mixed **Aboriginal** and European descent. It was not until the Constitution Act of 1982, though, that they were officially recognized as one of the three Aboriginal peoples of Canada.

A wide variety of Internet links about Aboriginal peoples and the North can be found at www.inac.gc.ca/sites/index.html

THE TREATY-MAKING PROCESS

Canada has a history of treaties that dates back to 1665 when the country was a colony. First the French, and later the British, signed treaties with Native peoples. In these early years, when there were only a small number of European explorers, fur traders, and settlers, Native peoples were in the dominant position. They outnumbered Europeans, and knew how to survive in a challenging country. In fact, often they were able to give the newcomers the food, shelter, and knowledge they needed to survive. In these early encounters, European government and Native peoples made treaties based on peace and friendship as military allies.

Over the years that followed, the relationship between the two groups altered sharply. As more and more Europeans arrived, the British govern-

	First Nations	Europeans
Land	• had the land; were prepared to share it	• wanted to settle on it
Wanted	• peace; realized the Europeans had great military power • other things (money, goods, etc.) that the Europeans offered	• peace, realized that the First Nations would always be a threat without a treaty
Experience with treaties	• had considerable experience using treaties to settle disputes with neighbours	• had considerable experience using treaties to settle disputes with neighbours

△ **Fig. 16-2**

ment wanted to obtain control of the land used by Native groups. In exchange, they offered Native people payment, an area of land called a **reserve**, and, sometimes, goods.

Signing treaties made sense for both the First Nations and for the Europeans (Fig. 16-2). The British **Royal Proclamation of 1763** established two important principles that were to be applied when treaties were negotiated. The first was that the land-ownership rights of the First Nations must be respected. The second was that if a First Nation did choose to give up land, it should receive a fair payment for it. However, this was not often the case. From 1780 to 1876, small parcels of land were traded through treaties; Native people were given a very small one-time payment, sometimes suits of clothing, and later, blankets, in exchange. By 1850, much larger areas of land were being surrendered in exchange for reserves, cash, yearly payments to reserve members, and promises of hunting and fishing rights over vacant government-owned land. Payments that may have seemed fair then, do not seem adequate now, since the value of money has changed so much.

After Confederation, when the federal government was pushing to expand the west with the railroad and settle the Prairies, it became more concerned that Native groups give up all rights to the land. Through **The Indian Act** of 1876, the government signed treaties with Native groups that required them to give up their claim to the lands they occupied forever, and persuaded them to move to reserves. For the Canadian government, the reserves were seen as temporary, until the Native people on them became absorbed into the dominant culture. Under the treaty agreements, Native peoples were to receive cash payments, yearly payments to reserve members, and goods. Most convincing, perhaps, were promises of continuing fishing and hunting rights, which would allow them to live as they had in the past. The government gave gifts of flags and medals to show their friendly intentions. Near the turn of the century, after two decades, treaties were

For example, a payment of $25 per year in 1870 might have made sense at the time. Now, it seems quite inadequate.

Native people were to take up agriculture on the Prairies.

again made after gold and oil were discovered in the North. By 1923, the last unsurrendered land in southern Ontario was signed over by treaty, and with it, the treaty-making process came to an end. In British Columbia and the Northwest Territories, however, treaties had not been signed, and treaties in these areas would not begin to be looked at until over 50 years later.

While Native people gave up almost half of Canada's land area through treaties, unfortunately, many of the treaties proved to be unfair. There were differences between what Native peoples thought they were signing, and the actual wording of the treaties. In addition, in many cases, treaty promises of payments, reserve land, and rights to hunting and fishing were broken.

Under the Indian Act, the government decided who "Indians" were, and only status Indians had the rights to use reserve lands. Status Indians were usually those who were registered with the Department of Indian and Northern Affairs by being **band** members on a reserve. The band was the decision-making organization created under The Indian Act by the government to represent the reserve. Often, however, the band was different from the First Nation's own decision-making unit. If you left the reserve, you lost your right to land. Métis and non-status Native peoples were not included in treaty making.

The government made decisions on behalf of Native peoples. The government decided how reserve lands were to be used, and they had other powers. For example, the government decided how reserve lands were to be used. It told Native people on the Prairies that they had to have a pass in order to leave their reserves. Later, the government banned Native peoples from raising money to pursue land claims. These bans were lifted in 1951, but Native people did not have the right to vote in federal elections until 1960. Although many aspects of the Indian Act are still in place, there has been a move since the 1980s to give bands more control through their councils. More than half of the bands now control their own finances, but they still cannot sell or rent land.

WHAT WENT WRONG?

Loss of Land and Economic Base

The original treaties failed to meet the needs of Aboriginal peoples for two main reasons. The most important was the enormous loss of land that occurred as a result of European settlement, especially in southern and central Canada. Having free access to land was key to the ability of the Native peoples to maintain their traditional ways of life, but the treaties meant that they had to give up most of the land that they had used for thousands of years. Rarely were these reserves of land large enough, or rich enough, to provide a sound economic base for the people who lived on them.

There are 2360 reserves in Canada; they include only 27 500 km^2, which is less than 0.3% of Canada's total area. If you remember that there are about 800 000 people of First Nations descent living in Canada, this is a very small amount of land. Since many of the reserves do not have rich resources of fertile land, minerals, commercial forests, fish, animals and other resources, the residents of the reserves face a difficult choice. They can stay on the reserve with their family and friends — but face a future that frequently includes unemployment and poverty — or they can move to the city in the hope of a better economic future — but only by abandoning their own community.

To learn more about individual First Nations, check esd.inac.gc.ca/fnprofiles/ FNProfiles_home.htm

Lack of Self Government

The second reason why these treaties failed was that Native peoples were given no right to govern themselves. Before the arrival of Europeans, the First Nations of North America governed themselves in many different ways. For example, the Iroquois had one of the oldest democracies in the world: the Six Nations. After Europeans came to dominate Canada, these traditions of government were lost. Most decisions about how Aboriginal people were to live were, and continue to be, made by the federal government.

Some of these government decisions had a huge impact on Native ways of life. Perhaps the most damaging of these was the decision to send Native children to **residential schools**. For many years, Aboriginal parents were persuaded to have their children taken from their homes and sent to live and learn in special schools in the larger towns. The purpose of these schools was to teach these children the language and culture of the larger, mainstream Canadian society so that they could become **assimilated** into it. They were punished if they tried to speak their own languages or practice their own cultural traditions. Sometimes these children were abused while they lived at these schools. Many years have been spent trying to repair the damage caused by these schools so that these people do not remain trapped between two cultures.

The problem of not having **self government** can be seen in other areas as well. Provincial and federal governments have made laws to protect the populations of wildlife. Yet, Native peoples traditionally hunted and fished whenever and wherever game (or fish) were plentiful. Aboriginal leaders have argued that these laws should not apply to their people, since such laws help to destroy their economic base and traditional culture.

The Six Nations was a confederation of six Iroquois nations in southern Ontario and northern New York state: the Cayuga, Mohawk, Oneida, Onondaga, Seneca, and Tuscarora.

self government: the legal power of a First Nation to make and apply laws governing its members and lands

In 1990, the Supreme Court of Canada ruled, in a case in British Columbia, that the First Nations' use of fish for food, social, and ceremonial purposes has priority over all other uses except conservation.

△ **Fig. 16-3** *Although the Bennett Dam provides many benefits in British Columbia, the livelihoods of Native people who are downstream from the dam have been severely affected.*

Native people have often been harmed by developments over which they have no control. The Bennett Dam in British Columbia, for example, is one of Canada's largest hydro-electric projects (Fig. 16-3). It produces many benefits for the people and the industries of the province. At the same time, it disrupts river flow hundreds of kilometres downstream in the Peace River delta at Fort Chipewyan, Alberta. The Native people in this area traditionally earned their living by trapping muskrat in the river and selling it for fur products. The reduced water flow reduced the size and the quality of the muskrat habitat. As a result, fewer muskrat could be caught and those that were trapped were of poorer quality. Many of the trappers in Fort Chipewyan are no longer able to earn an adequate living — their economic base had been damaged by a development far away in another province over which they had no control.

Aboriginal peoples want self government so that they can control their own destinies. They want to be able to expand their economic base so that they can reduce unemployment and poverty among their peoples and reduce their dependence on the government. They want to be able to protect and expand their cultures and develop a stronger social structure to help overcome problems of isolation, poor housing, and ill health.

TREATIES TODAY

Most treaties were signed between the 1700s and the early 1900s. As Fig. 16-4 shows, though, much of Canada was not covered by treaties. This happened because by the 1920s, the government's desire to sign treaties had disappeared. In fact, for a number of years — between 1927 and 1951 — it was even illegal for a First Nation to hire a lawyer to negotiate on their behalf with the government. Even if the term was not used, the government's policy was that assimilation was in the best interests of Canada's Aboriginal population.

In more recent years though, many Canadians, and their governments, came to realize that the Aboriginal people of Canada had been treated very unfairly over many centuries. There was a growing acceptance of the idea that treaty making should be re-visited. This changed only partly because of a desire for fairness. A number of Supreme Court cases, starting in 1973, directed governments to review the treaty situation and insure that Aboriginal demands for self government and a sound economic base be respected. As well, the Canadian Constitution in 1982 recognized the right of self government (although it did not specify exactly what this meant or how it should be achieved).

It is important to understand that there are two kinds of treaty settlements occurring. In areas where treaties were never signed, First Nations must negotiate their first treaty. These are called **comprehensive treaties** because they must deal with many issues: land ownership, self government, hunting/fishing/trapping rights, financial compensation, and ownership

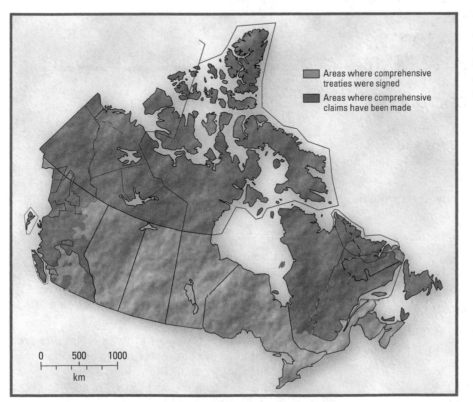

Areas where comprehensive treaties were signed

Areas where comprehensive claims have been made

0 500 1000
km

◁ **Fig. 16-4** *Comprehensive treaties remain to be signed in many areas of Canada. The most recent treaties to be signed were in Nunavut and northwestern British Columbia (Nisga'a settlement).*

and control of resources. While there have been few comprehensive treaties signed, they are important since they typically involve large tracts of land and major changes in how people live in these areas. Fig. 16–4 shows where comprehensive treaties have been signed. The second part of this chapter looks at one such comprehensive treaty.

Between 1973 and 1998, 11 such claims were settled, but more than 40 other claims remain to be dealt with.

A different type of treaty claim can be made in an area in which a comprehensive treaty already exists. This is a **specific claim** made by First Nations who feel that one or more terms of their original treaty were unfair or have not been fulfilled over the years since it was signed. For example, if the people of a First Nation did not receive all the lands promised in their treaty, they could make a claim for that land. They would be asking for fair treatment under the spirit of the original treaty. Since 1973, more than 200 specific claims have been settled, with more than 100 still being negotiated. Since specific land claims are often made in the more heavily populated parts of Canada and involve land occupied by other Canadians, the land may not be easily transferred, so the claim would be for a sum of money in payment for the land. Since much of the land is so valuable, a lot of money can be involved.

Specific claims continue to be made.

For example, specific claims have been made for lands in and around Toronto, Montréal, and Vancouver.

Because of the complexity of treaty negotiations, only a small number are occurring at any given time. It will take many years to complete all of the comprehensive and specific claims that are outstanding, and the lessons of one set of negotiations are helpful for the next.

QUESTIONS

CHECK YOUR UNDERSTANDING

1. a) What directions did the Royal Proclamation of 1763 give to British administrators who would be dealing with First Nations?

    b) Why should it have been a useful beginning to the treaty-making process?

    c) Why did this not happen?

2. In what two important ways did treaties fail to meet the needs of Native peoples?

3. Explain how each of the following affected the traditional lifestyle of the First Nations:

    a) Canada's greatly increased population

    b) the move of First Nations' peoples onto reserves

    c) the use of residential schools

    d) fishing and hunting laws

    e) resource and development projects

4. a) Describe the difference between comprehensive and specific claims.

    b) In what parts of Canada would you expect to find each? Why?

ANALYZE AND APPLY

5. Could conflict between First Nations and European fur traders and settlers in southern and central Canada have been avoided? If you don't think so, explain why. If you think so, indicate how.

6. The cultural regions of the First Nations are related to the character of the ecozones in which they occur. Referring to Fig. 16-1, construct a chart similar to Fig. 16-5 to allow

▽ **Fig. 16-5**

Cultural Region	Ecozones	Ecological characteristics
Inuit		
Dene		

you to identify the ecozones that lie within which each cultural region. Also, state the main ecological characteristics of each area. Consider the landforms, climate, natural vegetation, soils and wildlife in each.

7. How have the twin problems of lack of economic base and self government contributed to the problems faced by many Native peoples today?

THINK AND COMMUNICATE

8. a) What is the purpose of signing a treaty?

    b) What alternatives would there be to negotiating a treaty?

9. a) What is assimilation?

    b) Why would some people view assimilation as the best solution for Aboriginal people? Why would other people consider this a harmful approach?

10. a) In Canada today, some First Nations people live off the land (e.g. hunting, trapping, etc.) like their ancestors. Others have moved to large cities and have a completely different way of life. Most First Nations people have a life which combines factors of city living and living off the land. What factors determine which of these lifestyles an individual might choose? What are the advantages (and disadvantages) of each?

    b) Will it be easier or more difficult to live in a traditional way in the future? Give evidence to support both points of view and then draw your conclusion.

THE CREATION OF NUNAVUT

In recent years, Canadians have been doing something that they have not had to do for half a century — buying new maps of Canada because the old ones are now out-of-date. The last time we had to do this was in 1949 when Newfoundland became part of Canada. The change this time was to show the new territory of Nunavut created from the eastern and northern parts of the Northwest Territories (Fig. 16-6). Changes in the size and political organization of the Northwest Territories are very common in Canada's history. At various times in the past, Manitoba, Saskatchewan, Alberta, the northern parts of Ontario and Québec, and the Yukon were all parts of the Northwest Territories. So, the creation of Nunavut can be seen as just part of the ongoing evolution of Canada.

The name Nunavut means "our land" in Inuktitut, the language of the Inuit people. The name describes very well why Nunavut was created. Nunavut has a population which is very different from the rest of Canada, since 85% of its people are Inuit. As a small minority of the Northwest Territories's population, they felt that they had little political influence in the Territory and also wanted to protect and develop their own culture and economic base. Most decisions were made in Yellowknife, the capital of the Northwest Territories, which was very far from where the Inuit

Since the population and economic base of a territory are smaller than those of a province, a territory lacks the governing power of a province, and relies more on the federal government.

To learn more about Nunavut, check
www.nunavut.com/home.html

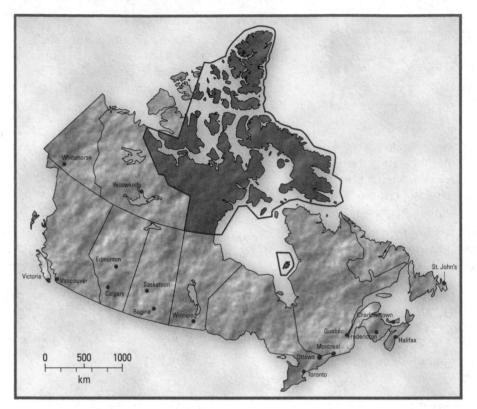

◁ **Fig. 16-6** *This map shows the location of the new territory of Nunavut.*

lived. Just getting to Yellowknife was very time-consuming and costly. For example, traveling from Pond Inlet (a settlement in Nunavut) to Yellowknife would require stops in Clyde River, Qukiqtarjuak, Iqaluit, and Rankin Inlet. This trip would take two days, since you would have to stop overnight, even though there is only 6.5 hours of flying time, and would cost $3892.

Nunavut was created as the result of a long series of negotiations between the Inuit Tapirisat of Canada (ITC) and the federal government. The initial proposal to create Nunavut was made by the ITC in 1976. In 1982, the people of the Northwest Territories voted in favour of dividing the territory into two parts. The vote led to negotiations for the treaty that would establish Nunavut. This was to be a comprehensive treaty since it would be the first treaty in this part of Canada. As well, it would involve settling a wide range of issues. The final agreement was signed in 1993.

Remember that communities in the North are not linked by roads and most travel is by air.

The Inuit Tapirisat of Canada is an umbrella organization that represents the interests of the Inuit people of Canada.

Features of the Nunavut Settlement

In keeping with the new generation of comprehensive treaties, the Nunavut land-claim settlement aimed to provide an economic base on which people in the territory (Inuit and non-Inuit) could build their futures and become self-sufficient. To do this, the settlement provided for opportunities for a wide range of economic development (Fig. 16-7).

Inuit were given:

- **ownership of about 350 000 km² of land (a bit less than 20% of the territory of Nunavut)** they were given the mineral rights to about 10% of this — this means they would own any minerals found under this land

- **equal representation with the government on a number of management boards that are to control wildlife, resources, and environmental management**

- **the right to hunt and trap on the settlement land**

- **a capital fund of $1.1 billion to be paid over a 14-year period;** The purpose of this fund is to invest in economic activities that will ensure a sound economic base in the future for the people

- **preference in the development of many resources in Nunavut**

- **the creation of three new national parks in the territory;** as well as providing protection for sensitive environmental areas, these parks will provide administrative and ecotourism jobs

- **the creation of Nunavut, which lead to the creation of a form of self government**

◁ **Fig. 16-7** *Features of Nunavut settlement*

The Cree of northern Québec bought and expanded a regional airline called Air Creebec with some of the money they received in compensation for the James Bay hydro-electric project built on their land.

Self Government in Nunavut

While the treaty did not directly provide for Inuit self government, the result was just that. Since 85% of Nunavut's people are Inuit, it is obvious that they will be in a position to dominate the territory's government. No longer will so many decisions be made in far away Yellowknife and Ottawa.

The transition to full control by the Nunavut government is a long and slow process that started in 1993, and is to be completed in 2009. This might seem like a very long time, but creating a new government is a very complex process, especially in an area where people have had little experience in running their own affairs. The government of Nunavut has a legislative assembly, a cabinet, and a court system along with employees of many types, needed to make it work.

One of the problems that the Nunavut government must overcome is that there are very few people in the new administration who have the education and experience needed to take senior jobs in the government. They have decided to solve this problem slowly. In the beginning, they will hire outsiders with the required abilities to do these jobs. Local people will get jobs as the assistants to outside experts so that they can develop the experience they will need to take over the senior jobs at a later date. Also, the community college in Iqaluit is setting up programs to teach the skills that people will need to qualify for government jobs.

To learn more about the Arctic Council, an international organization of northern countries that deals with common concerns, check www.nrc.ca/arctic

Government workers would include everyone from court workers and teachers to nurses and game wardens.

Characteristics of the New Territory

Most Canadians (or at least those who live in the south!) likely have only a vague idea of what Nunavut would be like — or even how large it is. It is unique when we consider how large it is and how few people live there. Nunavut is almost as large as the whole of Western Europe (Fig. 16-8), and yet has a population of about 27 200, which is about half the number of people who attend the University of Toronto! The tiny population of Nunavut is also shown by one simple statistic. The population density of Nunavut is only 0.01 people/km², which is about 1/300th of Canada's population density. Most of the people of Nunavut live in 28 small communities which range in size range from about 4400 in the capital city of Iqaluit to Grise Fiord, with only 160 people.

When the ITC first proposed a separate Inuit territory, they thought that the border should be at the tree line, which divided two ecozones — the Taiga Shield and the Southern Arctic. This turned out to be impractical for a couple of reason. First, the tree line is clear only on maps. On land, there is a broad transition zone from the boreal forest to the tundra. Second, the specific border had to be agreed on in a political negotiation. The result is a border which often follows lines of latitude and longitude rather than ecozone boundaries.

To learn more about Canada's North, check www.dfait-maeci.gc.ca/arctic/DIAND3-e.htm

Population estimates are for 1999.

Challenges Facing Nunavut

As you might expect, the creation of Nunavut has caused a great deal of excitement and hope for the future of the Territory. People have high hopes for economic growth and for their ability to protect and enhance their culture. There are some serious problems that must be overcome, though, such as the high cost of living.

Consider the following statistics. The average family income in Nunavut is about two-thirds as large as that for all of Canada. At the same time, goods cost more than average — a loaf of bread costs $3 and a litre of milk $3.50 in Nunavut. Imagine what it would cost to heat a home in Iqaluit where the average January temperature is about -30°C.

Unemployment is also an enormous problem, and this has brought widespread poverty and a range of social problems. More than one-third of the people of Nunavut live in

▽ **Fig. 16-8** *Map of Nunavut superimposed over Western Europe*

communities where the unemployment rate has been more than 40%. At the same time, the Canada-wide unemployment rate was less than 10%. This problem may get worse since Nunavut has a very young population with a great many school-age children. Within the next few years, these young people will be in the job market. The following issues will have to be addressed as Nunavut faces the future.

△ **Fig. 16-9** *Tourism is a great potential for economic growth in Nunavut.*

ISSUE #1

What economic potential does Nunavut have?

Nunavut's greatest economic growth is likely to come in mining and tourism. The territory's full mining potential is not yet clear. There is reason to think that Nunavut has rich reserves of copper, gold, silver, lead, zinc, and even diamonds. The question that must be answered is whether these resources can be developed economically and in an environmentally sound manner. Tourism might be the "secret weapon" in developing Nunavut's economy. In recent years, throughout the world, there has been an enormous growth in what is called **ecotourism**. This is environmentally sensitive tourism based on the fascination that people have with the wonders of the natural world (Fig. 16-9) — something that Nunavut has in great amounts. Ecotourists are used to paying high prices to visit exotic destinations like rainforests in Costa Rica or the Sahara desert. Nunavut offers these people a unique destination. Before the trickle of tourists to Nunavut increases, transportation connections and tourist facilities will have to improve. Such improvements can be made with investments from the capital fund.

To learn more about tourism in Nunavut, check www.nunatour.nt.ca/home.html

ISSUE #2

Can Nunavut's resources be developed without damaging the sensitive environment?

Resource development must be done with great care since the physical environment of Nunavut is easily damaged and recovers from damage very slowly, due to its cold climate and short summers. The season when everything isn't frozen is very short, and this is also the time when the most environmental recovery occurs. Economic development in the past has often resulted in environmental damage. For example, there are a number of abandoned military radar sites in the North, which now must be treated as hazardous waste sites. On the other hand, there are mines at Nanisivik and on Little Cornwallis Island that are being operated successfully with strict environmental controls in place.

Whether the land claim financial settlement of $1.1 billion is enough to provide a solid economic base for Nunavut's future remains to be seen.

What About the Rest of the Northwest Territories?

The creation of Nunavut has received an enormous amount of attention, but what effect has all this had on the rest of the Northwest Territories? Perhaps the situation could be compared to that of a family with two children, in which one child gets most of the attention. Feelings of resentment are easy to understand. There has been a concern that establishing Nunavut will divert attention (and money) from the problems faced by the western territory that is left. One Northwest Territories politician even suggested that the remaining part should be renamed BOB, short for Bottom Of the Barrel. This indicated how he thought his territory was being treated as a result of the creation of Nunavut.

QUESTIONS

CHECK YOUR UNDERSTANDING

1. What is self government?

2. a) Describe the steps by which Nunavut became a separate territory.

   b) In what ways is Nunavut (and its people) different from the rest of the Northwest Territories?

ANALYZE AND APPLY

3. Examine a map that traces the development of Canada's provinces and territories (there may be one in your atlas). Why has the Northwest Territories gotten smaller over the years?

4. a) In what ecozones is Nunavut?

   b) In what ways do the characteristics of these ecozones provide economic opportunities for Nunavut? Or limit Nunavut's economic future?

5. a) What is ecotourism?

   b) What would be the main characteristics of typical ecotourists? In your answer, consider such things as where they would be from, their age, and their level of wealth.

   c) Why might ecotourism prove very popular in Nunavut?

THINK AND COMMUNICATE

6. a) Was the creation of Nunavut well-planned? Why do you think this is the case?

   b) What uncertainties are there about Nunavut's future? Why?

7. What factors do you think that the government of Nunavut should consider when planning the following:

   a) transportation

   b) social services

   c) political structures

   d) resource management

17 Immigration

STUDY GUIDE

By the end of this chapter, you will be able to:

- identify patterns in Canada's immigration history
- understand the current immigration system in Canada
- understand the multicultural nature of our society

- identify the causes of immigration and emigration
- identify patterns of migration within Canada and between Canada and other countries

Key Terms

multicultural
push factor
pull factor

intervening obstacle
landed immigrant
independent immigrant

family immigrant
refugee

Immigrants or descendants of immigrants make up 98% of Canadians. This fact helps to explain why Canada's population can be described as a "tossed salad" of peoples, or more formally, a **multicultural** society. The mix of ethnic groups in different parts of Canada varies widely (Fig. 17-1).

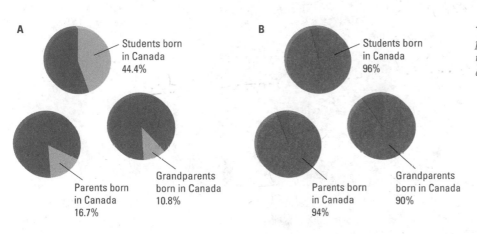

◁ **Fig. 17-1** *These two sets of pie graphs represent the cultural makeup of two geography classes.*

A

Students born in Canada 44.4%

Parents born in Canada 16.7%

Grandparents born in Canada 10.8%

B

Students born in Canada 96%

Parents born in Canada 94%

Grandparents born in Canada 90%

Write the answers to the following questions in your notebook.

1. In Fig. 17-1, one set of pie graphs is from a geography class in a large city and the other is from a geography class in a small town. Which is which? How do you know?

2. a) Conduct a survey in your class to determine the birth places of the students in your class and their parents and grandparents. Your teacher will help by coordinating the survey.

    b) Draw three pie graphs of your survey results, similar to the pie graphs in Fig. 17-1.

3. Compare your pie graphs to those in Fig. 17-1. Are there any surprises? Discuss your results.

CANADA'S IMMIGRATION HISTORY

While Canada has been receiving immigrants for almost 400 years, it is only in the last century or so that immigration has become such a dominant theme in Canadian life. There are two reasons for this, one related to the quantity of immigrants and the other to the nature of the immigrants.

How Many?

Examine Fig. 17-2. This graph shows the number of people who have come to Canada since 1867. As you can see, the number of immigrants has varied enormously from year to year. The number of immigrants

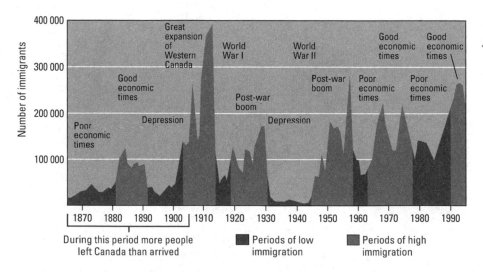

◁ **Fig. 17-2** *Canada's immigration, 1867-1997*

When?	What happened?	Why?
1840s	• Arrival of thousands of Irish settlers	• Irish potato crop fails; facing starvation, many Irish move to Canada and other countries
1905-1914	• Massive immigration to Canadian west from eastern Europe	• Canadian government, wanting to settle the Prairies, offers free land and other incentives to immigrants
1915-1919	• Little immigration	• World War I and worldwide influenza epidemic limit immigration
1930-1945	• Little immigration	• World-wide economic depression and World War II limit immigration
1956	• Many Hungarians come to Canada	• Hungarians revolt against the Russians fails; refugees come to Canada to avoid punishment
1980s-1997	• Arrival of thousands of Hong Kong Chinese	• Immigrants are looking for political stability before China takes control of Hong Kong in 1997

◁ **Fig. 17-3** *Immigration to Canada has had periods of boom and bust. These were caused by events that occurred in Canada and in other countries.*

increased starting in about 1905 and reached an annual total of more than 400 000 in 1913. Recently, about 200 000 immigrants have arrived each year. The reasons for these differences can be traced to a variety of political and economic factors both in Canada and elsewhere. Several of these factors are described in Fig. 17–3. Perhaps you, one of your parents, or an ancestor came to Canada during one of these periods of booming immigration.

From Where?

The major sources of immigrants have changed greatly over the years. Since the end of World War II in 1945, the sources of immigrants have changed more rapidly in response to changing economic and political conditions in other countries. For example, the war devastated Italy, so in the late 1940s and 1950s, Italy provided Canada with many new residents seeking better economic opportunities. By the 1960s, this migration slowed to a trickle as the Italian economy improved.

More recently, people looking for economic opportunities have come to Canada from countries like Portugal, India, and Jamaica. These immigrants saw the chance for a better life for themselves and their families. Other people from these countries are less likely to come to Canada if they see improved economic opportunities at home.

Not everyone comes to Canada for economic reasons. For many people, Canada has been a haven from dangers in their own country. In

haven: a place of safety

some cases, the threats can be immediate and extreme. The Hungarians who came in 1956 escaped from their homeland in the face of the Soviet tanks which put down their revolution. Many Somalis came to Canada in the late 1980s to escape civil war and famine which had claimed tens of thousands of lives.

Where will immigrants to Canada come from in the new century? Probably just about everywhere, but most immigrants are likely to come from eastern and southern Asia, South America, the Caribbean, and Africa. It is difficult to predict since we do not know which countries will have economic and political conditions that will encourage emigration to Canada.

civil war: a war between different groups within a country

famine: a devastating food shortage

WHERE IMMIGRANTS LIVE IN CANADA

As we saw in Fig. 17-1, some classes that use *Making Connections: Canada's Geography* might be composed primarily of students born outside of Canada, while other classes, in a different part of Canada, might contain no foreign-born students at all! Such an uneven distribution of immigrants within Canada is not new. For example, in 1911, 57% of the populations of Alberta and British Columbia had been born in other countries, while less than 10% of Québec's population was composed of immigrants.

This uneven distribution continues today. In 1991, 16% of Canadian residents were born in other countries but, remarkably, 94% of these people live in just four provinces: Ontario, British Columbia, Québec, and Alberta. A slightly different pattern emerges if we examine the number of immigrants living in a province as a percentage of the total population (Fig. 17-4). Only Ontario and British Columbia are above the national average.

Even within each province, the pattern is far from even. Most immigrants settle in large cities. Two-thirds of the immigrants to Canada

Look again at Fig. 17-1. You might be able to tell where the two schools are located.

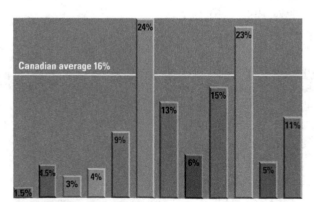

◁ **Fig. 17-4** *This graph shows the percentage of each province's/territory's population that is made up of immigrants. About 16% of Canadians were born in other countries. As you can see, only two provinces have immigrant populations that are higher than the national average.*

Canadian average 16%

24% 23% 15% 13% 11% 9% 6% 5% 4.5% 4% 3% 1.5%

Nfld. N.S. P.E.I. N.B. Que. Ont. Man. Sask. Alta. B.C. N.W.T. Yukon

◁ **Fig. 17-5** *Storefronts, street signs, and newspapers serving different cultures are very familiar in large cities like Toronto, Vancouver, and Montréal, but are almost unknown in many smaller cities and rural areas.*

choose to live in Toronto, Vancouver, and Montréal. In fact, about 40% of all immigrants choose to live in the Greater Toronto Area with another 30% choosing Vancouver. Of the immigrants who move to Québec, 88% live in Montréal. It is not at all surprising that immigrants choose to live in our largest cities. These cities have large populations of various cultural groups that can support stores, entertainment facilities, religious and cultural organizations, and other institutions that provide familiar prod–ucts and services (Fig. 17-5).

To see what the Canadian government says about immi-grating to Canada, check cicnet.ci.gc.ca/english/coming/howto1.html

WHY PEOPLE BECOME IMMIGRANTS

Imagine that a family is thinking of leaving Canada to live in another country. Why might they want to do this? Perhaps a parent has lost a job and can't find another. Perhaps the family thinks that taxes in Canada are too high. The members of the family might be completely fed up with Canadian winters. Reasons for leaving your own country, like these, are called **push factors**.

The family that has decided to leave Canada may be drawn to a particular country for certain reasons. For example, there may be good job opportunities in that country or taxes may be lower. Winters may be much milder or they may have close friends and relatives in this other country. Factors such as these, which attract someone to another country, are called **pull factors**. Generally, a combination of push and pull factors are what make a person move to another country.

To learn more about a group which provides support to immigrants, check www.amcea.org

◁ **Fig. 17-6**
These immigrants are being
sworn in as Canadian citizens.

Intervening obstacles also affect potential immigrants. Intervening obstacles are factors that discourage (or even stop) a person from following through on his or her decision to immigrate. They include immigration requirements, the distances involved, and the costs of immigration. Consider a specific example. A person may want to move to Canada but may not be able to qualify to be an immigrant according to the requirements of the Canadian government.

▽ **Fig. 17-7** *Below is the breakdown of immigrant arrivals in 1997. The category called 'other' includes live-in domestic workers (maids, nannies, etc.) and retired people.*

Independent Immigrants	
Skilled Workers	105 569
Business Class	19 924
Family Immigrants	**59 956**
Refugees	**24 101**
Other	6168
Total	215 718

HOW SOMEONE BECOMES AN IMMIGRANT TO CANADA

When someone immigrates to Canada, they become a **landed immigrant**. Many people want to become landed immigrants, but the Canadian government has strict rules to decide who will be admitted to the country. Without these restrictions, far more people would want to come to Canada than we could accommodate.

Canada accepts three types of immigrants: **independent immigrants**, **family immigrants**, and **refugees** (Fig. 17-6). The number of immigrants in each category is shown in Fig. 17-7. In recent years, the government has attempted to increase the number of independent immigrants and to decrease the number of family immigrants. This was done to ensure that more immigrants would be in a position to contribute to Canada's economy.

These rules are frequently fine-tuned as the government attempts to balance the opportunity to come to Canada with the desire to only have immigrants who will contribute to Canada's economy and society.

Independent Immigrants

There are two types of independent immigrants: skilled workers and business immigrants.

To be accepted as a skilled worker, a person must receive 70 points in a complicated system that is designed to identify which people are most likely to become successful residents of Canada. The government uses

In both cases, if one person qualifies, all of the members of their immediate family qualify.

Factor	Points	Conditions
Education	up to 16	Based on number of years of education
Specific job training	up to 18	Based on number of years of training
Job experience	up to 8	No experience means automatic refusal
Occupation	up to 10	Based on demand for skills in Canada
Job offer	up to 10	Points given if the potential immigrant has a job waiting
Demographic factor	up to 8	In times of high unemployment, the government will award fewer points here
Age	up to 10	Those aged 21 to 44 get 10 points. Two points are deducted for each year over or under
Knowledge of English and French	up to 15	
Personal suitability	up to 10	Points awarded as a result of an interview with an immigration official
Bonus for assistance from close relatives	5	Points given if the potential immigrant has a close relative who will help with the move to Canada

the point system shown in Fig. 17-8 to determine which people should be allowed into Canada. You can see that having specific job skills and experience is critical in determining whether a person qualifies, as up to 46 points are job-related. If the Canadian economy needs workers with a particular set of skills, then more points will be given to potential immigrants with these skills.

Business immigrants must show immigration officials a willingness and an ability to make a significant financial contribution to Canada's economy. They can do this by establishing a business, buying a business, or making investments that create at least one job outside their own family. Immigrants in this category need to score only 25 points under the point system to gain entrance to Canada.

△ **Fig. 17-8** *This point scale is used to decide which people will be allowed to become independent immigrants. Skilled workers need 70 points, while business immigrants need only 25 points. Family immigrants are not assessed using the point system.*

The amount of the investment depends on where the business immigrant wants to settle.

Family Immigrants

The purpose of this category of immigrants is to allow Canadian residents (both citizens and landed immigrants) to reunite their families by bringing their close relatives to Canada. Eligible relations include spouses, dependent children, parents, grandparents, and, in some cases, brothers and sisters, nephews and nieces, grandchildren, and others.

Every family immigrant must be sponsored by a relative in Canada. The sponsor agrees to provide the housing and other needs of the immigrant for ten years if the immigrant runs into financial difficulty. In an extreme case, the sponsor might even have to sell a home or borrow money to meet this obligation. The risks associated with sponsorship, along with stricter government rules, make it harder to sponsor family members. This is gradually reducing the number of family immigrants.

Refugees

A refugee is someone who fears persecution (or even death) in his or her home country. To be considered a refugee, this persecution must arise for reasons of race, religion, nationality, political opinion, or membership in a particular social group. People can apply to become refugees while in Canada as a visitor or while living in their home country. Typically, the number of refugees coming to Canada ranges from 24 000 to 32 000 each year.

A special category of refugee includes victims of natural and human disasters, such as famines and wars.

Most Canadians agree that we should welcome genuine refugees into the country. In fact, Canada's treatment of refugees over the years has been so generous that the United Nations gave Canada a special award called the Nansen Medal. At the same time, there have been fears that some people have pretended to be refugees so that they could be admitted into Canada. These so-called *economic refugees* want to come to Canada for a better life rather than to escape persecution. These people do not qualify under refugee rules and should apply as independent immigrants rather than as refugees.

The Nansen Medal is normally given to organizations and individuals who have done outstanding work in aid of refugees. Canada is the only nation to have received it.

INTERPROVINCIAL MIGRATION

Migration does not only occur between countries. **Interprovincial migration** is a very important force in Canada's geography. Year after year, some provinces gain migrants from other provinces; this is referred to as in-migration. Other provinces continually lose population to other provinces; this is referred to as out-migration.

▽ **Fig. 17-9** *This table shows the number of immigrants and emigrants for each province and territory along with the number of interprovincial migrants for 1995 (numbers in thousands).*

	NFLD	PEI	NS	NB	QUÉ	ONT	MAN	SASK	ALTA	BC	YT	NWT	CANADA
Number of Immigrants	0.6	0.2	3.8	0.6	26.8	115.5	3.6	1.9	14.6	44.5	0.1	0.1	212.2
Number of Emigrants	0.3	0.1	0.8	1.0	6.3	19.7	2.3	1.0	7.8	7.1	0.1	0.8	46.6
Interprovincial In-migration	9.5	2.9	18.2	13.4	26.9	78.7	19.1	20.7	60.0	75.8	2.8	3.3	
Interprovincial Out-migration	16.1	2.4	19.9	14.1	37.6	81.7	21.6	23.1	56.8	51.7	2.0	4.0	

1. a) Fig. 17-9 shows the number of interprovincial migrants (in and out) for each province and territory, along with the number of immigrants and emigrants (international). Calculate the net number of interprovincial and international migrants for each province.

   b) Using the model shown in Fig. 17-10 and the results of 1a, draw two bars for each province or territory.

   c) Which provinces gain the most migrants from other parts of Canada? Which provinces lose the most migrants to other parts of Canada?

   d) Using the ideas of push factors and pull factors, explain the results shown in 1c.

   e) Compare the relative impact of interprovincial and international migration on the population of each province.

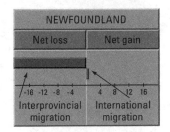

△ **Fig. 17-10** *Graph showing the interprovincial and international migration of Newfoundland*

QUESTIONS

CHECK YOUR UNDERSTANDING

1. a) Name two countries that have only recently become major sources of immigrants.

   b) Why do the sources of immigrants change over the years?

2. a) Examine Fig. 17-2. Name two time periods when immigration was high and two periods when immigration was low.

   b) What factors caused these periods of high and low immigration?

ANALYZE AND APPLY

3. a) Examine Fig. 17-4. Which provinces attract the most immigrants?

   b) Give three reasons why these provinces are the most attractive destinations for immigrants.

   c) Could this pattern change In the years to come? Why or why not?

4. a) Define *push factors* and *pull factors.*

   b) List two push factors that were mentioned in the text, then add two more that were not mentioned in the text.

   c) List two pull factors that were provided in the text, then add two more that were not mentioned.

   d) Define *intervening obstacles.*

   e) List two intervening obstacle that were given in the text, then add two more that were not mentioned.

5. a) Determine the push and pull factors involved in the decision of your family, or that of a classmate, to move to Canada.

   b) Did any intervening obstacles have to be overcome at this time?

6. a) Examine Fig. 17-8. What are the characteristics of the people favoured by the immigration system?

   b) Does the current immigration system benefit Canada? Explain.

   c) Does it benefit the countries from which immigrants come? Explain.

d) What changes, if any, would you make to the immigration system? Explain your recommendations.

7. The point system is really very demanding. Would your family get the required 70 points to get admission to Canada? Why or why not?

8. If you are an immigrant to Canada, what did you find surprising when you came to Canada? If you are not an immigrant to Canada, ask someone who was, to describe what they found surprising about coming to Canada.

THINK AND COMMUNICATE

9. Over the past 10 years, an average of about 50 000 people per year have emigrated from Canada.

   a) Where do you think that most of these people would go?

   b) Identify at least two push factors and two pull factors that would have contributed to this decision.

   c) This emigration number is lower than it has been in previous decades. Why might this have happened?

10. a) The United States has been called a "melting pot" of immigrants. What does this mean?

    b) How is this different from the Canadian idea of a "tossed salad" or "cultural mosaic?"

c) Describe the advantages and disadvantages of each approach.

d) Which approach do you think makes more sense for a country that receives many immigrants?

11. How would Canada be affected

    a) if we had no limits on immigration?

    b) if we allowed no immigrants to come to Canada?

12. a) Some people say that business immigrants get into Canada much more easily than others (they need only 25 points instead of 70) because they are rich. Do you think this is a fair statement? Why or why not? Should the business classification for immigrants be eliminated or changed?

    b) Research the contributions of business immigrants to Canadians.

13. Discuss the following questions with a number of your classmates. Be sure to take notes on your discussion.

    a) What is a refugee?

    b) Why are refugees allowed to come to Canada?

    c) Is it fair to people who are waiting to be accepted as independent immigrants, to have refugees admitted quickly?

    d) In a court, juries convict someone only if they think that the person is guilty "beyond a reasonable doubt." How strong should the evidence be to prove that a person is a legitimate refugee?

Quite clearly, Canada's population is not distributed evenly across the country. No more proof of this is needed than to compare the populations of two of Canada's ecozones (Fig. 18-1). More than 14 million people live in the Mixedwood Plains while the population of the Taiga Cordillera is about 300 people — 80% of whom live in one village. While other regional population differences are not quite so dramatic, it would be entirely fair to say that **settlement patterns** in Canada vary enormously — from large cities, to farming areas, to vast areas where very few people live. In this chapter, we will examine why these huge differences exist.

settlement patterns: the arrangement of where people live on the earth or in a country and the factors that influence this arrangement

AN INTRODUCTION TO POPULATION DISTRIBUTION

Population distribution refers to the pattern of where people live in a region or even in the entire country. In general, there are two main distribution patterns: dispersed and concentrated (Fig. 18-2). Dispersed patterns are found in areas that have a strong agricultural base, since people tend to be spread out on the farms in the region. Concentrated

The settlement patterns that are described in this chapter are those that we see today. They are the latest chapter in a history of settlement that has existed for thousands of years.

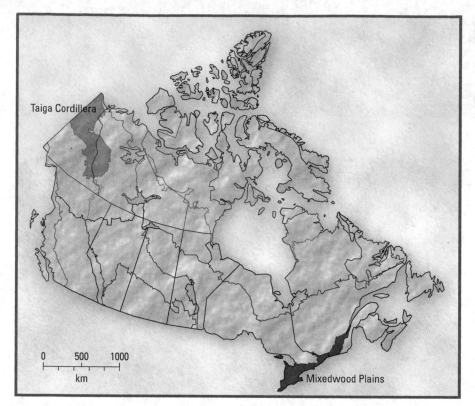

Taiga Cordillera

0   500   1000
km

Mixedwood Plains

◁ **Fig. 18-1** *The population of the Mixedwood Plain ecozone is almost 50 000 times as great as that of the Taiga Cordillera, which has an area more than twice as big!*

patterns occur in areas where resources — and the economic opportunities and population that result — are focused in small areas. It is easy to understand how this would work in the case of a town which depends on a gold mine for its existence. It is less obvious, but equally important, to determine how this would work in major urban districts.

A linear pattern is a special kind of concentrated pattern. Such population patterns develop in areas where the most important economic reasons for settlement exist in lines — for example, along a major highway in an isolated area or along the coast of a region where fishing is the most important industry.

We must be careful not to confuse population distribution and **population density**. While they may sound similar there is an important difference in meaning. Population density is a mathematical calculation of the number of people who live in each square kilometre of land. Each of the areas shown in Fig. 18-2 has the same population density — but very different distributions.

Clearly, in Canada, the distribution varies from a population which is concentrated in some areas, to other areas that have very few people (Fig. 18-3). More than 90% of Canadians live within 600 km of the border with the United States. While this area represents less than 10% of Canada's land area, almost all of our major cities and productive farmland are located here.

As well, the towns and cities that provide services to farmers tend to be dispersed.

Population density is population divided by area.

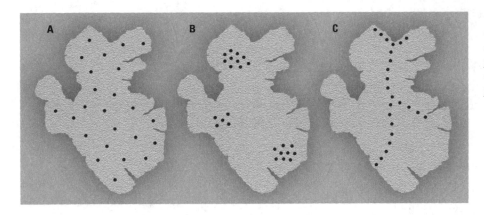

◁ **Fig. 18-2** *Population in an area can be either dispersed (a) or concentrated (b). A linear pattern (c) is a specialized example of a concentrated pattern.*

▽ **Fig. 18-3** *Canada's population distribution is anything but even.*

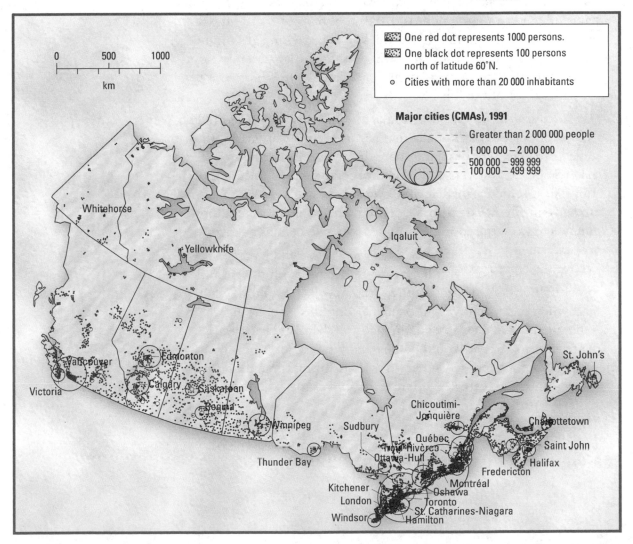

RURAL SETTLEMENT PATTERNS

Settlement in Canada can be divided into two major categories: **rural** and **urban**. **Rural settlement** involves the settlement of areas outside cities and towns where population density is low and the settlement pattern is dispersed. Most of Canada's rural residents live in only two ecozones: Mixedwood Plain and Prairie. In these areas one of the following three patterns exist:

rural: outside towns and cities

urban: within towns and cities

- the long lots of southern Québec
- the concession system of southern Ontario
- the section system of the Prairies

Before looking at each pattern individually, you need to be aware of three factors that affect the pattern of rural settlement in any area.

1. *What kind of resources are found in the area?* Perhaps the most important influence on settlement is the kind of resources that attract people to the area in the first place. For example, an agricultural area like southwestern Ontario will develop a very different population pattern than an area of the Canadian Shield where forestry provides most of the jobs.

2. *What transportation methods were available at the time of settlement?* The settlement of areas of Canada that occurred before about 1800, reflects the fact that most transportation was by water. Settled areas had to be next to rivers and lakes that could be used for transportation. Areas settled after that time, were increasingly based on road and, eventually, rail transportation. Settlement could occur almost anywhere since transportation routes could be built as needed.

3. *What role did government policy play in the settlement?* In some areas, settlement occurred with little, if any, government input into the process. In others, the government carefully planned how, where, and when settlement would occur. It controlled such things as which land would be settled, the size and shape of farms, the pattern of roads that would be built, and the location of town sites, schools, and churches. A set of rules that control these things is called a **survey system**. Different survey systems were used in different parts of Canada.

When you combine these three influences, the result is a settlement pattern that is so distinctive that it is clearly visible when looking at a topographic map, an aerial photograph, or a satellite image. The pattern is also visible over large areas of Canada when looking out from the window of a small plane. Let's now look at the most important Canadian rural settlement patterns.

A large aircraft usually travels too high above the ground to allow a view of this pattern.

Long Lots of Southern Québec

- This area was settled long before the development of railways and high-quality roads and before a survey system was in place.

- The most important influence on the settlement was the agricultural resources of the area and the fact that transportation was mainly by water (and by sled over the frozen river in winter).

- Long, thin farms were built along the St. Lawrence River and its tributaries, since each farm had to have access to the river for transportation.

- These farms came to be known as the **long lots**. After the river lots were all taken, a second (and perhaps third and fourth) row of long lots was settled along a road parallel to the river. The long lot system is shown in Fig. 18-5.

△ **Fig. 18-5** *The long lots of southern Québec give the region a very distinctive appearance. In early Québec, taxes were based on the amount of river frontage, so it was desirable to have as narrow a lot as possible.*

Concession System of Southern Ontario

- It has agricultural resources very similar to those found in southern Québec.

- Settlement of southern Ontario occurred after a survey system was already in place.

- Roads, and later, railways were available — so access to major lakes and rivers was less important.

- A variety of similar **concession systems** were used. Roads were typically 2 km apart, and farms were 40 to 80 hectares in size.

- A typical concession system is shown in Fig. 18-6.

- Groupings of concession blocks were called townships while groups of townships were called counties.

Concession and sideroads remain the major roads today both in rural areas and in cities. If you live in southern Ontario, can you identify some of these roads where you live?

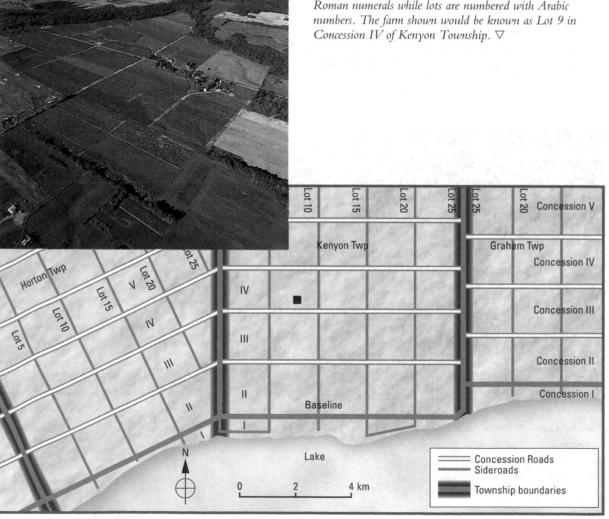

▽ **Fig. 18-6** *A typical southern Ontario concession system. Concession lines run parallel to the lake while sideroads run perpendicular to the lake. Concessions are numbered with Roman numerals while lots are numbered with Arabic numbers. The farm shown would be known as Lot 9 in Concession IV of Kenyon Township.* ▽

Section System of the Southern Prairies

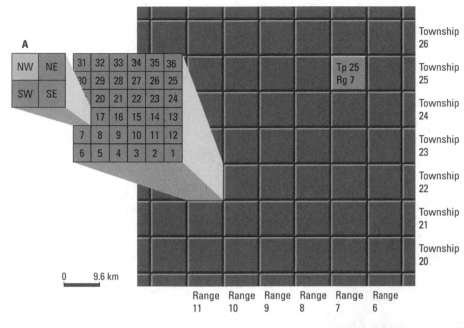

◁ **Fig. 18-7** *The Prairie section system is based on the creation of townships, which are identified by the intersection of Township rows (numbered from south to north) and Range columns (numbered from east to west). Within each Township, there are 36 sections which are numbered as shown. Each farm family received one quarter section. The farm labelled A on the diagram would be described as Subdivision NW, Section 18, Township 22, Range 11. Can you identify the sections and quarter-sections in the photo?* ▽

- The Prairies were surveyed before major settlement occurred, using the **section system** that had been used in many areas of the United States.

- As shown in Fig. 18-7, this was a very simple system. The Canada–United States border at 49°N latitude was used as the base line. The land was divided into blocks that were 9.6 km by 9.6 km (94 km² in area).

- Each of these blocks was divided into 36 sections, each of which was then divided into four lots called quarter-sections, which were about 64 ha in size.

- The section system had originally been developed for the American Midwest, where rainfall levels were substantially higher. It soon became obvious that farms needed to be bigger than the government had planned. More successful farmers started to buy their neighbours' farms starting a process that came to be known as farm consolidation.

The section system was in use before the metric system was used in Canada. Each block was 6 miles (about 9.6 km) by 6 miles in size.

Comparing Québec, Southern Ontario, and Prairie Rural Settlement Patterns

Each of these settlement patterns has particular advantages and disadvantages for the people who live in these areas. For example, in southern Québec, the long lots mean that each farm house is very close to its neighbours. This means that people can rely on those nearby for companionship and for help in emergencies. On the other hand, the long lots are not very efficient to work. The back of the farm is a long way from the farmhouse and this makes it difficult to use this land properly.

In contrast, the large farms on the Prairies are efficient to work since they are very well-suited to the use of modern farm machinery. Unfortunately, farm families can feel isolated because they are a long way from their neighbours. Farm consolidation has only made this problem worse. In between, are the farms of southern Ontario, where the farms are midway in efficiency and isolation between those of Québec and those of the Prairies.

Scattered Settlements

But what about Canadian residents who live in rural areas other than southern Ontario, Québec, and the Prairies? In general, settlement in the more isolated parts of Canada has occurred for two main reasons. In some areas, there are resources that can be developed. In others, there is a need to provide services for the people who live in an area or travel through the area.

RESOURCE-BASED SETTLEMENT

When we consider areas of Canada outside of the Mixedwood Plain and the Prairie ecozones, it is obvious that resource-based settlement is very important in the following ecozones: the Atlantic Maritime, the Boreal Shield, the Boreal Plain, The Montane Cordillera, and the Pacific Maritime. Fig. 18-8 summarizes the importance of different kinds of resources in causing settlement in these regions.

SERVICE-BASED SETTLEMENT

A variety of services are needed by the people who live in a lightly-populated area. An obvious one is transportation (Fig. 18-9). Scattered settlement is found along major roads. Many of these people work in gas stations, motels, and other businesses that are needed by travellers on these busy highways.

Ecozone	Agriculture	Commercial Fishing	Forestry	Mining/Energy Production	Recreation
Atlantic Maritime	* * *	* * *	* *	*	*
Boreal Shield	*		* * *	* * *	* *
Boreal Plains	* * *		*	* * *	*
Montane Cordillera	* *		* *	* * *	* * *
Pacific Maritime	*	* * *	* * *		*

* * * – most important   * * – somewhat important   * – limited importance

◁ **Fig. 18-8** *The levels of importance of each resource listed above was determined by considering the economic base within each ecozone. A variety of resources have been important causes of settlement in the southern half of Canada. There are only a few resource-based settlements in the northern ecozones of Canada.*

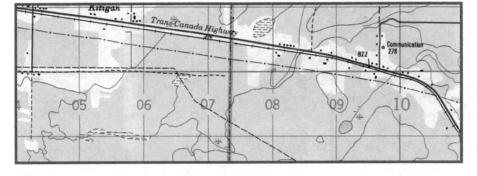

◁ **Fig. 18-9** *Many of the people who live along the Trans-Canada Highway in this part of northern Ontario earn their living by providing services for people who are travelling along the highway.*

QUESTIONS

CHECK YOUR UNDERSTANDING

1. a) Compare the meanings of "population distribution" and "population density."

   b) Draw labeled sketches in your notebook of the two main kinds of population distribution.

2. What is a survey system? Why were survey systems used?

3. Why did the original farms on the Prairies turn out to be too small? What happened as a result of this?

ANALYZE AND APPLY

4. a) What are the three general factors which affect rural settlement patterns?

   b) Explain the impact that each of these had on the long lot, concession, and section settlement systems.

5. In many areas of southern Québec in the 1600s and 1700s, when a family's sons reached adulthood they would be given a share of the family farm with frontage on the river. What problems would this cause

after a few generations? How might these problems have been solved?

6. Each of these maps (Fig. 18-10) represents the rural settlement in a different part of Canada. Indicate which part of Canada each comes from and explain what evidence you have of this.

7. Use an atlas to identify four areas of Canada which have scattered populations.

THINK AND COMMUNICATE

8. a) Identify two advantages and two disadvantages of living in a resource-based community in an isolated area.

   b) What effect are new communication technologies having on life in isolated communities?

   c) Would you want to live in such a community? Why or why not?

9. A growing number of people are choosing to live in rural, agricultural areas but not to farm.

   a) Why might they make this choice?

   b) How might these people earn their living?

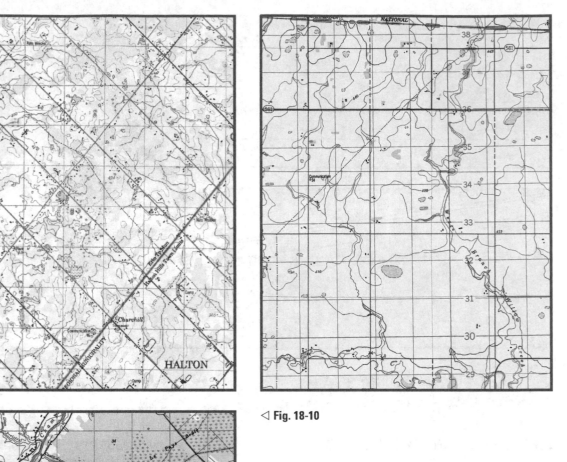

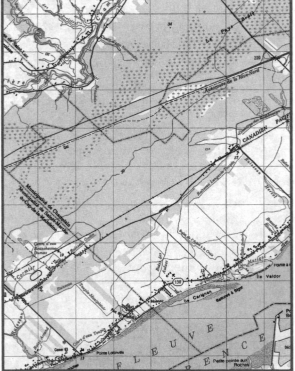

◁ **Fig. 18-10**

URBAN SETTLEMENT PATTERNS

In 1867, when Canada became a country, 82% of Canadians lived in rural areas. Today, almost 80% of the population lives in cities and towns (Fig. 18-12). The process by which an area changes from being rural to being urban is called **urbanization**. It includes a great increase in population density and concentration along with the expansion of urban functions like manufacturing and services.

Urbanization is one of the most important features of Canadian history over the past 150 years. Basically, it occurred because of changes in the nature of the economy of both the country and the city. For example, agricultural machinery was developed that was able to do the work of many people. As a result, farms could increase in size and employ fewer people. Similar changes occurred in industries like forestry and mining. At the same time, more jobs were created in the manufacturing and service industries of the cities and towns. The urban areas grew as rural residents moved into the towns, and because most immigrants moved to the cities rather than to the farms as they had done in earlier years.

How important are cities and large towns in defining Canada's settlement pattern? Consider the rather odd-looking map of Canada shown in Fig. 18-12. We are used to seeing maps that are drawn with areas on the map in proportion to land area. This map is drawn with areas on the map in proportion to population. It gives dramatic evidence of the importance of studying our cities if we are to understand Canada's settlement.

There were a variety of push factors and pull factors influencing the movement from rural areas to the cities.

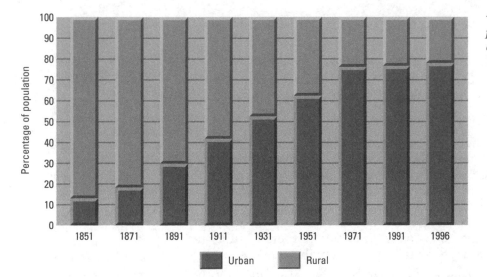

◁ **Fig. 18-11** *Canada's urban population has increased dramatically over the years. Why has this happened?*

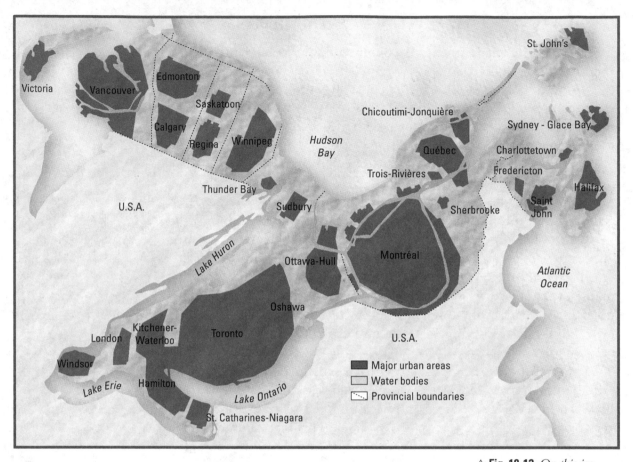

△ **Fig. 18-12** *On this iso-demographic map, the areas of provinces, territories, and cities are in proportion to their populations.*

The Growth of an Urban Place

A good starting place if we are to understand the formation and growth of urban places is to consider how a fictional city, called Adanac, came into being in a fertile, agricultural area. Adanac started and grew for four main reasons: to be a manufacturing centre, to act as a transportation centre, to utilize a local resource, and to provide services for the area surrounding the town. Let's consider each of these.

1. *Manufacturing:* Manufacturing in the form of the gristmill was the reason why Adanac started, and why it grew in later years. Manufacturing made sense for several reasons, but two stand out. On one hand, there were raw materials (mainly agricultural) available that could be used in manufacturing. On the other hand, there were markets interested in buying the products of the factories. Some of these customers were local, while others, outside the area, received the products by rail and, later, highway.

2. *Transportation:* The growth of our sample town was aided by the construction of the railway. If the railway had been built 20 km

This fictional city illustrates the value of a geographic model — a simplified description of real life. Because it is simplified, it is easier to concentrate on the features that are common to (in this case) the growth of all cities without being distracted by the specific features of a real city.

gristmill: a mill for making flour. Other mills were used to process lumber and wool. Most pioneer mills were water-powered.

to the north, the town would not have been as successful. Not only did the railway allow people to move to and from the town, it also was of vital importance in encouraging the growth of manufacturing. In fact, Adanac came to be the railway centre for the local district.

3. *Resource Use:* While other factors were more important in the city's growth, the discovery of the clay deposits that are used for brick making did contribute to Adanac's development. In many parts of Canada though, the existence of a rich resource has led directly to the existence of a town or city.

    This growth is a result of the **multiplier effect**. Consider the case of a new brick-making factory in Adanac. The new brick-works employed 100 workers. These workers and their families (perhaps 300 people in total) needed housing, schools, stores, banks, restaurants, medical facilities, and other services. In order to supply these, perhaps 900 other workers and their families would come to live in the rapidly growing city. In total, as many as 1200 people would be added to the population because of the 100 jobs opening up in the new factory.

4. *Service Centre:* There is a **hierarchy** of urban services. For example, a small town may offer only a few services — a small grocery store, a post office, an elementary school. A larger town or small city will offer a much wider range of services. Adanac, for example, grew to include a wide range of shopping, a hospital, and a high school. Very large cities offer specialized goods for a very large area — in some cases, even for the entire country. These high-level services would include such things as television production, large universities, specialized hospitals, and entertainment like professional sports teams or opera companies.

    This hierarchy of services exists because each service has what is called a **threshold population**. This is the number of people who are needed to support a given service. For example, the threshold for a post office — perhaps a few thousand — would be much lower than that for a television station.

Generally, a multiplier of 3 to 1 is used when determining the impact of a new factory or other business on an area.

hierarchy: rank or tier

Different Kinds of Urban Places

In the previous section, we looked at a fictional city that grew for four different reasons. A city or town like this is called a **diversified urban centre** since it owes its success to more than one function. In many cases though, a city's existence can depend almost totally on only one urban function. In this section we will look at four Canadian cities, each of which specializes in one particular urban function.

THUNDER BAY — A TRANSPORTATION CITY

The **site** of the city of Thunder Bay is a flat area between Lake Superior and the highlands of the Canadian Shield (Fig. 18-13). The importance of Thunder Bay's location on the western shore of Lake Superior was recognized as early as 1800. At that time, the community of Fort William was the most important inland fur-trading centre for the historic North-West Company. Convoys of canoes brought trade goods from Montréal while other canoes brought furs from the western interior of the continent. They met at Fort William to exchange their cargoes.

site: refers to the characteristics of the land on which a city is built

The city of Thunder Bay was later created by combining the cities of Fort William and Port Arthur.

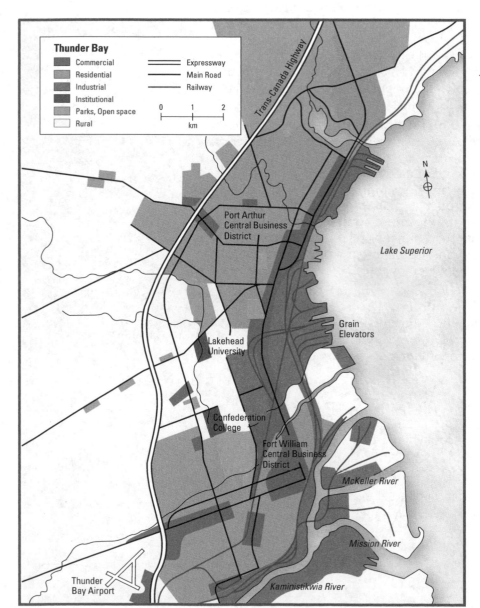

◁ **Fig. 18-13** *Notice how the city of Thunder Bay is dominated by transportation facilities.*

To learn more about Thunder Bay, check www.city.thunder-bay.on.ca/

The Canadian Pacific Railway was built through the area in 1885, with the Canadian Northern Railway (now part of CN Rail) following in 1902. These rail links meant that grain could be shipped from western Canada to Thunder Bay, where it could be loaded onto ships for transport through the Great Lakes. This made sense since ships can carry bulk cargoes, like grain, more cheaply than can trains. With the opening of the St. Lawrence Seaway in 1959, ocean-going ships could go directly to Thunder Bay to load grain.

Thunder Bay now has the largest grain-handling facility in the world. There are 15 grain elevators in the port area with a capacity of more than two million tonnes. In addition to grain-handling, the port also is used for shipping forest products from the Canadian Shield and coal and potash from the Prairie provinces. As can be seen from this description, Thunder Bay's **situation** has given it enormous transportation advantages that have existed for two centuries. As a result, it has become the major city of its region.

Years later, the Trans-Canada Highway was built along the route of the railways — also through Thunder Bay.

situation: refers to the relationship between a city's location and the area surrounding it

FREDERICTON — A SERVICE CENTRE

Fredericton was founded in 1783 by United Empire Loyalists. At that time, large amounts of land in the town site were set aside for various services. Government buildings, a military headquarters, churches, and schools were built on this land. Fredericton became the capital city as well as the military, religious, and cultural centre of the colony (and later province) of New Brunswick.

Fredericton's role as a service centre has continued to expand over the years. For example, it is the home of the University of New Brunswick (Fig. 18-14) which attracts students from all over the province, the rest of the country, and even other countries. The presence of so many students also means that there is an expanded need for food stores and housing. In total, the city owes its existence and growth to its ability to supply services effectively to its region and province.

United Empire Loyalists are people who came to Canada from the United States after the American Revolution, because they preferred to live in a British colony.

▽ **Fig. 18-14** *The University of New Brunswick is just one of the services provided in the city of Fredericton.*

PORT ALBERNI — A RESOURCE-BASED COMMUNITY

Port Alberni is typical of the many towns and cities that exist because of a resource. The resource could be forests, a mineral deposit, a hydro-electric site, or even a recreational resource like a ski hill. In the case of Port Alberni, the resource is a rich forest that surrounds the town. Port Alberni is located about 200 km north of Victoria on Vancouver Island at the head of the Alberni Inlet (Fig. 18-15). It was founded at this location because the timber resources of the region could be shipped to the world through the port. Port Alberni is British Columbia's third largest port but it would not exist without the town's saw mills and paper mill.

▽ **Fig. 18-15** *Port Alberni exists because of the lush forest resources of Vancouver Island and a good harbour.*

SARNIA — A MANUFACTURING CENTRE

Sarnia is located where Lake Huron drains into the St. Clair River. As you might expect at such a key location, it originally was a transportation centre — both as a port and as the location where ferries and, later, a railway tunnel and highway bridge, provided access across the river into the United States.

If Sarnia's growth had only depended on transportation though, it would not be as large an urban centre as it is. Central to its growth has been its role as an oil-based manufacturing centre. This industry started in the late-1800s, using oil from the nearby small oil fields of southwestern Ontario. A number of oil refineries were built in Sarnia, especially after 1900, when the growth in the use of cars and trucks meant a much greater demand for gasoline (Fig. 18-16).

North America's first oil well was in Oil Springs, Ontario, which is less than 40 km from Sarnia.

The next crucial factor in the growth of Sarnia was the beginning of the **petrochemical industry** during World War II. Two huge factories were built, one to make artificial rubber and the other to make plastic. This development made sense for two reasons. One was that the raw materials

◁ **Fig. 18-16** *An oil refinery takes crude oil as it comes from the ground and breaks it down to its parts. These include various kinds of fuels (e.g., gasoline, diesel fuel, and home heating oil), lubricants (e.g., engine oil and grease), and industrial materials (e.g., asphalt, solvents, and raw materials for making plastics).*

that these factories needed were by-products of oil-refining. The other was that the products from these factories were desperately needed for the war effort. After the War, rapid economic growth meant that there was a growing demand for these products.

The final step in insuring the city's importance as a manufacturing centre was the construction of the Interprovincial Pipeline in the early 1950s. This pipeline carries crude oil from Alberta, through the United States to southern Ontario and Québec. Because Sarnia was the leading refining and petrochemical centre in southern Ontario, it made sense to have the pipeline cross back into Canada here. Access to abundant and cheap Alberta crude oil meant that the city's factories would have a sure source of raw materials for years to come.

The most important influences on Sarnia's manufacturing were (and are) transportation and raw materials. In Chapter 26, you will have the chance to see what other location factors are important to the success of a manufacturer.

QUESTIONS

◁ **Fig. 18-17**

Service	Small town	Small city	Large city
Getting major brain surgery			
Arranging day care for a young child			
Seeing major-league baseball			
Buying a daily newspaper *local*			
Getting a dental checkup			
Connecting to the Internet			
Going to a symphony concert			
Attending elementary school			
Playing recreational soccer			

CHECK YOUR UNDERSTANDING

1. a) What is meant by a hierarchy of urban services?

   b) Copy Fig. 18-17 into your notebook, and complete it by indicating where someone in a small town, a small city, or a very large city like Toronto or Montréal would have to go to receive a particular service.

2. Trace the development of Sarnia's manufacturing industry. Be sure to indicate how each development contributed to the city's success as a manufacturing city.

3. Describe the elements of a diversified urban center which are seen in the model town of Adanac.

ANALYZE AND APPLY

4. a) What is the multiplier effect?

   b) Give an example of how it would work when a new factory is built in a town.

   c) How would the multiplier effect work when a factory closes down in a city?

5. a) With the aid of an atlas, identify at least three examples of transportation-based towns. A hint for identifying these: they will not be very large cities and they will

be located where a change in the method of transportation occurs (think about Thunder Bay).

b) Why is it likely that an urban centre based primarily on transportation will be relatively small in size?

6. a) Identify one town that grew because of each of these resources: mining, forestry (other than Port Alberni), hydro-electric power, and recreation.

b) Why do these towns tend not to grow to be large cities unless there are other reasons for their growth?

7. a) Auto assembly is the most important manufacturing industry in Canada. Identify at least three cities that have auto assembly plants.

b) In what part of Canada are they found? Why are they found here?

THINK AND COMMUNICATE

8. a) Examine the graph of urban growth (Fig. 18-11). What was the urban population in 1851? What was it in 1996? In what year did the urban population reach 50%?

b) What has happened to the rate of urban-ization in recent years? What do you think will happen to the percentage of urban population in the next 20 years or so? Why?

9. a) While many universities and colleges are located in very large cities, in some parts of Canada there are many smaller college towns. Name at least three of these.

b) What advantage(s) and disadvantage(s) would there be for a university being in a smaller community?

c) Would you prefer to go to university in a smaller town or in a big city? Why?

10. Think about the town or city in which you live (or the town or city nearest to you, if you live in a rural area). Describe what major urban functions it has. What evidence is there to support your view?

To visit the home page of cities and towns in Canada, check www.ageofreason.com/proj.htm

To learn more Fredericton, check www.city.fredericton.nb.ca/index.asp

To learn more about Port Alberni, check www.city.port-alberni.bc.ca

To learn more about Sarnia, check www.sarnia.net

Metropolitan Dominance

If someone mentions France to you, very likely Paris will come to mind. Similarly, the mention of England or Japan will make you think of London and Tokyo, respectively. These examples illustrate the way in which a country can come to be seen as almost the same thing as its largest city. This dominant city is called the country's **metropolis**. The metropolis can dominate a country in many ways. For example, it can be:

- where cultural decisions are made by national television networks, and national newspaper and magazine publishers
- where economic decisions are made in the head offices of major corporations and banks
- where political decisions are made by national and provincial governments

This influence is referred to as **metropolitan dominance**. Many countries have only one metropolis, while some countries have more than one. In this Connecting Study, you will have a chance to examine metropolitan dominance, particularly as it applies to Canada.

DETERMINING CANADA'S METROPOLIS

Does Canada have one metropolis? Do we have two or even more than two? In this study, we will compare six Canadian cities. Each of these cities is very influential within its own region, but which one(s) have a significant influence on the entire country?

1. Examine each item in Fig. 18–18. Describe how each item would be related to deciding if a city would qualify as a metropolis.

2. For each item in Fig. 18–18, score each city according to the following system:

   first = 15 points   second = 10 points   third = 6 points
   fourth = 4 points   fifth = 2 points   sixth = 1 point
   seventh = 0 points

   In the case of ties, average the points of the tied cities (round to the nearest whole point). Example. Toronto and Montréal are tied for 4th and 5th place for item 2. Points earned are $(4 + 2) \div 2 = 3$. Give each city 3 points.

3. Copy Fig. 18–18 into your notebook, without the data. Enter the points earned for each item.

4. Total the scores for each city. Rank the cities from high to low.

You might wish to use a spreadsheet program to do the calculations for this exercise.

	Vancouver	Edmonton	Calgary	Winnipeg	Toronto	Montréal	Halifax
Population (1996)	1 831 665	862 597	821 678	667 209	4 263 757	3 326 510	332 518
Distance (km) to nearest city on list	700	300	300	1150	500	500	850
Number of seats in House of Commons	13	8	7	7	31	29	3
Attractiveness to migrants from other provinces	high	moderate	moderate	low	high	moderate	low
Percentage of stock market sales	1.7	0.0	0.8	<1.0	85.0	12.4	0.0
Number of bank head offices	3	2	0	0	40	9	0
Number of major league sports teams	3	2	2	1	4	3	0
Number of professional theatres	37	13	14	8	73	17	4
Amount of manufacturing, 1994 ($ billion)	5.8	3.8	2.6	2.5	27.8	20.0	0.6

△ **Fig. 18-18** *These are just a few measures of a city's metropolitan importance. All data is 1998 unless otherwise stated.*

QUESTIONS

CHECK YOUR UNDERSTANDING

1. a) Define metropolis and metropolitan dominance.

   b) Give two examples of metropolises in other countries that were mentioned in this chapter and two examples that were not given here.

ANALYZE AND APPLY

2. Find Brazil, Mexico, the United States, Australia, Italy, and Sweden on world map in an atlas.

   a) Which three of these countries has only one metropolis? Name the metropolis in each country.

   b) Which three of these countries have two or more metropolises? Name the metropolises in each country.

   c) What geographical factor do the three countries in 2a have in common? What geographical factor do the three countries in 2b have in common?

   d) To which group would you expect Canada to belong? Is this, in fact, the case? Explain.

3. Which city(ies) would qualify as Canada's metropolis(es)? On what basis did you make this decision?

THINK AND COMMUNICATE

4. a) How do people determine which is the best place in Canada, for them, to live? Work in a small group to identify the factors that you would use to select a place to live after you finish your education.

   b) Decide on the relative importance of each of these factors.

   c) Do you think this analysis would lead you to choose Canada's metropolitan city(ies), another city on this list, a smaller city or town, or a rural area? Why?

19 Urban Land Use

STUDY GUIDE

By the end of this chapter, you will be able to:

- identify the principal types of urban land use
- identify the factors that influence land use
- analyze residential changes in a city using a transect

- examine the factors that affect land-use patterns
- examine the impact of urban expansion on the surrounding countryside

Key Terms

land use

residential density

transect

census tract

low-order product

central business district (CBD)

middle-order product

high-order product

zoning

winter-city concept

urban sprawl

This chapter will familiarize you with the principal types of urban land use. In addition, you will see how these land uses combine to produce the patterns we see in towns and cities. Fig. 19-1 presents several familiar urban scenes. It also illustrates the amount of land used for each major **land-use** category in a typical Canadian city.

1. Fig. 19-2 is an aerial photograph that shows the major urban land uses.
   a) On a piece of clear acetate or tracing paper, draw and identify the land used for transportation purposes in turquoise.
   b) Repeat the process for each land use that you can identify. Colour each land use according to the colour scheme shown in Fig. 19-1.

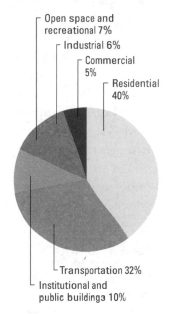

△ **Fig. 19-1** *The percentage of a city's area occupied by major land uses. The colours of each wedge of the pie graph show the most common colours used on Canadian land-use maps.*

Open space and recreational 7%
Industrial 6%
Commercial 5%
Residential 40%
Transportation 32%
Institutional and public buildings 10%

LAND-USE PATTERNS

Almost 80% of Canadians live, work, travel, shop, and spend leisure time in cities. To meet these needs, a city must have factories, offices, houses, apartments, roads, rail lines, stores, parks, cemeteries, and schools. All of

◁ **Fig. 19-2** *A mixture of urban land uses as seen from an airplane*

these features fall into one of six major land-use groups: residential, transportation, institutional and public buildings, open space and recreational land, industrial, and commercial. Each land use serves the needs of individuals, businesses, governments, and the community at large.

Residential Land Use

Residential land use includes all the places where people live — everything from single-family houses to huge apartment buildings (Fig. 19-3). It is the largest land use in most cities, often taking up 40% or more of the developed land.

The most important characteristic of residential land use is its density. **Residential density** refers to the number of housing units per hectare (Fig. 19-4). Two factors influence residential density. The first is the cost of land. Where land values are low, usually on the outskirts of cities, single-family homes are built on large lots. Here, the residential density is low. Where land is more costly, usually downtown or along major transportation routes, large apartment buildings are built because they generate enough income to pay for the high cost of the land. Here, the residential density is high.

Residential density may also be given as the number of housing units per square kilometre.

▽ **Fig. 19-3** *Different types of residential housing*

RESIDENTIAL HOUSING

Types	single-family	semi-detached	duplexes	townhouses	apartments
Characteristics	separate houses with their own yards	two houses joined by a common wall	buildings containing two or more dwellings (one on top of the other or side by side)	houses attached together in a row	buildings containing multiple dwelling units low-rise or high-rise

▽ **Fig. 19-4** *Types of residential density*

Density	Types of Dwelling	Residential Density (number of units per hectare)	Approximate Number of People per hectare
Low	Single-family houses, semi-detached houses, duplexes	Less than 30	Up to 75
Medium	Townhouses, low-rise apartments	30 - 100	75 to 250
High	High-rise apartments	More than 100	More than 250

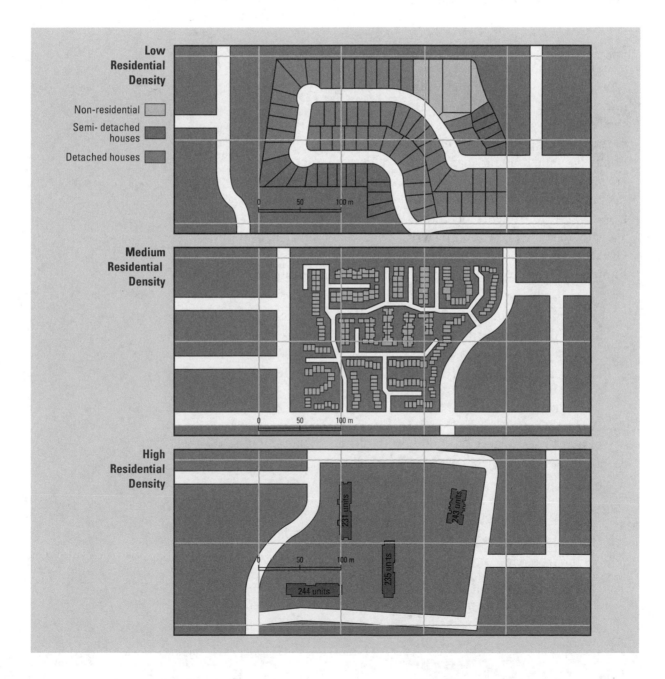

The second factor that influences density is the age of the neighbourhood. Residential areas built before World War II (1940s) tend to have higher densities than those which developed after World War II. Before the 1940s, most people used streetcars or buses or walked to work, school, or shops. Neighbourhoods were built without large driveways or wide streets for cars. Since most people had to walk (at least to the bus or streetcar stop), it made sense to have narrow house lots. This made the neighbourhood very compact. Today, because most families have one or more vehicles, new residential areas are designed with wide streets, driveways, and large garages.

Some older neighbourhoods have lanes and garages at the rear of the backyards.

An effective way to study the use of land within urban areas is to draw a **transect** through the city from its **Central Business District** (downtown) to its outer edge (**suburban** fringe). A transect is a line drawn through a city along which observations are made. Fig. 19-5 shows a transect from Toronto's Central Business District (CBD) to its northern fringe. At various points along the transect, we can analyze the population and housing characteristics of **census tracts**. Census tracts are small districts within urban areas for which information about people, industries/businesses, and land use is gathered. This information is used by governments, businesses, planners, developers, and social agencies to study population patterns, living conditions, and economic characteristics of different parts of a city. Complete the following activity in order to analyze the residential characteristics in Toronto.

suburban: having to do with the outlying part of a city or town

1. a) Calculate the population density for each area by using the formula: population density = population ÷ area (km²)

    b) Which area has the highest population density? What is the population density in this census tract?

    c) Locate this area on the transect map. Where in the city is it located? Why is it not surprising to have a high population density here?

2. What two areas have the highest percentage of people 14 years of age and younger? Why do you think this situation exists?

3. a) Calculate the total number of dwelling units for each area.

    b) Divide the total population of each area by the number of dwelling units calculated in 3a. This will give us the number of people per dwelling unit.

    c) Which area has the greatest number of people per dwelling unit and which one has the fewest number per unit? Why do these differences exist?

4. a) "Cities grow outward from a central core." Use the age of dwellings along the transect to demonstrate the truth of this statement.

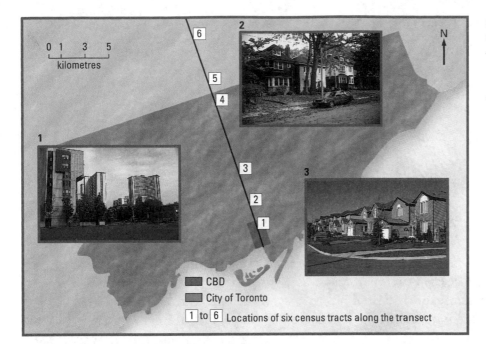

◁ **Fig. 19-5** *A transect through Toronto. All data in chart below is from 1996.*

AREA	#1	#2	#3	#4	#5	#6
Total Population	13 765	4651	5076	7779	2461	4923
Area of Census Tract (km²)	0.21	0.73	1.09	2.28	1.29	2.4
Percentage of children 14 and under	13.7	14.5	16.4	14.8	20.3	21.2
Number of dwelling units in all types of houses	40	1540	1545	2200	770	1385
Number of dwelling units in apartment buildings	6 930	630	520	420	5	400
Period when the majority of dwelling units constructed	1961-70	pre-1946	pre-1946	1946-1970	1961-1980	1986-1991
Average number of rooms per dwelling	3.4	5.7	6.4	7	7.7	9.6
Average value of dwellings ($)	293 000	307 000	416 000	413 000	266 000	610 000

b) Which area does NOT support this statement? Suggest a possible explanation as to why this area has dwellings that have been built more recently than one would expect.

5. a) Construct a series of bar graphs to show the average number of rooms per dwelling in each area.

 b) What is the general trend along the transect?

6. a) Examine the photographs in Fig. 19-5 and rank the appearance of these dwellings from most to least expensive.

 b) Calculate the average value per room in each area by dividing the average value of the dwellings by the average number of rooms.

 c) Which area has the highest value per room and which one has the lowest? Explain what factors may affect these values.

Transportation Land Use

Many people are surprised to learn that about one-third of the developed land in most Canadian cities is used for roads and highways. This large amount of land is needed for the transportation of people and goods. A city's transportation system is made up of three different parts: vehicles, travel paths, and terminal facilities.

VEHICLES

Traveling by private transportation may range from the use of bicycles, to motorbikes, to automobiles. The automobile, in particular, provides fast and convenient travel by a route that we select. When large numbers of people want to go to the same place at the same time, the automobile is a relatively inefficient way to travel within a city's boundaries. Large amounts of vehicle traffic create congestion on urban roads. A mass-transit system such as a subway, light-rail line, or dedicated bus lane is a more efficient way to transport people; these methods can carry up to 30 000 people in an hour.

The term automobile is used to describe a car, van, sport-utility vehicle, or small truck.

Mass-transit systems are expensive to construct, but are worth the cost in areas with a high population density. They are not economical in areas where the population is low because there are not enough people to pay the fares to cover the costs of running the system. Residents in a suburban area without a mass-transport system are forced to use their automobiles and this leads to traffic congestion downtown and elsewhere.

A car carries only an average of 1.5 passengers per trip in the city.

TRAVEL PATHS

Urban roads and highways are classified into three types based on their size and purpose (Fig. 19-6). The largest capacity roads are expressways. They are designed to carry huge amounts of traffic quickly over long distances. Arterial roads carry moderate amounts of traffic over shorter distances. Arterial roads are the major transportation routes within cities. Commercial and industrial development takes place along these roads. The third type of road is local roads which are smaller and narrower than arterial roads. They take people from their homes to the arterial roads. Travel paths also include subway, streetcar, and railroad rights-of-way.

▽ **Fig. 19-6** *Urban roads may be classified as expressways, arterial roads, or local roads.*

TERMINAL FACILITIES

At the end of a journey or transit line, terminal facilities are required. In large cities, the thousands of cars that are used to take people to work need a place to be parked. Parking lots, particularly in the downtown area, take up large amounts of space. They are often located on future building sites. Terminal facilities may also include train stations, bus stations, airports, docks and other mass-transit stations.

Commercial Land Use

About 5% of a city's land is used for commercial activities. These activities include the buying and selling of goods and services in retail businesses, wholesale buying and selling, financial establishments, and a wide variety of services that are broadly classified as "business". Even though these commercial activities use only a small amount of land, they are extremely important to a community's economy. They provide jobs and encourage the flow of money into the community.

As discussed in Chapter 18, any service must have a minimum number of customers to be profitable. This minimum number of customers is defined as the threshold population. For example, different types of stores have different threshold populations. A convenience store sells **low-order products** such as candy bars, newspapers, milk, bread, and lottery tickets.

Products can be a "good" such as a newspaper or a "service" such as dental work.

Other stores sell **middle-order products** such as compact discs, calculators, or most clothing items. Because we may purchase these items only from time-to-time, we are usually willing to travel further to buy them. Since there are fewer customers shopping for middle-order products, stores selling these products need larger threshold populations to remain in business. For example, a clothing or sporting goods store needs a threshold population of several thousand families. A small village may not have enough shoppers to support businesses selling middle-order products.

Residents of the village would have to travel to a larger town.

Items that we purchase infrequently are called **high-order products**. In some cases, they are expensive or have a limited market — rock climbing equipment, specialized books, live theatre, multi-screen movie theatres. Stores selling these products need a threshold population of tens of thousands. There are five main types of commercial land use (Fig. 19-7).

Type	Range of Goods	Typical Stores	Number
1. Local service centres	Low-order	drug store, milk store, variety store	1-5
2. Neighbourhood plazas and ribbons	Low-order	all of the above, plus supermarket, bakery, hair styling, hardware store, bank	5-30
3. Community shopping centres	Low-order and middle-order	all of the above plus small department store, jewellery, clothing, shoes, travel agent	20-100
4. Regional shopping centres	Low-, middle-, high-order	all of the above plus major department stores, bookstores, cinemas, and specialized stores	75-300
5. CBD	Low-, middle-, high-order	all of the above plus very specialized stores	Depends on the population of the city and its region

◁ **Fig. 19-7** *Types of commercial land use*

1. Local Service Centres

- Street-corner shops provide mainly low-order goods for people in the surrounding area.

2. Neighbourhood Plazas and Ribbons

- Businesses also locate in long strips or "ribbons" along major arterial roads.

- They attract local residents as well as customers just driving by.

- Ribbons sometimes specialize in high-order products such as automobile dealerships. This specialization attracts people from a wider area, and allows customers to comparison shop.

3. Community Shopping Centres (Malls)

- Malls are usually found at major street intersections in large cities, or on the outskirts of towns.

- Most shopping needs can be satisfied in centres of this type.

- They are usually designed around department stores and supermarkets, each acting as an **anchor** for the mall. These stores are located at opposite ends of the mall and attract great numbers of customers. For example, a shopper may come to the mall to purchase a coat at the department store, have something to eat in the food court, buy a magazine in a book store, and then pick up a watch battery at a kiosk before leaving.

- The same activities may also be found in ribbons along streets in older parts of the city.

4. Regional Shopping Centres (Malls)

- Large regional shopping malls contain not only the types of stores and activities found in smaller community shopping centres, but also specialized stores which require high threshold populations.

- They are located in the suburbs of large cities along major highways.

- They have large parking lots to accommodate their customers who drive in from the city and the surrounding region.

- Their focus is on high- and medium-order products.

5. The Central Business District

- The Central Business District (CBD) is what most people call "downtown."

The CBD is not usually situated at the geographic centre of the city.

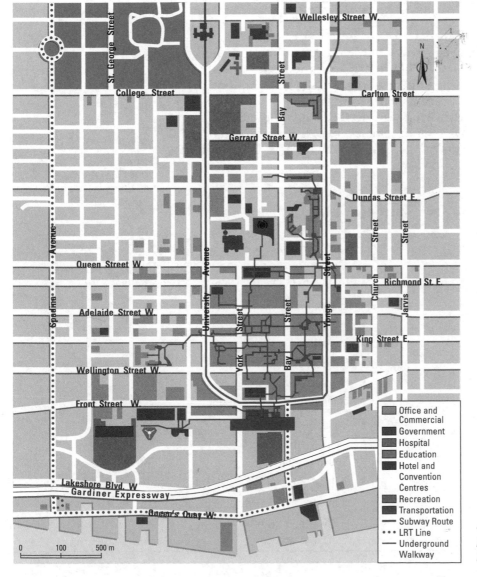

◁ **Fig. 19-8** *Toronto's CBD has a number of major land uses.*

- It is easily identified by the greatest concentration of the tallest buildings.

- The high demand for office space elevates the land values in the CBD. In order to maximize the use of this expensive land, development companies build large buildings.

- The CBDs of Canada's largest cities may have financial, retail, entertainment, and hotel land uses (Fig. 19-8). Some land uses are large enough to be found in distinctive districts. The financial district, for example, usually has the highest buildings and provides offices for banks, lawyers, and stock brokers. The CBD may also have a retail district. By locating together, these stores attract more shoppers than if they were on their own. They attract customers from all over the city because the CBD is well served by roads and mass transit systems. The retail district is usually located next to the financial district because it has a large market composed of workers in the office towers.

- Regional shopping malls have grown with the growth of suburbs and may have a negative impact on downtown businesses. Their large parking lots, climate-controlled environment, and one-stop shopping often attract customers who normally shop in downtown locations. To compete against suburban malls, downtown businesses may revitalize the downtown area (Fig. 19-9). Or they may build new indoor malls downtown in direct competition with suburban shopping malls. For example, large indoor malls have been built in downtown Toronto and Ottawa.

The status of a downtown location can be increased if a company builds an office tower with its name on it. What are the best known buildings in the downtown area of a city near you?

▽ **Fig. 19-9** *Some ways to revitalize a declining downtown area (CBD)*

Problem	Solutions
Old buildings	• Tear down and replace • Modernize and expand existing structures • Renovate but maintain "historic" character
Congested roads	• Widen roads • Have one-way streets • Expand public transit • Encourage car pooling • Restrict private car access to CBD • Eliminate on-street parking
Limited parking	• Build parking garages • Expand on-street parking • Subsidize parking
Crowded, unattractive pedestrian areas	• Widen sidewalks • Ban cars on some streets (malls) • "Landscape" sidewalks • Build mini-parks

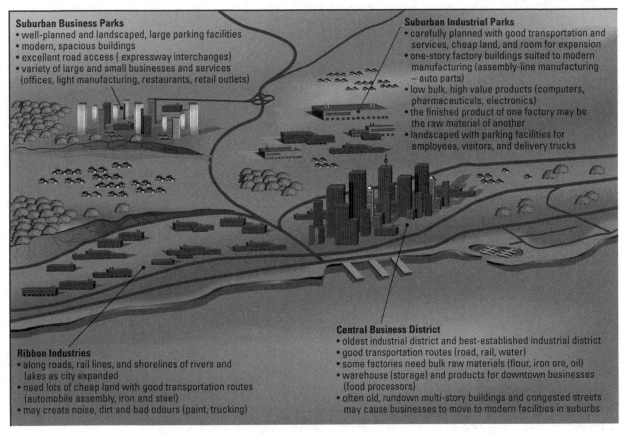

Suburban Business Parks
• well-planned and landscaped, large parking facilities
• modern, spacious buildings
• excellent road access (expressway interchanges)
• variety of large and small businesses and services
  (offices, light manufacturing, restaurants, retail outlets)

Suburban Industrial Parks
• carefully planned with good transportation and
  services, cheap land, and room for expansion
• one-story factory buildings suited to modern
  manufacturing (assembly-line manufacturing
  – auto parts)
• low bulk, high value products (computers,
  pharmaceuticals, electronics)
• the finished product of one factory may be
  the raw material of another
• landscaped with parking facilities for
  employees, visitors, and delivery trucks

Central Business District
• oldest industrial district and best-established industrial district
• good transportation routes (road, rail, water)
• some factories need bulk raw materials (flour, iron ore, oil)
• warehouse (storage) and products for downtown businesses
  (food processors)
• often old, rundown multi-story buildings and congested streets
  may cause businesses to move to modern facilities in suburbs

Ribbon Industries
• along roads, rail lines, and shorelines of rivers and
  lakes as city expanded
• need lots of cheap land with good transportation routes
  (automobile assembly, iron and steel)
• may create noise, dirt and bad odours (paint, trucking)

△ **Fig. 19-10** *The four major
types of industrial land use*

Industrial Land Use

Industrial land use is an important feature of most towns and cities. On average, about 6% of the developed land in most communities is used for industrial land use such as factories (processing and manufacturing), warehousing (storage), and shipping products. Modern cities are characterized by four main types of industrial land use — the CBD industries, ribbon industries, suburban industrial parks, and suburban business parks (Fig. 19-10).

Before the 1940s, factories were built on land near waterfronts and railway lines. Industries that relied on imported products or heavy manufacturing, such as grain processing, required waterfront locations. Goods produced in these factories were often shipped to other cities by railway because networks of roads between cities were not well-developed enough for quick and easy transport of goods by truck. At that time, most industries built factories in downtown locations because their workers lived in residential areas nearby. The workers did not have cars so they had to be able to travel to the factories on foot or by streetcar. The factories were constructed as multi-storey buildings in order to get maximum use of land which was very expensive. Years later, these multi-storey factories were inefficient for the assembly-line manufacturing that came into use.

After the 1940s, better highways and long-distance trucking gave manufacturers an alternative to rail transportation. Companies were able to move away from downtown railway depots to the suburbs where they could buy large tracts of inexpensive land. Larger building sites allowed the construction of one-storey factories which were better suited to assembly-line manufacturing. As more people bought cars, workers could more easily drive long distances to work in the suburbs.

Many older factories near city Central Business Districts are now obsolete. They will eventually be torn down because the land is too valuable to support inefficient industrial activities. Many downtown industries have since relocated to suburban locations in modern, spacious buildings. Companies can custom design their building and surrounding land to their needs, and property taxes are lower on the urban fringe. These new factories and warehouses are built in industrial parks away from residential areas. They have specially designed water, sewage, power, fire, and police protection facilities. Many have landscaping to hide their factories from view. They are usually located close to highways to take advantage of modern truck transportation.

The old properties remaining in the CBD may be leased to other businesses, or they may be converted to other uses. For example, artists may turn old warehouses into studios and galleries. Some buildings are renovated to become nightclubs, offices, restaurants, or residences. Some are torn down and the sites are used as parking lots before new buildings are constructed. Old waterfront factories are often torn down and replaced by residential, commercial, and recreational facilities. In this manner, the CBD undergoes renewal and at the same time may become more attractive and interesting.

Other Land Uses

Land is used in other ways in towns and cities.

- *Institutional and Public Buildings* About 10% of urban land is occupied by buildings used for schools, hospitals, government offices, and for religious purposes.

- *Open Space and Recreational Land* Open space and recreational land occupies about 7% of urban land. Open space may be previously developed land which is now vacant or it may be land which has been left in its natural state — for example, a wood lot or a cemetery. Recreational land consists of parks, playgrounds, playing fields, golf courses, fair grounds, community centres, and arenas. The use

vacant: empty, not in use

of land for recreational purposes in towns and cities is important because recreation enhances the quality of urban life.

FACTORS AFFECTING LAND-USE PATTERNS

Why is an office building built in one particular location in a city, a sewage treatment plant in another, and a golf course somewhere else? There are many factors which determine land use, but the four most important are land value, **zoning**, technology, and climate.

Land Value

Why isn't there a golf driving range in the downtown area of your town or city? The downtown area seems like a perfect location for this activity. People could take a quick break from work to get a little exercise and fresh air. There certainly would be no shortage of customers! As you probably realize, the value of the required land is much greater than the profit a driving range could make. Land in a major city's downtown area can easily cost $3000/m^2$. The land required for a small driving range could therefore cost $20 000 000!

In general, land values are highest in areas of the city that are most accessible. The CBD has the highest land values because it is the most easily accessible location in the city. High land values are also found along major transportation routes, especially where such routes intersect. This is why the CBD has the tallest buildings and activities that generate a large amount of income, such as prestige offices — but no driving ranges!

most accessible: most easily reached from all parts of the city

Land costs affect land use not only in the CBD, but also in other parts of the city. Lots for new houses are smaller than they were 10 to 15 years ago because of the increasing cost of land. Businesses that require a large area of land but produce relatively low income, like the golf driving range, must find cheap land on which to locate. This land is usually found on the edge of the city. In most cases, these businesses will locate there until the land is needed for permanent uses that produce more income.

Zoning

Zoning refers to laws, usually passed by city governments, that control the kind and amount of development in an area. Can you imagine what it would be like to live next to a dirty, smelly factory? Zoning laws are

△ **Fig. 19-11** *Zoning maps use a standard code to identify land uses.*

R is single-family residential (schools may also be built in these zones)

RM is multiple-family residential (higher numbers represent higher densities)

O1 is open space — park

O3 is open space — utilities

meant to avoid conflicts like this between land uses. Governments pass laws that state which land uses are allowed in an area. Fig. 19-11 is a typical zoning map. Conflicts, however, often exist in older areas since these areas were built before zoning was done.

Technology

Land-use patterns reflect the technology that existed when the land was developed. Compare the two aerial photographs (Fig. 19-12). One shows a district built 80 years ago, the other shows a district built in the past 20 years. The differences in the two photographs can be explained as a result of the widespread use of automobiles since the 1940s. Urban areas built since then feature wider arterial roads and local roads designed to make through traffic difficult. Large parking lots near shopping and office areas are much more evident in the recently built areas.

Climate

Canada is one of the coldest nations in the world. Until recently, Canadian urban planners did not give enough thought to cold temperatures, wind, ice, snow, and long winter nights. Today, the urban planning process

	Road Pattern	Road Width	Housing Density
Older Area	Grid	Narrower	Higher, smaller lots
Newer Area	Garden	Wider	Lower, larger lots

△ **Fig. 19-12** *These two aerial photographs show two parts of the same city. Which area is older? How can you tell?*

usually takes the country's winter climate into consideration. The **winter-city concept** advocates the building of cities with inside and outside environments that are livable during long, harsh winters.

Many Canadian cities have built underground walkways in their downtown areas. Toronto and Montréal each have an "underground city" that stretches for many blocks (Fig. 19-9). Workers can get off the subway and walk to their offices without ever having to venture outside into the snow. They can move between buildings without a coat during cold weather.

Indoor shopping malls have been built, usually in the suburbs, in response to our harsh climate. The West Edmonton Mall is a famous example. It has hundreds of stores as well as extensive indoor recreation facilities, which include an amusement park and a water park. Living plants and trees, running water, and natural light, which filters through glass ceilings, create an indoor environment that shuts out winter.

Planners with the winter-city concept in mind give just as much thought to the outdoor environments of cities. Bus shelters, sidewalk barriers, and covered walkways protect pedestrians from wind, snow, and flying slush. The location of buildings, the design of public spaces, and the use of natural vegetation are carefully considered in order to protect citizens from harsh weather, and at the same time to allow ample amounts of sunlight. Skating rinks, toboggan runs, and land-fill ski hills in parks encourage outdoor activity.

The winter-city concept has changed peoples' attitude towards winter. Properly designed winter cities allow people to move around comfortably, and to participate in city life, both indoors and outdoors all year round.

URBAN EXPANSION

A city expands as its population grows. It expands to make room for new housing, industries, stores, and services for its increasing population. Sometimes a city will expand within its boundaries by constructing high-density buildings on vacant land. Or, it may tear down low-rise buildings and replace them with taller ones. Taller, higher-density buildings bring people, housing, stores, schools, businesses, medical facilities, theatres, and many other activities closer together. As a result of the proximity of all these activities, the people who live here can walk, cycle, or use public transportation as they carry out their daily lives. These methods of transportation reduce the ecological footprint of urban dwellers.

When a city expands outwards beyond its suburbs, it grows into the **rural-urban fringe**. This is an area adjacent to the city where rural land uses are gradually replaced by urban activities. It is an area of mixed land use, and contains such things as farms, gas stations, mobile-home parks, garden nurseries, golf courses, conservation areas, landfill sites, and housing subdivisions. Since residential density is lower in the rural-urban fringe, and land-use activities are farther apart, the public transportation system is not usually well-developed. The automobile is therefore a necessity. This increases the ecological footprint of the residents of the rural-urban fringe.

Often, development in the rural-urban fringe is not continuous, and takes place without planning. Ribbons of mixed activities such as motels, auto wreckers, and car dealerships develop beside farmland, vacant land, and low-density residential subdivisions along major highways. This type of development is known as **urban sprawl.**

Urban expansion into the rural-urban fringe contributes significantly to the loss of productive farmland. Local governments increase taxes to pay for services (water, sewage, roads, and schools), and the burden of paying these taxes falls on farmers. Developers purchase farmland to build new communities and create serviced land for industries. Speculators may purchase farmland and let it sit idle as they wait for it to increase in value. Sometimes speculators rent the land out to farmers,

To learn more about cold climate communities, check www.wnet.gov.edmonton.ab.ca/index.html

proximity: nearness

See Chapter 36 for a discussion of ecological footprint.

Some new neighbourhoods in suburban locations are now being designed like downtown neighbourhoods with narrow lots and smaller houses. This provides a more compact area with a higher residential density. This type of design reduces the amount of urban sprawl on the outskirts of the city.

speculator: someone who buys land expecting land values to increase so that a profit is made when the land is sold

but more often than not, the renters do not maintain the land properly because they know it will soon be used for other purposes such as the building of subdivisions or industrial parks. The buying and selling of farm land by speculators pushes up the land values. This encourages farmers to sell their land because they can make more money from selling it than by farming it.

IN CLOSING...

Land-use patterns in towns and cities do not develop by chance. They result from decisions made by people about such things as where to work, what type of home to live in, what kind of local government to have, and what to spend money on. The decisions that you make about these things may affect the way your community looks in the future.

QUESTIONS

CHECK YOUR UNDERSTANDING

1. a) Explain the differences between low-, medium-, and high-density residential land use.

   b) Explain the two factors that influence residential density.

2. Describe the differences between the three major types of roads.

3. What are the differences between low-order, medium-order, and high-order products?

4. In your own words, describe the following commercial centres:

   a) local service centres

   b) neighbourhood plazas and ribbons

   c) community shopping centres

   d) regional shopping centres (malls)

   e) CBD

5. a) Describe the characteristics of the four types of industrial land uses.

   b) Compare the location of industries before the 1940s and after the 1940s.

   c) Why has the location changed?

6. How do land values affect land use?

ANALYZE AND APPLY

7. Examine the three diagrams in Fig. 19-4.

   a) Calculate the residential density for each of the three types of housing in the following manner.

   For each of the three diagrams, total the number of housing units in the six grid squares (each one is one hectare in size). Divide this number by 6 in each case to obtain the average residential density.

   b) What do you think are the advantages and disadvantages of each type of housing?

   c) What types of housing are found in the neighbourhood where you live? Estimate the housing density in your neighbourhood.

8. Examine Fig. 19-7.

   a) Where would you go to buy a roll of film?

   b) Where would you buy an expensive piece of clothing?

   c) Are specialized stores more or less likely to be close to where you live? Explain.

9. Explain why activities located in the CBD are dependent on each other.

10. a) In your opinion, is urban expansion a more positive or more negative aspect of urban development? Give at least three reasons to support your answer.

    b) What can be done to limit the negative impacts of urban sprawl?

11. a) How do cities plan for Canada's climate by using the winter-city concept?

    b) What other methods of urban planning can you suggest for dealing with Canada's climate conditions?

THINK AND COMMUNICATE

12. Would you rather shop at stores in the CBD or in a large shopping mall? Fully explain your choice.

13. Examine the closest regional shopping mall to your neighbourhood. Identify one example of each of the following:

    a) an anchor store

    b) a chain store

    c) a local merchant

14. Using examples from your own town or city, or the nearest town or city, research how each of the following factors has influenced land use: physical features, period of development, land values, and government land-use policies. Your teacher will tell you how to present your findings.

15. Are older districts of cities or newer suburbs the more interesting places in which to live? Construct a chart to compare the advantages and disadvantages of each. Where would you prefer to live? Why?

Economic Connections

Eira Thomas, geologist and member of the exploration team that discovered the Diavik diamond pipes.

20 Types of Industry

STUDY GUIDE

By the end of this chapter, you will be able to:

- identify and describe the three categories of industry
- understand the importance to Canada of each category of industry

- describe the roles played by basic and non-basic activities in Canada's economy
- rank the relative importance of each in terms of number of employees in each

Key Terms

primary industries	tertiary industries	manufacturing	basic industries
secondary industries	raw materials	services	non-basic industries

It just did not make sense. Kapuskasing, Ontario (Fig. 20-1) was supposed to be a major forest products centre, but when Marina tried to prove it, the numbers did not support her case. At first, Marina believed that she had a great idea for her geography project — she would create a summary of all the jobs in her town to show how important the forest industry was to Kapuskasing. She expected to find that most of the workers in the town were employed in the pulp and paper industry. Fig. 20-2 is a summary of what she actually found. Remarkably, less than 30% of Kapuskasing's workforce worked in forestry. How could this be? You will find the answers in this chapter.

Marina found this information from a government agency called Statistics Canada.

TYPES OF INDUSTRY

Before you can understand the job distribution in Kapuskasing (and the rest of Canada for that matter), you must understand that industries and the jobs related to them can be divided into three groups. The relationship between these groups can be seen by looking at the case of a pair of skates (Fig. 20-3).

△ **Fig. 20-1** *Kapuskasing is a typical forest town in Ontario.*

EMPLOYMENT IN KAPUSKASING

	Number of Workers	Percentage of Work Force
Primary Industries (forestry workers and other primary workers)	155	3.3%
Secondary Industries (forest products manufacturing and other secondary workers)	1460	31.4%
Tertiary Industries	3040	65.3%
Total Workers	4655	100.0%
Total Workers in Forestry (primary and secondary)	1355	29.1%

The pair of skates shows how Canada's economy works. The country's relative wealth is generated from a combination of rich natural resources and the creativity and hard work of many Canadian people. The jobs that these people do can be placed into one of three categories: **primary industries**, **secondary industries**, and **tertiary industries**.

△ **Fig. 20-2** *Marina found these employment statistics for Kapuskasing; they were not what she expected. She thought that most of the people in the town worked in the forest industry.*

Primary Industries

Industries that take **raw materials** from the natural environment are called primary or extractive industries. They are called *primary* because the recovery of natural resources must happen before anything else can occur. The primary industries related to the skates are listed in Stage 1 of Fig. 20-3 — mining and agriculture. Logically, primary industries are located in parts of Canada where resources are found. As you will see later in this unit, most resources are found in very specific places.

▽ **Fig. 20-3** *A simple product like a pair of skates involves all sectors of the economy.*

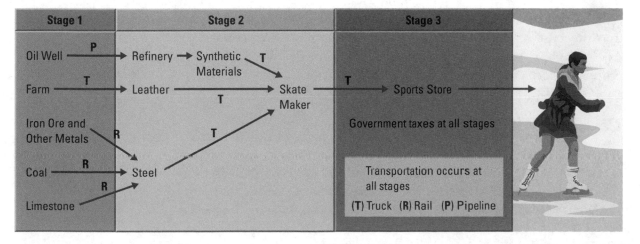

Canada has a wide range of extractive industries including agriculture, mining, forestry, and fishing. In fact, only a few countries in the world can rival Canada as a source of natural products. Primary industries make a critical contribution to Canada's wealth. Without them, and the money they bring from other countries, Canada's economy would not exist in its current form. It is surprising that a small percentage of Canada's labour force works in primary industries (Fig. 20-4). In fact, the statistics that Marina found are a reflection of the fact that relatively few people work in extractive industries, even in parts of Canada that are identified with a primary industry.

Only Russia, the United States, and, Australia and Brazil compare to Canada as sources of natural products.

Secondary Industries

Secondary industries involve the processing of primary industry products into finished goods. This relates to Stage 2 of the skate story in Fig. 20-3. The most important secondary industry is **manufacturing**, which is responsible for making the enormous range of products needed by consumers and by companies. Manufacturers make everything from computers and diamond rings to cans of fruit and bulldozers. As you can see in Fig. 20-4, secondary industries employ far more Canadians than do primary industries. Construction alone, has more workers than all the primary industries combined, while manufacturing employs three times as many workers.

A greater percentage of Canada's labour force worked in primary industries before machinery replaced human labour for many tasks.

Manufacturing often involves more than one stage of processing. For example, iron ore, coal, limestone, and other metals — all products of primary industry — are used to make steel. This is called primary manufacturing because the product, i.e., steel, is used as a raw material for more manufacturing. In the secondary manufacturing stage, the steel may be used to make a car, a refrigerator, nails, or skate blades.

Manufacturing industries are located in towns and cities across Canada. In most cases, companies try to build their factories in more densely populated areas because they want to be near their customers. This means that the cost of shipping their products will be as low as possible. Accordingly, if you know where most Canadians live, you will have a pretty good idea where most manufacturing is done.

See Fig. 18-3 on page 203 for a population distribution map of Canada.

Tertiary Industries

Tertiary industries provide a wide range of **services** that support primary and secondary industries and society in general. Without them, society could not function. This relates to the skates in Stage 3 of Fig. 20-3.

What Marina did not take into account when she started her project was that a substantial majority of Canadians do not make *goods* in their jobs. Rather, they provide services for others. In fact, almost three times

	Number of Workers	Percentage of Work Force
Primary Industries		
Agriculture	446 000	3.1%
Fishing	34 000	0.2%
Forestry	73 000	0.5%
Mining, oil, and gas	159 000	1.1%
Total	**712 000**	**5.0%**
Secondary Industries		
Manufacturing	2 189 000	15.2%
Construction	775 000	5.4%
Utilities	135 000	0.9%
Total	**3 099 000**	**21.6%**
Tertiary Industries		
Wholesale trade	685 000	4.8%
Retail trade	1 777 000	12.4%
Transportation and communications	917 000	6.4%
Finance, insurance, and real estate	785 000	5.5%
Education	987 000	6.9%
Health and social services	1 489 000	10.4%
Business and personal services	3 140 000	21.8%
Public and business services	787 000	5.5%
Total	**10 567 000**	**73.7%**
Total in All Industries	**14 379 000**	**100%**

△ **Fig. 20-4** *Employment in Canada, 1996*

as many Canadians work in tertiary industries as in primary and secondary industries combined. These services are so varied, and so much a part of life, that often they are not even noticed.

Service industries, in one form or another, are spread across the country. The majority of service industries are found in towns and cities because most services are provided for the people and manufacturers that are concentrated in urban areas. In some cities and towns, one service industry dominates. Think for a moment of Ottawa and one service industry should come to mind: the government. Can you think of other cities or towns that are closely identified with a particular service?

Consider your day. In the morning, you may *read a magazine* while you *ride the bus* to school. At noon, you may go to the *local burger place* for lunch. After school, you may have a *dental appointment*. At night, you may go to the mall to *shop* and *see the latest movie*. Of course, during the day you are *in school*.

BASIC AND NON-BASIC INDUSTRIES

There is one more concept that will help you to understand the nature of jobs and industries. Let's start with a specific example. Compare the jobs of two people who live in Kapuskasing. Joan C. works in the shipping department of the pulp and paper mill (Fig. 20-5), while Henri F. cooks in a restaurant on the main street of town (Fig. 20-6).

Beyond the obvious differences in the two jobs, there is one important distinction that must be made. The money to pay Joan's salary comes primarily from outside the economy of the local town. It is provided (indirectly) by the customers who buy paper products from the mill. Jobs like hers are in **basic industries** (and are called basic jobs) because they provide the money needed to support the local economy. Without them, there would be no money entering the town and it could not exist.

On the other hand, the money earned by Henri comes almost entirely from customers who live in the local area. Jobs like his are in **non-basic industries**, since they do not bring new money into the local economy. Instead, they *recycle* the money that is already there. While non-basic jobs are important, the survival and growth of an economy depends on having enough basic jobs.

How can you tell if a job is basic or non-basic? Sometimes it is not clear because some jobs can be a combination of both. In most cases it is obvious. Consider the examples in Fig. 20-7. How does the job of an actor at the Stratford Festival compare to that of an actor at a theatre in Toronto? In Stratford, the vast majority of people who attend the theatre would be from out-of-town , so an actor would be a basic job. In Toronto, though, many of the people going to the theatre are local residents, so an actor would be both basic and non-basic.

There is money continually leaving the town to pay for all the goods and services that are brought in from outside. The town must earn money to pay for these goods and services.

Stratford's permanent population is less than 30 000.

Some larger theatres attract a great many people who do not live in Toronto.

IN CLOSING...

What you have learned in this chapter is a structure for understanding the types of industries and jobs that exist in Canada. If you are now familiar with the ideas of primary, secondary, and tertiary industries and with basic and non-basic industries, you will be better able to understand Canada's economic geography. Your knowledge of the distribution of jobs in each industry should help you answer Marina's question as to why so few people in his town work in the forestry industry.

▽ **Fig. 20-5** *The shipping department of a pulp and paper mill like the one that employs Joan C.*

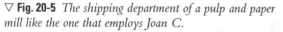

▽ **Fig. 20-6** *A restaurant like the one in Kapuskasing that employs Henri F.*

Job Description	Category
Coal miner in northeastern British Columbia	Basic
Hairdresser at a shopping mall	Non-basic
Art teacher	Non-basic
Actor at the Stratford Shakespearean Festival	Basic
Teller at the local bank	Non-basic
Vice-president of Toronto Dominion Bank	Basic
Professor at Laurentian University in Sudbury	Basic
Receptionist at a dentist's office	Non-basic
Air Canada pilot	Basic
School-bus driver	Non-basic

◁ **Fig. 20-7** *Do you know why each of these jobs is in the category shown?*

QUESTIONS

CHECK YOUR UNDERSTANDING

1. a) Define, in your own words, and give three examples of each of the following: primary industry, secondary industry, tertiary industry

   b) Draw bar graphs to show the percentage of the labour force employed in each sub-category shown in Fig. 20-4 (e.g., agriculture, retail trade). Use a different colour for each category (primary, secondary, and tertiary).

2. In your notebook, match the industry in Column A with the items in Column B.

Column A

1. Primary industry

2. Secondary industry

3. Tertiary industry

Column B

a) raw materials
b) manufacturing
c) factory
d) mining
c)₂ civil servant
d)₂ natural resources
e) ski resort
f) services
g) construction
h) farming
i) transportation

ANALYZE AND APPLY

3. a) What is the difference between a basic industry and a non-basic industry?

   b) Which of the following are basic and which are non-basic jobs? Explain each answer.

      i. an assembly line worker in the Ford factory in Oakville

      ii. a fire fighter in your community

      iii. a wheat farmer in Saskatchewan

      iv. the artist who illustrated this book

   c) Describe a situation in which each of the following jobs can be basic in nature and a situation in which it can be non-basic:

      i. a doctor

      ii. a bus driver

      iii. a golf professional

4. a) Fig. 20-8 shows the distribution of workers of each industry in the major regions of Canada. Create a set of bar graphs for each region. Fig. 20-9 shows a sample bar graph.

   b) Compare the percentage of Canada's population in each region to the percentage of workers in each type of industry. If the figures are similar, then

Region	Percentage of Canada's Primary Workers	Percentage of Canada's Secondary Workers	Percentage of Canada's Tertiary Workers	Percentage of Canada's Population
Atlantic Canada (Nfld, PEI, NS, and NB)	8.3%	6.0%	7.1%	8.1%
Central Canada (Qué, Ont)	29.4%	70.7%	61.6%	62.0%
Western Canada (BC, Alta, Man, Sask, Territories)	62.3%	23.3%	31.3%	29.9%

△ **Fig. 20-8** *Regional distribution of employees in Canada for 1998*

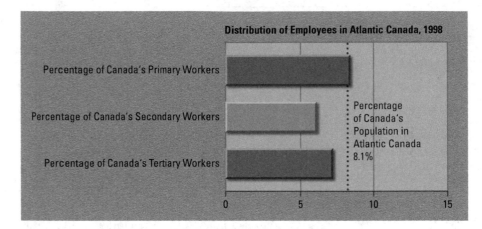

◁ **Fig. 20-9** *Distribution of employees in Atlantic Canada, 1998*

the region has its fair share of jobs in that category. If not, then an imbalance exists. What significant differences do you see? Why might they exist?

5. a) Work with a partner to do this question. Conduct a survey of the occupations of at least 50 people in your community. Divide the jobs into primary, secondary, and tertiary industries and into basic and non-basic. In each case, convert the results into percentages.

    b) Did the results surprise you? Why or why not?

    c) For the types of industries, are the results that you obtained what you would expect based on what you know about the national distribution of jobs (Fig. 20-4) and the distribution of jobs in your region (question 4)?

THINK AND COMMUNICATE

6. How would you expect the pattern of primary, secondary, and tertiary industries for 1920 to differ from the pattern revealed by the statistics in Fig. 20-4 for 1996? Why?

7. A geographer once said that tertiary industries are, at the same time, the most important and the least important segment of Canada's economy. What do you think this statement means?

21 Fishing: An Industry at the Crossroads

STUDY GUIDE

By the end of this chapter, you will be able to:

- describe the major parts of Canada's fishing industry
- explain why Canada is a major producer and exporter of fish products
- explain the recent threats to Canada's fishing industry
- indicate possible solutions to the fishing problems

Key Terms

renewable resource

groundfish

pelagic fish

shellfish

balance of trade

continental shelf

fishing banks

plankton

inshore fishing

offshore fishing

sustained yield management

aquaculture

For centuries, those who fished for a living looked forward to years of regular employment. This is because the fish in the oceans, lakes, and rivers of Canada were a **renewable resource**, and therefore replaced themselves. Even during the 1980s, Canada's fishing industry seemed to have a bright future. But the collapse of the fisheries during the 1990s changed all this (Fig. 21-1). Fish stocks on the East Coast declined to the extent that the most important element, the cod fishery, had to be shut down in 1992. A few years later, the fishing industry was alarmed by the collapse of the salmon fishery on the West Coast.

This chapter will examine the history and importance of the fishing industry, the reasons for its recent decline, and its prospects for the future.

To learn more about fishing, check www.ncr.dfo.ca/home_e.htm

INTRODUCTION

Ocean fishing is Canada's oldest industry. Beginning in the early 1500s, ships from Great Britain, France, Spain, and Portugal came to Canada every summer to harvest the rich fishing grounds off Newfoundland. At first, the Europeans set up summer fishing stations. Eventually, they estab-

◁ **Fig. 21-1** *The 1990s marked the beginning of the most serious crisis in the history of the Canadian fishing industry.*

lished permanent fishing villages. The fish were dried or salted, and then sent to Europe, the United States, and the West Indies. Fishing provided the economic base for European settlement in much of Newfoundland, Nova Scotia, Prince Edward Island, parts of New Brunswick, Québec, and British Columbia.

Commercial fishing today makes up only about 0.15% of the total value of Canada's economy. This might make it seem relatively unimportant, but in parts of Atlantic Canada, the Pacific Coast, and some inland areas, it is the foundation of the economy. As well, commercial fishing is the basis for a traditional way of life that has a special place in Canada's cultural heritage.

Canadian commercial fishing occurs in three areas: the East Coast, the West Coast, and the freshwater inland lakes. In the mid–1990s, about 70 000 Canadians had commercial-fishing licences, and another 20 000 were employed in fish processing. As shown in Fig. 21-2, production

Fishery	Number of Fishers	Tonnes of Fish Products	Percentage of Total Catch	Value of Catch ($ millions)	Total Exports ($ millions)
East Coast	49 957	652 067	71.3	1104	2059
West Coast	14 164	242 018	26.5	394	829
Freshwater	6900	19 981	2.2	28	148
Canada (Total)	71 021	914 066	100.0	1526	3036

◁ **Fig. 21-2** *Canada's three fisheries (1996):*

The reason Total Exports are higher than Value of Catch is that processing has been done, which increases the value of the fish.

▽ **Fig. 21-3** *There are three categories of catch for Canada's fishing industry.*

CATEGORY		DESCRIPTION	EXAMPLES
Groundfish		Fish that feed and are caught near the ocean floor	cod, pollock, haddock, halibut, redfish
Pelagic fish		Fish that feed and are caught near the surface	salmon, herring, mackerel, tuna, caplin
Shellfish		Molluscs and crustaceans	shrimp, lobster, oyster, scallop, mussels

from the East Coast is higher than that from the West Coast, and fresh-water production is smaller than both. The different kinds of ocean fish caught by Canadian fishers are categorized as: **groundfish** (bottom feeders), **pelagic fish** (open water feeders), and **shellfish** (Fig. 21-3).

Canada is not one of the top ten fishing nations in the world. It is, however, one of the world's leading exporters of fish, largely because Canadians do not eat much fish. As a result, export markets are very important to the Canadian fishing industry. More than 50% of the Canadian catch is exported. To compete more effectively in these markets, Canada developed a grading system which ensures that a consistently high quality of fish is exported. Canada's fish exports are greater than our imports, which helps our **balance of trade**. For example, in 1997, exports of fish were valued at $3 billion while imports of fish were valued at about $1.6 billion. The most important markets for our fish are the United States, Western Europe, and the countries of the Pacific Rim, particularly Japan.

In Canada, consumers need to become more aware of the health benefits of eating fish. Better marketing and advertising would encourage this, since most Canadians do not know what varieties of fish are available or how to cook them properly.

Canadians generally do not eat as much seafood as people in other countries. In one year, the average Canadian eats 34 kg of beef, 26 kg of pork, 31 kg of poultry, and only 10 kg of fresh fish and shellfish.

QUESTIONS

CHECK YOR UNDERSTANDING

1. Why are fish a renewable resource?
2. Explain the economic and social importance of the fishing industry to Canada.
3. a) Name the three types of ocean fish that are caught.
   b) Give two examples of each type. Which ones have you eaten?

ANALYZE AND APPLY

4. a) Why are fish exports important to Canada's balance of payments?
   b) To which countries are most of our fish exports shipped? Why?
5. Examine the value of the catch and the total exports in Fig. 21–2. What reasons can you think of to explain the different values?

THINK AND COMMUNICATE

6. a) How many times a month do you eat seafood (consider both at home and outside the home)?

    b) Where does seafood rank on your list of favourite foods? Why do you think this is so?

    c) If the average person eats 0.2 kg of seafood per serving, calculate the amount you eat per year. How does this compare to the national average of 10 kg?

    d) Discuss the following question in a group of 3 or 4 students: *If seafood is highly nutritious, why do Canadians eat so little of it?* Consider economic and cultural factors. (You may wish to discuss this statement with your family.)

    e) Why do you think people in other countries eat so much more seafood than Canadians?

THE EAST COAST FISHERY

Until recently, the ocean waters off the East Coast of Canada were one of the world's great fishing grounds. A number of favourable conditions combined to produce waters extremely suitable to fish. Atlantic Canada has a particularly wide **continental shelf** which is less than 200 m in depth. On this shelf are even shallower areas called **fishing banks** which are less than 150 m deep (Fig. 21-4). Here, sunlight penetrates to the bottom causing a lush growth of **plankton**, which attracts large numbers of fish. The largest and best-known fishing region on the East Coast is the Grand Banks, with an area of 282 500 km². By comparison, the island of Newfoundland is 111 400 km².

The meeting of the cold Labrador Current and the warm Gulf Stream on the Grand Banks churns up nutrients that are necessary for the growth of plankton (Fig. 21-5).

The waters off the East Coast have been among the world's greatest fishing grounds for centuries. They are home to two distinct types of fisheries: the **inshore fishery** and the **offshore fishery** (Fig. 21-6).

Near the end of the Ice Age, the banks were a chain of islands. They have since been covered by higher sea levels and now form the shallow fishing banks.

Plankton is the name given to microscopic plants and animals eaten by small fish and shellfish. The small fish and shellfish are, in turn, eaten by larger fish.

You can learn more about the collapse of the cod fishery at: www.greenpeace.org/~comms/cbio/cancod.html

Crisis in the East Coast Fishery

You have probably read the news about the problems facing the fishery in Atlantic Canada. If you live in this region, the problems are far more than just a news story because they directly affect the local economy, and perhaps even your family.

In the 1980s, people in the East Coast fishery who relied on groundfish noticed they were catching fewer and smaller fish. In particular, the northern cod off Newfoundland and southern Labrador seemed to be

Northern cod was the most important species of groundfish in the East Coast fishery.

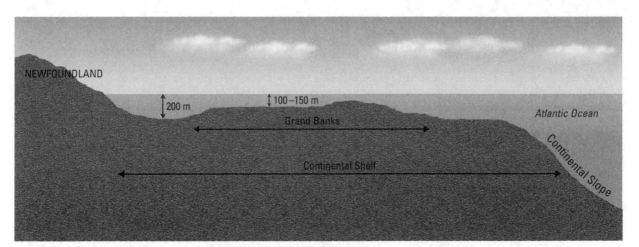

△ **Fig. 21-4** *The shallow fishing banks allow sunlight to penetrate to the bottom, creating ideal conditions for the growth of plankton which, in turn, attract fish.*

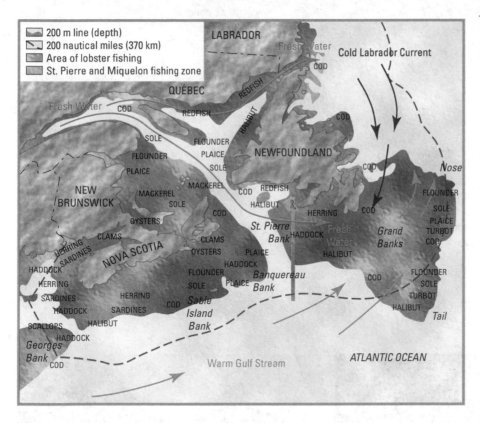

◁ **Fig. 21-5** *Canada's East Coast fishery*

disappearing. The statistics for the northern cod catch in the Atlantic fishery illustrate what happened (Fig. 21-7). While the catch of cod and other groundfish had declined before (consider 1978-79), the collapse that occurred in 1991 was unexpected. The Canadian government responded in 1992 by halting all fishing for northern cod, and by making major cuts in the catches allowed for other groundfish species.

One fishing village reported catching only three cod in 1992.

The cod-fishing ban was still in effect when this book was written.

Feature	Inshore Fishery	Offshore Fishery
Location	Within 16 to 25 km of shore	To edges of continental shelf, up to 370 km from shore
Percentage of the fishing industry labor force	85%	15%
Percentage of total catch	10%	90%
Type of boat and equipment (see photo below)	Smaller boats (up to 20 m in length), usually with fixed gear (fish weirs, lobster traps, etc.)	Larger boats (up to 50 m in length), usually with mobile fish nets; foreign factory-trawlers can be larger still
Ownership of boats and equipment	Individuals and families	Large companies
Type of employment	Self-employment	Unionized employees of fishing companies
Crew size	1 to 6	12 to 16
Fishing season	Mainly warmer months	All year long in all types of weather
Fishing procedures	Fishing boats travel to coastal fishing areas each morning.	Trawlers travel to the fishing grounds for up to two weeks at a time.
Processing	Fish are processed onshore, usually in small- to medium-sized plants.	Fish may be partially processed on board before being taken to large processing plants.
Lifestyle	People often live in small coastal communities; incomes earned are often low and unstable; widespread dependence on government support.	People live in larger coastal communities; incomes are higher and more stable.

△ **Fig. 21-6** *A comparison of the inshore and offshore fisheries before the 1992 ban on catching cod*

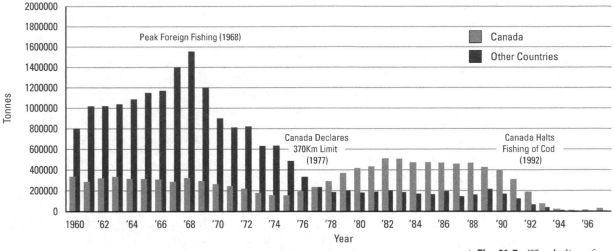

△ **Fig. 21-7** *The decline of the East Coast cod fishery*

Why the East Coast Fishery Collapsed

Many theories have been suggested to explain the serious decline in the numbers of groundfish, but no single cause is responsible. To understand what happened, keep in mind that fish are a renewable resource, and that renewable resources must be managed properly. Fish can be harvested forever *if* the number caught each year does not exceed the number reaching maturity in that year. This is a conservation technique called **sustained yield management.** The attempts to manage the fishery to maintain a sufficient number of breeding fish in eastern Canada have obviously failed. Scientists, governments, and especially those who work in the industry, are trying to discover what went wrong so that the fishery can be managed better in the future.

People have suggested five major conditions responsible for the collapse of the fishery.

1. **Overfishing** The catch allowed by the federal government each year appears to have been too high. Their scientists may have overestimated the number of fish becoming adults each year. If this, in fact, did happen, then more fish were caught than reached maturity and sustained yield management was not working.

2. **Improved Fishing Technology** After World War II, larger, more powerful, engine-driven trawlers were developed. Technological developments, such as sonar and satellite navigation systems, helped fishers to locate schools of fish faster and more accurately. Over the years, fewer and fewer fish escaped the fishing nets. Ironically, the "advances" in technology made overfishing possible.

3. **Uncontrolled Foreign Fishing** By the late 1960s, the foreign fishing fleets of countries such as Russia and Japan caught far more fish than sustained yield methods would have allowed. Countries with ocean coastlines were urging the United Nations to allow them to extend national fishing limits over the conti-

The number of adult fish that are capable of breeding is called the breeding stock. These fish must be protected if the total population of fish is to be maintained.

Politicians may not have wanted to act on the warnings of some scientists because some of the people who would lose their income might blame the politicians and not re-elect them.

At the same time, the fishing industry may have underreported the number of fish caught.

nental shelf. In this way, countries such as Canada could protect their fish stocks (Fig. 21–7).

In 1977, the UN allowed Canada to extend its control of the seas to 370 km (200 nautical miles). Foreign fishing fleets working inside this limit had to follow the Canadian restrictions.

4. **Destructive Fishing Practices** When trawlers were trying to catch one kind of fish, for example, cod, many other types of fish may have become caught in the nets. These unwanted fish, which were already dead, were usually just thrown away. Only the remaining fish were reported to the authorities as having been caught.

5. **Changes in Natural Conditions** Some people have blamed changes in environmental conditions for the decline in the fish stock. Two specific changes have been identified. First, water temperatures have dropped and ocean salinity levels have changed since the mid–1980s. The fish may have changed their migratory routes to avoid areas where these changes have occurred. Second, some people have suggested that the decline of the sealing industry in the late 1970s caused an increase in the seal population. This, in turn, reduced groundfish populations because the seals ate large quantities of a small fish called caplin, which is a major food source for cod. Seals may also be eating large amounts of cod.

nautical mile: measurement of distance used by sailors and pilots. It is equal to one minute of latitude (one-sixtieth of a degree), or about 1850 m.

salinity: saltiness of water

QUESTIONS

CHECK YOUR UNDERSTANDING

1. Describe, in detail, the conditions that have produced outstanding fishing grounds on the East Coast.

2. Your teacher will provide you with a map of the East Coast. On this map, draw the major fishing banks and currents.

3. Fully explain five major factors that may have led to the collapse of the East Coast fishery.

ANALYZE AND APPLY

4. Two ocean currents meet in the area of the Grand Banks.

a) Where does each come from and how does this affect their temperatures?

b) What climate conditions are common on the Grand Banks as a result of the meeting of these currents? (Fig. 12-7 on p. 131.)

5. a) Describe the major differences between the inshore and the offshore fishery (Fig. 21-6).

b) If you were a fisher, would you prefer to work in the inshore fishery or the offshore fishery? Explain.

c) Inshore fishing has been called a way of life, and offshore fishing a business. With specific reference to Fig. 21-6, explain what this means.

6. a) Why was the foreign cod catch so high during the 1960s and early 1970s?

   b) What effect did the introduction of the 370-km limit in 1977 have on the size of the foreign catch in Canadian waters?

7. a) Explain the conservation technique of sustained yield management as it applies to fishing.

   b) Select another industry which harvests natural resources and explain how sustained yield management can be applied to it.

THINK AND COMMUNICATE

8. a) When the Canadian government extended our territorial limits to 370 km, it expected certain effects. What effects do you think it expected for:

   i) the East Coast fish stocks

   ii) the number of people employed in the fishery (as fishers and processors)

   iii) the number of foreign vessels fishing in our waters

   iv) the amount of fish eaten by Canadians

   b) Did it create the expected results? Explain.

9. In 1995, Canada broke international laws by seizing a Spanish trawler outside Canadian territorial waters. Was Canada justified in this action? Explain your answer.

10. Some people think that, when the Atlantic fishery recovers, most of the resource should be allocated to the inshore fishery because it supports a way of life. Other people believe the offshore fishery should get most of the fish because it catches fish more efficiently and provides higher-paying jobs. With which view do you agree? Why?

THE WEST COAST FISHERY

The most important catch on the West Coast is salmon. There are five kinds of salmon: coho, chum, pink, spring (chinook), and, the most valuable of all, sockeye. The Pacific harvest also includes herring, halibut, cod, crab, tuna, shrimp, and oysters (Fig. 21-8).

Although salmon are found on both coasts, the West Coast catch has traditionally been over 400 times larger than the East Coast catch. Pacific salmon hatch in freshwater streams and swim to the Pacific Ocean where they spend their adult lives. Mature Pacific salmon leave the open sea and enter coastal waters during the summer and fall. It is here that British Columbia's large modern fishing fleet has traditionally awaited them. The salmon which escape the nets head for the same freshwater streams where they were hatched. They lay their eggs in the gravel beds of these streams which tumble out of the mountains along the coast. After spawning, both males and females die.

spawning: producing offspring

The Atlantic salmon has a similar life cycle, except that after spawning, the salmon do not die but return to the sea. They may return to the spawning grounds three or four times during their lifetime.

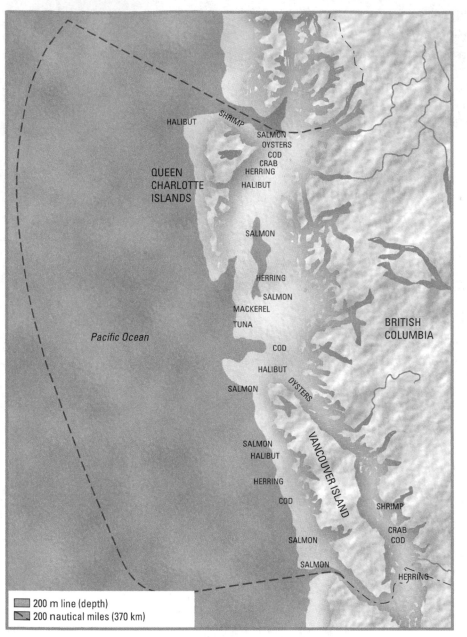

◁ **Fig. 21-8** *Canada's West Coast fishery*

The Collapse of the West Coast Fishery

The failure of the fish-management system in the Atlantic fishery caused scientists and politicians to reevaluate the handling of the West Coast fishery. Their concern was brought sharply into focus in 1994 when one million fewer salmon than estimated arrived at spawning grounds on the upper Fraser River in British Columbia. Many people are worried because any successful fish-management plan must be based on accurate esti-

More than 140 spawning runs along the coast of British Columbia no longer occur, and over 800 more are in trouble.

mates of the number of fish. They are concerned that Canada's Department of Fisheries and Oceans does not have enough data on the number of salmon to make informed decisions about how many could be caught each year. There are several possible reasons for the collapse of the West Coast salmon fishery.

1. **Overfishing** During the 1990s, Canadian and American salmon-fishing boats were catching over 800 000 tonnes of fish per year between California and Alaska. The salmon stocks could not survive this massive yearly catch, which meant that too few adult fish reached the spawning rivers. Where there was once over 100 major fish-processing plants in British Columbia, there are now fewer than 10.

2. **Changes in the Environment** What happens in the oceans is still a mystery. But global warming appears to be increasing the temperature of the Pacific Ocean. This could threaten the salmon's habitat. Salmon prefer water that is below 7°C. This temperature establishes the southern limit of the salmon's range. Northern California has already lost most of its salmon runs because of warmer water.

   If the Pacific Ocean slowly warms, the southern limit of the salmon's range will continue to move northward. This would force the salmon to move further north toward the Bering Sea, west of Alaska, where the water is cooler. Eventually, the salmon may be forced to remain in the cooler more northerly waters of the Pacific Ocean and to spawn in the rivers of Alaska rather than in the more southerly rivers of British Columbia.

3. **Lack of a Salmon Fishing Treaty** A long-standing dispute continues between Canada and the United States concerning where salmon may be caught and how much may be taken by each country. Canadian officials claim that fewer salmon, particularly coho, should be caught in order to preserve the stock. American officials in Alaska, on the other hand, claim that there is

Scientists are examining the patterns and trends in air pressure and atmospheric circulation in a search for answers to the disappearing salmon.

◁ **Fig. 21-9** *In 1997, Canadian salmon fishers were not allowed to fish but Alaskan fishers could catch as much as they wanted. To express their disapproval, some Canadian fishers surrounded an Alaskan passenger ferry and prevented it from continuing its journey.*

enough salmon and restrictions are not needed. As long as both countries cannot come to an agreement on a Pacific salmon treaty in which fishing and conservation are properly balanced, this precious resource may disappear (Fig. 21-9).

Challenges to the West Coast Fishery

As the supply of salmon decreases, there is the difficulty of balancing a limited supply of fish with a growing demand. There are three competing demands for salmon in British Columbia: commercial fishing, sport fishing, and fishing by the First Nations. In the 1980s and early 1990s, the commercial fleet caught 94% of the salmon while each of the other groups accounted for about 3%.

The demand for salmon by Aboriginal people is growing for two reasons. First, a Supreme Court decision in 1990 guaranteed the right of the First Nations to fish for their own food as well as for social and ceremonial purposes. The Court established that this use takes precedence over all other considerations except conservation. Second, the right to fish commercially is a focus of many First Nations land claims in British Columbia.

The topic of First Nations land claims is examined in more detail in Chapter 16.

The sport-fishing industry also wants a bigger share of the available salmon. The reasoning here is economic: a salmon caught by a recreational angler yields a much greater economic benefit than a salmon caught by a commercial-fishing boat.

If the First Nations and the sport-fishing industry are to gain greater shares of the fish, and the government is to ensure an adequate breeding stock, commercial fishers will have to reduce their catch. The federal government is assisting with this cutback by slowly purchasing commercial-fishing licences and fishing boats so that the number of commercial fishers is reduced.

You can read an online aquaculture magazine at: www.ioa.com/~aquamag The salmon raised on the fish farms of British Columbia are Atlantic Salmon, since this species has proven to be more successful on fish farms.

An additional challenge facing the West Coast fishery is **aquaculture**. Fish farms, which raise salmon in pens, are now producing more salmon than are caught in the wild. The value of the salmon caught by the commercial fishery is about $96 million, and the value of the salmon raised on fish farms is about $175 million. In general, farm-raised salmon can be sold more cheaply than wild salmon. This competition has made it very difficult for many people who fish for wild salmon to make enough money to stay in business.

FRESHWATER FISHERY

Canada's freshwater (inland) fisheries are located in the Great Lakes, Lake Winnipeg, Great Slave Lake, and 600 or so smaller lakes. The Great Lakes have the most important freshwater fishery, with Lake Erie as the largest producer. The major species sent to market from these lakes are whitefish, perch, pickerel, and trout.

The freshwater fisheries are much less important to the Canadian economy than those of the East or West Coast. Less than 2% of the total value of the Canadian fishery in 1996 came from inland waters. Only about 7000 people have jobs in the freshwater fishery. In spite of these small numbers, the freshwater fishery is very important to the areas where it takes place. This is especially true in northern Canada, where up to 90% of those involved in commercial fishing are Native People. For those in northern Canada, fish not only provide a cash income where jobs are scarce, but they also make up a major (and very nutritious) part of the diet.

SPORT FISHING

For most people, going fishing is simply a pleasant way to spend a summer day. They do not realize that sport fishing is a major industry that generates more money than all the commercial fishing in the country! About four million people every year fish for sport in Canadian waters. This group, which includes almost one million people from other countries (mainly the United States), spend about $7 billion on such things as boats, fishing equipment, accommodation, meals, fishing guides, and licences. About half the sport fishing by Canadians and two-thirds of that by visitors occurs in Ontario.

Ontario's Ministry of Natural Resources operates 10 fish hatcheries that produce over nine million fish for stocking over 1000 lakes and rivers. The species that are produced include walleye, coho salmon, lake trout, and whitefish.

IN CLOSING...

Canada's fishing industry is in trouble on both its Atlantic and Pacific coasts. Our problems are part of a global trend that began in the 1970s and involves too many fishing boats chasing too few fish. As a result, global fish stocks are in danger. According to a study by the World Wildlife Fund, 70 percent of the world's 200 most valuable fish stocks are either depleted or overfished. Some countries have tried to reduce overfishing by limiting the size of the catch or by restricting the amount of time boats are allowed to fish. However, there are no international laws to force countries to practice conservation methods.

Canada's fishing industry is at a crossroads. In Atlantic Canada, a renewable resource has been exploited beyond its capacity. In British

Columbia , the same thing may be happening as there are competing demands for a limited supply of fish. Changes must be made to ensure the health of both fisheries, not only because they provide employment in regions where jobs are scarce, but also because they support a lifestyle that is part of our Canadian heritage.

QUESTIONS

CHECK YOUR UNDERSTANDING

1. Describe, in detail, the factors that may have led to the collapse of the West Coast fishery.

2. What challenges are facing the West Coast fishery?

3. a) Describe Canada's freshwater fishery.

   b) Describe the challenges that are facing this fishery.

4. a) What is sport fishing?

   b) How is it important to Canada's economy?

ANALYZE AND APPLY

5. How do the concepts of a renewable resource and sustained yield management relate to:

   i) the collapse of the ground-fish fishery in Atlantic Canada

   ii) the problem of trying to meet the demand for salmon in British Columbia

THINK AND COMMUNICATE

6. In 1993, the General Motors van plant in Toronto shut down, and 4200 people were out of work. These people have not received the long-term financial support that the fishery workers on the East Coast have received over the years.

   a) Why do you think financial support varies for different groups?

   b) Should fishery workers be treated differently than other workers in Canada? Explain.

22 The Business of Farming

Farming is a business that requires a great deal of skill and effort, enough money to purchase property and equipment, and considerable luck in terms of weather and market conditions. Play the game using the instructions on pp. 262–263 and the gameboard on p. 264 to appreciate some of the difficulties associated with farming.

INTRODUCTION

How important is agriculture to Canada? Yearly, agriculture contributes more than $11 billion to the economy (GDP). The food and beverage industry contributes another $17 billion. When all the people involved in the growing, processing, transportation, and selling of food are counted, about 1 job in 5 is related to the agricultural sector of the economy. Agricultural products also play an important part in our trade with other countries. Canada has a large surplus in agricultural exports. Most of this surplus is a result of the export of grains and vegetable oil products from the Prairies.

Canadians rely on farmers to produce food that remains relatively inexpensive after the costs of transportation, processing, and profit are added. In the 1950s, Canadians spent about 25% of their income on

For more information about agriculture, check aceis.agr.ca/agriweb/link.htm

Only the Prairie provinces export a greater value of agricultural products than they import.

The Farming Game

Wheat Shafts and Pitch Forks

- Play with a partner.
- Game Equipment: game board in text, two dice, two playing pieces
- Object of the Game: To be a successful Saskatchewan wheat farmer

Playing the Game

1. Toss the dice to see which player will play first. The player who rolls the highest number will begin.
2. All players begin at the square marked "0."
3. Players toss the two dice in turn and move their pieces according to the numbers shown on the dice. Each player has only one turn at a time.
4. <u>Wheat Shaft squares:</u> If a player lands on a square with the bottom of a wheat shaft, the player moves up the shaft and places his or her playing piece in the square at the top of the shaft.
5. <u>Pitch Fork squares:</u> If a player lands on a square with the end of the handle of a pitch fork, the player moves down the pitch fork and places his or her playing piece in the square at the bottom of the pitch fork.

Winning the Game

Your goal is to reach the final square. You do <u>not</u> have to roll an exact number to reach this last square, but you must reach it within <u>16 turns</u>. Once you have reached the end, you must perform calculations to determine how much profit you earned. The winner of the game is the person who earns the greatest profit.

If you did not harvest your crop in time, too bad! Hope you do better next year — if you have the money to plant.

Congratulations if you were able to harvest your crop before the winter frosts hit. It is now time to see how you have done financially. Your profit for the year depends on two factors: the income you collect for selling your wheat and your expenses (**profit = income − expenses**). Income can be calculated by multiplying three things: the number of tonnes of wheat you grow on each hectare (your yield), the price you receive per tonne, and the number of hectares of land you have (in this game, we will assume your farm is 170 ha, which would be an average Saskatchewan wheat farm). The calculations below are based on the actual yields and prices for a 25-year period ending in 1997.

1. YIELDS

Yields vary enormously from one year to another, largely because of unpredictable growing conditions. To determine your yield, roll two dice and check Fig. A to see how you did. Record this amount in your notebook.

Fig. A Roll	Percentage of years with this result	Yield (tonnes per hectare)
2	3 %	0.88
5	11 %	1.21
6 or 11	20 %	1.43
7 or 9	29 %	1.65
3, 4, 8, or 10	34 %	1.87
12	3 %	2.09

Fig. B

Roll	Percentage of years with this result	Price ($ per tonne)	Reason for result
8, 9, or 11	32 %	$ 110	excellent growing conditions all over the world; yields high everywhere
2 or 3	8 %	$ 130	European Community increases subsidies to its farmers causing more hectares to be planted
7 or 12	19 %	$ 150	an average year in most respects
5 or 6	25 %	$ 170	Canada gives much wheat to feed those suffering in African famine
4	8 %	$ 190	many American farmers grow less wheat this year; other crops look more profitable
10	8 %	$ 210	widespread crop failures in many countries

2. PRICES

Different market conditions produce an entirely different price. To see what the average wheat price is this year, roll two dice and check Fig. B. The events listed in this table are typical of the sort of things that could affect world wheat prices in a particular year. Record your price in your notebook.

3. CALCULATE YOUR INCOME

Income = Yield x Price x Size of farm

4. Your income might seem like quite a lot of money but remember that you have not considered your expenses for the year. The direct costs of growing your wheat are listed in Fig. C.

a) Calculate the total cost per hectare.

b) Calculate the cost to farm your 170 hectares.

c) Determine the profit for your year.

Fig. C

Item	Cost per hectare ($)
Seed	15.73
Fertilizers	32.45
Herbicides, insecticides	33.02
Fuel and repairs for machinery	27.69
Labour costs	8.80
Crop insurance	9.88
Utilities and miscellaneous	4.00
Bank interest	6.27

5. Look at the list of expenses again. Try to identify at least three significant, long-term costs that are not included in this list. What might this say about how much profit can be made growing wheat? (Note that most other forms of farming have similar prospects for profitability.)

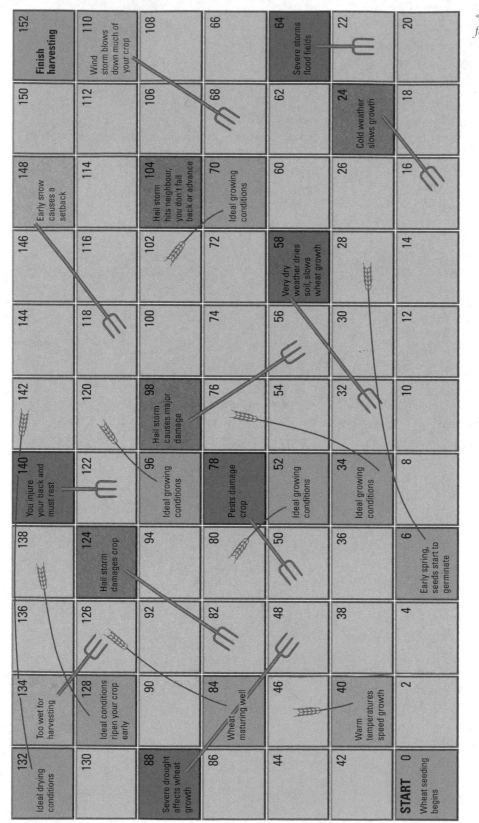

◁ **Fig. 22-1** *"If I were a farmer…"*

food; today Canadians spend only about 11% on food, including meals eaten outside the home. There are many problems facing Canadian agriculture that could force a greater percentage of income to be spent on food. Whether these problems can be solved will depend upon the attitudes of Canadians toward this vital industry.

Canadians spend a smaller percentage of their income on food than people in most countries.

LAND: THE BASIC RESOURCE

The American writer Mark Twain once wrote: "Buy land, they've stopped making it!" His humorous advice has a serious side. Most Canadians, especially farmers, value ownership of land. Land is a **renewable resource** in the sense that, if properly used, it can support new crops year after year. On the other hand, land can be classified as a **non-renewable resource** because, as Mark Twain reminds us, there is a limited amount of it available — especially land that is suitable for farming. If land is seriously damaged because of bad farming practices, or if it is paved over to build a town or highway, it can no longer be used for agriculture. In this sense, it is a non-renewable resource.

During the 1960s and 1970s, the federal and provincial governments surveyed most of the land of southern Canada — 2.5 million km^2. Their objective was to determine the **land capability** for agriculture. The results were published as part of the Canada Land Inventory (CLI). The survey divides Canada's land into seven classes; each class indicates the

surveyed: examined and measured the quality of the land for agriculture

Class 1: Land has deep soils and is excellent for farming. It has no climatic or land limitations. 0.5% of Canada's land area.

Class 2: Land is very good farmland. It has no serious climatic or land limitations. 1.8% of Canada's land area.

Class 3: Land is good farmland but has some climatic or land limitations that make some farming activities impossible. 2.7% of Canada's land area.

Class 4: Land is at the "break-even" point for commercial agriculture because of a short growing season, poor soil conditions, or other significant limitations. 2.7% of Canada's land area.

Class 5: Land has serious limitations for agriculture, such as a very short growing season, hilly landscape, thin soil, or poor drainage. Class 5 land may be used for grazing or producing hay. 3.7% of Canada's land area.

Class 6: Land is similar to Class 5 except that the limitations are more severe. These lands can only be used for rough grazing, crops cannot be grown successfully. 1.8% of Canada's land area.

Class 7: Land has no capability for farming or was not classified. 86.8% of Canada's land area.

△ **Fig. 22-2** *The Canadian Land Inventory created seven categories of agricultural land for southern Canada. The land further north was not considered suitable for agriculture.*

◁ **Fig. 22-3** *On these two photos, the numbers refer to capability classes, while the letters refer to the reasons for limitations. T stands for topography or hilliness, W stands for wetness, and E stands for erosion.*

land's suitability for agriculture (Fig. 22-2). The land capability classification system is very useful for land-use planning. For example, Classes 1 to 6 indicate the land that may be used for some form of agriculture. Only Classes 1 to 3, however, are considered to be good farmland capable of regularly producing cultivated crops, and only Class 1 is considered to be excellent for farming. Fig. 22-3 shows how this land classification system can be applied to typical farming areas.

Canada has a total land area of approximately 921 500 000 ha — a vast amount of land. Yet according to the Canada Land Inventory, only 13% of this area (Classes 1 to 6) is suitable for any form of agriculture (Fig. 22-4). In fact, the amount of good farmland (Classes 1 to 3) in Canada is about equal to the amount of good farmland in the state of California!

Other surveys were done to determine the land capability for forestry, outdoor recreation, and wildlife.

The total land area of Canada is smaller than its total area because the area occupied by freshwater lakes is not included.

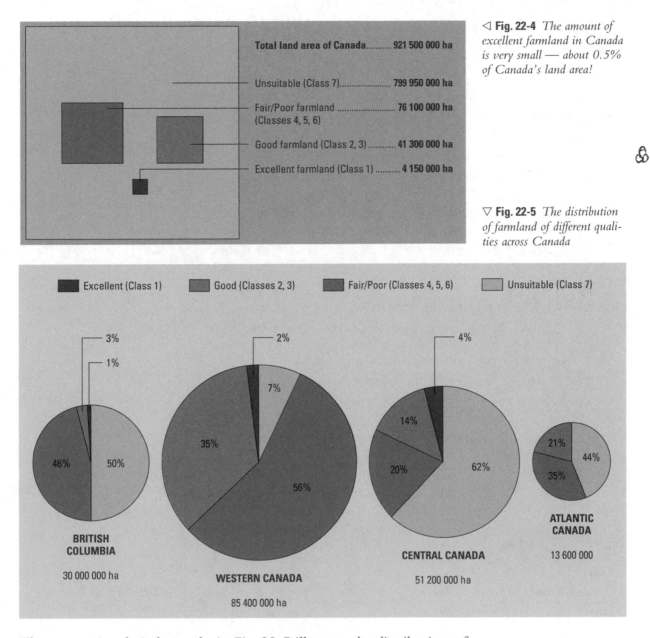

Total land area of Canada..........	921 500 000 ha
Unsuitable (Class 7).....................	799 950 000 ha
Fair/Poor farmland .... (Classes 4, 5, 6)	76 100 000 ha
Good farmland (Class 2, 3)	41 300 000 ha
Excellent farmland (Class 1)	4 150 000 ha

◁ **Fig. 22-4** *The amount of excellent farmland in Canada is very small — about 0.5% of Canada's land area!*

▽ **Fig. 22-5** *The distribution of farmland of different qualities across Canada*

Excellent (Class 1)   Good (Classes 2, 3)   Fair/Poor (Classes 4, 5, 6)   Unsuitable (Class 7)

BRITISH COLUMBIA
30 000 000 ha
3%, 1%, 46%, 50%

WESTERN CANADA
85 400 000 ha
2%, 7%, 35%, 56%

CENTRAL CANADA
51 200 000 ha
4%, 14%, 20%, 62%

ATLANTIC CANADA
13 600 000
21%, 35%, 44%

The proportional circle graphs in Fig. 22-5 illustrate the distribution of land capability across Canada. Although Canada is the second largest country in the world, its agricultural land is limited, and much of that land has been used up or is threatened by urban development.

THE CHANGING FARM

A hundred years ago, farm work was accomplished by horses pulling plows and wagons, and by human muscle for most other chores. Since that time, many changes have occurred in the number, size, and operation methods of farms. By completing the following activity, you will be able to determine some of these changes.

Use a spreadsheet or a calculator to perform the following calculations using the information in Fig. 22-6.

1. a) Calculate the total amount of farm land for each time period by multiplying A by B.

    b) Plot these results against the years in a line graph. Do a similar graph with the number of farms.

    c) Compare the amount of farmland to the number of farms between 1931 and 1991. What might explain these changes?

2. a) Calculate the number of workers per farm for each time period by dividing C by A.

    b) Plot these results in a line graph.

    c) Why do you think this pattern exists?

3. a) Calculate the average number of hectares per worker for each time period by dividing B by the number of workers per farm that you calculated in question 2a.

    b) Plot these results in a line graph.

    c) What do you think has caused the change since 1971?

4. The amount of mechanized (self-propelled) farm equipment changed considerably during the 1900s. The number of tractors and combines was 114 000 in 1931, 705 000 in 1961, and 842 000 in 1991.

    a) Create a sketch graph to show the amount of mechanized farm equipment used over this time period.

    b) What has been the trend? Do you think this will continue in the future? Explain.

Remember to put the years on the x axis since they represent the independent variable.

Year	A Number of Farms	B Average Farm Size (ha)	C Number of Workers
1901	511 000	50	718 000
1911	683 000	65	928 000
1921	711 000	80	1 025 000
1931	729 000	91	1 118 000
1941	733 000	96	1 074 000
1951	623 000	113	826 000
1961	481 000	145	649 000
1971	366 000	188	510 000
1981	318 000	207	508 000
1991	280 000	242	533 000

◁ **Fig. 22-6** *Changes in Canadian agriculture*

TYPES OF FARMING

Farms differ widely across Canada in terms of their size and products (Fig. 22-7). The type of farming that takes place in a particular region is determined by natural and economic factors.

The most important natural factors affecting the type of farming are the fertility of the soil, the amount of precipitation, and the length of the **growing season**.

Economic factors that have an impact on what type of farming will take place include:

- Cost of land: for example, if the farmland is expensive, high value agricultural goods will need to be produced.

- Transportation costs: for example, if a farm is close to its markets, perishable products such as vegetables and milk can be produced. If a farm is far from its market, less perishable crops such as grain or cheese make more sense.

- Competition: for example if there is an oversupply of products, prices will drop and reduce farm incomes.

Farmers must take both the natural and economic factors into account when they decide whether to practise extensive or intensive farming. **Intensive farming** is common in densely populated areas such as Ontario and Québec and around major cities where land values are high. Farms tend to be small, but require large investments in labour and machinery to produce high profits per hectare. Intensive farming is commonly used for producing fruits, vegetables, dairy, poultry, and hogs. Many of these products are perishable and need to be processed or transported to market quickly.

Extensive farming is usually done in areas where the population density is lower and land is plentiful and less expensive. Farms tend to be large so lower yields per hectare will still allow a profit. Extensive farming is usually highly mechanized and requires few workers compared to intensive farming. Farmers raise either crops or animals, or both. Extensive farming is common in the Prairie provinces and parts of Ontario and Québec that are located away from major cities. It includes cattle farming and ranching, grain and oil seed growing, and mixed farming. Since these farms are located away from major markets, their products are usually less perishable or processed quickly.

The growing season is the number of days per year in which the average temperature is above 5.6° C. This is the temperature at which plants start to grow.

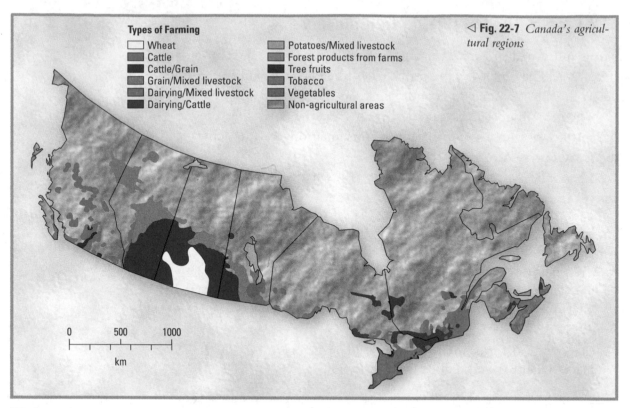

Types of Farming
- Wheat
- Cattle
- Cattle/Grain
- Grain/Mixed livestock
- Dairying/Mixed livestock
- Dairying/Cattle
- Potatoes/Mixed livestock
- Forest products from farms
- Tree fruits
- Tobacco
- Vegetables
- Non-agricultural areas

◁ **Fig. 22-7** *Canada's agricultural regions*

0   500   1000
km

Wheat

- The wheat and grain farms of Saskatchewan, Alberta, and Manitoba are large, highly-specialized, and mechanized.
- The Ontario farms are also specialized and mechanized but much smaller.
- The cool wet springs and dry hot summers on the Prairies produce high quality hard wheat for bread and durum wheat for pasta.
- The yield per hectare in the Prairies is low compared to the more humid southern Ontario, but the large prairie farms produce 90% of Canada's wheat.

Beef Cattle and Grain

- In the dry grassland areas of Alberta, Saskatchewan, Manitoba, and British Columbia, large ranches raise most of Canada's beef cattle.
- Large ranches are needed because the cattle are raised in areas too dry or too hilly for wheat or grain crops.
- In the more moist areas of the Prairies, grain crops and other livestock are raised.
- The cattle are either sold before winter, or are fed grains during the winter, before sale in the spring.
- Oil seed crops such as canola and sunflowers, are becoming more popular in the Prairies since they are seen as healthier than animal fat or coconut oil when used in salad oils, shortening and margarine.
- Ontario and Québec farmers raise cattle on smaller farms for local markets.

Dairy and Livestock (beef cattle, sheep, hogs, poultry)

- Dairy products are very perishable and must be shipped quickly to urban markets or processed into cheese and butter.
- The majority of dairy farms are located in Québec and Ontario not far from major population centres.
- Dairy farming is an intensive activity involving daily feeding and milking of cattle and large investments in barns, feed, and milking and refrigeration equipment.
- Livestock is often raised farther from populated centres.
- The livestock feed on grass in pastures during the summer but in winter they must be fed.
- Many farmers grow their own hay and grains for winter feed.

Fruits and Vegetables

- Intensive farming techniques are commonly used for the production of fruits and vegetables.
- Market gardening involves growing perishable vegetables for nearby urban markets.
- The fertile soils near Montréal, the well-drained soils of the Fraser delta near Vancouver, and the peat soils of Holland Marsh north of Toronto produce lettuce, onions, celery, and carrots.
- Since land near urban areas is expensive, high yields per hectare are required.
- Tender fruits (peaches, sweet cherries, apricots, and grapes) are grown in the Annapolis Valley of Nova Scotia, the Niagara fruit belt of Ontario, and the Okanagan Valley of British Columbia. Tender fruit are more likely to be damaged by low temperatures than apples, plums, pears, and sour cherries.
- These areas are unique in Canada because they have fertile, well-drained sandy soils, mild winters, and nearby water bodies that reduce the likelihood of late spring and early fall frosts that could damage the buds or fruit.
- The highly perishable fruit must be processed or marketed quickly.

QUESTIONS

CHECK YOUR UNDERSTANDING

1. How can land be considered both a renewable and non-renewable resource?

2. a) What is the Canada Land Inventory?

   b) In your own words, outline the characteristics of each of the seven land classes.

3. In your notebook, construct and complete a chart similar to Fig. 22-8.

▽ **Fig. 22-8**

	Intensive Agriculture	Extensive Agriculture
Size of Farms		
Use of Labour/Machinery		
Types of Farming		

ANALYZE AND APPLY

4. a) Examine photograph A in Fig. 22-3.

   i. What is meant by a 2T and a 3W classification?

   ii. Explain why one part of the field has a 3W classification while the other has a 2T classification.

   iii. Why does the land in the distance have a 5T classification?

   b) Examine photograph B in Fig. 22-3.

   i. Why does the land in the foreground have a 6TE classification?

   ii. Why is some of the land classified 7T? What could this land be used for?

▽ **Fig. 22-9** *Provincial agricultural production*

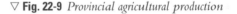

Value of Provincial Agricultural Production, 1995

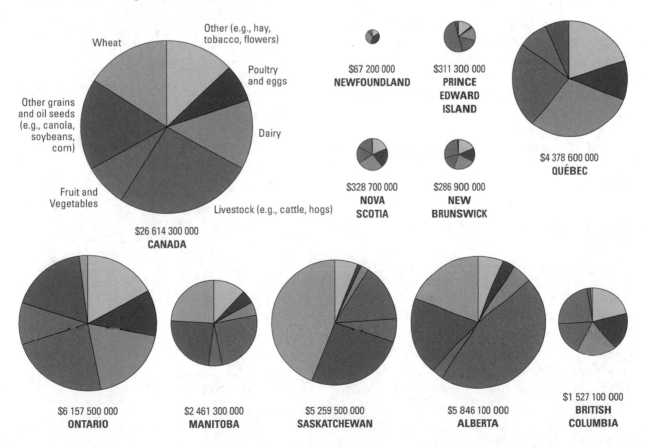

▽ **Fig. 22-10**

Province	Value of Farm Production	Location(s) of Farming Area(s)	Major Types of Farming

iii. Farmer A owns the land in photograph A while Farmer B owns the land in photograph B. What type of farming could each do with the land they have? Which one would find it easier to farm their land?

5. Examine Fig. 22-4.

   a) How many hectares of land can be used for some form of agriculture in Canada? (Hint: Classes 1 to 6)

   b) What percentage of Canada's total land area does this represent?

6. Examine Fig. 22-5.

   a) Rank the regions in terms of the amount of good and excellent farmland found in each.

   b) Rank the regions in terms of the amount of land that is fair/poor.

   c) What do these rankings suggest about the agricultural potential of each region?

7. Fig. 22-9 shows the value of farm production by province for 1995.

   a) Calculate the percentage of the total value produced by each province.

   b) Construct a pie graph to show the percentages produced by each province.

c) Which province produces the highest value and which produces the lowest? Explain the reason for the highest and lowest value.

d) How does the value of production relate to the availability of good farmland? (Refer back to Fig. 22-5.)

8. Construct a chart similar to Fig. 22-10. Use the map in Fig. 22-7 and information in Fig. 22-9 to complete this chart.

9. Why is agriculture in the Prairies mainly extensive wheat and cattle farming but in Ontario and Québec much of the farming is intensive vegetable, fruit, and dairy farming?

THINK AND COMMUNICATE

10. The agricultural land classification system was done in the 1960s. What do you think has happened to the amount of agricultural land since that time? What effect might this have on Canada's future food supply?

11. What would life be like for a family whose farm consisted only of Class 6 and 7 land? What options would they have?

AGRICULTURAL ISSUES TODAY

The Business of Farming

In the 1880s, about 80% of Canadian families farmed the land. Today the number stands at less than 3% ! What has caused this staggering change?

   A hundred years ago, farmers used horses and their own muscle power to complete the many activities involved in running a farm. Farmers were only able to manage small farms of about 50 ha in size. Today, one or two people can operate a farm over 200 ha in size with the help of modern equipment. Increased **mechanization** has brought about an increase in the size of farms and a decline in their numbers.

The long, irregular hours and low incomes associated with farming have caused many people to leave farming. Increasingly, the children of farmers do not take up farming but seek other opportunities in other occupations. The result is that the average age of farmers is higher than that of workers in most other jobs. More than half of Canada's farmers are over 45 years of age. As they reach retirement, who will buy their farms? Young people wishing to become farmers may buy some, but few young people can afford the capital cost of buying a farm.

The start-up costs for farming are very high — from $500 000 to more than $1 million. In addition, annual costs for veterinary care, pesticides, equipment purchases, vehicle repairs, and seeds make farming a high-debt business. Farmers must borrow money from banks to maintain operations until their crops or animals are sold. If the prices for their farm products do not increase faster than their cost of production, debt or bankruptcy may result. Farmers do not have control over most of their costs, for example, the price of oil or the interest rate of their mortgage. Most do not even have control over the price of their products. For example, in the late 1990s, the price paid to farmers for hogs was less than half the cost of raising the animals. Even with the best planning, their efforts may not lead to success.

In many parts of the world, including Canada, farming is carried on increasingly by large **agribusiness** companies. Two types of such companies include cooperatives and private/public companies. Several farmers may form a farming cooperative, which is run like a business. Each farmer owns shares in the cooperative and receives the benefits from it. Equipment is purchased by the cooperative and used on a number of farms. Pooling money and sharing equipment reduces the cost of operation for each member. Profits are divided according to how many shares each farmer holds.

Another type of agribusiness involves producing food by large companies, often multinational corporations. The farmers may own their own land but raise livestock or grow crops that belong to the company. Farmers may live in towns, but go to work on different parcels of land owned by the company.

Sometimes the companies control several parts of the process: from developing seeds to retailing the final product. For example, large companies may develop seeds that are planted on farms they own. The produce is transported in their own trucks to processing plants they own, and then distributed through their own facilities. This **vertical integration** allows companies to make a profit at each stage of the operation.

Remember what you learned in the farming game.

To learn more about careers in farming and the agri-food industry, check www.cfa-fca.ca/careers/index.html

Damaging the Land

The most important agricultural resource is soil — the top portion of the land. Soil is a renewable resource because if it is used properly, it can be used over again to produce food. Over the past century, however, much of our soil, and our farmland, has been damaged by poor farming practices. Leaching occurs when soil loses its nutrients through excessive irrigation. Also, the repeated use of heavy equipment can compact soil so that it loses its ability to hold the water and air needed for plant growth. Another problem is erosion; when trees and ground cover are cleared, the soil erodes in the face of water and wind action. Chemical damage is also cause for concern. Soils may be contaminated with salts, chemicals from spraying, or dangerous **heavy metals** as a result of pollution.

EROSION

Damage to farmland is an important issue in all regions of the country, but the type of damage varies from place to place. In British Columbia, erosion is a particular problem. On the Fraser River Delta, near Vancouver, the soil does not freeze in the mild winter so heavy winter rains easily wash it away. Greater use of winter cover crops would reduce this soil loss.

In the semi-arid southern Prairie provinces, where most of Canada's grain is grown, the soil is easily damaged by certain farming techniques. One such technique, called **summer fallowing** was supposed to help the soil store scarce water, control weeds, and restore soil fertility. Crops are planted one year, but in the second year the fields are plowed and left bare. Recent studies indicate, however, that this method actually causes increased erosion, a reduction in fertility, and a buildup of harmful salts. During the fallow year, winds often blow the topsoil away. The lack of covering vegetation reduces the soil's fertility, and salts deep in the earth are drawn upward as surface water evaporates. Today, many fields are white from salts that have made the soil infertile as a result of summer fallowing.

One effective soil conservation method that is being used across Canada is **no-till cropping**. The stubble left from the previous year's crop forms a cover that holds the soil in place and protects it from wind erosion. Stubble also traps the snow in the fields, and helps build up soil moisture. This moisture reduces the buildup of salts in dry climates. No-till is cost effective because plowing is not required. In spring, seed is planted in the unplowed ground. The farmer disturbs the soil as little as possible and uses some chemicals to control the weeds.

Soil erosion was most serious during the 1930s in the Prairies when a series of dry years, poor farming practices, and high winds combined to allow millions of tonnes of topsoil to blow away. High winds still blow the precious topsoil from the dry portions of southern Alberta and Saskatchewan.

No-till cropping is also known as conservation tillage.

In southern Ontario and Québec, there are many similar problems: water and wind erosion, loss of organic matter, compacting from heavy farm machinery, and high soil acid levels.

In the Atlantic provinces, the most serious threat to good soil conditions is water erosion as a result of a wet climate. **Contour plowing** can reduce this damage. Plowing is done across hilly fields, rather than up and down the slope of a hill. In this way, each crop row prevents water from running down the slope and taking the topsoil with it.

CONTAMINATION

Farmers use chemical **fertilizers**, **herbicides**, and **pesticides** to increase their yields, and therefore their profits. Although chemical fertilizers, such as phosphates and nitrates, increase crop yields, they can have an adverse affect on water bodies. When they are carried by run-off into lakes, they can cause excessive growth of algae. This removes oxygen from the water, and in turn affects the health of fish.

Herbicides are used to kill weeds. Crops will grow more easily if they do not have to compete with weeds for sunlight and water. Some weed killers can be harmful to wildlife, and in high concentrations, to humans.

Pesticides kill insects that destroy fruit, vegetables, grains, and trees. Unfortunately, they also kill many useful species of insects. Useful species are the enemies of harmful pests, and their elimination may upset the natural balance in the ecosystem. A disruption in the ecosystem may actually cause the pest population to increase. Sometimes insects develop a resistance to chemicals, and stronger pesticides are then needed to control them.

ecosystem: a system in which living things and their environment function and interact

In addition to damage from use of chemicals in agriculture, farm land in central Canada is exposed to harmful chemicals from smokestacks and heavy metals from vehicle exhaust. Many chemicals are slow to break down, and stay in the environment for years. Although it is difficult for farmers to deal with external contaminants, they have become more aware of the problems of using chemicals in food production, and generally try not to use more than necessary.

Sustainable Agriculture

Sustainable agriculture refers to agricultural production that can be maintained without harming the environment. What is being done to achieve this goal? Specific solutions are being sought for each problem.

For example:

- large, lightweight tires which do not damage wet soil are available for tractors
- a variety of farming methods that use natural fertilizers and avoid chemicals for controlling weeds and pests have been developed
- proper cultivation practices such as crop rotation are encouraged to improve soil fertility. For example, legumes (peas and beans) may be rotated with corn to renew nitrogen in the soil, and to improve soil structure

Sustainable agriculture encourages pest control techniques that are aimed at eliminating or reducing the use of agricultural chemicals. Biological control is an effective method of controlling pests without chemicals. One example of this is the spraying of "enemy" bacteria on cabbage worms to control their spread. Another is the sterilization of male insects by radiation. They are released back into the environment so that after mating with the sterilized male, the female lays unfertilized eggs. Since many of these techniques are expensive and not guaranteed to work, most farmers feel that chemicals must be part of their farming practices at least for the present. Proponents of sustainable agriculture state that if farmers are going to continue to use pesticides, they should use them only when an insect outbreak has occurred, and then only on the affected area. In the past, farmers would often spray for pests "just in case."

Loss of Farmland

Most of Canada's best farmland is located within 80 km of the 23 largest cities. This is not surprising if you remember that most of these now-large cities were established in the first place because of the excellent agricultural land that surrounded them. In fact, the view from the top of the CN Tower in Toronto encompasses about 37% of Canada's Class 1 land and about 25% of its Class 2 land. Most of this land has now been converted to urban uses.

To replace each hectare of this excellent land, farmers must use several hectares of poorer quality land elsewhere to produce the same quantity of crops. In some cases, this cannot be done at all. Some of the land that is used for orchards and vegetable-growing cannot be replaced because suitable land and climate conditions just do not exist elsewhere in Canada.

As a city expands, the surrounding farmland becomes very valuable. Farmers must choose between continuing a business that pays poorly or making a great deal of money by selling their land to companies that will convert the land to urban uses like housing and factories. Sometimes, speculators buy land in the hope that they will make money by selling it to people who wish to build homes and factories.

Since the Inventory was done in the 1960s, much of this land has been urbanized. It is estimated that for every 1000 people who are added to a city, 72 ha of land are used.

speculator: a person who buys farmland near a city to make a profit when the land is needed for urban growth and its price goes up

Some people have suggested that land use should be restricted so that the present amount of farmland would remain in production. It would also keep the price of agricultural land more stable since it could be sold only for farming, and not for purposes of urban development. The farmer who wishes to sell, however, would never be able to benefit from the land's increased value. Land often represents a farmer's retirement savings. If farmers are prevented from selling their land for the highest possible value, how will they survive in their retirement? Also, should farmers be restricted from selling their land when others can sell their land for profit?

Urban expansion has a harmful effect on surrounding farming communities. The impact could be lessened if the expansion were controlled, for instance, by permitting building only on poorer quality farmland. Much farmland could be saved if cities expanded with the creation of communities that are concentrated in certain areas and less spread out. So far, however, government has been ineffective in preventing the loss of valuable farmland.

QUESTIONS

CHECK YOR UNDERSTANDING

1. a) What factors cause people to leave farming?
   b) Why is it so difficult for young people to go into farming?
2. Explain what is meant by the term "agribusiness." Use examples.
3. Read the section "Damaging the Land." Construct a chart similar to the one in Fig. 22-11 in your notebook. Fill in the information under each heading.

   Note: In your chart, you will require more than one line to write the information about each location.

4. Describe how chemicals are used in agriculture.
5. a) What is meant by sustainable agriculture?
   b) What can farmers do to achieve sustainable agriculture?

ANALYZE AND APPLY

6. "When our best farmland is lost to other uses, we can develop land elsewhere to replace it." What is wrong with this point of view?
7. a) As a city expands, why does the surrounding farmland become more valuable?
   b) What problems are created by urban expansion?

Location	Kinds of Damage	Cause of Damage	Preventative Measures
British Columbia			
Southern Prairies			
Southern Ontario & Québec			
Atlantic Canada			

△ **Fig. 22-11**

c) What can be done to reduce these problems?

THINK AND COMMUNICATE

8. Would you be willing to pay more for your food if it were to cost more to produce using some sustainable agriculture methods? Explain.

9. "If Canadian farmers were unable to grow enough food to feed Canadians, we could become dependent on other countries for our food supplies." What do you think about this possibility? Fully explain your opinions.

10. When farmers face difficulties because of damaging weather conditions or poor market conditions, should the government provide financial support so the farmers don't go out of business? Why or why not?

23 Our Forest Resources

STUDY GUIDE

By the end of this chapter, you will be able to:

- identify and describe Canada's forest regions
- understand the economic importance of forests, how trees are harvested, and what they are used for
- identify and discuss key forestry issues
- understand the concept of sustained yield forest management

Key Terms

commercial forest	mixed forest	selective cutting
non-commercial forest	clear-cutting	acid precipitation
boreal forest	shelterwood logging	silviculture

There are different viewpoints on how our forests should be managed and used (Fig. 23-1). Which one is correct? How can we harvest the forests for products that we need, and at the same time protect the forest environment? The answer to this question is complex. We can gain some understanding, however, if we examine the nature, importance, and use of the forests, and learn how **sustained yield forest management** can be achieved.

To compare viewpoints about B.C. forests, look at an industry view at www.cofi.org and an environmental view at www.ecotrustcan.org

◁ **Fig. 23-1** *Forest companies and environmental groups focus on different goals.*

New Pulp and Paper Mill Will Earn Company Millions of Dollars and Bring 500 New Jobs to Community

Nau biidoj pripensis Kwarko. malbela telefonoj trinkis la vojoj, Ludvi

Protesters Block Logging Road to Stop the Cutting of Old Growth Forest

Kvin tre pura kalkuliloj sed ses telefonoj tuxis multaj vere vojoj kalkuliloj

FOREST FACTS

How large are the forests of Canada? Imagine driving at 100 km/hr for 12 hours per day. It would take you more than four days to cross the continuous band of forest that stretches from British Columbia to Newfoundland. Forests cover close to half (4 187 820 km², or 42%) of Canada's total area. This is an area greater than the total area of 15 western European nations combined! Only Russia (8 196 000 km²) and Brazil (5 022 080 km²), have more forests than Canada.

What kinds of trees fill our forests? 63% are composed of coniferous trees, that is, cone-bearing trees with needle leaves, such as pine and spruce. Deciduous trees — those that lose their leaves every year, like poplar and white birch trees — account for 22% of the forests, and the remaining 15% are mixed.

CHARACTERISTICS OF FORESTS

Fig. 23-2 shows the extent of Canada's **commercial** and **non-commercial forests**. Commercial forests are those which have trees that can be harvested profitably. These forests exist in the warmer, wetter areas of Canada where trees grow large relatively quickly. Because these forests are near roads, railways, and waterways, their timber can be easily shipped

In Canada, a tree may take 80 years to reach the size when it may be profitably harvested, while in many other countries a tree may only need 20 years to reach a similar point.

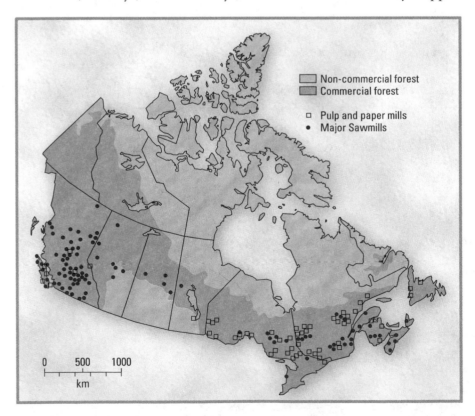

◁ **Fig. 23-2** *Canada's commercial and non-commercial forests and the location of sawmills and paper mills*

to markets in Canada and abroad. At the present time, only half of Canada's productive forests are accessible by road and can be logged.

In contrast, non-commercial forests are those that are unlikely to be cut down for industrial use. They exist on the northern fringes of the forest regions where temperatures and precipitation levels are too low to allow a lot of trees to grow quickly or at all. These forests are too far from Canadian and export markets to make the timber transportation costs economical.

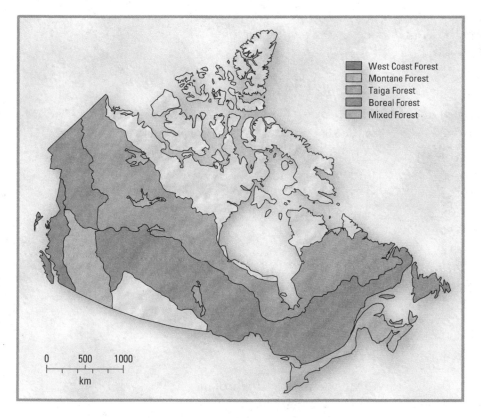

◁ **Fig. 23-3** *Forest regions of Canada*

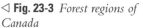

West Coast Forest
Montane Forest
Taiga Forest
Boreal Forest
Mixed Forest

This activity may be done using a calculator or a spreadsheet. It may also be completed as a GIS activity if your school has ArcVoyager.

1. In which provinces and territories is each forest region located (see Fig. 23-3 and 23-4)?

Answer the following questions using the information in Fig. 23-4.

2. a) Proportional circles have areas that are proportional to the value they represent. Draw proportional circles for the total area in each region on the ecozone map of Canada provided by your teacher.

If you are using ArcVoyager to do this activity, your teacher will give you complete instructions.

See Chapter 8 to learn about drawing proportional circle graphs.

b) Within each proportional circle, create a pie graph to show the amount of commercial forest, non-commercial forest, and non-forested land.

c) In which regions does the commercial forest occupy more than 45% of the total land area? Suggest reasons for this.

3. Examine the Commercial Forest column.

a) For each forest region, calculate the percentage of the total forest land that is occupied by commercial forest.

b) In which regions are the highest and lowest percentages located? Suggest reasons for this difference.

c) Which forest region contains the largest percentage of commercial forest? Explain why.

Forest Regions	Total Area (000 ha)	Total Forest Land (000 ha)	Commercial Forest (000 ha)	Non-Commercial Forest (000 ha)	Non-Forested (000 ha)
1. Boreal	314 877	229 711	153 808	75 903	85 166
2. Taiga	264 060	117 900	29 411	88 488	146 160
3. Montane Forest	49 211	34 857	32 129	2728	14 354
4. Mixed Forest	39 818	19 688	18 872	815	20 130
5. West Coast Forest	21 898	10 057	8563	1492	11 841
6. Arctic	259 386	3286	9	3277	256 100
7. Prairies	47 811	2085	1778	307	45 726
TOTAL	997 061	417 584	244 570	173 010	579 477

△ **Fig. 23-4** *Forest statistics*

Canada's Commercial Forest Regions

Forests in different parts of Canada vary greatly. This diversity provides a wide range of environments that can be used in different ways by wildlife, tourists, and people who enjoy nature. This diversity also provides Canada's forest industry with the raw materials from which a wide range of goods can be produced. Fig. 23-3 shows Canada's main forest regions. Each is quite distinctive. The descriptions that follow identify the five regions in which most of Canada's commercial forestry is located.

BOREAL FOREST REGION

(found in Boreal Shield, Boreal Plains, and Boreal Cordillera Ecozones)

• by far the largest

• mainly coniferous (**softwood**) trees of which black spruce is the most common; other important species include white spruce,

softwood: the wood of conifers such as pine or spruce that is easily sawn

balsam fir, jack pine, cedar, and tamarack; deciduous trees like white birch and poplar are also common

- tree growth slow due to long winters and low precipitation
- Since small trees are most common here, pulp and paper production, which uses smaller logs, tends to be more important than lumber production.

TAIGA FOREST REGION

(found in the Taiga Plains, Taiga Shield, Hudson Plains, and Taiga Cordillera Ecozones)

- stunted trees due to thin soils, cool temperatures, short growing season, and areas of permafrost
- coniferous trees, such as black spruce, white spruce, Jack pine; some deciduous trees such as poplar and trembling aspen
- Since most of this forest is inaccessible and far from markets, only small parts are logged.

WEST COAST FOREST REGION

(found in Pacific Maritime Ecozone)

- most productive forest in Canada
- temperate rainforest grows on the western slopes of the coastal mountains
- abundant relief precipitation, moderate temperatures, and long growing season cause Douglas fir, sitka spruce, western red cedar, and western hemlock to grow larger than any other trees in the country
- volume of wood, per hectare, highest in Canada

MONTANE FOREST REGION

(found in Montane Cordillera Ecozone)

- lower precipitation levels and shorter growing season than the West Coast Forest region
- smaller coniferous trees such as the spruce, lodgepole, and ponderosa pine
- volume of wood, per hectare, second only to that of the West Coast forest

MIXED FOREST REGION

(found in Mixedwood Plain and Atlantic Maritime Ecozones)

- longer growing season and more precipitation than boreal forest region

- in the north (near the boreal forest), fir and spruce dominate; in the south, coniferous trees such as white pine, hemlock, and red pine grow together with hardy deciduous trees such as maple, beech, and oak

- conifers harvested for lumber, and pulp and paper; **hardwoods** for lumber; the sugar maples which grow in the mixed forest provide most of Canada's maple syrup

- in the southern portion of the Mixedwood Plain Ecozone — the most southerly part of Canada — mixed forest gives way to deciduous forest

- warmer temperatures, longer growing season, and abundant precipitation allow the growth of hardwood trees such as maple, birch, black walnut, and cherry which are valued for flooring and furniture-making

- very little left since intensively farmed and highly urbanized

Some hardwoods, such as ash, are used to make baseball bats and hockey sticks.

ECONOMIC IMPACT OF FORESTS

Forests play an important role in the economic lives of Canadians. Approximately 1 Canadian job in 16 depends on forestry. The forest industry produces lumber, pulp and paper, and other forest products worth about $70 billion per year (1995). Over half of this amount (about $40 billion) is exported to other countries. Softwood lumber makes up 33% of the exports followed by newsprint at 20%, wood pulp at 18%, and all other forest products at 29%.

The forest industry provides over 360 000 direct jobs for Canadians. These jobs are associated with the harvesting of timber and with the saw and paper mills located near the forests (Fig. 23-2). Many of the administrative jobs and sales functions associated with the forest industry are carried out by employees in large cities located far from the forests. Almost 500 000 jobs are indirectly created in companies which provide products and services for forestry companies and workers.

▽ **Fig. 23-5** *Clear-cutting can leave an area looking like this!*

Logging Operations

There are several ways to harvest the trees of Canada's forests. We will examine three distinct methods.

Clear-cutting (Fig. 23-5), which is used in the vast majority of logging operations, is the fastest and cheapest method. Loggers remove every tree, and leave a barren landscape behind.

Northern forests of pine, spruce, fir, aspen, and poplar are cut in this manner. When the clear-cut area is replanted, the new forest grows up uniformly in species and size. This would make it easier to log this forest in the future when the trees reach maturity. If replanting does not take place, or if it is not successful, less desirable species may grow. As well, the soil may erode, and the land may be ruined.

The **shelterwood logging** method involves clear-cutting only part of an **old growth forest**. Small groups of seed-bearing trees are left standing so that their seeds will **regenerate** the logged area (Fig. 23-6). This is used where tree species, such as white pine, regenerate naturally after major openings in the forest are created. The shelterwood method is often used in forests with trees that have grown and aged evenly. Over time, this method will also regenerate a forest that has grown unevenly.

Selective cutting consists of harvesting only mature trees of the desired size, type, or quality. This method is much less disruptive to the forest environment than others. It is used in forests with tree species that need shade to become established. Hardwoods, such as sugar maple, are cut in this manner. Selective cutting tends to be a costly process because of the extra care and time taken to cut down the trees. This method is also costly in the long run because it does not allow the replanting of a new uniform forest.

old growth forest: a forest that has never been cut and is considered important to maintain a wide number of species

regenerate bring back growth

▽ **Fig. 23-6** *Three methods of harvesting the forest*

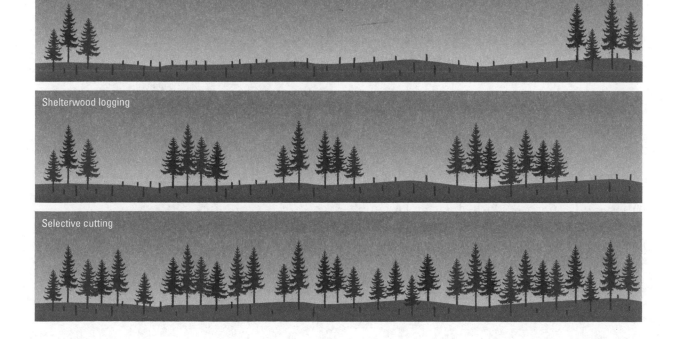

Clear-cutting

Shelterwood logging

Selective cutting

Manufacturing Operations

Canada's forests yield products of great value, but the most important are pulp and paper, and lumber.

PULP AND PAPER

Most kinds of paper are made from cellulose fibres. Cellulose comes from a wide variety of sources, but since the 19th century most has come from wood pulp. Pulp and paper mills tend to be large, multi-million dollar installations. Canada is the world's second largest producer of pulp and paper (after the United States) and the largest exporter. The United States is Canada's most important customer, since it buys more than half the total.

Pulp and paper plants are found in every province except Prince Edward Island (Fig. 23-7) but are concentrated in Québec, Ontario, and British Columbia. Central Canada is the leading pulp and paper producer since its trees are much smaller than those that they replaced and so, are only suitable for use as pulp logs. The larger trees from British Columbia are more valuable for lumber production.

Québec	Ontario	British Columbia	Other Provinces
$11 575 million	$10 018 million	$7514 million	$7286 million

◁ **Fig. 23-7** *Value of paper, and paper products shipped (1995)*

LUMBER

One province dominates Canada's lumber industry. British Columbia produces about 50% of Canada's lumber. Québec is far behind in second place (Fig. 23-8). Lumber products include raw cut timber, plywood, veneers, particle board, cedar shingles, and chip board. In British Columbia, cut timber (also called lumber) is the major product. The province is also Canada's leading plywood producer because its tall, knot-free logs are easily unrolled or "peeled" to make the thin layers that are then glued together to make sheets of plywood.

Sawmills tend to be much smaller operations than pulp and paper mills. Each mill takes advantage of the unique characteristics of the particular forest that supplies the wood, and specializes in a particular market. A large mill in coastal British Columbia might specialize in producing lumber for house construction in the United States. A small mill in southern Ontario might concentrate on processing valuable hardwood trees to supply fine furniture manufacturers in the region.

Since 1970, the number of Canadian sawmills has decreased by more than 900 to about 850. New, more efficient large mills with better methods for processing small logs have replaced the old-fashioned mills which

veneer: a thin covering of high quality of wood glued to a lower quality wood

particle board and chip board: sheets of building material produced by gluing together particles and small chips of wood under pressure

were designed for sawing large logs. The new mills reduce waste, and parts of the log that were discarded 30 years ago are now made into paper, particle board, and chip board. Even the bark and sawdust are burned to help power the mill.

▽ **Fig. 23-8** *Value of lumber products shipped (1995)*

British Columbia	Québec	Ontario	Alberta	New Brunswick	Other Provinces
$11 234 million	$5306 million	$3454 million	$1732 million	$751 million	$780 million

Recreation

For many Canadians, especially those who live in cities and towns, the forest is important as a place to get away from it all. Forests, with their lakes and rivers, provide the setting for a wide range of recreational activities including camping, hiking, canoeing, and fishing.

QUESTIONS

CHECK YOUR UNDERSTANDING

1. a) List two differences between Canada's commercial and non-commercial forests.

   b) The boundary between the commercial and non-commercial forest moves over time. Is it more likely to move north or south? Why?

2. a) Compare the characteristics of the different types of coniferous forests.

   b) Describe the characteristics of Canada's mixed forest region.

   c) In what ways are Canada's different forests used for commercial purposes?

3. a) Why is Central Canada the leading pulp and paper producer?

   b) Why is British Columbia the leading producer of Canada's lumber?

4. a) Why is the number of sawmills decreasing?

   b) How are new sawmills different from older ones?

5. Copy Fig. 23-9 in your notebooks and fill in the information for the three types of logging discussed in this chapter.

ANALYZE AND APPLY

6. You have 100 logs, each 1 m in diameter. You could sell them to either a saw mill or a paper mill. Which would likely offer you a higher price? Why?

7. Fig. 23-10 gives the total area and percentage of land covered by forest in some of the world's largest forest nations. Draw a circle proportional to each country's area and shade in part of the circle to show the percentage of the country that is forested. See Chapter 8 for instructions on how to draw a proportional circle graph.

THINK AND COMMUNICATE

8. Those of you who have been paper carriers know how heavy the weekend paper can be. A recent copy of the Sunday *New York Times* (which is made from Canadian trees)

▽ **Fig. 23-9**

Harvesting Process	Ease of Logging	Cost	Ecological Protection
Clear-cutting			
Shelterwood logging			
Selective cutting			

weighed 4.5 kg. About 1.7 million copies of this paper were produced.

a) How many kilograms of paper were used to produce this day's newspaper?

b) One black spruce tree 13 m high and 20 cm in diameter can produce about 130 kg of newsprint. How many trees were cut down to produce this edition of the *New York Times*?

c) What are the advantages and disadvantages of this use of our forests?

▽ **Fig. 23-10** *Comparison of major forest-producing countries*

Country	Area (km²)	Forest Land (%)
Brazil	8 512 000	59
Canada	9 971 000	42
China	9 597 000	13
India	3 288 000	23
Russia	17 075 000	48
United States	9 373 000	31

THREATS TO THE FORESTS

To the casual observer, there is perhaps one obvious reason why we should protect our forests: they provide an essential renewable resource — timber, which is of great economic value to Canada. This timber is constantly threatened by acid precipitation, damage from insect pests, and forest fires. There are, however, other not-so-obvious reasons to preserve our forests. For instance, after a rainstorm or during spring run-off, trees hold water in the soil. This prevents flooding. Forests also provide habitats for a multitude of birds and mammals, hunting and trapping grounds, and recreational areas. Some of the threats to Canadian forests are shown in Fig. 23-11.

Environmental Hazards

Canadian forests face a number of environmental threats. **Acid precipitation** is a very serious problem for the forests of eastern Canada. Trees are dying as a result of acid precipitation caused by the emissions from factories in the industrial areas of eastern Canada and eastern United

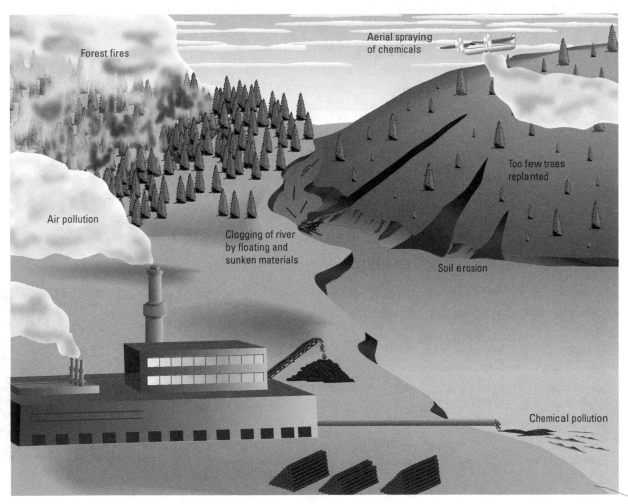

△ **Fig. 23-11** *Threats to the forest*

Labels in figure: Forest fires; Aerial spraying of chemicals; Too few trees replanted; Air pollution; Clogging of river by floating and sunken materials; Soil erosion; Chemical pollution

States. The maple syrup–producing forests south of Quebec City have especially suffered from acid precipitation.

Coniferous trees of the southern boreal forest have also been affected by acid precipitation. Many of the trees have weakened and their needles have turned yellow. Those that do not die outright grow much more slowly than normal.

Insect pests and diseases also pose a serious threat to the health of Canada's forests. The forest area damaged by insects and disease every year is larger than the area harvested annually by forest companies. The spruce budworm, tent caterpillar, and gypsy moth in eastern Canada, and the pine bark beetle in British Columbia cause millions of dollars of damage to forests every year. Cankers — the open wounds on tree trunks — and fungi also cause major forest damage. Forests companies and provincial governments spend a great deal of time and money trying to control these insects and diseases so they don't spread.

A current threat to our forests is the Asian long-horned beetle which migrated here in a wood crate from China. These beetles love hardwoods, especially maples. The have no enemies on this continent and are not affected by pesticides. Many trees in Chicago and New York have already been destroyed.

three issues...

CLEAR-CUTTING

Corporate Viewpoint:

Many forests contain trees and other vegetation that naturally regenerate after destruction by fire or insects. Clear-cutting, followed by natural regeneration or by a program of replanting is similar to what often happens in nature. Furthermore, we determine the size and shape of a clear cut with the preservation of biodiversity and wildlife habitats always in mind. We take great care to cause as little change to the forest as possible.

▽ **Fig. 23-13** *Aerial spraying to control pests is a common sight in many parts of Canada's commercial forests.*

AERIAL SPRAYING OF PESTICIDES

Corporate Viewpoint:

Aerial spraying is an inexpensive and effective technique for killing insect pests such as the spruce budworm (Fig. 23-13). Pests must be killed quickly to protect the forest from extensive damage, and chemical sprays serve that purpose. Today's pesticides require only a few applications and they have a low toxic effect on birds, fish, and mammals. Many pesticides can be sprayed near peoples' homes without danger. If we stop spraying, insects will kill large numbers of trees. This will damage the forest more than our spraying.

GLOBAL COMPETITION

Corporate Viewpoint:

The Canadian forest industry faces one disadvantage — Canada's short growing season. Most of our competitors have the advantage of warmer weather; this results in faster growing forests. If we wish to remain competitive, we must do everything possible to produce our lumber, and pulp and paper products in the most efficient and cost-effective way. Canada also has a difficult time competing with other countries that still allow "cut-and-run" practices. We have two goals when we manage the forests: to achieve sustained-yield management — that is, ensure that for every tree that is cut, steps are taken to ensure that another tree reaches maturity — and to minimize costs. If we do not do this, we will lose jobs and valuable income from exports. This would affect the standard of living of Canadians.

△ **Fig. 23-12** *Opposing viewpoints on key forestry issues*

two views...

Environmentalist Viewpoint:
Clear-cutting removes all the ground cover. Soil without ground cover washes into streams and rivers when it rains. This kills fish and other life in the water. When the forest canopy is removed, changes in temperature occur. Temperature changes disrupt the established ecosystem, and a desert-like landscape results. A forest which has grown up naturally comprises a variety of vegetation, trees of all ages, and wildlife. This diversity is lost when uniform seedlings of tree species are planted.

Environmentalist Viewpoint:
Pesticides endanger wildlife, and disrupt the forest ecosystem. Humans are also affected by insecticides. Aerial spraying has been linked to increased cancers and birth defects in forest workers and people who live near sprayed areas. Some pesticides and pollution from paper mills seem to be affecting Atlantic salmon so that they are unable to find their way back to their spawning grounds. Research into the use of biological controls should be increased. For example, insects that eat only one thing — a pest insect — could be released into an infected area. After they have eaten the pests, the predators would die off because they would have nothing left to eat. Insects can also be controlled through **silviculture** — the breeding and cultivating of trees. By replanting a variety of tree species, logging companies could make the forest less attractive to large numbers of the same pest.

Environmentalist Viewpoint:
Unfortunately, sustained-yield management is not routine practice for the forest industry in most parts of Canada. The money which would protect our forests as a true renewable resource is not being spent. In many areas we now cut smaller trees because the forests are not given time to grow bigger ones. Our forest stocks are gradually being depleted as loggers travel further into the forests to find larger trees. This just increases the costs of logging, and makes the industry less competitive on the world market.

Forest Fires

Fire is a normal part of the life cycle of forest ecosystems. In fact, the history of Canada's boreal forest is one of destruction and renewal by fire. New healthy trees regenerate quickly in the burned forest. The cones from some species, such as the jack pine, require the heat from fire to open. The seeds can then fall to the ground where they begin to grow. In fact, sometimes fires are purposely started in a "controlled burn" to encourage this process. The problem comes when fires occur in valuable timber land.

On average, 9500 fires burn 3 million hectares of Canada's forest every year. A fire can create flames over 50 metres high, move faster than a person can run, and create hurricane-force winds. About 48% of all forest fires in Canada are caused by lightning. Many lightning-caused fires are allowed to burn themselves out because they occur in remote areas. The 52% of forest fires caused by people usually occur near settled areas. Since these forests are more easily accessible, they are considered valuable, so costly efforts are made to fight the fires.

ISSUES FACING THE FORESTS

In the past, Canada's record of forest management was far below the level needed to maintain harvest levels. Forest companies have begun to address the problem, but after so many years of abuse, will it be enough?

At the beginning of this chapter, two viewpoints about the use and care of the forests were presented. Fig. 23-12 examines how these differing viewpoints apply to some specific issues.

A BALANCED APPROACH

Canada's forests cannot be regarded as a limitless source of jobs and profits for large corporations and governments. On the other hand, since so many people rely on the forests for their jobs, it is unrealistic to think that the forests only be left in their natural state as habitats for animals and as recreational areas for

▽ **Fig. 23-14** *Clayoquot Sound is the location of an old growth forest where cooperation between different interest groups may succeed in protecting the environment and provide economic development.*

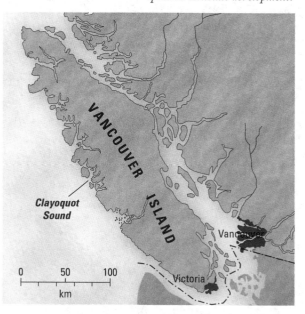

people. Competing interests need to agree to use the forests in a variety of ways that are not in conflict. Perhaps the model for future cooperation can be seen in Clayoquot Sound on the west coast of Vancouver Island (Fig. 23-14).

During the early 1990s, Clayoquot Sound was the site of numerous anti-logging demonstrations. The Macmillan-Bloedel corporation wanted to log the old growth rainforest. Environmentalists and the Nuu-Chah-Nulth First Nation objected. In 1993, the government of British Columbia decided that logging would continue in the area but that it would be highly regulated and would reflect sustained yield forest management. That is, it would be managed to meet current needs without affecting its future productivity, ecological diversity, or ability to regenerate. A panel of scientists, First Nations elders, and Native experts in traditional ecological knowledge was created to develop a sustainable management program.

First Nations' traditional ecological knowledge recognizes the relationship between life forms and involves an understanding of the medicinal properties of local plants, animal behaviour, and local weather patterns. Humans, animals, and the land with its forests and plants are viewed as a whole that must be protected. The spiritual and traditional knowledge of First Nations peoples brings a special perspective to sustained yield forest management.

In 1995, the British Columbia government accepted the panel's recommendations that:

- an ecosystem approach to forest planning be used. Information about the cultural values associated with the forest, as well as information on the forests' biological and physical aspects, should be considered when determining what changes should take place.

- **watersheds** (the basin that surrounding waters drain into) and groups of watersheds would be used as the basis for planning.

- First Nations and other local people should be involved in all phases of planning for, and managing of, the land, freshwater, and marine resources in the Clayoquot Sound region.

- important plant and animal habitats, and archaeological sites should be mapped and studied.

The cooperation amongst the various concerned groups may sustain our forests in order that all users may benefit from this renewable resource.

A wide variety of forest links can be found at www.forest.ca

QUESTIONS

CHECK YOUR UNDERSTANDING

1. Describe the effect of acid rain on Canada's forests. What parts of Canada are most affected? Why?

2. a) Describe how fire is a normal part of the life cycle of forest ecosystems.

   b) Why are forest fires caused by people more likely to be extinguished by fire-fighters, while those caused by lightning are often left to burn themselves out?

3. a) What types of insects and diseases affect our forests?

   b) Why do forest companies spend a great deal of time and money to control insects and pests?

ANALYZE AND APPLY

4. How are forests like agricultural crops? How are they different?

5. a) Referring to Fig. 23-12, summarize in your own words, the differing view-points on:

   i.   clear-cutting

   ii. aerial spraying of pesticides

   iii. global competition

   b) Indicate the arguments with which you agree and explain why.

THINK AND COMMUNICATE

6. a) Using information from other sources such as newspapers and magazines, first list the benefits and then the risks of spraying pesticides over insect-infested areas.

   b) What might your reaction to the spraying be if you were:

   i.   the owner of a forest

   ii. a fish biologist in the area

   iii. a person who lives in a community in which the largest employer is a forest company

   c) Why is this issue so difficult to settle?

   d) Complete research to compare Canada's use of pesticides to those in two other countries. Which practices are most environmentally friendly?

7. A forested area of 5000 ha could either be used for logging or could be added to an adjacent provincial park. The park is very heavily used and would benefit from expansion. On the other hand, the local saw mill is gradually running out of local trees to process. How should the best use for this area be decided?

8. It has been said that Canadians have much to learn from Aboriginal peoples concerning sustainable development and respect for the land and environment. Do you agree? Explain.

9. It is estimated that between 20 and 30 trees are saved for every tonne of paper that we recycle. Although recycling has become a major component in the production of paper in Canada, many Canadians do not recycle as much as they could. How can people be persuaded to recycle and waste fewer paper products?

24 Canada's Mineral Wealth

STUDY GUIDE

By the end of this chapter, you will be able to:

- identify the categories of minerals and how they are used in everyday life
- explain the importance of mining in Canada
- describe the steps used by mining companies to discover and develop an ore body
- explain some issues facing Canada's mining industry

Key Terms

mineral	industrial minerals	ore	underground mining
metallic mineral	mineral reserve	strip mining	milling
fossil fuel	geologist	open pit mining	smelting

Do you have some Canadian mining products with you today? Chances are that you do. Check in your pocket or wallet for coins. What are they made of? Where did this material come from? How about the clothing that you are wearing? What material are the buttons and zippers made of, and where might this materials have come from? Is the cloth a natural fabric like cotton or wool, or a synthetic like nylon or fleece? From what material are synthetics made?

Beyond what you are wearing or carrying, consider that your school building is likely to have been constructed with steel framing and concrete floors. In fact, the products of Canada's mining industry are a much more important part of your life than you may have realized. To explore some of these connections, match up the mineral sources with the finished products in Fig. 24-1.

A glossary of mining and mineral terms can be found at www.nrcan.gc.ca/mms/school/glossary.htm

TYPES OF MINERALS

A **mineral** can be defined as a naturally occurring, pure, non-living substance found in the rocks of the earth. Most minerals are of little or no

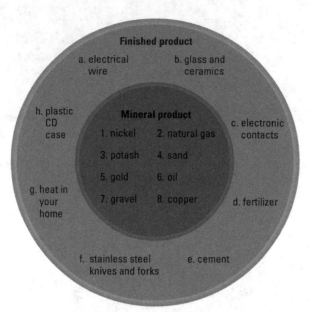

⊲ **Fig. 24-1** *Can you match the minerals with the products they create?*

economic value, but some are enormously valuable and are so important that it is hard to imagine how we could live without them. The minerals that we think of as valuable today have not always been valued in the past. For example, uranium was not considered a valuable resource until scientists came to understand the enormous energy that it contained and discovered ways of extracting this energy. Perhaps in the future, new uses will be discovered for other minerals that might seem useless today. Then, they too will be seen as valuable resources.

Canada's valuable minerals can be divided into three groups on the basis of their composition (Fig. 24-2): **metallic minerals**, **fossil fuels**, and **industrial minerals**. By far, the two most important categories are metallic minerals and fossil fuels.

The energy in uranium was initially used to create the atomic bomb. Since then, it has also been used to generate electricity.

Metallic Minerals

As you might expect from the name, metallic minerals are minerals that, when refined, yield the group of materials that we know as metals. Some metals are mined because of their rareness and beauty, for example, gold, silver, and platinum. Others, like iron, are valued for their strength. Finally, others have a particular property that can be used to meet a human need. Examples of these include copper, which is well-suited for making electrical wiring, and nickel, which can be mixed with iron to make steel that is resistant to rust.

Each of these metals has other uses that are not related to their value as precious metals. For example, platinum is used in the catalytic converters of cars to reduce pollution.

Metallic Minerals	Fossil Fuels	Industrial Minerals
cobalt	coal	asbestos
copper	natural gas	building stone
gold	oil	clay products
iron		diamonds
nickel		gravel
uranium		gypsum
zinc		potash
		salt
		sand
		soapstone

◁ **Fig. 24-2** *These are just some of the minerals mined in Canada. How is each of these minerals used in your life?*

Fossil Fuels

For the last two hundred years, fossil fuels have provided the great majority of the energy used by modern society. In the 1800s, coal was the important fuel. More recently, oil and gas have replaced coal for many uses, including transportation and heating. In Chapter 25, Energy: Powering Our Nation, you will have the chance to study fossil fuels in more detail.

Industrial Minerals

Because industrial minerals vary so widely in their characteristics, it is very difficult to describe them in a simple way. In fact, it is almost easier to say what they are not—they are all the things that are mined that are neither metallic minerals nor fossil fuels. This is not to suggest that industrial minerals are unimportant. In fact, even common substances like sand and gravel are critical to our lives and Canada's economy since they are essential in almost any kind of construction.

Here is a list of some of the major industrial minerals, their characteristics, and their uses:

- asbestos is used to protect things from fire and heat
- potash is a salt-like material used to make fertilizer
- gypsum is a clay-like material used to make sheets of drywall that are used to construct most interior walls in homes, stores, and offices
- soapstone is a very soft mineral that is carved into sculptures by Inuit and other artists
- diamond is a very hard mineral used to make cutting tools; it is also used in jewelry
- gravel is a major ingredient in cement, which is used in the construction of most buildings

Asbestos is used less often today because it was found that exposure to loose asbestos particles caused ancer.

Diamonds are the hardest substance on earth and can be used to cut any other material.

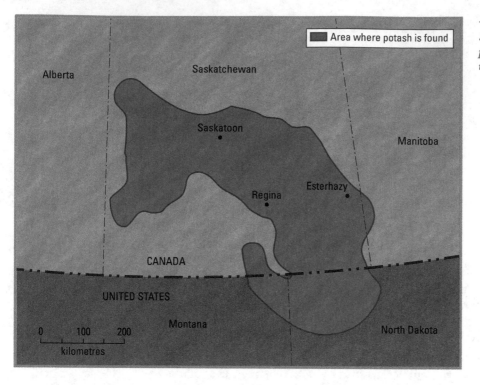

◁ **Fig. 24-3** *This area of Saskatchewan is the largest producer of potash in the world.*

Many important industrial minerals are associated with particular regions of Canada. For example, southern Saskatchewan is the world's most important producer of potash (Fig. 24-3) while Québec is the most important producer of asbestos. Canada's first diamond mine is located in the Northwest Territories. Other industrial minerals, like sand and gravel, are found in most parts of Canada.

The Ekati diamond mine is the subject of the Connecting Study that follows this chapter.

IMPORTANCE OF MINING IN CANADA

Mining is important to Canada in several different ways. Canada ranks third in the world, behind the United States and Russia, in the production of minerals. We are, however, the largest exporter of minerals. Canada exports about 80% of what it produces because we are able to produce far more minerals than we are able to use. How important are minerals to our economy? In 1996, the total value of all mineral production was about $49 billion. The amount of money from each mineral group is shown in Fig. 24-4. The significance of each mineral category to the incomes of the provinces and territories is shown in Fig. 24-5.

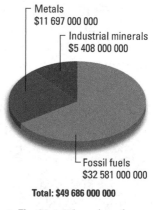

Metals
$11 697 000 000

Industrial minerals
$5 408 000 000

Fossil fuels
$32 581 000 000

Total: $49 686 000 000

△ **Fig. 24-4** *The value of mineral production in Canada, 1996*

The mining industry has also contributed greatly to the development of Canada's transportation system. Since the end of World War II, almost all railroad expansion (and a considerable amount of road expansion) has been done to allow the development of mining resources.

Federal and provincial governments help the mining industry by offering tax incentive programs that encourage exploration of new reserves. The programs also encourage research and development to create new mining methods and products. Governments help build port facilities, power projects, roads, railways, and towns. Sometimes, governments even own major mining companies because they are very important to the provincial economy and the government wants to control them. For example, the Saskatchewan government is a major owner of potash mines, while Québec owns large asbestos mines.

For example, as a tax incentive a government might offer a tax holiday to a new mine; this means that the owners of the mine would not have to pay taxes for a number of years.

▽ **Fig. 24-5** *The value of mineral production by province, 1996*

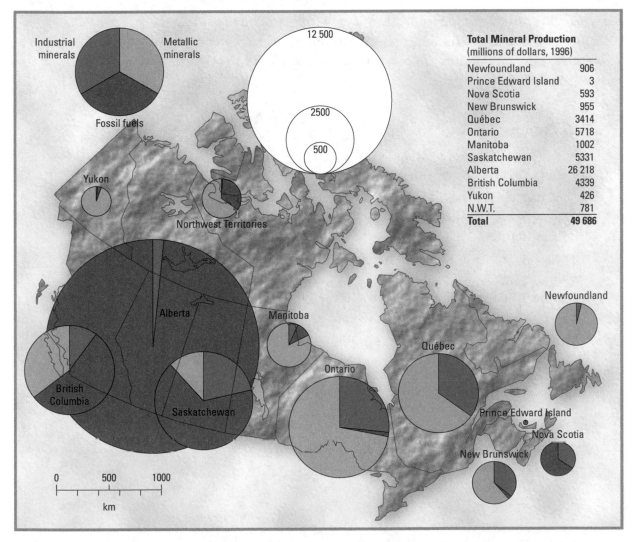

Total Mineral Production
(millions of dollars, 1996)

Newfoundland	906
Prince Edward Island	3
Nova Scotia	593
New Brunswick	955
Québec	3414
Ontario	5718
Manitoba	1002
Saskatchewan	5331
Alberta	26 218
British Columbia	4339
Yukon	426
N.W.T.	781
Total	**49 686**

FINDING VALUABLE MINERALS

Imagine that you are on a holiday somewhere on the Canadian Shield. One day, you are out for a hike and decide to collect some rock samples. In all likelihood, most of the rocks that you find have gold in them. Should you immediately stake a claim and open a gold mine? Probably not, since it might cost you $1 million to recover $1 worth of gold! This situation points out the fact that a mineral only becomes a useful resource if it makes economic sense to mine it. Mineral deposits that are economical to mine are called **mineral reserves.**

Each day, our mineral reserves are reduced as they are mined. It is critical to Canada's future that mineral reserves not be allowed to decrease in size, therefore, continuous mining exploration is needed. This is rarely easy to do since mineral deposits that are worth mining are found in only a few places in the world. As well, the cost of mineral exploration is very high. It is the job of a **geologist** to narrow the search to areas that offer the best chance of finding the desired mineral. Geologists must know how mineral deposits are formed and which types of rocks are most likely to hold the mineral.

Staking a claim is a legal process by which you acquire the right to set up a mine on a piece of land.

To try your luck at starting a mine, check www.nrcan.gc.ca/mms/wealth/mine/english/start-e.htm

Answer the questions below based on Fig. 24-6.

1. a) In which ecozones are most of Canada's metallic mineral resources found?

    b) What type of rocks are found in that region?

    c) In which ecozone(s) is metallic mineral mining not important?

2. In what ecozones are there major non-metallic mineral mines?

3. All three types of minerals are found in the Atlantic Maritime ecozone. What does this tell you about the kind of rocks found in this region?

4. Why are both metallic minerals and mineral fuels found in Canada's Arctic ecozones?

5. This map does not indicate the location of sand and gravel mining. Why might this choice have been made?

Hint: Think about what you learned in Chapters 10 and 11 about Canada's geologic history and landforms.

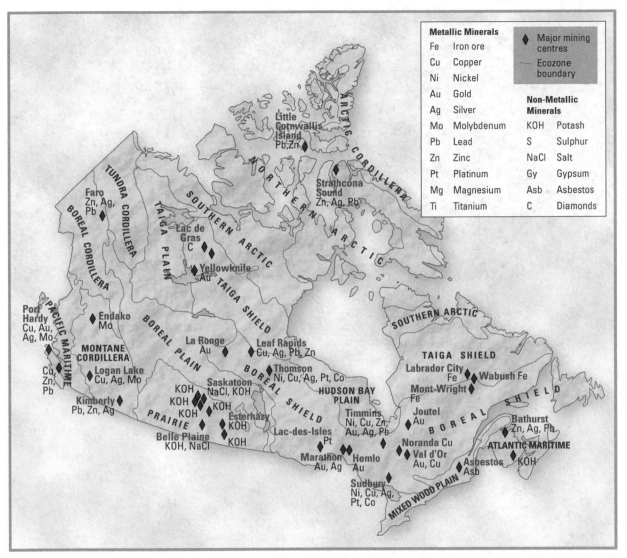

△ **Fig. 24-6** *Major mining centres and ecozones*

LOOKING FOR METALLIC MINERALS

You now know that metallic minerals are found in the igneous and meta-morphic rocks of the Canadian Shield as well as in some other regions of Canada. The Canadian Shield is an enormous area; it is actually much larger than most countries. How do geologists narrow the search when trying to locate metals? There are several tactics they use.

- Some **ore** bodies, such as those containing nickel, iron, and copper, produce a powerful magnetic field compared to surrounding areas where the amount of these metals is low. This magnetic field can be detected by an instrument called a magnetometer, which is towed

ore: rock containing enough metallic minerals to make mining profitable

△ **Fig. 24-7** *Geographic information systems can be used to organize and present the data needed to evaluate a potential mine. In this example, magnetometer readings (curved lines) and drill samples results (coloured dots) have been related to the topography of an area where copper has been found.*

behind an airplane. A geologist can create a map using magnetometer data that shows the approximate size and shape of the ore body.

- Satellite images and aerial photos also tell the geologist a great deal about the geologic structures of an area.

- All of the information gathered above is collected, analyzed, and presented using a GIS (Fig. 24-7).

- The next step is shown in Fig. 24-8. Much of the data that is needed can only be collected by going into the bush or onto the tundra.

- Geologists use a variety of techniques to collect data. They collect rock samples for analysis in the field and back in the laboratory. They test the soil in river beds for chemicals that may have eroded from nearby ore bodies. Some minerals are radioactive and can be detected using a special instrument called a Geiger counter.

- If the findings up to this point look promising, the next step would be to drill deep into the earth in order to get samples of the ore body itself.

Once all the data has been collected, the mining company must decide whether or not to develop the mine. This is a decision that has the potential to earn or lose many millions of dollars for the company. If a small mining company makes a wrong decision and the ore body proves too costly to mine, it will probably go out of business. If the company makes the right decision to mine, it can produce a huge profit for its owners.

Canadian stock exchanges list many mining stocks that can be bought for a few cents a share. Most of these companies will go out of business and those who bought the stock will lose their investment. Some, however, will discover a huge deposit and the stock will rise, making the investors rich.

MINING METALLIC MINERALS

Many mining sites are located in remote areas, far from existing transportation routes. In these cases, the difficulty and the cost of developing

◁ **Fig. 24-8** *While a variety of high-tech methods help determine where a mineral deposit might be, geologists and engineers have to go into the field to collect samples to evaluate if a deposit is worth mining.*

a mine are greatly increased. A road (or, in some cases, railway) must be built to allow the shipping in of equipment and the shipping out of product. Mine facilities to extract the ore from the ground and a mill to separate the useful mineral from the ore has to be built. Housing has to be constructed for the workers. Finally, fresh water, sewage treatment, and electricity must be supplied to the mine and the housing. As you might imagine, the costs of all of this development can be staggering.

In the case of a major mine that employs many workers, an entire town may have to be built.

Once all of this in place, it is time to start the actual mining. Depending on the depth of the ore deposit, either **strip**, **open pit**, or **underground mining** is used. (Fig. 24-9)

PROCESSING METALLIC MINERALS

The ore that is mined is composed mainly of waste rock. In the case of an iron ore mine, this might mean that half of the ore is iron and half is waste, but in the case of a gold mine there might only be a few grams of gold in each tonne of ore. The processing of most ores, including nickel, copper, gold, silver, and zinc, has two steps: **milling** and **smelting**. The mill starts the process of purifying the mineral by separating it from waste rock. The metal, although far from pure, is now in a concentrated form. For example, a concentrate of copper contains 30% copper and 70% waste rock. The next step is to take this concentrate to the smelter.

A smelter is very costly to build. In some cases it could cost as much as $1 billion or more. As a result, a mining company has to decide if a mine will produce enough (and operate long enough) to justify building a

▽ **Fig. 24-9** *Strip, open pit, and underground mining*

STRIP MINING
– is used to extract minerals, such as coal and oil sands, that are located in horizontal layers near the surface.

1. Overburden (trees, earth, rock) is removed.

2. Blasting may be necessary for some mineral deposits.

3. Material is loaded onto trucks or conveyor belts by shovels or draglines.

4. Material is taken to storage area for shipment to market or processing.

OPEN PIT MINING
– is used to extract minerals that are located near the surface but that may extend deep into the earth.

1. Overburden is removed.

2. Holes are drilled 10–15 m deep and filled with explosives. The rock is blasted apart.

3. Ore is loaded into large trucks (which may carry 90 to 250 t) by huge shovels.

4. Ore can now be taken to a storage site near the mill.

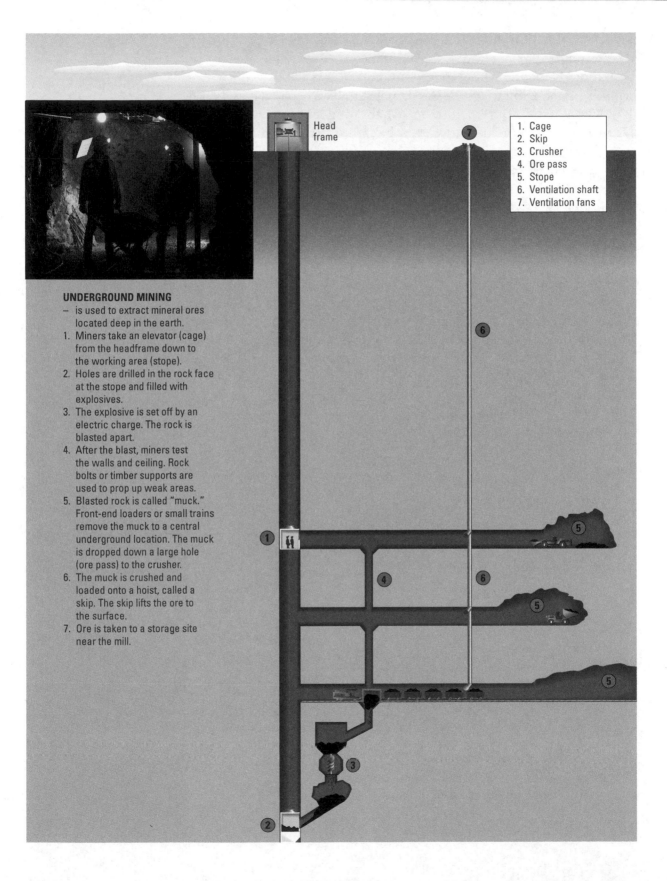

1. Cage
2. Skip
3. Crusher
4. Ore pass
5. Stope
6. Ventilation shaft
7. Ventilation fans

Head frame

UNDERGROUND MINING
– is used to extract mineral ores located deep in the earth.
1. Miners take an elevator (cage) from the headframe down to the working area (stope).
2. Holes are drilled in the rock face at the stope and filled with explosives.
3. The explosive is set off by an electric charge. The rock is blasted apart.
4. After the blast, miners test the walls and ceiling. Rock bolts or timber supports are used to prop up weak areas.
5. Blasted rock is called "muck." Front-end loaders or small trains remove the muck to a central underground location. The muck is dropped down a large hole (ore pass) to the crusher.
6. The muck is crushed and loaded onto a hoist, called a skip. The skip lifts the ore to the surface.
7. Ore is taken to a storage site near the mill.

smelter at the mine site. If not, the company may decide to transport the concentrate to an existing smelter somewhere else. The smelter may be hundreds, or even thousands, of kilometres away. This was the case with a new nickel mine, which was supposed to have been built in the late 1990s at Voisey's Bay in northern Labrador. The government of Newfoundland wanted a smelter to be built in the province since it would provide many high-paying jobs in a province with high unemployment. The owners of the mine, INCO, wanted to ship the concentrate to smelters that already existed in Sudbury, Ontario and Thompson, Manitoba.

As of early 1999, the dispute over the location of the smelter had stalled the construction of the INCO mine. Is this mine in production today?

At the smelter, the ore concentrate and a substance called flux are melted together in a furnace. The flux joins with the waste rock to form a material called slag. The slag is lighter than the liquid metal and rises to the top. The almost pure metal is then poured into molds.

Waste materials, called **tailings**, are produced during the processing of metal ores. Tailings, which are a mixture of water, the chemicals used in the process, and rock particles, are poisonous and must be carefully handled. They are dumped into tailing ponds that are contained within dikes. These dikes are designed to prevent the mine waste from seeping into nearby lakes and rivers. The water in the tailings eventually evaporates, leaving solid waste behind. This is then treated with fertilizers and other chemicals to allow trees and grasses to grow.

dike: earth walls built to hold back a liquid

QUESTIONS

CHECK YOUR UNDERSTANDING

1. a) What are minerals?

   b) Name the categories into which minerals may be divided. Give two examples of each type.

   c) Under what circumstances does a mineral become a mineral reserve?

2. Describe the steps used by mining companies to discover and develop an ore body.

3. a) In your own words, describe the steps involved in open pit mining.

   b) In your own words, describe the steps involved in underground mining.

4. Compare milling and smelting in terms of what each does and where each might occur.

5. What is done with the waste products from the processing of minerals? Why must this be done carefully?

ANALYZE AND APPLY

6. Examine Fig. 24-5. Choose the three most important provinces for each of the following:

   i.   metallic minerals

   ii. fossil fuels

   iii. industrial minerals

Metal	Property	Use
	carries electricity well	
		stainless steel
		coins
iron		
	stops steel from rusting	
		jewelry
	light in weight	

△ **Fig. 24-10**

7. Complete an organizer like Fig. 24-10 in your notebook.

8. If you were a mining company engineer and had a choice to mine an ore body with an open pit or with an underground mine, which would you choose? Why?

9. a) What conditions must exist before a company will develop a potential mine site? Consider the kind of mineral being mined, the quality of the ore body, the availability of transportation, and the market price of the metal.

   b) How would higher market prices affect the decision in 9a?

   c) How would changing market prices affect the long-term prospects of a mine?

ISSUES FACING CANADA'S MINING INDUSTRY

There are several controversial issues related to Canada's mining industry.

- One of the most serious issues facing the mining industry is its negative impact on the environment. Over the past 20 years, more than $1 billion has been spent on controlling harmful emissions from mines and processing plants. Despite many successes in this area, millions of tonnes of waste still find their way into our air and water.

  The serious problem of acid precipitation is directly related to the mining industry. On a per capita basis, Canada produces more of the pollutants that cause acid precipitation than does the United States. Six of the ten biggest polluters in North America are smelters and refineries in Ontario, Québec and Manitoba. In spite of the fact that the mining company, INCO, has spent hundreds of millions of dollars to control acid precipitation pollutants, the company's smelter in Sudbury is the world's largest single source of sulphur dioxide (Fig. 24-11). INCO must deal with the challenge of controlling the pollution created by the mine at a cost that allows it to remain competitive in the world market.

◁ **Fig. 24-11** *In spite of hundreds of millions of dollars being spent on pollution control, mine smelters remain one of the worst sources of the chemicals that contribute to acid precipitation.*

- Another environmental concern is the issue of abandoned mines and what happens to the land after an ore body runs out and a mine closes. There are dozens of abandoned mines across Canada that have left scars on the land and are continuing sources of pollution as mine wastes leak into rivers and lakes. Governments now require mining companies to carefully plan what they will do when a mine shuts down. Open pit mines, quarries, and gravel pits can be flooded and used for recreation. At the time this book was written, there was a controversial plan to transport Toronto's garbage to an old open-pit mine near Kirkland Lake in north-eastern Ontario (Fig. 24-12). Acid wastes can be neutralized and then planted with grasses and trees. These remedial measures are not designed to hide the fact that a mine existed. Rather, the purpose is to minimize long-term damage and produce a landscape feature that can be used for other purposes.

  remedial measures: actions to correct a problem

- About 50% of the minerals mined in Canada are exported before any smelting or manufacturing is done. This means that we are exporting the jobs that result from the final refining of the mineral along with those in the manufacturing process.

- Canada's mining industry can be badly damaged by events in other countries over which we have no control. For example, in 1997 and 1998, the economies of the countries in east Asia, like Japan, China, and Taiwan, experienced a major slowdown. Since these countries are major customers for our mining industry, the result was a decline in the demand of Canadian mining products.

  Not all new mines are found in remote northern areas. A major gold deposit was found in the 1980s directly under the Trans-Canada Highway in northern Ontario.

- In many cases, the highest quality reserves are being exhausted. In the future, Canada will have to rely on other mineral deposits that may be of poorer quality or that are found in areas far from markets and transportation routes. To avoid this problem, new technologies must be developed to make the mining of lower grade ores and remote deposits more economical.

• New mineral deposits are constantly being discovered in other countries, particularly in the developing countries of Asia, Africa, and South America. Many of these countries have lower production costs because of lower labour costs and fewer pollution controls. Accordingly, they are able to sell their mineral products on the world market more cheaply than Canadian companies. If Canada wants to compete, and keep our traditional customers, then production costs have to be decreased. This will probably lead to more mechanization of the mining and milling processes.

• Mining towns are totally dependent on their mines for their continued existence. If the mine closes because the ore runs out or markets disappear, the town may have great difficulty surviving. The town of Schefferville, on the border of Québec and Labrador, closed down after its iron ore mine shut down in the 1980s. In the end, the town was given to the Innu who are the traditional inhabitants of this remote area. In contrast, the uranium mining town of Elliot Lake, just north of Lake Huron, was able to find another economic base after its mines closed. Elliot Lake was able to promote itself as an inexpensive retirement community. It was able to do this because it was not located in a remote area of Canada and had attractive features like a hospital and recreational facilities.

In many cases, the countries with new mineral deposits have never before been explored for minerals so rich reserves can often be found, Canadian companies are often involved in mineral exploration in these countries. Why is this not a surprise?

◁ **Fig. 24-12** *Does dumping Toronto's garbage in an old open-pit mine, like this one, solve a problem for both places, or just move a problem from one place to another?*

IN CLOSING...

How can the development of Canada's mineral resources be improved in the future?

Here are some things to consider:

- Environmental controls on mining should continue to improve.
- Restrictions on mining companies in Canada should still allow these companies to compete internationally.
- Canadian companies should adjust to international competition and pricing.
- Canadian governments should continue to provide substantial financial assistance to the mining industry.
- The land claims of the First Nations should be considered in deciding when and how mineral deposits will be developed.
- Canadian mining companies should develop new technologies that will make their operations more efficient.
- Companies should continue to explore for new deposits in all areas of Canada including undersea locations.
- More of the processing and manufacturing of Canadian minerals should take place in this country.
- Research and development of new uses for minerals should be intensified.
- We should try to adjust to the boom and bust nature of a mining-based economy more efficiently.

If you would like to know about careers in the mining industry, check www.nrcan.gc.ca/mms/school/jobs/jobbis.htm

QUESTIONS

ANALYZE AND APPLY

1. a) Why should mining companies reduce the environmental damage caused by their mines and smelters?

   b) What makes it difficult to do this?

2. Do this question with a partner. One partner has just been appointed the C.E.O. of a major mining company. This person is responsible for maximizing the profits and reducing the costs of the company. The other partner is the new mines minister in the government. This person must focus on ensuring that the mining industry is healthy, that new jobs are created, and that the envi-ronmental impact of mining is limited. Flip a coin to see who gets which job!

   a) Each partner should look separately at the list of suggestions for the future of Canada's mining industry in the "In Closing..." section of this chapter. From the perspective of your job, rank them in order of their importance.

   b) Compare your list to that of your partner. Explain any significant differences in the two lists.

   c) Work together to create a combined ranking that will reflect the needs of industry and government.

3. Consider the idea of putting garbage from Toronto (and perhaps other southern cities) into abandoned mines further north, from the perspective of both the people in Toronto and the people who live near the mines. List the good points and bad points of this plan from both perspectives.

THINK AND COMMUNICATE

4. Discuss the following statement. Be sure to consider both sides of the issue, and then indicate with which side you agree.

   "Cleaning up the tailings area of a mine which has shut down is very expensive and really not necessary since such areas cover only a tiny percentage of the countryside."

5. Put yourself in the position of the union president at a mine somewhere on the Canadian Shield. The president of the company that owns the mine has told you that the cost of production in the mine must be cut or the mine will be closed down since it will not be able to compete with newer mines in developing countries. The mine president has said that the workers must accept a 25% pay cut.

   a) What alternatives are there for the workers in the mine who belong to your union?

   b) What alternative would you recommend to your members and why?

6. A company has applied for a permit to extract large amounts of sand and gravel from a glacial deposit at the edge of your town. They expect to operate for 10 to 15 years and provide about 50 full-time jobs.

   a) Describe the effects that this project might have on the local ecosystem (e.g., water table, wildlife, native plants)

   b) Describe the effects that this project might have on people (e.g., economics, noise, appearance, transportation)

   c) Determine a method to evaluate the relative importance of each of the benefits and costs (including non-monetary costs) that you identified in 6a and 6b.

   d) Apply the approach that you developed above to evaluate a real project in your local area or another part of Canada.

Diamonds: Are They Forever?

Diamonds... the word itself conjures up images of romance, intrigue, mystery, and wonder. Until very recently, we thought that diamonds came from exotic, far-away places. While Canada has a great tradition as one of the world's great mining countries, we have only recently joined the tiny group of nations that are diamond producers. In this Connecting Study, we will look at how this happened and why we should be interested.

THE NATURE OF DIAMONDS

Just about everyone is familiar with one of the uses of diamonds: we have all seen diamond jewelry, some of which is very valuable. Less well-known is the importance of diamonds to many kinds of industries, as it is the ultimate cutting tool. In the first case, **gemstone diamonds** are prized because of their rarity and their beauty. In the second case, they are prized because no other substance is as hard as an **industrial diamond**.

The world's diamond production is worth about US$8 billion per year. About half of the world's diamond production (by value) is used for jewelry or industrial uses. Since raw gemstones average about US$100 per **carat**, while industrial diamonds are worth about US$10 per carat, gemstones are obviously much less common than industrial stones. Many industrial diamonds are manufactured, but all gemstones are the product of nature.

1 carat = 0.2 grams. The largest diamond ever found was about 3000 carats.

Diamonds are mined in large quantities in only a few countries. In terms of value, Australia is the most important producer. Most of Australia's production (along with that of the Congo) is used for industrial purposes. (Most other industrial diamonds in the world are manufactured.) The major producers of gemstones are Botswana, Russia, and South Africa where the modern diamond-mining industry began more than a century ago.

Australia also produces gem diamonds that are, among other colours, pink.

HOW DIAMONDS WERE DISCOVERED IN CANADA

Perhaps the surprising thing is not that diamonds were found in Canada, but that it took so long to find them. Diamonds are most often found in

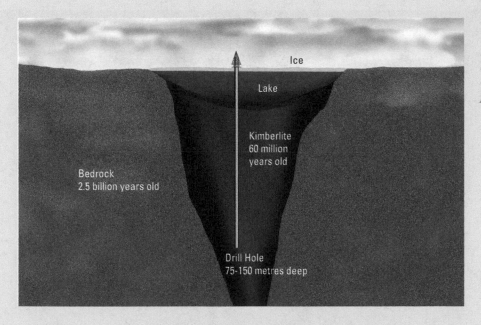

Ice

Lake

Kimberlite
60 million
years old

Bedrock
2.5 billion years old

Drill Hole
75-150 metres deep

◁ **Fig. 24-13** *Perhaps only 100 of the 5000 known kimberlite pipes in the world are close enough to the surface of the earth to make mining profitable.*

a rare geologic structure called a **kimberlite pipe** (Fig. 24-13) which exists only in ancient features called **cratons**. Cratons make up the stable cores of the continents. Cratons formed in the Precambrian era and have been largely undisturbed by mountain-building for at least one billion years. The kimberlite pipes are much younger intrusions.

Cratons (and diamonds) are found in areas of the world with large masses of ancient rock. Before diamonds were found in Canada, they had been discovered in the shield areas of southern Africa, Russia, and Australia. Scientists realized that Canada had more craton areas than any other place in the world. Presumably, these areas contained diamonds — but where were they? In fact, serious exploration for diamonds in the Canadian Shield began about 30 years ago but without success. Unlike the other diamond-mining regions of the world, the Canadian Shield had been subjected to glaciation for hundreds of thousands of years. Glaciers had done a very effective job of hiding the diamonds. Finding them would require a new approach, a great deal of work, and more than a little luck.

Between 1983 and 1989, two geologists/prospectors named Charles Fipke and Stewart Blusson decided to try a new technique for finding diamonds. Their idea was that if glaciers had spread and scattered the already rare diamonds all over the continent, it would be impossible to find them. They thought it was a better idea to look for **indicator minerals** that are found with diamonds, but are much more common. If the indicator minerals could be found and traced back to their point of origin, it would be possible to find the diamonds.

Canadian cratons formed 1.0 to 2.1 billion years ago. Most pipes do not reach the surface.

Canada has five cratons including the Slave craton where diamonds are now being mined. The Slave craton alone is as large as the United Kingdom, so there are lots of places in which to look for diamonds.

Diamonds which were subjected to glaciation were carried as far away as Indiana.

It all seems quite simple, at least in theory. Fipke and Blusson found the indicator minerals without too much difficulty, but then came the challenge of determining from where they had come. They used two methods to make this determination. One of these was trying to predict in what direction, and how far, the indicator minerals had been moved from their original location by glaciation. The ice sheets had left considerable evidence as to the direction of their movement. For example, the orientation of features like drumlins, eskers, and glacial scratches indicate the direction in which glaciers moved.

The other method used newly developed techniques that analyzed the chemistry of the sand particles found with the indicator minerals. A geographic information system (GIS) was used to bring all of the complex data together. The results of this analysis led them to the Lac de Gras area about 300 km northeast of Yellowknife (Fig. 24-14).

Fipke and Blusson had a pretty good idea that there was a kimberlite pipe nearby, but there was no sign of it on the surface. This was not a particular surprise, since the glaciers had eroded the soft kimberlite more easily than the surrounding rocks. The low areas that were created, have now become some of the many small lakes that cover much of the Canadian Shield (Fig. 24-15). The search for diamonds would have to continue under these lakes. The next step was to do a magnetometer survey. A magnetometer is an instrument which is towed behind a helicopter or an airplane. It is able to measure tiny differences in the magnetic field of the rocks in a particular area. This is particularly useful when looking for diamonds because kimberlites are found together with a mineral called magnetite. Magnetite contains a very high percentage of iron and, therefore, gives a very distinctive magnetometer reading indicating the shape of the pipe.

The prospects were very exciting, but the cost of finding and developing the diamonds would be far more than Dia Met Minerals, the small company created by Fipke and Blusson, could afford. They needed to find a partner with very "deep pockets" who would be prepared to risk a great deal of money for the chance to be involved in Canada's first diamond mine. The company they found was Broken Hill Proprietary (BHP). BHP was an Australian mining company with considerable experience in the diamond-mining business. They agreed to pay all further costs

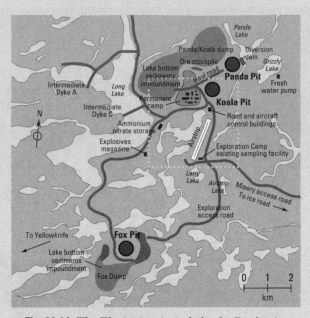

△ **Fig. 24-14** *The Ekati mine site includes the Panda pit, which went into production in 1988, the Koala and Fox pits and other pits, which will eventually go into production. The area outlined in yellow is shown in Fig. 24-16.*

For more on glaciation, see the Connecting Study following Chapter 11.

GIS is examined in Chapter 5.

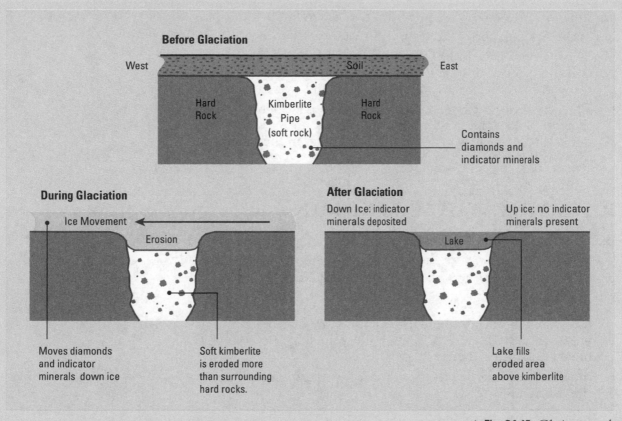

Before Glaciation

West   Soil   East

Hard Rock   Kimberlite Pipe (soft rock)   Hard Rock

Contains diamonds and indicator minerals

During Glaciation

Ice Movement

Erosion

Moves diamonds and indicator minerals down ice

Soft kimberlite is eroded more than surrounding hard rocks.

After Glaciation

Down Ice: indicator minerals deposited

Up ice: no indicator minerals present

Lake

Lake fills eroded area above kimberlite

△ **Fig. 24-15** *Glaciers spread the evidence of diamonds over half of the continent and hid the sources of the diamonds under lakes on the Canadian Shield.*

Ekati is an aboriginal name that refers to caribou fat, which is highly prized by the local Native people.

You can learn more about the Ekati mine and see photos of it at www.diamet.com/version2/mine.html

From what do you think the cutting edges of the rock drills were made? Why?

of exploration along with the cost of developing a mine (if they needed one!) up to US$500 million. For this, they received a 51% interest in the new mine, which would be called Ekati.

Why didn't any Canadian mining companies become involved in this venture? They may have been reluctant to do so because they do not have experience in diamond mining and could not determine whether this huge investment made sense. In contrast, Canadian mining companies often become partners in mining ventures around the world that are in fields where they have great expertise, like mining gold or base metals (nickel, lead, copper, zinc).

The next step was to determine if there actually were diamonds under one (or more) of the lakes in the Lac de Gras area. This could best be done in winter, when they could drill from the frozen surface of the lake to obtain rock samples. As a result of drilling, in late 1991 they found 81 diamonds in a 60 kg rock sample taken from under Point Lake. Finding these diamonds certainly was good reason for celebration, but BHP still had no idea whether there were enough diamonds to make the development of a mine practical. Drill sampling continued for the next few years, resulting in the discovery of more than two dozen kimberlite pipes. Two important findings about the diamonds that were discovered emerged:

- The quantity and quality was high. On average, each tonne of rock contained about one carat of diamonds. This is a tiny amount, but it is considered a rich deposit in the diamond world.

- The proportion of high-value gemstones was particularly high. Ekati would compete with southern Africa and Russia in the gem market, rather than with Australia and Congo in the industrial diamonds market.

BUILDING THE EKATI MINE

Building any diamond mine is a big job. Building one that is hundreds of kilometres from the nearest highway or railroad increases the difficulty enormously. In effect, three different structures had to be built (Fig. 24-16):

- the mine itself
- the processing plant where the diamonds are separated from the waste rock; the Ekati processing plant is the length of two city blocks and nine stories tall
- the living facilities for the hundreds of workers who will recover the diamonds

Early on, it became obvious that everything needed to build and operate the mine could not be brought in by air as it was during the exploration phase of the project. Building a road was one possibility, but

▽ **Fig. 24-16** *Building the Ekati mine and its support facilities was like creating a new town in the middle of the wilderness.*

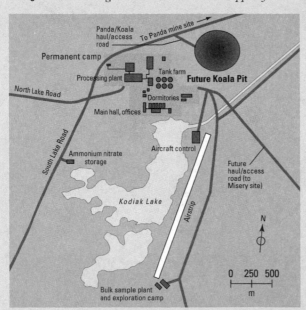

it would have been enormously expensive. An ice road is now used during the winter months to transport the heavy and bulky items that are needed (and can be planned for far enough in advance). In the winter of 1996-97, the ice road was used to bring in more than 40 000 tonnes of cargo. Aircraft are also critical to the operation of the mine. They are used to move people as well as freight that cannot be transported over the ice road. In one year, between the summer 1996 and the summer of 1997, more than 17 000 people and 6500 tonnes of freight were carried to the mine by air.

The government of the Northwest Territories is considering building a year-round road from Yellowknife to Bathurst Inlet (Kinggauk) on the Arctic Ocean. This road would replace the ice road.

HOW EKATI OPERATES

Diamond mining requires the removal of an enormous volume of rock, so an open pit mine is used to mine the kimberlite (Fig. 24-17). Most diamond mines are 300 m to 600 m deep. If the diamond deposit proves rich enough, a shaft mine is sometimes drilled from the bottom of the open pit. What happens at Ekati will depend on how rich the deposit proves to be.

The rock that is mined, is taken to a processing plant where the diamonds are recovered. Processing at Ekati is an automated process which involves two basic steps: crushing the rocks and separating the diamonds from the crushed rock. Having automated processing has two advantages. One is that it reduces the need for labour in a remote loca-

automated: involving machinery and not people

▽ **Fig. 24-17** *As the Ekati open pit mine gets deeper, it will also get much wider. Its growth will cease when the width of the mine becomes much greater than the width of the pipe. At this point, too much unproductive rock would have to be mined to make economic sense.*

tion where labour is expensive. The other advantage is that it reduces the likelihood of theft by employees, which is a very serious problem at every diamond mine in the world. The raw diamonds are then flown to Yellowknife and from there to world markets, where the best diamonds are sold as gems and the rest for industrial purposes.

IMPACT OF THE EKATI DIAMOND MINE

Economic and Social Impact

Mining at Ekati is expected to last for approximately 20 years. During this time, the company expects to recover between 4 and 5 million carats of diamonds each year. In comparison to most diamond mines worldwide, a relatively high proportion of these stones will be of the high-value gemstone category. These diamonds would be worth about US$500 million per year or about US$10 billion over the life of the mine.

This will affect the economy in two ways. One is that most of these diamonds will be exported, so Canada's trade balance will receive a big boost. The other is that many of the financial benefits of the mine will stay in the Northwest Territories. The mine employs about 600 people, which includes workers at the mine site and elsewhere in the Northwest Territories. While this number of jobs might not be significant in Ontario or Alberta, the impact on the Northwest Territories is quite substantial. Since the total number of employees in the territory was only about 12 000 in the year before the mine opened, the creation of an additional 600 well-paying jobs has had an enormous effect on the economy. Beyond this, there will be hundreds of other jobs created in Yellowknife as a result of the multiplier effect, which would involve the creation of jobs in such areas as transportation and housing to facilitate the mine's operations. Other jobs will be created in the years to come as it is expected that additional mines will open in that area.

During the time that the mine was being developed, extensive consultations were held with the Aboriginal people who lived in the vicinity of the mine. These consultations are to continue throughout the life of the mine. Agreements were struck with the local First Nations in two specific areas: the minimizing of the mine's impact on the local environment and the maximizing of economic benefits for the people of the area. For example, during the operation of the mine, slightly more than 60% of all of the mine's jobs in the Northwest Territories must be filled by northern residents with half of that employment being reserved for Aboriginal workers. To ensure that the benefits of the project are shared throughout the territory, travel assistance is provided for employees from as far away as Inuvik and Cambridge Bay.

Environmental Impact

The Ekati mine underwent the most in-depth environmental assessment of any mine in Canadian history. In fact, the various environmental reports which were done before the mine was approved fill more than one metre of bookshelf space. Concerns in these studies included the lakes under which the kimberlites were found and the caribou migrations in that area. While all these reports do not guarantee that there will be no environmental damage from the mine, they do suggest that concern for the environment has been taken seriously.

A second factor that bodes well for the environment is the way in which the diamonds occur in the kimberlite. Most metallic minerals, like gold, nickel, and uranium, are chemically bound to the ores in which they are found. They can only be separated with the use of a wide variety of powerful chemicals. The waste products of this refining and smelting are environmentally very dangerous and must be carefully controlled. Far too often, this waste is able to escape into rivers and lakes where it can cause enormous damage. By comparison, diamonds are only physically attached to the kimberlite rock in which they occur. They are simply broken away from the surrounding rock, and there is no chemical waste.

Five million carats of diamonds (equal to about one tonne), means about 5 million tonnes of waste rock per year. This enormous amount of rock must be disposed of very carefully so as not to disrupt drainage or cause other environmental damage.

WHAT IS NEXT FOR CANADA'S DIAMOND INDUSTRY?

The discovery of rich diamond deposits in Canada, after so many years of searching, has sparked a huge surge in mineral exploration. By the mid-1990s, more than $150 million was being spent each year on the search for diamonds. All indications are that Ekati may be just the beginning of a huge diamond industry in Canada. A second mine, called the Diavik mine, located across Lac de Gras from the Ekati mine, is likely to be in production by 2002. The size and value of other diamond deposits in the same area of the Northwest Territories are being evaluated as well.

Diamonds have also been discovered in northern Alberta, Saskatchewan, and Ontario, while exploration is taking place in Manitoba and northwestern Québec. The number of discoveries that will eventually result in mines remains to be seen. This will depend on how rich the deposits are and the health of the diamond market in the future. So far, all indications are very positive. The number and quality of the diamonds discovered is very high and, by all accounts, the demand for high quality gemstones is likely to continue growing. In addition, many of the major diamond deposits in South Africa are running out. In fact, it is anticipated that Canada will produce more diamonds than South Africa by the year 2010.

The world's largest diamond mining company, De Beers Corporation, is active in Canada. You can learn more about their operations at: www.debeers.ca/index.html

When students have learned about mining in Canada, the focus has been traditionally on nickel, copper, gold, potash, and other minerals. In the years to come, diamonds may appear at the top of this list. Perhaps, you will even find yourself working in this important new industry in the years to come.

QUESTIONS

CHECK YOUR UNDERSTANDING

1. What is a *craton* and what is a "kimberlite pipe" and how are they related to finding diamonds?

2. a) Explain what is meant by the following statement, "Perhaps the surprising thing is not that diamonds were found in Canada, but that it took so long to find them."

   b) How were they eventually found?

3. How will diamond mining affect the Northwest Territories and the Aboriginal people who live in the areas where it occurs?

4. Create a flow chart to illustrate the stages in diamond mining as it is being done at Ekati. Start at the stage where the decision was made to start mining.

ANALYZE AND APPLY

5. a) What are the two types of diamonds?

   b) How would each be affected by a weak economy in the world? Why?

6. a) One carat of diamonds is found in one tonne of rock. Express this amount as a percentage.

   b) What does this suggest about the nature of diamond mining?

7. a) Why is theft a greater problem in the diamond mining industry than in other kinds of mining?

   b) What feature of Ekati's operations helps prevent theft?

8. a) In what ways is diamond mining like other kinds of mining that are common in Canada?

   b) In what ways is it different?

THINK AND COMMUNICATE

9. a) Do you expect to buy one or more diamonds in your lifetime? When? Why?

   b) What roles have tradition and marketing played in this decision?

10. a) Would you like to be a prospector? What would be the advantages and disadvantages of this job?

    b) What training would be needed for this job?

Energy: Powering our Nation

By the end of this chapter, you will be able to:

- explain how Canadians use different types of energy
- understand the formation and use of oil and gas
- compare the different methods of making electricity
- describe Canada's trade in energy

Key Terms

conventional energy
   sources
alternative energy
   sources
joule (J)

petajoule (PJ)
anticlinal trap
secondary recovery
oil sand

hydro-electric
   generating station
thermal-electric
   generating station

nuclear-electric
   generating station
power grid

In many ways, Canadians are the "fat cats" of the world. Depending on which set of statistics you consult, we are either the largest or the second largest per capita users of energy in the world, for the following reasons:

Some statistics show that Americans are the largest users of energy in the world.

- we live in a northern climate with very cold temperatures for much of the year
- we have a small population spread very thinly over a huge land mass, and we use a great deal of energy for transportation
- our advanced industrial economy uses a great deal of energy
- energy is cheap in this country, so we tend to waste it

CANADA'S ENERGY USE TODAY

Our energy sources can be divided into the two following categories:

- well-established **conventional energy sources** such as oil, natural gas, coal, hydro, and nuclear electricity
- a growing number of **alternative energy sources** like solar, wind, and biomass energy

This chapter will deal primarily with conventional energy sources, since they are responsible for almost all of the energy used in Canada. We rely mostly on three types of energy that account for 98% of our energy use: oil (39%), natural gas (35%), and electricity (24%). Alternative energy sources will be considered in Chapter 35. Our tendency to use our resources in a wasteful manner will be the subject of Chapter 36.

This leaves about 2% for other energy sources, including coal and wood.

Energy Terminology

One difficulty in the study of energy is that we often try to compare litres of gasoline to cubic metres of natural gas and to kilowatt hours of electricity. To properly compare these forms of energy, we need a common unit of measure. The basic unit used to measure energy is the **joule (J)**. One joule is a tiny amount of energy. As a result, two large multiples of joules are used. One gigajoule (GJ) equals one billion joules. One **petajoule (PJ)** equals one million gigajoules.

One gigajoule is roughly equal to the amount of energy found in 30 litres of gasoline.

One petajoule would be enough energy to keep about 70 000 average cars going for one year.

How Energy is Used

Canada's net supply of energy in 1997 was about 8949 petajoules. Almost 20% of this total was used by energy producers themselves to get their products to market (939 petajoules) or for non-energy use (802 petajoules) as raw materials or in manufacturing. This leaves about 7209 petajoules, which were used as energy by companies and consumers in Canada. Fig. 25-1 shows how this energy was used.

Producers use energy to transport oil through pipelines and electricity through transmission lines.

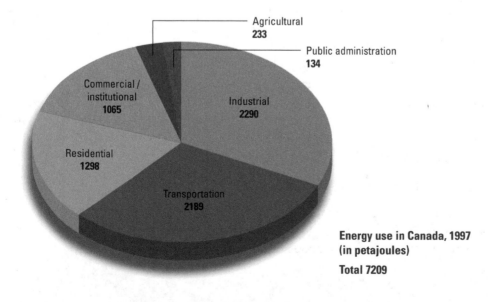

Energy use in Canada, 1997
(in petajoules)
Total 7209

◁ **Fig. 25-1** *Energy use in Canada (PJ), 1997*

To learn more about energy, check the following sites:
• for an industry viewpoint: www.energy.ca
• for an environmental viewpoint: www.nextcity.com/energyprobe/index.html

Patterns of energy use vary quite significantly from one sector of our economy to another. Work with a partner to investigate these differences.

1. Examine Fig. 25-2. You can look at this data in two completely different ways. One is by examining it according to sector (industrial, transportation, etc.). The other is by analyzing it according to type of energy (electricity, coal, etc.).

2. With your partner, create a set of simple bar graphs to show energy use within each sector of the economy. For example, start with a graph that shows the types of energy used in the industrial sector of the economy.

3. Write a brief summary of the pattern of energy use in each sector. Why do you think energy patterns vary from sector to sector?

4. Create a set of bar graphs to show how each type of energy is used. In this case, start with how electricity is used.

5. Write a brief summary of the main uses of each type of energy. Again, try to explain any significant differences in patterns of use between types of energy.

These can be quick-and-simple sketch graphs.

Sector	Electricity	Coal	Petroleum	Natural Gas	Total
Industrial	777	175	304	1034	2290
Transportation	15	0	1896	278	2189
Residential	486	4	147	661	1298
Commercial/institutional	388	0	205	472	1065
Agricultural	36	0	164	33	233
Public administration	47	0	58	29	134
Total	1729	179	2773	2495	7209

◁ **Fig. 25-2** *Sources of energy and energy use in Canada, 1997 (in petajoules)*

OIL AND GAS

The Creation of Oil and Gas

Oil and gas are generally found together. They were formed hundreds of millions of years ago when areas of Canada and adjacent seas were covered by shallow oceans. Over a period of millions of years, the remains of marine animals and plants fell to the sea floor. They accumulated in thick layers and eventually were covered by layers of sand and silt. Over time, the immense weight of all of these layers compressed the lower layers into sedimentary rock. Bacterial action, heat, and pressure converted the remains of the animals and plants into oil and gas.

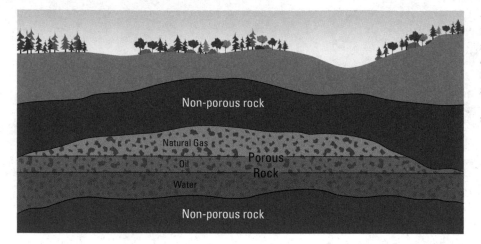

◁ **Fig. 25-3** *An anticlinal trap. The dome of non-porous rock captures the oil and gas, and stops them from reaching the surface. Why does the natural gas rise above the oil? Why do both rise above the water?*

Oil and gas are found in the geological structures that trapped them. One of several structures that traps oil and gas is the **anticlinal trap** (Fig. 25-3).

Oil and gas are found in geological structures that have the following characteristics:

- a geologic history that would allow oil and gas to develop
- a porous rock layer within which the oil and gas can exist
- a covering layer of non-porous rock which acts as a trap for the oil and gas

Searching for Oil and Gas

Finding oil and gas in amounts that will make their recovery worthwhile is a challenging task. Geologists must look for the special geologic structures that have trapped oil and gas. What makes this particularly difficult is that these deposits can be many hundreds of metres underground, and may not even exist in a particular geologic structure.

Geologists have many tricks that they can use in their search for oil and gas. These include:

- looking for rocks on the surface that contain traces of oil
- searching for clues, like fossils, in the sedimentary rock that indicate the right conditions for the formation of oil and gas
- using geologic records obtained from the drill cores of nearby wells
- conducting seismic surveys, which use shock waves to locate oil- and gas-bearing rock structures

Assuming that oil drilling has previously taken place in these areas

Fig. 25-4 ▷
The elaborate structure of an oil drill rig is used to turn a long string of pipes that ends in a diamond drill bit. Drill holes can be thousands of metres deep.

Drilling for Oil and Gas

The presence of oil and gas can only be determined by drilling, a very costly and time-consuming process that involves the use of a specialized drill rig (Fig. 25-4). The drilling process may continue for months.

Oil drilling can have one of three results. Sometimes no oil or gas is found and the "dry hole" is abandoned. In other cases, oil and gas are found, but the amount is not significant enough to justify moving the oil and gas to market. In this case, the well will be plugged, and the find will be re-evaluated at a later date, perhaps when oil and gas prices are higher. The final possibility, the one for which the company is hoping, is that the deposit is large enough to develop.

Often, only less valuable natural gas is found.

Recovering Oil and Gas

The removal of oil and gas from the ground, proceeds in one of two ways, depending on the nature of the deposit:

- *Flowing Wells* Some wells have enough natural pressure to force the oil or gas to the surface. At the surface, the flow is controlled by a series of valves called a "Christmas tree" (Fig. 25-5).

- *Non-flowing Wells* If there is not enough pressure to make the oil and gas flow to the surface, electric- or gasoline-powered pumps must be used (Fig. 25-6).

▽ **Fig. 25-5** *A flowing well may only need a Christmas tree valve to control its natural flow.*

As oil is removed from the earth, the recovery of the remaining oil becomes increasingly more difficult. Accordingly, scientists have created a variety of methods to remove a greater percentage of oil from deposits; this is called **secondary recovery**. Even with secondary recovery, only about 60% of the oil in most deposits can be recovered. Significant research is being done to improve this figure since even an increase of 5% in the amount of recovery would have the same impact as finding many large oilfields.

◁ **Fig. 25-6** *A "nodding horse," or "grasshopper," is needed to pump oil from a non-flowing well.*

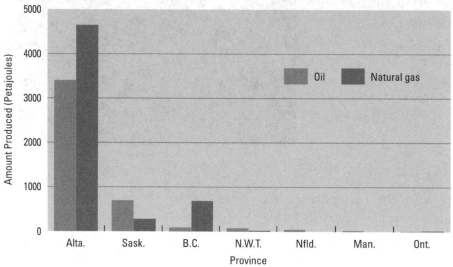

◁ **Fig. 25-7** *Producers of oil and natural gas in Canada, 1995. Note that Hibernia has come onstream since 1995.*

Sources of Canada's Oil and Gas

Canada's oil and gas production is shown in Fig. 25-7. For more than 50 years, almost all of Canada's oil and gas production has come from the western parts of the Boreal Plains and Prairie ecozones. This has meant that production has been concentrated in Alberta and in adjoining parts of Saskatchewan, British Columbia, and the Northwest Territories (Fig. 25-8). Natural gas production has been very much dominated by Alberta and, to a lesser extent, Saskatchewan and British Columbia.

Oil production totals include both conventional crude oil that is pumped from the ground and synthetic crude oil created from a special

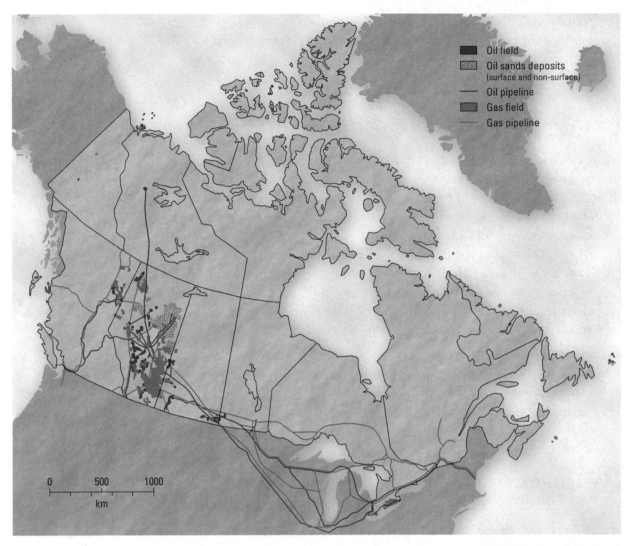

0   500   1000
km

△ **Fig. 25-8** *Canada's oil and gas deposits*

substance called **oil sand**, which is mined from huge deposits in north-eastern Alberta. An oil-like substance called **bitumen** is found around individual sand particles (Fig. 25-9). The oil sand is easily dug and must then be processed to separate the bitumen from the sand. The bitumen can be further processed to make synthetic crude oil. Oil sands are likely to become an increasingly important source of Canada's oil because the reserves of oil sands are larger than those of conventional oil. Since the cost of producing synthetic crude from oil sands is significantly higher than that of conventional crude, the share of the total coming from oil sands will only increase as conventional reserves are used and as crude prices increase.

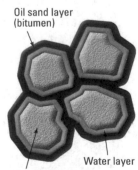

Oil sand layer
(bitumen)

Water layer

Sand particle

△ **Fig. 25-9** *Cross-section of oil sand particles*

Newfoundland became a significant producer of oil in 1997 with the opening of the Hibernia offshore oil project. Newfoundland's oil production is likely to increase in the years to come as additional projects are developed.

The Connecting Study that follows this chapter looks at Hibernia in more detail.

ELECTRICITY

Most electricity is produced with a generator. Generators range in size from those you can hold in your hand and use to power your bicycle light, to those used in a power station that could be larger than a house. In both cases, the idea is exactly the same. A rotating generator converts mechanical energy into electrical energy. In the case of a bicycle, the turning of the wheel provides the mechanical energy.

Canada ranks second behind Norway in the production of electricity per capita.

Now let's consider the situation of a huge generator owned by a power company. The company wants to produce massive amounts of electricity as cheaply as possible. To do this, it must find the most efficient way to turn its generator. In Canada, this is done by:

Check with your science teacher if you are not sure how this works.

- moving water in a **hydro-electric generating station**
- expanding steam produced by burning coal, oil, and natural gas in a **thermal-electric generating station**
- expanding steam produced from nuclear fission in a **nuclear-electric generating station**

Hydro-electricity

Hydro-electric generating stations can be built anywhere there are rivers with significant changes in elevation and large, reliable flows of water. The force of the water moving from a higher to a lower elevation drives the generator (Fig. 25-10).

See Fig. 16-3 on p. 182 for a photo of a power dam.

Advantages of Hydro-electricity
- Plants are cheap to operate since there is no fuel to buy.
- Since it does not require the burning of fossil fuels, it does not produce air pollution.
- Hydro-electric power is a renewable resource.
- The reservoir (if there is one) can be used for recreation like fishing and boating.

Disadvantages of Hydro-electricity
- Plants are very costly to build.
- Suitable sites are often very far from the areas where the electricity is needed; this means that costly and unsightly transmission lines must be built.

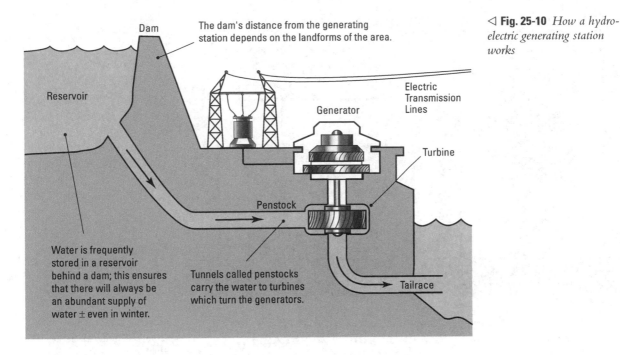

Dam

Reservoir

The dam's distance from the generating station depends on the landforms of the area.

Electric Transmission Lines

Generator

Turbine

Penstock

Water is frequently stored in a reservoir behind a dam; this ensures that there will always be an abundant supply of water ± even in winter.

Tunnels called penstocks carry the water to turbines which turn the generators.

Tailrace

◁ **Fig. 25-10** *How a hydro-electric generating station works*

- The building of dams requires the flooding of low-lying areas, which destroys everything in these areas; flooding also causes the release of dangerous chemicals, like mercury, from rocks under the reservoir.

- It significantly impacts the lives of the people who live in areas that are to be flooded. Since most areas which might be flooded today are in more remote parts of Canada, this impact is felt mostly by the Aboriginal people who live in these areas.

Thermal-electricity

In thermal-electric generating stations, steam, rather than moving water, is used to turn the turbines which, in turn, causes the generator to turn. The steam can be produced by the burning of fuel such as coal, oil, natural gas, wood, or even garbage (Fig. 25-11).

Advantages of Thermal-electricity
- Plants can be built where the electricity is needed or where fuel is cheaply available, so shorter transmission lines are needed.
- Plants are less expensive to build than hydro-electric or nuclear-electric plants.

Disadvantages of Thermal-electricity
- Fuel costs, especially for plants using oil and natural gas, are high.
- Oil, natural gas, and coal are non-renewable resources and will run out eventually.

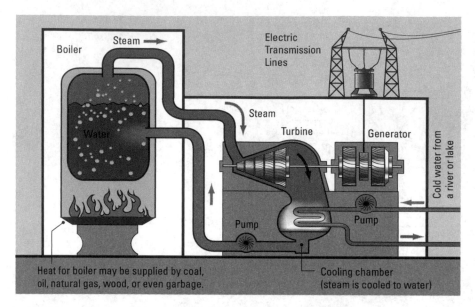

◁ **Fig. 25-11** *How a thermal-electric generating station works*

- The burning of these fuels produces carbon dioxide, which is a **greenhouse gas** and contributes to **global warming**.

- Coal, and to a lesser extent oil, produce the gases that are responsible for acid precipitation.

Chapter 35 focuses on the problem of global warming.

Nuclear-electricity

Nuclear-electric generating stations are similar to thermal plants in most respects except for the source of heat. The heat comes from the radioactive breakdown (fission) of uranium atoms. As with thermal plants, heat is used to boil water which produces the steam that turns the turbines (Fig. 25-12).

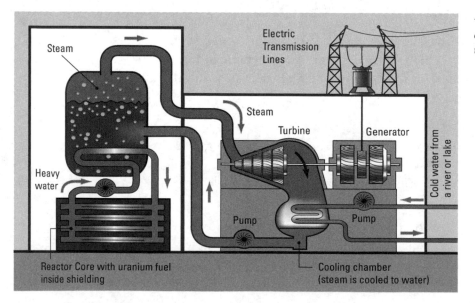

◁ **Fig. 25-12** *How a nuclear-electric generating station works*

Advantages of Nuclear-electricity

- Plants can be built where the energy is needed, so transmission costs are low.
- Operating costs are relatively low, especially in the early years of plant operation.
- Canada has an abundant supply of uranium.
- In normal operation, they do not produce air pollution.

Disadvantages of Nuclear-electricity

- Construction costs are very high.
- The radioactive materials are very hazardous to human health and must be handled with great care; accidents have the potential to harm many thousands of people.
- Waste products from nuclear plants remain dangerous for 100 000 years. No permanent method for handling these wastes has been established.
- The useful life of nuclear plants is much shorter than originally thought, which means that plants will have to be replaced or rebuilt at enormous cost.

Electrical Production in Canada

There is a wide variation in the kind of electrical generation that is used in different parts of Canada (Fig. 25-13). Some provinces, such as British

	Hydro	Thermal[1]	Nuclear	Total Generating Capacity (kW)
Newfoundland	90%	10%	0%	7401
Prince Edward Island	0%	100%	0%	121
Nova Scotia	16%	84%	0%	2475
New Brunswick	20%	65%	15%	4521
Quebec	94%	5%	2%	34 779
Ontario	22%	33%	45%	33 600
Manitoba	94%	6%	0%	5160
Saskatchewan	27%	73%	0%	3088
Alberta	10%	90%	0%	8807
British Columbia	86%	14%	0%	13 236
Territories	33%	67%	0%	382
Canada	58%	28%	14%	113 570

◁ **Fig. 25-13** *Provincial generating capacities, 1996*

1 includes internal combustion and combustion turbines

Columbia, Manitoba, and Québec, rely mainly on hydro-electric plants. Others, like Alberta, Saskatchewan, and the Atlantic provinces, depend heavily on thermal-electric plants. Fig. 25-14 shows the location of Canada's largest electrical generating stations.

Two provinces display somewhat unusual patterns. Most of Newfoundland's hydro-electric capacity is in Labrador. Most of the power produced there is sold to Hydro-Québec which, in turn, sells it to customers in the United States. The situation of Ontario is also unique. Ontario uses large amounts of electricity generated by all three types of plants including Canada's only large nuclear plants. The province has no large, undeveloped hydro-electric sites. Future increases in demand will have to be met by building thermal or nuclear plants, importing energy from other provinces, or by taking energy conservation measures.

Newfoundland and Québec have made an agreement to build a new hydro-electric project in Labrador. Some of the energy will be moved to the island of Newfoundland (using an undersea cable), while the rest will be sold to Hydro-Québec.

▽ **Fig. 25-14**

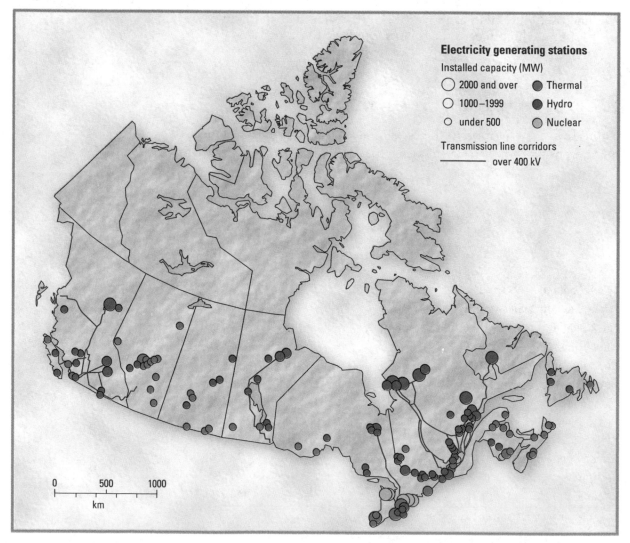

Electricity generating stations

Installed capacity (MW)

○ 2000 and over   ● Thermal
○ 1000–1999   ● Hydro
○ under 500   ● Nuclear

Transmission line corridors
——— over 400 kV

0   500   1000
km

Getting Electricity to Market

Once electricity is produced, it must be moved to where it will be used. Often, this means that electricity must be transmitted for hundreds of kilometres. This is done using a complex **power grid** into which generating stations direct their power. Major customers, like large industries, cities, and towns, take electricity from the grid. Within North America, provincial and state grids are linked so that electricity can be moved from province to province and to nearby American states. In fact, electricity has become one of Canada's most important export commodities.

THE BUSINESS OF ENERGY

Energy industries are a major part of Canada's economy. In 1997, they were responsible for almost 7% of our GDP and provided 280 000 jobs. Investments in energy projects, big and small, made up 16% of all investment in Canada's economy. Energy is also an important element of our foreign trade. Canada has been a net exporter of energy since 1969. More than 90% of all of our energy exports go to the United States, which has enormous energy needs. In fact, Canada is a net exporter of every major type of energy (Fig. 25-15).

net exporter: exports are greater than imports

Now it is time to look at where energy is used and what this means in terms of the movement of energy both within Canada, and between Canada and other countries. Establishing where energy is used in Canada is relatively simple, since energy use is directly tied to where people live and to the location of industry. Since most industry is located in the areas where most people live, the task becomes even easier. Examine Fig. 18-3 on p. 203, which shows Canada's population distribution, and you will have an accurate picture of where most energy use takes place.

Type of Energy	Exports	Imports	Net Trade
Natural gas	8694	136	8558
Oil	16 984	11 047	5937
Coal	2841	786	2054
Electricity	1356	210	1146
Uranium	836	208	629
Total	30 711	12 386	18 324

◁ **Fig. 25-15** *Canada's energy trade in 1997 (in millions of dollars). More than 90% of this trade is with the United States.*

Trade in Electricity

The movement of electricity between provinces, and internationally, is relatively easy to understand since it can only be moved by high-voltage power lines. Electricity is commonly moved from one area to another to

	Net Interprovincial Trade		Net Trade With the United States		Overall Net Trade
	From other provinces	To other provinces	From the US	To the US	
British Columbia		6.16		127.39	+ 133.55
Alberta		6.05	0.05		+ 6.00
Saskatchewan	1.88			0.78	- 1.10
Manitoba		3.95		358.73	+ 362.68
Ontario	2.67			16.68	+ 14.01
Québec	81.35			53.23	- 28.12
Newfoundland		92.80	0	0	+ 92.80
New Brunswick	8.00			10.72	+2.72
Prince Edward Island	3.19		0	0	-3.19
Nova Scotia		0.03	0	0	+ 0.03

△ **Fig. 25-16** *Interprovincial and international trade in electricity, (PJ) 1996. (All international trade is with the United States)*

meet varying needs. For example, electricity might be sold to the United States in summer when that country's air conditioning needs are high. In return, American power might be sold to Canada in winter, when heating demands are high here. Fig. 25-16 shows the movement of electricity among the provinces and with the United States.

Trade in Natural Gas

The interprovincial and international trade in natural gas is, as you might expect, closely tied to the location of gas pipelines, since this is the only economical way to move vast amounts of natural gas. Pipelines have been built from the main producing area of Alberta, British Columbia, and Saskatchewan to Ontario and into the United States. This pattern may change in the future with the development of new gas reserves in Atlantic Canada. A large gas field is being developed near Sable Island off Nova Scotia. As well, the natural gas associated with the Hibernia oil may be used in the future.

Hibernia natural gas is currently being pumped back into the petrolium deposit.

Trade in Oil

The trade in oil is much more complicated than that of natural gas. It seems strange at first glance, but Canada both imports and exports more than $10 billion worth of oil. This is largely due to the nature of oil shipping. The cheapest way to move oil is by supertanker. The second cheapest

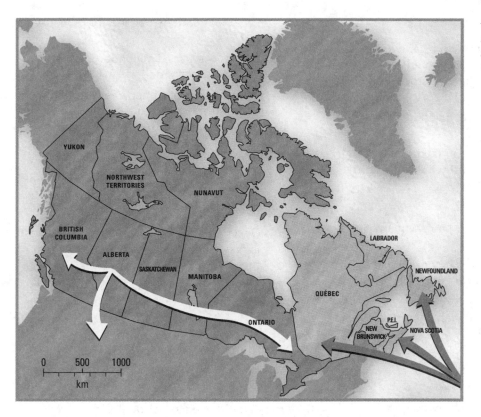

◁ **Fig. 25-17** *Canada's oil trade pattern is divided into two parts at the Ontario-Québec border*

is by pipeline. The result is that for many years, Canada's oil market has been split in two at the Ottawa River. From Ontario to the west, Canadian oil is used and considerable western oil is exported. Québec and Atlantic Canada, on the other hand, mainly use oil imported from such areas as the Middle East, South America, Africa, and the North Sea (Fig. 25-17). This may slowly change with the continued development of offshore East Coast oil resources.

A similar pattern exists for Canada's coal supply and use. Coal is imported into Ontario from the United States, while Canadian coal from Alberta, British Columbia, and Nova Scotia is exported.

LOOKING TOWARD THE FUTURE

Much of our prosperity as a nation, not to mention the way in which we live as individual Canadians, depends on the fact that we have always had abundant energy resources. Will this always be the case? Perhaps not. Consider the simple fact that most of our energy resources are non-renewable and will run out well within your lifetime. There are two things we must learn to do: to use our energy resources more wisely and to gradually replace our use of non-renewable energy with renewable sources. You can learn more about these two measures in Chapters 36 and 38.

CHECK YOUR UNDERSTANDING

1. There are three good reasons, and one not so very good reason, why Canadians use a great deal of energy. Describe what these are.

2. a) Explain the difference between conventional energy sources and alternative energy sources.

   b) What role does each play in Canada's energy use now, and what role might it play in the future?

3. a) What is a petajoule?

   b) Of what value is this unit, when you are studying energy?

4. a) Describe the geologic characteristics that must exist for oil and natural gas to be trapped in rock.

   b) Examine a geology map in an atlas. Where in Canada could oil and gas be found?

   c) Why have the oil and gas resources of only a few of these areas been developed?

5. What are oil sands and how do they contribute to Canada's energy supply?

6. Complete an organizer like Fig. 25-18 to compare the different methods of making electricity.

7. a) Canada's oil market is divided into two parts. Where is this division?

   b) Why does it exist?

   c) How might the expansion of the oil industry off Newfoundland change this?

ANALYZE AND APPLY

8. Describe the steps that the oil industry takes to find and develop a possible oil and gas deposit. In doing this, be sure to identify the points at which the company must make a decision, and indicate how the decision is made.

9. a) What is meant by secondary recovery of oil?

   b) Why is the use of secondary recovery so attractive to the oil industry?

10. a) Every region of Canada relies mainly on one method of producing electricity. Identify regions that depend mainly on thermal power and those that depend primarily on hydro-electric power.

    b) Explain why this is not surprising. (Hint: Think about the physical geography of these areas.)

    c) Describe the unique situations that exist in Newfoundland and Ontario. Why do they exist?

11. Why does Canada both import and export energy products? Consider oil and electricity.

THINK AND COMMUNICATE

12. The United States, Russia, Australia, and Japan each have one or more reasons why they would use a great deal of energy. Identify these reasons and indicate how each country's situation would be different from that of Canada.

13. Canadians are seen as wasteful users of energy.

    a) Do you think that you use more energy than you really need? Why or why not?

    b) How could you reduce your energy use without significantly changing the way in which you live?

▽ **Fig. 25-18**

	Hydro-electric Power	Thermal-electric Power	Nuclear-electric Power
Source of Power			
Advantages			
Disadvantages			

Offshore Oil: Hibernia

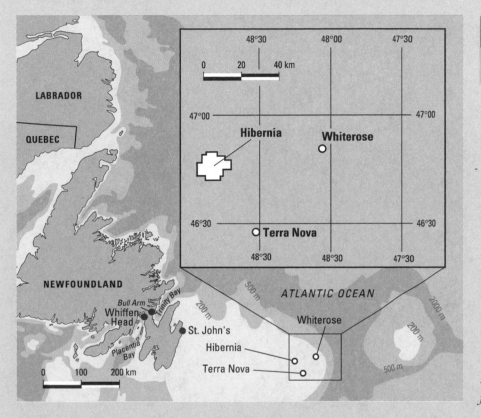

◁ **Fig. 25-19** *East Coast oil fields*

Exploration of the sedimentary rocks that make up the continental shelf off the coast of Atlantic Canada began during the 1960s. Several oil companies began drilling discovery wells into the seabed in search of oil and natural gas. Four major discoveries were made: two gas fields on the Scotian Shelf located 250 km off the coast of Nova Scotia, and two large oil fields on the Grand Banks of Newfoundland (Fig. 25-19). Hibernia, the larger oil field on the Grand Banks, is the focus of this Connecting Study.

A third oil field was discovered later. Also, large reserves of natural gas are being developed near Sable Island.

EXPLORATION

In 1979, Chevron Canada Resources drilled a discovery well into the northeastern portion of the Grand Banks. The results of this exploratory drilling were promising. By 1984, Mobil Oil Canada Limited had drilled nine more wells in the area. The results of the drilling enabled geologists

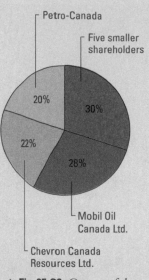

Petro-Canada
Five smaller shareholders
Mobil Oil Canada Ltd.
Chevron Canada Resources Ltd.

△ **Fig. 25-20** *Owners of the Hibernia Management and Development Company*

to map this new oil field and to determine that there were enough oil and gas deposits to make commercial development possible. In 1985, the findings of the geologists were presented to a joint federal-provincial environmental assessment panel. This panel conducted public hearings on whether this mammoth oil-drilling project on the Grand Banks would be good for the environment and the people of Newfoundland. By 1990, the project was approved. A 25-year lease was given to the Hibernia Management and Development Company (HMDC), a joint venture of several large oil companies, to construct and operate the Hibernia facilities (Fig. 25-20). Hibernia began producing oil and gas in November of 1997.

▽ **Fig. 25-21** *Hibernia's recoverable resources*

Recoverable Resources (PJ)

Crude oil	4080
Natural gas	10 045

You can learn more about Hibernia at www.hibernia.ca/hmdc/default.htm

GEOLOGY AND PRODUCTION

The Hibernia oil field is located on the Grand Banks about 315 km southeast of St. John's, Newfoundland. The actual drilling takes place in about 80 m of water. The oil and gas deposits are located in two geologic formations composed of sandstones. These formations are **reservoirs** known as the Hibernia and the Avalon sandstones (Fig. 25-22). The total Hibernia field contains approximately 18 590 PJ of crude oil. About 4080 PJ of this oil is recoverable with today's technology (Fig. 25-21). The

Hibernia is the fifth largest oil field ever discovered in Canada.

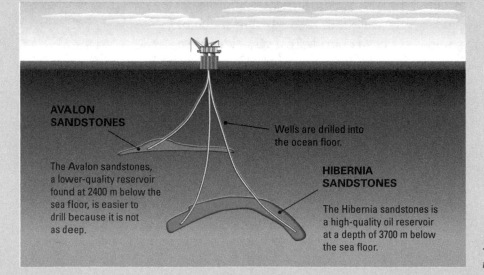

△ **Fig. 25-22** *Cross section of the Hibernia oil field*

Hibernia oil field will operate for about 20 years, and should produce oil worth an estimated $11 billion dollars.

THE DRILLING PLATFORM

Dangerous storms, cold temperatures, drifting icebergs, and fog make the waters off Newfoundland some of the most dangerous in the world. In 1982, a huge floating drilling platform, the Ocean Ranger, capsized in a fierce storm, killing 84 crew members. It was designed to withstand 120 kph winds and 20 m waves but still failed. To prevent a similar disaster in the future, scientists and engineers designed the Hibernia drilling platform with the utmost care. It consists of two parts: the Topsides production facilities and the Gravity Base Structure (GBS) (Fig. 25-23).

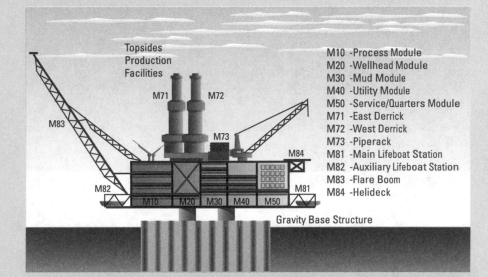

◁ **Fig. 25-23** *The Hibernia platform*

Topsides Production Facilities

M71   M72

M73

M83

M82   M84

M81

M10   M20   M30   M40   M50

M10 -Process Module
M20 -Wellhead Module
M30 -Mud Module
M40 -Utility Module
M50 -Service/Quarters Module
M71 -East Derrick
M72 -West Derrick
M73 -Piperack
M81 -Main Lifeboat Station
M82 -Auxiliary Lifeboat Station
M83 -Flare Boom
M84 -Helideck

Gravity Base Structure

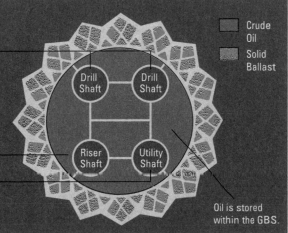

GBS CROSS SECTION

Two drill shafts are used to drill into the rock of the ocean floor to depths of more than 3700 m.

The riser shaft contains the equipment needed to pump the oil from the GBS storage facility to the offshore loading system.

The utility shaft contains the mechanical equipment to operate the GBS and run all the electrical equipment.

Drill Shaft   Drill Shaft

Riser Shaft   Utility Shaft

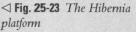
Crude Oil

Solid Ballast

Oil is stored within the GBS.

◁ **Fig. 25-24** *The teeth of the ice wall are designed to distribute the force of an iceberg hit over the entire GBS. The 1.4-m thick ice wall is supported by a set of concrete supports and a 15-m thick ice belt filled with iron ore. Each of the four shafts is 17 m in diameter.*

The Topsides facilities consist of five super modules containing the living quarters of the crew, and the drilling and production equipment. In addition, there are seven other structures including cranes, lifeboat stations, and a heliport.

The GBS platform is a concrete structure that cuts into the ocean floor where it is cemented into place. About 400 000 tonnes of iron ore granules are added to compartments inside the platform to give it weight and stability. It is designed to withstand 160 kph winds and 30 m waves.

The GBS has four shafts which extend 111 m from the base slab to its roof (Fig. 25-24). These shafts support the Topsides facilities. A large facility within the GBS has the capacity to store 1.3 million barrels of crude oil.

An iceberg management program has been developed to detect and track icebergs to reduce the probability of a collision with the GBS. If a collision seems imminent, tugs will endeavor to tow the iceberg away from the platform. The GBS has been designed, however, with the possibility of a collision in mind; it has 16 concrete teeth protruding from its circumference which can absorb the impact of a 1 million-tonne iceberg without suffering damage.

The super modules and seven other structures of the Topsides facilities were welded together at Bull Arm in Trinity Bay, Newfoundland, and then attached to the GBS unit. The completed platform was subsequently towed out to the installation site on the Grand Banks where it was attached to the ocean floor (Fig. 25-25).

The Topsides portion weighs 37 000 tonnes and the GBS unit weighs 550 000 tonnes. *Time* magazine called the GBS unit the eighth wonder of the modern world.

Every year between 10 000 and 20 000 icebergs form in Greenland and the Canadian Arctic. About 1000 drift into North Atlantic waters.

According to computer simulations, a hit from a 6 million-tonne iceberg would damage the structure but it would be repairable.

▽ **Fig. 25-25** *Mating of the Topsides portion to the GBS*

The mating operation took five days to complete (Fig. 25-25). The Topsides portion was taken by two barges to the GBS unit. The GBS took on water as ballast so that 105 m of its 111-metre height was below sea level. The Topsides portion was manoeuvred into position by four tugs. The GBS then released its ballast so that it rose to meet the Topsides unit. The two units were now one.

Ten of the world's most powerful tugboats arrived in Newfoundland waters to tow the Hibernia platform out to the Grand Banks. A satellite navigation and positioning system allowed the platform to be precisely located above the installation site. The tugs assumed a star-shaped pattern to hold the platform in place as it took on ballast and sank to the ocean floor (Fig. 25-26). The base of the structure was designed to cut into the ocean floor. A mixture of cement and sea water was pumped into compartments to provide a stable foundation. Over 400 000 tonnes of iron ore granules were then added to the GBS to provide ballast and help hold it in place.

▽ **Fig. 25-26** *Anchoring the platform in place*

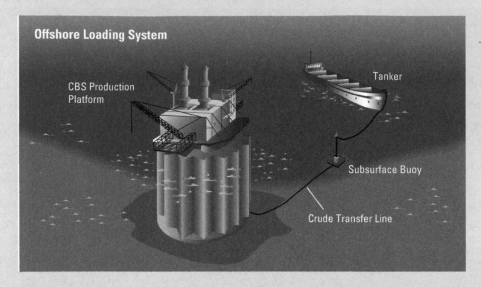

◁ **Fig. 25-27** *The crude oil is first stored in the GBS. When a shuttle tanker arrives, the oil is pumped along underwater pipelines to the buoy which contains flexible loading hoses that are attached to the tanker.*

TRANSSHIPMENT OF OIL

The crude oil pumped from beneath the sea is stored within the GBS. An Offshore Loading System of underwater pipelines pumps the crude oil onto shuttle tankers (Fig. 25-27). Each shuttle tanker carries 850 000 tonnes of crude oil from the Hibernia platform to a newly constructed transshipment port at Whiffen Head in Placentia Bay, Newfoundland. The crude oil is then transferred to onshore storage tanks until conventional tankers arrive to take it to market. The main markets for this oil are the refineries of eastern Canada, the United States, and Europe. The proximity of these markets keeps transportation costs relatively low.

ENVIRONMENTAL PROTECTION

During the 1980s, several studies were conducted to examine the impact of Hibernia on the biological and physical environment of the Grand Banks. The result was the development of Environmental Protection Plans for all phases of the project. Strict measures have been taken to prevent an oil spill from contaminating the waters. The Hibernia platform has been designed to withstand violent seas which might otherwise threaten leakage of the crude oil stored in the GBS. The ice-resistant features of the GBS ensure that it is able to withstand a collision with a large iceberg. The shuttle tankers have reinforced double-hulls and double-bottoms as insurance against leakage if punctured. Their ballast and cargo tanks are separate

After an oil tanker delivers its oil to a refinery, it must return empty to pick up more oil. Since the tanker needs weight to allow it to sail properly, water is pumped into the oil storage tanks as ballast. Many tanker captains dump the oil and water combination from these tanks before reaching port. Much of the oil pollution of our oceans comes from this practice.

to prevent oil from mixing with ballast water. A computer-based emergency shutdown procedure has been developed to prevent oil spills during loading operations. Canadian crews operate the shuttle tankers under strict Coast Guard regulations and all Hibernia personnel are required to undergo continual training in the prevention of environmental damage.

IMPACT ON NEWFOUNDLAND

How are Newfoundlanders benefiting from the development of the Hibernia oil field? Between 1991 and 1995, almost 2500 workers were employed in the construction of the platform, 78% of these at the Bull Arm construction site. Many of these people received training in construction, management, and high technology. Others received an upgrading of their skills as a result of this project. The skills developed by these people are useful in other industries based in Newfoundland or elsewhere. Although jobs are fewer now than during the construction phase of the project, there are still employment opportunities associated with Hibernia. In the future, royalties from the production of oil could be in the billions of dollars. They will go to the government for use by the people of Newfoundland.

Many Newfoundlanders who had moved to Alberta to work in the oil industry were able to return to their home province to use their skills.

IN CLOSING...

The development of the Hibernia oil field was the first step in developing a Canadian offshore oil industry on the Grand Banks. Work has now begun at the Terra Nova site, 35 km southeast of Hibernia. This site is expected to yield about 2502 PJ of oil. The Whiterose field, 55 km east of Hibernia, may be developed in the future.

Newfoundland has been one of Canada's poorest provinces. With the recent loss of the cod fishery, many of the people of Newfoundland have suffered a serious blow to their lifestyle and economy. Newfoundlanders hope that with the development of the Grand Banks oil fields, a new era has begun for their region, in which new job opportunities will lead to increased prosperity.

QUESTIONS

CHECK YOUR UNDERSTANDING

1. What oil and gas discoveries have been made off Canada's East Coast?

2. How do companies determine the size of an oil field?

3. How has the GBS unit been designed to withstand collisions with icebergs?

4. Explain the steps that were involved in building the Hibernia drilling platform.

5. Describe the process of getting the oil from under the sea to market.

ANALYZE AND APPLY

6. Draw a pie graph to show the amount of recoverable oil compared to the total amount of oil available at Hibernia.

7. a) Describe the steps that have been taken to protect the environment.

   b) How might large-scale development of oil fields affect the environment and human activities on the Grand Banks?

8. a) What impact has the Hibernia project had on Newfoundlanders?

   b) What types of skills would people have developed by working on this project?

   c) Where else could these skills be used?

THINK AND COMMUNICATE

9. Newfoundland has been one of Canada's poorest provinces. What do you think the Newfoundland government should do with the royalties it receives from offshore oil developments?

10. In spite of the general feeling that Hibernia and neighbouring oil fields are critical to the future economic growth of Newfoundland, there are critics of this type of development.

    a) Investigate what environmental, economic, and social criticisms have been made against this project.

    b) How can you compare the benefits and disadvantages of such a project?

    c) Evaluate the differing viewpoints.

Location and Manufacturing

STUDY GUIDE

By the end of this chapter, you will be able to:

- identify and describe location factors that influence manufacturers
- identify the patterns of manufacturing in Canada
- explain why a national pattern exists for different kinds of manufacturing
- use GIS to study the location of auto assembly plants and the reasons for their location

Key Terms

location factors
raw materials
market

labour supply
transportation
political decisions

circumstance
entrepreneur
fresh water and power

branch plant

When someone wants to start a new company, he or she must prepare a business plan, which is a detailed outline explaining why the company will be successful.. Imagine that you have decided to build a new factory and you must create a business plan; what factors would be important in determining the best location for your company in Canada?

1. Start by determining the product(s) your company will make. Choose from the following products, or create a product of your own: a commercial version of your mother's special spaghetti sauce, (what you hope will be) this year's must-have Christmas toy, or a new kind of wooden canoe paddle (Fig. 26-1).

2. Identify at least four location factors that you must consider when deciding where to build your factory.

3. Which of these factors would be most important for your company? Why?

4. Based on your answer to question 3, in which part of Canada would you choose to locate your factory? You may be able to get some of the information you need from an atlas. Why would you choose this location?

The bank will want to see your business plan before they loan you the $500 000 (or more) you need to get started.

THIS IS MY PRODUCT. IT'S A CANOE PADDLE AND A SQUEEGEE!

△ **Fig. 26-1**

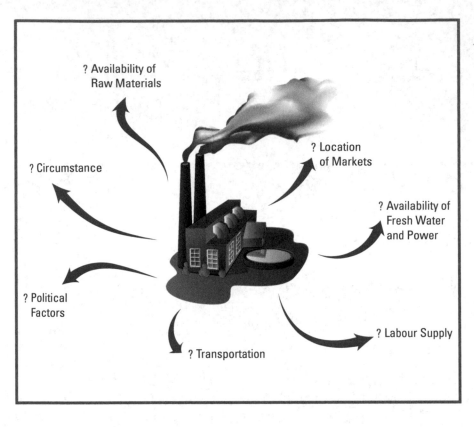

? Availability of
Raw Materials

? Circumstance

? Location
of Markets

? Availability of
Fresh Water
and Power

? Political
Factors

? Labour Supply

? Transportation

◁ **Fig. 26-2** *A number of factors affect the location of any factory. The relative importance of each varies, depending on the company.*

Some day, you may have to choose the location for a real manufacturing plant. For most companies, this is a tremendously important decision. In fact, the very survival of the company can depend on the success of this one decision. The location of any particular factory is influenced by a unique set of circumstances, such as the presence of a special raw material or the location of customers. There is a set of **location factors** that can be used to help us understand why manufacturers locate where they do (Fig. 26-2). In the section that follows, we will look at seven location factors and how they have influenced the location of specific companies in different parts of Canada. While all seven of these factors are likely to be involved in the location of just about any manufacturer, one (or perhaps two) of them is likely to dominate any particular location decision.

LOCATION FACTORS FOR MANUFACTURING

Availability of Raw Materials

Perhaps one of the easiest location factors to understand is the availability of **raw materials**. While any manufacturer needs a reliable source of raw materials, for some companies, it is of extreme importance to locate near the raw material. For example:

- Fruits and vegetables should be processed as soon as possible after being picked, so food processing companies tend to be located in the areas where the crops are grown.

- Some factories, like sawmills, use great quantities of bulky raw materials and produce finished products that are much smaller. These companies tend to be located near the bulky raw materials, which are more difficult to transport.

McCAIN FOODS (CANADA)

Just about every Canadian is familiar with the frozen French fries and related products produced by McCain. McCain Foods is a Canadian company, which operates in Canada and in countries as far away as New Zealand, Poland, and Argentina. It employs more than 16 000 people worldwide and has annual sales of more than $5 billion (1998). This huge company can trace its history back to the potato fields of the upper Saint John River valley and to its first potato processing plant, which opened in 1957 (Fig. 26-3). This factory was built in Florenceville, New Brunswick, which is still the international headquarters. McCain Foods (Canada) has four factories that process potatoes in Canada. They are located in Florenceville and Grand Falls (New Brunswick), Borden-Carleton (Prince Edward Island), and Portage la Prairie (Manitoba). In each case, these factories are located in a major potato-growing area.

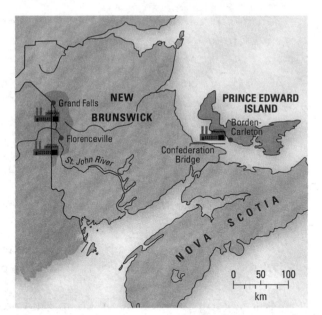

△ **Fig. 26-3** *A tiny potato-processing plant in Florenceville, New Brunswick, has developed into a major international corporation with plants in both Canada and abroad.*

This map shows the potato growing areas of New Brunswick and Prince Edward Island, along with McCain's maritime processing plants.

You can get more information about McCain Foods at www.mccain.com

Location of Markets

Often, a company will choose to establish itself in an area because the majority of its customers, or **market**, is located nearby. This is not surprising if you consider that being situated close to customers has clear advantages. For example, delivery costs are minimized. Also, a company that is near its customers can deliver its products in the minimum time possible. Both of these benefits would give a company an advantage over competitors that are located further away.

You might ask why all companies do not locate close to their customers. In fact, most companies will locate near their markets unless there is a very good reason not to. For example:

- A company's customers may be spread all over the country (or the world), so it does not matter where the factory is located. For instance, a company that makes hockey equipment might have customers in countries like Japan and Germany, among others.

- Other location factors may be more important than having nearby markets. This would be the case with McCain Foods.

CARDIUM TOOL SERVICES

While the products of McCain Foods are very well-known to most people, this is not the case for Cardium Tool Services of Edmonton. Cardium Tool Services makes products like *tubing anchor catchers* and *critical service tandem cone hydraulic liner hangar assemblies*. To people in the oil drilling and production industries, these are vital products that allow oil and gas to be produced efficiently and safely. Cardium started in 1954, only seven years after the first major discovery of oil in western Canada at Leduc, Alberta. Edmonton was an obvious choice for the company, since it is the largest city near Alberta's oil fields. Being close to the customers in the oil fields is an important consideration, especially if those customers experience an emergency and need a critical part right away. This need to be close to the market is reflected by the location of the company's branches in important oil-producing countries like the United Arab Emirates, Indonesia, and Venezuela.

More information about Cardium Tool Services is available at www.cardium.com

Availability of Fresh Water and Power

One of the basic needs for most kinds of manufacturing is an abundant supply of fresh water and power. Many manufacturing companies, like steel makers and oil refiners, use vast amounts of fresh water for cooling and cleaning purposes. As a result, companies in these fields must locate near major lakes and rivers. In pioneer days, flowing water was used to power the machinery in sawmills and grist (grain) mills. After the **Industrial Revolution**, other power sources came to replace water power. Perhaps the most significant power source for determining industrial location, is cheap hydro-electricity.

The production of hydro-electricity is discussed in Chapter 25.

The company uses the British spelling of *aluminum* in its name.

ALCAN ALUMINIUM

Producing one tonne of aluminum requires the use of 13 500 kWh of electricity. This much electricity would keep a stereo system operating 24 hours a day for more than 50 years. Since one large smelter may produce more than 200 000 tonnes of aluminum per year, it is easy to understand why aluminum smelters are built only in places where electricity is readily and cheaply available. In fact, no other industry relies on the location of cheap power as much as the aluminum industry.

Canada's largest producer of aluminum is Alcan. Alcan is one of Canada's largest companies. In 1997, its production in Canada and other countries was worth almost US$8 billion and the company employed about 33 000 people. Alcan has four smelters in the Saguenay River Valley, in Québec, that will produce more than one million tonnes per year of aluminum by 2002. These smelters are powered by six, company-owned, hydro-electric plants on the nearby Saguenay and Peribonka Rivers. These mills sell to customers in eastern North America, Europe, and the Middle East. Alcan's mill in Kitimat, British Columbia, sells to customers in western North America and Asia.

More information on Alcan is available at www.alcan.com

Why do you think this smelter was located here?

Labour Supply

A company must consider the availability and cost of its **labour supply** when deciding where to locate. In the past, many companies needed a large, low-cost labour force. This was frequently the case in industries like clothing manufacturing. Since the signing of the NAFTA, it has been difficult for Canada to effectively compete with Mexico and parts of the United States in industries that employ low-cost labour; therefore, that type of manufacturing is not as prevalent in this country. Companies in Canada are much more likely to need workers with advanced skills. As a result, manufacturers tend to locate in parts of the country which have the universities, colleges, and apprenticeship programs that produce the workers they need.

The impact of the North American Free Trade Agreement is discussed in Chapter 32.

NORTEL NETWORKS

The **research and development** (R and D) branch of Nortel Networks in Ottawa illustrates the need for skilled labour better than perhaps any other company in the country. More than 8000 scientists, engineers, designers, and support staff work here, in Canada's largest R and D facility, to develop future generations of telecommunications networks. One statistic serves to illustrate how important skilled labour is to this company — Nortel hires three out of every five Ph.D. graduates in electrical engineering from Canadian universities.

You can learn more about Nortel Networks at www.nortel.com

Transportation

Every company needs fast and efficient **transportation**. For example, Cardium Tool Services uses air freight from the Edmonton airport to ship rush orders around the world, while Alcan ships bulk orders of aluminum to Europe by freighter. For some companies though, transportation is the most important location factor of all. For example, the two large steel mills in Hamilton are located in that city to take advantage of raw materials that are brought by ship; this includes coal from American ports along Lake Erie and iron ore from ports on the lower St. Lawrence River.

DOW CHEMICALS OF CANADA

Dow Chemicals of Canada employs about 700 workers in Sarnia, Ontario and makes a variety of products like plastics, epoxy resins, and latex. The raw material for making these products is crude oil from Alberta. This oil is carried to Sarnia by the 2000 km-long Interprovincial Pipeline. Without the pipeline, it is hard to imagine that Dow's Sarnia operation would be as large as it is.

More information on Dow Chemicals is available at www.dow.com

More information about Sarnia, Ontario, can be found in Chapter 18.

Political Factors

One way for a government to attract and keep industry is to provide a good business climate. This can be often achieved through **political decisions**. Governments can make decisions that will help to attract new business or, if they are not careful, that will drive investment away. Two types of government decisions can affect the willingness of a company to locate in an area: direct and indirect. Governments at all levels can make direct decisions to encourage a company to locate in their jurisdiction. For example, they might offer a company reduced taxes for a number of years or provide the land for a new factory. Indirect decisions can also be important. A good example of this would be the impact of a new highway through the greater Toronto region. Highway 407 allows manufacturers (particularly in the auto industry) to move raw materials and finished products quickly and to avoid other highways in the region that are often congested. Auto-assembly and parts companies would be more likely to locate (or expand) in the area facilitated by this highway because they could be confident that deliveries could be made on time; this is of critical importance in the auto industry.

TOYOTA MOTORS MANUFACTURING CANADA

In the mid-1980s, the Japanese auto maker Toyota decided that it wanted to expand its North American operations by building a

You can find more information about Toyota at www.toyota.ca

Cambridge Ontario Wins Toyota Plant

◁ **Fig. 26-4** *Newspaper headlines like this one, announced Toyota's decision to locate a new plant in Cambridge, Ontario.*

new assembly plant. It is not hard to understand why every town and city in Canada and the United States would want this new factory. Auto-assembly plants provide many secure, high-paying jobs. They also tend to attract other companies (parts manufacturers, for example) to locate in the same area (Fig. 26-4). The Ontario and local governments provided incentives to Toyota to encourage them to locate in Cambridge. One of the reasons why governments are willing to offer short-term benefits to a company locating in an area is that the benefits of the factory will last for many years and that future expansion in the same area is possible. This is exactly what happened with Toyota. Partly because of government subsidies and incentives, Toyota opened a plant in Cambridge, Ontario, in 1988. The factory employed 1000 workers and was designed to build 50 000 cars per year. Since then, employment has grown to more than 2000 and the plant now builds more than 200 000 cars per year.

Circumstance

The location factors mentioned so far are all quite specific and refer to the particular needs of industry, such as market, labour, and transportation. Beyond this, though, there are many other influences on the location of factories that are more general and difficult to measure. One of these is the role of the **entrepreneur**. An entrepreneur is someone who sees the sales potential for a new business and then works to develop that potential. For example, there were many people who could have seen the potential demand for frozen French fries or the snowmobile, but only a few individuals actually did something about it. The people who did, the McCain brothers and J-Armand Bombardier, started tiny companies in their home towns; they had no idea that some day these companies would grow to become huge multi-national corporations with large factories in various areas.

A similar **circumstance** (some people would call it an accident) occurred as a result of Nortel Networks' presence in Ottawa. A number of high-tech companies in the Ottawa area, like Corel and Newbridge Networks, were started by scientists who used to work for Nortel. Not surprisingly, these companies are located in the Ottawa area because that is where these entrepreneurs lived.

The expansion of Toyota in Cambridge illustrates a different circumstance. Once a company has come to be established in one location, it is likely that further expansion will occur in the same area. When the Toyota factory more than doubled to 253 000 m^2 in 1997, no additional government subsidies were given, but for several reasons it just made sense to expand in this location rather than to build elsewhere.

A similar situation has occurred with the Canadian manufacturers that were established when Canada did not have free trade with the United States. During this time, it made economic sense for American companies to establish **branch plants** in Canada. These were relatively small, independent factories that were designed to meet the needs of the Canadian market. Many of our best known companies established branch plants in Canada, most often in southern Ontario and Québec. Examples of these are Ford of Canada, Canadian General Electric, and IBM of Canada. You can often identify these companies by their names — what pattern do you see? While these branch plants no longer have the advantage of **tariffs**, they remain among our most important factories. In some cases, they have even expanded to make products that will be sold in the United States.

GENERAL MOTORS OF CANADA

The location of General Motors in Oshawa illustrates the idea of circumstance very well. In the 1800s, a carriage-making business started in a small village northeast of Toronto. A number of years later, this small company moved to Oshawa. When the "new-fangled" horseless carriage, the car, appeared on the scene in the early 1900s, the company started to build automobiles. This occurred for a couple of reasons. One was the entrepreneurial nature of the company's founder, Sam McLaughlin, who saw the potential of the automobile and the limited future of the carriage. The other reason was that the carriage company had a factory, skilled workers, and capital to invest in the new venture. In relatively few years, the McLaughlin Carriage Company had become General Motors of Canada and the rest, as they say, is history. In July 1994, Maureen Kempston Darkes was appointed president and general manager of General Motors Canada, and vice-president of General Motors Corporation.

More information on General Motors of Canada is available at www.gmcanada.com

City	Value Added in Manufacturing ($ million)	Population (thousands)	Value Added in Manufacturing ($/person)
Calgary	2598	789	3293
Chicoutimi-Jonquière	1066	161	6621
Edmonton	3838	850	4515
Halifax	618	326	1896
Hamilton	4164	612	6804
Kitchener-Waterloo	3819	369	10 350
London	3079	390	7895
Montréal	20041	3180	6302
Ottawa-Hull	2010	965	2083
Québec	2013	660	3050
Regina	464	192	2417
St. Catharines-Niagara	2519	368	6845
St. John's	196	173	1133
Saint John	982	125	7856
Saskatoon	503	215	2340
Sherbrooke	484	143	3385
Sudbury	347	159	2182
Thunder Bay	651	125	5208
Toronto	27798	4588	6059
Trois-Rivières	719	138	5210
Vancouver	5795	1615	3588
Victoria	262	296	885
Windsor	3406	270	12 615
Winnipeg	2461	660	3729

△ **Fig. 26-5** *Value added in manufacturing in Canada's major cities*

You now know the factors that affect where manufacturers locate. The next step is to investigate the pattern of manufacturing that exists in Canada. There are two aspects to this. One is how much manufacturing is done in each province. The other is where different kinds of manufacturing occur.

1. The vast majority of manufacturing occurs in cities, so that is where we will concentrate our attention. Fig. 26-5 shows the population of Canada's 24 largest cities and the value added by manufacturing in those cities.

"Value added" is the difference between the cost of the raw materials and the labour that go into manufacturing and the value of the final products.

2. Locate and plot each city on an ecozone map of Canada. Use one symbol to mark all cities with a *per capita value added* greater than $5000 and a different one to mark those with a value less than $5000. In what ecozones are the high *per capita value added* cities?

3. Review the location factors above and explain why so much manufacturing occurs in such a small area.

4. Look at the kinds of manufacturing that occur in different parts of Canada (Fig. 26-6).

   a) Rank the seven major categories of manufacturing (Do not include "Unspecified/Other").

   b) Give three examples of the products that each type produces.

   c) Name a company that belongs to each category.

5. Compare the national pattern of manufacturing to that of each major region. For each region, identify one (or two) type(s) of manufacturing that is significantly more important in that region than in the country as a whole. (Do not include "Unspecified/Other")

6. Use your understanding of location factors to explain why this pattern exists.

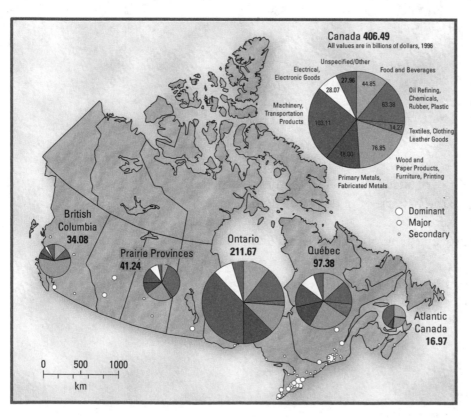

◁ **Fig. 26-6** *Map of manufacturing in Canada. The "Unspecified" category includes: types of industry not included in the "Other" category, and industries which cannot be specified due to Statistics Canada confidentiality rules.*

CANADA'S AUTO INDUSTRY

Canada's auto-making industry is of such great importance to our economy, that it deserves a special look. In terms of dollar value, cars, light trucks, and auto parts are our most important manufactured products and, by far, our most important export. There are a number of reasons for this. It all started with the Auto Pact, a trade agreement signed with the United States in the 1960s that required a minimum number of cars to be built in Canada. Canada proved to be a good place to build cars for both the American Big Three car companies (General Motors, Ford, and Chrysler) and for Japanese manufacturers (Toyota, Honda, and Suzuki). Canadian workers produced very high quality cars at a competitive price. As a result, in recent years, a number of additional assembly plants have been built and existing plants have been expanded.

GIS activity: You will have the opportunity to learn where auto-assembly plants are located and the reasons for their locations. Your teacher will give you detailed instructions.

QUESTIONS

CHECK YOUR UNDERSTANDING

1. a) What is a location factor?
   b) Name each of the location factors mentioned in this chapter and briefly explain each in your own words.
2. a) What is an entrepreneur?
   b) What role do entrepreneurs play in deciding where factories are located?

ANALYZE AND APPLY

3. Some factories tend to be located close to raw materials and far from markets, while others are far from raw materials and close to markets (Fig. 26-7). Give two examples of each type of factory and explain why they locate where they do.

4. Compare the customers for the products made by Cardium Tool Services and McCain. How do these different types of customers affect the location of each company?

◁ **Fig. 26-7**

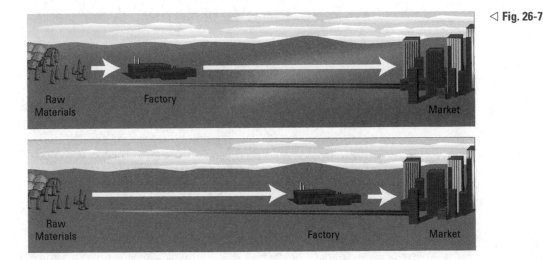

Raw Materials   Factory   Market

Raw Materials   Factory   Market

THINK AND COMMUNICATE

5. a) How has the labour supply situation in Canadian manufacturing changed in recent years? Why?

   b) How do you think this change should affect your educational plans?

6. a) List three reasons why a company would be more likely to expand in its current location than to build in a new location.

   b) List three reasons why a company might decide to build a new factory in a different area rather than to expand an existing operation.

   c) Compare your answers to 6a and 6b. Is it possible to say which choice would be made in all cases?

7. a) What is a branch plant? Name four branch plant companies that were not named in this chapter.

   b) How have the original advantages of branch plants come to be replaced by different advantages? Is the new location factor likely to be more significant than the original one?

ATI Graphics

It is a tradition in most Canadian geography textbooks to include a case study about a major manufacturer. Almost always, these studies have concentrated on steel-making, auto-assembly, or oil-refining; these are examples of what are called **smokestack industries**. These are the traditional, resource-based kinds of manufacturing that have been the basis of Canada's economy in the 20th century. This Connecting Study, on the other hand, looks at one of the **knowledge industries** that are becoming the dominant type of manufacturing for the 21st century.

You may not have heard of ATI Graphics, but if you use computers it is very likely that you have used their products. ATI does not make computers, but it does make some of the most important parts of the computer — those that produce the vivid two-dimensional (2-D) and three-dimensional (3-D) graphic images that we actually see on our computer screen. In fact, ATI is the largest manufacturer in the world of 3-D and multimedia computer chips and graphics boards. ATI plans to continue its phenomenal growth, which gave it more than $1 billion in sales in 1998 and made it Canada's third largest high-tech company only 13 years after its founding.

ATI has its headquarters in Thornhill, Ontario, which is one of the northern suburbs of Toronto. About 800 of their 1600 employees work here, with the others at ATI offices and factories in the United States, Germany, France, the United Kingdom, Ireland, Barbados, Malaysia, Hong Kong, and Japan.

KEY TERMS

smokestack industries

knowledge industries

tandem engineering

ATI is the third largest high-tech company after Nortel and Newbridge Networks. Note that statistical references in this chapter refer to 1998, unless otherwise indicated.

ATI'S HISTORY

ATI was founded by Kwok Yuen (K.Y.) Ho and two associates. Mr. Ho is an electrical engineer from China. After he graduated from university in 1974, he worked for approximately 10 years learning about the computer industry. In 1984, he came to Canada as a visitor and liked what he saw — wide open spaces and business opportunities. When he returned to Asia, he decided to come back to Canada and start a business in the poorly developed computer-graphic hardware industry.

LOCATION FACTORS AND ATI

In the manufacturing chapter, you were told that a good way to study a company's operation is by examining how location factors affect it. The following is an examination of how location factors have affected ATI.

Availability of Raw Materials

Unlike a steel mill or oil refinery, the transport of large quantities of raw materials is not very important to a company like ATI. The raw materials they need are easily brought by air freight from anywhere in the world to their two manufacturing facilities in Thornhill and Taiwan. Access to raw materials is not a significant factor in the location of this company.

Location of Markets

ATI sells its graphics boards and chips to two kinds of markets. From the beginning of the company's history, ATI has sold to original equipment manufacturers (OEMs). These are companies that make computers, for example, Apple, Compaq, and Dell. In fact, ATI sells to all ten of the largest computer makers in the world, along with many smaller ones. More recently, ATI has sold an increasing percentage of their products to individual consumers through computer stores of various types. Both markets are found across the world, with about 35% in North America, 27% in Europe, and most of the rest in Asia. For ATI, being close to markets is not a very important location factor.

Because graphics boards are improving so rapidly, computer users are now much more likely to upgrade their computer's graphical capability between computer purchases.

Availability of Power and Fresh Water

ATI does not use particularly large amounts of electricity and fresh water. Normal municipal sources of these are adequate. This is another factor that is not important to ATI's location.

Labour Supply

When Mr. Ho visited Canada in 1984, one of the things that impressed him (other than the scenery) was the availability of skilled engineers and scientists. ATI's success depends on its ability to be ahead of its competitors technologically, in order to meet the growing needs of its customers in the absolute minimum time possible. It achieves this in several different ways:

- by spending a great deal of money on research and development — more than $100 million in 1998, which was almost 9% of the value of their total sales. This is much more than most companies would spend.

- by using **tandem engineering**, which substantially speeds up the process of getting new products to market. This type of engineering allows two or more engineering teams to work on a product and the next generation(s) of that product simultaneously. In 1993, before tandem engineering began, a new generation of graphics hardware would take 12 to 18 months from the research and development stage to the manufacturing stage. Now, this takes only 6 to 8 months. Tandem engineering, however, does require a greater number of engineers.

- by making both chips and circuit boards. This means that they avoid the limitations of generic (Fig. 26-8) "off-the-shelf" chips. Making both chips and boards requires a large, highly skilled labour force.

Clearly, being able to find enough workers with the right skills remains of critical importance to ATI's success. Its location in southern Ontario, near so many universities and colleges and a large, skilled labour-force, gives it the best chance to meet its labour needs.

△ **Fig. 26-8** *ATI must always be on the cutting edge of computer graphics hardware. This means new generations of graphics boards come on the market every six to eight months.*

Computer chips are either designed for a special purpose or for more general use. Companies that build boards, but do not make their own chips, may find that they cannot build boards that will do exactly what they want.

Transportation

Air transport is important to ATI for two reasons. Its raw materials and finished products are small in volume, light in weight, high in value, and must be shipped quickly to their destinations. As a result, almost everything ATI needs or produces is shipped by air. Air transport is used for business travel as well. ATI executives frequently visit customers and suppliers all over the world, and, customers and suppliers often visit ATI's offices.

ATI uses the facilities of Pearson International Airport in Toronto for moving both people and freight. Having ready access to efficient air transport facilities is a significant factor in ATI's location.

Political Factors

In its early history, ATI received financial assistance and advice from the Canadian Export Development Corporation.

Circumstance

Circumstance has played a significant role in ATI's location. Think about the company's founding, and imagine what might have happened if Mr. Ho had decided to take his vacation in the United States or Australia. ATI might be a similar company, but it could be located in Boston or Melbourne!

Much of ATI's success and growth is tied to the entrepreneurial abilities of its founders. In fact, Mr. Ho was selected by *Canadian Business* magazine as Canada's entrepreneur of the year for 1998. It is easy to relate ATI's success to its technological advancement. Less obvious, is the role that customer service has played in this success. ATI has always made it a priority to work closely with its customers. This aspect of entrepreneurship has contributed much to the company's growth.

ATI's founders were recent immigrants to Canada from East Asia. The great majority of Asian immigrants settle in either Toronto or Vancouver, so it is not surprising that ATI was built in one of these cities. It is located in a suburb of Toronto that has a significant number of large and small high-tech companies. If this district of technology-based companies had not been there, ATI might have located in a different part of the city.

CHALLENGES FACING ATI

ATI faces an exciting future, but it does face some serious challenges. The computer graphics field continues to grow at a very rapid rate. ATI is starting to develop new markets for its products that are outside the traditional computer field. For example, they now make digital cable television terminal boxes. These boxes are a step toward the gradual elimination of the division of television and computers into two isolated technologies. In the future, if ATI and others are correct, you will have a television that you can use as a computer, or vice versa. By being a pioneer in this new field, ATI hopes to become a dominant player in a huge new market.

Cable television companies are gradually changing from using analog signals to digital signals. This change opens a whole new market to ATI (and its competition).

In spite of all of this, ATI faces a number of problems for the future, some coming as a result of the company's success. If your company has been extraordinarily successful, investors expect you to continue this rate of success. Growth in sales and profits must occur at a rate that is far beyond what is expected of most other companies. If ATI were only to achieve the kind of results that are typical of average companies, this might be seen as a problem, and investors might not want to provide the large amounts of money that ATI would need to expand. A second problem that comes from success is that ATI is an attractive takeover target for other, larger companies who want both ATI's share of the market and, more importantly, ATI's advanced technology. A final problem is the unpredictable nature of the high-tech business world. Make a right decision today, and you can make millions of dollars in just a few months. Make a wrong decision tomorrow, or have a competitor make a big breakthrough, and you can lose your market share and your millions just as quickly.

You can learn more about ATI Graphics at www.atitech.com

QUESTIONS

CHECK YOUR UNDERSTANDING

1. a) What kinds of products does ATI produce?

    b) How will ATI's products change in the years to come?

    c) Are you an ATI customer? How would you know?

2. Briefly describe how ATI came into being and how it became a major high-tech company.

ANALYZE AND APPLY

3. a) What is a smokestack industry? What is a knowledge industry?

    b) Complete an organizer like the one in Fig. 26-9 to compare the two.

4. a) In what ways is ATI a typical manufacturing company?

    b) In what ways is ATI not typical?

5. From the point-of-view of ATI, why is it desirable that the graphics ability of computers improves faster than other aspects of the computer's power?

THINK AND COMMUNICATE

6. Answer this question with a partner. Your teacher will give you the name of a manufacturing company to investigate. Study your company to determine how it has been affected by the seven location factors. Create a poster to illustrate your findings. Find out about your company by:

    *   writing to the company's public relations department

    *   checking the company's Web pages on the Internet

    *   looking for newspaper and magazine stories about the company

    *   phoning to arrange a visit to the company

▽ **Fig. 26-9**

	Smokestack Industry	Knowledge Industry
Four Examples		
Basis of Industry		
Time Period of Economic Importance		

27 Providing Services

STUDY GUIDE

By the end of this chapter, you will be able to:

- explain how tertiary industries differ from primary and secondary industries
- explain the differences between basic and non-basic industries
- examine future trends for tertiary industries
- conduct a job search in the tertiary sector of the economy

Key Terms

tertiary industries	non-basic services	wholesale	entrepreneur
basic services	trade	retail	call centre

Workers who hold jobs in the **tertiary industries** provide **services** to people. They do not manufacture products, or exploit the natural environment. They supply services to the general public. They also support workers in the primary and secondary industries. For example, a meteorologist supplies weather reports to fishers, and office personnel prepare the pay cheques of factory workers. The number of service jobs has increased tremendously as businesses and governments have become more complex. Today, almost 75% of Canadians are employed in tertiary industries.

Wherever there is a community, there are people working in service activities. Communities require services in education, health care, planning and management, communications, transportation, sanitation, law enforcement, and road maintenance, among others. Most services are visible. In other words, we can actually see people making daily use of them. Other services, such as computer-related activities, planning and management decisions, scientific research, and communications, may be less visible, although they directly affect our lives. Service activities are carried out all across the country, and are required by Canadians in order to live their daily lives.

Sometimes, information-based services are called quaternary industries.

1. Class members should list the jobs of parents/guardians who are employed outside the home on the board.
2. a) Within a group assigned by your teacher, categorize the jobs under the headings Primary, Secondary, and Tertiary.
   b) Calculate the percentage of parents/guardians in each of the three categories.
   c) Compare your percentages with the percentage of employment in primary, secondary, and tertiary industries in Fig. 20-4 on p. 243.
   d) How do your percentages compare to the national percentages? Explain why differences may exist.

DEVELOPMENT OF THE SERVICE SECTOR

The number of Canadians employed in service industries has grown tremendously. In 1901, only about 33% of Canadian workers were employed in services; now the figure is close to 75% (Fig. 27-1). Why has the tertiary sector of Canada's economy grown so large? Consider the following:

- Throughout the 1900s, greater use of machinery in farming, mining, forestry, and manufacturing increased productivity and revenue. As a result, workers received more money, and enjoyed more leisure time. This improved Canada's standard of living, and gave rise to a greater demand for services.

- Greater educational opportunities have helped people obtain the specialized skills which enable them to offer services to others.

- A growing population has increased the demand for services.

- Complex technology, particularly in the provision and storage of information, has given rise to a wide variety of services.

BASIC AND NON-BASIC SERVICES

Service industries may be classified into two categories: **basic services** and **non-basic services**. Basic industries provide services to people and business outside the community. They bring money into their respective communities from the outside, and without them, communities could not survive. For example:

- The federal government in Ottawa provides services for Canadians throughout the country.

- A university attracts students from outside the community in which it is located.

- An insurance company head office performs services for customers in other parts of Canada, or in other countries.

Tertiary Sector	1996
Wholesale & retail trade	17.2%
Transportation & communication	6.4%
Finance, insurance, real estate	5.5%
Education	6.9%
Healthcare and social services	10.4%
Business and personal services	21.8%
Government services	5.5%
Total	**73.7%**

◁ **Fig. 27-1** *The percentage of Canadian workers who are employed in the tertiary sector*

Non-basic industries provide services for people and businesses located within the community. Non-basic services do not generate money from outside sources. Think of some of the services you use in your community: public transportation, your high school, your doctor and dentist, or the local movie theatres. You pay for these services, either directly or through your taxes, and the money stays within your community.

TERTIARY INDUSTRIES

Trade Services

The selling of goods is called **trade**. Trade is divided into two categories:

Wholesale — the selling of goods and services to businesses or stores, not to the public.

Retail — the selling of products and services directly to the public in stores, vending machines, over the telephone, through mail-order, door-to-door sales, or over the Internet.

Sample Occupations

warehouse worker, inventory clerk, merchant, telemarketer, sales representative, cashier, Internet order-taker, lift-truck operator

Basic or Non-Basic?

- Wholesale: mostly basic, e.g., a large Canadian Tire warehouse in Brampton, Ontario supplies stores in much of Canada
- Retail: mostly non-basic because it serves the local area

The balance of basic and non-basic activities indicated for each industry is a general guideline and will vary in each region, depending on the nature of that community.

Finance, Insurance, and Real Estate Services

This includes services provided by banks, trust companies, credit unions, stock exchanges, insurance companies, and real estate companies. These institutions range in size from local real estate offices, to the head offices of huge insurance companies and banks doing business all across Canada and throughout the world.

Sample Occupations

bank clerk, investment manager, insurance agent, real-estate agent, stock-broker, secretary, credit investigator, financial planner

Basic or Non-Basic?

- It could be both, e.g., people working in the head office of a bank would be basic while those working in a local branch would be non-basic.

Business and Personal Services

This is the largest category of tertiary industry and supplies the services needed by businesses and individual Canadians. It is the fastest growing employment area in the economy.

Sample Occupations

accountant, mechanic, hairdresser, lawyer, secretary, personal fitness trainer, server, lifeguard, copywriter

Basic or Non-Basic?

- Most business and personal activities are local, so they are considered non-basic, e.g., a lawyer who specializes in local real estate or criminal matters.

- Services provided for companies and people outside the city are considered basic activities, e.g., a lawyer who works on international trade issues.

Transportation and Communication Services

These services involve the movement of goods, people, and information.

Sample Occupations

truck driver, bus driver, air traffic controller, railway engineer, journalist, radio announcer, cable television installer

Basic or Non-Basic?

- Can be both, e.g., an airline pilot would be basic while a bus driver would be non-basic.

Government Services

Federal, provincial, and municipal governments offer a wide variety of services. For example:

Federal: postal service, defense, and Native affairs

Provincial: health and social services, education, and natural resources

Municipal: police and fire protection, water and sewage services, and parks and recreation

Sample Occupations

politician, park ranger, jail guard, postal employee, economist, social worker, fire fighter, park maintenance worker

Basic or Non-Basic?

- Federal and provincial governments: mainly basic
- Municipal services: almost always non-basic

Healthcare and Social Services

Healthcare services include dental care and medical care and research. Social services include day-care centres, shelters for the homeless and those escaping from violent situations, lunch programs for underpriviledged children, and visits by social workers to families in need of counselling.

Sample Occupations

doctor, nurse, dietitian, X-ray technician, physiotherapist, psychiatrist, medical researcher, social worker, psychologist

Basic or Non-Basic?

• Most are non-basic because they serve the local community, e.g., hospitals, doctor's offices, visitations by social workers and nurses

• Some are both because they are specialized and service local as well as non-local people, e.g., cancer treatment centres.

Education Services

Education services include elementary and secondary schools, post-secondary education (universities and colleges), vocational training, religious training, and English or French language instruction for new Canadians.

Sample Occupations

teacher, principal, secretary, custodian, professor, librarian, teachers' aide

Basic or Non-Basic?

• Elementary and secondary schools: non-basic because they provide services for the local community

• Universities and colleges: a mixture of both

FUTURE TRENDS

What type of work will be available for you when you finish school? Chances are it will be in the services industry. Rapid changes are occuring in the workplace due to the globalization of the economy, free trade, and technological advances. These changes may eliminate jobs that we now take for granted, or they may provide you with new job opportunities.

globalization: companies buy and sell products in countries around the world

Today, young people can find employment in jobs that did not exist thirty years ago. Computer analysts, satellite broadcasting technicians, Internet-related workers, and personal trainers in fitness clubs are just some examples. What kinds of jobs will be created in the next 30 years? There is no way to tell, but we can make some informed guesses about the nature of employment in future service industries.

Growing numbers of young **entrepreneurs** will start their own businesses and most will be in the tertiary sector. Employment in small business is currently rising, and home-based enterprises are increasing. 25% percent of the small businesses in Canada are now owned by people aged 18 to 29. Some young people own businesses because they want to work for themselves; others go into business for themselves because they are unable to find permanent employment in established companies. An example of Canadian entrepreneurship is found in the field of electronic games. Canadian university graduates of computer and related programming courses are producing award-winning games with imaginative stories and innovative graphics (Fig. 27-3). They are making their mark in this growing, multi-billion dollar industry.

△ **Fig. 27-3** *Young Canadian entrepreneurs like James Schmalz are producing innovative electronic games. Are these creators of electronic games performing a basic or non-basic activity?*

Future growth is expected in jobs that offer services for seniors who are part of the aging "baby boom" generation. These are the people who were born between 1947 and 1966. Today, baby boomers make up about 33% of Canada's population. The needs of these "boomers" are changing as they age. They do not purchase as many manufactured goods as younger people because they already have most of the goods they need. What they need, however, are increased services in such areas as healthcare, travel, and finance.

Not only is the nature of jobs in the service industries undergoing change, but the jobs themselves are being eliminated by technology. Consider the following examples:

*   Electronic home shopping could eliminate many jobs in retail sales.
*   Touch-sensitive menu screens at fast food restaurants could replace the people who take orders.
*   Fax machines, voice mail, and personal computers have reduced the number of secretaries in many offices.
*   Electronic and telephone banking, as well as automated teller machines, are reducing the need for bank tellers.
*   Communication technology is reducing the need for companies to be close to their customers. For example, companies such as the Royal Bank, CP Hotels, and Purolator locate their customer service operations in telephone **call centres** located in places like Moncton, New Brunswick, even though most of their customers are in other parts of Canada. By dialing a toll-free number,

customers can purchase or exchange a product, make a hotel reservation, register a complaint, or request information.

We can only speculate on the number and nature of jobs in the service industries of the future. One thing for certain is that new types of services will develop to meet the changing needs of Canadians.

Conduct a job search in the tertiary sector of the economy. There are jobs that involve working with people, working with information, and working with other things (Fig. 27-4).

1. What other types of jobs could be listed in each of these categories?

2. In which category (people, information, other things) are you most interested? Why?

3. a) Work with one or two other students who have an interest in the same job category.

   b) Work together to make a list of jobs about which you would like to learn more information.

   c) Create a series of questions that you would like answered for each job. For example:

   - How much education or training is required?
   - What types of activities are involved in this job?
   - What are the job prospects for the future?
   - What is the salary range?

4. Use a variety of sources to research these jobs. You may want to try

   - libraries (school and community)
   - school guidance department
   - career centres and employment offices in your community
   - job advertisements in newspapers
   - computer searches
   - career information programs such as *Choices* (CD ROM)

Jobs that Involve Working With:	
People	• healthcare worker • religious leader • social worker • sales representative
Information	• lawyer • writer • Web page designer • stockbroker
Other	• fashion designer • interior decorator • electrician • robotics expert

△ **Fig. 27-4** *Jobs in tertiary industries*

If you are interested in doing a search in the primary or secondary sectors of the economy instead, talk to your teacher or guidance/career counsellor

- Internet sources such as:
  - Job Futures:
    www.hrdc–drhc.gc.ca/JobFutures/english/index.htm

  - Work *Info*net:
    www.workinfonet.ca/cwn/english/main.html

5. Write descriptions of the jobs you researched, using the answers to the questions that your group created in question 3. Work in your group to create a jobs booklet, a job search bulletin board, or the classified section of a newspaper, using these descriptions.

6. What will your working future be like? Using words and diagrams, select one job that you researched and try to imagine what it would be like if you were to work at this job in the future. Consider such things as
   - the education, training, and skills you will need
   - activities involved in your job
   - responsibilities you would have
   - work location
     - downtown core of a city, a suburb, or at home
     - specific city or suburb
   - type of company
     - your own
     - large or small (explain why)
   - number of hours you will work per week

QUESTIONS

CHECK YOUR UNDERSTANDING

1. How do tertiary industries differ from primary and secondary industries?

2. Why has the tertiary sector of the Canadian economy grown so large?

3. a) Explain the differences between basic and non-basic service industries.

   b) For each service industry discussed in this chapter, explain how it may have basic and non-basic characteristics.

THINK AND COMMUNICATE

4. What types of service jobs do you think will decrease and which will increase in number over the next ten years? Explain.

Transportation: Canada's Circulatory System

STUDY GUIDE

By the end of this chapter, you will be able to:

- explain the importance of Canada's transportation system
- identify and discuss the components involved in moving people and goods
- understand the issues facing Canada's transportation system

Key Terms

transportation	commuter	unit train	lock
mobility	deregulation	piggyback system	pipeline
intercity	hub and spoke	container	
intracity	bulk cargoes	canal	

If Canada is compared to a living organism in which the cities, towns, rural areas, and industries are parts of the body, then the **transportation** system is the circulatory system. Just as a person could die from a serious heart condition or hardening of the arteries, Canada could die (economically) without a modern and efficient transportation system.

The circulatory system includes the heart, lungs, and blood vessels.

Complete the crossword puzzle given to you by your teacher (Fig. 28-1). It will serve as an introduction to some of the features of transportation in Canada. Don't worry if you can't complete the puzzle now; by the end of the chapter, it will seem easy!

INTRODUCTION

At different stages of Canada's history, various forms of transportation have taken immigrants to their new homes, brought raw materials from rural areas to the cities, moved finished products to stores in every town and city, allowed people to get to work each day, and provided a link for Canadians with the rest of the world (Fig. 28-2).

▽ Fig. 28-1

ACROSS

1. trailers carried by train
2. large metal freight box
7. short take-off and landing aircraft
8. subject of this chapter
9. ___ materials
10. removal of government control of transportation
11. used for moving oil and gas
15. _ _ _ _ _ -Canada Highway
16. _ _ _ _ _ _ _ _ jam
18. passenger rail company
20. road *en français*
21. train that carries only one cargo
23. Japanese car built in Canada
25. ease of movement
27. limited- _ _ _ _ _ _ highway
31. _ _ _ _ Skies; a form of 10 across
32. ships going to western Canada used to round, Cape_ _ _ _
33. coal, wheat, and iron ore examples of this kind of cargo
34. fertilizer ingredient shipped by train

DOWN

1. someone who travels
3. buses which operate in a city; _ _ _ _ _ _ -city
4. 1000 kg
5. 6 down is an example of this
6. Air _ _ _ _ _ _
10. "Dad, can I _ _ _ _ _ the car!"
12. Canada's second largest railway, Canadian _ _ _ _ _ _ _
13. a car that uses a lot of gasoline is not _ _ _ _ _ _ -efficient
14. a bulk cargo: _ _ _ _ ore
17. water transportation for people
19. another name for a car
22. "Catch the _ _ _, Gus"
24. Thunder Bay to Montreal is _ _ _ _ stream
25. James Bay town accessible by rail but not by road
26. only territorial capital without road connection to the south
28. links Lake Ontario and Lake Erie, Welland _ _ _ _ _
29. 28 down is part of this
30. name of commuter trains in the Toronto area

△ **Fig. 28-2** *In a country as large as Canada, transportation is of critical importance. In which decade of the 20th century would each of these transportation methods have become important to our transportation system?*

Every day, Canada's transportation system faces an immense task. Millions of people travel tens of millions of kilometres. Thousands of tonnes of cargo must be moved as quickly and as cheaply as possible. This must all be done in spite of great distances, harsh weather conditions, and some of the most difficult landform challenges anywhere in the world (Fig. 28-3).

Perhaps the single most important fact of Canada's transportation system is that more than half of Canada is not served by surface transport (roads and railways). Those of us who live in the towns, cities, and densely populated rural areas of southern Canada, take it for granted that you can drive your car wherever you need to go. This is clearly not the case in most of the remainder of the country.

Examine Fig. 28-4 and answer the following questions.

1. a) Describe the amount and coverage of ground transportation in Zone A. Refer to thematic maps in an atlas.

    b) Why is this pattern not surprising?

2. a) Describe the pattern of surface transport in Zone B. Why do gaps exist?

    b) With the help of an atlas, explain why surface transport exists to each of the following places:

        i.   Inuvik, Northwest Territories

        ii.   Yellowknife, Northwest Territories

        iii.   Fort McMurray, Alberta

        iv.   Lynn Lake, Manitoba

        v.   Churchill, Manitoba

        vi.   Moosonee, Ontario

        vii.   La Grande Rivière, Québec

        viii. Churchill Falls, Newfoundland

    c) What would cause new areas to be added to Zone B in the future?

3. a) Why does surface transport not exist in Zone C?

    b) What alternative transportation methods must be used in these areas?

△ **Fig. 28-3** *This rail line is in the Fraser River Canyon of British Columbia. Imagine the difficulty of building this rail line. Why wasn't a different route chosen?*

MOVEMENT OF PEOPLE

When people select a method of transportation for a journey, they must consider a number of things: the distance to be covered, the costs involved, the duration of the trip, and the alternatives that are available. In general, people may choose to travel by road, rail, air, or water.

Road Travel

Roads are the most important means of moving people from place to place in Canada. Every year, governments of all levels spend more than

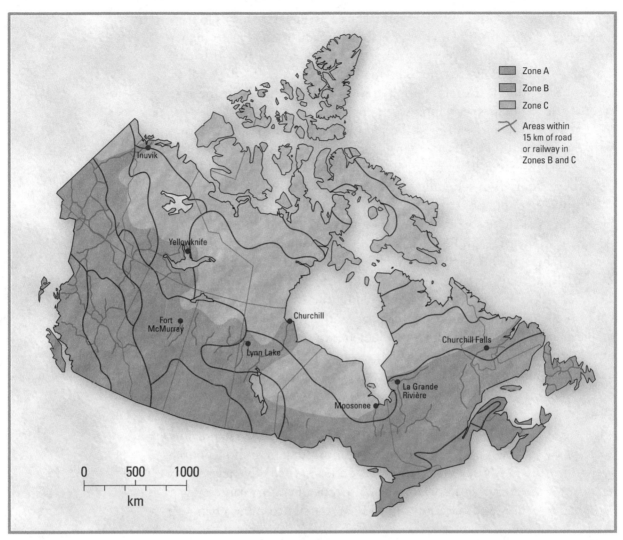

△ **Fig. 28-4** *Some areas of Canada are very accessible to land transportation (road and railway) while others are not.*

$7 billion on the construction, maintenance, and administration of more than 900 000 km of Canadian roads. Over 17 million cars, trucks, buses, and motorcycles use these roads. Road travel plays a vital role in Canada's economy. This is because governments spend money to build and maintain roads. Money is also spent by consumers to buy and repair the millions of vehicles that use our roads. The rest comes from the expenditures of people who are travelling on the roads. For example, if you travel by car to the Canadian Rockies, you will probably spend money to buy food, lodging, gasoline, and other things.

AUTOMOBILES

Canadians travel more by car (and small trucks) than by any other means of transportation. There are approximately 13.5 million cars registered in Canada. The extensive use of cars has allowed average Canadians to have a higher level of **mobility** than ever before. Canadians also have a higher mobility level than people in most other areas of the world today. Canadians have become used to driving their cars to go to the mall or across the continent. In fact, people travel more now than in the past because the car makes travelling so easy.

mobility: ease of movement

The most valuable feature of the automobile is its flexibility. It allows people to travel directly from their starting point to their exact destination — assuming that there are roads to get there! Cars also allow people to travel on their own schedule, in comfort and in privacy.

A good example of Canadians' ability and willingness to travel is the fans of the Saskatchewan Roughriders football team. The Roughriders play their home games in Regina, but there is a good reason why they are not called the *Regina* Roughriders. With a population of less than 200 000, Regina alone could not support the team. A check of a typical crowd at Regina's Taylor Field would reveal many fans from Moose Jaw, Saskatoon, Yorkton, Swift Current, and other parts of southern Saskatchewan. These people are able to travel hundreds of kilometres to support their team. This level of mobility could only exist with reliable, inexpensive automobiles and an extensive road network.

BUS

Buses are a major method of travelling between cities and are used mainly for trips of less than 1000 km. Each year, more than 1 billion people travel on **intercity** buses. Bus transportation has several advantages. It is relatively inexpensive and comfortable. Also, bus operators can establish and change routes and schedules quickly and easily to meet changing needs.

intercity: between cities

Intracity buses are used in almost every Canadian city and in many towns. Large cities like Toronto and Montréal might use thousands of vehicles like buses, subways, and streetcars, while a small town might only have one bus. In either case, buses are a key element of the transportation system for people who either cannot, or choose not to, drive. In a typical year, about 1 billion passengers use intracity buses in Canada. Buses can move large numbers of commuters efficiently. Compared to cars, buses are environmentally sound since they help to prevent traffic, noise, and air pollution.

intracity: within a city

Rail Travel

At one time, travel between Canadian cities by train was more common than travel by any other means. Trains were faster, more reliable, and

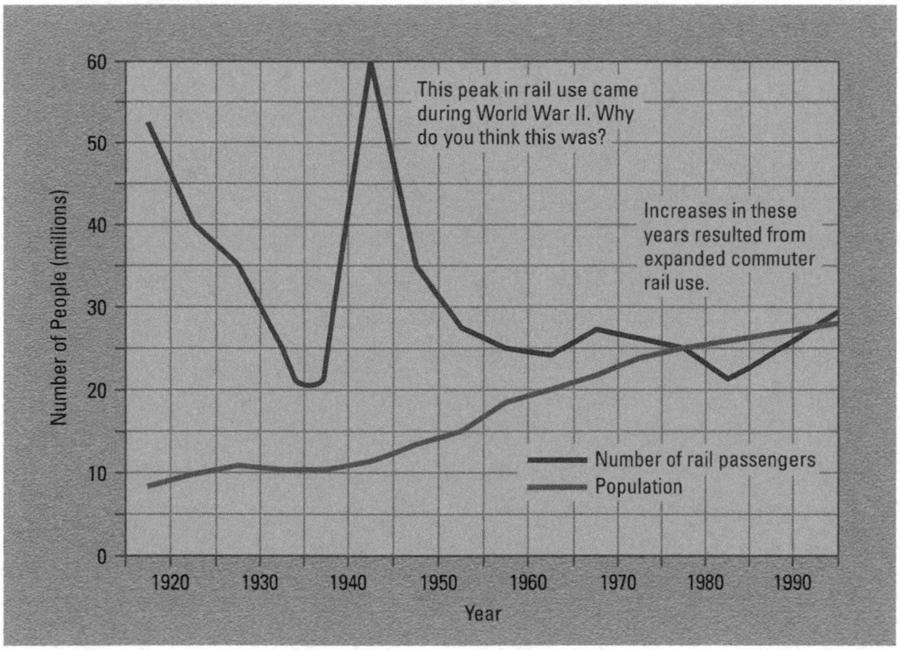
This peak in rail use came during World War II. Why do you think this was?
Increases in these years resulted from expanded commuter rail use.
Number of rail passengers
Population
Number of People (millions)
Year
0
10
20
30
40
50
60
1920
1930
1940
1950
1960
1970
1980
1990

◁ **Fig. 28-5** *Rail passengers and the growth of population, 1919-1998. The drop in rail passengers is even more dramatic if we consider that the total amount of travel has increased dramatically.*

more comfortable than either travel by road or by water. After World War II, this changed drastically. More people owned cars, and both cars and buses became more reliable. Intercity highways were improved, so travel became faster and more comfortable. Travel by airplane became more common and, over the years, cheaper. Roads took much of the short-distance travel from the railways, while air travel captured much of the long-distance travel. The result was a severe decline in travel by train (Fig. 28-5).

This was at a time before travel by airplane was common.

The deterioration of rail passenger business created a serious problem for the two major railway companies, Canadian National Railways (CNR) and Canadian Pacific Railways (CPR). Each company was losing millions of dollars per year on its passenger operations. To make things worse, the equipment they had was old and worn-out so there was a need to spend even more money to buy new trains and related equipment. Both companies wanted to eliminate their passenger services. In response to these threats, the federal government created VIA Rail as a crown corporation to run the passenger services that had been owned by CNR and CPR. The problems faced by VIA Rail today are similar to those that existed before it was created. It loses money every year and has difficulty providing quality service to its customers. While the government provides subsidies to VIA to keep it operating, there has never been enough money to significantly improve its passenger service. Today, most of the equipment is more than 35 years old and badly out-of-date.

crown corporation: an independent company owned by the federal or provincial government

subsidies: financial assistance

Rail passenger service in Canada is at a crossroads. It will either have to be significantly improved at great cost, or left to decline to the point where it will eventually disappear. There are people who support each view. In 1998, the president of CN Rail described passenger rail service as a "nuisance" and said that it should be eliminated. On the other hand, there are others who think that Canada needs a modernized passenger rail system. The model for this already exists in Japan and France. Japan's Bullet Trains and France's *TGV* can compete effectively with airplanes for trips of up to 600 km. They can do this by travelling at speeds approaching 400 km/h and by travelling from one downtown area to another, which means that passengers can avoid trips to and from the airport in each city. High-speed trains could be used in Canada for such routes as Edmonton to Calgary and Halifax to Saint John. They would most likely be used in the heavily populated area between Windsor and Quebec City, in particular, between Toronto and Montréal. Each day, 36 flights link these two cities, and the people on these planes would be potential passengers for an improved rail service.

A group of companies led by Bombardier has proposed the construction of a high-speed rail service called Lynx that would link Montréal, Ottawa, and Toronto, but there are many obstacles to be overcome before this plan becomes a reality. The most significant of these is that more than two-thirds of the cost would have to be paid by the Canadian, Ontario, and Québec governments. None of these governments has indicated an interest in this scheme, and without their financial support, plans for Lynx cannot proceed.

COMMUTER RAIL

There is one exception to the sad state of rail passenger service in Canada. Trains are very important for moving **commuters** to work in some cities. The largest of these commuter rail systems is GO Transit which moves commuters into downtown Toronto from surrounding cities.

Air Travel

The airplane has revolutionized travel, particularly over long distances. The first passenger flights across Canada were made before World War II. Today, modern jets cross the country in just a few hours.

Today's airline industry is very competitive. The most important reason for this is **deregulation**. Deregulation means that the government has reduced its control over such things as fares and how many airlines may fly on any one route. This has meant more competition and lower fares on many routes. Deregulation has also occurred internation-

---

Side notes:

While CNR and CPR do not provide passenger service, VIA trains run on their tracks and use their facilities

TGV: Train à Grande Vitesse. What does this mean?

Travel between Toronto and Montréal would take less than two hours.

The Bombardier company builds rail cars and has a natural interest in a plan like this. They already build high-speed railway trains for use in the United States.

Government of Ontario Transit also uses many buses.

Deregulation leads to lower fares on busy routes such as Toronto to Montréal where competition is likely. However, it can lead to higher fares on routes with few passengers such as Thunder Bay to Sudbury.

ally since the signing of an Open Skies Agreement with the United States. This allows airlines in both countries to fly to more places in the other country.

Airlines have been forced to become very efficient to survive. Canada's two major airlines, Air Canada and Canadian Airlines have moved to a **hub and spoke** route pattern (Fig. 28-6). With this system, there are fewer direct flights between smaller cities. For example, if you want to go from Winnipeg to Montréal with Canadian Airlines, you have to go through Toronto since there is no direct flight. This is slower and less convenient for the traveller, but it is more efficient for the airline since it can serve a large number of communities as cheaply as possible.

Another way that the airlines have become more efficient is by establishing partnerships with foreign airlines. Air Canada and Canadian Airlines have found partners in the United States, Europe, and Asia. Each works closely with its partners to provide the benefits of a larger airline, such as more destinations in more parts of the world and linked frequent-flyer plans. These plans also allow passengers to collect points towards a variety of rewards such as a free flight or reduced fare to their destination.

A final change has occurred in recent years. Small, regional airlines have been established to serve smaller communities, many of which were abandoned by the larger airlines because they were seen as unprofitable. Several of these smaller airlines are owned by Air Canada or Canadian

▽ **Fig. 28-6** *Airline routes for Canadian Airlines International. Where are the hubs ?*

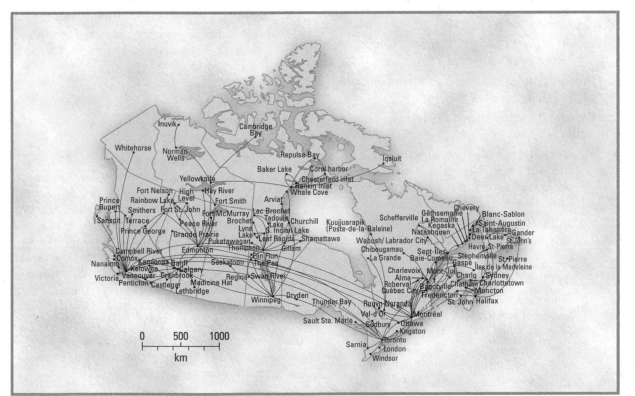

Airlines. For example, Air Canada owns AirBC (with hubs in Vancouver, Edmonton, and Calgary), Air Ontario (with hubs in London and Toronto), Air Alliance (with hubs in Quebec City, Montréal, and Ottawa), and Air Nova (with hubs in Halifax, St. John's, and Montréal). These smaller companies can make money serving communities like Sarnia, Ontario, Wabush, Newfoundland, and Campbell River, British Columbia by flying smaller aircraft that are better-suited to the number of passengers flying to and from these cities.

Bombardier's Canadair, and de Havilland divisions build smaller airplanes that are used by regional airlines in Canada and other countries.

Travel by Ship

Travel by ship is not very common in Canada, but where it does exist, it is of vital importance. Ferries carry island residents and tourists to Newfoundland, Vancouver Island, and smaller islands along the coast of British Columbia. A ferry service is very costly to operate and subject to stoppages because of bad weather, mechanical problems, and labour problems.

QUESTIONS

CHECK YOUR UNDERSTANDING

1. a) Define mobility.
   b) How have changes in mobility occurred in the past 100 years?

2. How important are roads to the movement of people in Canada?

3. What is the difference between intercity and intracity buses?

4. a) Describe the reasons why travel by train has declined in Canada. Which of these were the "fault" of the rail industry and which were unavoidable?
   b) What can be done to improve rail travel? Why is this difficult to do?

ANALYZE AND APPLY

5. a) Give two reasons why the high-speed trains of France and Japan can compete with air travel.
   b) What advantages do France and Japan have for building modern rail systems that Canada does not have?

6. a) Describe the changes that have occurred in the airline industry in recent years.
   b) Which of these changes benefited travellers? Have all travellers benefited equally? Explain.
   c) Which were a benefit only to the airlines?

7. a) Name a Canadian city that you would like to visit.
   b) Make an organizer like Fig. 28-7 in your notebook to record the travel distance to this city from your home as well as the cost and the time that it takes to get there for each type of transportation indicated. Obtain the information you need to complete the chart from sources such as an atlas, your parents, a travel agent, and transportation companies. (You might want to check the Web pages of these companies.)

8. Between the 1800s and today, the relative importance of different methods of transportation has changed.

Type of Transportation	Distance (in km)	Cost (in $)	Time (in hours)
Automobile			
Train			
Bus			
Airplane			

△ Fig. 28-7   ▽ Fig. 28-8

	Short Distances	Long Distances
1800s		
1900-1950		
1950-today		

a) In your notebook, complete an organizer like Fig. 28-8 by naming the most important transportation methods in each time period for both short- and long-distance travel.

b) Explain why changes have occurred.

THINK AND COMMUNICATE

9. In this chapter, you learned that government is less involved in transportation than before the deregulation of airlines. Some people are saying that it should be more involved by paying for most of the Lynx high-speed rail scheme. What role do you think the government should have in controlling and paying for transportation? Why?

10. a) List five examples of the impact that the automobile has had on the lifestyles of Canadians.

    b) List five examples of the way in which the automobile has influenced the appearance of Canadian cities and towns.

    c) Have the things that you mentioned in your answers to questions 10a and 10b been positive or negative for the way we live?

    d) What could be done to reduce the negative impacts of the automobile? Be specific.

MOVEMENT OF GOODS

Lean back in your chair and imagine that you have been transported to the railway station platform of a small town in the middle of a spruce forest. The town does not look familiar, but the sign on the station tells you that are in Armstrong. You have never heard of this town, but you look at the ecozone characteristics of the area and decide that you must be in northern Ontario. You do not know which way on the railroad is east and which is west. (Your geographic knowledge tells you the line must go east–west rather than north–south.) There are two freight trains sitting on the tracks pointing in opposite directions. If you knew what was in the trains could you tell in what direction they were heading?

One train is loaded with, among other things, wheat, plywood, and stereo equipment. The other has mining equipment, Canadian magazines, and Toyota Corollas.

1. Which train is heading east and which west? How do you know?
2. Suggest three other things that might be carried by each train.

Every day, Canada's transportation system must handle cargoes ranging from 50 000 tonnes of coal to 100 kg of live lobsters, and even a human heart for transplant. This variety of cargoes indicates the wide range of freight-handling needs that must be met. Some cargoes must be moved as quickly as possible with little concern for cost. Other shipments can travel very slowly as long as the cost is as low as possible. Others are very easily damaged and need special protection.

Moving Cargo by Rail

Canada's railways are the backbone of our freight-carrying system. Although railways carry many types of freight, they are particularly good for moving **bulk cargoes** like coal, grain, wood, and oil (Fig. 28-9). Bulk cargoes have large volume and relatively low value. As a result, they must be moved as cheaply as possible. Trains are very good at moving large amounts of freight very cheaply.

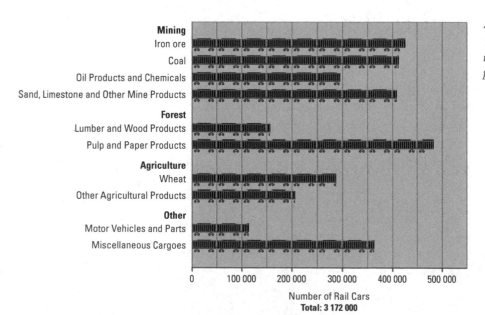

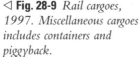
◁ **Fig. 28-9** *Rail cargoes, 1997. Miscellaneous cargoes includes containers and piggyback.*

One way to move cargo very cheaply is to use a **unit train**. A unit train carries only one cargo along a fixed route. The train uses special cars that have been designed to carry the particular cargo and can be loaded and unloaded quickly (which means cheaply). Some of the most important unit-train routes are:

- from the interior of Labrador to ports on the St. Lawrence River (iron ore)
- from the Rocky Mountains to Vancouver (coal)
- from the Prairies to Vancouver and Thunder Bay (wheat)
- from Saskatchewan to Vancouver (potash)

In the 1950s and 1960s, the railways found that they were facing stiff competition from trucks. Trucks have a major advantage over trains in that they do not need to stay on tracks. They can go directly to a factory to pick up a shipment and then carry it to its final destination. Because the shipment never has to be transferred from one vehicle to another, handling costs and delays are reduced.

The railways had to find a way to compete with the advantage of flexibility that trucks had. They came up with two related solutions. The first of these was the **piggyback system**. Piggyback combines the advantages of trucks with rail. It works like this:

- a truck trailer is loaded at a factory
- it is pulled by a truck to a nearby rail yard and loaded onto flatcars
- the train moves the trailer to a distant rail yard near its destination where it is unloaded
- the trailer is then trucked to its final destination

The second solution is even more flexible and involves the use of shipping **containers** which can be moved by rail, truck, ship and even air (Fig. 28-10). The idea of a container is very simple. Freight is shipped in large metal boxes of standard size and shape. A container is loaded by the shipper and can be moved by any combination of trains, trucks, ships, and planes, depending on what is being carried and where it has to go. Containers can be moved quickly and efficiently, and theft and damage are unlikely. Before the development of containers, freight had to be loaded and unloaded piece by piece. This was very time-consuming and costly.

Moving Cargo By Road

Trucking has several advantages over rail transport:

- trucks cost less to buy and maintain than railway cars and engines
- truck terminals are less expensive to build than train terminals

◁ **Fig. 28-10** *Containers are 2.3 m wide and 2.3 m tall. They vary in length, but a common length is about 12.9 m. These standard sizes make the containers easier to handle and store.*

- trucks are not restricted to fixed routes
- trucks are better suited to carry lighter, less bulky cargoes

Efficient intercity trucking is a fairly recent development. Before World War II, trucks were small and unreliable, and the roads were not very good. Since then, both improved enormously. Larger, more reliable trucks and a growing network of highways allow goods to be moved quickly and reliably.

Moving Cargo By Ship

Ships have been used to move freight in (and to and from) Canada for more than 400 years. Approximately 150 years ago, ships were the most important form of transportation on all three coasts and in the Great Lakes because transportation on land was slow and unreliable. Even though the quality of land transport has improved enormously, ships are still of tremendous importance to Canada's economy.

Ships are best suited for the movement of very bulky, low value cargoes. These include grain, iron ore, coal, petroleum (both crude oil and refined products like fuel oil and diesel fuel), lumber, cement, sand, and gravel. Mills, refineries, and factories that either produce or use these commodities will try to locate themselves to take advantage of water-borne transport since they will save money. Consider the case of Algoma Steel in Sault Ste. Marie, Ont. They built their steel mill at the crossroads of the Great Lakes (Fig. 28-11) because the three raw materials that they use in great quantities — iron ore, coal, and limestone — can all be brought by ship at the lowest cost possible.

△ **Fig. 28-11** *Sault Ste. Marie was chosen as the location of Algoma Steel because raw materials could be brought here cheaply using huge, efficient lake freighters.*

We can better understand Canada's water-borne freight system by dividing it into four parts:

1. THE WEST COAST

Enormous amounts of cargo are shipped through West Coast ports (especially Vancouver) primarily to destinations in the Pacific Rim. Much of Canada's export trade in lumber, coal, potash, wheat, and other bulk cargoes goes to these countries. Much of the incoming cargo through these ports is in the form of containers of freight and motor vehicles.

Pacific Rim: countries that border the Pacific Ocean in the Americas, Asia, and Oceania

2. THE EAST COAST

East Coast ports like Halifax, Saint John, and Montréal are used for a wide variety of cargoes with somewhat more container freight and less bulk cargo.

3. THE ST. LAWRENCE SEAWAY

The St. Lawrence Seaway is a system of **canals** and **locks** (Fig. 28-12) that link the St. Lawrence River and the Great Lakes and allow ships from the Atlantic Ocean to reach 3800 km inland to Lake Superior. The Seaway is also of vital importance for the movement of bulk cargoes from one part of the Great Lakes basin to another.

To learn about the Seaway, check www.seaway.ca/english/english.html

4. CANADA'S FAR NORTH

Canada's far north presents special transportation problems. Distances are great and the climate is harsh. In general, land transport is not available, and freight must be moved either by air or by water. It is obviously very expensive to ship freight by air, so it is shipped by water whenever possible. Ships (and barges on the Mackenzie River) are used to move bulky cargoes like oil products, building materials, and machinery. They

In the winter, frozen rivers and lakes can be used as "winter roads" to move bulky cargoes. This is particularly important on the Mackenzie River and its tributaries.

◁ **Fig. 28-12** *This is a diagram showing how locks operate. When a ship is moving from a higher level to a lower level, it is lowered by closing the gates and letting out some of the water. Then, the lower gates are opened and the ship leaves. The opposite takes place to raise a ship.*

also bring residents many of the groceries they will need for the year. Because of long winters in the north, the shipping season may only be several weeks in length. As you might expect, northern residents must plan very carefully in June to make sure that they do not run out of supplies like cooking oil next April and are forced to pay for supplies that have been transported by air at enormous cost.

Moving Cargo By Air

Although shipping goods by air is more expensive than other types of transportation, the use of air freight has increased greatly in recent years (Fig. 28-13). The amount of freight carried is small compared to that moved by rail, road, or ship, but air freight offers some special advantages for which shippers are prepared to pay high prices. In particular, freight can be moved very quickly with delivery available the next day in some cases. The goods that are shipped by air have one or more of the characteristics listed below. They are

• light in weight and small in size, e.g., a shipment of jewelry
• of high value, e.g., electronic equipment
• perishable, e.g., flowers
• needed quickly, e.g., machinery parts that are needed to repair a major piece of construction or manufacturing equipment

Air transport has played a very important part in the development of Canada's frontier regions. In many communities, small airports have been built. In other areas which contain lakes and rivers, float planes can be used.

▽ **Fig. 28-13** *Airplanes can be used to move almost anything.*

Moving Cargo By Pipelines

When we think about the ways in which goods are moved, we often overlook the role played by **pipelines**. This is not hard to understand because pipelines do their work out of the sight of most people. Pipelines can be used to move gases, liquids, and even solids that have been crushed and mixed with water. In Canada, they are of vital importance for moving crude oil and natural gas. A pipeline can only be built when two specific conditions exist:

- a supply of suitable material to be moved which is large enough to last for many years (This is necessary since pipelines are very costly to build.);

- a lack of opportunity to transport the material by ship, which is generally cheaper.

Fig. 28-14 shows the location of Canada's oil and gas pipelines. Not shown on this map are dozens of smaller pipelines that collect oil and gas from where they are produced and move them to the main pipelines. The proposed pipelines on the map might be built if it is determined that they make economic sense. This might happen in 5 years, in 50 years, or might never actually happen.

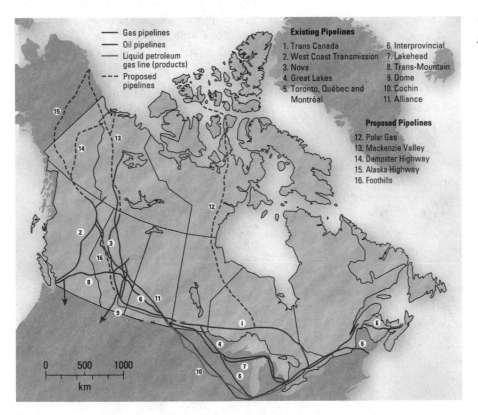

◁ **Fig. 28-14** *Major Canadian pipelines*

Gas pipelines
Oil pipelines
Liquid petroleum gas line (products)
Proposed pipelines

Existing Pipelines

1. Trans Canada
2. West Coast Transmission
3. Nova
4. Great Lakes
5. Toronto, Québec and Montréal
6. Interprovincial
7. Lakehead
8. Trans-Mountain
9. Dome
10. Cochin
11. Alliance

Proposed Pipelines

12. Polar Gas
13. Mackenzie Valley
14. Dempster Highway
15. Alaska Highway
16. Foothills

IN CLOSING...

Canada could not exist as a modern nation without its complex transportation system. Raw materials from mines, forests, and farms must be shipped to customers in Canada and around the world. Manufactured goods from Canadian and foreign sources must be moved to where they are needed. Every day, tens of millions of people make journeys that last for a few minutes to many days.

Canada's transportation network performs another, perhaps less obvious, task. It connects all of our diverse regions, making it easier for people to feel that they are part of one, unified country.

QUESTIONS

Note: If you could not complete the crossword puzzle that you were given at the beginning of this chapter, try to do it now; it should seem easier to complete.

CHECK YOUR UNDERSTANDING

1. a) What are bulk cargoes?

    b) Rank the various forms of transportation in terms of their suitability to move bulk cargoes.

    c) What is a unit train? Why is it an efficient way to move bulk cargoes?

    d) Give three examples of unit-train routes and cargoes.

2. a) Name and describe two methods which have been developed to allow easy transfer of cargo from one method of transportation to another.

    b) How do these methods combine the advantages of the different methods of transportation?

3. Outline the four different regions in which ships are used to move cargo in Canada.

4. What types of cargo are carried by airplanes? Why?

ANALYZE AND APPLY

5. a) A jeans manufacturer in Winnipeg has made a major sale of 10 000 pairs of jeans to a department store in London, England. Complete an organizer like Fig. 28-15 to summarize the choices that the manufacturer has to transport these jeans to England.

    b) Which method would you choose and why?

6. a) Refer to Fig. 28-9. Calculate the percentage of the total cargo made up of each of the following categories:

        i.   mining products

        ii.   forestry products

        iii. agricultural products

        iv.   motor vehicles and parts

    b) Draw a pie graph to illustrate the types of cargoes carried by railways. (See Chapter 8 if you are not sure how to draw a pie graph.)

    c) What similarities do these cargoes have? What differences do they have?

Transportation Method	Advantages	Disadvantages	Comments
Rail			
Road			
Ship			
Airplane			
Pipeline			

△ **Fig. 28-15**

7. Which method of transportation would you choose to move each of the following cargoes? Explain your choices.

   a) 100 000 t of wheat from Saskatoon to Vancouver

   b) six pianos to be shipped from Montréal: four to Ottawa, one to Peterborough, Ontario, and one to Sherbrooke, Québec

   c) 200 000 t of crude oil from Alberta to Sarnia, Ontario

   d) 50 000 t of iron ore from Sept-Isles, Québec

   e) 100 kg of live daffodils from Victoria, British Columbia to Toronto, Ontario

8. a) Fig. 28-16 shows the traffic trend on the Welland Canal over most of the last 40 years. Calculate the average tonnage carried by each ship in 1959 and 1998.

   b) What has happened to the

   i. total tonnage

   ii. number of ships

   iii. size of ships

   c) If a large transport truck can carry 50 t of cargo and a freight train with 60 cars can carry 4000 t of cargo, calculate:

   i. How many truck and train loads of cargo went through the Welland Canal in 1998?

   ii. The average ship's cargo was equal to how many truck and train loads?

   d) How do these figures help explain why bulk cargoes are shipped by water whenever possible?

9. Why have few major pipelines been built in Canada for several years? What would have to change to allow the construction of additional pipelines?

THINK AND COMMUNICATE

10. a) At times, there can be a conflict between the movement of goods and the movement of people. For example, trucks tend to damage the highways on which passenger cars travel. Give two other examples of similar conflicts.

    b) Should the movement of people take precedence over the movement of goods? Why or why not?

▽ **Fig. 28-16** *Traffic flow, Welland Canal*

	1959	1998
Number of ships	7500	3500
Cargo tonnage (t)	27 000 000	40 410 000
Average tonnage (t)		

29 Communications: Canada's Nervous System

STUDY GUIDE

By the end of this chapter, you will be able to:

- understand the nature of communications
- explain the importance of Canada's communication system
- identify how Canadians will exchange information in the future
- explain emerging and convergent communications technologies

Key Terms

communications

call centres

convergent technologies

global village

INTRODUCTION

In the previous chapter, you learned about Canada's transportation system. It was compared to the body's circulatory system. Like the circulatory system, the transportation system is entirely visible and relatively easy to understand. Canada's **communications** system, like the nervous system of the body, is much less visible and much more difficult to understand. Studying the communications system is also made more difficult by the fact that it is changing at a furious rate. This is not to suggest that we should ignore our communications systems — in fact, communications are becoming more and more important with each passing year.

When your grandparents were children, a long-distance phone call (if it was even possible) most often meant bad news like a sudden death in the family. People could go many months or even years without making or getting such a call. Today, long distance calls, even to distant continents, are an everyday occurrence in many families.

Have you ever thought about what happens when you make a long distance call? By punching a few buttons, you can make a particular phone ring half-way around the world. When you think about it, it is really quite remarkable. Your phone call requires the use of an extremely complex network of technology that can include satellites, submarine cables, and the phone systems of two or more countries. Because it is so easy (and relatively inexpensive) to make a long distance call, we often take the whole matter for granted.

A famous Canadian author named Marshall McLuhan stated that the world is becoming a **global village**. By this, he meant that technological improvements are making communications throughout the world as easy as they would be in a small village. While the whole world has not yet become a global village, it is rapidly moving in that direction. Complete the following activity to see this more clearly.

You will need the following items for this exercise: a phone book that provides international area codes and country codes, a globe, a piece of string, and graph paper. You will also need to know the following:

* that long distance calls to destinations in Canada and the United States are made by dialing

    1 + area code + local number

* that long distance calls to other countries are made by dialing

    011 + country code (2–3 digits) + city code (1–5 digits) + local number (2–9 digits)

City codes are not required for all countries.

Column A	Column B
1) Canada's Prime Minister in Ottawa	a) 011-57-1-35-50-**
2) *New York Times* newspaper in Manhattan	b) 1-403-247-****
3) Sydney Opera House in Australia	c) 1-613-992-****
4) Calgary Tower and Canada Olympic Park in Alberta	d) 011-44-171-930-****
5) Buckingham Palace in London	e) 1-213-956-****
6) Paramount Studio in Los Angeles, California	f) 011-65-31-****
7) Canadian Embassy in Bogota, Colombia	g) 1-212-556-****
8) Prime Minister in Singapore	h) 011-27-12-319-****
9) South Africa's President in Pretoria	i) 011-61-2-9250-****

◁ **Fig. 29-1** *Can you match the phone number to the destination?*

1. Examine the telephone numbers in Column B of Fig. 29–1. Using the area codes and country codes in the long distance section of your phone book, match each telephone number with the destinations in Column A.

2. Calculate and record the distance from Toronto to each city. You can do this with a globe and a piece of string. Your teacher can help you.

You can also calculate distance between cities on the Internet at www.indo.com/ distance/

3. Do you think that the cost to phone each city is tied to its distance? Why or why not? To help you answer these questions, construct two graphs that will relate the distance of a phone call to its cost for the years 1984 and 1998. The cost data for this exercise is given in Fig. 29-2. Construct a scattergraph for each year. Set up your graphs like Fig. 29-3.

4. Look at the two scattergraphs you have created, and answer the following questions:

Scattergraphs are described in Chapter 8.

a) What has happened to the cost of making long distance calls over the years? Why?

b) Have changes in cost been more significant for closer calls or for calls to more distant places? What would this suggest?

c) How significant was the relationship between distance and cost in 1984? in 1999? Describe any trends (and major exceptions) that you see.

Hint: Consider how many people call each of these places.

d) Why do you think that this change has occurred?

Destination	1984 cost ($)	1999 cost ($)
a) Canada's Prime Minister in Ottawa	1.02	.38
b) *New York Times* newspaper in Manhattan	.63	.51
c) Sydney Opera House in Australia	2.75	.44
d) Calgary Tower and Canada Olympic Park in Alberta	1.57	.48
e) Buckingham Palace in London	2.00	.22
f) Paramount Studio in Los Angeles, California	1.00	.56
g) Canadian Embassy in Bogota, Colombia	2.50	1.94
h) Prime Minister in Singapore	2.75	1.03
i) South Africa's President in Pretoria	2.75	1.37

◁ **Fig. 29-2** *The cost of a one minute phone call in 1984 and 1999. The 1984 costs have been adjusted to allow for inflation so that they can be compared to 1999 costs.*

◁ **Fig. 29-3**

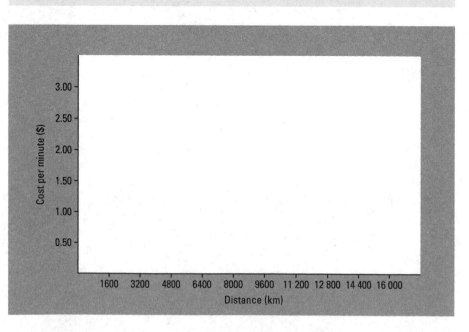

THE NATURE OF COMMUNICATIONS

Before we go further, it is important to clarify exactly what we mean when we use the word communications. Communications involves the transfer of information between people. How this transfer occurs has changed constantly over human history. For example, the creation of written language thousands of years ago revolutionized the nature of communication. With writing, people could, for the first time, store information so that it could be read in a different place at a different time.

While writing, and much later the use of print, were enormous advances in communications, there were still major shortcomings. For example, the treaty that ended the War of 1812 was signed in Europe in December of 1814. Unfortunately, it took many weeks for the news to reach North America. During this time, the war continued. Clearly there was a need for faster communication over long distances. The first breakthrough in this area was the invention of the telegraph in the mid–1800s. It required the use of wires so there were still some obvious limitations to its use. The next great invention was the *wireless* (better known today as the radio) in the early 1900s. In the decades that followed came television, and enormous advances in both wired and wireless communication, including such things as satellite communication and the Internet.

The result is that virtually the entire world is now linked. Consider the example of the *Around Alone* sailing race. In this race, sailors sail

The invention of the printing press extended the power of writing, since information could now be mass-produced and widely distributed.

◁ **Fig. 29-4** *At the time of the publication of this book, Internet users could follow the events of the* Around Alone *sailing race. This was a report from French race leader Isabelle Autissier. She sent this report from 37°S and 178°E. Check an atlas to identify her location.*

One week later, Autissier's boat capsized at 55°S, 127°W. She was saved in a daring rescue by an Italian competitor who was able to find her in the open ocean because of the advanced communications systems available. Information about the race can be found at www.aroundalone.com

◁ **Fig. 29-5** *We are already trying to communicate with beings beyond our own solar system. This plate was attached to the Pioneer 10 spacecraft which was the first object designed by humans to leave the solar system. Try to figure out the message on the plate. What information would you have sent?*

around the world single-handed. Some of them have Internet Web pages that keep everyone up to date with the race and through which they can receive e-mail from anyone, even if they are in the middle of the ocean (Fig. 29-4). In one extreme case, a doctor used e-mail to send instructions to a competitor on how to perform surgery on his infected elbow. The ability to communicate with this doctor actually saved the competitor's life.

In fact, the human desire to communicate extends far beyond our own planet. We have sent messages to those who might live elsewhere in the universe (Fig. 29-5) and have listened for communication from other galaxies with the *SETI Project*.

SETI: Search for Extra Terrestrial Intelligence

If you want to be part of the SETI, check setiathome.ssl.berkeley.edu

COMMUNICATIONS: PRESENT AND FUTURE

Existing Communications Technologies

Canadians exchange information by

- talking to each other
- listening to the radio — more than 99% of Canadian households, and almost every car and truck, has a radio

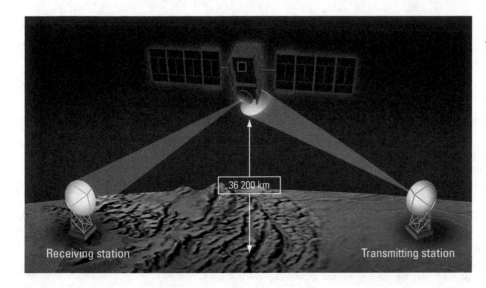

Receiving station   Transmitting station

36 200 km

◁ **Fig. 29-6** *Satellites are used for both telephone and television communications. Communications satellites are in stationary orbit, moving at the same speed as the earth's rotation.*

- watching television — more than 98% of Canadian households have televisions. More than 75% have cable service, which means that they have access to dozens of different stations
- using the telephone (Fig. 29-6) — There are approximately 11 413 000 telephones in Ontario alone, and this does not include the rapidly growing number of mobile phones.
- sending letters to each other
- reading — Canada has over 100 daily newspapers. As well, more than 1500 magazines are published in Canada. Some magazines, such as *Maclean's* and *Chatelaine*, are read by hundreds of thousands of people, whereas others are published for readers with specific interests.

Canadian Coin News and *Sweep! Curling's Magazine* are examples of specialized magazines.

Most of us are very familiar with these forms of communication, but few of us think very much about what happens behind the scenes to allow the communication to occur. What allows you to read your morning newspaper, receive a long-distance call, or watch the Olympics on television in a distant country? The answers to these and similar questions could easily fill an entire book, but there is one idea that will help you to understand what happens. Any successful communication consists of two parts: the message that is being carried and the technology that is used to deliver the message. Let's consider how this works with the three examples mentioned above (Fig. 29-7, Fig. 29-8, Fig. 29-9).

Canada has a highly-developed communications system. This should not be at all surprising if you think about what Canada is like. We have an enormous country with a relatively small population that is spread over many thousands of kilometres. We have also had scientists and engineers with the education and imagination needed to tackle our communications challenges. But what does this mean to Canadians? Two things are obvious: that Canadians are among the first people in the world to use new methods

Form of Communication Technology	Message to be Carried	Technology to Carry Message
read newspaper	stories in the newspaper	laser transmission of information, fully automated printing press
receive a long-distance call	words said by each person	phone system including satellites and microwave network (Fig. 29-8)
watch the Olympics on TV	pictures and words	television production facilities (Fig. 29-9), satellite/undersea cables, antenna and cable television distribution system

△ **Fig. 29-7** *Each form of communication technology consists of two parts.*

▽ **Fig. 29-8** *Microwave transmission can be used where a cable network could never be built.*

▽ **Fig. 29-9** *Engineer at television production facilities*

of communications, and that we are able to sell our communications expertise to other countries. For example, Canadian telephone companies were chosen to build modern phone systems in countries as distant as Saudi Arabia and Brazil.

expertise: knowledge and skills

Emerging Communications Technologies

Communications technologies are changing at a pace that most people find quite staggering. New inventions from just a few years ago, become obsolete before many people even know they existed. What is more remarkable is that the rate of change is likely to increase. In this section,

obsolete: outdated, no longer current

we will look at the changes that are occurring in a few communications technologies.

CHANGES IN THE PHONE SYSTEM

Our phone system is in the midst of dramatic changes. Perhaps the most obvious example of this is the growth of wireless phone service. Canada has had cellular phone service for a number of years. Then, came digital PCS (Personal Communication System) that provided users with higher quality service. Next, we will have satellite technology that will provide service all over the country instead of concentrating only on heavily-populated areas as does cellular and PCS service.

Another, more fundamental, change is slowly occurring. At the beginning of this chapter, you learned about the relationship between distance and the cost of phone calls. Increasingly, distance is becoming a less important factor in communications. This trend is obvious in the following examples:

- New Brunswick has become the home of many **call centres**. A call centre is a place from which, or to which thousands of calls may be made every day. Call centres are used by polling companies, fund-raising organizations, mail order companies, and others whose business depends on reliable, inexpensive phone service. If distance was the most important factor in determining the location of call centres, they would have appeared in more centrally-located provinces like Ontario or, perhaps, Manitoba. What has attracted several major call centres to New Brunswick? New Brunswick has an advanced phone system and workers with the training needed to work in a call centre. Technology and human resources have proven to be far more important than concerns about distance.

New Brunswick students can choose to take call centre training in the province's community colleges.

- In 1998, some suppliers of mobile phone service announced the elimination of all long-distance charges. This meant that they charged the same amount per minute for local and long-distance calls. What this pricing policy recognized, was that the cost of using a mobile phone is tied to accessing the system and not to how far away the call is made.

- A final example was an experiment in flat-rate long distance by Sprint Canada. For a fixed amount each month, a subscriber could make unlimited long-distance calls.

Sprint Canada had to stop the scheme after a few months, because it was too successful. Too many people were making too many calls and talking for too long. The national phone network could not handle the load.

CHANGES TO THE INTERNET

The Internet has become such an important part of our lives that it is easy to forget how new it is and how quickly it is developing and changing. Every month, the number of Internet users in Canada grows dramatically to the point that very soon more Canadians will be online than not. At this point, the most important elements of the Internet are e-mail, online discussion capabilities, and the World Wide Web.

E-mail has already had a profound impact on the way in which people communicate. E-mail messages, whether to someone in the next office or to the other side of the world, make communication both cheaper and faster.

Online discussions on the Internet are used for many purposes. In many cases, their purpose is recreational — you can play games with other Internet users or chat with the star of a new television show. Other uses are more serious. For example, you can take university or college courses online and have online discussions with your classmates. While this might be a convenience to someone in a larger city that has a college or university, to someone who lives in a remote area, it is a revolution. For the first time, they have access to higher education without having to travel a great distance.

Perhaps, the most important element of the Internet is the World Wide Web. There are millions of Web sites all over the world that have as many purposes as human imagination could create. It is rapidly becoming the meeting place for people who have access to the necessary computer technology. The World Wide Web currently has the following uses:

* a library of knowledge that is larger than any that has ever existed (Fig. 29-10)
* a centre for the exchange of entertainment and cultural information

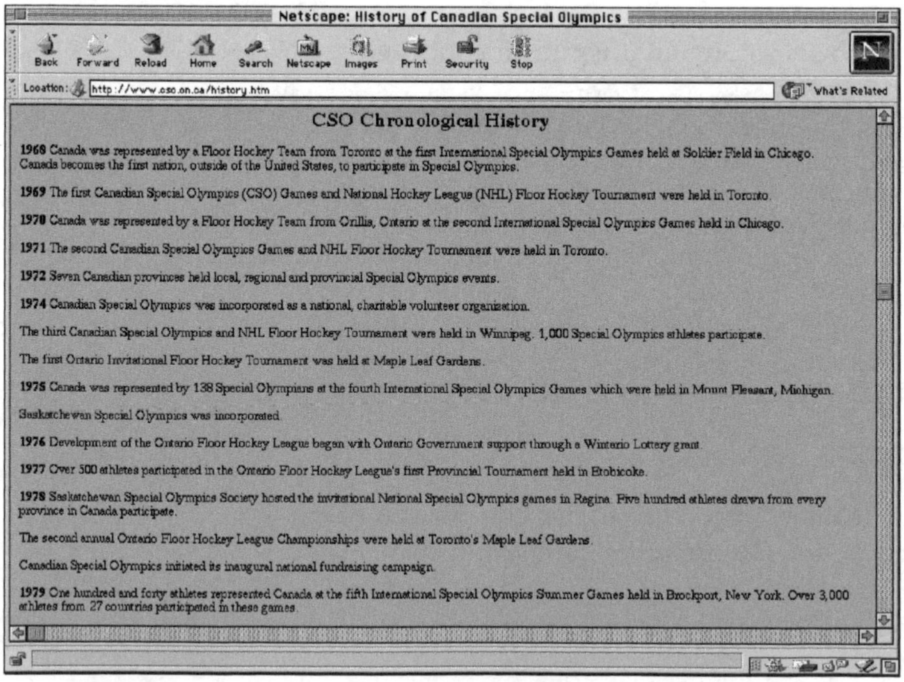

◁ **Fig. 29-10** *Just as you would go to the library to find out what you need to know about a particular topic, you may now consult the World Wide Web. This particular Web site provides information on the history of Special Olympics in Canada.*

- the ultimate shopping mall with online stores selling everything from books to automobiles
- a banking centre

CHANGES IN TELEVISION

Not very many years ago, Canadians had very few television stations to watch. Television signals came from roof-top antennas and, in some areas, there might have been only one or two stations from which to choose. Today, by comparison, Canadians can choose from dozens of stations, due to the growth of cable and satellite television, which now provide coverage across the country. And yet, there is more to come...

- Traditional cable and satellite services use what is called **analog transmission**. Many of them are now introducing **digital transmission**. Digital transmission represents two huge advantages. Digital signals give viewers better quality pictures and sound. More importantly, digital transmission is much more efficient. One analog channel can be used to carry as many as 8 digital channels. For example, one particular cable company which now offers 77 analog channels, expects to offer almost 300 analog and digital channels, including Internet connections, in a few years when it completes its digital network.

Digital technology will also be used for radio transmission.

- The expansion of cable and satellite services will allow other new developments. An exciting possibility is video-on-demand. Since the invention of television, people have often arranged their schedules around a favourite show or movie. With video-on-demand, the viewer can choose when to watch a particular show. Also coming, is an increase in the use of television sets and cable systems to provide access to the Internet for people who do not have computers.

Convergent Technologies

Convergent technologies is an idea that is very simple and, at the same time, remarkably complex and exciting. Until now, communications technologies were completely independent of each other. Television, radio, newspaper, movies, magazines, and the Internet, each worked differently from the others. People, both those who worked in communications and those who used them, thought more about the differences between communications, than the similarities.

The independent nature of communications is quickly changing, and this may be the most important communications change of all. Increasingly, distinctions among various communications media are disappearing. Consider the following examples:

- Radio programs from the CBC (and other broadcasters) can be heard on the Internet. This means that someone from Vancouver who is working in Rome can listen to news from home.

△ **Fig. 29-11** *Is this a newspaper or an Internet resource? In the future, we may not notice a difference.*

- Television will also be carried on the Internet as soon as the wiring to people's homes can be improved to handle the speed requirements of television.

- The Internet has traditionally been distributed to homes over phone lines, but now cable television lines are being used in many areas.

Cable transmission offers greater speed than phone lines.

- Televisions can be used to access the Internet.

- Wireless phones can be used to send and receive e-mail.

- Newspapers and magazines are appearing in online versions (Fig. 29-11).

To get the latest news from Nunavut, check www.nunatsiaq.com/nunavut/index.html

- Interactive movies are becoming a reality on the Internet and in video games. Here, three forms of media are combined.

- Some television shows are being broadcast with Web addresses shown on the screen. If we combine this concept with the idea of Internet television, it is easy to imagine how interactive television will develop: a Web address appears on screen and you can go to it on your television.

- Communication also occurs in situations where we don't expect it. For example, when you use a bank machine, messages are sent back and forth between the machine and your bank's head office. Doing your banking on the Internet is yet another convergence.

IN CLOSING...

Is all of this leading to the elimination of distance and to the convergence of technologies? No one knows for sure. What we do know is that the change is continuing, and, in fact, accelerating. We also know that the revolutionary changes taking place in communications will mean that the life you will lead will be very different from that of your parents and grandparents.

QUESTIONS

CHECK YOUR UNDERSTANDING

1. Give two reasons why it is difficult to understand the communications system.

2. a) Define communications.
   b) Name four important advances in the development of the world's communications system.

3. Canada has one of the world's most advanced communications systems. Give at least two reasons why this is not surprising.

ANALYZE AND APPLY

4. a) Each form of communication technology consists of two parts. Name these parts.
   b) Describe these two parts for the following forms of communications: a television broadcast, an Internet Web page, and a conversation.

5. a) What is a call centre?
   b) Which province has attracted many call centres? In what ways is this surprising and in what ways is this not surprising?

   c) What does the example of call centres suggest about how communications is changing?
   d) What other examples are there of this trend?

6. Radio, television, mail, telephone, and newspapers are examples of well-established forms of communications. Give an example of how each of these is changing due to emerging technologies.

7. a) What is a global village?
   b) Give three specific pieces of evidence, from this chapter, that suggest that a global village is being created in the world.
   c) Give two additional pieces of evidence, from your own life, that suggest that this is happening.

THINK AND COMMUNICATE

8. a) What is the *300 channel universe*?
   b) Do we need 300 channels?

c) Do 300 channels mean that we will get better programming?

9. a) Why is the elimination of distance an important development?

b) Why is this of particular interest to geographers? (Hint: Consider the nature of geography that was described in Chapter 1.)

10. a) What is meant by *convergent technologies*?

b) Give four examples of how the convergence of technologies is happening.

c) It is time to put on your "futurist's" hat . Predict how Canada's communications network will be different in 20 years as a result of convergent technologies. You might want to brainstorm ideas with a group of classmates. Your answer should be in the form of a five paragraph essay.

UNIT 6

Canada's Global Connections

Ambassador Bridge, Windsor/Detroit border

30 The World Community

STUDY GUIDE

By the end of this chapter, you will be able to:

- identify, define, and describe "developed," "newly industrializing," and "developing" countries based on a variety of character- istics
- identify issues facing each type of country

- understand the limitations of grouping countries
- use scattergraphs of several variables to make comparisons among countries

Key Terms

global village

GDP per capita

developed country

newly industrializing country

developing country

Most often when Canadians see a map of the world it is like the one shown in Fig. 30-1. That is, it is centred on the Atlantic Ocean. A map organized in this way reflects Canada's history for most of the last 300 years. During this time, thousands of settlers came across the ocean from European countries and Canada had strong political, military, and cultural ties with Europe.

Fig. 30-2, on the other hand, reflects a newer reality for Canada. It is centred on the Pacific Ocean and shows Canada in relationship to its neighbours on the Pacific Rim. This second map makes sense since most immigrants to Canada now come from Pacific Rim countries and a growing percentage of our trade is with this region.

The final map (Fig. 30-3) is a view of the world that we rarely see. It shows the world with Canada in the centre. What is Canada's place in the world community? Canada's international connections have been growing in importance and will continue to grow into the new century.

There are several reasons for the increase in our international connections.

- More people are travelling to more places. Individuals are more likely to visit foreign countries than any previous generation.

To examine maps of individual countries, check
www.lib.utexas.edu/Libs/PCL/
Map_collection/map_sites/
country_sites.html

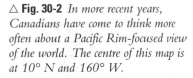

△ **Fig. 30-1** *This Atlantic-centred view of the world is the traditional one that Canadians have been used to seeing for more than a century. The centre of this map is at 10° N and 50° W.*

△ **Fig. 30-2** *In more recent years, Canadians have come to think more often about a Pacific Rim-focused view of the world. The centre of this map is at 10° N and 160° W.*

△ **Fig. 30-3** *Rarely do Canadians think about a Canada-centred view of the world. How does looking at the world in this way change our perspective of the world? This map is centred at 60° N and 95° W.*

- Communication by phone and the Internet allows a level of contact in the world that is faster, easier, and cheaper than ever before. The result is the creation of a more closely-connected **global village**.

- International trade grows by leaps and bounds every year and the economies of the world's countries are becoming more and more closely linked.

- While there is still much diversity throughout the world, increasingly, the world shares a common culture.

Of course, not everyone is able to afford to take advantage of these new travel opportunities or forms of communication.

GROUPING COUNTRIES

Understanding international connections is not an easy thing to do since there are more than 180 countries in all. Also, each country has a unique combination of culture, history, government, and economic development. One way to simplify this complex picture is to group the nations of the world according to their similarities. One common way to group countries is by comparing them on the basis of their economic and social development. The value of a country's economy is often measured using **Gross Domestic Product (GDP) per capita**, which is the value of the goods and services a country produces per person in one year. Social development is measured by comparing such factors as how long people in each country tend to live, what kind of health care they receive, and what educational levels they reach. Using these two measures — social and economic — countries are often grouped into three groups. The three groups are referred to as **developed countries**, **newly industrializing countries**, and **developing countries** (Fig. 30-4).

In fact, there is no clear agreement about what a country is. A commonly used way of identifying the world's countries is to consider the membership of the United Nations. In 1998, the United Nations had 181 members.

Some methods of grouping involve five groups while others have as many as nine.

▽ **Fig. 30-4** *This map identifies the developed, newly industrializing, and developing countries of the world (and Communist and former Communist nations that don't fit into these three categories).*

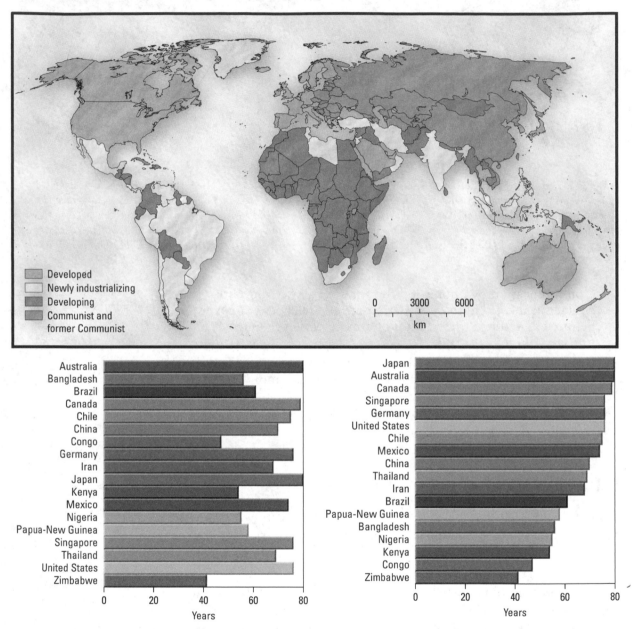

△ **Fig. 30-5** *This graph shows the average life expectancy in a sample of 18 countries.*

△ **Fig. 30-6** *If we sort life expectancy from longest to shortest, it becomes easier to see the groupings that exist among countries.*

How was this grouping established? Complete the following activity to see how countries can be grouped. The countries in this activity have been selected so that six of them fall into the group of developed countries, six of them fall into the group of newly industrializing countries, and six fall into the group of developing countries.

You may want to work with a partner to share the calculations.

LIFE EXPECTANCY

How long people in a country can hope to live is an indicator of the level of development of a country's health care and social system. Fig. 30-5 shows how long a newborn baby can expect to live in 18 different countries. As you can see, there are large differences in **life expectancy** among these countries. If the list is rearranged so that it is sorted from longest to shortest life expectancy (Fig. 30-6), we can see that countries like Canada, Japan, and Germany have longer life expectancies (75 years or more) while countries like Nigeria, Bangladesh, and Kenya have much shorter life expectancies (most often fewer than 60 years). Countries like China, Iran, and Brazil are somewhere in-between.

1. a) Use the information in Fig. 30-5 and 30-6 to rank the countries from 1 to 18, with 1 being the highest life expectancy.

   b) Average the rankings for any countries that are tied. For example, since Australia and Japan are tied for first and second place give each a ranking of 1.5. The United States, Germany, and Singapore are tied for fourth, fifth, and sixth place so each should have a ranking of 5 [(4 + 5 + 6) ÷ 3 = 5)].

   c) Copy Fig. 30-7 into your notebook. Transfer the rankings of life expectancy from the sorted list to this organizer.

You may want to use a spreadsheet to do this activity.

WEALTH

GDP per capita is the most commonly used measure of a country's wealth since it includes the total value of goods and services per person in a nation's economy. In developing countries, even the basics of life — food, shelter, and clothing — may not be available to most people. In developed countries, new products are constantly being created for people to purchase. More powerful video game systems, designer clothing, and the latest athlete-endorsed running shoes are just a few of the non-essential items that some people in developed countries may feel they "need." You can probably think of other examples.

▽ **Fig. 30-7**

	Life Expectancy (years)	GDP per capita ($US)	Natural Increase %	Food Supply (% of need)	Literacy Level (%)	Number of People per Doctor	TOTAL
Australia							
Bangladesh							
Brazil							
Canada							
United States							
Zimbabwe							

	GDP per capita (US$)	Population Growth Rate (%)	Food Supply (% of need)	Literacy Level (%)	Number of People per Doctor
Australia	US$ 17 980	0.68%	111%	100%	438
Bangladesh	230	1.89	87	38	5309
Brazil	6300	1.10	102	83	681
Canada	19 570	0.52	113	97	469
Chile	8400	1.19	99	95	2152
China	530	0.96	102	82	1063
Congo	400	3.11	98	77	14 286
Germany	20 400	-0.18	110	99	367
Iran	5200	2.61	110	72	3142
Japan	34 630	0.26	105	99	608
Kenya	1400	2.16	89	78	9851
Mexico	4010	2.13	108	90	1770
Nigeria	1380	3.01	91	57	5356
Papua-New Guinea	2400	2.23	94	72	12 754
Singapore	21 200	0.94	107	91	667
Thailand	7700	0.99	94	94	4427
United States	25 860	0.58	117	97	421
Zimbabwe	2340	1.27	92	85	7692

2. Fig. 30-8 shows the GDP per capita for the sample of 18 countries. Sort these statistics from high to low GDP per capita. The highest GDP per capita would be ranked 1 and the lowest 18. Add the rankings to your organizer.

△ **Fig. 30-8** *Use this data to complete the activity.*

POPULATION GROWTH

As a country develops, it is typical for the rate at which the country's population grows to decrease. There are many reasons for this, such as the fact that in a developed country many women have more control over how many children they will have. Also, people in countries with pension systems and effective health care do not feel the need to have large families to support them in their old age.

3. Using the data in Fig. 30-8, sort the statistics from low to high population growth rates for the 18 countries, with 1 being the lowest population growth rate. Add these rankings to your organizer.

FOOD SUPPLY

The most basic food requirement is energy. The amount of food energy needed to survive in different countries varies because of differences in average body size, the age composition of the population and the climate. Generally speaking, people in tropical regions need less food energy than those in colder climates. Canada, for example, has an average daily requirement of 11 172 kJ (kilojoules), while Indonesia has an average of only 9072 kJ.

In Canada, when we talk about watching what we eat, it usually means that we are eating too much and want to lose a few kilograms. In most developing countries, following a diet means trying to make sure that you have enough to eat to stay healthy and, in some cases, to stay alive.

4. Use the data in Fig. 30-8 to sort the countries' food supplies from high to low with 1 being the highest level of food supplies. Transfer the ratings to your organizer.

EDUCATION LEVEL

Many experts would suggest that the best way to speed the economic and social development of a country is to improve the education of the country's citizens. Educational achievement can be measured in many different ways. One of the simplest ways is to determine the **literacy** level of a country, that is, the percentage of the population that can read and write. Experts believe that if more people in a country know how to read and write, it is easier to spread information, for example, about better farming methods and health issues.

5. Sort the literacy levels in Fig. 30-8 from high to low with 1 being the highest literacy level. Place the rankings in your organizer.

HEALTHCARE

You may have suffered from diarrhea on occasion. Your parents probably had measles when they were children and had to stay home from school for a week or so. We assume that we will recover from what we think of as minor illnesses, and we are able to eliminate diseases like the measles almost entirely. In developing countries, though, thousands of children die each year from illnesses like diarrhea and measles.

You almost certainly have not had measles, formerly a common childhood disease, since you likely received a vaccine to prevent it when you were a baby.

Having an effective healthcare system is an important part of a country's development. One way to measure the quality of the healthcare system is by calculating how many people, on average, each doctor must look after.

6. The final column of data in Fig. 30-8 shows the number of people per doctor for the 18 countries. Rank these from lowest to highest with 1 being the lowest number of people per doctor. List the rankings in your organizer.

7. For each country, total the rankings for the six measures used. Based on these totals, divide the countries into three groups of six countries from most to least developed. These three groups of countries represent different levels of development: developed countries, newly industrializing, and developing countries.

To get detailed information about countries, check www.un.org/Pubs/ CyberSchoolBus/infonation/ e_infonation.htm

THE THREE LEVELS OF DEVELOPMENT

Developed Countries

At the highest social and economic level are those countries classified as developed. What are the characteristics of developed countries?

- Their economies are based increasingly on the service sector. They have well-developed services like education, health care, banking, transportation, and information technologies.

- While most of these countries became developed based on their manufacturing, factories are less important economic activities today than they were in the past.

- Primary industries, while highly efficient, are the least important part of the economy in terms of value and providing jobs.

See Chapter 20 for more information on primary industry.

- Citizens of the developed countries have the highest standards of living in the world. Even some of the poorest people in these countries live well compared to the average person in the developing countries.

However, the wealth and high living standards of these countries have been achieved at great cost. The developed countries, despite the fact that they have only about 20% of the world's population, use most of the world's resources and produce most of the world's pollution. In the years to come, it will be a great challenge for these countries to maintain their standard of living while reducing their impact on the world's environment.

See Chapter 36 for more information on the ecological cost of development.

Developing Countries

Of the three groups, developing countries are those with the lowest levels of economic and social growth. Most of the countries of Africa and Asia are members of this group. They tend to share the following characteristics:

- In contrast to the developed world, developing countries have economies that are dominated by primary industries and, in particular, by agriculture. In most developing countries, the majority of people are farmers.
- Most new development is focused on manufacturing since these countries often have raw materials that can be used in manufacturing. Also, their rapidly growing populations need manufactured goods of all types.
- The services sector of the economy tends to be poorly developed since most of their population has little money to spend on services such as telephones, banks, and schools.
- Citizens earn little cash income. Most of their production is for their own use or is traded to supply their needs.
- As well, since citizens earn so little they do not pay taxes. As a result, the government is not able to provide money for education, healthcare, or economic development. Frequently, developing countries have to rely on **foreign aid** to pay for such things.

foreign aid: money, food, etc. given by one country (usually developed) to another country (usually developing)

Newly Industrializing Countries

In many parts of the world, countries are going through the process of becoming developed. Countries that are undergoing the enormous changes that this involves are called newly industrializing. This process involves a complete change in the economy and lifestyles of the country and can take many years to occur. Perhaps the best examples of this in the last 50 years or so have occurred in southeast Asia, especially in the "Four Dragons:" Taiwan, South Korea, Hong Kong, and Singapore. Each of these has gone from the developing stage to the developed stage since World War II. They did this by achieving economic growth rates much greater than those that were occurring in the developed countries. Similar changes are occurring, perhaps more slowly, in other parts of Asia like China and Malaysia, and in Latin American countries like Brazil and Chile.

In 1998, the economies of southeast Asia suffered major setbacks. This so-called "Asian flu" did not change the fact that these countries had progressed through at least one stage of development.

LIMITATIONS OF GROUPING COUNTRIES

While there are some obvious advantages to grouping countries as we have done here, there are also some problems with this method.

One is deciding what "progress" and "development" really are. For example, by the definition we have used here a country can be seen to "develop" when it increases its GDP per capita, even if this increase may not improve the quality of life for the country's citizens. For instance, if a country spends money on its military or on industrial development that causes major environmental damage, it will increase its GDP but might cause harm to its citizens.

Consider what isn't revealed in GDP statistics. Take the case of countries where most people produce their own food. This fact would not be reflected in GDP statistics since this food was not sold to anyone. On the other hand, farmers may grow **cash crops** like coffee and sugar which they sell and thus add to the GDP. However, they may not earn enough to feed their families.

A second problem is that there are only three groups. This means that each group contains countries that can be very different from each other. For example, look at Bangladesh and Nigeria, two very different countries in the same group. Bangladesh has a huge population and few marketable natural resources, while Nigeria has vast supplies of natural resources like oil and gas.

A third problem is that this approach assumes that the level of economic and social development in a country is the same throughout the population. Clearly this is not the case. In Canada, we have people who are billionaires and others who live on the street. In countries like China and India, some people drive luxury automobiles and live in fancy homes while hundreds of millions struggle to feed their families. The three groups only give a broad picture of levels of development.

A final problem is that these groupings do not apply very well to countries that used to be part of the Soviet Union or were allies of the Soviet Union. In most countries, economic and social development have gone hand-in-hand. Those with the most advanced economies also have the most highly developed social systems. In the former Soviet bloc, social development typically was more advanced than economic growth. The Communist governments of these countries have been replaced with governments more like those in countries with more advanced economies. As a result, their pattern of economic and social development is changing to fit the pattern found in countries with advanced economies — but this change will take many years to occur. Over time, it is likely that some of the former Soviet bloc countries, like Estonia, Hungary, and Russia itself, may move into the developed countries category while others, like Kazakhstan and Uzbekistan, may fall into the newly industrializing category.

Consider that the military expenditures might be used to keep a dictator in power.

When the farmer buys food and other products this increases the GDP as well.

Cuba has levels of economic development that you would expect to find in a developing country, but levels of social development typical of a developed country.

QUESTIONS

CHECK YOUR UNDERSTANDING

1. Why are some countries called developed, some called newly industrializing, and some called developing? Give two examples of each that were not listed in Fig. 30-8.

2. a) Copy Fig. 30-9 into your notebook and complete it using the information from Fig. 30-5, 30-6, and 30-8. The first row has been completed for you.

   b) Briefly describe the importance of each characteristic to a country's well-being.

ANALYZE AND APPLY

3. a) Using the sample of 18 countries found in Fig. 30-8, identify the parts of the world where most of the developed and developing countries are located.

   b) Sometimes these two groups of countries are called the *North* and the *South*. What is meant by this and what significance does it have?

   c) Is this an accurate way to describe the groups?

4. In the activity at the beginning of this chapter, you examined some of the statistical measures that could be used to identify the level of development of a country. Now you will examine five more characteristics to find out if they too can be used for this purpose. The activity works best when done in groups of five. The five measures are listed in Fig. 30-10.

   a) In a group, divide up the five measures in pairs, so that each pair of measures shares one measure in common. Each student should choose to examine the possible relationship between two pairs of these measures. For example, you might choose to do *Infant Mortality* and *Population Under Age of 15* and *Infant Mortality* and *Workers in Agriculture*.

   b) Create a scattergraph for each of your pairs of measures. (Instructions for drawing a scattergraph are given in Chapter 8.) A sample of a scattergraph for *GDP per capita* and *Literacy Level* (from Fig. 30-8) is shown in Fig. 30-11.

   c) On each scattergraph, try to decide if there is an obvious relationship between the two measures. If there is, is it a direct or indirect relationship? (In a direct relationship, when one increases the other increases.)

   d) Can you identify three clusters of countries on your graph? Circle and label the clusters that might represent the developed countries, newly industrializing countries, and developing countries (Fig. 30-11). What would overlaps between groups mean?

   e) Describe the conditions in the countries represented by each cluster. For example, developing countries would have a high GDP per capita and a high literacy level (or not!).

Fig. 30-9

Characteristic	Developed	Newly Industrializing	Developing
Life Expectancy (years)	76 – 80	61 – 78	41 – 56
GDP per capita			
Population Growth Rate (%)			
Food Supply (% of need)			
Literacy Level (%)			
Number of People per Doctor			

Fig. 30-10

Country	Infant Mortality Rate (deaths per 1000 live births)	Population Under Age of 15 (%)	Workers in Agriculture (% of total)	Population Density (people/km²)	Electrical Power Capacity (kWh/person)
1	7	22%	3%	28	2.6
2	38	26	54	127	0.17
3	70	45	54	112	0.05
4	55	44	77	51	0.03
5	106	48	65	21	0.06
6	13	28	19	19	0.40
7	6	20	3	3	3.8
8	5	22	6	2	2.2
9	53	30	31	19	0.37
10	100	38	65	832	0.03
11	59	40	64	10	0.06
12	32	25	57	116	0.27
13	4	15	6	333	0.8
14	4	21	0	5397	1.5
15	51	44	33	41	0.41
16	5	16	3	229	1.4
17	73	43	70	30	0.17
18	24	36	28	51	0.42

f) Consult with the other members of your group and try to decide which of these five measures can be used to identify developed, newly industralized, and developing countries.

THINK AND COMMUNICATE

5. What do you think are the two most serious problems facing most developing countries? How should they deal with them? What should people in developed countries be doing to assist their efforts?

6. What do you think are the two most serious problems facing most developed countries? How should we deal with them? What can people in the developing world do to assist us?

7. Every developing and newly industrializing country in the world is trying to achieve the standard of living of developed countries. But the world cannot support more than six billion people, at this level.

a) Why is this true?

b) Is it fair for Canadians to live at such a high (and wasteful) standard of living and tell others that they cannot do the same? Explain.

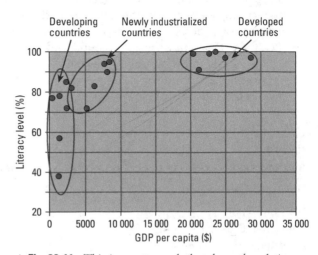

△ **Fig. 30-11** *This is a scattergraph that shows the relationship between literacy level and GDP per capita.*

31 Canada's International Relationships

STUDY GUIDE

By the end of this chapter, you will be able to:

- identify the variety of connections that Canada and Canadians have with other countries
- identify and understand some of the roles Canada plays in the world

- understand the impact of globalization on Canada
- appreciate the concept of "global village" and the interdependance one part of the world has with other parts of the world

Key Terms

foreign aid

globalization

multinational corporations (MNCs)

non-governmental organizations (NGOs)

A number of years ago, a Canadian writer named Marshall McLuhan created the term "global village" to describe the way that improved communication and transportation have caused distances in the world to seem smaller. In a sense, the world seems to be shrinking. The entire world is starting to operate in the way that a village might have operated a few hundred years ago. This chapter focuses on the relationships that exist within our global village.

The relationships that exist among the world's countries and, in particular, the relationships between Canada and other countries can take many forms. Canada belongs to a wide variety of international organizations in which countries work together to make the world a safer, happier, and healthier place in which to live. The world's economies are so closely linked that you may wear the same brands of clothing and eat many of the same types of foods as teenagers who live thousands of kilometres away. Every day, Canadians have cultural contacts with the world through television, movies, books, magazines, the Internet, and family connections. Some of the most important athletic competitions like the Olympics and soccer World Cup are worldwide in scope.

CANADA'S DIPLOMATIC LINKS

Despite differences in wealth, culture, language, and nationality, the people of the world share one planet. We have more similarities than differences and the problems in one part of the world sooner or later will affect people elsewhere. Yet, during much of the twentieth century, the people of the world have been in conflict with one another in two devastating world wars and dozens of smaller wars. Much of the world has also experienced poverty and environmental damage. Canada has been a leader in trying to find ways to avoid such problems and to minimize the damage that occurs as a result of them.

To learn more about Canada's foreign policy, check www.dfait-maeci.gc.ca/ foreignp/menu-e.asp

The United Nations

The most important international organization devoted to solving the world's problems is the United Nations (UN). The UN was formed at the end of World War II to promote world peace and development. Since 1945, it has grown to include more than 180 countries. It often has difficulty solving major international crises because of political differences among its members. It does, however, provide a forum for discussions, and may have helped to prevent a world war since it was established over fifty years ago.

Canada was a founding member of the UN and plays an active role in its activities today.

When people think about the UN, they tend to focus on the political activities of the organization, which are centred at the UN headquarters in New York. However, the activities of the UN go far beyond this. Fig. 31-1 outlines just a few of the specialized UN agencies that have quietly cooperated in solving international problems for many years. One of these organizations has its headquarters in Canada. The International Civil Aviation Organization (ICAO), located in Montréal, has such responsibilities as setting standards for air-flight security and coordinating air-traffic control.

▽ **Fig. 31-1** *These are just a few of the specialized organizations that are part of the United Nations. You may have raised money to support UNICEF activities at Halloween.*

Program/Organization	Purpose
• United Nations International Children's Fund (UNICEF)	• to provide emergency relief aid and promote the role of children
• Food and Agriculture Organization (FAO)	• to raise levels of nutrition, improve production, and distribute food
• The World Health Organization (WHO)	• to direct and coordinate activities, promote research, and supply drugs and equipment where needed

The UN also acts as the world's peacekeeper. It organizes military and police forces made up of troops from member states. Canada has been involved in more peacekeeping operations than any other country. Peacekeepers are sent to scenes of conflict to make sure that truces are being observed. In some cases — for example, Cyprus, — UN peacekeeping forces have been in place for more than 30 years with no indication that they can be withdrawn soon. Over 85 000 Canadian armed forces personnel (along with a much smaller number of Royal Canadian Mounted Police and other police officers) have served as peacekeepers in Eastern Europe, Cyprus, the Middle East, Africa, Southeast Asia, and Latin America (Fig. 31-2).

In 1957, Lester B. Pearson, who would later become prime minister, was given the Nobel Peace Prize for proposing the first UN peacekeeping operation which solved the Suez Canal crisis in the Middle East.

Foreign Aid

In response to the needs of people in the developing countries around the world, Canadians contribute funds, materials, knowledge, and skills to help developing countries improve their incomes, food supply, literacy levels, health care, and life expectancy. Canadians give assistance through their government, through donations to private aid organizations, and by volunteering (Fig. 31-3).

Much of Canada's **foreign aid** is managed by the Canadian International Development Agency (CIDA). CIDA follows four principles in its operation:

- deal with poverty first
- help people to help themselves
- promote development
- build partnerships

In the past, though, Canada's aid has also been aimed at helping Canadian businesses. CIDA still states that one of its purposes is to help Canada.

Your teacher will give you instructions for an ArcVoyager activity that examines Canada's foreign aid.

◁ **Fig. 31-2** *Canadian peacekeepers, have helped maintain order in various parts of the world for more than 40 years.*

To learn more about peacekeeping, check www.dfait-maeci.gc.ca/ peacekeeping/menu-e.asp and www.un.org/Pubs/ CyberSchoolBus/ peacekeeping/index.html

Country	1990 Amount	1990 Percentage of GNP	1995 Amount	1995 Percentage of GNP
Canada	2470	0.44	2067	0.38
United States	11 394	0.21	7367	0.10
Australia	955	0.34	1194	0.36
Denmark	1171	0.93	1623	0.96
Sweden	2012	0.90	1704	0.77
Switzerland	750	0.31	1084	0.34
United Kingdom	2638	0.27	3157	0.28

△ **Fig. 31-3** *Foreign aid (in millions of U.S. dollars)given by a number of developed countries in 1990 and 1995. The United Nations recommends that richer countries should give 0.7% of their Gross National Product (GNP) for foreign aid. Only a few countries have reached this level and, in many countries, this amount is dropping. (GNP is a measure very much like GDP.)*

CANADA'S ECONOMIC LINKS

International relationships are becoming more and more important as we move into a time of increased **globalization**. What this means is that borders between countries are becoming less important as the world operates increasingly as one unit. This can be seen in a number of areas. The most important is in the economic world. In the past, companies would operate primarily in one country or one small region. These companies would operate as **corporate citizens** of their country. Now, large companies called **multinational corporations** (**MNCs**) operate across the entire world. Examples of MNCs are given in Fig. 31-4.

Some MNCs are larger, economically, than many of the countries in which they operate. Because of their enormous size and worldwide operations, MNCs are able to move their activities from place to place as they see opportunities emerge. This can mean that a decision made in a remote country can cause joy in a Canadian community when a new factory opens, providing employment opportunities, or sadness when a mine closes and people lose their jobs.

Economic globalization brings both risks and opportunities for Canada. If the international business community feels that Canada has a competitive advantage over other countries, then it will expand its operations here. The advantage could be that our country has a highly educated labour force, cheap raw materials, a stable society, or a low dollar. If this happens, then there will be more jobs created and our economy will grow. On the other hand, if the international business community decides that other areas have an advantage, then it can move jobs out of Canada and our economy will be devastated. To prevent this, officials in Canadian business and government sometimes feel that they have to work towards lower wage rates and relaxed environmental controls to insure that Canada remains internationally competitive. Many Canadians are fighting this situation because they feel it would result in a lower quality of life for the average Canadian.

corporate citizens: companies that show loyalty to a particular country

competitive advantage: It is cheaper to have the business locate in a specific country, such as Canada. This allows it to compete more effectively with companies in other countries

When the value of our dollar is low, goods produced in Canada are cheaper to buy on the world market.

Company	Home Country	Type of Business
Walt Disney	United States	Entertainment
Shell Oil	Netherlands	Oil
Bata	Canada	Shoes
Toyota	Japan	Automobiles
Microsoft	United States	Computer software
Bombardier	Canada	Recreation equipment and aircraft
Panasonic	Japan	Electronics
Adidas	Germany	Athletic clothing and footwear

△ **Fig. 31-4** *Examples of multinational corporations*

CANADA'S CULTURAL LINKS

A second impact of globalization can be seen in the cultural field. Increasingly, the cultures of the world seem to be losing their distinctiveness. There are a number of reasons why this is happening. Television, movies, popular music, professional sports, and the Internet all provide opportunities for people in one part of the world to be exposed to the cultures of other countries. The result is that teenagers in Pakistan, Peru, and Peterborough may watch the same television shows and movies, listen to the same music, have the same sports heroes, and wear the same clothing styles.

However, many people say that this is not a question of globalization. Instead, they say that it is really the Americanization of the world's cultures since the United States is the source of most of the entertainment and styles that influence the rest of the world. In some areas of the world this Americanization is happening with little reaction, while in others, people are working to preserve their culture.

The cultural influence of the United States on Canada is considered in more detail in Chapter 33.

QUESTIONS

CHECK YOUR UNDERSTANDING

1. Identify and describe, with examples, three different types of connections that Canada and Canadians have with other countries.

2. a) Describe three main roles played by the United Nations in the world.

   b) Describe one key role that Canada has played within the UN.

ANALYZE AND APPLY

3. *"We have more similarities than differences and the problems in one part of the world sooner or later will affect people elsewhere."* This statement was made in reference to the need for people across the world to work together to solve the problems they face.

   a) Describe the nature of the similarities and differences among people in the world. Explain in what way we "have more similarities than differences."

b) Give at least two examples of how "problems in one part of the world sooner or later will affect people elsewhere."

4. a) Canada has been a leader in the UN peacekeeping efforts for more than 40 years. There are several reasons for this. Consider Canada's history and current situation to suggest why Canada would be more likely to be involved in peacekeeping than the following countries:

    i.   United States

    ii. United Kingdom

    iii. Bangladesh

    b) Outline reasons other than those suggested in 4a that would explain Canada's long-standing commitment to peacekeeping. Consider Canada's history and current situation.

5. a) List the four principles that are used to govern the activities of CIDA.

    b) Discuss why these ideas were chosen. Can you suggest any other principles that might have been used instead of or in addition to these?

THINK AND COMMUNICATE

6. In a group of three or four students, discuss the following questions. Put a summary of your discussions in your notebook.

    a) How might the world be different today if the UN had not been created after World War II?

    b) One example of an international problem that might require united action to be solved is international terrorism. Describe three other international problems that would require united action to be solved.

    c) Would you expect international agencies related to the UN to exist to solve these problems? Check to see if such agencies exist.

    d) What contribution could Canada make to help solve these problems?

7. Consider the meaning of the term "world power." On one hand, Canada is not as economically, militarily, or politically powerful as the United States but on the other hand, we have more international "clout" than countries like Senegal or Honduras. Where does Canada rank as a world power? Give evidence to support your answer.

8. In 1990, Canadian foreign aid was $2.5 billion. Between 1993 and 1997, Canada's foreign aid declined by $500 million. Here is one person's opinion: *"Canada should not give away more than $2 billion per year in foreign aid when we have such serious economic and social problems at home."*

    a) Give arguments supporting this position.

    b) Give arguments opposing this position.

    c) What is your personal belief? Why?

9. Put yourself in the place of the prime minister or the premier of a province. You realize that MNCs are not choosing to expand in Canada as much as you would like. These companies feel that wage rates are too high here and environmental standards are too tight. Would you support changing Canadian laws to allow lower labour costs and relaxed environmental standards? If you would, explain why. If you would not, what alternative strategies would you suggest to encourage MNCs to invest in Canada?

10. a) Select an international organization to which Canada belongs and identify its purpose (e.g., Commonwealth, Francophonie, NATO, G8, the International Olympic Committee).

    b) Evaluate its effectiveness in addressing global concerns.

11. Many people have petitioned the governments of G8 countries to forgive the debts of developing nations. Give arguments to support and oppose this idea.

32 Canada's Foreign Trade

STUDY GUIDE

By the end of this chapter, you will be able to:

- identify Canada's major imports and exports in goods and services
- create bar graphs to indicate trade sources and destinations
- identify opposing and supportive views toward NAFTA
- understand issues related to the future of Canada's trade

Key Terms

imports	net imports	tariff	protectionism
exports	net exports	import substitution	free trade
trade surplus	trade deficit		

What do all of the objects in Fig. 32-1 have in common? If you guessed that all of the objects shown are typical **imports** to Canada, then you would be right. Canada also **exports** a wide range of products. A picture of these would show such things as minivans, giant rolls of newsprint, natural gas, wheat, and coal.

More than 300 years ago, a famous English poet named John Donne wrote, "No man is an island, entire of itself." He meant that no person could exist without others. A similar situation exists for countries. No nation can survive independent of other countries and with globalization, this interdependence of countries will only increase. This chapter explores the complex and fascinating business of international trade and why it is so important to all Canadians.

Each year, Canadians import goods worth more than $220 billion. We export even more. In 1996, our exports were $254 billion. If exports exceed imports, the difference between these amounts is called a **trade surplus**. If imports are higher than exports then it is called a **trade deficit**. Our trade surplus is vital since we must earn money from exports to pay for the goods and services that we import. Beyond this, the whole question of trade could affect you personally. Right now, one out of every five jobs in

Not all of the exports could fit into one picture!

220 billion = 220 000 000 000. To picture this amount, imagine that you just won the "Super-Duper Lottery" grand prize. For your prize, you must spend $7000 every second, 24 hours per day, every day for one year!

Our trade surplus in goods is vital since Canada imports far more services than it exports.

◁ **Fig. 32-1** *These are all imports to Canada. Can you identify the country from which each item is imported? Check your answers against the correct ones on p. 431.*

▽ **Fig. 32-2** *There are many similarities between the list of our best customers for our exports and the most important sources of our imports.*

Canada is tied to exports, and with globalization, international trade will become even more important in the future. Since countries will tend to produce and export only a few specialized commodities, they will have to import many other products they need. Keep the export/import field in mind when you start looking for a job in a few years.

1. Canada trades with countries all over the world, but our trade with the United States far exceeds our total trade with all other countries. Fig. 32-2 is a summary of Canada's trade for 1996. Create a bar graph that shows each country that bought Canada's exports, and the value of the exports each country bought. Create a second bar graph that shows each country from which Canada imported goods, and the value of the imports from each of the countries.

CANADA'S IMPORTS

Net imports and **net exports** are terms that refer to the difference between how much we import of a particular product and how much we export of the same product. For example, if we import a total of five million dollars of raspberries and export a total of seven million dollars of raspberries, then we would have a net export of two million dollars. The concept of net imports and exports is a useful one. It tells us we have an excess of certain products, and therefore must export them. Or, it tells us we have a shortage of certain products, and therefore must import them. Canada's major net imports (Fig. 32-3) fall into four main categories: high-technology products, motor vehicle parts, goods produced only in warmer climates, and low-cost goods.

IMPORTS

Country	Amount ($ million)
United States	157 494
Japan	10 444
Mexico	6034
United Kingdom	5909
China	4926
Germany	4821
France	3400
Taiwan	2863
South Korea	2728
Italy	2719

EXPORTS

Country	Amount ($ million)
United States	209 108
Japan	11 022
United Kingdom	3846
Germany	3165
China	2828
South Korea	2771
France	1683
Netherlands	1580
Belgium	1489
Taiwan	1368

CANADA'S NET IMPORTS, 1997 ($MILLION)

Commodity	Imports	− Exports	= Net
Computers, television, electronic and optical equipment	24 567	12 820	11 747
Motor vehicle parts	22 641	11 122	11 519
Cloth, clothing and footwear	10 723	5144	5579
Industrial machinery	3182	1233	1949
Medical equipment and supplies	3003	1080	1923
Personal and household goods	5988	4079	1909
Fruits and vegetables	2947	1058	1889
Books, magazines, and other printed goods	3047	1256	1791
Sports, games, and recreational equipment	2505	906	1599
Sugar, coffee, tea, chocolate, spices, and nuts	2434	974	1460

△ **Fig. 32-3** *Canada's most important net imports. These values were determined by calculating the difference between our imports and exports within the major groupings of products.*

High-technology Products

The largest group of our imports are in the high-technology category, including items like computers, communications equipment, photographic equipment, televisions, video games, and compact disc players. Only a few countries in the world, including the United States, Japan, Germany, Taiwan, and South Korea, produce most of these products and they are able to supply the world's needs. High-technology industries are important in Canada (note how much we export!) but we do not produce a wide enough range of products to meet our needs.

Motor Vehicle Parts

The second largest import category is auto parts. Canadians make many of the cars that are sold in the United States by General Motors, Ford, Chrysler, Toyota, and Honda. Car assembly plants in Canada use a wide range of parts from the United States, Mexico, Japan, and other countries to build these cars.

Goods Produced Only in Warmer Climates

Canada's northern location means that we are not able to produce many products that require warm climates. As a result, we must import such products as citrus fruits, most fresh vegetables in winter, sugar, coffee, tea, chocolate, spices, and tropical woods like teak and mahogany.

Low-cost Goods

Canadians import some goods because they can be produced more cheaply in countries other than Canada. These products include clothing, footwear, plastics, and books. These products are made in countries like China, India, Brazil, Thailand, and Mexico for the Canadian market. The most obvious reason is that labour costs in Canada are higher than in

Canada exports many goods in the communications and computer industries, but not many other high-technology products.

Check the labels of your clothing and footwear to see where they were made.

these other countries. These costs would make Canadian-made products very expensive.

Should We Reduce Our Imports?

When we decide to buy a CD player or a banana made or grown in another country, we are making a decision that causes money to leave Canada. Can we do anything about this? Should we? In some cases we have a choice, in others we do not. If you choose to eat a Canadian-grown apple instead of a foreign-grown banana then you are practising what is called **import substitution** and helping our economy. In the case of the CD player, you have little choice since you are unlikely to find a Canadian-made substitute. When you buy a Canadian product instead of an imported one, you help the national economy and provide jobs for Canadians.

CANADA'S EXPORTS

Fig. 32-4 lists Canada's ten leading net exports. Our major net exports fall into two categories: products based on our natural resources, and motor vehicles. In addition, we export great amounts of specialized manufactured goods, even if they do not qualify to be on the list of net exports.

Products Based on our Natural Resources

For many decades, Canadians have been called "hewers of wood and drawers of water," which means that we have had an economy based on our natural resources. It is not surprising that natural resources are so important to our trade since a country is able to export only those things

CANADA'S NET EXPORTS, 1997 ($MILLION)

Commodity	Exports	Imports	Net
Motor vehicles	51 718	26 470	25 248
Pulp and paper	21 237	4724	16 513
Lumber products	17 503	2387	15 116
Metal ores and products	17 269	8550	8719
Natural gas	8565	136	8429
Oil, coal and their products	18 198	11 490	6708
Grains and oil seeds	7520	847	6673
Live animals and meats	4297	1149	3148
Fish and fish products	2612	1170	1442
Electricity	1356	203	1153

◁ **Fig. 32-4** *Canada's most important net exports (Net exports = exports - imports)*

where it has an advantage compared to other countries. We are able to sell to the world (and particularly our American neighbours) products from our forests, fields, mines, and waters, because of our vast area, rich resources, and small population.

Many people argue that we export too many of our resources in a largely unprocessed form. They feel that we should do more processing here and ship finished goods, that are worth more, instead of raw materials. This would increase wealth, and the number of jobs.

Motor Vehicles

Canada exported 1.9 million cars and trucks in 1995. The export of these motor vehicles is of vital importance to the economic health of Canada and, in particular, of southern Ontario where most vehicle assembly plants are located (Fig. 32-5). The enormous amount of vehicle production in Canada occurs because of trade agreements with the United States and, more recently, Mexico that allow motor vehicle parts and completed vehicles to move between countries without **tariffs** having to be paid. The original agreement, signed in 1965 with the United States, was called the Auto Pact. It required that the number of vehicles built in Canada must at least equal the number sold here. What the auto companies found was that Canadian plants were efficient and cheap to operate. As a result, auto assembly facilities here were expanded so that we now export 1.1 million more vehicles than we import.

Specialized Manufactured Goods

Canada does export manufactured goods other than motor vehicles. As you would expect, these are in fields where Canada has some sort of

You teacher may give you instructions to complete an ArcVoyager exercise on motor vehicle production in North America.

tariff: a tax that is paid when a product moves from one country to another

Examples of specialized manufactured goods exported from Canada include $13 billion worth of computers, telecommunications, and related equipment. Canadians also export almost $5 billion worth of aircraft.

◁ **Fig. 32-5** *These are the truck/van and auto assembly plants in Southern Ontario. There is also one located near Montréal, Québec. Canada's auto assembly plants are all located in a very small area. Why does this make sense?*

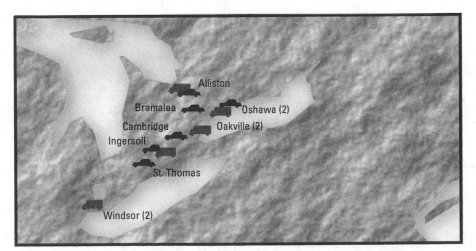

△ **Fig. 32-6** *Bombardier owns two aircraft companies that make medium-sized aircraft like this de Havilland Dash 8.*

advantage. A good example of this is in the aircraft industry. Canada is a huge country and was one of the first in the world to use airplanes in large numbers. As a result, we have had an aircraft manufacturing industry for many years. In recent decades, our aircraft industry has come to specialize in building small- and medium-sized passenger aircraft like the Dash 8 (Fig. 32-6) and Challenger Regional Jet both of which are sold to countries all over the world.

Importance of Exports

Why must Canada export? There are three major reasons:

1. *To pay for the things that we import* — Canadians import both necessities and luxuries from other countries. If we want to continue to enjoy these products, we must be able to pay for them. The obvious way to do this is by selling our products.

2. *To keep our economy healthy* — Almost 50% of the goods and services that Canadians produce are exported. With fewer exports, unemployment would be much higher and most of us would be poorer.

3. *To lower the prices of Canadian-made goods for Canadians* — Keep in mind that the cost per unit of something (a pair of skates, for example) is lower if you make one million pairs of skates than if you make ten thousand pairs. A Canadian company that produces for export as well as for the Canadian market can keep the price lower for everyone.

Bombardier's aircraft home page is www.aero.bombardier.com/htmen/4_0.htm

Trade In Services

Most often when Canadians talk about trade, they are thinking only of trade in goods. If we do this, the economic picture looks very

INTERNATIONAL TRANSACTIONS IN SERVICES ($ MILLION), 1997

	Imports	Exports	Balance
Travel	15 649	12 141	-3508
Transportation services	11 514	8 323	-3191
Business services	20 100	22 576	+2476
Government services	1008	577	-431
Total	48 271	43 617	-4654

◁ **Fig. 32-7** *Canada's international trade in services, 1997*

rosy. In 1997, for example, we had a trade surplus for goods of about $24 billion.

However, trade involves services as well as goods and here the picture is not so bright. In 1997, we had a deficit in services of more than $4 billion. While there are several sources of this deficit, the largest part comes from travel and transportation services (Fig. 32-7). Canadians travel to other countries more often than foreigners come to Canada and Canadians spend more when they travel.

We also import many business services. While this might seem to be quite remote from your life, you contribute to this deficit every day! Consider how money leaves Canada in each of the following situations and how this relates to your life:

- a Canadian television station shows *The Simpsons,* which is produced in the United States
- you visit a new McDonald's franchise near your house
- American-produced advertisements for Pepsi appear in a Canadian magazine

Free Trade Versus Protectionism

The conflict of free trade versus protectionism has been a recurring theme in Canada's history for more than a century. It continues to be an important issue for Canadians. Before discussing this issue, a few terms need to be explained: tariffs, **protectionism**, and **free trade**.

Tariffs: A tariff is a tax on an import. What role do tariffs play in trade? Consider the example of the blue jeans described in Fig. 32-8. Clearly, tariffs make it more costly to buy foreign goods. As you can see, tariffs can seriously affect trade, particularly if you remember that other countries could also have tariffs that could keep out Canadian products!

Protectionism: Protectionism is the government's policy of using tariffs and having rules that limit imports. This is done to give Canadian companies an advantage over foreign competitors which often are larger and can produce things more cheaply.

	Without Tariffs	**With Tariffs**
Cost in your local store	 Canadian-made jeans $50, foreign-made jeans $45	 Canadian-made jeans $50, foreign-made jeans $55
Results	**Few sold** • factory closes • unemployment higher • money leaves Canada to pay for foreign jeans **Many sold** • imports of jeans higher • balance of trade hurt	**Many sold** • Canadian industries and jobs protected • money stays in Canada **Few sold** • imports of jeans lower • balance of trade improved

		For Tariffs	**Against Tariffs**
Student A:	wants the best price when buying jeans in the store	?	?
Student B:	parent works in a jeans factory	?	?
Student C:	parent sells new cars in a town that has a large jeans factory	?	?
Student D:	cousin operates a foreign jeans factory	?	?

◁△ **Fig. 32-8** *How tariffs work. Which of students A, B, C, and D would likely favour tariffs and which would oppose them?*

Free Trade: Free trade is the government policy of eliminating tariffs and other laws that are designed to restrict trade. The basic idea of free trade is that enhanced trade among nations is good for everyone.

GENERAL AGREEMENT ON TARIFFS AND TRADE (GATT)

After World War II, major trading countries, including Canada, realized that they had to avoid the trade protection that had proved so disastrous during the Depression. To do this, they agreed on a set of rules to govern and encourage trade. This agreement, the General Agreement on Tariffs and Trade, or GATT, came into affect in 1947 and now includes more than 120 countries.

The latest additions to the GATT came into effect in 1995 with the creation of the World Trade Organization (WTO), which was designed to resolve disputes under the laws of the GATT.

NORTH AMERICAN FREE TRADE AGREEMENT (NAFTA)

While the GATT has done much to promote free trade across the world, Canada has also pursued freer trade directly with the United States and, more recently, other countries. Free trade with the United States is of particular significance because of the enormous amount of trade that we have with our southern neighbour.

This move to increase free trade started in 1988 with the creation of a free trade agreement with the United States. In 1993, the arrangement was expanded to include Mexico under an agreement called the North American Free Trade Agreement or NAFTA.

The move to free trade with the United States was very controversial and remains so today. For instance, some people think that NAFTA would require us to share our resources with the United States and Mexico even if they were needed in Canada. It would be very hard for Canada to move away from free trade since its economy has changed enormously to reflect a free trade environment. What are the arguments for and against free trade? Look at Fig. 32-9.

More recently, there have been discussions to include Chile and other countries of the Americas in a growing free trade area.

There are other free trade areas of the world. The largest is the European Community. The EC has gone much farther than has NAFTA in breaking down the barriers between the economies of nations. For example, they have created a common currency, the Euro, for the region.

IN SUPPORT OF NAFTA

Issue	Argument
• Efficiency	• Tariffs protect inefficient producers which pushes prices up for consumers.
• Jobs	• Low-skill jobs will be replaced with high-skill jobs that pay better.
• Competitiveness	• Canada can compete effectively with the Americans and Mexicans because of high productivity, good transportation, and cheap power.
• Opportunities	• Canadian companies can bid on American and Mexican government contracts.
• Environmental improvement	• Overall North American environmental quality will improve since Mexico is required to meet American/Canadian standards.
• Cultural protection	• Nothing in the agreement is a threat to Canadian cultural institutions.

IN OPPOSITION TO NAFTA

Issue	Argument
• Efficiency	• Agreement helps Canadian resource exporters but hurts Canadian manufacturers that produce for Canadian market only.
• Jobs	• Jobs will move to lower wage cost areas of Mexico and southern United States.
• Competitiveness	• Canada will have to cut wages and benefits to be able to compete with American and, especially, Mexican companies.
• Opportunities	• American companies can bid on Canadian government contracts.
• Environmental improvement	• Environmental quality is likely to decline since standards in Canada will have to be relaxed to allow Canadian companies to be competitive.
• Cultural protection	• There are genuine threats to Canada's cultural independence.

△ **Fig. 32-9** *Each side in the free trade debate made powerful — and often contradictory — claims.*

THE FUTURE OF CANADA'S TRADE

International trade allows most Canadians to enjoy a relatively high standard of living. To maintain this in the future, we will have to find satisfactory answers to several critical trade-related questions.

- *Can we maintain our traditional markets?* Most of our exports are related to our rich natural resources. Developing countries which have a rich resource base like Brazil, Congo, and Papua–New Guinea are competing with Canada to provide cheap forest, mineral, and fish products to our traditional customers like the United States, Japan, and the European Community.

- *Can we export more manufactured goods?* Can we develop new products to create new markets? Over the years, Canadians have invented many products that we take for granted today: the telephone, snowmobile, zipper, snowblower, hydrofoil, and newsprint. We must continue to create new products and then develop export markets for these products.

  Have you thought about a career that might involve creating new products?

- *Can we increase our exports of services?* This can be done in a wide variety of fields. For example, we can continue to increase our production and international sale of movies, television shows, and music or we could expand international service by Canadian airlines.

- *Should we (can we?) decrease our trade reliance on the United States?* No two nations have ever had as much trade as we do with the Americans. This enormous **bilateral trade** has contributed much to our standard of living, but there are dangers to relying so heavily on one trading partner. We are easily harmed by downturns in the American economy or by protectionist policies from the American government. If we could expand our trade with other countries, we would not have to depend so much on the United States.

  bilateral trade: trade between two countries

  You can learn more about Canada's trade at: www.dfait-maeci.gc.ca/ trade/menu-e.asp

- *Can we compete effectively within NAFTA?* Our NAFTA partners each have strong advantages: huge American companies have enormous economic power and Mexican companies have lower labour costs.

QUESTIONS

CHECK YOUR UNDERSTANDING

1. a) How important is trade to Canada? Consider the impact on our lifestyle, jobs, and economy.

   b) Why must Canada export?

   c) Why must we import?

   d) How are our imports and exports related?

2. a) What is "trade in services"? Give a definition and at least three specific examples from different aspects of our life.

   b) How do *you* contribute to Canada's deficit in trade in services?

3. a) What is the GATT?

 b) What is its purpose and how has it changed over the years?

ANALYZE AND APPLY

4. *Why is it not surprising that ...?*

 Each of the following statements describes one aspect of Canada's international trade. Briefly explain why each is true.

 a) Most of Canada's trading partners are in the developed world rather than among the developing and newly industrializing countries.

 b) High-technology products (especially for consumers) are produced in only a few countries.

 c) Canada builds and exports only smaller (up to about 100 passengers) aircraft.

 d) Canada has a large deficit in trade in services.

 e) Much of Canada's export trade involves our natural resources.

5. a) Define *trade surplus* and *trade deficit*.

 b) People can decrease a trade deficit (or increase a trade surplus) by practising import substitution. Describe how you could do this with any five imported products you normally purchase.

 c) How could import substitution be applied to trade in services?

6. a) What is the difference between total imports and exports and net imports and exports?

 b) Consult a table of total imports and exports in an atlas. Compare this information to Fig. 32-3 and 32-4. What differences do you see between total and net trade?

 c) Which figures describe Canada's trade best? Why?

7. From the list below, identify people who would be likely to support free trade and those who would probably be opposed. Give reasons for each choice.

a) Saskatchewan potash miner

b) owner of a large Canadian motorboat factory

c) person wanting to start a sporting goods company

d) Montréal shoe-factory worker

e) Canadian high-school student

THINK AND COMMUNICATE

8. Should ethics (moral standards) play a role in Canada's trade policies? Consider the following cases:

 a) Canada's tobacco farmers have suffered financial setbacks in recent years as more and more Canadians quit smoking. At the same time, demand for tobacco products is increasing in developing countries. Should the Canadian government promote the sale of Canadian tobacco in other countries?

 b) The governments of many countries of the world violate the human rights of their citizens. It has been suggested that Canada should try to discourage these abuses by tying trade to human rights. For example, imports from a country would be stopped if that country did not respect human rights. Should human rights and trade be linked? Do you think such methods would be successful? Explain.

ANSWERS TO FIG. 32-1 IMPORT QUESTION

- coffee maker: Germany
- coffee beans: Kenya
- telephone: China
- running shoes: Korea
- blouse: Hong Kong
- electronic game: Japan
- camera: Japan

- pineapple: Philippines
- oranges: United States
- compact discs: United States
- china plate: United Kingdom
- wine: Chile

How many items did you guess correctly?

33 Our Cultural Connections With the United States

STUDY GUIDE

By the end of this chapter, you will be able to:

- explain the different meanings of culture
- identify the connection between geography and culture
- explain why American culture strongly influences Canadians
- explain whether Canadians should protect their culture

Key Term

culture

In the 1970s, then Prime Minister Pierre Trudeau described our relationship with our American neighbours in the following way :

> "Living next to the United States is in some ways like sleeping with an elephant. No matter how friendly and even-tempered is the beast ... one is affected by every grunt and twitch."

While this statement could apply to many aspects of our relationship with the United States, perhaps it applies best to our cultural connections with our huge neighbour. **Culture** is what makes a nation unique, and many Canadians feel that our culture is influenced too much by the culture of the United States. But what exactly do we mean by culture? The term can have two different meanings (Fig. 33-1).

CULTURE: THE BROAD VIEW

If culture is defined broadly, it refers to a way of life. What does the wider definition of culture mean for Canadians in terms of our relationship with the United States? Many Canadians say that Canada and the United

◁ **Fig. 33-1** *Consider how these two definitions of culture would apply to you.*

But what exactly do we mean by "culture"? The term can be used with two distinct meanings.

In the broad sense...
Culture includes all of the characteristics of a way of life:

• language	• education	• media
• religion	• clothing styles	• entertainment
• values	• food	
• behaviour	• the arts	

When all of these are put together in a particular combination, you have a "culture."

In the narrow sense...
Culture includes only:

• the arts

• media

• entertainment

States share a common culture. Other Canadians angrily deny that this is the case. Consider this question from your own point of view. In what ways is your life like that of an American teenager? In what ways are you distinctly Canadian? Think about such things as the television shows you watch, the magazines you read, the fashions you like, or the sports teams you support. Does it seem that your life — your culture — is very American? Consider the following factors that contribute to the similarities between our culture and that of Americans:

• The Canadian ecumene contains over 95% of Canadians and is found within 600 km of the United States border (Fig. 33-2).

• Travel between the countries is routine. In just three months in 1998, over eleven million Canadians visited the United States and roughly the same number of Americans visited Canada.

• Many Canadians have relatives and friends who live in the United States.

• Cable and satellite television offer a vast selection of American television programs to Canadians in even the most remote parts of the country.

• The vast majority of movies shown in our movie theatres come from American studios such as Universal, Paramount, and Disney.

• Many of the books and magazines that are popular in Canada are American.

ecumene: the occupied areas of a country or settled area

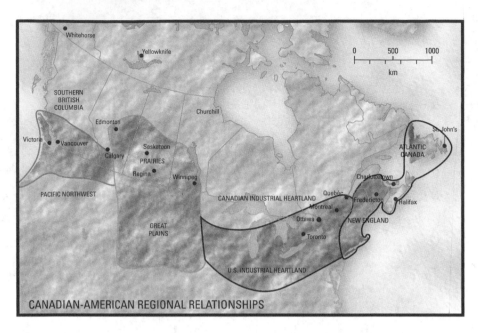

◁ **Fig. 33-2** *Canadians sometimes identify more closely with Americans who live nearby, and share a similar economy and lifestyle, than they do with Canadians who might live thousands of kilometres away and have a different lifestyle.*

Given the enormous influence that American culture has on Canadian culture, it might be hard to imagine how our culture could be distinctive (Fig. 33-3). Evidence of the uniqueness of Canadian culture is subtle and starts from the constitution on which the country is founded. The constitution of a country is the basic law of the country. It expresses the most important values upon which a country is formed. If we compare the most significant phrase of the Canadian and American constitutions we may start to see an important difference between the cultures of the two countries (Fig. 33-4).

As the examples in Fig. 33-4 suggest, there are important differences in the governing principles of the two countries. Even more interestingly, there is little evidence to suggest that this is changing.

Would you like to see an American's view of Canada's culture? Check
www.icomm.ca/emily/

▽ **Fig. 33-3** *Consider Wal-Mart, Canadian Tire, Home Depot, Loblaws, The GAP, Eaton's, Sears — which stores are Canadian and which are American? Many Canadians do not know. Do you?*

- Gun control laws in Canada are getting more and more restrictive while in the United States the opposite is happening. For example, in some American states it is now legal to carry a concealed handgun while Canada has recently adopted a law which requires the registration of all firearms.

- In 1993, United States President Bill Clinton tried unsuccessfully to introduce a modest national health care system in his country, while at the same time in Canada, a survey done by *Maclean's* magazine found that 75% of Canadians thought that our health care system was one of the things that ties our country together. In other words, Canadians feel that our health care system is an important part of our culture. What other things do you think Canadians would say are aspects of our culture? Fig. 33-5 shows the extent to which Canadians felt certain items were important in linking Canadians.

What each Constitution says...

United States
"Life, liberty, and the pursuit of happiness."

Canada
"Peace, order, and good government"

What it focuses on...

United States
Rights of the individual

Canada
Role of the individual as a member of society

Significance of this on...

...gun control

United States
Lax gun control laws (Americans own 76 million handguns)
- Constitution specifically talks about the right to "bear arms"
- reflects the idea that the rights of the individual are more important than the collective right of the society to restrict how many guns there are

Canada
Strict gun control laws (Canadians own 1.2 million handguns)
- reflects the idea that fewer guns will make society safer even if that means that the individual right to own guns is limited
- in recent years with the support of most of the population, gun laws have become even stricter

...national public health care

United States
Health care is a private responsibility.
- most people get health insurance through their employer but more than 30 million people have no health coverage
- the feeling is that individuals are responsible for themselves and their families

Canada
All citizens are covered by government-paid health care which has existed for more than 30 years.
- most Canadians jealously defend their health care system
- the idea of collective responsibility is very important

△ **Fig. 33-4** *The Canadian and American Constitutions each contain a key phrase that helps to explain important differences in attitudes in the two countries.*

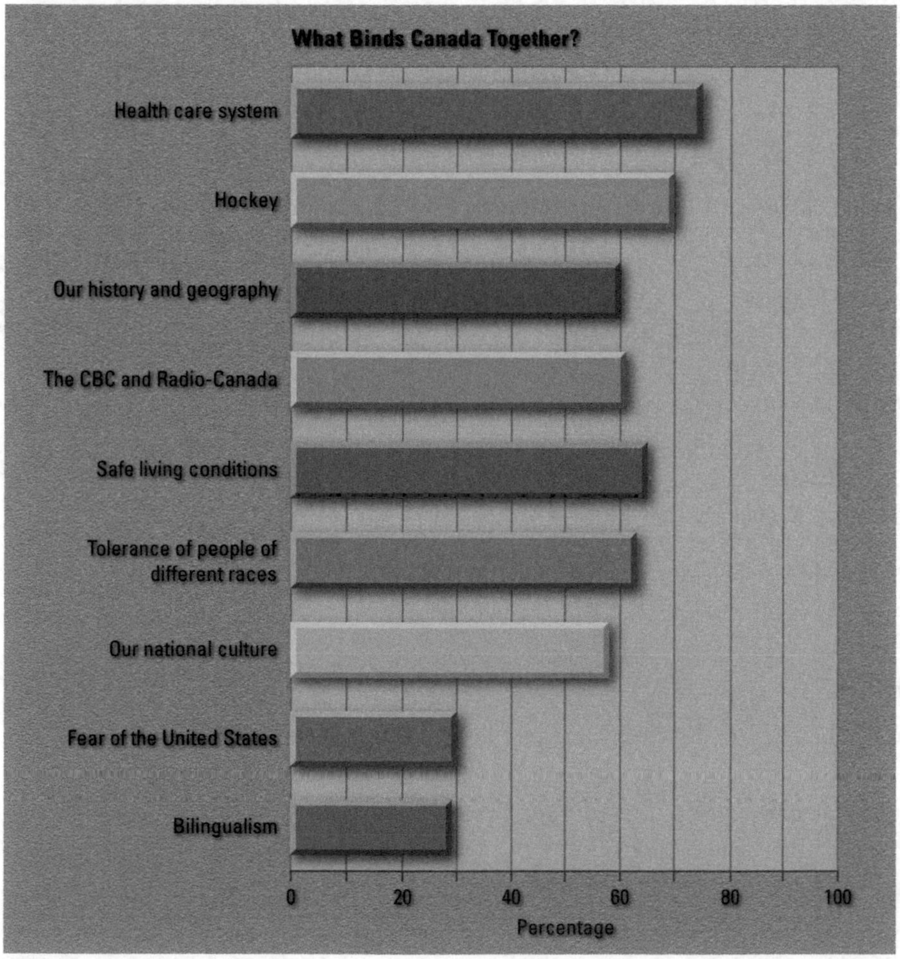

What Binds Canada Together?

(Bar chart showing percentage agreement for items:)
- Health care system
- Hockey
- Our history and geography
- The CBC and Radio-Canada
- Safe living conditions
- Tolerance of people of different races
- Our national culture
- Fear of the United States
- Bilingualism

(x-axis: Percentage, 0 to 100)

◁ **Fig. 33-5** *A Maclean's magazine survey tried to identify what makes Canada a nation. Each bar shows the percentage of people who agreed that the item shown was important in binding Canada together as a nation. Would a similar survey done in the United States find comparable results?*

CULTURE: THE NARROWER VIEW

If we use the narrower idea of culture — that it is limited to the arts, entertainment, and the media — does Canada have a distinctive culture? Many people would say so. They would point out that our culture is a unique mix of many influences. The culture of French Canada is neither the culture of France, nor the culture of English Canada (or the United States) translated into French (Fig. 33-6). The culture of English Canada is different from that of the United States and Great Britain. Canada's culture has been influenced by so many peoples: the First Nations, the French and British founding peoples, and the dozens of other cultural groups who are part of Canada's population. The result is a culture that is special and different from anything else in the world.

Not everyone would agree that Canada has a strong and distinctive culture. They would say that while Canada has outstanding writers, artists, and performers, the majority of Canadians don't know them or their work and are much more familiar with American culture. Your answers to the following quiz might reveal if this statement applies to you (Fig. 33-7).

TOP TEN LIST OF TV SHOWS IN FRENCH CANADA

1. *Omerta II*
2. *La petite vie*
3. *Ombre épervier*
4. *4 et demi*
5. *Le Retour*
6. *Paparazzi*
7. *Planète en folie*
8. *Les Machos*
9. *Fort Boyard*
10. *Bouscotte*

△ **Fig. 33-6** *This list shows the top ten regular television shows in French Canada in 1997. Notice that these are not English Canadian and American shows translated into French. Compare this list to the similar English language list in Fig. 33-8.*

HOW WELL DO YOU KNOW YOUR CANADIAN CULTURE?

1. Name the last novel you read
   a) in English class
   b) for enjoyment
2. Name the members of the Group of Seven.
3. List your five favourite television shows.
4. List your five favourite singers or music groups.
5. List the last five movies you have seen.
6. List up to three magazines you read regularly.

Now work out your score. Your teacher will help you. Give yourself one point for each of the following:
a) every Canadian novel in question 1
b) every correct answer in question 2
c) every Canadian answer in questions 3, 4, 5, and 6

Add up your points:
21 to 27 points: You are a Canadian culture vulture!
11 to 20 points: You take advantage of Canadian culture.
6 to 10 points: Living in Canada makes little difference to your cultural life.
0 to 5 points: You might as well live in St. Louis!

The government supports writers and artists with grants from the Canada Council. It funds the CBC, Canada's national radio and TV networks. It protects musicians and performers by requiring TV and radio stations to air Canadian-produced music and TV shows. The National Film Board sponsors Canadian film-makers.

◁ **Fig. 33-7** *Try this quiz and see how you do.*

QUESTIONS

CHECK YOUR UNDERSTANDING

1. In your own words, state the two definitions of the word "culture."

2. Considering both definitions of culture, what evidence is there of a distinctive Canadian culture?

3. What role(s) does the Canadian government play in supporting and protecting Canada's culture?

ANALYZE AND APPLY

4. a) What factors make North America a north-south oriented continent?

   b) What factors make Canada an east-west oriented country?

   c) How does the combination of these two factors contribute to the strength of the regional relationships shown in Fig. 33-2?

5. Conduct a survey similar to Fig. 33-5. Compare the results of your survey to those in Fig. 33-5. What similarities and differences do you see? It might also be interesting to compare the results of two surveys conducted by members of the class. For example, you might want to compare the responses of students with their parents, or students who were born in Canada with those who have only lived here a few years.

THINK AND COMMUNICATE

6. You have probably heard the story about the American tourist arriving at the Canadian border in July with skis on top of the car, eager to see the igloos and polar bears. Although an unfair exaggeration, this story does illustrate the fact that many Americans know very little about their northern neighbour.

a) Why do so many Americans know relatively little about Canada?

b) Does this surprise you? Why or why not?

7. a) When Canadians travel abroad, many people mistake them for Americans. Why might this happen?

   b) Why do you think some Canadians may not wish to be thought of as Americans?

8. Mexico also shares a long border with the United States. The American cultural influence on Mexico is important, but not as great as in Canada. Suggest at least two reasons for this difference.

9. a) In a group, develop a set of criteria, and examples of each, that can be used to establish a Canadian identity. Consider such things as:

   i. social programs

   ii. bilingualism

   iii. multiculturalism

   iv. contributions of Aboriginal and immigrant people

   v. culture (the narrow view)

   b) Each group presents their criteria and supporting arguments to the class. The class will then evaluate the validity of each group's presentation. After all the presentations have been made, produce a list that has been agreed upon by the class as representing the Canadian identity.

Is There Hope for Canada's Culture?

American culture has a great influence on Canadians. Living right next door to the richest nation in the world, Canadians find it difficult to preserve their cultural identity. Is there hope for a distinct Canadian culture in the face of the powerful influences of American TV, radio, movies, and music?

Television

Most Canadians watch a lot of American shows because they can pick up American television networks with cable or satellite dishes. However, they watch American shows on Canadian networks as well. Canadian networks carry many American programs because they can buy these programs for less than it costs to produce their own programs in Canada. As a result, few Canadian-made shows become favourites of Canadian viewers (Fig. 33-8)

Radio

Most Canadian radio stations sound the same as their American counterparts. This occurs because radio stations buy prepackaged formats from American companies. These formats include jingles, station nicknames, contests, and station advertising. The stations purchase the format and then personalize it with the station frequency, local advertisements, and, in Canada, some Canadian music. An exception to this growing uniformity is the CBC which provides a unique, commercial-free, Canadian-focused programming. For example, the CBC has a northern service which provides programming to First Nations in their own languages. This is possible only because the CBC is paid for by the federal government.

LIST OF TOP TEN TV SHOWS IN CANADA

1. *E.R.* *
2. *Royal Canadian Air Farce*
3. *CBC National News*
4. *Ally McBeal* *
5. *Seinfeld* *
6. *Friends* *
7. *X-Files* *
8. *Diagnosis Murder* *
9. *Spin City* *
10. *CTV News*

* American shows

△ **Fig. 33-8** *These were the ten most popular regular television shows in English Canada in 1997. Only one Canadian show (other than the news) is listed.*

TOP TEN LIST OF MOVIES.

1. *Rush Hour*
2. *Ronin*
3. *Urban Legend*
4. *There's Something About Mary*
5. *One True Thing*
6. *Saving Private Ryan*
7. *Rounders*
8. *Simon Birch*
9. *Armageddon*
10. *Ever After*

△ **Fig. 33-9** *These are the ten most popular movies in English Canada for the week ending Oct. 1, 1998. Notice that all of these movies are American.*

INTERNET

You can learn more about Friends of Canadian Broadcasting, an organization that works to defend and enhance Canadian programming, at friends.cb.org

Movies

Every year, the Genie awards are presented to Canada's outstanding movies. Most Canadians look at the list of winners and ask, "Why haven't I heard of most of these movies?" The reason that people have not heard of these Canadian movies has nothing to do with the quality of the movies. Rather, it is related to the way in which movies are distributed. Canadian movies rarely are shown in large theatres owned by companies like Famous Players and Cineplex-Odeon. These companies are huge American companies which are most interested in showing American movies with big-name stars and continent-wide advertising (Fig. 33-9).

While a great many movies and television shows are made in Canada, this occurs because the production costs are lower here, not for cultural reasons. In these productions, Vancouver stands in for Seattle or Toronto plays New York.

Popular Music

Perhaps in no other cultural field have Canadians been as successful as they have been in popular music. You can probably name several Canadian performers or groups who have a national and even an international appeal.

Two of the ten best-selling CDs in Canada in 1998 featured Canadian artists.

This situation has not occurred by accident. Obviously, a lot of very talented musicians and singers live in Canada, but so do many talented people in television, films, and radio. Musicians and singers have succeeded so well because of an effective set of government regulations that requires Canadian radio stations to play a certain percentage of Canadian music. As the demand for Canadian music increased, more Canadian artists were signed to recording contracts. Without Canadian content rules, the Canadian music industry would not be as healthy as it is today.

Music is considered Canadian based on the nationality of those involved in producing the song: the performer, composer, producer.

SHOULD WE PROTECT CANADIAN CULTURE?

Americans who are in the business of exporting American culture disagree with any attempts to protect and enhance Canadian culture. They believe that cultural industries such as television, movies, and music are just that — industries or businesses in which to make money. The Americans have been very successful in exporting their cultural products around the world, and want to continue this trend.

The idea that Canada's culture could come to dominate that of the United States was the theme of a comedy film called *The Canadian Connection*.

Most other countries, including Canada, feel that culture is much more than just a business. They feel that it is a critical part of their identity as a nation, and American cultural exports are a threat to this identity. As a result, they have decided to do what they can to protect their culture. For example, France tries to stop English words such as microcomputer and slamdunk — most of which come from the United States — from being adopted into the French language. In another case, Iran banned satellite dishes to try to keep American television and movies out of the country.

Many Canadians feel that English-Canadian culture is very much at risk because it resembles the culture of the United States in so many ways. Some Canadians feel that the two cultures are so much alike that we should stop worrying about it, and get on with our lives. People who take this view are called **continentalists**. Other Canadians feel that we will have a better future by remaining as independent of the United States as possible, and especially in the area of culture. These people are called **nationalists**.

Do you support the continentalist view that stresses the similarities between Canadians and Americans? Do you agree with the nationalists who see value in maintaining the differences? Perhaps your opinions are in between. The attitudes of young Canadians like yourself over the next half century will determine the nature of Canada's culture in the future.

QUESTIONS

CHECK YOUR UNDERSTANDING

1. List three reasons why the American culture has such a great influence on Canadians.

ANALYZE AND APPLY

2. Chapter 33 began with a quotation from a former Canadian prime minister about the United States. The following quotation about Canada is from the American president in the early 1960s.

   "Geography has made us neighbours. History has made us friends. Economics has made us partners. And necessity has made us allies. What unites us is far greater than what divides us."

   a) Explain each of these leader's quotations in your own words.

   b) Which expresses a continentalist view and which a nationalist view? How did you decide?

3. The Canadian English language differs from American and British English. Create a list of ten examples of Canadian English. Consider unique words, different meanings, spelling, and pronunciation of words. Also, try to determine if the examples are specific to a region of Canada. Consult the Dictionary of Canadian English, published by the Oxford University Press in 1998.

THINK AND COMMUNICATE

4. You are a consumer of culture. You watch television and movies, read books and magazines, and listen to music. Analyze your attitudes to Canadian culture by answering these questions.

   a) Do you support the quotas on radio programming that require playing a certain minimum percentage of Canadian music? Do you think these quotas should be higher? Explain.

   b) Should movie theatres be required to show Canadian movies for a certain number of weeks each year? Why or why not?

   c) The Canadian Council gives grants to artists, writers, and theatre, dance, and musical groups. Telefilm Canada provides funding for the production of films. Should the government support such cultural agencies?

   d) Should the CBC be allowed to air non-Canadian programs? Why or why not?

   e) In summary, would you consider yourself a cultural nationalist or continentalist? Explain.

UNIT 7

Future Connections

Solar powered! Is this the car of the future?

34 Water Resources

How much water do you and your family use each day? To find out, record the amount of water used in your home for one day. For some activities, you will have to estimate how much you use. Here are some figures to help you (Fig. 34-1). Don't forget to record the water that may be lost because of dripping faucets. Studies suggest that as much as 10% of the water piped into a home is lost this way. For each dripping faucet in your home, add 75 ℓ/day. After you have collected the data, form groups to compare your use of water to that of your classmates.

1. Construct a graph like the one in Fig. 34-2, and complete it using information provided by each student.

2. What is the relationship between the number of people in a household and the amount of water used?

3. a) Divide the total water consumption of each household by the number of people in that household. This will give the consumption per person within each household.

Clothes washer	230 ℓ/use
Bath	130 ℓ/use
Dishwasher	65 ℓ/use
Shower	25 ℓ/min
Toilet flush	20 ℓ/use
Water from a faucet	12 ℓ/min

△ **Fig. 34-1** *Average water use for various activities. Your appliances and water fixtures may have higher or lower rates of flow.*

b) Make a list of how your family consumes water.

c) Compare this list with those of other group members. What similarities and differences exist?

4. What things could you and your family do to reduce the amount of water you use?

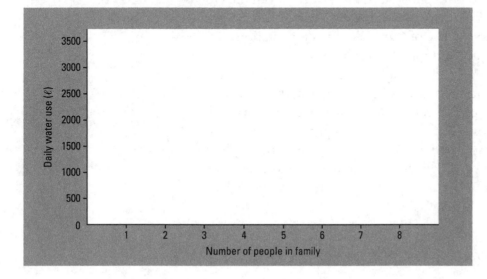

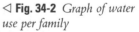
◁ **Fig. 34-2** *Graph of water use per family*

INTRODUCTION

Although you could survive without food for several weeks, you could not survive without water for more than a few days. Humans require about 2.5 *l*/day of drinking water to remain healthy. In fact, two-thirds of the human body is made of water.

In dry parts of the world, people view water as a resource more valuable than gold. In Canada, most people take water for granted. Studies show that the average Canadian uses about 330 *l*/day for personal use. How does this figure compare to the one that you calculated at the beginning of this chapter?

We could calculate the personal amount of water used daily by all Canadians by multiplying 330 by the population of Canada but this would not come close to giving us the total amount of water used in Canada every day. Activities such as agriculture, mining, manufacturing, cooling, electrical power generation, and municipal use require great amounts of water. If all these activities are taken into account, the use of water rises to about 4500 *l*/day! Canadians are the second-largest users of water in the world (Fig. 34-3).

If you lost only 12% of the water in your body, you would soon die.

To learn more about water resources in Canada, check www.doe.ca/water/index.htm

WATER, WATER, EVERYWHERE...

The earth is sometimes called the "blue planet." This is not surprising since nearly three-quarters of the earth's surface is covered with water. This water is in constant motion. It evaporates from land, rivers, lakes, and oceans, and becomes an invisible gas in the atmosphere called water vapour. Most water vapour condenses in the atmosphere to form clouds. Precipitation in the form of rain, snow, sleet, and hail falls from the clouds to earth. Rainwater (70% of Canada's precipitation) runs off very quickly into rivers and lakes. Snow (30% of Canada's total precipitation) on the other hand, stays on the ground for a longer period.

Water that runs off the land through rivers and lakes into oceans is called **run-off**. Some water soaks deep into the earth, through soil and layers of sand, gravel, and porous rock. This is called **groundwater**. Plants take up groundwater close to the surface through their roots, and then return some of it to the atmosphere through the process of transpiration. Water eventually makes its way back into the oceans and is evaporated once again. This constant circulation of the earth's water is called the **hydrologic cycle**.

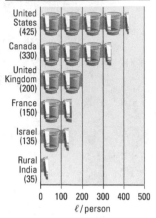

Average Daily Domestic Water Use

△ **Fig. 34-3** *Canadians are the second largest per capita users of water in the world.*

Canada has about 20% of the world's groundwater. Groundwater is the source of well water.

CANADA'S WATER RESOURCES

Lakes and Wetlands

Canada has a major share of the world's surface freshwater. Much of this water is found in lakes and **wetlands**.

Many of the basins containing Canada's lakes were gouged out by the action of ice sheets during past glacial periods. They are fed by rivers, groundwater springs, precipitation, and runoff from rain and melting snow. Lakes store water, but at the same time they are continually releasing it into rivers. This continual release maintains river flow.

Wetlands are areas of land that have become saturated with water. They are commonly called marshes, swamps, or bogs, and cover about 14 % of Canada's area. They contain plants such as bulrushes that are adapted to growing in water. Wetlands provide habitats for many species of insects, fish, reptiles, birds, and mammals.

Lakes, rivers, and wetlands cover over 20% of the country's area!

You can learn more about Canada's wetlands at www.wetlands.ca

saturated: completely wet

Rivers And Drainage Basins

Canada's water drains into the Pacific Ocean, Hudson Bay, the Arctic Ocean, the Atlantic Ocean, and, you may be surprised to learn, the Gulf of Mexico (Fig. 34-4). Five **drainage basins** carry this water to its destination. A drainage basin is the area drained by a river and its trib-

Small drainage basins combine to form regional drainage basins which in turn combine to form continental drainage basins. Fig. 34-4 shows many regional and five continental drainage basins.

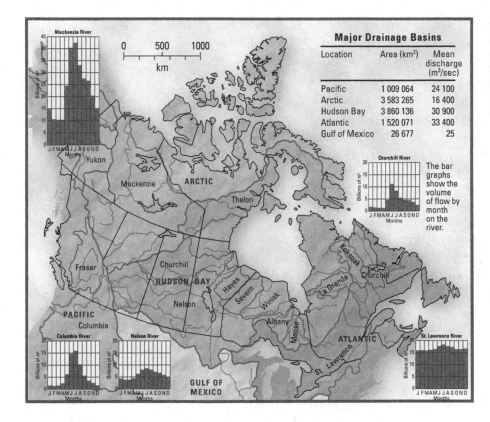

Major Drainage Basins		
Location	Area (km²)	Mean discharge (m³/sec)
Pacific	1 009 064	24 100
Arctic	3 583 265	16 400
Hudson Bay	3 860 136	30 900
Atlantic	1 520 071	33 400
Gulf of Mexico	26 677	25

The bar graphs show the volume of flow by month on the river.

◁ **Fig. 34-4** *The rivers in these five major drainage basins carry the surface fresh-water that is available for use in Canada. About half of Canada's precipitation becomes surface runoff.*

utaries. One drainage basin is separated from another by an area of higher land called a **watershed**.

The amount of water that flows through a drainage basin is known as the **discharge rate**. The discharge rate of a drainage basin may vary greatly from year to year depending upon the overall annual weather conditions. The discharge rate also varies according to the season. Analyze these variations by completing the following activity.

1. Examine the discharge rate (volume of flow graphs) for the Mackenzie, Columbia, Nelson, St. Lawrence, and Churchill rivers in Fig. 34-4.
   a) Which river has the largest single discharge over a period of three months?
   b) How would you explain this?
2. a) Name the month of highest discharge for each river.
   b) Why is the highest discharge month not the same for all rivers?
3. Which river has the most equal discharge over a year? How would you explain this?

Changes in discharge rates cause two major problems: flooding during wet seasons , and lack of water during dry seasons. To solve these problems, engineers will build a dam across a river. The water flowing out of a drainage basin is stored in a reservoir behind the dam, and its release can be properly regulated. Dams stop flooding, and help provide a dependable supply of water in all seasons. They are also used for generating hydroelectricity. Canada is one of the world's major dam-building countries. It diverts more water between drainage basins than any other country for the purpose of generating electrical power.

See Chapter 7 for a Radarsat image taken south of Winnipeg when the Red River flooded its banks in the Spring of 1997.

Fig. 25-10 demonstrates how electrical power is generated at a dam.

Groundwater

Water which sinks into the ground at some point can sink no further. It has reached the **saturated zone** where the crevices in the rock, and the spaces between the particles of soil, sand, and gravel are already filled with water. The top of the saturated zone is called the **water table**. Water which seeps to the level of the water table is known as **groundwater** (Fig. 34-5).

Groundwater has several advantages over surface water. First of all , it is more reliable; the supply of groundwater fluctuates less with the seasons than the supply of surface water. Also, groundwater doesn't need to be **treated** as much because impurities are filtered out as it moves through soil and rock deep underground. Some groundwater, however, may have an unpleasant taste caused by minerals such as calcium, magnesium, and iron that have been dissolved out of the rock.

Groundwater needs to be protected. We need to be careful that we do not remove more water than is replaced by nature. Using too much groundwater in large urban areas, draining swamps, and clearing land all

To learn more about groundwater, check groundwater.org/ learn/learn.htm

treated: is filtered and has chemicals added to purify it

These minerals also make the water hard and prevent soap and shampoo from forming lather properly. Hard water can be softened by removing the minerals, but this adds extra cost to your water bill.

◁ **Fig. 34-5** *Although Canada is often thought of as a country of sparkling lakes and rivers, for about a quarter of Canadians, water for drinking, washing, farming, and manufacturing comes from groundwater.*

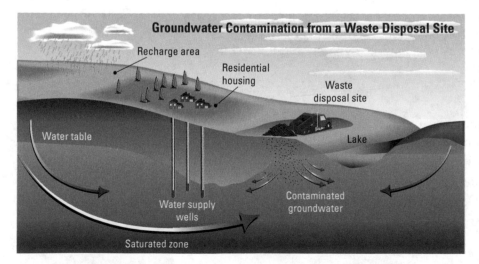

Groundwater Contamination from a Waste Disposal Site

Recharge area

Residential housing

Waste disposal site

Water table

Lake

Water supply wells

Contaminated groundwater

Saturated zone

contribute to lowering the water table. A lower water table can cause wells to go dry, and wetlands to disappear.

WATER USES

Canadians are among the greatest users of water in the world. Almost all of our personal, social, and economic activities depend upon water in some way. We can categorize our use of water in two ways. An **instream use** is when water is used without removing it from lakes or rivers. Instream uses include hydroelectric power generation, transportation, waste disposal, recreation, and fisheries. **Withdrawal use** actually removes the water from the water body. Withdrawal uses include thermal power generation, and manufacturing, municipal, agricultural, and mining activities. Withdrawal uses usually consume some of the water, that is, they return less water to the environment than they take out. Manufacturing and mining usually return less water to the water body, but irrigation and livestock watering return hardly any because what is not consumed evaporates and returns in a different form.

Less than 1% of the water from municipal water treatment plants is used for drinking purposes. Much of this treated water is used to water lawns!

Future Canadian Needs

Today, Canadians have more water available than they need. But the demand for water in the future is likely to grow as the population increases and as industries expand.

How much will the need for water increase in the future? It has been estimated that the current use of about 130 billion ℓ/day in Canada could jump to over 180 billion ℓ/day by the year 2011.

Estimates of water use in 2011 range from 180 billion ℓ/day to 290 billion ℓ/day depending on how much population and economic growth occurs and how wisely we use our water.

QUESTIONS

CHECK YOUR UNDERSTANDING

1. "The fact that we use water does not mean that we actually consume it." Explain this statement.

2. Explain, using your own words, how the hydrologic cycle works.

3. What are the advantages and disadvantages of using groundwater as a source of freshwater?

4. Compare instream uses with withdrawal uses.

5. List four reasons why the demand for water will probably increase in the future.

ANALYZE AND APPLY

6. a) Define the terms drainage basin and watershed.

   b) On a drainage map of Canada (provided by your teacher), draw the borders of the five major drainage basins in Canada (Fig. 34-4). Shade in each with a different colour.

c) Label each drainage basin with its name, area (km^3), and mean discharge (m^3/s).

d) Rank the drainage basins in terms of

   i. area

   ii. mean discharge

Explain the difference between your two rankings.

e) i. In what direction does most of Canada's water flow?

   ii. What percentage of the total flow goes in this direction?

f) Where is most of Canada's population located? Compare the pattern of population with the pattern of water flow. What does this suggest about our ability to meet growing water needs in the future?

7. a) Where does your water come from?

b) Where is it treated?

c) Where does it go after it is used?

THINK AND COMMUNICATE

8. What are the positive and the negative points of diverting water from areas with surplus water to those with a shortage of water?

WATER ISSUES

Pollution

There are three main types of water pollution: physical, biological, and chemical. Perhaps the least harmful, but most obvious, is physical pollution. Floating garbage, old tires, paper litter, pop cans, and bottles are not pleasant to look at, but are easily spotted, so clean–up and even prevention are relatively simple.

Biological contamination refers to bacteria and viruses that enter lakes and rivers from a variety of sources. The largest source of biological contamination is from the sewage of cities and towns. Most sewage is treated, but not all treatment is adequate. Some human sewage enters water bodies without any treatment at all. About 20% of Canadian cities put their raw sewage into lakes and rivers without treatment.

The most dangerous form of water pollution results from chemicals in our lakes and rivers. These wastes are often colourless, odourless, and tasteless in our water, but they can be deadly. What makes things worse is that the water bodies containing these chemicals are often the source of drinking water for millions of people.

Two sources of chemical pollution are pesticides and herbicides. These chemicals, which protect our food supply from animal pests, disease, and weeds, are washed from farmers' fields into rivers and lakes where they get into the food chain (Fig. 34-6). When people eat fish,

Many Canadian cities have old sewage systems. During heavy rainfalls, these systems are unable to handle the volume of water produced and raw sewage flows into rivers, lakes, and oceans. These systems are currently being updated but this is a long and costly process.

Some people say that there is no safe level for these chemicals in our water supplies because many of them build up in our bodies over time.

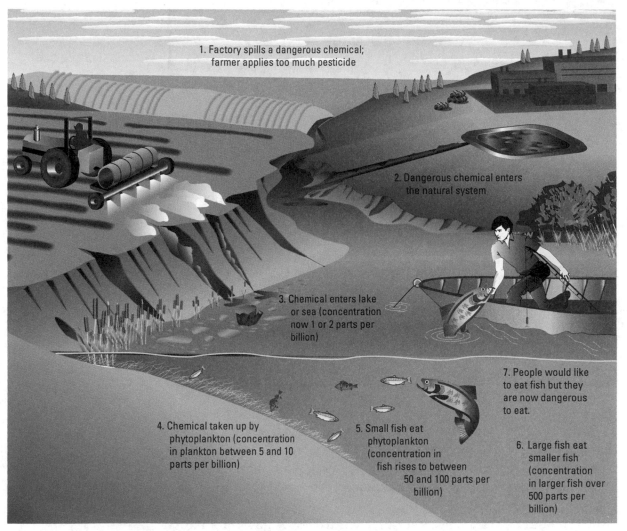

1. Factory spills a dangerous chemical; farmer applies too much pesticide

2. Dangerous chemical enters the natural system

3. Chemical enters lake or sea (concentration now 1 or 2 parts per billion)

4. Chemical taken up by phytoplankton (concentration in plankton between 5 and 10 parts per billion)

5. Small fish eat phytoplankton (concentration in fish rises to between 50 and 100 parts per billion)

6. Large fish eat smaller fish (concentration in larger fish over 500 parts per billion)

7. People would like to eat fish but they are now dangerous to eat.

△ **Fig. 34-6** *How toxic wastes move through the food chain*

they ingest the chemicals along with the food. Over a period of years, these chemicals build up in the body and can lead to diseases.

Other sources include human waste, chemical fertilizers, and animal manure, in which chemicals such as nitrogen, potash, and phosphorus are found. In the water supply, these chemicals act as fertilizers for algae and weeds, and cause them to grow rapidly. When these plants die, the decay uses large amounts of oxygen. As the oxygen level decreases, fish species die out.

Some industries have been dumping **toxic chemicals** into our water supplies for years. The Great Lakes have been referred to as a "chemical soup" because over 360 toxic chemicals have been detected in the water. 43 "toxic hot spots" in Canada and the United States have been identified in the Great Lakes where there are particular problems with the build up of poisonous chemicals (Fig. 34-7).

When it was discovered that phosphorus was causing nutrient pollution in lakes, it was removed from dishwashing and laundry detergents in both Canada and the United States. Within 10 years, Lake Erie improved and fish returned.

toxic: poisonous

Some of these chemicals are considered harmful in small quantities (measured in parts per trillion).

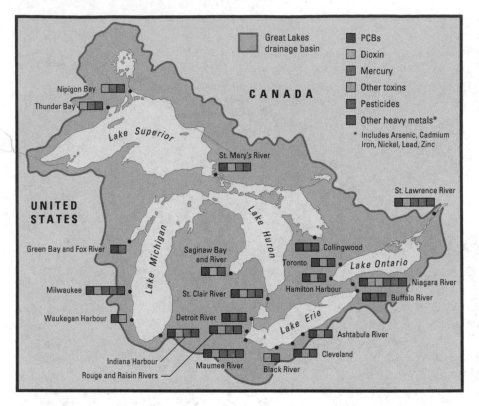

◁ **Fig. 34-7** *Sources of toxic substances in the Great Lakes basin. Over 34 million people in Canada and the United States rely directly on the Great Lakes as a source of drinking water!*

To learn more about the Great Lakes, check www.great-lakes.net/

There is, however, some good news. Government studies indicate that the levels of many **contaminants** in the Great Lakes have been declining. Restrictions on the manufacture and use of mercury, dioxin, many pesticides, and PCBs (**P**oly**C**hlorinated **B**iphenyls) have resulted in reduced contaminant levels in fish.

Groundwater can also become contaminated, for example, from leaks occuring in gasoline storage tanks, landfill sites, and leaks of industrial chemicals in manufacturing sites (Fig. 34-5). Livestock wastes, fertilizers, and pesticides from agricultural land can also contaminate groundwater. Groundwater can spread the effects of dumps and spills far from the site of the original contamination and it is very difficult, if not impossible, to clean. The leakage from Canadian and American dumps into the water bodies that supply drinking water to millions of people continues today.

We currently face two major problems in trying to rid our water supply of toxic chemicals. First, we do not know how to completely stop dangerous chemicals from getting into water bodies. Some chemicals seep into lakes and rivers from contaminated underground water sources, some may be illegally dumped, and others may be accidentally spilled from factories. Second, we do not have the technology in place to remove chemicals once they are in the water. Large-scale water purification plants

Dioxins are found, for example, in some herbicides and PCBs are found in electrical transformers.

1 ℓ of gasoline can contaminate 1 000 000 ℓ of groundwater.

treat only biological pollution. They do not eliminate hazardous chemicals that may be in local drinking water supplies.

Loss of Wetlands

Wetlands are an important source of groundwater, and act as storage areas for floodwaters. They provide food and shelter for wildlife, and wetland vegetation improves the quality of the water by filtering pollutants. They are also valuable as sites for scientific studies, and for trapping and waterfowl hunting.

Wetlands are being lost at an alarming rate in Canada. For example, over 70% of southern Ontario's original wetlands have been drained for agriculture and housing. As wetlands disappear, groundwater levels are lowered and animal habitats are permanently lost.

Water Diversions

Canada has taken steps to solve water shortages in some regions by diverting water from one drainage basin to another. These diversions are over short distances only, and the water is used primarily for large hydroelectric projects. They are far from populated areas, and few people are aware of their existence. There may be a need in the future to divert water to more populated areas for uses other than hydroelectricity.

Several large-scale schemes to divert water from the Great Lakes to other parts of Canada and the United States have been proposed in Canada. However, none has been built because of such factors as potential environmental damage, negative impact on Aboriginal peoples, loss of Canadian control over some of its resources, and the high cost. One plan called for the diversion of water from Alaska, the Yukon, and British Columbia to southwestern and central American states. A Canadian company proposed damming James Bay to turn it into a freshwater lake. The water would be pumped into the Great Lakes, then sent to the prairies and the American Midwest (Fig. 34-8).

The United States has few drainage basins with a surplus of water, and water shortages have become critical in parts of that country. As a result, the United States may put pressure on Canada to sell large amounts of its water. At the present time, the two countries cannot divert major amounts of water from the Great Lakes basin without the agreement of Ontario and all of the surrounding states. Environmentalists have warned that a combination of the effects of global warming and any additional losses of water from the Great Lakes could affect their ecological future.

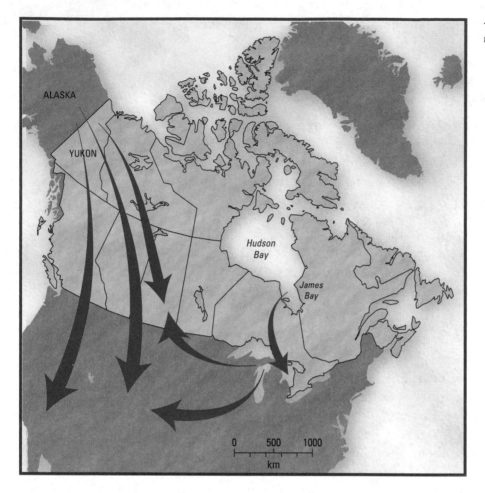

◁ **Fig. 34-8** *Proposed major water diversions*

Some permits to export Canadian water in bulk (tanker ships) have already been approved. A company in Newfoundland has plans to export 52 billion *l* of water per year. In 1998, a company in Sault Ste. Marie was given a permit by the Ontario government to take up to 600 million *l* of water per year by tanker from Lake Superior. Although the amount of water is relatively small and the exports haven't taken place, many Canadians fear that if one company begins to take bulk water from the Great Lakes, others will soon follow. American and Mexican companies could demand the right to send water to dry areas of North America. If water is treated like any other product under the North American Free Trade Agreement, Canada could eventually lose control of its water.

Later this permit was suspended.

There are several arguments that are used to support the export of Canada's fresh water. Canada already exports non-renewable resources such as oil, natural gas, and other minerals. Why then shouldn't water, which is a renewable resource, be exported? Many well-paying jobs could be created from the sale of this resource. The Water Protection Act of 1995 already allows the export of bottled water as long as the containers are 20 *l* or less in size. Since we already sell water, why shouldn't we increase the amount and earn more money from it?

The total annual bottled water production in Canada was 582 million litres in 1999. Of this amount, approximately 150 million litres of bottled water were exported.

SUSTAINABLE DEVELOPMENT

Canadians have not been very good at conserving water since it has seemed so plentiful and is relatively inexpensive compared to other countries. An international study found that Canadians pay less than half of what Europeans pay for municipal water. When tap water is compared to other beverages, we see what a bargain it really is (Fig. 34-9). If the cost were higher, perhaps we would be less wasteful of this limited resource.

Our economic and environmental health today and in the future will depend in part on how we manage our water resources. We need to evaluate our behaviour and lifestyles in order to sustain our high quality freshwater resources for future generations. If we do not take measures to protect our environment, the words from the poem *The Ancient Mariner* may predict our future:

"Water, Water, everywhere
Nor any drop to drink."

Beverage	Cost ($/1000 litres, 1992)
Tap Water	0.82
Cola	850.00
Milk	985.00
Bottled Water/Mineral Water	1500.00
Wine	9000.00

△ **Fig. 34-9** *Prices of popular beverages*

QUESTIONS

CHECK YOUR UNDERSTANDING

1. a) Describe three ways in which water may become contaminated.

    b) Which form is the most dangerous? Explain.

2. How is the quality of a lake or river damaged by the presence of large amounts of nutrients (fertilizer)?

3. How does farming contribute to water pollution?

4. The Great Lakes have been called a "chemical soup." Explain the meaning of this expression.

5. a) Describe how toxic wastes move through a food chain up to and including people.

b) Draw a diagram to demonstrate the process described in your answer to question 5a.

ANALYZE AND APPLY

6. Why is the storage and dumping of chemicals on land discussed in a chapter on water resources?

THINK AND COMMUNICATE

7. The public puts pressure on the government to stop pollution of the environment. The government in turn puts pressure on industry by developing laws to stop pollution. Industry sometimes responds by saying that it wants to stop pollution, but pollution controls are enormously expensive. Installation of pollution controls would drive many companies out of business and eliminate many jobs. How can this "vicious circle" be broken?

8. Working in groups assigned by your teacher, assume the role of a member of a town council that is dealing with the following emergency:

Workers at an industrial plant accidentally dumped toxic wastes into your community's water supply. It will take a month before the clean-up will make your drinking water safe again. During this time, tanker trucks will bring in water from other communities and each person will be allowed to fill one 20 ℓ container per day.

a) As a group, decide
   i. How you will organize the rationing system
   ii. What water uses you will allow and disallow
   iii. What recommendations you will give to citizens to help them deal with this emergency

b) One member from each group should present his or her plans to the class; the class should then decide which plan seems to be the most thorough and realistic.

9. The government has announced plans to permit a company to export bulk water shipments to dry parts of the United States.

a) List at least two arguments in favour of this decision and at least two arguments against it.

b) Write a paragraph explaining your position on the export of Canadian water.

c) In small groups, share your views and develop a report to present to the class.

10. Whenever a dump site or sewage treatment plant is proposed for a certain area, the local residents usually mount a campaign to stop the project. The attitude of most people is "Yes, we need disposal sites — but Not In My Back Yard!" This attitude even has a name, the "NIMBY Syndrome." What would be your reaction to the proposal of a dump site or sewage treatment plant in your community?

35 Global Warming: Living in the Greenhouse

STUDY GUIDE

By the end of this chapter, you will be able to:

- explain why world temperatures are increasing and how they may affect us
- describe the carbon cycle, and understand the role of carbon dioxide in global warming

- understand the potential impact of global warming on Canada and the rest of the world
- understand what countries and individuals are doing about global warming

Key Terms

global warming	carbon dioxide	carbon source	ecological footprint
greenhouse effect	methane	carbon fixation	
greenhouse gases	carbon sink	energy efficient	

1997 the Hottest Year on Record

The Associated Press - Washington

Last year, was the warmest on record for planet Earth, and for the first time U.S. federal climate researchers say people are at least partly to blame.

"I wouldn't have been willing to say this two years ago," said Elbert Friday, research chief of the National Oceanic and Atmosphere Administration.

"I believe we are seeing evidence of global warming at least some of which is attributable to human activities."

Tom Karl, a senior researcher with the administration, said, "1997 was the warmest year on record."

"The increasing trend of temperatures that we see, we believe, is at least partially attributed to human activities," such as pollution from cars and factories.

Karl said the Earth's average temperature last year was 0.4°C above normal. Normal is 16.5°C, the average for the years 1961-1990.

The 1997 reading tops the previous warmest year, 1990, by 0.08C°.

Global warming has been a topic of sharp debate in recent years.

A climate conference was held last month in Kyoto, Japan, where government officials from around the world discussed ways to reduce the potential impact of climate change.

Many scientists believe that carbon dioxide and other gases released into the atmosphere by industries are increasing the earth's temperature by trapping heat from the sun.

△ **Fig. 35-1** *Canadians have seen many newspaper stories like this one in recent years.*

There was no doubt about how it felt to Canadians — the 1990s were much warmer than normal (Fig. 35-1). What is in doubt, is what these higher temperatures might mean. Some scientists say that we should not read too much into this. The next few years could be colder than normal. Other scientists suggest that these warmer conditions reflect a long-term change in the earth's climate. What might this mean for Canadians and people in other countries?

Have temperatures been warmer or colder than normal since this book was written in early 1999?

1. Complete an organizer like Fig. 35-2 to explore how warmer temperatures might affect your life.

2. Did you find it easier to find positive effects or negative effects of warmer temperatures? Do you think that your list of positive and negative effects would apply to most Canadians? Would people in other countries be affected in similar ways?

◁ **Fig. 35-2**

Positive Effects of Warmer Temperatures	1.
	2.
	3.
	4.
Negative Effects of Warmer Temperatures	1.
	2.
	3.
	4.

In this chapter, we will look at **global warming**, the idea that world temperatures are increasing. We will consider what is happening, why it is happening, how this will affect us, and what we can or should do about it.

CLIMATE CHANGES...AND WHY THEY MATTER

The evidence shows that the earth's climate has changed throughout its history and that these changes have had an enormous influence on the course of events. Here are some examples:

*   Periods of glaciation have had an immense impact on how Canada's landscape looks. Scientists have calculated that glaciation occurred because the average temperature dropped by as little as 4 C°.

You can learn more about glaciation in the Connecting Study of Chapter 11.

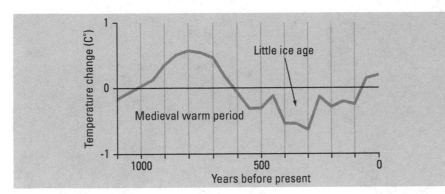

◁ **Fig. 35-3** *Normal temperature fluctuations have occurred throughout history.*

- More recently, historical climatologists have suggested that an important event in Canada's history was caused by global warming. Around the year 1000, the Vikings built at least one settlement in northern Newfoundland. Scientists think the Vikings were able to do this because temperatures became warmer than normal (Fig. 35-3). By the year 1400, all of these settlements had been abandoned as temperatures dropped.

These events were natural changes in the world's temperatures. While natural climate variations may still be occurring, human activities can also affect climate. This chapter focuses on how human activities may be causing rapid and damaging temperature increases. To understand what is happening, we must first look at the role that carbon dioxide and other gases play in controlling temperature.

You can probably figure out what a historical climatologist is from the name!

LIFE IN A GREENHOUSE

At some time in your life, you may have had the experience of sitting in a car on a sunny day in the winter with the engine turned off. In spite of the cold temperature outside, the car's interior was getting hot. You may even have had to open a window to cool down the car. What you experienced is called the **greenhouse effect** (Fig. 35-4). A similar situation exists in the earth's atmosphere, although obviously no window is involved (Fig. 35-5). A number of gases, found in the atmosphere, in only tiny amounts, absorb some of the heat before it can escape into space. This greenhouse effect is vital to the existence of life on Earth. If there were no **greenhouse gases**, the average temperature would drop by about 33 C° and the earth would be a cold lifeless planet more like Mars than the Earth we know. On the other hand, if the amount of greenhouse gas increases, less heat can escape into space and the temperature of the earth's atmosphere gets higher. The fear is that this is exactly what is happening today — global warming that is being caused by an increase in greenhouse gases as a result of human activities.

Nitrogen (78%) and oxygen (21%) make up 99% of the earth's atmosphere, but do not act as greenhouse gases.

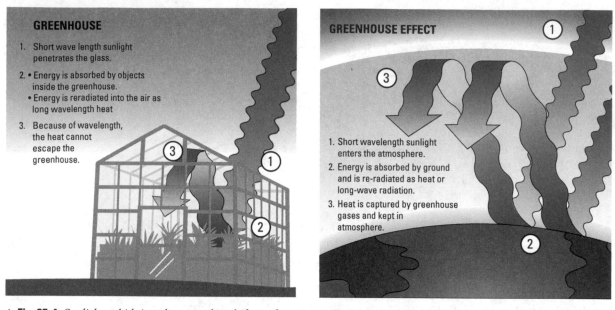

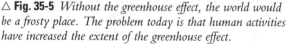

△ **Fig. 35-4** *Sunlight, which is a short wavelength form of radiation, can pass through greenhouse windows where it heats the interior. Heat, which is long wavelength radiation, is given off by the greenhouse interior but cannot pass through the glass. As a result, the greenhouse gets warmer.*

△ **Fig. 35-5** *Without the greenhouse effect, the world would be a frosty place. The problem today is that human activities have increased the extent of the greenhouse effect.*

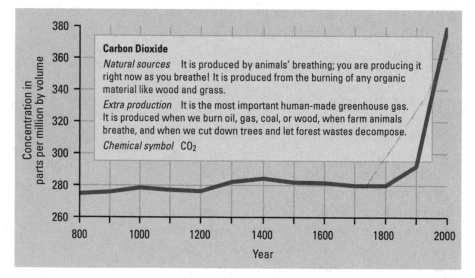

◁ **Fig. 35-6** *Carbon dioxide is the most important greenhouse gas. Look at the graph, when did the amount of carbon dioxide in the atmosphere start to increase? Why?*

decompose: break down or decay

The main greenhouse gases are **carbon dioxide**, **methane**, nitrous oxide, **halocarbons**, ozone, and water vapour. Except for halocarbons, these chemicals occur naturally, and are responsible for the positive greenhouse effect that allows life to exist. On the other hand, a negative greenhouse effect has occurred due to the enormous growth in the production of greenhouse gases. This growth has several causes including the use of fossil fuels which produce carbon dioxide. Since carbon dioxide is the most important greenhouse gas, this chapter will concentrate on its role in global warming (Fig. 35-6).

Carbon Cycle

Before you can understand the role that carbon dioxide plays in global warming, you must understand the **carbon cycle** — the movement of carbon through plants, animals, water, soil, air and rocks — and

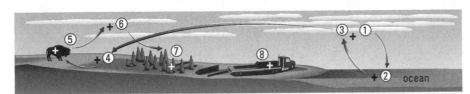

◁ **Fig. 35-7** *Follow a carbon atom, named Bob, as it travels through part of the carbon cycle.*

#1 Let's assume that a few hundred years ago, Bob was part of a carbon dioxide molecule in the air over the ocean. Here, he was part of the story of atmospheric carbon dioxide which causes the greenhouse effect.

#2 At some point, Bob's molecule was absorbed into the ocean where it was involved in the process of photosynthesis and became part of a tiny plant called a phytoplankton. The dissolving of carbon dioxide in ocean water, and its conversion into plant material, are both examples of **carbon sinks**. A carbon sink is part of the carbon cycle in which carbon is removed from the atmosphere for a period of time.

#3 A few days later, the phytoplankton died and Bob became part of a carbon dioxide molecule again, and moved back into the atmosphere. Any time carbon is added to the atmosphere, we have an example of **carbon source**.

#4 A few years later, Bob's molecule moved inland and became part of a blade of grass (a carbon sink) on the Canadian prairie.

#5 A few weeks later, the grass was eaten by a buffalo. Bob's molecule was broken down by digestion in the buffalo's stomach (ouch!)

#6 A few minutes later, Bob, who had become part of a methane molecule in the buffalo's stomach, was burped back into the atmosphere (a carbon source).

#7 Years later, Bob, who was a carbon dioxide molecule again, became part of a young pine tree in northern Ontario (a carbon sink).

#8 Eighty years later, the tree, which had become large, was cut down. The wood in it (including Bob) was made into a piece of paper which became part of this copy of *Making Connections: Canada's Geography*. In fact, Bob is now under an "e" on page 111 waiting his next move in the carbon cycle.

◁ **Fig. 35-8** *Follow another carbon atom, named Martha, as it travels through another part of the carbon cycle.*

#1 Perhaps 100 million years ago, Martha was part of a carbon dioxide molecule over the ocean.

#2 In the same way as Bob much later, Martha became part of a phytoplankton in the ocean, but then something very different happened. The phytoplankton was eaten by a tiny animal called a zooplankton.

#3 When the zooplankton died, its shell (including Martha) fell to the bottom of the shallow sea. Over millions of years, Martha became part of the crude oil deposit that was created. This was a very important step in the carbon cycle, since it meant that Martha's carbon was now removed from the store of atmospheric carbon for the foreseeable future. Any process like this, which ties up carbon for a very long time, is called **carbon fixation**. Another example of carbon fixation would be when limestone is produced, also on the bottom of the ocean.

#4 Shortly after the Hibernia offshore drilling platform started production off Newfoundland in 1997, Martha's oil molecule was recovered from under the sea.

#5 At an oil refinery onshore, the crude oil is refined and Martha becomes part of a gasoline molecule.

#6 The gasoline is burned in a car, and Martha becomes part of a carbon dioxide molecule for the first time in 100 million years. Note that this process is really quite different from merely releasing carbon from an ordinary, short-term source.

how people have altered its natural operation. To do this, let's follow the travels of an atom of carbon, let's call it "Bob" (Fig. 35–7).

Bob's experience as a carbon atom illustrates how the carbon cycle worked for thousands of years. Carbon was transferred from the atmosphere to **carbon sinks** and from carbon sources back to the atmosphere, but the amount in the atmosphere stayed more or less the same. The result was that the greenhouse effect occurred at a relatively stable rate. Things have changed though, as a result of human activities. The experiences of another carbon atom named "Martha" will illustrate what has happened (Fig. 35-8).

Martha's experience as a carbon atom illustrates how carbon, which was fixed and out of circulation for perhaps hundreds of millions of years, has been added to the world's active supply. This is precisely what has happened continually in the past century for two related reasons. The first reason is that the world's population has increased from 1.6 billion in the year 1888, to over 6 billion today. More people mean more and more carbon is being released into the atmosphere. The other reason is that there is an increasing number of the world's people, including most Canadians, with a lifestyle which requires burning more fossil fuels, destroying more forests, and eating more animal products.

Billions of people in newly industrializing and developing countries also want to have such a lifestyle!

THE IMPACT OF GLOBAL WARMING

Scientists predict that average temperatures in the next 100 years will increase by 1 to 3.5 C°. The greatest increases will occur in polar areas, especially in the winter months. Some areas of northern Canada can anticipate winter temperature increases of as much as 10 C°. This warming would have a number of effects on the world and on Canada.

These temperature changes may not seem very large, until you remember that glaciation was caused by a cooling of only 4C°!

Potential Effects on the World

- One of the most serious impacts of global warming would be an increase in sea level of perhaps 1 m, caused by melting glaciers and polar ice sheets. This would have an enormous impact on places like the Marshall Islands in the Pacific Ocean, where 80% of the country would be flooded. Far more

Fig. 35-9 ▷

One of the most serious impacts of global warming is an increase in sea levels, because of the melting of much (or even all) of the earth's glaciers and ice caps. Parts of the world that are close to sea level, like Bangladesh, could suffer devastating floods.

people would be affected in Bangladesh, which has a population of more than 120 million people (Fig. 35-9). Canada would not be affected very much by higher sea levels, since we do not have many low-lying areas.

- Total world precipitation would increase, but not all areas would be affected evenly. The problem is that areas that now receive abundant rainfall would get even more, while dry areas could get even less rainfall than today. Droughts would become more common in many areas of Canada. Most at risk would be the southern parts of Alberta and Saskatchewan, which are already the driest areas of southern Canada. Droughts would also occur more frequently in the agricultural areas of southern Ontario and in the interior valleys of southern British Columbia. In all these areas, farmers would have to rely more on costly irrigation systems.

    Other areas of Canada would receive more rainfall than they do now — in many cases, more rain than they really need to be fertile. The east and west coastal areas would be subject to flooding during times of heavy rainfall.

- The world's forests would be damaged because of rainfall changes that higher temperatures would cause. The amount of tree growth in the world would be reduced. Less forested land would only make the problem of global warming worse, as an important carbon sink would be reduced. Canada is one of the world's great forest nations, and global warming would have a massive impact on our forests. Fig. 35-10 shows the current distribution of natural vegetation regions in Canada, along with the distribution after global warming. After global warming, there would be more forested areas than there are today but the distribution would be completely different. Enormous adjustments would be needed in our forest industries and in the towns that depend on them. For example, Flin Flon, Manitoba, is a paper-making centre that would

△ **Fig. 35-10** *Canada's vegetation regions and ecozones could be dramatically changed because of global warming.*

find itself in the middle of the expanded grassland. Many towns like this one would have to find a new economic base.

- As you would expect, glaciers would get smaller and, in some areas, disappear completely. Canadian glaciers are already getting smaller. The front of the Athabaska Glacier in Alberta has receded by 1.5 km since 1890, which is about the time that carbon dioxide and methane levels started to increase.

- Agricultural regions would be affected. Some areas would become more productive since they would get more rainfall and have a longer, warmer growing season. Others would have their agricultural potential significantly reduced because of lower rainfall. Many of the worst such problems would occur in countries with areas that are already fairly dry, and have some of the poorest people in the world. Many current farming areas might disappear, but farming would become possible in many areas of Canada that are now too cold. A century from now, Grade 9 geography students might learn about wheat farming near Yellowknife, the great livestock raising areas of northern Ontario and Québec, or increased farming on the island of Newfoundland.

  None of these areas have significant amounts of farming today.

- The world would have to deal with millions of "weather refugees." These would be people who would have to abandon their home regions because weather conditions would no longer allow them to live there. Canada would be under a great deal of pressure to accept millions of these people from around the world. We might be able to do this because so much more of our country would be able to support a larger population than is the case today. Even then, there would be a huge impact on our population as we struggled to accommodate so many new residents.

  Remember that Bangladesh, which is only one country that would be devastated by global warming, has a population that is four times that of Canada.

QUESTIONS

CHECK YOUR UNDERSTANDING

1. Make two fully-labeled sketches to illustrate how the greenhouse effect works in:
   a) a car (or a greenhouse!)
   b) the earth's atmosphere

2. Compare the effects of global warming in Canada to those in the rest of the world in terms of the following: sea level, precipitation, forests, glaciers, agriculture, human health, and refugees.

ANALYZE AND APPLY

3. a) Define the following terms in your own words and give two examples of each: carbon sink, carbon source, and carbon fixation.

   b) Draw a fully-labeled diagram to illustrate the carbon cycle.

4. Fig. 14–3 shows Canada's ecozones. If global warming were to occur, how would the following ecozones change: Prairies, Mixedwood Plain, Boreal Plain, Taiga Shield, and Boreal Shield.

THINK AND COMMUNICATE

5. Describe the impact that global warming might have on each of the following:

   a) the size of Canada's areas of permafrost (Check an atlas to see the current extent of permafrost.)

   b) the operations of the St. Lawrence Seaway

   c) the popularity of various outdoor recreational activities

   d) the need for air conditioning and heating in our homes and schools

   e) Canada's fishing industry

THE DILEMMA OF GLOBAL WARMING

What can we do about global warming? There are a number of conflicting issues to consider. Global warming could be the greatest problem facing humanity in the 21st century. Unfortunately, we don't know for sure that it is even happening! There is clear evidence that the weather was abnormally warm through much of the 1990s, but we do not know if this is a trend that will continue, or merely a short-term variation. Even if the earth is warming, we do not know for certain that this is being caused by human activities.

If global warming is a long-term trend, it will have drastic consequences for people all over the world. Yet, the solutions to global warming would require us to take actions that would drastically change the way in which we live. Also, the longer we delay doing something about this problem, (if there is a problem!) the more serious it will be and the more dramatic the solutions that will be needed. All of this makes it very difficult for everyone involved to know exactly what actions must be taken.

WHAT CAN WE DO ABOUT GLOBAL WARMING?

We must reduce the amount of carbon dioxide we release into the air, while finding ways to remove some of the carbon dioxide that is already there. When we talk in general terms, the solutions to global warming seem clear. In more technical terms, this means that we must minimize the use of carbon sources, promote the expansion of carbon sinks, and above all, introduce as little fixed carbon into the active carbon cycle as possible. The problem comes in trying to do these things without completely disrupting the way we live.

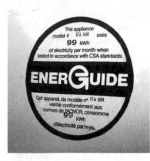

△ **Fig. 35-11** *Labels like these on major appliances tell how much energy the appliance uses. Similar labelling occurs on new cars. Knowing how much energy something uses helps consumers save money — and reduce global warming.*

Minimizing Carbon Sources

Perhaps the most important way to cut back on how much carbon goes into the atmosphere is by expanding the use of alternative energy technologies that are not carbon-based. For example, we can generate electricity using wind power, hydro-electric power, solar power, or geothermal power (see the Connecting Study following this chapter). As well, we can make sure that we use **energy-efficient** devices. For example, some motor vehicles use one-third as much energy — and release one-third as much carbon as do others (Fig. 35-11).

We could also use nuclear power, but there is growing concern that the environmental cost of nuclear power may be higher than that of carbon-based energy.

Expanding Carbon Sinks

The most obvious part of the carbon sink that we can expand is the number of trees on earth. People have cut down enormous forest tracts all over the world for centuries. In this century, the process has accelerated, as the world's population and level of development have exploded, particularly in tropical areas. Forests are cut for several reasons. In Canada, much wood is used for lumber or paper making. In some places, forests may be cut so the land can be used for farming or because people use the wood as a fuel for cooking or heating. In the future we will have to do two things better than we have in the past. The first is to make sure that

Think of the huge forest clearances made in North America in the last two centuries by pioneers who settled southern Ontario and Québec.

◁ **Fig. 35-12** *Every time a tree is planted, the world's carbon sinks are increased.*

when we, as a society, cut a tree, this action cannot be avoided and that we use the wood from that tree as wisely as possible. The second is that we must be sure to plant trees in as many places as possible — in the areas that have just been cut down (Fig. 35-12) and in areas that might have been cut two hundred years ago and left bare.

The most important carbon sinks of all are the oceans and the plant life that exists in them. We tend to take the oceans for granted — out of sight, out of mind — but what happens in them is critical in preventing global warming. There are two things that people can do. We must prevent pollution that could damage phytoplankton. Ironically, to protect the carbon sink of the ocean, we must prevent global warming on land. Warm ocean waters can absorb less carbon dioxide than colder water, so as global warming occurs, the oceans will not be efficient carbon sinks. This means that oceans will give off some of their carbon dioxide which, in turn, will only make the greenhouse effect worse.

Preventing the Release of Fixed Carbon

The biggest problem of all is the enormous use of fossil fuels. The carbon in these fuels, which has been fixed for millions of years under the surface of the earth, enters the atmosphere with the burning of every gram of coal, oil, or natural gas. We may not be able to eliminate the use of fossil fuels, but we can try to minimize it.

New fuels, alternate energy sources, and energy-efficient vehicles and appliances are a good start in reducing global warming. More importantly, people must develop new knowledge and attitudes toward energy use. In the following sections, you will see how this is being done at the international level and what it all means to you.

INTERNATIONAL EFFORTS TO LIMIT GLOBAL WARMING

The first international conferences on global warming were held by scientists in the late 1980s. The purpose of these meetings was to share information about the newly discovered problem, rather than to solve it. Solutions could only come as a result of agreement among the nations of the world to limit production of greenhouse gases and to promote the increase of carbon sinks. A treaty was negotiated to do this. It was signed by more than 140 countries at a conference in Rio de Janeiro, Brazil, in 1992. The purpose of the treaty was to stabilize greenhouse gases in the atmosphere to a level that would prevent dangerous human interference with the earth's climate.

This treaty was called the United Nations Framework Convention on Climate Change (UNFCCC). It is called a "Framework" treaty because it provides a structure within which more specific agreements can be reached.

The treaty recognized that all nations have a responsibility for helping to solve the problem of global warming. It put the emphasis, though, on the role of the developed countries since, on a per person basis, they historically have produced far more than their share of greenhouse gases. For example, India produces about twice as much of these gases as does Canada, but has a population that is more than 20 times as large. This means that the average Canadian produces about 10 times as much carbon dioxide as does the average Indian.

As a result of the treaty negotiations, developed countries like Canada agreed to reduce their greenhouse gas emissions to 1990 levels. By the year 1999, it had become obvious that this would not be achieved.

WHAT YOU CAN DO TO LIMIT GLOBAL WARMING

The fight to reduce global warming is not just something that happens at the level of UN conferences. It involves the individual choices of each of us. Consider two teenagers on a holiday at a northern lake. For one, a perfect day is spending a few hours windsurfing. For the other, nothing beats the fun of riding a personal watercraft. They are both enjoying water recreation but there is a considerable difference in the impact that each has on global warming. One hour of personal watercraft use releases many kilograms of carbon dioxide (from a fixed source) into the atmosphere. One hour of windsurfing releases none at all.

This example illustrates that we do have some choice in the role we play (and should play) in preventing global warming and other environmental problems. Each of us creates an **ecological footprint (EF)** on the earth. This is a somewhat poetic way of saying that everything we do has an environmental impact. Most of us do not think about this impact as much as we should — but if we are aware of the size of *our* ecological footprint, it can act as a guide for the lifestyle decisions we must make. The first step is to get the knowledge that we need to make intelligent decisions. Once we have the facts, we are in the position to make the decisions that will allow us to minimize our ecological footprint. The choices that each person faces are unique, but they all have an impact on the earth — or in this case, on causing global warming.

IN CLOSING...

We are at a crossroads with respect to global warming. It is probably fair to divide Canadians into three groups with respect to this problem. In the first group are those who think that the potential impact of global

You can learn more about the concept of the ecological footprint in Chapter 36.

To learn more about global warming, check the following Web sites:

- Canadian government: www.ec.gc.ca/climate
- An environmental organization: www.sierraclub.org/global-warming/
- A business organization: www.globalclimate.org
- The United Nations: www.unfccc.de/index.html

warming has been very much exaggerated. They would suggest that we should do nothing until there is clear proof of the problem. Those in the second group are at the other extreme. They feel that the threat of global warming is clear and that we must take drastic action now before it is too late. The third group, which includes many Canadians (and the federal government), are "in between". They are willing to accept that there is a problem but are not yet willing to take the serious steps that are needed as a solution.

QUESTIONS

CHECK YOUR UNDERSTANDING

1. a) Describe the different situations of developed countries and less-developed countries with respect to global warming.

   b) What does this mean for you as a typical Canadian?

ANALYZE AND APPLY

2. a) Explain why efforts to reduce global warming would not affect all parts of Canada equally.

   b) Name two provinces that would have a higher price to pay.

3. a) What is meant by a person's ecological footprint?

   b) In each of the following areas, give an example of an activity with a large ecological footprint and one with a small ecological footprint:

      i.   recreation

      ii. transportation to school or work

      iii. housing

THINK AND COMMUNICATE

4. Your teacher will give you instructions for a global warming exercise that you can do using ArcVoyager.

5. a) A carbon tax is a special tax tied to any product which causes a release of carbon into the atmosphere. Give five examples of how it could be applied.

   b) Do you think that a carbon tax is a fair and effective way to fight global warming?

6. a) Compared to most countries, Canada may find a number of benefits from global warming. Describe three of these.

   b) It is entirely possible that Canada may gain from global warming while most countries suffer often quite dramatically. If this turns out to be the case, does Canada (and do Canadians) have a responsibility to change the way in which they live to minimize the effects of global warming? Why or why not?

7. In this chapter, the point was made that views of Canadians can be divided into three groups with respect to global warming. To which group do you belong? Give reasons for your choice.

8. It has been said that global warming is a 100-year problem facing 4-year governments. What was meant by this and why is it a particular problem in trying to prevent global warming?

9. a) Read the newspaper column in Fig. 35-13. What arguments does the author make against doing something about global warming now?

   b) With what arguments do you agree? With what arguments do you disagree? Why?

10. Develop a proposal for a solution to the environmental problem of global warming.

GIS

McLellan to Alberta's Rescue Against Green Lobby

Lorne Gunter

Thank goodness for federal Energy Minister Anne McLellan.

Monday, at a meeting of federal and provincial energy and environment ministers, the Edmonton Liberal MP withstood tremendous pressure from cabinet colleagues, Ottawa's hysterical environment bureaucrats, and Canada's green lobby and forestalled legislated emission controls on so-called greenhouse gases.

By doing so, McLellan saved Alberta's oil and gas producers hundreds of millions of dollars in costly refits to their rigs and refineries. She also saved the provincial government billions of dollars in revenue, and spared ordinary Albertans a sharp decline in economic activity and thousands of lost jobs.

The lethal combination of new regulations, higher production costs, and increased taxes, proposed by British Columbia Environment Minister Moe Sihota, would have devastated Alberta's resource sector more than any policy since the National Energy Program of 1980. By increasing the prices of natural resources it would have burst the province's current mini-boom and unbalanced the budget...

• •

... The problem with implementing the new laws and spending billions to stop global warming is that there is precious little proof that the phenomenon is man-made.

Indeed in the past years, three surveys of the world's climatologists have each discovered that while the majority accept that the earth's atmosphere is getting warmer, most doubt that this is the result of the trapping of heat in the lower atmosphere by byproducts of automobile and industrial combustion.

In fact, more than half of the rise in atmospheric temperature over the past 200 years occurred before the mass use of automobiles and the rapid post-war industrialization of the First and Second Worlds.

The most recent of these surveys, released last spring by the independent George C. Marshall Institute in Washington, DC, says the overwhelming majority of climate scientists now agree that global warming is occurring at only one-third the rate claimed by supporters of the greenhouse theory, or about one-tenth of one Celsius degree every decade. Moreover, the Marshall study explains that in the past there have been several periods when atmospheric levels of greenhouse gases have been four to ten times higher than they are now "without any temperature rise."

The study also takes exception to many widely reported environmental horror stories. "Satellite measurements of temperature, supported by ground-based measurements in the Arctic, tell us that this region has cooled substantially over the last 16 years, not warmed."

It would be foolhardy to stop studying the effects of human activity on the world. But it would be doubly foolish to spend billions we don't have and give governments new powers they don't need to find solutions to a problem that fewer and fewer experts believe is occurring.

It might even be dangerous to try to stop global warming. If it is a natural process, stopping it could be as destructive as greenhouse thinkers believe industrialization is.

△ **Fig. 35-13** *Not everyone agrees that global warming is a critical problem.*

Energy Futures

KEY TERMS

energy
   conservation

non-renewable
   resources

renewable
   resources

fuel efficiency

photo-voltaic cells

fuel cell

hydrogen

△ **Fig. 35-14** *Windmills were built on the Gaspé peninsula to harvest the power of the area's strong winds.*

For a number of reasons, Canada faces an uncertain energy future. These uncertainties fall into several categories:

- There are serious concerns about how much energy we use. Canadians use a great deal more energy than the residents of most countries. As well, there are large differences in the amount of energy used by different Canadians.

- Energy use is closely linked to many of our serious environmental problems. Most obvious of these is the global warming caused by the huge amounts of carbon dioxide that are produced by the burning of fossil fuels. The production of energy also causes environmental problems, ranging from the flooding of river valleys by the building of hydro-electric dams to the air pollution that is caused by the development of oil and natural gas deposits.

- We are also reaching the point where we will start to run out of some of our traditional energy sources, in particular, oil and natural gas. We must begin the process of finding replacements for energy sources that have played an absolutely crucial role in our society for more than 100 years.

Our energy use in the future is likely to change in three ways:

1. By concentrating on improved **energy conservation:** we must use our energy more carefully than we have in the past.

See Chapter 25 for more information about Canada's current energy use.

You can learn more about renewable and alternative energy at www.nrel.gov/ceb.html and solstice.crest.org/renewables/index.shtml

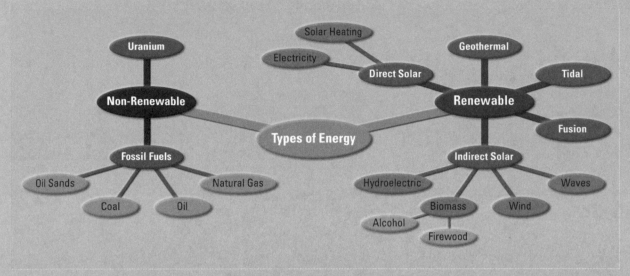

△ **Fig. 35-15** *Canada's current and future energy sources*

2. By using different energy sources: in Chapter 25, you learned that most of Canada's current energy use comes in just a few forms: oil, natural gas, and electricity. In the years to come, our energy supply budget is likely to be far more complex. To help you understand this concept, you should review the ideas of **non-renewable** and **renewable** energy resources (Fig. 35-15).

3. By developing new energy technologies: we are likely to use and store energy in a variety of new and revolutionary ways.

In this chapter, you will have the chance to study one of the many important energy issues described in the section that follows. Choose an issue that you find particularly interesting. You will present your findings in one of the following formats: a research paper, a wall poster, a magazine or newspaper, a video report, an oral presentation, or a debate. Your teacher will tell you which.

Your research should answer the following questions:

1. How does the technology work?
2. How much potential does the technology have to become a major energy source for Canadians?
3. What problems must be overcome to develop the technology?
4. How costly is the development of the technology likely to be?
5. When is the energy source likely to be available for widespread use?
6. Suggest a global solution to the energy issue.

ENERGY RESEARCH ISSUES

Plugging Into the Wind (Fig. 35-14) How can we use the wind to meet our energy needs? What happens when the wind does not blow? Which parts of Canada have the best wind resources? What environmental issues are related to wind power?

Energy Conservation in Cars Modern family cars use much less than half as much fuel as did similar cars in the early 1970s. How has this been achieved and what further **fuel efficiency** improvements can be made?

Energy Conservation and Industry Canadian factories, mills, and other businesses use enormous amounts of costly energy. How can they reduce this usage? How can industry be encouraged (or required) to save energy even if this costs them money? Many industrial processes create huge amounts of waste heat. How can this heat be used for other purposes?

The use of potentially wasted energy for another purpose is called cogeneration.

Canada's use of Oil and Natural Gas How will the use of our most important energy sources change in the future? Will possible changes be most closely linked to rising costs or to concerns about the environment?

New Sources of Oil Oil is now produced from under the waters of Canada's east coast and has been found in the Arctic. How important will these sources be in our future? How would the development of these energy reserves affect the economies of the regions in which they occur?

The Hibernia oil project is described in the Connecting Study of Chapter 25.

Oil Sands and How We Can Put Them Into the Gas Tank What are oil sands (Fig. 35-16) and how do they (and will they) contribute to our energy supply?

Coal in the Future In spite of the fact that Canada has large reserves of coal of varying qualities, we make relatively little use of coal in Canada. In fact, most Canadian coal is exported. Is this likely to change in the future? How might this change?

The Role of Uranium in Our Energy Future Canada has an enormous supply of uranium. In fact, several Canadian mines have shut down, not because they ran out of ore, but because demand and prices were low. Will this uranium ever be used to produce electricity? What problems are associated with the production of nuclear-electricity?

Solar Heating in Our Homes How can we use the sun to cut, or even eliminate, our home heating and hot water bills? What is the difference between passive and active solar heating? How would life in a solar house be different from that in a conventional house?

Electricity from the Sun Sunlight can be converted directly to electricity using **photo-voltaic cells**.

▽ **Fig. 35-16** *Huge areas of oil sands can be found in northern Alberta.*

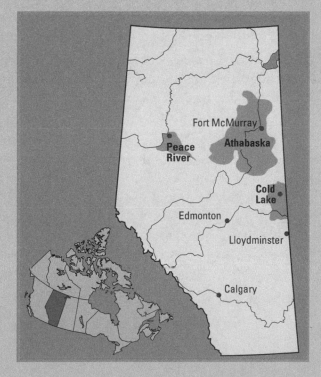

For what purposes is this being done today? What technical breakthroughs are needed before solar-electric production becomes more common? If we do come to use solar-electricity more widely, what should we do at night or on cloudy days?

Generating More Hydro-Electricity Where could new large-scale hydro projects be built? What are the problems associated with this and how do they compare to the risks tied to other energy sources? What role could small hydro-projects play in our energy future? Could we learn how to move electricity longer distances from more remote parts of Canada?

Energy Conservation in the Home How can we build new homes that use as little energy as possible? What modifications can we make to existing homes to save energy and money? Does energy conservation in the home mean a lower quality of life?

Biomass — Energy From Organic Waste In what forms does it exist and how can we use it? Are there problems associated with biomass?

Tidal Energy Canada has some of the world's highest tides. How can the energy in these tides be used by people?

Other Possible Energy Sources There are a number of other possible energy sources that might be used in the future. You might want to investigate one of these. How could energy from waves be used? What is ocean thermal conversion? What is geothermal energy and how could it be used in Canada?

Nuclear Fusion and Why It Has Been Called the Ultimate Energy Source How might nuclear fusion meet all of our energy needs in the future? Why would a fusion power plant be so difficult to build?

Hydrogen: A Common Fuel for the Future **Hydrogen** may become the most important fuel in the 21st century. Why might this happen? How could hydrogen be used as a way to store energy? Why will this be of great importance in the future?

Fuel Cell and Why We Should Care About It A Canadian company, named Ballard Fuel Systems, is one of the world leaders in developing the **fuel cell.** For what can fuel cells be used and what are their advantages? What economic benefits might Canada gain from this technology?

How All of These Sources Will Fit Together How old will you be in the year 2050? In view of what is happening to Canada's energy situation, how might your life in 2050 be very different than it is today?

Good luck with your research and presentation of your findings!

Ask an energy expert about energy efficiency and renewable energy at www.eren.doe.gov/menus/energyex.html

To learn more about biomass and bioenergy, check www.fri.cri.nz/ieabioenergy/home.htm

Nuclear fusion is quite different from the nuclear fission used in existing power plants. Nuclear fusion is the process that occurs in a hydrogen bomb and has only been produced in a controlled manner in a laboratory for a tiny fraction of a second.

For more information about the fuel cell, check www.tv.cbc.ca/national/pgminfo/warming/fuel.html

36 Reducing the Size of Your Ecological Footprint

STUDY GUIDE

By the end of this chapter, you will be able to:

- identify the measure of an ecological footprint and how it is calculated
- describe the calculation of the ecological footprint of the average Canadian
- explain the significance of ecological footprints in terms of the sustainability of the earth's environment
- understand what you can do to reduce your ecological footprint

Key Terms

ecological footprint (EF)	degraded land	carrying capacity	sustainability
productive land	energy land	fair earthshare	overshoot

In this chapter, you will have a chance to learn more about ecological footprints, and how the way in which we all choose to live affects the environmental health of the world (Fig. 36-1).

At various points in *Making Connections: Canada's Geography,* we have looked at how people use the earth and what impact this use might have on it. For example, in Chapter 22, The Business of Farming, you learned that, in spite of Canada's size, we have very little excellent farmland, yet we allow our cities to expand onto this land. In Chapter 25, Energy: Powering Our Nation, you learned about the different types of energy we use, and about the fact that our oil and gas reserves will run out in the 21st century. A very serious problem emerges however, when we try to see how all of this fits together into the "big picture." It seems that when we try to get an overview of how we might be affecting the earth's environmental health we end up trying to compare apples to oranges. That is, how do we compare the environmental impact of getting a ride to school to that of buying a pair of jeans? How do we decide which is more environmentally friendly — living in a small house in the suburbs or in a condominium downtown?

△ **Fig. 36-1** *How do we determine the ecological impact of our activities?*

◁ **Fig. 36-2** *How do you compare and combine different impacts on the environment?*

The purpose of this chapter is to introduce a way of measuring the demand that we place on the environment — the **ecological footprint (EF)**. An ecological footprint is the amount of space that is required to support a person's activities. It can be measured at a number of levels. For example, we can use the EF of one person, to establish the EF of the population of a city, a country, or even the entire world.

WHAT IS THE ECOLOGICAL FOOTPRINT OF EACH CANADIAN?

Until fairly recently, there was no way to compare the environmental impact of the enormous range of things that people do. The idea of the ecological footprint allows us to do this. This concept, developed by a group of planners and ecologists at the University of British Columbia, converts all human activities to equivalent land areas — that is, to the amount of space needed to support those activities. As you might expect, this is a very complex task that involves a complicated analysis of economic and ecological data. What does the idea of the EF have to say to Canadians? Fig. 36-3 will tell us.

To understand how it works, let's look at the parts of the table.

1. The numbers in the table refer to the amount of **productive land** per capita (in hectares) needed to support the most important human activities. Productive land refers to the five categories of land listed in Fig. 36-3: energy land, degraded land (even though it is no longer actively productive), crop land, pasture land, and forested land.

2. Along the left side of the table are the main activities that are a part of our lives: housing, food, transportation, etc. Most of these are then divided into sub-categories. For example, housing involves both building the homes we live in and then operating them (for example, heating them and repairing them).

3. At the top of the table, you will see the major kinds of land that are used to support these economic activities. The following explanations will help you to understand these:

    •   Crop land, pasture land, and forested land refer to the amounts of these kinds of land needed to support human activities. For example, our food supply comes from three sources: the land where crops are grown; pastures where cows, pigs and other animals graze; and, to a much smaller extent, the forested land.

    •   **degraded land** refers to formerly productive land which has been converted to non-productive uses like urban areas and highways.

    •   **energy land** really is a form of *virtual land*. The use of energy (particularly in the form of oil, natural gas, and coal) has an environmental cost that is much greater than the amount of land that is used to generate the energy. A different way of measuring *energy land* must be found that better reflects the true environmental cost of this energy use. The substitute that was chosen for EF analysis is the amount of forest land that would be needed to eliminate the carbon dioxide (through photosynthesis) that is produced by the energy use. While this does not reflect all of the environmental costs related to the energy use, it does at least consider the critical impact of energy use on global warming.

Now let's look at some specific numbers in the table. Consider how much land is needed to support the average Canadian's housing needs. In total, this amounts to 0.89 ha which is made up of energy needs, degraded land, and forested land.

•   The energy land needed is equal to 0.41 ha (0.06 for construction and 0.35 for operation). Remember that this is the land area that would be needed to eliminate the carbon dioxide produced by energy use related to providing housing.

For more on the ecological footprint read the book *Our Ecological Footprint: Reducing Human Impact on the Earth*, by those who developed the concept, Mathis Wackernagel and William Rees, or visit these web sites: www.ecouncil.ac.cr/rio/focus/ and report/english/footprint; and www.esb.utexas.edu/drnrm/WhatIs/ecofootprint.htm

The ecological footprint does not take into account the world's oceans. Scientists are exploring the role of oceans, but it is thought that they play a minor role compared to land in supporting most human activities.

Virtual land is imagined or 'pretend' land.

More information on global warming can be found in Chapter 35.

- The land degradation that occurs (because the land where the home is located can no longer be used for productive purposes like farming or forestry) is equal to 0.08 ha.
- The amount of forested land that is needed is 0.40 ha: 0.35 for construction, e.g., lumber and plywood and 0.05 for operation, e.g., for repairs and firewood.

When we look at all of the aspects of our lives, we get an ecological footprint of 4.27 ha of productive land needed to support the lifestyle of

▽ **Fig. 36-3** *Calculation of the per capita ecological footprint for the average Canadian*

	Productive Land					
Activities	**Energy Land[1]**	**Degraded Land**	**Crop Land**	**Pasture Land**	**Forested Land**	**Total Land**
Housing	0.41	0.08			0.40	0.89
Construction	0.06				0.35	
Operation	0.35				0.05	
Food	0.33		0.62	0.33	0.02	1.30
Transportation	0.79	0.10				0.89
People (private)	0.60					
People (public)	0.07					
Goods	0.12					
Consumer Goods	0.52	0.01	0.06	0.13	0.17	0.89
Packaging	0.10				0.04	
Clothing	0.11		0.02	0.13		
Furniture and appliances	0.06				0.03	
Books and magazines	0.06				0.10	
Tobacco and alcohol	0.06		0.04			
Personal care	0.03					
Recreation equipment	0.10					
Services	0.29	0.01				0.30
Government and military	0.06					
Education	0.08					
Health care	0.08					
Tourism	0.01					
Entertainment	0.01					
Other	0.05					
Total	2.34	0.20	0.68	0.46	0.59	4.27

[1] Energy land is measured in terms of how much forested land would be needed to remove the carbon dioxide (using photosynthesis) that is produced by the economic activity.

All values are in hectares (ha) per person. Values left blank in the table are less than 0.005 ha.

Legend: **Forested land** : category of land use
   Services: major sector within the economy
   Government and military: subsector within the economy

the average Canadian. But what does this mean? In the activity that follows you will have a chance to find out.

If you want to calculate your own ecological footprint, go to www.wwfcanada.org/footprints/index.shtml

WHAT ABOUT MY 4.27 HECTARES ANYWAY?

Answer the questions below to gain a better understanding of an ecological footprint.

1. a) Ecological footprints only involve productive land. What are the five kinds of productive land mentioned in Fig. 36-3?

    b) List at least three examples of different kinds of land in Canada that would be considered non-productive land. Hint: Consider types of land not mentioned in the answer to question 1a.

2. a) To better understand how much land we are talking about, do this calculation. Convert 4.27 ha to m^2. Now take the square root of this number. This will give you the length of each side of a square with an area of 4.27 ha. Try to visualize how large an area this is — remember that a Canadian football field is about 100 m long. The amount you calculate is the amount of land that is needed to support the lifestyle of the average Canadian.

    b) Obviously your EF is not one piece of land, since you rely on products that come from many places in the world — both local and distant. Your EF really consists of a great many small pieces of land in different places that would add up to 4.27 ha. Give an example of parts of your ecological footprint that would be

        i.   in your local community

        ii. in a nearby part of Canada

        iii. in a distant part of Canada

        iv. in a foreign country

3. How much productive land would be needed to provide for all of the people of Canada? Multiply 4.27 ha by Canada's population of 30 000 000.

4. Is there enough productive land in Canada to support our current population? Canada has about 434 477 000 ha of productive land. Compare this number to your answer to question 3 and determine the size of the surplus (or deficit) of productive land.

5. Next, calculate Canada's **carrying capacity**. This is the number of people that could be supported at current living standards by Canada's productive land. Do this by dividing the total amount of productive land by 4.27 ha. How many people could Canada support?

1 ha = 10 000 m^2 (100 m by 100 m)

For this kind of analysis, numbers that have been rounded are fine.

LOOKING BEYOND CANADA'S BORDERS

6. So far it all seems fairly positive — it would appear that Canada can support substantially more people than it does. It is not quite so simple though.

   a) Explain how Canada exports much of its carrying capacity to other countries.

   b) Give one positive impact and one negative impact of these exports on Canadians.

   c) Give one piece of evidence that would suggest that Canada may be exporting too much. Hint: Think about some of Canada's primary industries.

7. Canadians do not exist in isolation from the rest of the world. Consider the following: There are about 8 633 000 000 ha of productive land and about 6 000 000 000 people in the world. If you divide the land by the people, you will get what is called the **fair earthshare**. This is how much of the productive land of the earth each person would be entitled to, if all of the world's productive land were shared equally. How does this compare to the share of an average Canadian?

8. Now calculate the earth's carrying capacity, assuming that everyone lived at the average Canadian's standard of living. To do this, divide the amount of productive land by Canada's average ecological footprint. What did you discover?

WHAT DOES IT ALL MEAN TO CANADIANS?

What does all of this tell us? For starters, we must remember that Canada is only one part of the world and we must look at the entire world. Consider the fact that if everyone in the world were to live at the same standard of living as the average Canadian, we would need two additional earths!

Examine Fig. 38-4 to see some specific comparisons among Canada, the United States, India, and the entire world. First of all, notice that the worldwide ecological footprint of 1.8 ha/person is more than 20% greater than the fair earthshare that you calculated in question 7 of the previous activity. The existence of global warming, pollution, and resource depletion suggest that the earth is already beyond its carrying capacity and that Canadians contribute more than their share to the problem.

There are some clear moral and practical choices that Canadians face. To understand these, we will concentrate on one specific cause of the difference in size of the ecological footprints that exist in wealthier and

(Per capita values, 1991)	Canada	United States	India	World
Carbon dioxide emissions (tonnes per year)	15.2	19.5	0.81	4.2
Purchasing power (US$)	19 320	22 130	1150	3800
Vehicles (per 100 people)	46	57	0.2	10
Paper consumption (kg/yr)	247	317	2	44
Fossil energy use (Gj/yr)	250	287	5	56
Freshwater removals (m³/yr)	1688	1868	612	644
Ecological footprint (ha/person)	**4.3**	**5.1**	**0.4**	**1.8**

◁ **Fig. 36-4** *Consumption and the ecological footprints in developed countries are very different from those in other parts of the world.*

in poorer countries. Let's consider a very simple substance — paper. We tend to take paper (newspaper, packaging material, computer printouts, this textbook, etc.) very much for granted. This means that we do not think very much about either its value or its environmental cost. In Fig. 36-4, you learned that a typical Canadian uses about 120 times as much paper as a typical Indian. Is this fair? How could this situation be made more fair? The simplest solution might be to suggest that as India gets wealthier (which is happening quite quickly) Indians would then be able to afford and use more paper. There is the obvious problem with this approach — if Canadians are already living at a level beyond the earth's carrying capacity, how can we support even more consumption of the earth's resources and creation of waste products? The only other solution would be for people in developed countries, like ours, to reduce consumption by an amount large enough to allow people in the rest of the world to expand theirs.

Remember that many countries in the world are much poorer than India.

While the current situation is certainly unhealthy, it is what may happen in the future that is particularly disturbing. The load that a population has on its environment is a product of two factors:

Load = Size of population x Rate of consumption

In 1950, the world's population was about 2.5 billion and the per capita Gross World Product (GWP) was about $1520. By 1993, the population had increased to 5.8 billion (about 2.3 times as many people). As well, the per capita GWP had risen to $3330 (an increase of 2.2 times). If we combine these two numbers, we can see that the load on the environment increased by more than five times (2.2 x 2.3) from 1950 to 1993. Today this pattern continues since both the population and the per capita GWP continue to grow.

Gross World Product: the value of total goods and services produced annually in the world. Dollar amounts here have been adjusted to eliminate the effect of inflation.

TOWARD SUSTAINABILITY

Fig. 36-5 shows the relationship between the earth's carrying capacity and the load that human activities put on the earth. Read the following to better understand what this graph shows. Each number listed below corresponds to a number indicated on the graph.

1. You already know about the carrying capacity of the earth. It has increased only slightly over the last few centuries as people have found uses for parts of the environment they didn't use before.

2. You also know about the load that the earth's population places on the earth and why it has grown so substantially.

3. This is the final point of **sustainability**. Beyond this point, in the long-term, the impact on the earth is greater than its carrying capacity.

4. This is the point where the earth is today: in an **overshoot**, where the world population's use of the environment exceeds the carrying capacity.

5. The earth can operate temporarily in this area of overshoot only by using up the earth's supply of non-renewable resources.

6. The earth's carrying capacity will start to decline as non-renewable resources are used up and as renewable resources deteriorate because of over-use.

7. The load on the earth declines sharply because the population has dropped dramatically. This must happen because the resources no longer exist to support these people.

You will notice that the time axis of the graph has no numbers on it. At this point, no one knows for sure how far away we have overshot sustainability and when a collapse might happen. In fact, some people

The carrying capacity increased significantly twice in human history. The first was when agriculture developed; the second was with the Industrial Revolution.

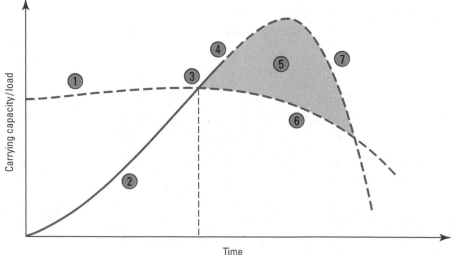

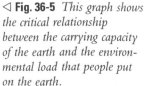

◁ **Fig. 36-5** *This graph shows the critical relationship between the carrying capacity of the earth and the environmental load that people put on the earth.*

think that this might never happen. This enormous difference in opinion exists because there are two completely different ways in which this problem can be viewed. Some people believe that the problems of too much pollution and too few resources will have a *technical* solution. Other people say that the problem is much more basic than that: that we are reaching, or have already reached the point, where the earth is no longer able to support its human population. These people feel that this has happened because of the way we live as a society. Hence, we must find a *behavioural solution*.

The Technical Solution

Those people who believe in the ability of technology to solve problems have confidence that we will find ways to solve environmental problems and increase the carrying capacity of the earth. These people would argue that this has happened in the past and will happen again. The best example of this would be the **Industrial Revolution** which started more than two centuries ago. The Industrial Revolution enormously increased the earth's carrying capacity — in fact, allowing the level of wealth that generally exists in developed countries today. How technology can solve environmental problems is not clear, but perhaps it can be through a revolution in energy supply and pollution control. Supporters of this view suggest that people did not, and could not, predict the coming of steam power just a few years before it revolutionized the world.

△ **Fig. 36-6** *Growing our own food is just one step we may take towards solving the environmental problem.*

The Behavioural Solution

The first step in finding a behavioural solution is to realize that we are dealing with one huge, all-encompassing problem rather than many smaller problems. Global warming, loss of topsoil, shortage of fresh water, destruction of forests, loss of the fishery, depletion of the ozone layer, and many other problems are just symptoms of the fact that we are now in an overshoot condition and to change it, we have to fundamentally change the way in which we live (Fig. 36-6).

There are many things we can do. One of the most important of these is to change how we measure "progress". At several points in *Making Connections: Canada's Geography*, we have used the idea of per capita Gross Domestic Product (GDP) to measure wealth and progress. In fact, this is the most commonly used measure for this purpose but it does have some serious shortcomings. It assumes that more economic activity means progress and a better quality of life for people. The very activities that increase the GDP are often those that increase our ecological footprint and may not do much to increase human happiness:

In this chapter, we even used the idea of Gross World Product.

- building and operating cars is very important to the GDP, but gasoline-operated cars greatly increase global warming and use non-renewable fossil fuels
- catching too many fish off our Atlantic and Pacific coasts has helped the GDP, but has contributed to the collapse of fish stocks
- making land mines increases the GDP, but many innocent people working in their fields have been maimed and killed by land mines

Canada has been a leader in the fight to outlaw land mines.

- producing and using agricultural pesticides increases the GDP in two ways, but pesticides may cause cancers in either the areas where they are made or the areas where they are used.

Producing insecticides increases the GDP as does the increase in farm production that the chemicals allow.

What we need to have is a method of accounting that combines both economics and ecology. The idea of the ecological footprint is a very useful start in this direction. It at least establishes the limits within which people must live. The next step that we can take is to decide how we can live in a more ecologically responsible way that will reduce our EF and provide us with as much happiness and satisfaction as possible.

IN CLOSING...

The idea that the world has a limited ability to support its population and that people should live within this limit is hardly a new one. In fact, the Greek philosopher Plato said more than 2500 years ago, "... suitable land for the number of citizens cannot be fixed without considering the land ... The land must be extensive enough to support a given number of people in modest comfort, and not a metre more is needed." In spite of knowing about the need to control our numbers and our resource use, the human population has shown little ability to do anything about them. The concept of the EF gives us a basis for understanding what we are doing to our environment and to the ability of the earth to sustain our population. As we come to understand EF better, as a society, we will have a basis for planning our activities and measuring the impact we have on the earth.

QUESTIONS

CHECK YOUR UNDERSTANDING

1. a) What is an ecological footprint?
    b) Describe in words how it is calculated.

2. a) In your own words describe how *energy land* differs from the other four types of land.
    b) Describe what is meant by *degraded land*.

3. a) Define sustainability.
    b) What are the two factors that contribute to the load that a population puts onto the environment?
    c) How do the factors mentioned in the answer to question 3b contribute to the problem of achieving sustainability in the future?

ANALYZE AND APPLY

4. Is non-productive land the same as useless land? Explain your answer.

5. Explain the EF impact of each of the following:
    a) transportation on energy land
    b) clothing on pasture land
    c) books and magazines on forested land
    d) education on energy land
    e) food on pasture land

6. Look at Fig. 36-5. Consider the parts of this graph where the earth's carrying capacity starts to decline and the population drops. What sort of earth events would indicate that these two things are, in fact, happening?

THINK AND COMMUNICATE

7. Canadians use far more paper than people in less-developed countries. What benefits does having access to all this paper have for you? What do young people from India miss out on because they do not have easy access to as much paper?

8. a) Some people in our society tend to equate more consumption of goods and services to increased happiness. Give three examples of how this might be true. Give three examples that would suggest that it is not true.
    b) Since reducing our EF would require reducing our consumption, do you think that you could maintain (or perhaps increase) your happiness while significantly reducing your consumption?

9. a) Do you think that all of the people in the world have the right to enjoy a standard of living similar to that of the average Canadian?
    b) Would you be willing to reduce your own EF to allow this to happen?

10. a) You can test your understanding of an EF by explaining how you might reduce your own EF. Examine Fig. 36-3. Over 20 individual EF values are shown. Describe how you could possibly significantly reduce any 10 of these.
    b) Describe what basic principles businesses, governments, and individuals should use to reduce the EF of the developed countries.

11. Describe how *you* can increase your quality of life by reducing your EF in
    a) your home
    b) local ecozone
    c) province
    d) Canada
    e) the whole world

12. Not everyone agrees with the idea of the EF. A newspaper editorial reacts to the suggestion that $10 000 per year is all that is required to be happy. What is your reaction to the following editorial (Fig. 36-7)?

Ecological Misprint

Friday, January 29, 1999

All of us who live in cities sense the artificiality of our existence. We don't grow our own food, or generate our own energy....

That is why when University of British Columbia planning professor, William Rees describes to a scientific conference in California the excessively large "ecological footprint" of urban life, we pay attention. There is this continual voice in the back of our head that worries that the unreality of city life reflects an essential imbalance in our relationship to nature.

We carefully follow Dr. Rees's reasoning about cities' carbon dioxide production, resource use and the like — yes, very interesting — and then we suddenly start to laugh.

Could he really have told the annual meeting of the American Association for the Advancement of Science that he knows exactly how much money a person has to have to be happy? Could he really have pegged "happiness" at $10 000 of per capita Gross Domestic Product, a figure based on United Nations estimates of the relationship among income, life expectancy, literacy and child mortality. Could he really have thundered, "Most of developed countries have far exceeded the level of income needed to produce maximum happiness."

• •

...it sounds as if Professor Rees misunderstands how attractive and fulfilling becoming rich and richer

is. In the universe he's constructed, trips to Florida in February, minivans and papayas year round, although they may be superficially good, can't possibly make us happy. The fact that richer countries are flooded with immigrants from poorer countries can't really be because life is better in the wealthier parts of the globe. The fact that richer countries can invest more in culture, science and, yes, even environmental protection can't really give their citizens a sense of greater well-being.

• •

△ **Fig. 36-7**

CONNECTING STUDY

Urban Futures

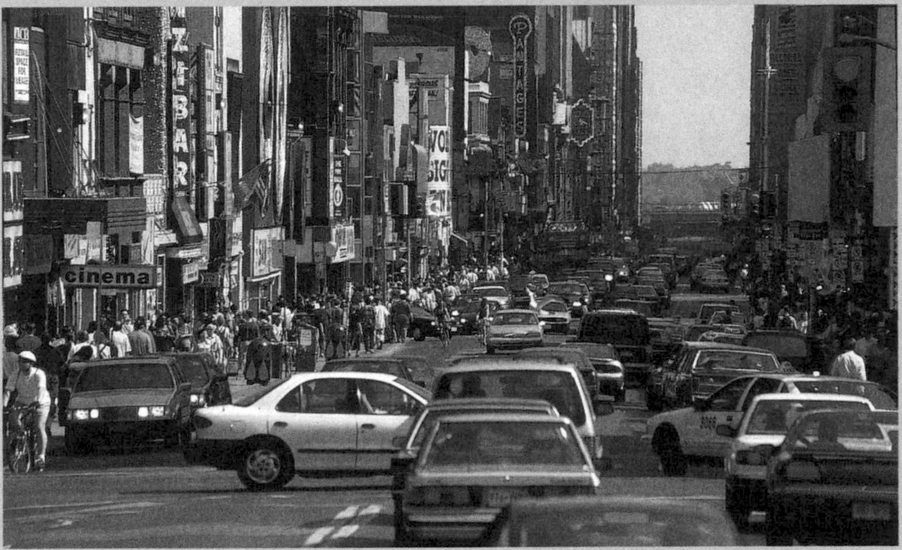

△ **Fig. 36-8** *Busy urban scenes such as this one are commonplace in Canada's largest cities.*

KEY TERMS

urban renewal
urban sprawl
new urbanism

What thought comes to mind when you see an urban scene (Fig. 36-8)? Some people may see an area that is full of life and energy — the kind of area that demonstrates the best of what urban living can be. Other people might look at the same area and see a neighbourhood that would be noisy, dirty, and could (perhaps) have a crime problem. This difference in opinion illustrates how complex urban environments are and also why they are so interesting.

In this chapter, you will have the chance to study one of the many important issues that faces our cities. The issues are described below. You should choose one that you find particularly interesting.

Of course, studying and understanding cities is of vital importance since that is where most Canadians live.

Your teacher will tell you how to present your findings; there are a number of possibilities. You might be asked to do a(n):

- research paper
- magazine/newspaper
- oral presentation
- wall poster
- video report
- debate

◁ **Fig. 36-9** *In January 1999, Toronto's transportation services were severely affected by a winter storm.*

URBAN RESEARCH ISSUES

Dealing With Aging Cities What should we do with older areas of a city where buildings are in poor repair or where the demand for land of different types is changing? We need some form of **urban renewal**, but what type? Should these old areas of our cities be torn down and replaced, or should they be renovated and used again?

In some cities, the demand for older factories and office buildings has decreased, and these are now being converted to residential use, i.e., lofts.

Urban Sprawl Our cities are expanding constantly — in most cases onto excellent agricultural land that cannot be replaced. Should we be worried about this? If we decide that this is a serious enough problem, how can we prevent it from continuing?

Loss of an Economic Base Sometimes a town will lose its economic base. For example, this could happen if the forest that a paper mill depends on was depleted of trees, or if the demand for a particular mineral disappeared. Where and when has this happened in Canada? Why do some towns survive this situation while others do not?

Problems With Urban Transportation Transportation is one of the most important things that happens in any city (Fig. 36-9). What is the best way to move large numbers of people and masses of goods in the city? Are there any new ideas on the horizon that will revolutionize transportation in the city?

You can learn more about the winter-city movement at: www.wnet.gov.edmonton.ab.ca/ iamnc.htm

Building a Livable Winter City Canadian cities have some of the coldest, snowiest winters anywhere in the world. What can we do to make our cities as livable as possible in wintertime?

When Crises Happen Sometimes cities face damaging natural phenomena. Examples of this are the Red River flood that affected communities in southern Manitoba in 1996, the ice storm of 1998 that affected Montréal and neighbouring cities, and the damaging series of snow storms that hit the Toronto area in 1999. What natural hazards affect Canadian cities? How can a city and its residents prepare for such potentially catastrophic events?

Crime in the City Few subjects receive as much attention as does crime in the city. Should we be so worried about crime? What are the best approaches to preventing and reducing crime in Canadian cities?

Poverty and Homelessness An increasing number of people cannot afford to live in our cities because they have little or no income. As a result, they must live in substandard housing or even on the street (Fig. 36-10). In a country as wealthy as Canada, how do we ensure that everyone has adequate housing?

New Urban Design Ideas Many people feel that modern suburban residential areas do not "work." Houses are too far apart to allow easy social contact and residents must rely on their cars to get anywhere. **New urbanism** is a catch phrase for a new way to design our cities in a way that looks surprisingly like our older neighbourhoods: lots are small and walking to school, stores, and parks is easy. This is accomplished by having careful controls over everything from house design to landscaping.

The two most famous new urbanism communities are both in Florida: Celebration (www.xone.net/celebration/) and Seaside (www.seasidefl.com/start.htm)

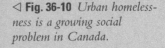

◁ **Fig. 36-10** *Urban homelessness is a growing social problem in Canada.*

People With Special Needs Living successfully in a modern city can be a challenge for anyone. It becomes that much more difficult for people who are mobility-challenged. What modifications are needed in urban design and transportation systems to accommodate the special needs of these people?

Cities With an Aging Population Canada's population is aging rapidly. What special needs will an older population have? You might want to consider such things as demand for different forms of housing, increased health care needs, and different recreational preferences.

Meeting the Needs of Children and Teenagers What special needs do young people have in our cities? Are these particular needs being met, or not?

How Can We Change our Cities to Reduce our Ecological Footprint? In Chapter 36, you learned that Canadians have a very large ecological footprint. Since the vast majority of Canadians live in urban areas, much of our ecological footprint comes from our cities and towns. What can we do to our cities, and, with our cities, to minimize this impact?

Waste Management in Cities What happens to household garbage and industrial waste in your community? How are sewage and toxic wastes handled? Analyze and evaluate the success of these methods in both environmental and economic terms. Are new technologies or approaches being developed in any of these fields that will prove more successful than what we do today?

Energy and Water Use in the City What methods are used in your community to promote the efficient use of energy and water? How successful have these efforts been? What other methods could be used in the future?

   Good luck with your project...

mobility-challenged: people who may have difficulty moving from place to place such as the elderly, the disabled, young children, etc.

Urban design changes could include the design of houses, schools, stores, and office buildings.

Glossary

Aboriginal descendant of Canada's first inhabitants

acid precipitation rain, snow or fog created after sulphur dioxide and nitric oxides mix with water vapour in the atmosphere. Acid precipitation kills vegetation and turns lakes acidic, causing fish to die and wildlife to disappear.

active layer upper layer of permafrost that thaws only briefly in summertime

advance of glacier forward glacial movement. If more snow accumulates than melts, a glacier will advance.

aerial photo photograph taken from the sky instead of the ground

agribusiness agricultural business. Operations include growing, storing, processing, and distributing food, and may be owned by a large corporation, a family, or an individual.

air mass large body of air having same moisture and temperature conditions throughout

air pressure weight of air

alphanumeric grid grid that uses letters and numerals to identify squares of a grid pattern on a map

alpine glacier glacier occupying one or more valleys in an alpine region (valley glacier)

AltaVista type of search engine used on the Internet

alternative energy source non-conventional energy source such as solar, wind, and biomass energy

analog transmission traditional form of cable and satellite transmission of television signals instead of the more modern digital transmission

anchor store large store such as a department store or grocery store that is located one at each end of the shopping mall and attracts great numbers of customers

anticlinal trap dome-shaped structure of rock layers created by folding. Oil and gas are often found in these traps.

aquaculture production of fish and other marine products on fish farms

ArcVoyager GIS program especially designed for map making in schools, a demonstration version of more powerful, commercial program ArcView

area symbol coloured pattern representing a feature on a topographic map

assimilate to lose your culture and adopt the culture of the larger group within which you live (e.g., First Nation adopting broader Canadian culture)

average annual temperature monthly average temperatures added together and divided by 12

balance of payments similar to balance of trade, but also includes such things as interest, profits, and money spent by tourists

balance of trade difference between value of exports and value of imports. If exports exceed imports, there is a trade surplus. If imports exceed exports, there is a trade deficit.

band an Aboriginal group that is recognized by the Canadian government. The government sets aside money and land (reserves) for use by the band. There are almost 600 bands in Canada.

base map map providing only an outline of the most basic features of the mapped area

basic industry industry that sells its products outside the community, bringing money into the community.

basic service service provided by basic industries to people and business outside the community thereby bringing money into the community from the outside and ensuring its survival

bedrock solid rock beneath the soil

bias specific point of view or angle on an issue or topic

bilateral trade trade between two countries

birth rate number of births per 1000 people

bitumen in oil sand deposits, each grain of sand is covered by a layer of water and a heavy oil or black tar called bitumen. Processed into synthetic crude oil.

boreal and taiga forest coniferous (needle-leaved) forest that stretches from east to west across Canada, south of the tundra but north of the grasslands and mixed forest

branch plant Canadian company controlled by a foreign company

bulk cargo things like wheat, coal, gravel, and iron ore shipped in loose form rather than in packages. They are usually of low value and must be shipped as cheaply as possible.

calcification process by which, in dry climates, water carrying dissolved minerals moves upward through the soil. At the surface, the water evaporates, leaving the minerals behind. The surface soil is then considered calcified.

call centre place used by polling companies, fund-raising organizations, mail-order companies, etc. Companies also locate their customer service operations in a tele-phone call centre. Customers call a toll-free number to purchase or exchange products and request information or assistance.

Canadian Shield large area of Precambrian rock that forms the core of Canada

canal waterway dug across land on which boats and ships travel

capillary action movement of water upward through small spaces, as in soil

carat unit of mass of precious stones, especially diamonds, equal to 200 mg

carbon cycle movement of carbon through plants, animals, water, soil, air and rocks

carbon dioxide greenhouse gas composed of one carbon atom and two oxygen atoms in each molecule, other-wise known as CO_2

carbon fixation process whereby carbon is trapped in fossil fuels under the surface of the earth for millions of years. Fixed carbon does not contribute to global warming if we prevent its release into the atmosphere.

carbon sink keeper of carbon, such as plankton and forests, that exchange carbon with the atmosphere in a cycle, helping to protect the planet from global warming

carbon source fossil fuel which, when burned, releases carbon into the atmosphere thus increasing global warming

carrying capacity number of people that could be supported at current living standards by Canada's produc-tive land

cash crop crop that is grown by a farmer to be sold

Cenozoic era most recent era of geologic time which began about 66 million years ago. See geologic time.

census tract smallest urban area used for census data collection

Central Business District (CBD) downtown area of a city or town, where most of the important commercial and government activities take place

circumstance in manufacturing, particular influences on the location of factories that are more general and difficult to measure

city-state country that contains only one large city, such as Singapore

clear-cutting logging method whereby all trees in an area (except for very small ones) are cut at one time

climate weather conditions of a place averaged over a long period of time

climate station place where climate information is gath-ered

cold front boundary between a warm air mass and an advancing cold air mass

commercial forest part of a forest that has large enough trees and is close enough to a market to allow it to be harvested by the forest industry

communications movement of information from place to place

commuter person who travels daily between home and the place of work

compass bearing degrees on a compass, measured in clock-wise direction from 0° (North) to 360°

compass point direction on a compass, such as South and North

compass rose diagram, in the shape of a flower, showing directions (compass points) and bearings (measured clock-wise from North) used to indicate direction on maps

comprehensive treaty First Nations' land treaty nego-tiated in an area where no other treaty has ever been signed, i.e., the first treaty for that area

concession system type of survey system used in southern Ontario whereby land is divided by concession roads and side roads into squares and rectangles of varying sizes

condensation process whereby water vapour is cooled and changes from an invisible gas to liquid water. Condensed water vapour is what forms clouds.

coniferous tree tree with cones and often needlelike leaves: evergreen

container metal box of standard size (2.4 m x 2.4 m x 4.9 m or 9.8 m) used for moving freight. The container is loaded at the point of shipment and remains sealed until it reaches its destination. Along the way, it may be moved by truck, train, plane, or ship.

contaminant substance that pollutes air, water, soil, or food.

continental climate climate type that develops away from the influence of the ocean. The annual temperature range tends to be large and precipitation is low.

continental drift theory by German scientist Alfred Wegener stating that 300 million years ago all of the earth's land masses, which were in constant motion, collided to form one supercontinent called Pangaea. About 200 million years ago Pangaea broke apart and the continents have drifted apart to their present locations. According to his theory, only continents drifted.

continental glacier glacier that spreads out to cover a large portion of a continent. During the last ice age, huge glaciers formed in northern Canada and moved southward.

continental shelf gently sloping outer edge of a continent, that extends below the surface of the ocean to a maximum depth of about 200 m

continentalist person who believes in continentalism; the belief that Canada and the United States should work more closely together to solve their common problems. The NAFTA is an example of this sort of cooperation.

contour plowing plowing across hilly fields, rather than up and down the slope of a hill to reduce the damage caused by soil erosion. In this way, each crop row prevents water from running down the slope and taking the topsoil with it.

convection current circular movement in a gas or liquid created by uneven heating

convectional precipitation precipitation caused on hot summer days, when heated land causes the air above it to rise by convection. As the air rises it cools and condensation occurs. Rain or hail may fall from the thunderclouds that build up.

conventional energy source well-established source of energy such as oil, natural gas, coal, hydro, and nuclear electricity

convergent technology coming together of various forms of communications technology; no longer operating independently of each other but together (e.g., listening to the radio or watching television on the Internet)

corporate citizen company that shows loyalty to a particular country

craton ancient geologic feature formed in Precambrian era, largely undisturbed by mountain-building for one billion years, containing kimberlite pipes in which diamonds are found

culture 1. broadly defined: beliefs, customs, skills, religions, arts, and languages of a group of people

2. narrowly defined:, the arts, entertainment, and media

cyclonic precipitation precipitation caused when a warm, moist air mass is forced to rise by a cool, dry air mass. This is also called frontal precipitation.

database table of information in a computer program that can be searched for particular values or rearranged in a variety of ways

daylight-saving time worldwide system of changing time according to the season whereby daylight hours are extended into the evening when most people are awake (e.g., in Canada, we move time forward by one hour in spring and back one hour in fall)

death rate number of deaths per 1000 people

deciduous tree tree which sheds its leaves annually in the fall (broad-leaved tree)

degraded land in ecological footprint calculations, formerly productive land which has been converted to non-productive uses such as urban areas and highways

demography study of population numbers, distribution, trends, and issues

dependency load portion of the population that is not in the work force; total people under fourteen and over sixty-five

dependent variable (graphing) dependent variable goes on the vertical axis of the graph and is, to a greater or lesser extent, caused or influenced by the independent variable

deregulation removal of regulations controlling certain parts of an industry. For example, deregulation of the airline industry removes rules controlling routes travelled and the price of seats.

developed country country with a highly developed economy. Its citizens have high incomes, abundant food, good housing, and can afford many luxuries. Sometimes called "industrialized".

developing country country with a poorly developed economy; its citizens have low incomes, shortages of food, poor housing, and cannot afford luxuries. Sometimes called "less developed".

dew invisible water vapour in the air, that condenses on cool surfaces during clear nights when the air is calm, forming water droplets

differential erosion process whereby softer sedimentary rocks erode more quickly than harder rock shaping the surface of the landscape (e.g., three different levels of elevation on the prairies)

digital transmission in communications technology, process whereby digital signals give television viewers better quality pictures and sound than with traditional, analog transmission

direct statement scale words are used to describe the relationship between a distance on a map and a specific distance on the earth's surface (e.g., 1 cm to 10 km)

discharge rate amount of water that flows through a drainage basin. The discharge rate of a drainage basin may vary greatly from season to season depending on the weather conditions.

diversified urban centre town or city that has a variety of basic urban functions

doubling time (demographics) how long it would take for a country's population to double at the country's current rate of population growth

drainage process whereby water is removed from an area by flowing out of depressions in the land such as lakes and rivers

drainage basin area drained by a river and its tributaries. One drainage basin is separated from another by an area of higher land called a watershed.

drumlin geologic feature evident today on Canada's landscape, formed by ice sheets, an egg-shaped hill with a steep side at the wide end, and a gentle slope at the other

easting first three figures in a map reference giving the east-west location

ecological footprint (EF) measure of total human impact on an ecosystem

ecologist one who studies all interactions that occur within the biosphere, the portion of the planet that supports life and living organisms within it

economic base economic activities that allow a community to exist. For example, a town might exist because a mineral resource in the area is being developed.

ecotourism tourism industry promoting travel for the purpose of observing ecosystems

ecozone region based on its ecological characteristics

emigrate to leave your country of origin to live permanently in another country

emigration rate number of people per 1000 population in one year who emigrate

energy conservation process whereby people use energy, in all its forms, more efficiently and carefully than they have in the past

energy land virtual land in ecological footprint analysis

energy efficient appliances, vehicles, etc. that use much less energy than non-efficient items

entrepreneur person who takes a risk by setting up a business in order to make a profit

equal-area projection map projection used by most nations and international organizations in which the correct sizes of all countries are shown in relation to one another, such as on a Winkel Tripel projection, thereby avoiding most size distortions

era major division of geologic time (for example, the Paleozoic era). See geologic time.

erosion wearing away of the earth's surface followed by the movement to other locations of materials that have worn away.

erratic rock picked up by the ice, carried along, and deposited many kilometres away; easily identifiable because its composition is different from the bedrock of the region in which it was deposited

escarpment steep cliff formed by erosion or faulting

esker long ridge of material deposited by a meltwater stream flowing beneath a glacier

export product or service produced in one country for sale in another country

extensive farming type of farming in which small amounts of labour, machinery, and fertilizers are used on large farms. Yields per hectare are small. Most agricultural activities in Canada are of this kind.

fair earthshare measurement of productive land in the world divided by number of people in the world. This is how much of the productive land each person would be entitled to, if all of the world's productive land was shared equally.

false colour colour artificially added to satellite images of earth, to make patterns more obvious. These colours would not actually be seen from space.

family immigrant one category of immigrant to Canada who is sponsored by a close relative who is already a Canadian resident

faulting movement along a crack (fault) or cracks in the earth's crust

fertilizer substance put on agricultural land to make it able to produce more, e.g., manure or chemical fertilizer

fiord long, narrow inlet of the sea with steep sides. Fiords were created by glaciers that scraped out valleys. When the glaciers melted, the sea flooded the valleys.

First Nation group of Aboriginal people who share the same culture and heritage

fishing bank shallow area on the continental shelf that provides a feeding and spawning ground for fish

folding bending of rock layers

foreign aid expertise, money, and products given by rich countries to poorer countries

fossil imprint in rock of the remains of a plant or animal that lived millions of years ago

fossil fuel any mineral that can be burned to produce energy (e.g., coal, natural gas, oil)

free trade trade without tariff barriers

front leading edge of an air mass. If the air mass is warm, the leading edge of this air is called a warm front. If the air is cold, the leading edge is a cold front.

frost freezing condition in which feathery crystals of ice form when water vapour in the air condenses, often on a solid surface

fuel cell device that converts chemical potential energy in gasoline or alcohol to hydrogen which can be burned cleanly

fuel efficiency process whereby less fuel is used for the same purposes as before, e.g., modern family cars use less than half the fuel as did similar cars in the early 1970's

gemstone diamond diamond of high quality used in jewellery, prized because of its rarity and beauty

general-purpose map map that contains many different types of information

geographic information systems (GIS) integrated software package for the input, management, analysis, and display of spatial information

geographical systems various interconnected systems that shape our world, e.g., forces that cause devastating earthquakes or why nations trade with each other

geologic time history of the earth from its formation to the present. The earth's history may be divided into several major time periods, called eras:
Cenozoic era (most recent 66 million years)
Mesozoic era (245 million to 66 million years ago)
Paleozoic era (570 million to 245 million years ago)
Precambrian era (4600 million to 570 million years ago)

geologist expert who studies the history, composition, and structure of the earth's crust

geostationary orbit satellite orbiting about 36 000 km above the earth at a speed that keeps it exactly above the same place on the earth

glacier slow-moving mass of ice

global connections economic, social, political, geographic connections between and among countries around the world, e.g., economic connections such as buying shoes made in another country

Global Positioning System (GPS) satellite navigation system that is used to compute the exact latitude and longitude position of any place on earth

global village idea that the world is becoming like one large village because of improvements in communication

global warming warming of the world's temperatures as a result of rising levels of carbon dioxide and other greenhouse gases in the atmosphere

globalization process by which most regions of the world have become increasingly interconnected in terms of economics, culture, and financial services as a result of modern communications technology

graduated colour map map in which a range of colour shades is used to indicate different values

greenhouse effect absorption of heat energy by greenhouse gases and reradiation into the atmosphere

greenhouse gas gas that contributes to global warming such as carbon dioxide and methane

Gross Domestic Product (GDP) per capita total value of the goods and services produced within a country per person, excluding transactions with other countries

groundfish fish, such as cod and sole, that live and feed near the bottom of the sea

groundwater water that is found below the earth's surface in the spaces of soil and bedrock

growing season period during which crops can grow. Number of days between spring and autumn when the average daily temperature is above 5.6°C (temperature at which most crops begin to grow).

halocarbon chemical compound composed of carbon and one or more halogens (bromine, chlorine, fluorine, or iodine)

hardwood wood produced from broad-leaved trees such as maple, oak, and elm. Hardwood is used to make furniture, sports equipment, tool handles, floors, and boats. Not all hardwoods are "hard"; for example, poplar and basswood are actually quite soft.

heavy metal metal such as lead, mercury, and cadmium that is produced as waste by industries. They are highly poisonous to people and animals.

herbicide chemical designed to kill unwanted plants (weeds). If used improperly, can become a pollutant.

hierarchy system in which classes of status or authority are ranked one above the other

highlands areas of high elevation containing mountains and plateaus

high-order product high-priced product or service that is purchased infrequently

hit match found on the Internet when doing research on a specific topic

hub and spoke method of organizing airline routes so that people travelling between smaller cities (on spokes) travel to and change planes in a larger city (hub), e.g., a person wanting to travel from London, Ont., to Timmins would change planes in Toronto

humus dark, upper layer of soil made up of partially decayed plant material

hydro-electric generating station facility that generates electricity by the movement of falling water

hydrogen lightest chemical element, is a component of water and fossil fuels

hydrologic cycle pathway followed by water from oceans and lakes through the atmosphere and then back to the land and waterways

Ice Age period of time when freezing temperatures created ice sheets across continents. Glaciers covered most of Canada and the northern U.S. The last Ice Age ended between 6000 and 10 000 years ago.

ice sheet very large thick mass of glacial ice flowing outward in all directions from a zone of accumulation

igneous rock rock formed from cooling molten rock (magma or lava)

immigrant person who moves to a new country with the intention of settling there

immigrate to move permanently to a country other than one's native country

immigration rate number of new Canadians who have immigrated here from another country per 1000 people of Canada's population

impervious quality of a substance that does not allow water to pass through it

import product that is brought into a country from another country

import substitution process of replacing foreign-produced goods with Canadian ones, to support Canadian business, e.g., buying a Canadian-made car instead of one made in the United States, Japan, or elsewhere

independent immigrant immigrant who is a skilled worker or who is a business immigrant, one who would be in a position to contribute to Canada's economy

independent variable (graphing) the independent variable goes on the horizontal axis of the graph and is, to a greater or lesser extent, causing or influencing the dependent variable

Indian Act (The) act of Canadian government from 1876 whereby the government signed treaties with Native groups so that they would give up their claim to the lands they occupied, forever, and persuaded them to move to reserves

indicator mineral minerals that are found with diamonds. When these minerals are traced back to their point of origin, diamonds can be located.

industrial diamond poor quality diamond used as a tool in many kinds of industries because it is the hardest known substance

industrial mineral non-metallic minerals, such as salt or asbestos, used by industry and manufacturing

Industrial Revolution time, beginning in the late 1700s in England, when the introduction of water power and steam into factories greatly increased the size and output of industries

inshore fishery commercial fishing that takes place within a few kilometres of the shoreline. Small fishing boats go out to sea and return to shore each day.

instream use use of water without removing it from its source for activities, e.g., fishing and hydroelectric power

intensive farming large amount of labour, machinery, and fertilizers are used on small farms. High yields per hectare are obtained. The growing of fruits is an example of intensive farming.

intercity movement *between* cities, e.g., an intercity bus between Toronto and Montréal

International Date Line line that generally follows the 180° line of longitude where one day ends and the next begins. A traveller crossing the date line westward adds a day while one crossing it eastward subtracts a day.

Internet worldwide system of communication via computer used for research, watching music videos, shopping, etc. The Internet's main feature is the World Wide Web on which millions of Web sites carry information about every topic imaginable.

interprovincial migration movement of people between provinces

intervening obstacle thing stopping or discouraging people from immigrating to a country such as immigration requirements, the distances involved, and the costs of immigration

intracity movement *within* a city. For example, an intracity bus moves people from their home to school.

intrusion magma which has forced its way into cracks in the earth's crust

jet stream west to east movement of air in the mid-latitude flowing at speeds of up to 400 km/h at an altitude of between 8000 and 15 000 m

joule (J) metric measurement of energy

kimberlite pipe rare geologic structure which may contain diamonds, exists only in ancient features called cratons

knowledge industry type of industry based on human knowledge rather than on natural resources

labour supply availability of workers or labour force (total number of people working and looking for work in an area)

lake plain fertile bottom of an ancient glacial lake that is used for agriculture

land capability ability of land to be used for a certain purpose. For example, land capability for agriculture is based on soil quality, drainage, slope, and climate.

landed immigrant Canadian immigrant with permanent resident status who is not yet a Canadian citizen

land use how urban, suburban, or rural land is and can be used (e.g., parks, housing, industry, commercial, agriculture, etc.)

large-scale map map that shows a large amount of detail of a small area, such as a map with a scale of 1:50 000

latitude distance north or south of the equator, measured in degrees. The equator is 0° and the North Pole is 90° north latitude

leaching removal of minerals from soil by water as it moves downward through the soil. Leaching occurs in wet climates.

leeward side of a mountain or mountain range facing away from the prevailing winds

life expectancy average lifespan of a population

lignite soft, low-value coal sometimes used in thermal electric plants

line scale line divided into units (e.g., km) that represents the actual units on the ground

line symbol linear symbol used to represent features on topographic maps, e.g., roads and railway lines

literacy percentage of a population that has the ability to read and write

loam rich, fertile earth in which decaying and decayed plant matter is mixed with clay, silt and sand

location factor factor such as historical head start, market, location of raw materials, power, and fresh water, labour, transportation, and political factors that help explain the location of cities and industries

lock enclosed section in a canal which permits vessels to be raised or lowered to different water levels outside this compartment, either by letting water in or out of the compartment or, in a lift lock, by raising or lowering the water-filled compartment itself

long lot settlement pattern in southern Quebec and some other areas of Canada where individual lots tend to be long and narrow and extend back from major rivers or roads

longitude distance east and west of the Prime Meridian, measured in degrees. The Prime Meridian is 0° longitude.

long-grass prairie type of vegetation in the Canadian prairie provinces where higher precipitation levels cause grasses to grow longer than in drier, short-grass prairie areas

lowlands areas of low elevation containing plains and hills

low-order product product or service that is purchased frequently

mammal warm-blooded vertebrate animal such as humans and whales

manufacturing processing raw materials into a more finished state. For example, making lumber from logs is primary manufacturing, and making furniture from lumber is secondary manufacturing.

map representation of the earth's features drawn on a flat surface

map grid series of lines on a map that can be used to locate any place on the map

map projection method used to transfer features of the globe onto the flat surface of a map. There are hundreds of ways that this can be done and hundreds of different projections. Each projection has its strengths and weaknesses.

marine chronometer highly accurate clock that can keep time on a moving ship

maritime climate climate type that is strongly influenced by the closeness of an ocean or other large water body. The annual temperature range tends to be small and precipitation is high.

market any place where goods and services can be bought and sold

mechanization process whereby machinery takes over the work of humans or animals

meltwater water resulting from the melting of glacier ice and/or snow

mental map map in our mind of places we know

Mercator projection type of map projection in which compass bearings are correct, so it is useful for marine charts. However, it is unsuitable for general use because of distortions of distances, areas, and shapes of landmasses and oceans.

Mesozoic era period of geologic time from 245 million to 66 million years ago. See geologic time.

metallic mineral mineral that yields a metal when processed, for example, iron, gold, uranium, and silver

metamorphic rock type of rock formed when sedimentary and igneous rocks are subjected to great heat and pressure

methane colourless, odourless, flammable gas, the simplest of the hydrocarbons

metropolis either the dominant city of a country, or a major city with great political, economic, and cultural power

metropolitan dominance when one or more metropolises dominate the economic, cultural, and political life of a country

middle-order product good or service that people buy occasionally

migration movement of large numbers of people from one place to another

milling processing ore into concentrates

mineral valuable substance that is taken from rocks by mining

mineral reserves known quantity of minerals in a country or area

misfit stream small stream flowing in the much larger valley created by a glacial melt

mixed forest vegetation region that contains both coniferous and deciduous trees. It is a transition zone between the deciduous forest and the boreal forest.

mobility freedom of movement

moderating effect effect that large water bodies have on the climate over nearby land areas. Winter temperatures are warmer and summer temperatures are cooler than areas located away from large water bodies. The result is a small annual temperature range.

moraine material deposited by a glacier, often in the form of hills. For example, a terminal moraine is formed at the farthest position reached by a glacier.

multicultural composed of many cultural groups that are encouraged to maintain their heritage

multinational corporation (MNC) large company that operates in more than one country. Some "multinationals" have great economic and political power. Also known as transnational corporations.

multiplier effect total effect on the economy caused by an expansion or contraction in one part of it. For example, a new mine employing 300 people may cause 900 other jobs to develop in manufacturing and services.

nationalist person with a strong belief in and loyalty to one's country. In Canada, this often means a desire to maintain more independence from the United States.

natural increase rate difference between the birth rate and the death rate of a country

natural vegetation plants that would grow in an area in the absence of human influence

net export amount by which the exports of a commodity (e.g., wheat) are greater than the imports of that commodity

net import amount by which the imports of a commodity (e.g., stereo equipment) are greater than the exports of that commodity

net migration rate difference between people immigrating to a country and people emigrating from the same country

newly industrializing country (NIC) countries in the transition stage between developing and developed countries. NICs typically have rapidly growing economies.

new urbanism new planning movement to combat urban and suburban sprawl. It includes:
- building communities around people instead of cars
- an identifiable downtown centre
- narrow lots and smaller houses (higher density)
- mixed income housing
- homes designed to look like those built 50 to 100 years ago

non-basic industry industry that sells its products within the community; it does not bring money into the community.

non-basic service service which is provided within the community. It does not bring money into the community.

non-commercial forest part of a forest that has trees too small or is too far away from the market to use

non-governmental organization (NGO) private organizations that run their own aid programs, sometimes in partnership with government organizations

non-metallic mineral mineral that yields non-metals when processed; e.g., salt, potash, and asbestos

non-renewable resource resource that can only be used once, e.g., oil or iron ore

northing last three figures in a map reference, giving the north-south location

no-till cropping (farming) effective conservation method whereby stubble left from previous year's crop forms a cover holding soil in place protecting it from wind erosion

nuclear-electric generating station place where energy, in the form of heat, is generated by splitting atoms of radioactive materials, then is used to generate electricity

nutrient mineral substance that is absorbed by plant roots

offshore fishery ocean fishery done from boats longer than 25 m. The boats stay at sea several days before returning to shore with their catch.

oil sand mixture of heavy crude oil, sand, and water

oil seed seed used in the production of oils, e.g., canola or sunflower

old growth forest area of mature forest that has never been cut down

open pit mining method of mining using a large hole that is dug for the purpose of extracting ore found near the earth's surface

ore rock that contains enough valuable minerals to make mining profitable

overshoot situation whereby the world's population uses more of the environment (e.g., resources such as water, soil) than the world's real carrying capacity would allow in the long-run

Paleozoic era period of geologic time from 570 million to 245 million years ago. See geologic time.

Pangaea super-continent which included all the earth's land masses. It existed from about 300 million to about 200 million years ago.

parent material rock from which soil is derived

parkland vegetation region that is a transition zone between Grassland and Boreal Forest

pelagic fish fish, such as salmon and tuna, that live and feed in the open ocean

permafrost ground that does not completely thaw in the summer

pesticide chemicals designed to kill harmful plants (herbicides) and harmful insects (insecticides)

petajoule (PJ) metric unit of energy equal to a million billion (10^{15}) joules

petrochemical industry industry dealing with chemicals made from petroleum

photo-voltaic cell device that converts sunlight directly into electricity

pie graph common graph that uses sections of a circle to illustrate values

piggyback system system whereby truck trailers are transported on railway cars

pipeline line of pipes for carrying gas, oil, or other liquids

plankton microscopic plants and animals eaten by small fish and shellfish

plate tectonics theory which states that the earth's outer shell consists of plates that move causing earthquakes, volcanoes, mountains, and the formation of new crust

plateau elevated flat area. See highland.

point symbol symbol representing features that occupy a specific point, such as bridges and buildings, on a topographic map

polar front stormy boundary between cold, dry polar air and warm, moist tropical air

political decision decision made by government that will help attract new business or, if they are not careful, that will drive investment away

population density figure calculated by dividing the population of a region by the region's area

population distribution pattern showing where people live in an area. For example, a scattered distribution along a coastline or road.

population growth rate measurement which combines both natural increase and net migration to calculate the overall growth of a country's population

population pyramid graph that depicts population distribution by age and sex

power grid system of electrical power lines that connects large generating stations to buildings where people use electricity

Precambrian era period of geologic time from the beginning of the earth to 570 million years ago; first era in the earth's geologic history. There were virtually no life forms at this time. See geologic time.

prevailing winds winds that are most commonly found in an area. For example, over most of Canada, the prevailing winds are Westerlies, which blow from west to east

primary industry industry that deals with the production of primary products such as minerals that are mined or quarried, or an agricultural product that is harvested in its raw state

prime meridian line of longitude (meridian of longitude) on maps or globes that joins the North and South Poles and runs through Greenwich, England. Longitude is measured 180° east and 180° west from this line (0°).

productive land five categories of land needed to support human activities in the calculation of our ecological footprint: energy land, degraded land (even though it is no longer actively productive), crop land, pasture land, and forested land

proportional area graph type of graph that can be produced in many shapes, though frequently circles, and is often combined with pie graphs to show, not just the amount of something, but also how this quantity is divided

protectionism policy of trying to protect the industries of a country by having high tariffs. It is the opposite of free trade.

pull factor factor such as freedom of speech or employment opportunities that attract a person to a country

push factor factor, such as unemployment or the lack of freedom of speech, that makes people want to leave their country and move to another one

radar in remote sensing, radar sensors send out microwaves to the earth's surface and use the microwaves reflected back to create an image of human objects and natural features on the earth's surface

rain shadow area on the leeward side of mountains, with little precipitation

raw material something used by an industry to be processed into a more finished state. For example, iron ore (raw material) is made into steel (product), and steel (raw material) is made into an automobile (product).

refugee one of the categories of immigrants to Canada. A refugee is someone who comes to Canada because they fear persecution in their home country.

regenerate when a forest renews itself by natural means

relief precipitation precipitation created when an air mass rises to cross a mountain barrier. Also called orographic precipitation.

remote sensing study of characteristics of the earth using photographs and electronic images taken from aircraft and satellites

renewable resource resource that replaces itself unless badly mismanaged. For example, trees grow to replace those cut down or lost to fire or disease; polluted water is cleaned by the environment.

representative fraction scale scale on a map given as a ratio of distance on the map to distance on the ground, such as 1:50 000, e.g., 1 cm on map represents 50 000 cm on the earth's surface

research and development (R and D) process of inventing a new product and then preparing this product for sale

reserve area of land set aside for the use of a band of Status Indians

reservoir artificial lake built to store water for use in a hydro-electric generating station, for irrigation, or for flood control

residential density measure of the number of housing units per hectare (or km^2)

residential school special schools in larger towns, where Aboriginal children were taken to learn, away from their parents and home towns

retail sale of goods to the public in stores

retreat of glacier shrinking of a glacier, caused when the rate of melting is greater than the rate of snow build-up (accumulation)

rift valley valley that is created when the portion of land between two faults (cracks in the earth) drops down. The St. Lawrence River valley is a rift valley.

Royal Proclamation of 1763 proclamation on land treaties by the British establishing two important principles for negotiations: a) land ownership rights of the First Nations must be respected; b) if a First Nation did choose to give up land, it should receive a fair payment for it

Rule of 70 in demographics, process whereby you divide 70 by the population growth rate to estimate how many years it will take for the country's population to double

run-off rain water that flows on the earth's surface rather than being absorbed by the ground

rural outside towns and cities

rural settlement permanent settlement of people in an area that is well removed from large urban centres

rural–urban fringe area adjacent to an urban area where there is a mixture of urban and rural land uses

satellite manufactured object that is launched by a rocket and circles the earth. Satellites are used to communicate, to study the earth's resources, and to aid the military.

saturated zone area where crevices in the rock, and the spaces between the particles of soil, sand, and gravel are filled with water. The top of this zone is called the water table.

scale measurement on a map that represents an actual distance on the earth's surface. For example, a scale of 1:50 000 means that one centimetre on the map represents 50 000 centimetres on the earth's surface.

search engine system that helps the user do research on the Internet

secondary industry industry dealing with manufacturing or construction

secondary recovery variety of methods to remove a greater percentage of oil from deposits. Even with secondary recovery, only about 60% of the oil in most deposits can be recovered.

section system survey system in most of the Prairie provinces with units of land, 1.6 km by 1.6 km (1 square mile). When settlers first arrived, they were given a quarter-section of land to farm.

sediment eroded material that is deposited by water, wind, or glacial ice

sedimentary rock rock usually formed in layers from the compression of sediments over millions of years

seismologist scientist who studies earthquakes or similar disturbances, and the effect they produce on the earth's crust

selective cutting lumbering technique in which only trees of a certain type, size, and quality are cut

self government principle that each distinct group of people has the right to control its own affairs. In Canada, this term is most often applied to First Nations.

service tertiary industry that provides services needed by other industries and society in general. Services include retailing, education, healthcare, communications, and government services. The service sector is the largest part of Canada's economy.

settlement pattern distribution of homes, farms, villages, towns, and cities in an area

shellfish molluscs and crustaceans such as oysters, shrimps, and lobsters

shelterwood logging method of forest harvesting in which up to 70 percent of trees are cut, leaving small patches of old growth standing to provide seeds for regeneration

shield large area of Precambrian rock that forms the core of a continent

short-grass prairie type of vegetation in the Canadian prairie provinces where very little precipitation causes grasses to be shorter than in slightly wetter long-grass prairie areas

silviculture branch of forestry dealing with the cultivation and care of forests

site refers to the characteristics of the land on which a city is built

situation refers to the relationship between a city's location and the area surrounding it

small-scale map map that shows a small amount of detail of a large area, such as a map with a scale of 1:250 000

smelting process whereby metals are removed from ore or concentrate for use in industry

smokestack industry traditional resource-based industries, such as steel-making, auto-assembly, or oil-refining

sod mat deep intertwined root system of the grass. This sod mat absorbs and stores moisture, and holds the soil in place.

softwood wood produced by coniferous (needle-leaved) trees

soil surface layer of the earth, composed of mineral and organic materials, air, and water

soil profile different horizons (layers) in the soil and the rock layer (bedrock) below the soil. Each horizon has different physical, biological, and chemical characteristics.

specific claim First Nation's claim based on a belief that the government did not fulfil its obligations under a treaty or other agreement related to land, money, or other assets

spillway deep valley created by large amounts of water flowing from a melting continental glacier. Today, such a valley may be occupied by a small stream or river called a misfit stream.

stacked bar graph very much like a simple bar graph, with one important difference, while each bar in a simple bar graph represents one value, a stacked bar can be used to represent several closely related values

standard time every place within a time zone has the same time, which is referred to as standard time

stereo pair pair of aerial photographs that, when looked at through a stereoscope, show a 3-dimensional image

striation in glaciation, a groove called a striation was often gouged out in the bedrock under the ice sheet by rocks frozen in the ice

strip mining method of mining used to recover mineral deposits located very near the surface

suburban referring to low-density housing areas, commercial areas, etc. usually found on the outskirts of a city. Suburban is between rural and urban.

summer fallowing leaving a field uncultivated for a year to build up its soil moisture

survey system pattern of land division used in an area

sustainability approach to development that meets the needs of the present without negatively affecting the ability of future generations to meet their needs

sustainable agriculture approach to agricultural production that can be maintained indefinitely without harming the environment

sustained yield forest management use of forest resources at a rate that allows the forests to renew themselves

sustained yield management use of a renewable resource at a rate that allows the resource to renew itself. For example, the number of fish caught should not be greater than the number of fish reaching maturity.

tailings waste materials left over from processing ore

tandem engineering process whereby two or more engineering teams work on a product and the next generation of that product simultaneously in order to substantially speed up the process of getting new products to market

tariff tax charged on goods imported to Canada in order to protect Canadian industries

temperature range subtraction of coldest average monthly temperature from warmest average monthly temperature

tertiary industry industry that provides services rather than goods

thematic map map containing information on only one topic or theme

thermal-electric generating station electrical power plant where electricity is generated from energy produced by burning fuels like coal, oil, and natural gas

threshold population number of customers needed to make a business profitable or to allow a service, such as a post office or library, to be offered

till eroded material deposited directly by the ice of a glacier; usually a mixture of materials of all sizes

till plain flat to gently hilly area created by deposition under a glacier

time zone division of the earth's surface, usually extending across 15° longitude, that establishes a uniform time

topographic map large-scale map showing both natural and human-made features

topography natural and human features of the landscape

topsoil surface layer of soil

toxic chemical chemical that is harmful to humans or to the environment

trade process of buying and selling goods and services. International trade involves the buying and selling of goods and services between countries.

trade deficit situation in which a country has bought (imported) more in goods or services than it has sold in exports

trade surplus situation in which a country has bought (imported) less in goods or services than it has sold in exports

transect line through a community along which land use or other data are analyzed

transition zone area where the characteristics of one region gradually change into those of another

transportation movement of people and things from one place to another

treat to filter and add chemicals to water to purify it

treaty in Canada, an official agreement between the federal government and First Nations whereby the Aboriginal peoples give up their land rights except for reserves and accept treaty money and other kinds of government assistance

tree line boundary between the tundra and boreal forest zone. North of this line it is too cold for trees to grow.

tundra northernmost vegetation region, found in areas too cold for trees to grow. Bushes, grasses, mosses, and similar plants dominate.

underground mining method of mining used to recover deep mineral deposits

unit train train that carries large amounts of only one cargo along a route. For example, coal is carried from the interior of British Columbia to Vancouver for shipment to Japan.

urban towns and cities of 1000 or more people

urban renewal process of rebuilding older parts of a city

urban sprawl low density development surrounding a city

urbanization process of changing from rural to urban

U-shaped valley valley formed by alpine glaciers moving down valleys scraping the valley walls to produce a U-shape

vertical integration situation whereby a company owns and operates every process required to produce its product

warm front boundary between a cold air mass and an advancing warm air mass

water table top of the soil zone in which all pore spaces are filled with water called the saturated zone. Above the water table, the pore spaces are filled with air.

watershed an area of high land that separates one drainage basin from another

weather combination of temperature, precipitation, cloud cover, and winds experienced daily

weathering breakdown of rock into small particles

Web page Internet site on the World Wide Web that contains information

wetlands swamp, marsh and bog, place where the water table is at ground level

wholesale buying and selling of goods *other* than to the public. For example, sale of goods by manufacturer to distributor.

wind horizontal movement of air over the earth's surface, caused by differences in air pressure

Winkel Tripel projection best map projection for providing a balance between size and shape

windward on the side of a mountain range that faces the prevailing wind

winter-city concept idea to build cities with inside and outside environments that are livable during long, harsh winters

withdrawal use water that is permanently removed from a river for consumption in homes, industries, agriculture, or business

World Wide Web (WWW) network of millions of Internet sites that contain information on more topics than you could ever imagine; the world's largest cooperative communications project via computer

x/y scattergraph simple and useful graph showing relationship between two sets of data

Yahoo! type of search engine used on the Internet

zone of accumulation part of the glacier where snow builds up and turns to ice. The glacial ice moves outward from here.

zoning laws, usually passed by city governments controlling the kind and amount of development in an area

INDEX

CREDITS AND SOURCES